ARIZONA
DISCOVERY GUIDE

A remarkably useful travel companion
for motorists, RVers and other explorers

By Don W. Martin & Betty Woo Martin

ORIGINALLY PUBLISHED AS *THE BEST OF ARIZONA*
COMPLETELY REVISED, UPDATED AND EXPANDED

Pine Cone Press, Inc. • Columbia, California

BOOKS BY DON AND BETTY MARTIN
NEVADA DISCOVERY GUIDE • 1996
ARIZONA DISCOVERY GUIDE • 1996
ADVENTURE CRUISING • 1996
UTAH DISCOVERY GUIDE • 1995
WASHINGTON DISCOVERY GUIDE • 1994, 1996
THE ULTIMATE WINE BOOK • 1993
NORTHERN CALIFORNIA DISCOVERY GUIDE • 1993
OREGON DISCOVERY GUIDE • 1993, 1995, 1996
THE BEST OF THE WINE COUNTRY • 1991, 1994, 1995
INSIDE SAN FRANCISCO • 1991
COMING TO ARIZONA • 1991, 1993
SAN FRANCISCO'S ULTIMATE DINING GUIDE • 1988
THE BEST OF THE GOLD COUNTRY • 1987, 1990, 1992
THE BEST OF SAN FRANCISCO • 1986, 1990, 1994

Library of Congress Cataloging-in-Publication Data
Martin, Don and Betty —
The Best of Arizona
Includes index.
1. Arizona—Description and travel
2. Arizona—history

ISBN: 0-942053-20-6
Library of Congress catalog card number: 95-92753
Cartography • **Vicky Biernacki**; cover design **Dave Bonnot,** Columbine Type and Design, Sonora, Calif.
Photography • **Betty** or **Don Martin**, unless otherwise credited
Chapter illustrations • **Bob Shockley,** Bob Shockley Designs, Mariposa, Calif.

THE COVER • *Mission San Xavier del Bac near Tucson, the "white dove of the desert," glistens in a warm Arizona sun.* **— Don W. Martin**

WALK SOFTLY

It began decades ago with the simple, almost naive phrase: *Take nothing but photographs; leave nothing but footprints.* It has evolved into a new travel consciousness called *eco-tourism*. The message remains the same: As you tread this planet on your journeys of discovery, respect its fragility. Tourism by its very nature promotes crowding and intrusiveness. Crowds tend to litter, trample and tax an area's resources. Here's how you can help make the world a better place to visit and therefore a better place in which to live:

1. Walk softly wherever you travel. A million footprints have preceded yours and millions more will follow. Try to impact an environment as little as possible, whether it be a hiking trail or an old village street. If you can, avoid peak seasons when resources of popular tourist areas are heavily impacted; seek out places less visited.

2. As a hiker, don't leave established trails and never cut switchbacks; it creates ugliness and erosion. When you see others doing so, tactfully tell them why it's not a good idea.

3. Obviously, you shouldn't litter, but go a step beyond. Pick up what others have left behind. If you see someone littering, offer to carry it out. Perhaps they'll have second thoughts the next time. And remember, cigarette butts are litter—the ugliest kind. If you're on the water, never toss anything overboard.

4. Practice no-trace camping in the wilderness and even in established campgrounds. Don't leave a fire pit full of garbage for the next camper. Don't gather or cut firewood unless signs permit it. This strips vegetation and robs soil of important decomposing nutrients.

5. Protect all natural and manmade sites and resources. Avoid gathering "souvenirs" from the wild or from ghost towns or historic sites. A single bit of adobe or beach shell will be missed if thousands of people take one. If you discover a prehistoric artifact, leave it alone. If you move it, you may accidentally erase the story it has to tell.

6. Never put your initials, graffiti or any kind of mark on any structure, cave wall or cliff, tree or stone. And for heaven's sake, please don't deface ancient writings or structures.

7. Respect the traditions and privacy of others. Take time to learn their ways and learn what offends them. There's a difference between honest curiosity and boorish intrusiveness. Ask whose who live in a place if they mind having their picture taken.

8. Recycle and use recycled or recyclable materials whenever possible. When disposing of something, seek out and use recycling bins.

9. Support environmental groups with your actions and your donations, and patronize companies that practice eco-tourism.

10. Most importantly, teach your children these things by word and by example. They are the tourists of today and tomorrow.

Take time to see the sky; find shapes in the clouds
Hear the murmur of the wind, and touch the cool water.
Walk softly; we are the intruders
Tolerated briefly in an infinite universe.
— Jean Henderer, National Park Service (retired)

CONTENTS

MAPS

FINDING THE BEST OF ARIZONA

After publishing several regional guides to California, we compiled our first statewide guidebook in 1990, calling it *The Best of Arizona.* It has been quite successful through the years and in fact, was our best seller. We have since changed our focus somewhat, writing comprehensive statewide driving guides geared to folks in the family sedan, rental car or RV. We call them Discovery Guides, for they steer people to every corner of the state, helping them discover both the obvious and the obscure.

Thus, this complete revision and update of *The Best of Arizona* has become the *Arizona Discovery Guide.* We give you not only the best of the Grand Canyon State, but all of the rest. It is written for the way you travel, taking you along highways and backways, suggesting what to see and do, and where to eat and sleep. With this book and a good road map, Arizona is yours to explore.

If you travel with an RV or trailer, this book is the ideal vehicle, for it offers **RV advisories** on roads and parking conditions, and it suggests numerous RV parks and campgrounds.

While it's comprehensive, this book isn't an encyclopedic tome that merely lists facts. We garnish our data with opinion, insight and a bit of wit, to give you a sense of place, and to make it a "good read." Vignettes and backgrounders help bring Arizona to life; look for them in shaded boxes on the pages ahead.

Arizona and I have been carrying on a flirtation since the 1950s. Back when Phoenix was a manageable size and smog never smudged its skies, I commuted frequently from California. My purpose wasn't tourism; I was wooing a pretty young accordion teacher. That affair never worked out, but it did launch my love affair with the Grand Canyon state. And I hadn't even seen the canyon yet.

More than two decades ago, as associate editor of a San Francisco-based travel magazine, I often sought Arizona assignments. I wrote about Phoenix and Scottsdale, Tucson, dude ranching, Yuma Territorial Prison, Sedona and Oak Creek Canyon and those two cactus preserves—Organ Pipe and Saguaro. I still hadn't made it to the Grand Canyon.

I finally made a brief visit while en route to somewhere else, but lacked the time to explore it. A bit later, when Betty and I were in Las Vegas, partying in the name of journalism, we booked a Grand Canyon scenic flight. Although we were disturbed by our aerial intrusion into this wilderness, we were awe-struck by its complex beauty. Later, we took an 18-day river trip with Grand Canyon Dories, then owned legendary conservationist Martin Litton. We were hooked. We decided to write a book about the canyon—and the rest of the wonderful state which slopes grandly away to the south.

Let our *Arizona Discovery Guide* take you by the hand and lead you through one of America's most interesting states. Take your time and be selective. Stop to smell the cactus flowers and the pine needles. Explore Arizona as we have, section by section, and savor all of its wonders. You might even want to save the Grand Canyon for dessert. It took many million years to get here, and it isn't going anywhere soon.

Don W. Martin
Cape Royal lookout, North Rim, Grand Canyon National Park

The look of Arizona — Cactus garden at Tonto National Monument

THE WAY THINGS WORK

The *Arizona Discovery Guide* takes you mile by mile, with attendant maps, from one corner of this state to the other. Along the way, we suggest interesting stops and detours to little discoveries that other guidebooks may have missed. In towns with visitor appeal, we review the attractions and activities and we suggest places to eat, sleep and camp.

Don't rely too much on hours and prices listed in this book, since many places change them more often than a deadbeat changes his address. Often, hours are shorter during the off-season, which means summer in southern Arizona and winter in the north. If you're going out of your way to visit an attraction or try a recommended restaurant, call to ensure that it's open.

☺ *Special places:* Our little smiling faces mark Arizona's special places—the best visitor lures in each area. These range from major attractions and excellent museums that belong on your "must see" list, to undiscovered jewels. Several restaurants and lodgings earn grins in addition to their regular ratings because of their particular charm, exceptional facilities, food, great views or other distinctive features.

DINING

Our intent is to provide a selective dining sampler. We focus on restaurants in or near visitor attractions, so we won't send you to a neighborhood shopping center in search of a Navajo taco. (What's a Navajo taco? See Chapter one, page 29.) We *do* recommend tucked away diners that have become legend for their food and atmosphere. Restaurants suffer a high attrition rate, so don't be crushed if one that we recommend has become a laundromat by the time you get there.

Choices are based more on overviews of food, service and ambiance, not on the proper doneness of a specific pork chop. We try to offer the typical regional dining experience, which in Arizona may be cowboy steak, spicy Mexican fare or Southwestern cuisine. Of course, one has to be careful when recommending restaurants. People's tastes differ. Also, the cook might have a bad night, or your waitress might be recovering from one. Thus, your dining experience may be quite different from ours.

We graded the restaurants with one to four stars, for food quality, service and ambiance.

☆ **Adequate**—A clean café with basic but edible grub.

☆☆ **Good**—A well-run restaurant that offers reasonably good food and attentive service.

☆☆☆ **Very good**—Substantially above average; excellent fare, served with a smile in an interesting dining environment.

☆☆☆☆ **Excellent**—We've found culinary heaven, and it even has a good wine list!

Price ranges are based on the tab for an average dinner, including soup or salad (but not wine or dessert). Obviously, places serving only breakfast and/or lunch are priced accordingly.

$—Average dinner for one is $9 or less
$$—$10 to $14
$$$—$15 to $24
$$$$—$25 to $34
$$$$$—Did you say you were buying?

LODGING

Our sleeping selections are somewhat arbitrary, since the book can't list them all. Nor does it attempt to; the idea is to recommend facilities near points of interest as you drive through Arizona. We suggest clean, well-run accommodations in all price ranges. In choosing pillow places, we often rely on the judgment of the American Automobile Association because we respect its high standards. We also include some budget lodgings that may fall short of Triple A ideals, but still offer a clean room at a fair price. Of course, one can't anticipate changes in management or the maid's day off, but hopefully your surprises will be good ones.

Bed & breakfast inns and mountain dude ranches are part of the Arizona vacation experience, and we've made a point of seeking these out. To earn a spot in our book, a B&B must offer three or more guest rooms or cottages. Folks who rent out the spare bedroom while daughter Conchita is away at the University of Arizona, and those who offer single-unit vacation home rentals, aren't included.

Again, we look to the stars to rate selected lodgings:

☆ **Adequate**—Clean and basic; don't expect anything fancy.

☆☆ **Good**—A well-run establishment with comfortable beds and most essentials.

☆☆☆ **Very good**—Substantially above average, with facilities such as a pool and spa.

☆☆☆☆ **Excellent**—An exceptional lodging with beautifully appointed rooms, often with a restaurant and various resort amenities.

☆☆☆☆☆ **Superb**—One of the very best in the nation.

Ø—**Non-Smoking rooms** are available, or the entire facility is smoke free (common with bed & breakfast inns). Incidentally, most B&Bs do not allow pets. Inquire when you make reservations so your poor pooch doesn't have to spend the night tied to a saguaro cactus trunk.

Our price ranges are based on figures provided by the establishments and should reflect the range for the high season (although we're sometimes misled). All prices are subject to change—inevitably upward. Incidentally, lodging prices drop radically during the summer in Tucson, Phoenix and other sunbelt vacation areas, often as much as 50 percent.

Price codes below reflect the range for a standard room during high season. Call ahead to confirm current prices and availability. It has been our experience that the lower end rooms are the first to go.

$—a double room for $35 or less

$$—$36 to $49

$$$—$50 to $74

$$$$—$75 to $99

$$$$$—$100 and beyond

It's always wise to make advance reservations, particularly during weekends and local celebrations (listed at the end of most community write-ups).

Two organizations in the state provide B&B lists; the second operates a reservation service:

Arizona Association of Bed & Breakfast Inns, 3101 N. Central, Room 560, Phoenix, AZ 85012; (602) 227-0775.

Mi Casa-Su Casa, P.O. Box 950, Tempe, AZ 85280-0950; (602) 990-0682.

RV ADVISORIES ● To assist folks who drive motorhomes or tow trailers, we've scattered RV Advisories through the book. They point out steep climbs, bumpy roads, hairpin turns and other conditions that might challenge larger rigs. We also try to help you find a parking place in congested areas. The advisories come from warning signs we've observed and from experiences with Ickybod, our 21-foot Mini-Winnie. Of course, our judgments are subjective and based on our driving ability, which may differ from yours. Further, conditions can change radically after a storm. Use our suggestions only as a general guide and always check locally for possible changes in road conditions.

A BIT ABOUT THE AUTHORS

The Martins have authored more than a dozen guidebooks, mostly under their Pine Cone Press banner. When not tending to their publishing company, they explore America and the world beyond, seeking new places and new experiences for their readers. Both are members of the Society of American Travel Writers.

Don, who provides most of the adjectives, has been a journalist since he was 16, when classmates elected him editor of his high school newspaper. (No one else wanted the job.) After school, he left his small family farm in Idaho, wandered about the country a bit, and then joined the Marine Corps. He was assigned as a military correspondent in the Orient and at bases in California. Back in civvies, he worked as a reporter, sports writer and editor for several West Coast newspapers, then he became associate editor of the California State Automobile Association's travel magazine. He now devotes his time to writing, photography, sipping fine Zinfandel and—for some odd reason—collecting squirrel and chipmunk artifacts.

Betty, a Chinese-American who's varied credentials have included a doctorate in pharmacy and a real estate broker's license, does much of the research, editing and photography for their books. She also has sold articles and photos to assorted newspapers and magazines. When she isn't helping Don run Pine Cone Press, Inc., she wanders the globe—with or without him. Her travels have taken her from Cuba to Antarctica.

A third and most essential member of the team is *Ickybod*, a Toyota-chassis "Mini Winnie," the Martins' home on the road. Without *Ick*, they might be tempted to solicit free lodging and meals, and their guidebooks wouldn't be quite so candid.

TRAVEL TIPS

Whether you travel by car, RV or commercial transit, these tips will help make any trip more enjoyable and economical.

Reservations ● Whenever possible, make advance room reservations. Otherwise, you'll pay the "rack rate," the highest rate that a hotel or motel charges. Also, with a reservation, you won't be shut out if there's a convention or major local celebration.

Car rentals ● The same is true of rental cars; you'll often get a better rate by reserving your wheels ahead. **Important note:** Car rental firms may try to sell you "insurance" (actually collision damage waiver) to cover the vehicle. However, you may already have this protection through your own auto insurance company. Check before you go and take your policy or insurance card as proof of coverage.

Trip insurance ● If you're flying, trip insurance may be a good investment, covering lost luggage, accidents and missed flights (essential if you have a no-refund super saver). Most travel agencies can arrange this coverage.

Medical needs ● Always take spare eye glasses or contacts. Take the prescriptions for your lenses and any drugs you may be taking. Don't forget sun protection, such as a wide brimmed hat and sun block, since you may be spending more time outdoors than usual.

Cameras and film ● If you haven't used your camera recently, test it by shooting a roll of film before you go. Test and replace weak camera and flash batteries. If you're flying, hand carry your camera and film through the security check.

Final checklist

There's more to trip departure than putting out the cat. Check off these essentials before you go:

____ Stop newspaper and other deliveries and put a hold on your mail.

____ Lock off or unplug your automatic garage door opener.

____ Arrange for indoor plant watering, landscaping and pet care.

____ Make sure your phone answering machine is turned on; most of these devices allow you to pick up messages remotely.

____ Don't invite burglars by telling the world via answering machine or voice mail that you're gone. Put several lights on timers and make sure newspapers and mail don't accumulate outside.

____ If you're going on a long trip, arrange for future mortgage and other payments to avoid late charges.

____ Take perishable food from the refrigerator and lower the fridge and water heater temperatures to save energy.

____ Double check the clothes you've packed (extra shoes, matching belts); make sure your shaving and cosmetic kits are complete.

____ Take more than one type of credit card, so you won't be caught short if one is lost or stolen.

____ Get travelers checks and/or take your bank debit card.

____ Have your car serviced, including a check of all belts, tires and fluid levels. For long desert stretches, take extra water and oil.

____ Turn out the lights, turn off the heat and put out the cat.

THANK YOU—

In a sense, guidebooks are written by committee. The thousands of facts must come from many sources, and they're checked by many more. We are greatly indebted to scores of helpful Arizonans, particularly those from chambers of commerce, Indian tribal councils, U.S. Forest Service offices and various national parks and monuments. In compiling our original *Best of Arizona* and this revised *Arizona Discovery Guide* version, we received considerable help from these people and organizations:

Lawrence L. Hilliard, vice president, communications, Phoenix & Valley of the Sun Convention & Visitors Bureau; **Carol Downey**, resources librarian, Arizona Department of Library, Archives and Public Records; **Brian C. Catts**, Office of Public Service, University of Arizona; **Glen E. Henderson**, superintendent, Montezuma Castle and Tuzigoot National Monuments; **Navajo Tribe** office of tourism; **L. Greer Price,** Division of Interpretation, Grand Canyon National Park; **Barbara Peck,** public relations manager, Metropolitan Tucson Convention & Visitors Bureau; **Fred Shupla,** Office of Research and Planning, the Hopi Tribe; **Karen Whitney,** management assistant, Glen Canyon National Recreation Area; **Barry D. Wirth,** regional public affairs officer for the Bureau of Reclamation's Salt Lake City office; **Jo Masterson,** manager of Yuma Territorial Prison State Historic Park; **Mitzy Frank,** chief of resources education, Organ Pipe Cactus National Monument; **Pat Quinn**, Petrified Forest National Park; and **Ellen Bonnin-Bilbrey**, public information officer, Arizona State Parks.

CLOSING INTRODUCTORY THOUGHTS:
Keeping up with the changes

Nobody's perfect, but we try. This guidebook contains thousands of facts and a few are probably wrong. If you catch an error, let us know.

Information contained herein was current at the time of publication, but of course things change. Drop us a note if you find that an historic museum has become an auto repair shop or the other way around; or if a restaurant, motel or attraction has opened or closed. Further, we'd like to know if you discover a great undiscovered attraction, café or hideaway resort. And we certainly want to learn if you have a bad experience at one of the places we've recommended.

All who provide information that's particularly useful for future editions of this guidebook will earn a free copy of a Pine Cone Press publication. (See listing in the back of this book.)

Address your comments to:

Pine Cone Press, Inc.
P.O. Box 1494
Columbia, CA 95310
e-mail address: pinecone@sonnet.com

PHOTO TIPS: PRETTY AS A PICTURE?

As we travel, we've watched scores of people take hundreds of photos and shoot thousands of feet of videotape. We can tell by their setups that most of the shots will be poor and they'll be disappointed when they get back home. By following a few simple steps, you can greatly improve your images. These pointers won't make you a pro, but they'll bring better results the next time you point and shoot.

Still cameras

Most of these suggestions work with the simplest fixed focus cameras, even the disposables, in addition to more complex ones:

1. Get the light right. In photography, light is everything. Avoid shooting objects that are hit by direct sunlight; it washes them out. Try to catch light coming from an angle to accentuate shadows, giving more depth and detail to your subject. Photo light is best from sunup to mid-morning and from late afternoon to sunset.

2. Frame your photos. Before you shoot, compose the image in the viewfinder. Eliminate distracting objects such as signs or utility poles by changing your position. Or, line up your shot so the offending sign is behind a bush. When shooting people, make sure a utility pole or tree isn't sprouting from a subject's head.

3. Create depth, not clutter. If you're shooting scenery, give dimension to the photo with something in the background (craggy mountains), the middleground (someone in the meadow) and the foreground (a tree limb to frame the photo). On the other hand, if you're focusing on a specific object such as wildlife or an intriguing rock formation, keep the photo simple; don't clutter it.

3. Take pictures, not portraits. Endless shots of Auntie Maude standing in front of the scenery and squinting into your lens are pretty boring. Everyone already knows what she looks like, so let professionals at home shoot the family portraits.

4. Put life in your lens. On the other hand, people *do* add life to scenic photos. Instead of posing them in front of the scenery, let them interact with it. The kids can enliven a river or lake shot by playing in the water instead of standing in front of it. Ask your mate to stroll from the historic building or peer carefully over the canyon rim. Aunt Maude can extend a tentative finger toward the prickly cactus. Also, have people wear bright clothes to add splashes of color to the photo.

Video cameras

1. Follow the above principles for lighting, framing and posing. You may want to create your own titles by shooting identifying signs.

2. Plan ahead. Think of what you're going to shoot before you pull the trigger. Be a good director and plot each sequence.

3. Hold her steady. You're shooting *moving* pictures, which means that the subjects should be moving, not the video camera. Keep it steady and let people walk in and out of the picture. Limit your panning; give viewers a chance to focus on the scenery.

4. Don't doom your zoom. A zoom lens is a tool, not a toy. Keep your zooming to a minimum, or you'll make your audience seasick.

Arizona

UTAH

NEVADA

CALIFORNIA

NEW MEXICO

MEXICO

N

Four Corners Monument

Pipe Spring National Monument

Lees Ferry

Page

Monument Valley Navajo Tribal Park

Navajo National Monument

Kayenta

Canyon de Chelly National Monument

LAKE MEAD

Hoover Dam

LAKE MEAD NATIONAL RECREATIONAL AREA

Colorado River

GRAND CANYON NATIONAL PARK

Grand Canyon Village

Tuba City

Second Mesa

Keams Canyon

Window Rock

LAKE MEAD NATIONAL RECREATIONAL AREA

Bullhead City

Kingman

Grand Canyon Caverns

Seligman

Williams

Ash Fork

Flagstaff

Wupatki National Monument

Sunset Crater National Monument

Winslow

Holbrook

Chambers

PETRIFIED FOREST NATIONAL PARK

Colorado River

Lake Havasu City

Sedona

Tuzigoot National Monument

Cottonwood

Jerome

Walnut Canyon National Monument

Meteor Crater

Montezuma Castle National Monument

St. Johns

Parker

Prescott

Heber

Show Low

Springerville

Quartzsite

Wickenburg

Payson

THEODORE ROOSEVELT LAKE

Alpine

Phoenix

Tonto National Monument

Globe

Scottsdale

Tempe

Mesa

Superior

Apache Junction

Clifton

Gila River

Gila Bend

Casa Grande Ruins National Monument

Florence

Safford

Yuma

San Luis

Casa Grande

Ajo

SAGUARO (East) NATIONAL PARK

SAGUARO (West) NATIONAL PARK

Tucson

Willcox

Benson

Chiricahua National Monument

Organ Pipe Cactus National Monument

Sonoita

Tombstone

Tubac

TUMACACORI NATIONAL PARK

CORONADO NATIONAL PARK

Sasabe

Nogales

Bisbee

Douglas

Agua Prieta

15 67 89 98 160 264 191 64 180 66 40 93 40 93 89 17 60 60 10 95 10 60 70 8 10 19 86 80 80 191 180

MONUMENT VALLEY

Chapter one

ARIZONA!

The call of the Canyon—and other places

With beauty before me, I walk;
With beauty behind me, I walk;
With beauty beneath me, I walk;
With beauty above me, I walk;
With beauty around me, I walk.
—A Navajo night chant

EVERY YEAR, more than 25 million people vacation in Arizona, leaving behind more than $10 billion dollars. A great many of these folks seek solace from icy winters back home, and they head for Arizona's Sunbelt. Others are drawn by summertime lures, and many of them—over four million—head for the Grand Canyon. Presumably, as you thumb through this book—hopefully after purchasing it—you plan to join these millions of Arizona visitors. Maybe you're already there.

Perhaps more than any other state, Arizona is a year-around vacation location. Those who *really* know the area say the best times of all are spring and fall, when the climate is great nearly everywhere and both the summer and winter crowds are gone.

Arizona is an amazingly diverse state, with pine forests as well as cactus deserts, so selections abound. If you seek retreat from winter chill, you have three broad choices—Phoenix and the Valley of the Sun, Tucson and its southern Arizona neighbors, and the Colorado River corridor along the Arizona-California border. Retired? You may want to join the growing ranks of Snowbirds who temporarily swell the state's numbers by a million or so every winter. The Valley of the Sun gets around 200,000 of them and Yuma's population nearly doubles when 40,000 Snowbirds put down temporary roots. In some communities, such as Quartzsite, winter visitors greatly outnumber permanent residents. We devote a special chapter to Snowbird retreats later in this book.

Incidentally, if you don't mind the summer heat—which is dry and quite tolerable in Arizona—you can get great vacation bargains in the Sunbelt areas. Many resorts, motels, golf courses and other facilities drop their rates by 50 percent and even more. Phoenix, which has a "No Sweat" off-season promotion, reports that 78 percent of its summer visitors say they'll return.

We can testify from personal experience that summers in an air conditioned desert can be great. Hit the tennis courts, golf course or bike trail early in the morning, then laze at the pool or prowl temperature controlled shopping malls, museums and other attractions during midday. Desert summer evenings, with their balmy breezes and low humidity, are *wonderful*.

Arizona's peak winter season is November to March. Obviously, this is the most crowded period for visitors and locals in the Sunbelt areas. Since their kids are still in school, local families usually don't take vacations then. They're commuting to work, sharing highway space with tourists. Thus, urban areas experience their heaviest traffic in winter.

THE LAY OF THE LAND

Asking people to define Arizona is like asking folks to describe an elephant in the dark. It depends on what part they're feeling. The state fits its desert stereotype. Indeed, two thirds of it is arid. It's the only state in the Union with two federal preserves named for and devoted to varieties of cactus—Saguaro National Park and Organ Pipe National Monument.

At the same time, Arizona defies this stereotype. Humphreys Peak north of Flagstaff is one of America's highest, at 12,670 feet. Nearly a fourth of the state is covered by forest, and it shelters the largest stand of virgin ponderosa pines in the country. And of course it contains the world's deepest gorge, which is Arizona's grandest stereotype of all. (Chambers of commerce in Oregon and Idaho claim that their Hells Canyon of the Snake River is deeper than Arizona's Grand Canyon. But they measure from the tops of peaks that flank the ravine, and we think that's cheating. Grand Canyon's 5,700-foot depth is measured from the rim of the great Kaibab Plateau.)

The shape of Arizona was summed up rather well by Reg Manning, Pulitzer Prize-winning cartoonist for Phoenix's *Arizona Republic*. In his whimsical book, *What Is Arizona Really Like?*, he says the state's topography can be taken in three bites, starting from the Four Corners area in the northeast.

The first bite is a remote, often hauntingly beautiful semi-arid plateau containing the large Navajo and Hopi reservations, Monument Valley and the Painted Desert. The second semi-circle, curving from the north central to the southeastern corner, is a green belt of ponderosa pines, including the forest-rimmed Grand Canyon. The Mogollon Rim, a fault extending in a 200-mile arc, marks the edge of this high country.

The final bite—consuming nearly two-thirds of the state—is a great sweep of desert, reaching from the northwest to the southeast corner and ranging from sand dunes to flowering cactus gardens. This is the Sunbelt, a term that originated in Arizona and now is used to describe just about any-place south of a Minnesota blizzard.

Although most of Arizona is desert, it isn't necessarily scalding hot. Much of this arid land—particularly in central and northeastern areas—is high desert that's often quite cold in winter. Naturally, the northwestern mountain regions get regular snowfall. Even in the southern Sunbelt, it's best to bring a warm evening wrap for your winter vacation.

Nearly 85 percent of Arizona's people live in this warm belt. Some say too much of it is focused there. Phoenix, with a million residents, has taken on the sprawl of Los Angeles and in fact is slightly larger in area. More than two million of the state's 4.2 million people live in the Valley of the Sun. Some boosters of the Tucson area—population 700,000—seem determined to catch Phoenix. We think they would be wise to settle for second place.

These metropolitan centers are not what make Arizona wonderful. Yes, we love to luxuriate at poolside in the resorts of Phoenix and Scottsdale. We have a great affection for sunny, laid-back Tucson. And we like the outdoor patios of Phoenix and Tucson pubs. In winter, Arizonans sip their Corona Extra in the sunshine, while San Franciscans and New Yorkers are huddled indoors, nursing their martinis.

Although its cities are appealing, Arizona's greatest charms lie in its open spaces and scenic wonders; in its small towns with their affable wanna-be-cowboy attitude. We found our Arizona in the high, silent reaches of the San Francisco Peaks and the hidden depths of the Grand Canyon; in the dignity of the Indian nations and the scruffy charm of Mexican border towns; in the solitude of a wilderness cactus garden reached only by a dusty road.

We'll take our bottle of Corona in El Tovar's cocktail lounge on the rim of the Grand Canyon. We will have earned it by hiking up from Rio Colorado, that great mother river of the Southwest.

GETTING THERE AND GETTING ABOUT

DRIVING ● Arizona is ideal for the highway traveler and RV wanderer. Uncrowded freeways will get you there in a hurry, then smaller and frequently scenic routes lead to the state's lures. Two and a half interstate freeways traverse the state from east to west. I-40 travels across the top, through Kingman and Flagstaff, exiting near Gallup, New Mexico, following much of the route of historic Highway 66. Interstate 10 is the Sunbelt route, coming across California's Mojave desert and then making a bee-line for Phoenix; it then droops southeast through Tucson and continues into southern New Mexico.

Interstate 8 takes the deep southern route, traveling from San Diego through Yuma to Casa Grande. And there it ends, halfway across the state, merging into I-10. There is no complete north-south freeway. Interstate 17 drops south from Flagstaff to Phoenix, where joins I-10, which continues southeast to Tucson. From there, I-19 makes a run for the border, terminating at the twin towns of Nogales, Arizona and Mexico.

FLYING ● Most folks who fly to Arizona set down in either Phoenix or Tucson, which are served by most major American and several international carriers. Local airlines serve the Grand Canyon, Flagstaff, Prescott and Yuma.

TRAINING ● **Amtrak** provides east-west service through Arizona, linking it to Los Angeles, Chicago, New Orleans and other points east. The *Southwest Chief* runs daily through Kingman, Flagstaff and Winslow, following the general route of I-40. The *Sunset Limited* calls on Yuma, Phoenix, Tucson and some smaller towns, running three times a week. For information and reservations, call (800) USA-RAIL.

BUSING ● Arizona is reached and breached by **Greyhound** along I-40, I-10 and I-8, connecting most towns big and small en route; (800) 231-2222. **Nava-Hopi Tours** links the Grand Canyon with Flagstaff and Phoenix, including Sky Harbor Airport; (800) 892-8687 or (520) 774-5003.

Fishing and hunting

In-state and non-resident fishing and hunting license fees and various bag limits are listed in publications of the **Arizona Game & Fish Department**, 2222 W. Greenway Rd., Phoenix, AZ 85023; (602) 942-3000. Arizona's Indian reservations have their own game laws and bag limits, and a reservation permit—not a state license—must be obtained for hunting and fishing on Native American lands.

Fore!

Arizona just may be the golfing capital of the world, with more than a hundred courses scattered about the state. Most are in the Sunbelt, although northern cities such as Flagstaff, Kingman, Yuma and Colorado River corridors have courses as well. About fifty of these are featured in the brochure, *Golf Arizona,* available free at many tourist information centers and published by Golf-Market, 15704 Cholla, Fountain Hills, AZ 85268; (602) 837-2184. However, it lists only courses in the major tourist areas of Phoenix, Tucson and Sedona. Individual chambers of commerce, listed in the "Trip Planner" box at the start of each chapter, can steer you to local courses.

Winter sports

The main winter sport in Arizona is getting a suntan. However, there are a couple of ski areas. Largest is the Arizona Snowbowl above Flagstaff; see page 122 in Chapter five. The White Mountain Apache tribe operates a fine winter and summer resort at Sunrise in east central Arizona; see page 361 in Chapter twelve. Even the sunbelt city of Tucson offers a small ski area, at Mount Lemmon, just above the cactus; see page 269 in Chapter nine.

What to wear

It's easy to pack for Arizona, since dress codes are rare in this informal state. Summer visitors to most areas will be comfortable in shorts. Toss in long pants or slacks and a jacket or sweater for cool evenings, particularly on the Grand Canyon rims. Remember that the planet's ozone layer is thinning, so keep those backs and shoulders protected with a light shirt or blouse on hot days. And always wear head protection outdoors. A billed cap or visor will keep you from squinting into Arizona's bright sun.

You'll want to be more dressy for Phoenix and Tucson cultural events and for evenings at some major resorts. Also, you should cover your sunburned knees in the state's nicer restaurants, including those grandly rustic dining rooms at the north and south rims of the Grand Canyon.

Cold winter and spring winds can cut right through you, even on mild days, so add a windbreaker to your off-season wardrobe, particularly for the highlands of the Colorado Plateau and east central Arizona. Skiers, especially those used to California's Sierra Cement and damper climate, will discover that the air is thinner and crisper and the powder's deeper at the Arizona Snowbowl and Sunrise. The layered look is the way to go.

GETTING CAMPED

Arizona is a great state for campers and RVers. Campgrounds abound and many state and federal camping areas are in spectacular settings, with canyon or red rock views. Campsites may be nestled among the pines or tucked among saguaro cactus. Although state and national park camping spaces often fill up on summer weekends, you generally can get a spot if you arrive before noon.

Commercial RV parks and campgrounds also are plentiful in the state, particularly near national parks, along the Colorado River corridor and in most towns of any size. For a brochure listing many of the state's commercial RV parks and campgrounds, with directions and lists of amenities, contact: Arizona Travel Parks Association, P.O. Box 11090-275, Phoenix, AZ 85061-1090; (602) 230-1126.

Although they're designed primarily for long-term visitors, some of the mobile home parks in Snowbird roosts around Phoenix, Tucson and the Colorado River corridor accept RVs for brief stays, but rarely tents.

STATE PARKS • Many of Arizona's 24 state parks and recreation areas offer camping, in addition to preserving a variety of recreational and historic sites. Campsites often are spacious and beautifully situated, rivaling those in national parks and forests. They often have more amenities, including hookups and showers. Fees are generally $13 to $15 with hookups and $8 to $10 without. Day use fees for most parks and recreation areas are $3 to $5 per vehicle (with up to six people) and $1 or $2 for walk-ins, motorcycles and bicyclists.

State parks do not offer campsite reservations, although you can call (602) 542-4174 to find out about potential availability. If you plan to visit a lot of parks, you can get an annual day use pass for $35. They're available at any state park or contact: Arizona State Parks, 1300 W. Washington, Phoenix, AZ 85007. The internet website is http://www.pr.state.az.us. Directories of state parks are available at many visitor information centers, or you can contact the main office in Phoenix.

NATIONAL PARKS, MONUMENTS & RECREATION AREAS • Generally, campsites at federal reserves in the state are on a first come, first served basis. However, there are some exceptions. Camping at Grand Canyon National Park may be reserved by calling (800) 365-CAMP; sites can be reserved with a MasterCard or VISA. In summer, sites are difficult to get without reservations, which should be made as far in advance as possible. Arizona has two large national recreation areas, which it shares with neighboring states—Lake Mead and Lake Powell. Both have commercially operated RV parks which can be reserved, and federally run campgrounds which cannot.

Day use admission to federal parks, recreation areas and Bureau of Land Management facilities vary from free to $10 per vehicle. All are free for holders of annual Golden Eagle passes (available for $25 from any federal preserve), Golden Age passes ($10 for anyone 62 and over) or Golden Access passes (free to the handicapped). Holders of these "Golden" passes can camp at national forest, national recreation area and Bureau of Land Management campgrounds for half price.

U.S. FOREST SERVICE ● There are dozens of national forest campgrounds in Arizona, and several take reservations, up to 120 days in advance. Call the National Forest Reservation System at (800) 280-CAMP; sites can be reserved up to 120 days in advance, with a MasterCard or VISA for a $7.50 fee per family. Reservations-by-mail forms are available at Forest Service offices and many tourist information centers. Personal checks, money orders or MC/VISA credit card numbers are accepted for mail-in reservations. For a list of national forest campgrounds in Arizona and elsewhere that accept reservations, call (505) 842-3292. Forest Service sites rarely have hookups, and many have chemical toilets. However, the price is right—from $10 down to nothing, and many rival state and national park campgrounds in the beauty of their settings.

Forest Service "Camp Stamps" save about 15 percent of campsite costs. They're also convenient, since you don't have to worry about having the right currency to poke into those little slots. You can purchase any amount in denominations of $1, $2, $3, $5 and $10. Send a check or money order to: Camp Stamps, U.S. Forest Service, P.O. Box 96090, Washington, DC 20090-6090.

BUREAU OF LAND MANAGEMENT ● Vast areas of Arizona's landscape are managed by the BLM, particularly in the southern deserts, Colorado Plateau and central highlands. Many of these areas offer campsites. Like Forest Service campgrounds, they have either flush or pit potties, and no hookups. Fees range from free to $8.

Casual camping ● Self contained camping and, in some cases, tent camping may be permitted on Forest Service and BLM lands outside regular campgrounds. This is allowed only in certain areas, so check with the regional Forest Service or BLM office. In all such areas, no- trace camping is required. Tent sites or RV rigs should be completely clear of any road, no matter how primitive it appears to be. You may wind up snoozing in the path of a loaded logging truck! On the other hand, as you move clear of the road, make sure your rig doesn't get stuck in mud or soft sand.

Arizona's **roadside rests** permit weary travelers to snooze for up to eight hours, but only in self-contained RVs or cars; tent camping isn't allowed. Rolling out sleeping bags on the grass is frowned upon, although we've seen some people do it. If you're tempted, stay clear of the pet areas.

Camping tips

● Take plenty of dollar bills when you go campground hopping. Some fees at state and national parks and Forest Service campgrounds are in odd amounts, and most don't accept checks. Also, many are self-registering and there's no one around to make change.

● At most public campgrounds, a stub from your camping envelope is clipped to a post at your site, indicating that it's occupied. It's also a good idea to leave a highly visible but expendable object on the picnic table, or have some "Campsite occupied" signs printed. You don't want to return from a day of hiking to find a big fifth-wheel rig comfortably settled in your space. ("What stub? I didn't see any stub. Look, Mac, we're right in the middle of dinner here...")

● Many state and national parks limit the use of generators to certain hours and/or restrict them to specific areas of the campground. Generally, they may not be run during "quiet hours," which are 10 p.m. to 7 a.m. in state parks.

● If you're driving one of those huge motorized condos, fifth wheelers or trailer rigs, note that many campgrounds have length limits. Check for a size limit sign before entering the camping loop; you may find it difficult to maneuver back out.

● As you lumber down the highway in your RV, pull over to let the more nimble traffic pass. In most states, it's required. Conversely, if you're a motorist fuming impatiently behind a slow motorhome, don't follow too closely. If you can't see the rig's mirrors, the driver probably can't see you and may not realize that you're back there.

INDIAN RESERVATIONS

Arizona has more Indian lands than any other state, and the largest Native American population in America—more than 160,000. Twenty reservations cover more than 19 million acres—a combined area larger than some states. They all welcome visitors and many have specific tourist attractions.

The most popular are the huge Navajo reservation—largest in America—and the smaller Hopi reservation surrounded by Navajo lands. Attractions there include Canyon de Chelly and Navajo national monuments, the splendor of Monument Valley and the ancient Hopi villages, perhaps the oldest continually occupied communities in America.

Other areas with significant tourist lures are the Fort Apache Reservation, with camping, hiking, hunting and fishing and a major ski resort; and the Hualapai and Havasupai reservations, which preserve and provide access to rarely visited areas of the Grand Canyon of the Colorado River.

For a brochure listing the state's Native American reservations and their attractions, contact the Arizona Commission of Indian Affairs at 1645 W. Jefferson, Phoenix, AZ 85007, (602) 542-3123; or the Arizona Office of Tourism, 1100 W. Washington St., Phoenix, AZ 85007, (602) 542-8687.

HANDICAPPED TRAVELERS

People with mobility problems can get permits to use handicapped parking spaces by applying at any Motor Vehicle Division office. Proof of impairment must be provided. These permits aren't limited to the driver; they can be used if any regular occupant of the car is physically impaired. Incidentally, there is a stiff fine if able bodied persons park their vehicles in handicapped spaces.

Golden Access Passes, available free to handicapped persons at national park, U.S. Forest Service and BLM offices, provide half price camping at national forest, national recreation area and BLM campgrounds, and free admission to all national parks and monuments.

Among agencies that handicapped travelers will find useful are: **Travel Information Center,** 12th Street and Tabor Rd., Philadelphia, PA 19141, (215) 329-5715; **Society for the Advancement of Travel for the Handicapped,** 26 Court Street, Brooklyn, NY 11242; (718) 858-5483; **American Foundation for the Blind,** 15 W. 16th Street, New York, NY 10011; (800) 323-5463; and **Mobility International USA,** P.O. Box 3551, Eugene, OR 97403. Two federal government pamphlets, *Access Travel* and *Access to the National Parks,* are available by writing: **U.S. Government Printing Office,** Washington, DC 20402.

An extremely helpful publication is *Access to the World—A Travel Guide for the Handicapped* by Louise Weiss. Available at many bookstores, it's published by Holt, Rinehart & Winston of New York.

SENIOR TRAVELERS

Anyone 62 or older can obtain a **Golden Age Pass** for $10 that's good for life. It provides half price camping in Forest Service, national recreation area and BLM campgrounds, and free admission to national parks and monuments. Nearly every attraction and museum in Arizona and the rest of the country offers senior discounts. They're also available on most public transit systems, and many restaurants and hotels offer reduced rates as well.

A fine organization that serves the interests of seniors is the **American Association of Retired Persons,** 1919 K Street Northwest, Washington, DC 22049; (202) 872-4700. For a nominal annual fee, AARP members receive information on travel and tour discounts and other stuff of interest to retired folk.

Elderhostel, which specializes in learning vacations for seniors and often uses college dorms and classrooms, offers some Arizona travel programs. If you're 60 or older and you love to learn while traveling, contact Elderhostel at 75 Federal Street, Boston, MA 02110-1941; (617) 426-8056.

BEATING THE HEAT

Arizona isn't all desert, as we've established, and it's not the driest state in the Union. It ranks third, behind Nevada and Utah. However, more than half the state is considered desert, including the two major metropolitan centers of Phoenix and Tucson. And it does get *hot* in summer. The thermometer can top 120 in Phoenix; Tucson is a bit higher and generally lags about five degrees behind. While 120-plus temperatures are unusual in these metropolitan areas, they are routine long the Colorado River corridor, which is the lowest area of the state. Arizona's heat is the dry kind, so you won't suffer too much if you take proper precautions. Humidity is the main culprit in heat discomfort, since it slows surface evaporation from your skin, which is nature's cooling device.

Hot weather vacations require special precautions for man, woman, beast and vehicle. Follow these steps to keep your cool when the weather's not:

• Don't be a mad dog or an Englishman. Plan active outdoor activities in the early morning and evening.

• Avoid dehydration by drinking plenty of water. And we mean *plenty*. A gallon a day will keep heatstroke away. If you're hiking—and you'll want to do a lot of that in the Grand Canyon—take all the water you can carry. If there are water sources along the trail, carry a ceramic water filter to replenish your supply. *Never* drink untreated stream or spring water, even if it does look like Evian.

• In desert areas, the ground absorbs and then radiates the sun's rays, so temperatures may remain high until sundown and even beyond. It's best to do your summer hiking in the morning. In the Grand Canyon, we mean *early* in the morning. Trails there begin on the rim and descend, meaning that the end of your hike is always uphill. While it may be cool on the rim, the inner canyon has a desert climate. People have died of heatstroke down there.

• Avoid sweet drinks or alcohol, which speed up dehydration. Besides, you chubby little rascal, soft drinks contain about *twelve teaspoons* of sugar!

• Don't take salt tablets, despite what they told you in boot camp. Salt causes you to retain water, and you *want* to perspire. That's what keeps you cool. You should keep plenty of fluid circulating through your system.

• Don't exert yourself on a hot day. Your body will lose more fluid than it can replace.

• Wear light colored, reflective clothing—preferably cotton or linen. Avoid nylon and polyester, since these fabrics don't "breathe" and this traps body heat against your skin.

• If you must work outdoors in the heat, dip your shirt or blouse in water frequently. The garment's evaporation, along with that from your body, will help keep you cool.

Shielding the sun

Southwestern states such as Arizona have high skin cancer rates. Because of the southern latitude, clear air and relatively high altitude, more of the sun's damaging ultraviolet rays reach the earth. With the ongoing depletion of our ozone layer, scientists tell us that the skin cancer rate is increasing dangerously. It can develop late in life, even years after you've stopped getting your annual tan. One form—melanoma—can be fatal. Even if you don't get skin cancer, which is nearly 100 percent preventable, constant sun exposure will lead to premature wrinkling.

Some drugs increase the skin's sensitivity to the sun, so check with your pharmacist. Among the suspect items are hormone based drugs including birth control pills, some tranquilizers, diuretics, sulfa drugs and antibiotics such as vibramycin and tetracycline. Even some artificial sweeteners and perfumes are suspect.

Take these precautions to keep your hide from being fried:

• Use sunscreen with a high PABA content; it ranges from five to 33 percent (which is a virtual sunblock). Even if you're working on a tan, use sunblock on sensitive areas, such as your lips, nose and—yes—the tops of your ears. If you have a bald pate, remember to protect that—preferably by wearing a hat instead of a sun visor. In case you're curious, PABA stands for *para-aminobenzoic acid*. (No wonder people use the acronym!) A few individuals are allergic to PABA; if a rash appears, try something else.

• Bear in mind that suntan lotion will rinse off when you swim or perspire, so re-lather yourself after swimming or exercising.

• Always wear a broad brimmed hat or visor outdoors. It'll protect your eyes from sun glare and shield your face from sunburn. There's some evidence that sun glare may be a cause of cataracts. The *vaqueros* knew what they were doing when they created the sombrero.

• If you spend a lot of time outdoors, some specialists recommend getting a careful, light tan. Moderately tanned skin will resist sunburn—up to a point. You can still get singed from prolonged exposure. Get your tan *very slowly*. Limit initial exposure to a few minutes a day. Do your tanning in the morning or late afternoon when the sun's rays are less direct. Take Rudyard Kipling's advice; avoid the noonday sun.

We prefer to keep moving when we work on tans—hiking, swimming, bike riding and such. If you baste yourself in the sun, you may doze off and get too much exposure. Besides, it's boring. Incidentally, clouds don't block all ultraviolet rays. Also, reflections from sand, pool decks or water can intensify burning. Wet T-shirts may look rather fetching on the right bodies, but they offer almost no sun protection, despite their cooling effect.

If you *do* get burned, ease the pain with a dip in the pool or a cool shower, then use one of those over-the-counter anesthetic sprays. Antihistamine will relieve the itch. That's right; the same stuff that you take for the sniffles. And keep your skin out of the sun until it's fully healed.

Avoiding "heat sickness"

Heat exhaustion and its lethal cousin heatstroke are real dangers on hot summer days. Both are brought on by a combination of dehydration and sun.

Signs of heat exhaustion are weariness, muscle cramps and clammy skin. The pulse may slow and you may become unusually irritable. If left untreated, heat exhaustion can lead to deadly heatstroke. The skin becomes dry and hot, the pulse may quicken and you'll experience nausea and possibly a headache. Convulsions, unconsciousness, even death can follow.

At the first sign of heat sickness, get out of the sun and into the shade. Stay quiet and drink water—plenty of water. If you're near a pool, faucet or stream, douse your face and body with water, and soak your clothes to lower your body temperature quickly.

Driving and surviving the desert

Arizona's deserts occupy thousands of square miles of open spaces; population is thinly scattered. These can be intimidating places if you're stranded. If you're tempted—as we often are—to explore this remote and beautiful world, save the urge for fall or spring, when it's not so darned hot. Winters can be biting cold in higher desert elevations, creating hypothermia risks if you become stranded.

When you venture into the wilds, let someone know where you're going, and when you intend to return. Keep these pointers in mind if you wander off well-traveled asphalt:

• First, foremost and always, take plenty of water. Water to drink, to soak your clothes, to top off a leaky radiator. It's cheap, it's easily portable and it can save your life.

• Give your car, four-wheel-drive or RV a physical before going into the boonies, to ensure that it'll get you back. Take extra engine oil, coolant and an emergency radiator sealant. Include spare parts such as fan belts, a water pump, radiator hoses—and tools to install these things. Toss an extra spare tire into the trunk, along with a tire pump, patching and sealant.

• Take food with you—stuff that won't spoil. If your vehicle breaks down, you may be out there for a while. Also pack matches, a small shovel, aluminum foil (for signaling), a can opener, a powerful flashlight and a space blanket so you can snooze in the shade of your car. The shiny side of a space blanket also is a good signaling device.

• A CB radio or cellular phone can be a lifesaver. Remember that channel 9 is the emergency CB band, monitored by rescue agencies.

• *Never* drive off-road, particularly in an on-road vehicle. Loose, sandy desert soil can trap your car in an instant, even if the ground looks solid. We don't leave established roadways as a matter of principle, because tires are hell on the fragile desert environment.

• Even if you keep to the roads, you might get stuck in an area of blowing sand or a soft shoulder. It could happen when you leave the road to set up camp. Carry a tow chain and tire supports for soft sand, like strips of carpeting. An inexpensive device called a "come-along"—sort of a hand winch—can get you out of a hole, if you can find something for an anchor.

● If you become stranded in the desert, stay in the shade of your car—*not* in the vehicle itself. If you're far from civilization and not sure of your bearings, don't try to walk out, particularly during the heat of the day. Besides, a vehicle is easier to spot than a lone hiker. Use a mirror, foil or space blanket as a signal device if you see a plane approaching, and build a signal fire. A spare tire will burn, and a douse of oil will make the fire nice and smoky. Start your blaze in a cleared area away from your vehicle. You don't want to launch a wildfire that might compound your predicament.

● If you're on a road and you know that you can reach civilization on foot, do your walking at night. Take plenty of water, a flashlight and some food for nibbling.

Heat isn't your only problem in the desert. Flash floods can roar down dry washes and across roadway dips, particularly during spring and summer rain squalls. If you're driving or hiking in the desert and a sudden rainstorm hits, keep to the high ground until it passes. Storms can be unpredictable, so avoid camping in dry washes.

THE WAY IT WAS

Arizona is one of the youngest states in the union, admitted as the last of the lower forty-eight in 1912. Yet, river-runners and hikers in the Grand Canyon will see two-billion-year-old pre-Cambrian schist, some of the oldest exposed rock on Planet Earth. Native Americans have occupied Arizona's deserts and high plateaus for about 20,000 years.

Its first residents were nomadic hunters who drifted down from the Great Plains. When droughts drove the mammoths and antelope away, they swapped their spears for plowshares and became—about eleven centuries ago—North America's first farmers. Freed from the constant search for food, they developed complex societies and built large pueblos whose ruins survive today. The state is a treasure-trove of archaeological sites.

Anthropologists call these early people Hohokam, Anasazi, Sinagua and Mogollon. We don't know what they called themselves, for they left no written language. Like most ancient tribes, they probably just referred to their kind as "The People." Through the centuries, they evolved into highly-developed societies, occupying great pueblos of adobe or stone atop mesas or tucked into hidden canyons and precipitous cliffs. They dug irrigation canals and became excellent farmers. Their pottery, weaving and other crafts were among the most advanced of the time.

About eight centuries ago, this highly developed society began coming apart at the seams. The great pueblos were abandoned and left to weather away in the hot sun. Scientists speculate that a persistent drought may have driven them from their corn and bean fields. Some experts blame their downfall on disease, soil depletion or the arrival of more aggressive tribes.

People identify Navajos and Apaches with Arizona, yet these were latter-day arrivals, coming from the cold north. They were Athabaskans who drifted down from Canada, starting about six hundred years ago. Warlike hunters, they may have driven off many of the native tribes. Ironically, they adopted some of the original residents' farming and weaving techniques, particularly those who would become Navajos. Scientists have been unable to pinpoint the ultimate fate of the Hohokam, Sinagua or Mogollon. Similarities in culture and crafts suggest that today's Hopi may be Anasazi descendants.

Historians have fun feuding over the origin of Arizona's name. There are four Indian versions: Arizuma, an Aztec word for "silver bearing"; *Ali shonak* or *Ari-son*, meaning "small spring" or "young spring," which were names of Pima settlements; and a Papago term, *Aleh-zone,* also meaning young spring. Basque settlers insist that Arizona comes from *Aritz ona,* their term for "good oak." This name was given to a silver strike site in 1736. Some unimaginative scholars suggest that "Arizona" is merely a derivation of "arid zone."

The name "Arizona" first appeared in print in a 1750s document by one Padre Ortega, a Spanish missionary.

Spaniards were the area's first European visitors, and they got here by accident. In 1528, a group led by Alvar Núñez Cabeza de Vaca set out to explore Florida's west coast. Part of the group became lost after an Indian attack and spent more than eight years wandering through what is now Texas, New Mexico, Arizona and northern Mexico. Some accounts say they were befriended and protected by other Indians, after De Vaca convinced them that he was a powerful medicine man. When four surviving members of the group finally stumbled across some of their countrymen in western Mexico, they reported Indian legends of fabulously wealthy cities which lay to the north.

Antonio de Mendoza, viceroy of New Spain, knew of an eighth century Moorish legend about seven golden cities, hidden somewhere in the unexplored world. Could these be the same? In 1539, with golden greed glittering in his eyes, he dispatched a party of explorers from Mexico City to find these treasure-laden towns. It was led by Franciscan Father Marcos de Niza. Accompanying the group—probably reluctantly—was a Moorish slave named Estévan, one of the survivors of the De Vaca trek.

The legend of Cibola

As the Spaniards entered present-day Arizona, local Indians said the area through which they traveled was called "Cibola." Thus, the legend of the Seven Cities of Cibola was born. Learning that a Zuni pueblo lay ahead, Father de Niza sent an advance party to investigate, led by Estévan. The Zunis weren't very nice hosts; they killed the visitors.

An intimidated Father de Niza kept his distance. But he drew near enough to see that the pueblos glittered in the sun. He returned home and advised the Viceroy of Mexico that he may have found one of the golden cities. However, the good padre had been fooled by the glitter of mica, embedded in the adobe.

A year later, that great and brutal explorer, 30-year-old Francisco Vásquez de Coronado, traveled north to continue the search. He found no gold, pillaged a few pueblos and explored as far north as Kansas. After two years, he returned to Mexico City empty-handed. More than a century passed before the curious Spanish again began pestering natives of the Southwest. Then in the late 1600s, Father Eusebio Francisco Kino and other padres came to establish missions. Thousands of Indians were converted to Christianity. They were most likely encouraged by accompanying soldiers who set up military presidios to protect the missions.

Most of the Indians did not yield their land or their free spirits easily. Angered by abusive treatment from the Spanish intruders, they staged several violent revolts. The Hopi emptied their pueblos of Spaniards in a savage rebellion in 1680. Spanish occupation—punctuated by Indian uprisings—continued into the early 1800s. When Mexico won its independence from Spain in the 1820s, most of the soldiers were withdrawn from this northern outpost. In the absence of the military, Indians—primarily Apaches—again went on the warpath, driving frightened settlers to the safety of the walled cities of Tucson and Tubac.

Much of what is now Arizona and New Mexico was ceded to the United States in the 1848 Treaty of Guadalupe Hidalgo, at the end of the Mexican War. Sandwiched between California and Texas, they were lumped together as the New Mexico Territory. However, as far as the original residents were concerned, this was still their land and warfare with the intruders continued. In the late 1800s, more than a dozen U.S. Army forts were built to protect American settlers. Not until Geronimo surrendered in 1886 was the area considered safe for settlement.

A major force

Today, Native Americans are a major force in the state, culturally and politically. Vast tracts of land were set aside as reservations, which have become self-governing entities. The Navajo and Hopi nations occupy a huge chunk of northeastern Arizona. Combined with other reservations, they comprise a fourth of the state's land area.

The California gold discovery in 1848 spurred the greatest human migration since the Crusades. Many gold-seekers traveled south through the New Mexico Territory to avoid the precipitous Sierra Nevada range that formed a barrier on California's eastern edge. Part of this southern route dipped into Mexico, so the government decided to make it all-American by negotiating the Gadsden Purchase. In 1854, cash-poor Mexico sold 30,000 square miles of its northern desert for $10 million. This would become a large chunk of southern Arizona.

Four years later, the government awarded the Butterfield Overland Stage Company a contract to forge a mail a route through this area, from St. Louis to San Francisco. It was needed to link fast-growing California with the rest of the U.S., which then ended at the Missouri border.

The New Mexico Territory, settled primarily by Southerners, sided with the South during the Civil War. A Texas militia seized Mesilla, New Mexico, in 1861. The Texans claimed all of the land from the Rio Grande to the Pacific as Confederate territory. But a column of Union-sympathizing Californians soon put an end to that. In 1862, the Confederates were routed in the Battle of Picacho Pass, south of Phoenix. Little more than a skirmish with only eight casualties, it was the Civil War's westernmost battle. The following year, President Lincoln signed a bill creating separate Arizona and New Mexico territories.

For the next two decades, the Arizona Territory epitomized the Wild West. Cattle barons battled over water and grazing rights and knocked down sod-busters' pesky fences. Tombstone and its O.K. Corral shoot-out and Yuma's infamous Territorial Prison became the stuff of which legends—and certainly movies—were made. Then in the 1880s, several minor gold strikes, major copper discoveries and Mormon migrations from Utah brought a more settled brand of citizens to the territory. The railroad arrived late in the century to complete the taming of this last outpost of the Wild West. Then on St. Valentine's Day in 1912, portly President William Howard Taft signed the proclamation making Arizona the last of the 48 contiguous states.

Hampered by lack of water, the new state grew slowly in the first half of this century. Several military air bases were built in its wide open spaces during World War II, and many GIs who trained here returned at war's end. In the Fifties, Arizona's numbers began to swell, aided by air conditioning, the creation of the Snowbird cult, and a court ruling granting it a larger share of Colorado River water.

And suddenly, Arizona was on a roll. It grew by a whopping 53 percent during the 1970s, second only to Nevada in percentage increase; in the next decade it added another 35 percent, outgained only by Nevada and Alaska. In numbers of people, it is considerably larger than both, with an estimated population of 4,201,000 in 1995. Among Western states, only California and Washington have more people. Phoenix has blossomed into a major city. Its suburbs of Mesa, Glendale and Chandler doubled their populations between 1970 and 1980. Growth tapered toward the end of the 1980s and early 1990s, with fewer than 50,000 a year migrating to the state, compared with more than 100,000 annually a few years earlier. However, migration picked up again in the middle 1990s. As the millenium approached, Phoenix and several other Arizona communities again were numbered among the fastest growing cities in the nation.

THINGS ARIZONAN

Several things—cultural, historic or climatic—are distinctly Arizonan, or at least distinctly Southwestern.

Bola tie • This curious form of neckware, with a braided cord drawn through some kind of Western ornament, was born in Arizona and hopefully will die there.

Cowboys • The American cowboy's roots are mostly Mexican, and the cowboy himself originated in Arizona, New Mexico and west Texas. His standard gear—wide-brimmed hat, lariat, saddle with a horn (used for snubbing the lariat) and chaps are all of Mexican *vaquero* origin. The rodeo originated in Mexico and the guitar that cowboys like to strum is Spanish. Levi's were contributed by Californian Levi Strauss. We have no idea why all those Southern country singers dress like cowboys and play guitars. Round 'em up and head 'em out to—Nashville? (See box in Chapter eight, page 235)

Howling coyotes • That coyote, wearing a neckerchief and howling at the moon, is a typical object on Arizona jewelry and ceramics. No one seems to know where he came from.

Native American casinos • A phenomenon of recent years, Indian casinos are cropping up all over Arizona. They range from a small slot machine parlor above Pipe Springs National Monument on the Arizona Strip to the large, handsome Mazatzal Casino just outside Payson. Since reservations are sovereign territories, Native Americans are free to establish casinos and there is of course an abundance of native land in Arizona. Most gaming parlors are small by Las Vegas standards, offering primarily slot machines, video poker and keno. Some, however, are quite elaborate. The largest, which rivals some of the big Nevada resorts, is the Avi Hotel and Casino operated by the Fort Mohave Tribe. Although the tribe has land in Arizona and Nevada, the casino itself is in Nevada, challenging the gaming resorts of Laughlin, just to the north.

Silver and turquoise • The Navajo and Hopi of Arizona and Zuni of New Mexico are noted for their beautiful silver and turquoise jewelry. The Hopi work primarily with silver while the Navajo jewelry often combines silver with turquoise, particularly in the "squash blossom" necklace. However, it is not native to their culture, despite their love of adornment. The turquoise-

INDIAN TACO: A CULINARY CURIOSITY

If Arizona's Indians had developed this weapon a century ago, they might not have lost their war with the white intruders. The U.S. Army would have been too bogged down to attack the Apaches, pursue the Papagos or nab the Navajos.

The Indian taco is a delicacy of dubious pedigree. Its calorie and cholesterol content would bring the editor of the *Nutrition Action Healthletter* to tears. It is neither Indian nor taco, but a sort of Italian-Mexican tostada. The base is Indian fry bread, a puffy and pleasantly chewy dough akin to soft pizza crust. Upon this is layered pinto beans—sometimes with chili—and ground beef, plus grated cheese, chopped onions and shredded lettuce. Diced tomatoes and other salad veggies are optional.

Once devoured, the beans and crust unite in your stomach and begin expanding. Perhaps it is some mystical amalgam unknown to nutritional science. An hour after consuming an Indian taco, you feel like you've been force-fed a Thanksgiving dinner after winning a watermelon-eating contest. You won't need another meal for hours—perhaps days.

---

silver concept was introduced to them by none other than Fred Harvey, who had gotten his start by developing Southwest tourism in the late 1800s. It was crafted then as it is now—primarily to sell to tourists.

Southwest cuisine • The *nouveau* cuisine movement started about 20 years ago in California, featuring fresh ingredients simply prepared, interestingly spiced and lightly cooked. Chefs in Arizona and New Mexico, where fresh year-around vegetables are abundant, started adding chili peppers and *polenta* to these recipes and *voile!* Southwest cuisine.

Southwestern architecture • The look is earthy, squarish and adobe, with salmon and turquoise as the preferred colors. Probably more of New Mexican origin than Arizonan, it was inspired by a combination of Hopi and Zuni dwellings and Frank Lloyd Wright's earthy, geometric architecture. Wright spent his final years at Taliesen West, near Scottsdale.

Saguaro cactus • Pronounced *sa-WHA-ro,* this large and thick-limbed plant is often portrayed as a "typical" cactus in illustrations, cartoons and Western souvenirs. Yet its habitat is strictly limited; it grows only in the Sonoran Desert of southern Arizona and northern Mexico. It's also found frequently on bola ties.

JUST THE FACTS

Size • 113,909 square miles; sixth largest state; about 340 miles wide by just under 400 miles deep.

Population • About 4,201,000; largest city is Phoenix with just over a million residents. Tucson is the second largest city with just under half a million. Arizona's population density is 27.1 per square mile; ranks 40th among the states.

Elevations • Highest point, Humphreys Peak north of Flagstaff, 12,633 feet; lowest point, Colorado River as it enters Mexico below Yuma, 70 feet.

Admitted to the Union • February 14, 1912, as the 48th state; capital—Phoenix.

Time zone ● Mountain; one hour later than the West Coast, two hours earlier than the East. Except for the Navajo Reservation, Arizona doesn't switch to summer Daylight Saving Time; apparently those warm desert evenings are long enough!

Area codes ● (520) for all of Arizona except the Phoenix metropolitan area, which is (602).

Official stuff ● **State motto**—*Didat Deus* (God enriches); **state seal** depicts the five "Cs" of copper, cotton, climate, citrus and cattle; **state bird**—cactus wren (medium brown with speckled breast, likes to hang around saguaro cactus); **state flower**—saguaro cactus blossom (white with yellow center); **state tree**—paloverde (desert tree identified by green limbs, which is what *palo verde* means in Spanish); **state gem**—turquoise.

State nicknames ● The Grand Canyon State; the Copper State (appropriate, since it produces more than half of America's copper supply).

Alcohol ● None may be imported from another state (although there are no border checks). It's sold by the bottle in any licensed store; minimum drinking age 21, Legal bar hours 7 a.m. to 1 a.m.

Motorists' laws ● Safety belts required for drivers and front seat passengers. Children under five or weighing less than 40 pounds must be secured by child restraints in vehicles. Helmets required for motorcyclists under 18. Speed limit is 65 to 70 mph (as posted) on rural freeways and 55 mph on most urban freeways and other highways. Highway patrolmen use radar, and to even the score, radar detectors are permitted.

Road conditions ● Call (602) 279-2000 and punch R-O-A-D to learn about driving conditions.

Hunting and Fishing ● Out-of-state hunting and fishing licenses are available at most sporting goods stores. Anyone over 14 may get one; fees vary. State licenses aren't required on Indian reservations, but each has its own laws and permit fees; check before you go.

To learn more about Arizona, contact:

Arizona Office of Tourism, 1100 W. Washington St., Phoenix, AZ 85007; (800) 842-8257 or (602) 542-3618.

Arizona Game & Fish Department, 2222 W. Greenway Rd., Phoenix, AZ 85023; (602) 942-3000.

Arizona Wine Commission, 1688 W. Adams, Phoenix, AZ 85007; (602) 542-0968. (For a brochure listing the eight wineries in the state.)

Arizona State Parks, 1300 W. Washington St., Phoenix, AZ 85007; (602) 542-4174.

Arizona Travel Parks Association, P.O. Box 11090-275, Phoenix, AZ 85061-1090; (602) 230-1126.

Native American Tourism Center, 4130 N. Goldwater Blvd., Suite 114, Scottsdale, AZ 85281; (602) 945-0771.

U.S. Bureau of Land Management, 3707 N. Seventh St., Phoenix, AZ 85014; (602) 650-0504.

THE WATCHTOWER

Chapter two

THE GRAND CANYON
Meeting America's greatest gorge

WE BEGIN our Arizona exploration with the state's most famous attraction—that magnificent 227-mile chasm across the northwest corner. It has become, through the years, our favorite place on the planet.

Yet, when we first visited Grand Canyon National Park many years ago, we were vaguely disappointed. We dutifully drove to Mather Point at the South Rim, shouldered up to the railing between six tour bus groups and looked down. There it was, just the way we figured it would be. It was impressive but we'd already seen it a thousand times—on postcards and posters, in TV travelogues, and on poorly composed slides at our next-door neighbor's house.

It's difficult to be dazzled by something that has been paraded before your eyes since childhood. Or perhaps we were simply overwhelmed at seeing it in full dimension. Naturalist Joseph Wood Krutch, on viewing the canyon for the first time, also had a curious reaction:

At first glance the spectacle seems too strange to be real. Because one has never seen anything like it, because one has nothing to compare it with, it stuns the eye but cannot really hold the attention. For a time it is too much like a scale model or an optical illusion. Because we cannot relate ourselves to it, we remain outside, very much as we remain outside the frame of a picture. *

*From *The Grand Canyon: Today and All Its Yesterdays*, written in 1957; © 1989 by the University of Arizona Press

31

Our first visit to the canyon was was brief—a stopover enroute to somewhere else. Later we came for a better look and, at the suggestion of a ranger, we drove to Hopi Point to watch the sunset. Here, on this peninsula projecting into the chasm, we were no longer merely on the edge. The canyon seemed to reach up and surround us. We watched the most incredible light and shadow show we'd ever seen. The receding light turned the Grand Canyon into a palette of colors—red and blue-gray and burnt orange and soft yellow; purples, pinks and tawny browns too subtle for a camera. Deep shadows accented the canyon's complex shapes. This stunning scene changed constantly—like time-lapse photography—as the light and shadows shifted. Finally, the canyon was veiled in dark purple and the sky was as pink as Mae West's *boudoir*.

Through the years, we've flown above and hiked down into the chasm; we've run the turbulent waters of Rio Colorado. We've hiked rim-to-rim in both directions. We have discovered a complex and ever-changing wonderland—not a canyon, but hundreds of canyons, weaving a fantastic webwork of terraced buttes, pinnacles and ridges. If you explore *El Grande* as we do—from within as well as from the edge, at sunup and sundown, in sunshine and in rain—you will never see the same view twice. You will never tire of nature's grandest spectacle.

"To get into the picture," Krutch wrote, "one must relate oneself to it..." And certainly, we have.

If we were visiting the Grand Canyon for the first time, we'd arrive after dark and go straight to our lodgings. We'd get a good night's sleep, rise before dawn and catch our first view of the chasm at first light. We'd watch the canyon come alive before our eyes.

Showing its age?

How does one determine the age of the Grand Canyon? Do we begin with the Vishnu schist, the two-billion-year-old Precambrian rock at the bottom? Or was the canyon born only a few million years ago when the Colorado River began carving a path through the Kaibab Plateau?

Geologists agree that this dramatic canyon was created by the river's cutting action, and the gradual uplifting of the Kaibab Plateau allowed it to cut much more deeply than if the land had been stable. The Kaibab is part of the great Colorado Plateau, whose restless shifting has created magnificent landforms in northern Arizona, Nevada, Utah and New Mexico. The plateau isn't flat; it's slightly domed and sloping to the southwest.

A question is still unanswered regarding the canyon's formation: How did the river get over the hump to ultimately reach the Gulf of California? One theory holds that two rivers, the ancestral Colorado and the Hualapai, flowed in opposite directions, each originating high on the plateau. The Hualapai reached the Gulf of California while the Colorado emptied into a huge inland sea that geologists call Bidahochi. As the rivers flowed, they eroded further back into the Kaibab until only the crest of the plateau separated them. Then, the Colorado backed up from its inland sea and spilled over the crest, where it was "pirated" by the Hualapai. This may have occurred about twelve million years ago.

Geologists call this the "Stream Piracy Theory." And it's still just a theory, not accepted by all scientists or park naturalists.

However it was formed, it is the most extraordinary geological feature on the planet. Nowhere else has more than a billion years of the earth's calendar

TRIP PLANNER

IMPORTANT: Reserve *very early* for Grand Canyon lodgings and camping in summer, particularly for Phantom Ranch—up to a year in advance.

WHEN TO GO ● Best of all, you'll love the fall, when the park is uncrowded and the weather is crisp and clear. The South Rim is open year around. Elevation is 7,000 feet so take a warm wrap, even in summer; it often snows in winter. The North Rim, one to two thousand feet higher, is closed in winter. Its facilities are open mid-May through mid-October and park roads remain open until closed by snow, generally by December. The road to Jacob Lake, U.S. Highway 89, is kept open. The park entrance fee is $10 per vehicle or $4 per biker or hiker without a vehicle, good for seven days. Free for holders of Golden Age (senior citizen) or Golden Access (handicapped) passes.

WHAT TO SEE ● On the North Rim, viewpoints at Bright Angel, Point Imperial, Angel's Window and Cape Royal. At the South Rim, viewpoints at (reading from west to east) Hermits Rest, Hopi Point, Yaki Point, Mather Point, Grandview Point and Desert View. Also, catch the show at the Grand Canyon IMAX Theater in Tusayan and check out the visitor center museum and Yavapai Geological Museum.

WHAT TO DO ● On the North Rim, hike the Cliff Springs, North Kaibab and Ken Patrick trails; relax in a rocking chair on the flagstone patio of Grand Canyon Lodge and watch the light change in the canyon. At the South Rim, hike the South Kaibab, Grandview, Hermit and Rim trails. Also, take the Grand Canyon Railway from Williams to Grand Canyon Village.

☺ *Indicates an attraction, restaurant or lodging with special appeal.*

USEFUL CONTACTS

Superintendent, Grand Canyon National Park, P.O. Box 129, Grand Canyon, AZ 86023.

Backcountry Office, P.O. Box 129, Grand Canyon, AZ 86023 (Backcountry hiking and camping reservations only by mail or in person.)

Grand Canyon National Park Lodges (South Rim, Trailer Village and Phantom Ranch reservations), P.O. Box 699, Grand Canyon, AZ 86023; (520) 638-2401 or (520) 638-2631.

TW Recreational Services, Inc. (North rim reservations), P.O. Box 400, Cedar City, UT 84720; (801) 586-7686.

Essential phone numbers (520 unless otherwise indicated)

South Rim park information—638-7888/638-7770
North Rim park information—638-7864
South Rim lodging reservations—638-2401
North Rim lodging reservations—638-2611 or (801) 586-7686
South Rim camping reservations—(800) 365-CAMP.
Park road conditions (recorded)—638-2245
Scheduled activities (recorded)—638-9304

AREA RADIO STATIONS: North Rim

KCCK-FM, 101.1, Kanab, Utah—Country, popular.
KREC-FM, 98.1, St. George, Utah—Light rock, top 40.
KUVR-FM, 90.1, Salt Lake (local booster)—National Public Radio.
KXAZ-FM, 93.5, Page—Easy listening and new wave.

South Rim

KSGC-FM, 92.1, Tusayan—old and new top 40.
KMGN-FM, 93.9, Flagstaff—Talk, news & popular music.
KNAU-FM, 89.7, Flagstaff—National Public Radio.
KAFF-FM, 92.9, Flagstaff—Country & Western.
KVNA-FM, 97.5, Flagstaff—Light rock.
KVNA-AM, 690, Flagstaff—"Golden oldies."

been exposed to public view with one gigantic slash of nature's knife. The cutting of the river created not only the world's deepest gorge but two distinct regions. Because of elevation differences and the river barrier, unique species developed on each side of the canyon. For instance, the higher, wetter North Rim is home to the Kaibab squirrel, a black-coated critter with a glowing white tail. Found nowhere else on earth, it's an obvious evolutionary cousin to the dark brown Abert squirrel, which scampers about the South Rim.

Since the North Rim is higher—at nearly 9,000 feet—and catches more rainfall, it is much more eroded than the lower South Rim. And because the plateau slopes from northeast to southwest, rainfall along the North Rim flows *into* the canyon, while South Rim rain flows *away* from it. A cross-section would show a lopsided ravine, with the south side much more precipitous than the north. The river is twice as far from the North Rim as it is from the south. Any cross-canyon hiker who has strolled down the gently convoluted side canyons of the North Rim, then gasped and struggled up steep South Rim switchbacks, can verify this fact.

Patient canyon-watchers say the Grand is getting six inches wider every year, with four inches eroding off North Rim cliffs and two inches coming off the southern edge. The canyon, on average, is about ten miles wide.

This gap separates northwestern Arizona from the rest of the state. And it separated many early travelers from their appointed destinations. In fact, some explorers didn't think the big ravine was grand at all. Many considered it a pesky wasteland and an obstacle to travel.

A Nineteenth century explorer, Reverend C.B. Spencer, wrote: "Horror! Tragedy! Silence! Death! Chaos! There is the awful canyon in five words." He'd obviously had trouble getting across. A contemporary of his, C.S. Gleed, agreed, dismissing it as "the grave of the world."

No one knows what prehistoric men and women thought as they descended the canyon's depths. Their petroglyphs depict hunting scenes and the passage of time, but they make no mention of canyon esthetics. A projectile point found in the park suggests that humans may have visited this area as far back as 10,000 years before Christ. A nomadic hunter-gatherer group identified as the "Desert Culture" occupied the area between 6,000 and 2,000 B.C. As evidence of their passing, they left small animal figurines made of split willows. One has been radiocarbon dated to around 2145 B.C.

Sometime before the birth of Christ, the Anasazi—probably descendants of the Desert Culture folks—began occupying both rims of the canyon and living in its depths as well. Hundreds of sites have been found here and elsewhere in northern Arizona. A clever group, the Anasazi practiced agriculture, allowing them to subsist deep within the gorge for extended periods. They grew seed grasses on riverside sand bars and on canyon mesas. Cliffside granaries and ruins of their stone houses have been found in several areas. Around the 12th century A.D., most of the Indians abandoned the chasm, probably because of drought or harassment by hostile neighbors.

The first Europeans to see the canyon, and much of the rest of the Southwest, were Spanish conquistadors. Exploration was prompted by rumors of golden cities that lay to the north of Mexico. As Francisco Vásquez de Coronado made his epic trek through present-day Arizona in 1540, he dispatched García López de Cárdenas to find an Indian village supposedly situated near a great river canyon. Guided by Hopi Indians from a pueblo called Tusayan,

This Grand Canyon panorama is from Horseshoe Mesa, off Grandview Trail.

Cardenas and his group hiked for 20 days and finally reached the South Rim. They were unable to reach the river itself and, after several attempts, they returned to the main party.

More than two centuries passed before another group of outsiders—also Spanish—concerned themselves with the Grand Canyon. In June, 1776, Father Francisco Tomás Garcés visited the canyon while trying to find a land route between Mission San Xavier del Bac, south of Tucson, and Mission San Gabriel in southern California. Passing near Rio Colorado, he came across a group of Havasupai Indians and accompanied them to their village in the canyon. He obviously didn't care much for the trip down. He fussed in his diary that he had to follow a dangerous path with "a very lofty cliff" on one side and "a horrible abyss" on the other. Today's trail into that same Havasu Canyon has been considerably improved.

Frey Eusebio Francisco Kino, who spent 24 years establishing missions in the Southwest, never visited the canyon. However, he is credited with naming the river which formed it, after crossing the stream near present-day Yuma in 1701. Rio Colorado—Red River—was inspired by the reddish silt churned up by the swift-moving current.

One James Ohio Pattie may have been the first American to see the canyon. He and a party of French and American trappers bumped into the North Rim in 1826. Like the Spanish, he didn't care much for it. After spending 13 days in a futile search for a crossing, he wrote:

The river emerges from these horrid mountains, which so cage it up, as to deprive all human beings of the ability to descend to its banks, and make use of its waters.

There are no mountains—horrid or otherwise—flanking the canyon. He may have been referring to the complex buttes and ridges cut into the rugged north rim. It was daring, one-armed Civil War veteran John Wesley Powell who finally put the Grand Canyon on the map, with his famous down-river trip in 1869. Powell had lost his right forearm during the Battle of Shiloh. He went on to serve with valor at Vicksburg and Nashville before being discharged from the Union Army with the rank of major. He kept the title and headed west for an exploration of the Rocky Mountains.

Intrigued by the great Western wilderness, he sought government sponsorship of an expedition down the Colorado River. The Feds showed little interest, but President Ulysses S. Grant did authorize him to draw Army rations for the trip. With Army chow and $500 contributed by a science academy and two Illinois universities, Powell began his trip on the Green River, the Colorado's major tributary.

Ten men left Green River, Wyoming, on May 24, 1869, but only six completed the historic run through the Grand Canyon. One quit early, after a boat capsized on the Green. Toward the end of the trip, three more, frightened and demoralized by the Grand Canyon's wicked rapids, decided to hike out to a Mormon settlement. Powell and his five remaining companions completed the run without incident, for they had already passed the worst of the rapids. The three hikers were never seen again. They may have been killed by Shivwits Indians, possibly as revenge because some white prospectors may have abused their women.

Powell and his men completed their epic voyage on August 30, taking out at the mouth of the Virgin River, about 50 miles southeast of Las Vegas. They had covered 1,048 river miles in 98 days, including 24 days in the Grand Canyon. His crew didn't run all of the Grand's rapids—a feat accomplished routinely by river-runners today. His heavy plank boats, difficult to handle in white water, were portaged around or roped down most of the larger cataracts. But he did accomplish what none had done before: He had traveled the length of the Grand Canyon.

The one-armed adventurer made another trip in 1871. Later, he became director of the U.S. Geological Survey and a founder of the Geological Society of America. He died in 1902 at the age of 68.

Then came the tourists

Grand Canyon tourism began with the arrival of a lively, tale spinning character named John Hance in the early 1880s. He built a log cabin on the South Rim, near the present Grand Canyon Village, and led tours into the canyon. In 1901, the Santa Fe Railroad completed a spur line to the South Rim from Williams. A fellow named Fred Harvey, who'd gotten his start by opening a restaurant in a Topeka railroad station, built the elegantly rustic El Tovar Hotel and other facilities. Soon, tourism was in full swing. It hasn't abated since, drawing nearly five million visitors a year. The Fred Harvey Company, now under different corporate ownership, remains the main concessionaire. El Tovar, still open for business, has been designated as a National Historic Landmark.

Despite its popularity, the Grand Canyon didn't become a national park until February 26, 1919. President Theodore Roosevelt, impressed after a visit to the area, created Grand Canyon Game Preserve in 1906. It was given national monument status two years later. Through the years, its size has been doubled to its present 1,904 square miles.

"Do nothing to mar its grandeur," Teddy said. "Keep it for your children and your children's children, and all who come after you, as the one great sight which every American should see."

Grand Canyon
National Park

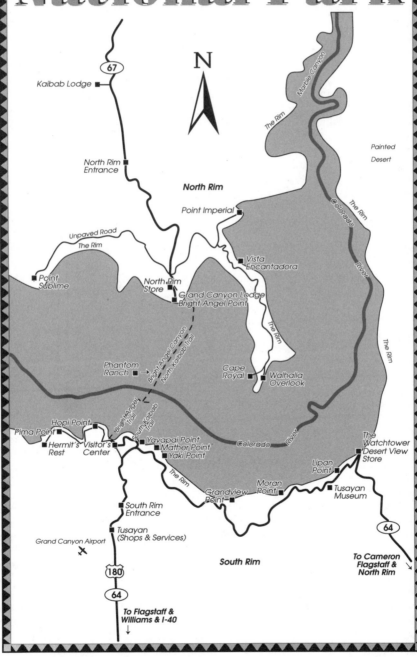

THE CANYON TODAY

Like most older national parks, Grand Canyon provides a plentitude of developed visitor facilities. (Some say it's overdeveloped. Does a national park really need a dozen gift shops?)

Visitor complexes at the north and south rims offer lodging, camping, restaurants, ranger programs and hikes, mule rides and all those gift shops. In addition, the village of Tusayan (pronounced *TOOSIE-yan*), just outside the South Rim entrance, has more lodging, camping and restaurants and a wide screen movie about the canyon. And, good grief, there's even a McDonald's.

Squadrons of airplanes and helicopters provide scenic flights over the canyon (more than 100,000 a year!), from Grand Canyon Airport at Tusayan, as well as from Williams, Page, Las Vegas, Flagstaff and even far-away Phoenix. Because of strong objections by environmentalists and a couple of tragic crashes, flights are restricted to certain areas of the canyon, and planes cannot dip below the rim.

Does this place sound busy? It is! Particularly in summer, when swarms of American tourists rub elbows with thousands of foreign tourists, all jockeying for a better view of the Hopi Point sunset. It's difficult to have a wilderness experience while hearing the babble of many tongues and inhaling diesel exhaust from tour buses.

There are better ways—beautiful ways—to experience the Grand Canyon. Try to go during the off-season. Fall is wonderful and spring is nice, too. The South Rim can be both peaceful and stunning in winter, when snow dusts the parapets of the great canyon. Bring your down jacket.

Leave the popular viewpoints and walk the Rim Trail, particularly along the West Rim. Or, simply walk a few hundred feet down one of the trails from the rim, find a peaceful perch and drink in the grandeur. (This doesn't work on the Bright Angel Trail. In summer, it's as busy as San Francisco's Market Street.)

Actually, the best way to avoid the crowds is to visit the North Rim, which gets one-tenth as many visitors as the South Rim. It's our favorite side of the canyon. And because we play favorites in this book, that is where our exploration begins. This must be a spring through fall trip, since winter snow closes the North Rim road at Jacob Lake.

RV and camping advisories

North Rim parking ● The climb to the North Rim is gradual and easily negotiable for any size rig. Midsized RVs will will fit in most parking lots, although North Rim parking is rather limited for big rigs, trailers and fifth wheels.

North Rim camping ● Sites can be reserved in advance at the North Rim campground by calling (800) 365-CAMP. Sites outside the park are avilable at De Motte and Jacob Lake forest service campgrounds on Highway 67 and Kaibab Lodge Camper Village at Jacob Lake. Without reservations, the best odds are Jacob Lake Campground (arrive before noon) and Camper Village. De Motte, closer to the park, fills up very early. (See specifics under "Where to camp" below.)

South Rim parking ● A parking lot below Thunderbird Lodge near the railroad station will accommodate RVs. To reach it, follow the main drive west past the park lodges to the West Rim Drive interchange (at the West

Rim shuttle stop) and loop back along the railroad tracks, following signs with RV icons. However, the lot isn't reserved *specifically* for RVs and often fills up with passenger cars. In a pinch, retreat to the large Babbitt general store parking lot across the main road from park headquarters. Turn south toward Mather campground and then left into the parking lot.

South Rim camping ● Mather Campground in the park is a tough ticket without reservations, which must be obtained far in advance by calling (800) 365-CAMP. Some spots may be available at Trailer Village, operated by the Fred Harvey Company, (520) 638-2401. Outside the park, try Grand Canyon Camper Village in Tusayan, which accepts reservations. The U.S. Forest Service Ten X campground, two miles south, is on a first-come basis; sites generally are available if you arrive before noon. Expansion of the campground is planned in the near future.

THE NORTH RIM
Elevation: 7,450 to 8,800 feet

The North Rim approach will be from the Arizona Strip, that remote slice of rolling desert in the state's northwestern corner. We explore this area in detail in the next chapter. Crossing the strip on U.S. 89A, you'll leave the desert and begin climbing into thick piñon-juniper woodlands and attractive meadowlands of Kaibab National Forest. At the small settlement of **Jacob Lake**, pick up State Route 67 and head south and uphill into the park, which is still more than 40 miles away.

Note: If it's summer and you haven't made camping or lodging reservations in the park, you may still be able to find space at Jacob Lake Inn or one of the campgrounds in the area. The large Forest Service campground fills up daily in summer, although generally not until afternoon. Also, space is often available at the commercial Kaibab Lodge Camper Village, which offers full hookups. (See "Where to recline" and "Where to camp" below.)

Continuing on to the park, the first thing you should do is scan through a copy of *The Guide,* which you'll get at the entrance station. This seasonal newspaper, with special editions for the north and south rim, lists ranger activities, lodging, camping, transportation, food and drink, medical services, lost and found, backcountry hikes, background information and maps. *The Guide* is so complete that you almost don't need this book. But you'd miss the clever writing.

The main difference between the north and south rims, other than crowds and elevation, is that most North Rim vista points are on peninsulas that thrust out into the main chasm. They were formed by deep side canyons cut by centuries of erosion. The South Rim is more of an long, irregular amphitheater. The north side, incidentally, comprises sixty percent of the park area. Only ten to eleven miles separate the two rims here, as the canyon raven flies. However, it's 215 road miles to the South Rim, via Lees Ferry. Shuttles between the rims are available in summer. (See "Transit" listings in the South Rim section.)

North Rim visitor facilities are clustered around Bright Angel Point. Although they aren't nearly as extensive as those across the gorge, they provide all of the basic needs. The center of North Rim activity is Grand Canyon Lodge, one of those rustically elegant log castles typical of our older national parks. It provides splendid views from its flagstone terraces and dining room; see listings below under "Attractions" and "Where to dine." It also serves as

GRAND CANYON CROSS-SECTION: A SLICE OF THE SOUTH RIM

FORMATION	FEET THICK	LANDFORM	DEPOSITS	DESCRIPTION	GEOLOGIC TIME ERA	PERIOD
MOENKOPI FORMATION	400	GENTLE SLOPE, CONCAVE	TIDAL FLAT	Canyon rim: light red to dark brown siltstone, shale and mudstone. Reptile tracks.	Mesozoic	Triassic
KAIBAB LIMESTONE	300	SHEER FACE	MARINE	Light gray limestone; marine fossils	Paleozoic	Permian
TOROWEAP FORMATION	250	SHEER FACE	MARINE	Mix of grayish limestone, siltstone beds, mudstone and sandstone; marine fossils.	Paleozoic	Permian
COCONINO SANDSTONE	300	SHEER FACE	DESERT SANDS	Cross-bedded light tan sandstone; fossil tracks.	Paleozoic	Permian
HERMIT SHALE	300	STEEP SLOPE	SAVANNAH	Reddish shale, siltstone and mudstone; fossil plants.	Paleozoic	Permian
SUPAI GROUP	900	LEDGES AND SLOPES	FLOOD PLAIN	Red-colored sandstone, siltstone, shale and limestone; fossil plants and animal tracks.	Paleozoic	Permian and Pennsylvanian
REDWALL LIMESTONE	500	SHEER FACE	MARINE	Limestone stained red by overlying Supai sandstone and Hermit shale; marine fossils and limestone caves.	Paleozoic	Mississippian
TEMPLE BUTTE LIMESTONE	30	SHEER FACE	MARINE	Limestone, soft purple to pinkish gray; fossils rare.	Paleozoic	Devonian
MUAV LIMESTONE	600	CLIFFS, LEDGES, SLOPES	MARINE	Yellow-gray limestone and siltstone; triobite fossils and wave-action ripples.	Paleozoic	Cambrian
BRIGHT ANGEL SHALE	350-400	LOW SLOPE BENCH	MARINE	Gray-green shale; trilobite and brachiopod fossils; tracks and trails of trilobites and sea worms.	Paleozoic	Cambrian
TAPEATS SANDSTONE	100-300	CLIFF	MARINE	Textured brown sandstone; marine animal track fossils.	Paleozoic	Cambrian
GRAND CANYON SUPERGROUP	UNKNOWN	INNER GORGE	MARINE	Mix of sandstone, limestone, siltstone and shale.	Precambrian	Late
VISHNU SCHIST	UNKNOWN	COLORADO RIVER	MARINE, METAMORPHISM, MOLTEN INTRUSIONS	Dark Precambrian schists and gneisses; intrusion from pink and white granite dikes and sills.	Precambrian	Early

the North Rim visitor center and the booking office for mule rides and other activities. A saloon, curio shop, rustic cabins and motel-type units complete the lodge complex. Other North Rim facilities include a gasoline station, groceries and national park campground. Ranger programs and hikes are available during the North Rim's mid-May to mid-October season.

ATTRACTIONS

Of course, the canyon is the attraction. You can observe it from several viewpoints reached by auto or on foot. A 21-mile road winds easterly from the visitor area to several vista points.

☺ **Bright Angel Point** • *Reached by a quarter-mile walk along a paved path from Grand Canyon Lodge, or from the visitor area parking lot.* ☐ Projecting into Bright Angel Canyon, Bright Angel Point is a fine place to witness the sunrise or sunset, with lots of formations to capture the moving shadows. From this vantage point you can see—and hear—Roaring Springs far below in Roaring Springs Canyon. The springs provide water for north and south rim visitor facilities.

Roaring Springs empties into Bright Angel Creek, named by Powell because of its crystalline waters. Bright Angel and Garden Creek on the South Rim are part of a fault line that form major side-canyons. Lest you become confused, the North Kaibab Trail follows Bright Angel Canyon down from the North Rim. It connects with the Bright Angel Trail, which follow Garden Creek Canyon up to the South Rim. And yes, the names are confusing.

☺ **Point Imperial** • *Eleven miles from the lodge.* ☐ Point Imperial is the highest vantage point in the park, at 8,803 feet. It offers a panoramic sweep of the eastern end of the Grand Canyon and Marble Canyon to the northeast. You can see the great Marble Platform—flat as a table top—and the abrupt drop- off of Marble Canyon. Pastel hints of the Painted Desert are farther to the east. To the north are the Vermilion Cliffs, a dramatic red escarpment that extends for 50 miles across the Arizona Strip.

☺ **Cape Royal and Angel's Window viewpoints** • *About 23 miles from the lodge.* ☐ From Point Imperial, retreat to a "Y" intersection, then follow another winding road to Cape Royal, about 23 miles from the lodge. The end-of-road parking area leads to a pair of lookouts—Cape Royal and Angel's Window. Like Point Imperial, Cape Royal provides a large slice of the eastern Grand Canyon, projecting far out onto the Walhalla Plateau. Angel's Window, reached by the same trail, is a giant peephole through a long, narrow ridge. You can stroll onto the ridge—above the window—for more canyon vistas.

Several turnouts on the way to Point Imperial and Cape Royal are worthy of a stop. At **Vista Encantadora** on the road to Cape Royal, a great razorback ridge rises in the foreground, with buttes and pinnacles beyond. The picture is equally impressive from nearby **Walhalla Overlook**; across the road are the ruins of a five-room Anasazi condo.

Toroweap • *Outside the main park area, reached by bumping 65 miles over a dirt road.* ☐ The route to Toroweap overlook branches south from State Highway 389, nine miles west of Fredonia and about 80 miles from the North Rim entrance station. Watch for a sign reading "Mt. Trumbull 53 miles." In good weather, it's navigable by a carefully driven car, but you'd feel more comfortable in a 4-wheel drive, and it's *not* RV country. It's impassable in wet weather. Your reward for all that bumpity driving is an uncrowded overlook with an impressive canyon view. The gorge falls away 3,000 feet and the river glistens directly below. You can camp free at a primitive site near the overlook. Spaces are on a first come, first served basis. There is no water, provisions or gasoline along this route, so go prepared. Snow may block the road in winter and summer thunder showers can render it temporarily impassable.

Fall color ● The North Rim becomes a spectacular showplace of aspen in the fall, with white bark and yellow leaves glittering against the canyon background. The slender, shimmering trees line the roads to Point Imperial and Cape Royal. Highway 67 leading through Kaibab National Forest also has splashes of color. Because of the high elevation, fall color comes early— usually by mid-September.

☺ **Grand Canyon Lodge ●** This is one of those classic national park hotels built of log and stone, earlier in this century. A rough stone fireplace dominates the lobby, and the ceiling above is a fascinating webwork of log trusses. The lobby and dining room are perched on the edge of the canyon; tall picture windows offer awesome views. Also, one can adjourn to a stone patio and enjoy the vistas from wicker rocking chairs.

THE BEST HIKING TRAILS

Several trails follow the peninsular contours of the North Rim. The North Kaibab Trail ventures deep into the heart of the canyon, and links with the Bright Angel Trail to permit a rim-to-rim hike, taken by hundreds every year. The hike usually takes two to three days and reservations are required for overnight camping or Phantom Ranch lodging. They must be obtained *far in advance;* see "Trip Planner" at the front of this chapter. Pick up a copy of the *Back Country Trip Planner* for details on hiking and overnight reservation requirements.

WARNING: When hiking into the canyon, *always* carry plenty of water and food snacks to maintain your energy level, and wear a shade hat. This is vitally important in summer, particularly if you leave the rim, since you'll be hiking down into desert climate zones where temperatures routinely top 100 degrees. Every year, hundreds of hikers are toppled by thirst and heat-exhaustion; some have died.

Wear clothes in layers that can be peeled and added, since temperatures can change quickly. Allow sufficient time for your uphill return. The rule of thumb, if you're in average shape, is to figure twice as much time to climb out as it took to go down. You don't want to be caught stumbling up a narrow trail in darkness. Finally, remember that a permit is required from the Backcountry Office for any overnight trips into the canyon.

☺ **Cliff Springs Trail ●** *Moderately easy hiking; about three miles round trip. Trailhead is a third of a mile from the Cape Royal parking area.* ⊓ Cliff Springs is our North Rim favorite, and the most unheralded trail in the park. You have to be watchful for the trailhead. Look for a small brown sign on a sweeping turn in the road just before the Cape Royal parking lot. There's limited parking available at a turnout.

The trail begins modestly, passing through a shallow forest ravine. Then it tucks under the dramatic overhang of a redwall cliff for several hundred yards before reaching the dripping springs for which it was named. The trail ends here although you can continue farther on an unmaintained trail. It follows a red rock ridge into a rough-hewn side canyon, offering great views of

THE CANYON FROM RIM TO RIM

For a total canyon experience, hike from one rim to the other. The North Kaibab and Bright Angel trails meet at the Colorado River to offer this popular rim-to-rim trek. And don't worry; there's a bridge across the stream. We'd recommend hiking north to south, since the North Rim is more than a thousand feet higher than the South Rim.

A cross-canyon hike requires advance planning. It's a two or three-day trip, covering more than 23 miles, so you'll need somewhere to spend the night. Phantom Ranch has rustic accommodations in rooms or dormitories, and meals. Backpackers can camp at Bright Angel Campground or other designated camping sites in the inner canyon. *Reservations for Phantom Ranch or inner canyon campgrounds must be made months in advance.* And of course, you'll have to arrange for a cross-canyon shuttle; see below.

The hike down from the North Rim descends through pine forests to Bright Angel Creek, which leads to Phantom Ranch and the Colorado River. It's 14.2 miles from the North Kaibab trailhead to the river, and you'll drop more than a mile in elevation. You'll want to get an early start the next morning, since it's 9.3 miles from Phantom to the top of Bright Angel Trail. And nearly eight miles of it is uphill. The steepest part comes at the end—a grueling series of switchbacks. Fortunately, there are water and rest stops at Indian Garden about halfway up, then every mile and a half until you each the top.

Phantom Ranch reservations (including meals) • Grand Canyon National Park Lodges, P.O. Box 699, Grand Canyon, AZ 86023; (520) 638-2401. Cabins are $53 for one or two and dormitory beds are $19 each. Meals are $8.50 for breakfast, $6.50 for a sack lunch, $14 for a stew dinner or $23.50 for a steak dinner. Because of heavy booking, give several alternate dates. The best way is to phone and see what dates are available. Meals, which must be arranged in advance, are available for campers as well as for those who stay in the cabins or dorms.

Inner canyon camping reservations • Backcountry Office, Box 129, Grand Canyon, AZ 86023. Again, get a copy of the *Backcountry Trip Planner,* apply early and have alternate dates.

Cross-canyon shuttle • You can catch the daily Trans Canyon shuttle between the north and south rims for $60 one way (or $100 round trip), May through October, or until the North Rim closes. It departs the North Rim's Grand Canyon Lodge at 7 a.m., arrives at the South Rim's Bright Angel Lodge at 11:30, starts for the North Rim at 1:30, arriving at 6 p.m. For reservations, call (520) 638-2820, or you can book at any transportation desk or write: Trans Canyon, P.O. Box 348, Grand Canyon, AZ 86023.

sculpted limestone and sandstone formations. Since it's not maintained, this portion is a bit rough, although it's navigable, with care.

North Kaibab Trail • *Steep, some cliff exposure in the upper part; about 15 miles to the river. Trailhead is just over two miles north of the visitor area on the main road.* ☐ From the rim, this trail takes you along a dramatic cliff edge to Roaring Springs. It then enters Bright Angel Canyon, following Bright Angel Creek into the Precambrian schists of the inner canyon. After about 13 miles, you'll reach Phantom Ranch and Bright Angel Campground. It's another mile and a half to the river.

Don't try to make it to the river and back, unless you've made overnight arrangements at Phantom Ranch or an inner canyon campground. However, shorter sections of the trail provide rich variety for day-trippers. If you're in good shape, you can probably make it from the North Rim to Cottonwood Campground, a 14-mile round trip. Cottonwood has fresh water, and a staffed ranger station in summer. For the rest of us, the 9.4-mile round trip to Roaring Springs will be a good day's work. You'll have to recover an elevation loss of more than 3,000 feet.

An unpleasant aspect of this trail is the constant parade of mules that take riders down to Roaring Springs. Hikers must stop frequently to let them pass, and they've turned sections of the trail into an open sewer. We've often wondered why the concessionaires aren't required to use some of their profits to clean up their mess.

Ken Patrick Trail ● *Easy hiking; ten miles one way. Trailhead is in the North Kaibab parking lot.* ☐ This rather level path follows the rim to Point Imperial, ducking in an out of forests with frequent canyon views. It's an ideal day hike if you have a car shuttle. If you want to go only part way on the trail, start your hike at the Point Imperial end. This offers the best canyon vistas. The trail was named for Ken Patrick, who once served at the Grand Canyon, then was transferred to Point Reyes National Seashore near San Francisco. There, he became the first ranger in the history of the National Park Service to be murdered in the line of duty. He was killed when he encountered some poachers.

Other trails

Widforss Trail ● *Moderately easy; some elevation change; ten-mile round trip. Trailhead is 2.7 miles north of the visitor area, then half a mile west on a dirt road.* ☐ This trail takes hikers to little-visited areas of the canyon and is thus refreshingly uncrowded. However, much of the route is buried in thick forest. It does allow occasional vistas of Transept Canyon. It then emerges onto the rim of the main canyon and passes incredible pinnacles that look like carelessly stacked building blocks, ready to fall. At Widforss Point, you see a pleasant—if not awesome—view of North Rim formations and the pencil-line ridge of the South Rim across the chasm. If you're short on time, hike to the pinnacle area, then start back just before the trail swings away from the rim to re-enter the forest. The round trip will take two to three hours.

Uncle Jim Trail ● *Easy hiking; five-mile round trip.* ☐ This is a loop trail to a canyon overlook, which spurs off the Ken Patrick Trail about a mile from the North Kaibab trailhead. After passing through a forest, it emerges for nice views of Roaring Springs Canyon and the eastern reaches of the Grand Canyon. In case you wondered, the trail was named for Jim Owens, a friendly uncle of a man who was the first warden of the Grand Canyon Game Preserve until it became a national park.

ACTIVITIES

Bike tours ● *Backroads, 1516 Fifth St., Berkeley, CA 94710-1740; (800) 462-2848 or (510) 527-1555.* ☐ This firm, which specializes in active vacations, offers guided bike tours from Utah's Brian Head, Zion and Bryce Canyon nationl parks to the Grand Canyon's North Rim. Both camping and hotel versions of the trip are available; accompanying vans carry guests' gear.

North Kaibab mule rides • *Contact Grand Canyon Trail Rides, c/o Grand Canyon Lodge, (520) 638-2292, or P.O. Box 128, Tropic, UT 84776.* ☐ Full day trips to Roaring Springs are $85 per person, including lunch. Half-day trips to Uncle Jim's Point are $35 and one-hour rides along the rim are $12.

Cross-Country skiing • *North Rim Nordic Center at Kaibab Lodge, c/o Canyoneers, Inc., P.O. Box 2997, Flagstaff, AZ 86003; (800) 525-0924 or (520) 526-0924.* ☐ From December 1 to April 1, Canyoneers has cross-country skiing on a 60-K trail system, plus two to four night all inclusive ski vacations, including some to the North Rim. Several other winter packages are available, such as rooms and meals at North Kaibab Lodge, snowvan tours and overnight yurt tours. Write or call for a detailed brochure.

Hikers shuttle • During the summer, a shuttle runs between Grand Canyon Lodge and the North Kaibab trailhead, from 6 a.m. to 8 p.m. daily. The cost is $5 for one person, plus $2 for additional members of your group. Get tickets at the lodge.

Whitewater raft trips • Seventeen national park service concessionaires offer rafting trips; they're listed in the park's *Trip Planner* publication.

WHERE TO DINE

Grand Canyon Lodge Dining Room • ☆☆☆ $$

☐ *In Grand Canyon Lodge, North Rim; (520) 638-2612, ext. 160. American; full bar service. Also an informal cafeteria. Breakfast 6:30 to 10 a.m.; lunch 11:30 to 2:30; dinner 5 to 9:30; reservations advised for dining room. Major credit cards.* ☐ Plan at least one meal in this grand old high-ceiling dining room with its picture-window views of the canyon. It serves hearty breakfasts and lunches and a variety of American and continental multi-course dinners. For thrift, try the cafeteria.

Jacob Lake Inn Dining Room • ☆☆ $$

☐ *Jacob Lake, AZ 86022; (520) 643-7232. American; wine and beer. 6:30 a.m. to 9 p.m.; shorter hours in winter. Major credit cards.* ☐ This informal, woodsy dining room serves generous portions of homestyle cooking.

☺ Kaibab Lodge Dining Room • ☆☆ $$

☐ *HC 64, Box 30, Fredonia, AZ 86022; (520) 638-2389. American; wine and beer. Breakfast from 6:30, dinner 6 to 9; dinner reservations required. Major credit cards.* ☐ Attractive alpine style dining room featuring babyback ribs, chicken fajitas and fish, steaks and chops.

WHERE TO RECLINE

Prices reflect high season rates and may be lower at other times. Most were provided by the management and are subject to change; use them only as a guide.

☺ Grand Canyon Lodge • ☆ to ☆☆☆ $$ Ø

☐ *C/o TW Recreational Services, P.O. Box 400, Cedar City, UT 84720; (801) 586-7686. Cabins and motel units, $53 to $82 for couples and singles, $69 to $97 for families. Major credit cards.* ☐ Grand Canyon Lodge has assorted accommodations, ranging from modern motel rooms to rustic cabins; some have canyon views. The lodge essentially serves as the North Rim's visitor center, with a transportation desk, saloon, ranger programs (not in the saloon, of course), park service information desk, dining room (listed above) and cafeteria.

Jacob Lake Inn ● ☆☆☆ $$

◻ Jacob Lake, AZ 86022; 643- 7232. Couples and singles $60 to $70; two-room units for families $75 to to $85. Major credit cards. ◻ Located in Kaibab National Forest at junction of highways 89A and 67, about 45 miles from the North Rim, Jacob Lake Inn has motel style units and some weathered cabins in a pleasant forest setting. **Dining room** (listed above); also a country store with groceries and provisions; playground. **Note:** The highway is kept open to Jacob Lake all year, although winter snow may close it temporarily.

☺ Kaibab Lodge ● ☆☆ $$$$

◻ HC 64, Box 30, Fredonia, AZ 86022; (520) 638-2389. For winter lodging and programs, contact Canyoneers, Inc., P.O. Box 2997, Flagstaff, AZ 86003; (800) 525-0924 or (520) 526-0924. Couples and singles $65 to $73, family units $78 to $95. Major credit cards. ◻ Attractive main lodge and several log cabins with private baths; tucked among the trees, five miles from the park boundary and about ten from the rim. Appealingly rustic **dining room** listed above. Reservations required for dinner.

The adjacent North Rim Country Store has fuel (including diesel), groceries and camping gear. Extensive winter ski-lodging-dining programs available through the North Rim Nordic Center.

WHERE TO CAMP
In the park

North Rim Campground ● Reservations available by calling (800) 365-CAMP; MC/VISA may be used to confirm space. ◻ Shaded spots with picnic tables and fire pans; no hookups; showers available nearby. Reservations should be made well in advance for summer. If you have no reservations, get there early in the day and hope for a spot to be vacated.

Outside the park

Demotte Campground ● C/o Kaibab National Forest, P.O. Box 248, Fredonia, AZ 86022; (520) 643-7395. RV and tent sites, no hookups, $10; half price for Golden Age and Access cardholders. No reservations. ◻ This is a national forest campground on the west side of State Highway 67, abc·:t 24 miles south of Jacob Lake and 20 miles from the North Rim. It has pit potties, picnic tables and barbecues. Open May to October; it fills up early on summer days.

Jacob Lake Campground ● C/o Kaibab National Forest, P.O. Box 248, Fredonia, AZ 86022; (520) 643-7395. RV and tent sites, no hookups, $10; half for Golden Age and Access cardholders. ◻ National forest campground across from Jacob Lake Lodge, at the junction of State Highway 67 and U.S. 89A; 44 miles from the North Rim. Potties, picnic tables, barbecues; dining room and groceries at nearby lodge. Open May to October. Spaces generally available in summer early in the day.

Kaibab Lodge Camper Village ● At Jacob Lake; mailing address P.O. Box 3331, Flagstaff, AZ 86003; in summer call (520) 643-7804; in winter (800) 525-0924 or (520) 526-0924. Full hookups $20 to $22, no hookups $12, tent sites $10. MC/VISA, DISC for reservation confirmation; cash only on site. ◻ Some pull-throughs, showers, picnic tables and fire pits, dump station, North Rim Country Store and hiking trails nearby. Located in a forested area near Jacob Lake Inn, just south of Jacob Lake Junction. Open mid-May until closed by snow.

THE SOUTH RIM
Elevation: 5,750 to 7,400 feet

When man sets about to preserve a wilderness, can civilization be far behind?

As you approach the park's south entrance on U.S. Highway 180, you'll pass through a commercial area called Tusayan, situated in Kaibab National Forest. It's basically in business to catch the overflow from park facilities. Busy Tusayan offers a campground, several motels, service stations, restaurants, a bowling alley and a restaurant-gift shop-theater complex called the Grand Canyon Experience, housed in ugly brown domes. And, yes, there's that McDonald's.

In Tusayan, you can book helicopter and fixed-wing canyon flights, which depart from chopper pads or from the nearby Grand Canyon Airport. Tusayan also is home to an excellent giant-screen movie, *Grand Canyon: The Hidden Secrets*. It offers a fine preview of what you're about to experience in the park.

Before entering the national park, you can pick up information on the surrounding Kaibab National Forest at the **Tusayan Ranger Station** near Moqui Lodge just outside the gate, open weekdays 8 to 10; (520) 638-2443.

Passing through the park gate, you might head for Mather Point for your first view—unless you've followed our earlier advice and arrived in the dark, to savor the canyon at sunrise. It isn't the most impressive canyon vista, but it will certainly whet your appetite. Then head west to the visitor center, or to the Yavapai Observation Station. You can learn about ranger walks, talks and campfire programs, inner canyon hiking, sunset and sunrise times, camping availability and just about anything else you need to know. *The Guide* newspaper, which probably was thrust into your hands at the gate, lists whatever the visitor center folks might have overlooked.

ATTRACTIONS
In the park

☺ *Sunups and sundowns* • *Various points along the canyon rim.* ❑ It may seem odd to list sunrises and sunsets as attractions, but then, this is an unusual guidebook. And certainly, the canyon is most beautiful during those times. Because you're on a plateau with no mountains or buildings to ruffle the horizon, sunups and sundowns are as clearly defined as they are at sea. Don't wait until the last minute to catch a sunset. The dramatic canyon lighting starts developing about two hours before. And in the morning, hang around for an hour after you've seen the sun peek over the horizon.

Several turnouts along the east and west rim drives provide fine sunup/sundown vantage points. Hopi Point is particularly popular for sunsets, while Yaki Point features spectacular sunrises. Our personal preferences are Hopi Overlook (a couple hundred yards beyond Hopi Point) for sunsets and Grandview Point for sunrises. Hopi Overlook is much less crowded than Hopi Point itself, and it offers a wonderful mix of formations to catch the late light. At Grandview Point, the sun bathes a great proscenium of the canyon with light and shadow. And you see a glittering bit of the Colorado River, like a distant jewel, far below you.

☺ *East Rim Drive* • *Grand Canyon Village to Desert View.* ❑ This 26-mile drive skirts much of the canyon's south rim, with frequent overlooks for

HOW TO SPEND YOUR SOUTH RIM DAYS

Half day • If this is all you can invest in Nature's grandest design, perhaps you don't deserve to see it. See the IMAX production, *Grand Canyon: The Hidden Secrets* at Tusayan, then go back to where you came from. Well, maybe you should drive out to Mather Point for a quick look, then follow the East Rim drive 26 miles to the Desert View exit. This will provide sufficient vistas to tempt you to return.

First day • Catch the IMAX show then stop at the visitors center for a park orientation; see the interpretive exhibits and slide shows there. Walk the 1.2-mile South Rim Trail from the visitors center to the Yavapai Observatioin Station; take the West Rim drive (via shuttle bus in summer) to Hermits Rest.

Second day • Experience a sunrise and sunset; take in one or more ranger walks and lectures. Walk the South Rim Trail from the visitors center west to Grand Canyon Village. There, view historic structures such as El Tovar Hotel, Bright Angel Lodge, Hopi House, Kolb Studio and Lookout Studio; walk at least a portion of the West Rim Trail.

Third day • Take a hike. Either of these will occupy most of a day: Hermit Trail to Lookout Point (eight-mile round-trip) or Grandview Trail to Horseshoe Mesa (six-mile round-trip), with a pause for a picnic lunch at your turn-around point.

Fourth day • Resting up from yesterday's hike, visit the Fred Harvey history museum in the Bright Angel Lodge. Drive to Tusayan to prowl the gift shops and arrange a horseback ride or Grand Canyon flight there; do a couple more ranger talks.

Fifth day • You're in good shape now, so it's time for a *serious* hike! Take the South Kaibab Trail to the Tonto Trail junction, cross the Tonto Platform to Indian Gardens, then climb the Bright Angel Trail. Total distance 13 miles.

---

a better peek. Among its premier view areas are Yaki Point, which thrusts beyond the rim for an outstanding look at canyon formations; Grandview Point, with its great wide-angle vista; and Lipan Point, where every eroded geological layer of the canyon can be seen.

Before reaching Lipan, watch on your right for a sign indicating the **Tusayan Museum** and ruin. Trails lead through Ponderosas to wall fragments and rough outlines of a Anasazi pueblo built around 1185 A.D. It was probably occupied by an extended family of 25 or 30 people. The small museum has exhibits on both the Anasazi culture and contemporary Native Americans of the area. It's open daily 8 to 6 in summer and 9 to 5 the rest of the year. Thirty-minute guided tours of the ruins are scheduled in summer.

The East Rim Drive ends at Desert View. Here, you can see a great serpentine section of Rio Colorado. The park's east entrance station is just beyond here.

☺ ***Desert View and the Watchtower*** • *About 26 miles east of Grand Canyon Village, off East Rim Drive. Tower open daily 9 to 6; admission is 25 cents.* ◻ The Desert View visitor complex offers gift shops, a general store, service station, campground, visitor information station and restaurant. The river is dramatically close here, since this is the upper end of the canyon where it hasn't cut so deeply. Appropriate to its name, this overlook also has a view of the Painted Desert's pastel hues, just to the east.

The area's focal point, other than the canyon view, is the 70- foot stone Watchtower. It was built in 1932 by the Fred Harvey Company as a rather fanciful interpretation of Southwest Indian architecture. The ground level houses a gift shop, and for a quarter you can climb up the three floors of the tower. It's the best 25-cent investment you can make. Walls are decorated with sand paintings and other bright trim, depicting Indian legends. As you climb, you'll get fine views of the canyon, particularly from the observatory on top. On the second floor, step onto the balcony and peek into those odd-looking boxes called Reflectoscopes. Sections of the canyon are reflected into black- glass mirrors, clearly defining their assorted awesome shapes.

☺ **West Rim Drive** ● *Grand Canyon Village to Hermits Rest. Closed to motor vehicles in summer; access by free shuttlebus.* ⛏ This eight-mile drive stays closer to the edge than the East Rim Drive for a greater variety of canyon views. The best way to savor the changing canyon panorama is to walk the Rim Trail instead of driving. In summer, free shuttles scurry over the drive every 15 to 20 minutes, so you can hop aboard when you've run out of energy. Shuttles don't run in the off-season and the drive is open to motorists. Summer shuttles also serve various points in Grand Canyon Village.

At Maricopa Point, you'll see ruins of the Orphan Mine with its towering headframe. The Powell Memorial here is an impressive granite column dedicated to the pioneer river-runner. Mohave Point is one of the viewpoints from which you can see a stretch of the Colorado River. That tiny bit of white foam far below is Hermit Rapids. At the end of the drive is Hermits Rest, a curio shop and refreshment stand in a rough-hewn stone building.

Visitor Center ● *Open daily 8 to 6 in summer and 8 to 5 the rest of the year.* ⛏ This fine museum traces man's intrusion into the canyon, from prehistoric Indians and Spanish explorers to Major Powell, early prospectors and today's tourists. It also exhibits stuffed critters native to the area. Slide shows and films help you become better acquainted with the park, and you can buy an assortment of books, maps and videos. Rangers at the information desk here can answer all your Grand Canyon questions.

☺ **Yavapai Observation Station** ● *Near Yavapai Point. Open 8 to 8 in summer, 9 to 5 in the off-season.* ⛏ Perched on the lip of the canyon, it offers some of the best vistas in the park, enhanced through polarized windows. "Vista identification panels" help you pick out features below the rim, such as Phantom Ranch and the Colorado River. It also houses one of the most complete bookstores in the park, staffed by members of the Grand Canyon Association.

Fred Harvey History Museum ● *Grand Canyon village, in the Bright Angel Lodge. Open daily 9 to 5.* ⛏ Situated off the Bright Angel Lodge lobby, this interesting mini-museum tells the story of the Fred Harvey Company with old photos and memorabilia. Harvey, tired of awful meals he was getting on trains, convinced the Santa Fe to let him open a restaurant in the Topeka, Kansas, railroad station in 1876. From this came a string of "Harvey Houses"—hotel/restaurants along the Santa Fe line. When the railway opened a spur to the Grand Canyon in 1901, Harvey began building many of the dramatically bold log and stone buildings that still house hotels, restaurants and gift shops. In the museum, you learn that the company's friendly but prim "Harvey Girls" worked for $17.50 a month plus room and board.

Women were scarce in the west, and girls left their jobs for marriage so frequently that Harvey began withholding half of their first year's wages. According to humorist Will Rogers, "Fred Harvey Kept the West in food and wives." Also of interest here is the Geological Fireplace. It's built of layered stone corresponding to strata in the canyon, from vishnu schist for the hearth to Kaibab limestone atop the ten-foot chimney.

Hopi House ● *Grand Canyon Village, near El Tovar. Open daily 9 to 5.* ☐ Another of the historic stone structures built by the Harvey Company, Hopi House sells Southwest Indian arts and crafts. It also has several museum-quality artifacts on exhibit. Built in the style of a Hopi pueblo, it's worth a visit even if you aren't in a shopping mood.

☺ **El Tovar Hotel** ● *Grand Canyon Village.* ☐ Described as "the most expensively constructed and appointed log house in America," El Tovar is perhaps the grandest of the grand hotels built in the early days of the national park system. Completed in 1905 at a cost of $250,000, it is a bold four-story edifice of Kaibab limestone and Douglas fir from Oregon. Dark-stained log columns and beams hold up the lofty ceiling; plush carpets cover the floors. It's an elegant blend of the rustic American west and a luxury Swiss chalet. Stop by to prowl the lobby, have a drink in the cozy cocktail lounge or really indulge yourself with dinner in the canyon-view dining room.

In Tusayan

☺ **Grand Canyon IMAX Theatre** ● *In Tusayan, seven miles from the south gate; P.O. Box 1397, Grand Canyon, AZ 86023-1397; (520) 638-2203. Shows hourly on the half hour from 8:30 to 8:30 daily; shorter hours in winter; $7 for adults, $4 for kids under 12. Gift shop, fast food outlets and flight reservation service.* ☐ Beautifully photographed, *Grand Canyon: The Hidden Secrets*, is one of the finest films of this type we've seen. The monster screen draws you right into the ravine, hurls you through the rapids and takes you on dizzying flights between the walls.

Tracing the history of man in the canyon, the movie begins with scenes of rather nubile Indian maidens, then moves on to some outstanding shots of J.W. Powell guiding his long wooden boats through Rio Colorado's violent rapids. Using replicas of the Powell boats, the cast actually ran many of the rapids that the early explorer bypassed. Closing footage of an ultra-light plane flitting in and out of the canyon shadows like a giant dragonfly is simply smashing.

Grand Canyon Experience ● *Daily in summer 7 to 11; shorter hours the rest of the year; MC/VISA.* ☐ Housed in a glob of brown domes, this facility has a café, gift shop, small museum, information and reservations desk and a movie theater. Regular films are shown nightly at 8, with matinees at 1 on weekends. A film about the canyon and its history, *The Grand Experience* is shown weekdays at 10, 12 and 2 for $2.

THE BEST HIKING TRAILS

We begin by repeating our advise from the North Rim section: When hiking into the canyon, *always* carry plenty of water and food snacks, and wear a shade hat. This is vitally important in the summer, since you'll be hiking down into desert climate zones where temperatures top 100 degrees. Every year, hikers are toppled by thirst and heat-exhaustion. Some have perished.

During the off-season, wear clothes in layers that can be peeled and added, since temperatures can change quickly. Allow enough time for your uphill return. The rule of thumb, if you're in average shape, is to figure twice as much time to climb out as it took to go down. You don't want to be caught stumbling up a narrow trail in darkness. Finally, remember that a permit is required from the Backcountry Office for any overnight hikes into the canyon. This hiking advise is particularly important on the south side trails, for the South Rim is much more precipitous and the climb out can be debilitating on a hot day. Also, the Tonto Platform crossed by the Tonto Trail is a burning desert in summer.

☺ **South Kaibab Trail** • *Steep incline, a tough climb out; 4.4 miles to Tonto Trail Junction and 6.4 miles to the Colorado River. Trailhead is near Yaki Point.* ◻ The Kaibab is our personal preference among the South Rim hikes. Starting in a narrow, shaded side canyon, it descends steeply down Cedar Ridge. It weaves between dramatically eroded formations before leveling out on the Tonto Platform. From here, you can cut across on the Tonto Trail to Indian Garden, and then hike up the Bright Angel Trail for a round-trip of around 13 miles. During the cool offseason, a strong hiker can make the 11-mile round trip from the Kaibab trailhead straight to the river and back in one day (*not* via the Tonto Trail). But don't try it in summer! The Kaibab's final climb-out is a torturous switch-back.

☺ **Grandview Trail** • *Steep descent; rough climb out; three miles to Horseshoe Mesa. Trailhead is at Grandview Point on the East Rim Drive.* ◻ The Grandview spirals right down the face of the South Rim, providing impressive panoramas as you hike. You then pass through narrow side canyons, where you're surrounded by razor ridges, pinnacles and those wedding cake buttes. The trail emerges onto broad, gently-sloping Horseshoe Mesa, where you'll encounter the ruins of the Last Chance Copper Mine and remnants of prospector Pete Berry's stone cabin. Hike out to the edge of the mesa, and a great amphitheater of canyon opens up around you. If you're doing a day hike, this is a good place to sit with lunch and camera before starting back.

Although it's listed as "not regularly maintained," most of the Grandview Trail is well-defined and safely terraced. We had no problems with it between the South Rim and Horseshoe Mesa. From the mesa, the trail merges with the Tonto Trail East and Cottonwood Creek trails. Routes leading down off the plateau are very rough and sometimes confusing because of a web-work of unauthorized "goat trails," so stay alert.

Hermit Trail • *Steep descent into the canyon, tough climb out; 8.9 miles to the Colorado River, four miles to Lookout Point. Trailhead is just beyond Hermits Rest.* ◻ The trail wigs and wags in serpentine twists down through Kaibab limestone to redwall formations. It then follows a dizzying but safe cliff edge route along a side canyon and emerges onto Lookout Point. This is a nice lunch spot and turn-around for a moderate one-day hike. You don't see a lot of the main canyon unless you go well beyond Lookout Point, but the side canyon scenery is fine.

The Hermit climb-out is wearying, so only a seasoned hiker can make the 17-mile round trip to the river. And again, don't try it in summer. Like the Grandview, Hermit is not regularly maintained, although most of the route is in good shape. You'll encounter a few minor rock slides, but nothing you can't step over.

South Rim Trail • *Easy stroll, four-mile round-trip. Trailhead near Bright Angel Lodge.* ◻ This paved trail follows the rim for about two miles through the main visitor area. It takes you past the monumental log and stone buildings of Grand Canyon Village, then along the rim to Grandeur Point and the Yavapai Geologic Museum. A half-mile continuation reaches Mather Point. As you walk this trail, note the old copper sighting tubes, through which you can spot the canyon's various geological features. About midway to Yavapai Observation Station, a spur to the south takes you to the park's amphitheater and main visitor center.

☺ *West Rim Trail* • *Easy—if lengthy—stroll along the canyon rim; about eight miles from Grand Canyon Village to Hermits Rest. Trailhead near Bright Angel Lodge.* ☐ This is the most pleasantly easy trail in the park. It offers wonderful canyon vistas, very little elevation change and it can be taken in manageable sections, depending on your physical shape.

Although it roughly parallels West Rim Drive, the trail hugs the canyon more closely than the road, giving you a wonderful assortment of views. The rim here is much more irregular than on the East Rim Drive, so you'll find yourself hiking out onto peninsulas, then swinging inland to skirt side canyons. The trail becomes a bit irregular and rough as it approaches Hermits Rest, and gets mixed in with an old road. Probably the most interesting section is between Bright Angel Lodge and Pima Point. It's paved from the Yavapai Observation Station to Maricopa Point.

OTHER HIKES

Bright Angel Trail • *Steep descent but well maintained, tough climb out; 4.6 miles to Indian Garden, 7.8 miles to the river, 9.7 miles to Phantom Ranch.* ☐ No, the Bright Angel Trail didn't make our list of favorites. It's too heavily traveled, particularly by mules. We dislike having to stand obediently to one side as the endless mule trains pass, and we particularly dislike having to sidestep what they left behind.

Views from the Bright Angel are certainly impressive, although they don't change much from the rim as you descend. Indian Garden, a spring-fed oasis,

A national park ranger delivers a "rock talk" at Yavapai Point.

is a welcome rest stop. From here, you can hike another mile and a half across the Tonto Platform to an overlook, where you're just 1,500 feet above the mighty Colorado. A trip from the rim to the overlook and back make a good day's workout.

Dripping Springs • *Steep descent, tough climb out; six-mile round trip; start at Hermit trailhead.* ⊓ Dripping Springs is a pleasant sylvan glen far back in a side canyon at the head of Hermit Creek. Follow the Hermit Trail 1.5 miles to the Dripping Springs junction, then go another mile and a half to the springs. You're away from the main gorge here, but some of the side canyon formations are quite impressive. Incidentally, the springs barely drip, so take your own water.

Tonto Trail • *Long, irregular trail, some level, some steep; varying lengths. No rim trailhead.* ⊓ Tonto is the long, long trail a-winding that parallels the canyon for an amazing 92 miles. It's a real trekker's trail, winding in and out of side canyons, with everything from river vistas to broad expanses of sloping desert of the great Tonto Platform. Two popular places to pick up this route are the from South Kaibab trail at the Tonto Junction, and the Bright Angel trail, just below Indian Garden.

ACTIVITIES

Air service • Two firms have scheduled service between Las Vegas and the Grand Canyon Airport—Scenic Airlines (800) 634-6801 or (520) 638-2436; and Air Nevada, (800) 604-6377 or (520) 638-2441 and (702) 736-8900 in Nevada.

Canyon flights • They're offered by no less than 40 different companies, operating from as far away as Phoenix and Las Vegas. The granddaddy of the group is Grand Canyon Airlines, which began more than 60 years ago with Ford Tri-motors. Flying out of Grand Canyon airport near Tusayan, the firm now uses more modern equipment. Outside Arizona, call (800) 528-2413 for schedules and prices; locally, call (520) 638-2407.

Other carriers operating from Grand Canyon airport or heli-pads at Tusayan include Air Grand Canyon, (800) 247-4726 or (520) 638-2686; Air Nevada, (520) 638-2441; AirStar Helicopters, (800) 962-2622 or (520) 638-2622; Kenai Helicopters, (800) 541-4537 or (520) 638-2412; Papillon Grand Canyon Helicopters, (800) 528-2418 or (520) 638-2419; Windrock Airlines, (800) 247-6259 or (520) 638-9591 and (520) 638-9570;

Guided tours • *Grand Canyon National Park Lodges, P.O. Box 699, Grand Canyon, AZ 86023. Call (520) 638-2401 for reservations and (520) 638-2631 for information.* ⊓ Among these "Harveycar" tours are two-hour trips to Hermits Rest for $11; a four-hour Desert View tour for $17; combo six-hour Hermit-Desert View for $20; Sunset Tour to Yaki Point for $7.50; all-day Monument Valley Tour for $80; all-day "smooth water" raft excursion through Marble Canyon for $65; and an all-day tour to Wupatki, Sunset Crater and Walnut Canyon national monuments for $80. In all of the above, rates are half price for children under 12.

☺ **Historic steam train rides** • *Between Williams and Grand Canyon Village; $49 round trip for adults and $23 for kids 3 to 16; Upgrades to "Club Class" $12 per person; to "Chief Class" $50 per person. Canyon rim tours available at additional cost. Contact Grand Canyon Railway, 123 N. San Francisco, Suite 210, Flagstaff, AZ 86001; (800) THE-TRAIN or (520) 773-1976; Williams depot (520) 635-4000. Major credit cards.* ⊓ Using turn-of-the-century steam locomotives and 1923 Harriman coaches and upgraded Club and Chief cars, Grand Canyon Railway has resumed the historic 65-mile run between Williams and the park. The excursion includes a Western shootout before departure from Williams, on-board entertainment and free refreshments.

Trains run daily except December 24 and 25, departing Williams Depot at 9:30 a.m., arriving at the grand Canyon at 11:45. They depart the canyon at 3:15, returning to Williams at 5:30. Steam engines are used from Memorial Day weekend through September, and then vintage diesel locomotives operate for the rest of the year. AMTRAK's cross-country service stops at Flagstaff, with a connecting bus to the Grand Canyon Railway in Williams; call (800) USA-RAIL for schedules.

Grand Canyon rail service originally began in 1901, then was discontinued in 1968 because of increased auto use. Ironically, the run has resumed to alleviate traffic congestion at the South Rim, where as many as 4,000 vehicles gather on a summer day.

Horseback/mule rides ● *Stables at Moqui Lodge; contact Apache Stables, P.O. Box 158, Grand Canyon, AZ 86023; (520) 638-2891.* ☐ Offerings include a four hour East Rim ride for $57.50, one hour $22, two hour $36; campfire trail ride $27 or campfire wagon ride $7.50. Some age and weight restrictions may apply. Most of these activities occur around Tusayan in Kaibab National Forest, just outside the park.

Mule rides ● *They must be reserved months in advance; contact Grand Canyon National Park Lodges, P.O. Box 699, Grand Canyon, AZ 86023; (520) 638-2401.* ☐ Rides down the Bright Angel Trail to Phantom Ranch, including one night's accommodations and meals at the ranch, are $250.25 (less per person for two sharing lodging at Phantom). One-day round-trip mule rides down the Bright Angel Trail to Plateau Point are $64 per person, including lunch. Duffel portage (30 pounds or less) is $34 from rim to river and $25 river to rim. And no, we have no idea why it costs less to pack it out than to take it down.

Riders must weigh under 200 pounds (dressed), be at least four-foot-seven, and not pregnant. The brochure says they also must be fluent in English. Apparently the mules aren't bilingual.

☺ **Whitewater raft trips** ● The Grand Canyon of the Colorado River is the world's premier whitewater run, with scores of rapids on its 227-mile length. Lava Falls, Hermit and Crystal Falls are the rapids of legend. These whitewater battles are only a small part of the experience, however. River runners enjoy camping on the banks (no motels down here), hiking side canyons, visiting ancient Indian ruins and learning about the flora, fauna, history and geology of this wonderous chasm.

Trips range from a few days to three weeks, using a variety of inflatable rafts and pontoon boats. Some are motor-powered; others use oars only. Most trips put in at Lees Ferry in Marble Canyon and full-length runs take out at one of several Lake Mead beaches. Some of the shorter trips go only to Phantom Ranch, and patrons hike the Bright Angel Trail to the rim; others begin their run at Phantom. Currently, 17 operators run commercial trips down the canyon. Private trips are available, although they require a permit and hopeful river-runners must wait for years. For details on private trips and a list of companies running the Colorado, contact: River Sub-district, Grand Canyon National Park, P.O. Box 129, Grand Canyon, AZ 86023; (520) 638-7843.

TRANSIT—RAPID & OTHERWISE

Transportation desks at Bright Angel, Maswik and Yavapai lodges on the South Rim and Grand Canyon Lodge on the North Rim can book many of the services listed below. Or contact the firms directly.

Bus service is provided between the South Rim and Flagstaff or Williams by the Nava-Hopi Tours. Operating out of Flagstaff, the company also has sightseeing tours in the area; (800) 892-8687 or (520) 774-5003.

Shuttle service operates between Tusayan, the airport and Grand Canyon Village, hourly from 8:15 a.m. to 7:10 p.m.; more frequent service in the summer. Rates are $5 one way and $8 round trip for adults; $3 and $5 for kids 6 to 12. Call Tusayan-Grand Canyon Shuttle at (520) 638-0821 or 638-0871. The firm also operates taxi and charter service.

Free park shuttles are operated in the summer, when the West Rim Drive is closed to vehicle traffic. The West Rim shuttle runs from the West Rim interchange near Bright Angel Lodge to Hermit's Rest, every 15 or 20 minutes. The Village Loop runs from the West Rim interchange to various points in the village, and as far east as Yavapai Point, every 15 minutes. Check for specific schedules, which can vary from year to year.

Hiker's shuttle to the South Kaibab trailhead leaves Bright Angel Lodge in summer at 6:30, 8:30 and 11:30 a.m., with stops at Maswick Lodge and the Backcountry Office near Mather Campground; the fee is $3. Returns from the trailhead are 7:10 and 9:10 a.m. and 12:10 p.m.

Rim to rim shuttle service is operates daily between the north and south rims from May through October, or until the North Rim closes; one way $60, round trip $100. Contact Trans Canyon Shuttle, P.O. Box 348, Grand Canyon, AZ 86023; (520) 638-2820. (See "The Canyon rim to rim" box on page 43.)

Car rentals are available from Budget (638-9360) and Dollar Rent-A-Car (638-2625), operating out of Grand Canyon Airport.

Taxis can be summoned by calling (520) 638-2822.

Other services

Babbitt's General Store, a bank, post office branch, service station and quickie film processing are located in Grand Canyon Village, across from the main visitor center. Laundry, ice machines and coin showers are adjacent to the Backcountry Office, near Mather Campground. Car repairs are available in Grand Canyon Village and there's a beauty parlor in the Bright Angel Lodge. Because of the long haul, prices for groceries and other staples are somewhat higher than in towns outside the park.

WHERE TO DINE
In the park

Arizona Steakhouse ● ☆☆☆ $$

◻ *Grand Canyon Village; (520) 638-2401. American; full bar service. Daily 5 p.m. to 10 p.m. Major credit cards.* ◻ In the historic Bright Angel Lodge; Western style interior. Also a coffee shop, open 6:30 a.m. to 10 p.m.

☺ *El Tovar Dining Room* ● ☆☆☆☆ $$$

◻ *Grand Canyon Village; (520) 638-2401. Southwest regional; full bar service. Meals from 6:30 to 11 a.m., 11:30 to 2 and 5 to 10 p.m.; reservations strongly advised. Major credit cards.* ◻ Situated on the rim of the Grand Canyon in the elegant El Tovar Hotel, this is one of the Southwest's finest restau-

DINING ON THE RIM

A canyon-view dinner for two at the elegant El Tovar dining room is probably worth the $60 to $80 tab. However, you can dine with the same view for nothing, although you must bring your own food. Several unmarked turnouts between Mather Point and Grandview Point on the East Rim Drive make great meal stops for RVers or picnickers. They're particularly handy for RVs, since parking is parallel and you can enjoy splendid views from your own personal dining room window. The vistas are particularly imposing during breakfast and dinnr, when shadows accent the canyon.

Traveling eastbound, you'll see the first vista point about half a mile after turning from the main park road onto East Rim Drive. Coming from Desert View, look for the first turnout about two miles from Grandview Point. Several more are scattered between these points. Our favorite—with perhaps the best view—is a twin overlook about midway between the Yaki Point and Grandview turnouts.

These spots are virtually empty in the morning, although you may find them busy just before sunset. They're never as crowded as the more popular Grandview, Yaki and Mather turnouts, however.

rants. An award winning chef, innovative menu and grand setting combine for an outstanding dining experience.

Grand Canyon Village has informal dining and cafeterias at the Maswik Lodge, Yavapai Lodge and in Babbitt's General Store. There's cafeteria style dining at Desert View.

In Tusayan

Coronado Dining Room ● ☆☆ $$

Best Western Grand Canyon Squire Inn; (520) 638-2681. American-Southwestern; full bar service. Daily 6:30 to 10 p.m. Major credit cards. ◻ Attractive Southwest style restaurant serving a variety of Southwestern and other regional American dishes; adjoining cocktail lounge. The adjacent Squire Coffee Shop is open 6:30 a.m. to 5 p.m.

Moqui Lodge Restaurant ● ☆☆ $$

Moqui Lodge; (520) 638-2401. Mexican and American; full bar service. Daily 6:30 a.m. to 10 p.m. ◻ Rustic-modern dining room with adjacent cocktail lounge. Also an outside dining area, open 5 p.m. to 8 p.m. in summer.

The Steak House ● ☆☆ $$

South end of Tusayan; (520) 638-2780. American; full bar service. Lunch 11:30 to 2, dinner 5 to 10. MC/VISA, AMEX. ◻ Appealing, properly rustic Western style place with checkered tablecloths, serving mesquite grilled steaks, chops and chicken.

WHERE TO RECLINE

Prices reflect high season rates and may be lower at other times. Most were provided by the management and are subject to change; use them only as a guide.

In the park

Bright Angel Lodge and Cabins ● ☆☆ $$ to $$$$ ∅

P.O. Box 699, Grand Canyon, AZ 86023; (520) 638-2401. Couples and singles in lodge or rustic cabins $40 to $51, rim cabins $89 to $111. ◻ The Bright Angel is an historic log and stone structure dating back to the turn of the century, located on the rim. Gift shops, cocktail lounge, transportation desk, dining room (listed above) and coffee shop.

☺ *El Tovar Hotel* ● ☆☆☆☆ *$$$$$* Ø

P.O. Box 699, Grand Canyon, AZ 86023; (520) 638-2401. Couples and singles $111 to $167, suites $183 to $270. Major credit cards. ◻ The premier national park lodge; a national historic landmark, with a dining room (listed above), cocktail lounge, patio, gift shops and other amenities. Located on the rim; some rooms with view.

Kachina and Thunderbird Lodges ● ☆☆☆ *$$$$$* Ø

P.O. Box 699, Grand Canyon, AZ 86023; (520) 638-2401. Couples and singles $96, canyon-side $106. Major credit cards. ◻ These twin contemporary lodges just off the rim have modern accommodations; some with canyon views.

Maswik Lodge ● ☆☆ *$$$$$* Ø

P.O. Box 699, Grand Canyon, AZ 86023; (520) 638-2401. Couples and singles $98 to $103. Major credit cards. ◻ Motel type units and some rustic cabins in Grand Canyon Village, a short distance from the rim. Cafeteria, cocktail lounge and transportation desk.

Yavapai Lodges ● ☆☆ *$$$$* Ø

P.O. Box 699, Grand Canyon, AZ 86023; (520) 638-2401. Couples and singles $79 to $89. Major credit cards. ◻ Yavapai East and West are motel- type units in Grand Canyon Village, near the visitor center, a short walk from the rim. Cafeteria, transportation desk and cocktail lounge.

In Tusayan

Best Western Grand Canyon Squire ● ☆☆☆ *$$$$* Ø

P.O. Box 130, Grand Canyon, AZ 86203; (520) 638-2681. Couples and singles $90 to $125. Major credit cards. ◻ Attractive resort with 250 rooms; TV, phones; swimming and wading pools, sauna, spa, tennis courts, bowling alley and coin laundry. **Coronado Dining Room** listed above.

Moqui Lodge ● ☆☆☆ *$$$$* Ø

P.O. Box 699, Grand Canyon, AZ 86023; (520) 638-2401. Couples $89, singles $74; closed January-February. Major credit cards. ◻ A Fred Harvey lodge in the north end of Tusayan, just outside the park gate. Dining room, cocktail lounge, horseback rides (see "Activities" above).

Quality Inn Grand Canyon ● ☆☆☆ *$$$* Ø

P.O. Box 520, Grand Canyon, AZ 86023; (520) 638-2673 or (800) 221-2222. Couples and singles $68 to $98; Major credit cards. ◻ A 176-room inn with TV movies, room phones; heated pool, indoor spa, atrium bar and restaurant (listed above).

Seven Mile Lodge and Gift Shop ● ☆☆ *$$$$*

P.O. Box 56, Grand Canyon, AZ 86023; (520) 638-2291. Couples and singles from $80. MC/VISA, AMEX. ◻ Nicely kept inn with TV, room phones; Indian arts and crafts shop.

WHERE TO CAMP
In the park

Mather Campground ● *Near Babbbitt's General Store. For reservations, call (800) 365-CAMP. RV and tent sites, no hookups, $10. MC/VISA.* ◻ Flush potties, water, RV dump station; coin-operated showers and laundry nearby.

Mather is heavily booked in summer, so make reservations as early as possible. It's located in a pleasantly wooded grove with barbecues and picnic tables. Open all year.

Desert View Campground • *Near Desert View Lookout. RV and tent sites, no hookups, $10. Flush potties, water. Reservations through (800) 365-CAMP. RV and tent sites, no hookups, $10. MC/VISA.* ❑ This campground, 26 miles from Grand Canyon Village in the park's eastern end, is open May through October.

Trailer Village • *P.O. Box 699, Grand Canyon, AZ 86023; (520) 638-2401. RV sites, full hookups, $17. Reservations accepted; major credit cards.* ❑ Flush potties and water; showers nearby. Operated by Fred Harvey Company; located in a woodsy setting beyond Babbitt's General Store. Open all year.

Outside the park

Flintstone Bedrock City • *In Valle, 30 miles south of the park on U.S. 180. Mailing address: Star Route, Williams, AZ 86046; 635-2600. Tent and RV sites, some pull-throughs, full hookups, $12 to $16. Reservations accepted; MC/VISA.* ❑ Showers, restaurant, groceries, Propane and dump station. Flintstone-themed "Prehistoric Park" adjacent, along with a movie theater, train ride and gift shop. Open April 1 through October 15.

Grand Canyon Camper Village • *Tusayan, Grand Canyon, AZ 86023; (520) 638-2887. Full hookups $22, water and electric $20, electric only $18, tent sites $15, teepees $18. MC/VISA.* ❑ Coin operated showers, picnic tables. Early reservations are advised, particularly in summer. Groceries, restaurants and other Tusayan facilities are nearby. Open all year.

Ten X Campground • *C/o Kaibab National Forest, Tusayan Ranger District, P.O. Box 3088, Tusayan, AZ 86023; (520) 638-2443. RV and tent sites, no hookups, $10; half price for Golden Age and Access pass holders. No reservations.* ❑ National forest campground located two miles south of Tusayan, with water, pit toilets, barbecues and picnic tables. Open May 1 to October 30. Space often is available here when other camping areas are full.

RAINBOW BRIDGE

Chapter three

GRAND CANYON NEIGHBORS

Looping the canyon: North and south of the rims

WHILE CERTAINLY the focal point of northwestern Arizona, the Grand Canyon has some interesting neighbors as well. To the north is the Arizona Strip, isolated from the rest of the state by the canyon, plus great swatches of Ponderosa pines in Kaibab National Forest and the aquatic playground of Glen Canyon National Recreation Area. To the south, Hualapai and Havasupai Indians have gotten into the tourist business with their holdings near the South Rim.

If you approach this region from California and Nevada, you'll likely head east from Las Vegas on Interstate 15, cross Nevada's southern tip and then clip a small corner of Arizona. Travelers coming to Arizona from the east generally find themselves on I-40. In Flagstaff, a turn north onto U.S. 89 gets them to northwestern Arizona and the Grand Canyon.

Since this is a driving guide, we'll take you on a loop trip around the canyon, North Rim to South. As mentioned in the previous chapter, the rims are only ten to eleven miles apart, yet more than 200 road miles a required to get from one to the next. We'll aim you eastward across the Arizona Strip, past the Jacob Lake gateway to the North Rim. You'll pass through Marble Canyon and visit Page and the Glen Canyon National Recreation Area, then drop south on U.S. 89 and swing west on State Highway 64 to the South Rim.

NORTH OF THE NORTH RIM:
The Arizona Strip

The Nevada-Arizona border town of Mesquite provides I-15 travelers with their last or first chance at gaming, depending on their direction. Once a scattered farming town in the green oasis of the Virgin River's Moapa Valley, Mesquite is coming together as a mini gambling center. Three mid-sized casino resorts offer the usual games, lodgings, restaurants and inexpensive buffets.

The newest—and the first encountered by Arizona-bound travelers—is **Players Island Resort**, a tropical theme complex opened in 1995 by Merv Griffin and other investors; (800) 896-4567. Just beyond in downtown Mesquite is the **Peppermill Oasis Resort Hotel,** with similar gaming-dining-lodging facilities, plus an 18-hole golf course on the Arizona side; (800) 621-0187. If you continue through Mesquite on the I-15 business route (Mesquite Boulevard) and then swing left under the freeway, you'll happen upon **Virgin River Hotel Casino.** It's an attractive Southwestern style gaming resort on a bluff overlooking the town and river valley. It has a full-hookup RV park and movie theater complex; (800) 346-7721.

Take time for a pause at the small rock-walled **Desert Valley Museum** at 31 W. Mesquite Blvd.; (702) 346-5705. Open Monday-Saturday 8 to 5, it presents a pleasant disarray of pioneer regalia, old phones and an "ancient" 1945 TV set.

Construction dust was flying when we last passed through Mesquite, so expect more gaming and lodging facilities in the near future. Just across the border at I-15's Littlefield exit is the **Beaver Dam Resort,** a vacation home and RV complex with a golf course, pro shop and Arizona Café open to the public; (520) 347-5000 or (800) 626-5006.

☺ Continuing east, I-15 nips a particularly attractive corner of Arizona as it veers through the **Virgin River Canyon**. Tilted strata, wedding cake buttes, a pinnacle or two and sheer canyon walls mark the river's twisting course through this little-known gorge. (Unfortunately, some of those sheer walls were carved not by erosion but by freeway engineers.) About midway through this eleven-mile canyon, hop off at the Bureau of Land Management's **Virgin River Recreation Area.** Facilities include a rest stop, picnic and no-hookup campground alongside the river.

Since I-15 heads northeast to St. George, Utah (and our *Utah Discovery Guide*), you'll need to abandon it to get back into Arizona. About ten miles north of St. George, fork right onto State Route 9 toward Hurricane. (Hurricanes hardly ever happen here; in fact not at all. The Mormon settlement got its odd name after a sudden wind gust practically blew a visiting church official out of his buggy.)

At Hurricane, turn right onto State Route 59 at the town's only stoplight and begin a steep climb onto the Colorado Plateau. Upon this great uplift, time and nature have shaped canyons, buttes and redwall escarpments, including the Grand Canyon and southern Utah's Bryce, Zion and Capitol Reef. This also is the platform for the Arizona Strip, which lies just ahead.

RV advisory • The long climb out of Hurricane is rather gentle, following sweeping curves and well-engineered grades, easily negotiable by any size RV or trailer rig.

TRIP PLANNER

WHEN TO GO ● Summer is peak season for the Arizona Strip and Glen Canyon to the north, and the Indian country to the south. Spring and fall are our favorite times to prowl these areas. Glen Canyon National Recreation Area gets crowded in summer, and it's usually wall-to-wall boaters over the Fourth of July, so make reservations well in advance. The climate varies widely, from cold winters with deep snow around Jacob Lake and hot summers on the Arizona Strip and Indian reservations below the South Rim.

WHAT TO SEE ● Virgin River Canyon; Pipe Spring National Monument; Lonely Dell Ranch at Lees Ferry; Powell Memorial Museum in Page and Carl Hayden Visitor Center in the Glen Canyon National Recreation Area; Cameron Trading Post and the Little Colorado River overlook; Planes of Fame Air Museum in Valle.

WHAT TO DO ● Stroll across the old Navajo Bridge at Marble Canyon; tour Glen Canyon Dam, guided or on your own; take a boat cruise on Lake Powell to Rainbow Bridge National Monument; dine with a lake view in the Rainbow Room at Wahweap Lodge; tour Grand Canyon Caverns; hike down Havasu Canyon.

☺ *Indicates an attraction, restaurant or lodging with special appeal.*

USEFUL CONTACTS—north of the North Rim

North Kaibab Ranger District, Kaibab National Forest, P.O. Box 248, Fredonia, AZ 86022; (520) 643-7395.

Page-Lake Powell Chamber of Commerce, P.O. Box 727 (106 S. Lake Powell Blvd.), Page, AZ 86040; (520) 645-2741.

Glen Canyon National Recreation Area, P.O. Box 1507, Page, AZ 86040; (520) 645-2511.

South of the South Rim

Tusayan Ranger District, Kaibab National Forest, P.O. Box 3088, Tusayan, AZ 86023; (520) 638-2443.

Havasupai Tourist Enterprises, Supai, AZ 86435; (520) 448-2121.

Hualapai Tribal Council, P.O. Box 168, Peach Springs, AZ 85634; (520) 769-2216.

RADIO STATIONS—North Rim area

KONY-FM, 101.1, Page—Country
KREC-FM, 98.1, St. George—Old and new top forty
KJUL-FM, 104.3, Las Vegas—"Soft hits"
KCKK-FM, 100.1, Page—Top forty
KXAZ-FM, 93.5, Page—Variety; light rock
KPGE-AM, 1340, Page—Country

South Rim area

See listings for Flagstaff area in Chapter five.

The winding ascent takes you through pleasing Colorado Plateau rock formations, red and otherwise, and then into prairie country. In this lonely borderland between Utah and Arizona, cattle roam free and ranch houses sit in the shade of cottonwoods. Settlements are few and tiny and we suspect the folks here like it that way.

Colorado City

Elevation: 5,000 feet   **Population: 3,000**

At the border, you'll pass through the twin farm towns of Hilldale, Utah, and Colorado City, Arizona. Both are clean scrubbed, no-nonsense Mormon settlements at the base of red sandstone cliffs. They're rather prim looking places, brightened somewhat by ruddy-cheeked school girls wearing pretty homemade dresses. Colorado City was settled by fundamentalist Mormons who left Utah to escape polygamy prosecution. Gossips say that plural marriage is still practiced here, although federal officers haven't raided the town for several years.

For a brief look at this little settlement and its modest yet prosperous looking homes, swing left from the highway at the city center sign and go left again after a few blocks onto Central Street. The Food Town Cooperative Mercantile, a service station and post office comprise the tiny business district. And don't expect to find a Bud Light in the busy, well-stocked general store. This is a dry town!

From Colorado city, you'll follow Arizona's State Route 389 across the Arizona Strip, backdropped by the Vermilion Cliffs, the area's most imposing landform. Stretching for more than 50 miles, the cliffs earned their name from their habit of turning to pleasing shades of crimson and hot pink in late light. Sixteen miles of brushy desert accented by occasional rock formations takes you onto the small Kaibab Indian Reservation and an excellent national monument that recalls the Arizona Strip's early Mormon days. Just beyond is a facility of quite a different stripe—a small casino operated by the Kaibab tribe.

☺ ***Pipe Spring National Monument*** ● *HC-65, Box 5, Fredonia, AZ 86022 (520) 643-7105. Visitor center/museum open daily 8 to 4:30; ranch buildings open until 5. Admission $1; free with Golden Eagle, Golden Age or Golden Access pass.* ☐ This small facility preserves the imposing fortified ranch headquarters of an early Mormon cattle spread. Nicknamed Windsor Castle after its English ranch superintendent Anson Perry Windsor, it was created for the Mormon Church's southern Utah "tithing herd." These were cattle tithed to the church; one cow in ten went on the collection plate.

Indian raids had killed earlier settlers here, so the ranch complex was built as a fort, with two stone buildings linked by thick walls. A spring—from which the monument takes its name—created an oasis of cottonwoods, fruit trees and cattle ponds in this dry country. The fort became a popular way station for travelers from the 1870s until after the turn of the century. Later sold by the church, it was given by its new owners to the National Park Service in the 1920s as a "memorial to Western pioneer life."

The sturdy main structure is little changed from its pioneer days. A self-guiding tour takes visitors through rooms furnish in early Americana, with oval rugs, rocking chairs and softly ticking grandfather clocks. In the kitchen, chairs are reversed and plates are upside down, awaiting the supper prayer. Gun ports are cut through the three-foot-thick walls, so this was indeed a

Northwestern Arizona

NEVADA

UTAH

Davis Dam

Lake Mohave Recreational Area

Lake Mead National Recreational Area

Bullhead City

68

Boulder City

Willow Beach

Temple Bar

Lake Mead National Recreational Area

LakeMead

15

93

168

169

Glendale

Mesquite

15

Littlefield

St. George

Hurricane

Colorado City

389

Pipe Spring National Monument

Kaibab Indian Reservation

Fredonia

89

93

Dolan Springs

Kingman

Hackberry

Quarter-master Point

Meadowview

GRAND CANYON NATIONAL PARK

Lake Mead National Recreational Area

N

Valentine

40

Hualapai Indian Reservation

Grand Canyon Caverns

18

Colorado River

Hualapai Indian Reservation

Fort Rock

64

KAIBAB NATIONAL FOREST

Seligman

Ash Fork

Tusayan

South Rim

Desert View

North Rim

GRAND CANYON NATIONAL PARK

67

Jacob Lake

89 ALT

Marble Canyon

89 ALT

Glen Canyon Dam

89

Pine Springs

Williams

64

180

Valle

KAIBAB NATIONAL FOREST

Little Colorado River Gorge

The Gap

Page

Lake Powell

Flagstaff

40

89

180

Gray Mtn.

Cameron

64

Echo Cliffs

fort. It was never attacked, however. Outbuildings contain a blacksmith and harness shops and other ranching essentials. Authentic farm chickens wander about the yard, along with some the fattest geese we'd ever seen. Ducks occupy a tree-shaded, spring-fed pond out front. A short loop trail leads up sandstone cliffs behind the house, providing an impressive view of the lonely, wind-ruffled Arizona Strip.

During summer months, park rangers and docents recapture the spirit of Western pioneers with living history activities such as spinning and weaving, gardening and baking. Adjacent to the visitor center is a gift shop, snack bar and bookstore operated by the Zion Natural History Association.

Pipe Spring Resort Casino ● *Just above Pipe Spring; mailing address HC 65, Box 3, Fredonia, AZ 86022; (520) 643-7777 or (801) 559-6537. Sunday-Thursday 8 a.m. to 12:30 a.m., Friday-Saturday open 24 hours. RV park with full hookups, $5.* ◻ This small casino offers several ranks of slot and video poker machines. A deli features breakfast fare, an all-you-can-eat salad bar, Indian fry bread, Indian tacos and other snacks. The adjacent RV park has picnic tables and partial shade.

Fourteen miles beyond Pipe Spring, Highway 389 leaves the Kaibab reservation and terminates at the small settlement of **Fredonia**, which provides little reason to pause. Turn southeast onto U.S. 89A and begin a long, gentle climb up the Kaibab Plateau's North Rim Parkway. As it slopes upward and into Kaibab National Forest, prairie grasses give way to the piñon and Ponderosa pines. Campgrounds, hiking trails and wilderness areas attract outdoor enthusiasts. The woodsy settlement of **Jacob Lake** offers a Kaibab Plateau visitor center, Forest Service campground, private RV park, lodge, restaurant and store. For specifics, see the "North Rim" section of the previous chapter.

Presumably, you'll continue from here to the North Rim of the Grand Canyon, having gotten this close. After your park visit, as you press eastward from Jacob Lake, you'll spiral quickly out of the piñon-juniper woodlands of Kaibab National Forest and drop back into prairie country. As you drop, watch for a turnout that presents a splendid view of the Vermilion Cliffs and the tawny-gray desert at its feet. Crossing this desert, you'll encounter tiny blips on the map that are essentially motel-restaurant-service station complexes—**Cliff Dwellers, Vermilion Cliffs** and **Marble Canyon**. Each offers basic travelers' services and each is poised prettily at the base of those cliffs. Just beyond Cliff Dwellers, note the adobe and stone ruins of the original lodge on the left, built into a sandstone overhang way back in 1890. Nearby, looking rather out of place, are several huge boulders that have tumbled down from the cliffs above. Softer soil around the bases of some have eroded away, leaving fat toadstool shaped formations.

Marble Canyon and Lees Ferry

The lonely drive across the Arizona Strip ends in dramatic fashion at Marble Canyon, which marks the upstream beginning of the Grand Canyon of the Colorado River. This steep-walled chasm was named by river-runner John Wesley Powell, who mistook its glossy hard granite walls for marble. The adjacent community of Marble Canyon has a lodge, restaurant, landing strip, small store and service station. At Marble Canyon Lodge (see below), you can book river trips and Indian country tours.

☺ Immediately beyond the tiny town, before you cross the river, turn left to visit the remnants of **Lees Ferry**, an early Mormon outpost. This was the last crossing on the Colorado River before it plunged into the 227-mile-long Grand Canyon. Sitting below red rock cliffs, this historic site is now a thumb of Glen Canyon National Recreation Area and a favored starting place for river runners. A campground (listed below) offers river-view sites; a ranger station occupies a hill just beyond. It's open daily 8 to 5.

The river flows crisp, cold and turquoise-clear here, issuing from the innards of Glen Canyon Dam just upstream. A sandy, rock- strewn beach lures fisherpersons and sun-bathers, but few swimmers. Nearby are several large parking areas for river runners, and the ruins of the original Mormon settlement, called Lonely Dell Ranch. To view remnants of this outpost, turn left onto a dirt road just short of a small bridge, less than half a mile beyond the ranger station. The complex consists of an old stone, metal-roofed ranch house, a couple of squared log outbuildings and a mixed fruit orchard. Walk past the ranch yard and you'll encounter a pioneer cemetery and an old pump site on the Paria River. Although a peaceful place, the ranch marked the final chapter of the most bizarre story in Mormon history.

The original outpost was built by Warren Johnson and his son in 1873. However, the site carries the name of a considerably more notorious individual. In 1857, about 300 miles away in southwestern Utah, several Mormon zealots joined with a band of Paiute Indians and slaughtered 120 members of a California-bound wagon train. Only a few children—too young to bear witness—survived this Mountain Meadows Massacre. The attack was blamed on the Paiutes, but federal investigators learned years later that Mormons were involved, led by John Doyle Lee, director of Indian affairs for southern Utah.

Banished to the wilderness

Although horrified by this revelation, church officials sheltered Lee by sending him into the wilderness in 1872 to establish a ferry crossing at the Johnson outpost. It was one of Lee's wives who named this remote area Lonely Dell. Finally, 20 years after the massacre, Lee was arrested, taken to the site of the killings and executed by firing squad. He was the only participant ever brought to justice.

If you're a serious hiker, you can trek the 35-mile **Paria Canyon Wilderness trail**, which starts near Kanab, Utah, and emerges just above Lonely Dell Ranch. In some areas, the gorge towers 2,000 feet overhead. Permits are required and the hike is only allowed downstream (from Kanab), so that updated weather information can be imparted. There's a risk of flash floods launched by summer thunder showers. For hiking permits, contact: **Kanab Area Office, Bureau of Land Management**, 320 N. 100 East (P.O. Box 459), Kanab, UT 84741; (801) 644-2672.

☺ Continuing beyond Lee's Ferry, you soon encounter the steel arch **Navajo Bridge** that carries Highway 89A across Marble Canyon. It's the last highway crossing of the Colorado River until Hoover Dam, more than 240 miles southwest. A new $13.9 million span was opened in 1995 and the original bridge has been converted into a pedestrian walk, with parking areas on either side of the river. Interpretive exhibits and a shaded picnic area occupy the west bank. The stream is 300 or more feet below—an imposing and dizzying view as you stroll across the old span.

The original bridge was built in 1927 to replace the ferry which had operated since the days of John D. Lee. It was the first bridge to cross the Colorado River on its 400-mile trek through northern Arizona. Two more have since been added—the Hoover Dam roadbed and the steel-arch bridge adjacent to Glen Canyon Dam near Page.

Whitewater rafting • One of the west's senior river outfits, with Colorado and other whitewater outings, and still being run by descendants of the founder, is Don Hatch River Expeditions, HC-67, Box 32, Marble Canyon, AZ 86036; (800) 433- 8966 or (520) 355-2241.

WHERE TO DINE ON THE ARIZONA STRIP

Cliff Dwellers Restaurant • ☆☆ $$

☐ *Highway 89A, eight miles west of Navajo Bridge in Marble Canyon;* (520) 355-2228. *American; Full bar service. Daily 6 a.m. to 9 p.m. MC/VISA, DISC.* ☐ Generous portions of rural fare are served in a knotty pine dining room that's decorated with old license plates and other knickknacks. Part of Cliff Dwellers Lodge.

Marble Canyon Lodge Restaurant • ☆☆ $$

☐ *Marble Canyon; (520) 355-2225. American; full bar service. Daily 6 a.m. to 9 p.m. MC/VISA.* ☐ Part of the Marble Canyon Lodge, the attractive knotty pine restaurant serves Western style American fare and some vegetarian dishes.

Vermilion Cliffs Bar and Grille • ☆ $$

☐ *Highway 89A, three miles north of Marble Canyon; (520) 355-2231. American; full bar. Daily 6:30 a.m. to 10 p.m. MC/VISA.* ☐ This rustic, Western style dining room is adjacent to Lees Ferry Lodge. Features include home-baked pies, homemade soups. If you bring in a fresh-caught trout, the chef will cook it.

WHERE TO RECLINE

Prices reflect high season rates and may be lower at other times. Most were provided by the management and are subject to change; use them only as a guide.

Cliff Dwellers Lodge • ☆☆ $$$

☐ *Eight miles west of Navajo Bridge in Marble Canyon; mailing address is HC 67-30, Marble Canyon, AZ 86036; (520) 355-2228. Couples and single $60 to $80.* ☐ A contemporary 21-unit motel has replaced historic Cliff Dwellers Lodge, which was built under the overhang of a huge balanced rock. Its ruins can still be seen, a few hundred feet east of the present lodge.

Lees Ferry Lodge • ☆ $$

☐ *HC67-Box 1, Marble Canyon, AZ 86036; (520) 355-2231. Couples and singles from $45. MC/VISA.* ☐ A rustic stone and timber motel located in Vermilion Cliffs, on U.S. 89A, three miles southwest of Marble Canyon; **Vermilion Cliffs Restaurant** listed above.

Marble Canyon Lodge • ☆☆ $$

☐ *Highway 89A at Navajo Bridge, Marble Canyon, AZ 86036; (520) 355-2225. Couples $55 to $60, family bunkhouse, cottage or apartments, $75 to $125. MC/VISA.* ☐ Nicely restored 1920s resort. **Dining room** (listed above), trading post and gift shop, landing field nearby.

WHERE TO CAMP

Mad Rabbit Campground • *State Highway 389, c/o Fredonia, AZ 86022; (520) 643-5545. Tent and RV sites, $10 with hookups, $5 without. No credit cards.* ☐ On the Kaibab Indian Reservation, just north of Highway 389.

Water, flush potties, showers; convenience market and laundromat nearby. Hiking trails and petroglyphs.

Lees Ferry Campground ● *C/o Glen Canyon National Recreation Area, P.O. Box 1507, Page, AZ 86040; (520) 645-2511; Lees Ferry ranger station (520) 355-2234. Tent and RV sites, no hookups; $8 (half price for holders of Golden Age and Golden Access passes). No credit cards or reservations.* ☐ Located near the Lees Ferry boat launch, the campground has water, flush potties and wind and shade shelters. It's nicely situated among red rock formations. Some sites have river views.

Virgin River Canyon Recreation Area ● *Seventeen miles west of St. George, Utah. Tent and RV sites, no hookups, $6. No credit cards or reservations.* ☐ The camping area comes in two sections—one at riverside and another on a bluff overlooking the river canyon. This Bureau of Land Management campground has flush potties, barbecues and picnic tables. Many sites have canyon views. Some are pull-throughs.

Page & Lake Powell

Elevation: 4,380 feet　　　　　　**Population: 6,500**

From Lees Ferry, Highway 89A dips southward, skimming the edge of the crimson Echo Cliffs, then it dissolves into route 89. Turning northward, you climb through a dramatic cleft in those cliffs and head across a desert tableland. Your destination is Glen Canyon Dam and Lake Powell, a pair of statistical rivals to Hoover Dam and Lake Mead. Although arid, the setting is dramatic—layer upon sculpted layer of pink Navajo Sandstone rising above Page and the turquoise glow of Lake Powell below.

When U.S. Army Lt. Joseph C. Ives explored this sandstone wonderland in 1858, he concluded that it was a "profitless locality," beyond the reach of development. Major Powell, battling Glen Canyon rapids in his longboats, wondered if such a wild river could ever be useful.

More than a century and one million barrels of concrete later, Glen Canyon Dam was built as the capstone of the upper Colorado River flood control, water storage and hydroelectric project. Hundreds of thousands of visitors now come to play in this "profitless locality." They water ski across Lake Powell, pull fat bass from its depths, hike its surrounding deserts and wonder what the canyon must have been like before it was flooded. It was beautiful, the old timers say, more then than now.

Glen Canyon did not surrender easily to concrete and steel. Conservationists issued predictable cries of protest when the dam was proposed in the 1940s. Once in place, it would drown a beautiful upstream chasm and change forever the flow of the Colorado River through the downstream Grand Canyon. After many delays, construction finally began and the dam was completed in 1964 to the trumpet call of engineering statistics—710 feet high, 300 feet thick at the base, containing eight zillion pounds of concrete, enough wiring to link every ghetto-blaster in South Central L.A., etc., etc. Lake Powell (which didn't fill until 1980, then overflowed in 1983 to bring havoc downstream) is America's second largest reservoir, after Lake Mead. With hundreds of finger-like side canyons, it has three times as much shoreline—1,960 miles. And are you now prepared for the ultimate statistic? The lake can hold nine trillion gallons of water.

River runners, always vocal about these projects, regard the dam with mixed emotions. Water storage has given them a longer, more predictable

Although the construction of Glen Canyon Dam filled a beautiful canyon, it created new beauty in Lake Powell, such as this near-perfect mirror image.

whitewater season in the Grand Canyon. On the other hand, surge releases dictated by hydroelectric demands are eroding the canyon's beaches. Incidentally, since water is released deep within the face of the dam, it comes out icy cold and clear—too cold for swimming.

The reservoir set the stage for the huge Glen Canyon National Recreation Area, providing easy boating access to the hidden enclaves and serpentine chasms of Lake Powell. It extends 186 miles upstream like a gnarled, multi-fingered hand. Most of the recreation area is in Utah, although the dam and largest marina complex—Wahweap—sit near the border on the Arizona side.

Lake Powell is probably America's best recreational boating reservoir, with hundreds of narrow side canyons to explore and thousands of sandstone shapes to admire. Visitors can splash off the summer heat in swimming bays and even don Scuba gear and explore underwater formations and drowned Indian ruins. Houseboating is popular; even on busy summer days, boaters can find a secret cove to lay in for the night.

Page came into being in 1956 as a construction camp for the dam site. Like many other such towns, it didn't go away after the job was finished. Sitting high on a red dirt shelf above Lake Powell, it thrives on the tourist business lured by Glen Canyon National Recreation Area.

PAGE-GLEN CANYON DRIVING TOUR

As you approach Page, look to the northeast and you'll see two striking landmarks—one natural, the other very manmade. From some angles, one is superimposed over the other. The huge coal-fed Navajo Generating Plant thrusts its smokestacks into the blue desert sky. Far beyond but appearing rather close is the imposing butte of 10,388-foot Navajo Mountain, highest peak in the region.

On the outskirts of Page, you can catch an impressive glimpse of the dam and the canyon which is overlooked by most visitors. Follow Highway 89 past the Page Golf and Country Club, turn left onto a bumpy dirt road and drive down to an overlook. Park and walk to the vista point, perched dizzily on rippled slickrock, several hundred feet above the chasm. Upstream, you see the great concrete plug of Glen Canyon Dam, with the steel-arch Glen Canyon Bridge before it, 700 feet above the water. When completed in 1959, it was the highest bridge in America.

Now, backtrack briefly on Highway 89 and turn left onto Lake Powell Boulevard (89L) at a Walmart complex. After about a mile, turn right onto State Highway 98, and follow it out to **Big Lake Trading Post and Museum** on your left, and a few miles beyond that, the massive **Navajo Generating Plant**. Accused of polluting the skies above the Grand Canyon, it rises from the desert like the superstructure of a monster ship. It burns 24,000 tons of coal a day, brought by rail from nearby mines, producing enough electricity for a city of three million. Its smokestacks are higher than Glen Canyon Dam, thrusting 775 feet skyward. The plant's name comes from its site on the edge of the Navajo Reservation; it's owned by a consortium of Western states power companies.

Return to Lake Powell Boulevard and follow it into the business district. The **Page-Lake Powell Chamber of Commerce** is on the left, adjacent to a Safeway supermarket in Page Plaza. It's open daily in summer 7 to 7 and weekdays only 8 to 5:30 the rest of the year; (520) 645-2741.

A long block and a half beyond, on the right, is the excellent **John Wesley Powell Memorial Museum,** which also houses a regional visitor center. Lake Powell Boulevard completes a loop through downtown Page and deposits you back on Highway 89. Turn right, go north briefly and follow it across the **Glen Canyon Bridge.** On the opposite shore, the Glen Canyon NRA's circular **Carl Hayden Visitor Center** offers fine views of dam, reservoir and surrounding countryside. Tours of the dam, guided or self guiding, begin here.

Continue on Highway 89 a few miles to the turnoff to **Wahweap Marina,** the main activity center for this part of the recreation area (see below, under "Attractions", "Activities", "Where to dine" and "Where to recline"). You'll encounter a couple of scenic turnouts en route. One contains an historical marker discussing the frustrations of the 1776 Domínguez-Escalante expedition that searched for nine days for a safe crossing of the Colorado River. From Wahweap, Highway 89 continues north into Utah and to assorted other elements of Glen Canyon NRA. These are covered in detail in our *Utah Discovery Guide.*

PAGE-LAKE POWELL ATTRACTIONS
In order of appearance

Big Lake Trading Post and Diné Bí Keyah Museum ● *1501 N. Highway 98, Page; (520) 645-2404. Store open daily 6 a.m. to 1 a.m.; donations accepted for museum.* ☐ TV performer Chris Robinson, a collector of Indian artifacts, opened this combination museum, gas station and general store several years ago to exhibit his collection and other artifacts. The Diné Bí Keyah Museum and Indian crafts shop occupy a balcony above the store. Here, visitors can view ancient Indian pots and buy modern ones. The museum collection isn't large and there's no attempt at interpretation, but it does contain some rather interesting artifacts.

☺ *John Wesley Powell Memorial Museum* ● *P.O. Box 547 (corner of N. Lake Powell Boulevard and N. Navajo Drive), Page; (520) 645-9496. Monday-Saturday 8 to 6 and Sunday 10 to 6, April through October; weekdays only 9 to 5, November through February (closed Dec. 15 to Feb. 15); free. Book store, gift shop and visitors bureau.* ⊓ This fine little museum traces Powell's epic voyages down the Green and Colorado rivers in 1869 and 1871. An oversized but accurate replica of the Powell's longboat, which starred in Disney's *Ten Who Dared* is parked out front. Within the museum are sketches, photos and other memorabilia of Powell's trips, along with the usual collection of Indian and pioneer artifacts. Other exhibits focus on the geology of the canyons cut by the Colorado, and the history and development of Page. Films on Lake Powell, dam construction and such are shown on request. The museum serves as a booking agency for river and lake trips, scenic flights, tours and hikes offered by local operators.

☺ *Carl Hayden Visitor Center* ● *At Glen Canyon Dam; daily 7 to 7 in summer, 8 to 5 the rest of the year. Self-guiding tours 7 to 6 and guided tours 8:30 to 5:30 on the half hour in summer; shorter hours the rest of the year.* ⊓ This attractive curved structure at cliff's edge above the reservoir is a good place to begin your Glen Canyon NRA exploration. Inside, nicely done graphics, displays and videos tell you about the dam, the reservoir and their creation. You learn that Glen Canyon Dam is the world's fourth highest, at 710 feet, and that it cost $145 million.

A read-out in the visitor center reminds you that it was a good investment as it totes up the value of electricity sold to cities as far away as Nebraska and Wyoming. From the visitor center, guided or self guiding tours take you via elevator deep into the dam's innards, past ranks of humming turbines. Back outside, you can walk the dam's crest and stare carefully over the 710-foot drop to the canyon.

Wahweap Marina ● *P.O. Box 1597 (six miles northwest of town), Page, AZ 86040. For concessionaire information and reservations, call (520) 645-2433 or (800) 528-6154.* ⊓ Wahweap, a Ute Indian word for "bitter water," is the major activity center for Lake Powell. A concessionaire has a marina, houseboat and speedboat rentals, boat tours, lodging, gift shop, restaurant, service station and a trailer park (see dining, lodging and camping listings below). The national park service provides a ranger station, campground, boat launch, picnic shelters, rest rooms, a fish-cleaning station and an amphitheater for ranger programs.

ACTIVITIES

Bike and sea kayak rentals and tours ● Red Rock Cyclery offers mountain bike rentals and tours and sea kayak rentals and tours on Lake Powell; 819 N. Navajo Dr., Page, AZ 86040; (520) 645-1479.

Boat rentals ● Speedboat, ski-boat, jet ski, fishing boat and houseboat rentals are available from Lake Powell Resorts and Marinas, P.O. Box 1597, Page, AZ 86040; call (520) 645-2433 or (800) 528-6154. Boat rentals, particularly houseboats, should be booked early during the summer season. (See "Lake Powell cruises" below for boat tours from Wahweap Marina.) Other boat rental outfits in Page include Powell Personal Watercraft Rentals, 148 Sixth Ave., (520) 645-5258; High Image Marine Center, 920 Hemlock, (520) 645-9323; Lake Fun Rentals, 18 N. Lake Powell, (520) 645-9837; and Outdoor Sports, 861 Vista, (520) 645-8141.

CRUISING THE LAKE

☺ If you aren't inclined to rent a boat, you can get a good sampler of the area by taking a Lake Powell cruise. Half-day and full-day trips leave daily from Wahweap and less frequently from other marinas. During winter, cruises may be canceled unless an adequate number of people show up, so it's best to check in advance.

These water tours take you several miles up the lake, past red rock buttes, pinnacles and other shapes that might have been sculpted in a Disney studio for *Fantasia.* The boatman eases his craft into serpentine canyons, slipping between vertical walls so close that passengers can reach out and touch them. You discover that one of the most awesome things about Lake Powell is the perfect reflections of rock formations cast in the surface, creating geological ink blot tests.

The highlight of the trip is a stop at **Rainbow Bridge National Monument,** the world's largest natural arch. It could be reached only by a 14-mile hike until Glen Canyon Dam backed water within a few hundred feet of it. When the reservoir is full, a finger of the lake actually extends under the structure. Geologists were concerned that the rising water might undermine the base of this great 275-foot arch, but it apparently isn't at risk.

The salmon-pink arch—aptly described by Indians as a "petrified rainbow"—spans Bridge Creek, which trickles into Glen Canyon. During the cruise stop, you can hike up to this natural wonder and even scramble down into the creek bed and pass under it. Appearing fragile from afar, it becomes a massive structure as you approach—42 feet thick and high enough to arch over the nation's capitol.

Float trips ● All day and half-day float trips down the Colorado River below Glen Canyon Dam are provided by Wilderness River Adventures, P.O. Box 717, Page, AZ 86040; (800) 528-6154 or (520) 645-3279. They're also available from Lake Powell Resorts & Marinas, P.O. Box 56909, Phoenix, AZ 85079; (800) 528-6154 or (520) 645-2433

Golf ● Glen Canyon Golf and Country Club, Highway 89 between Page and the river; (520) 645-2175; 18 holes, pro shop, restaurant and lounge.

Jeep tours ● Lake Powell Jeep Tours, P.O. Box 1144 (108 Lake Powell Blvd.), Page, AZ 86040; (520) 645-5501. Guided tours with geology and Native American themes in the Lake Powell area, Grand Canyon, Paria River and Monument Valley.

Lake Powell Cruise ● Departing from Wahweap and other marinas. Call (800) 528-6154 or (520) 645-2433. (Details in box below.)

Scenic flights ● Flights over Lake Powell, the Grand Canyon, Monument Valley and other area sites are offered by Scenic Air at Lake Powell Airport, P.O. Box 1385, Page, AZ 86040; (520) 645-2494.

Tours ● Overland trips to nearby areas of interest are provided by Grand Circle Tours, (520) 645-5088.

Whitewater rafting ● These local outfits have rafting on the Colorado and other area rivers—Diamond River Adventures, P.O. Box 1316, Page; (520) 645-8866 and Wilderness River Adventures, P.O. Box 717, Page; (520) 645-3296 or (520) 645-3279.

ANNUAL EVENTS

Creative Driftwood Contest, first Saturday of March; Lake Powell.
Page Rodeo, third weekend of May.
Pioneer Days Parade, second Saturday of July in Page.
State Championship Fire Fighter Muster, late September in Page.
Page-Lake Powell Air Affair, in early October, with hot air balloon launch, aerobatic flying and aircraft displays.
Festival of Lights Boat Parade, early December, Wahweap Marina.

WHERE TO DINE
Page and Wahweap Marina

Bella Napoli ● ☆☆ $$

☐ 810 N. Navajo, Page; (520) 645-2706. Northern Italian; wine and beer. Dinner nightly from 5 p.m. MC/VISA, DISC. ☐ Cozy chef owned bistro featuring chicken herb tortellini, baked ziti (mostaccioli noodles with riccota cheese and egg plant or Italians sausage), seafood cannelloni and pizza; patio dining. Extensive wine list.

☺ Porter's Sunset Grille ● ☆☆ $$

☐ 125 S. Lake Powell Blvd., Page; (520) 645-3039. Southwest cuisine; wine and beer. Breakfast, lunch and dinner daily. MC/VISA. ☐ Lively ranch style place serving Southwestern and "Tex-Mex" fare, with indoor and outdoor dining. Texas T-bone steaks are a specialty. Happy hour with free appetizers from 5 to 7 nightly.

☺ Rainbow Room of Wahweap Lodge ● ☆☆☆ $$$

☐ Wahweap Marina; (520) 645- 2433. American, Southwest; full bar service. Daily 6 a.m. to 10 p.m. in summer, 7 to 9 in the off-season. Major credit cards. ☐ This large circular dining room has impressive views of Lake Powell and the menu is a cut above standard resort fare. Specialties include honey roasted loin of pork, chicken fajitas, steaks and several seafood dishes. Also a buffet dinner with a Native American show, nightly.

Strombolli's ● ☆☆ $

☐ 711 N. Navajo, Page; (520) 645-2605. Italian; wine and beer. Lunch and dinner daily from 11. MC/VISA. ☐ Italian café and pizzeria with indoor and outdoor dining. Seafood pasta, shrimp marinara, stuffed eggplant and other dinner entrées, all under $10, plus the usual pizza assortment.

Zapata's Mexican Restaurant ● ☆☆ $

☐ 614 N. Navajo, Page; (520) 645-9006. Mexican and Southwest; full bar service. Lunch weekdays 11 to 2 and dinner nightly from 5. Major credit cards. ☐ Popular with locals, serving Sonora style Mexican fare, plus southwestern specialties such as New Mexico green chile rellenos and baked breast of chicken in green chile sauce. Assorted margaritas from the bar.

WHERE TO RECLINE

Prices reflect high season rates and may be lower at other times. Most were provided by the management and are subject to change; use them only as a guide.

Page and Wahweap Marina

Antique Arbor Bed & Breakfast ● ☆☆ $$ ∅

☐ P.O. Box 3172 (1020 N. Navajo), Page, AZ 86040; (520) 645-9518. Two units with private baths; full or continental breakfast; $35 to $85. No credit cards. ☐ Ranch home near downtown Page. Rooms done in a mix of antique and modern furnishings; living room with piano; patio with barbe-cue, picnic table and organic garden; bikes available.

Best Western Arizona Inn ● ✰✰ $$$ Ø

⌂ *P.O. Box C (716 Rim View Dr.) Page, AZ 86040; (800) 826-2718 or (520) 645-2466. Couples $66 to $92, singles $64 to $69. Major credit cards.* ⌂ TV movies, phones; pool, spa, lounge, coin laundry, conference room. Some rooms with view of Glen Canyon Dam and Lake Powell. Rates include continental breakfast.

☺ Courtyard by Marriott ● ✰✰✰ $$$$$ Ø

⌂ *600 Country Club Dr., Page, AZ 86040; (800) 443-6000 or (520) 645-5000. Couples and singles $99 to $109. Major credit cards.* ⌂ Handsomely ap-pointed hotel with Southwestern décor, on a bluff overlooking Lake Powell and the dam; 153 rooms with TV movies, phones and coffeemakers. Pool, spa exercise room. **Peppers Restaurant** serves Southwest fare and pasta; 6 a.m. to 11 p.m.; dinners $14 to $20; full bar service.

Holiday Inn/Lake Powell ● ✰✰ $$$ Ø

⌂ *P.O. Box 1867 (287 N. Lake Powell Blvd., downtown), Page, AZ 86040; (800) HOLIDAY or (520) 645-8851. Couples and singles $59 to $89. Major credit cards.* ⌂ TV movies, free coffee, balconies; some rooms with lake views; pool, outdoor barbecue, lounge with large-screen TV, gift shop. Lake-view **restaurant** serves 6 a.m. to 10 p.m.; dinners $7 to $15; full bar.

Lake Powell Motel ● ✰✰ $$$

⌂ *Highway 89 at Lakeshore Drive, Page, AZ 86040; (800) 528-6154 or (520) 645-2433. Reservations address: Lake Powell Resorts and Marinas, P.O. Box 56909, Phoenix, AZ 85079. Couples and singles from $70; family units $132.50. Major credit cards.* ⌂ Small motel on a bluff overlooking Wahweap Marina with TV and room phones.

Wahweap Lodge ● ✰✰✰ $$$$$

⌂ *Wahweap Marina, Page, AZ 86040; (800) 528-6154 or (520) 645-2433. Reservations address: Lake Powell Resorts and Marinas, P.O. Box 56909, Phoenix, AZ 85079. Couples and singles $109 to $129, suites $189. Major credit cards.* ⌂ A 350-unit Lakeside resort with gift shop, marina, swimming pool. Rooms have TV movies, phones, some lake views. **Rainbow Room restaurant** listed above.

WHERE TO CAMP

Wahweap RV Park ● *100 Lakeshore Dr. (at Wahweap Marina), Page, AZ 86040; (800) 528-6154 or (520) 645-2313. RVs and tents, 123 sites; full hookups $20.50. Reservations accepted; major credit cards.* ⌂ Some pull-throughs; showers, coin laundry, mini-mart, snack bar, fuel, dump station. Full marina facilities and Wahweap Lodge and restaurant adjacent.

Wahweap Campground ● *Lakeshore Drive (P.O. Box 1507), Page, AZ 86040; (520) 645-2471. National Recreation Area campground with RV and tent sites, no hookups; $8.50.* ⌂ Shaded sites above Wahweap Marina near NRA rangers office; flush potties, tables and barbecues, water.

Page to the South Rim

The drive south from Page on U.S. 89 takes you along the western rim of the huge Navajo Reservation and past a little heralded area called the Painted Desert. Overshadowed by the better known Painted Desert near Petrified Forest National Park, this is an area of softly contoured pastel hills between the Echo Cliffs and the Grand Canyon. Most of the desert's colored formations are some distance from the highway; the view is better from the Grand Canyon's Desert View area. Only one access road, a bumpy strip of dirt from the tiny hamlet of Cedar Ridge, provides a closer approach from Highway 89.

RV ADVISORY ● This rough, poorly maintained road, which reaches about 20 miles through the Painted Desert into the edge of Grand Canyon National Park, isn't recommended for RVs or trailer rigs.

The Echo Cliffs end as you press southward, although distant vistas of the Painted Desert continue. This section of the Navajo reservation is relatively unsettled although it isn't wilderness. Hamlets of **Bitter Springs, Cedar Ridge** and **The Gap** have small trading posts with fuel and basic essentials. Roadside Native American craft stands crop up frequently, selling silver and turquoise jewelry, sand paintings, pottery and weavings.

Immediately below **Cameron,** swing west onto State Route 64 to complete your north-to-south-rim loop. First however, you may want to pause at the Cameron Trading Post, about a mile north of the junction. Dating back to 1916 as a Navajo trading center, it's a popular stopover for Grand Canyon-bound visitors. A large curio shop occupies the stone and brick building, with pole ceilings and whitewashed walls. It also has a place to dine and recline:

☺ *Cameron Trading Post* ● *P.O. Box 339, Cameron, AZ 86020; (602) 679-2231. Motel rates are $40 double and $30 single. Overnight at the RV park, with hookups, is $12.60; MC/VISA.* A woodsy-looking **restaurant** beyond the curio shop is set off by a large fireplace and an unusual pressed tin ceiling. The area also has a post office, art gallery and an RV park.

Heading west from Cameron on route 64, you'll begin a slow climb that delivers you to the southern section of Kaibab National Forest. Before reaching the trees, pause at an interesting overlook to the Little Colorado River. You'll encounter it about 12 miles west of Cameron:

☺ *Little Colorado River Gorge Navajo Tribal Park* ● Even if you aren't canyon-bound, this overlook is worth the ten mile detour from U.S. 89. Barely more than a creek, the Little Colorado River and couple of even smaller tributaries have managed to cut near vertical gorges several hundred feet into the nearly level desert surface. It's one of the most striking examples of table-top erosion you'll see on the Colorado Plateau. When you've finished staring down from the security of a safety rail, you can stroll across the gravel parking lot and browse at a large outdoor market of Navajo jewelry, blankets and other crafts.

The Little Colorado River accompanies you for several miles and the highway provides a couple of more turnouts—with and without jewelry stands—as you press westward. About 20 miles from Cameron, the uptilted desert surrenders to the piñon and junipers of Kaibab National Forest. A short distance beyond—the Desert View section of the Grand Canyon.

SOUTH OF THE SOUTH RIM:
Valle, Hualapai and Havasupai

. The broad Coconino Plateau sweeps southwesterly from the Grand Canyon. It's a remote, untamed land of Joshua trees, bunchgrass and pine forests. Much of the Colorado River's southern edge is bordered by the million-acre Hualapai Indian Reservation. The Havasupai Reservation, with its hidden canyon village of Supai, occupies a 188,077-acre wedge just south of the Grand Canyon National Park boundary. Both tribes have gotten into the tourist business.

To reach this area from the South Rim, head down Highway 180/64 through Tusayan. After 28 miles, as you drop slowly from forest to desert, you'll reach the 180/64 junction at **Valle.** U.S. 180 swings southeast toward Flagstaff while State Route 64 continues south to Williams. Since most of the South Rim's traffic passes through here, a couple of motels and cafés have cropped up, along with a pair of amusements:

Bedrock City Prehistoric Park ● *HCR 34, Box A, Williams, AZ 86046; (520) 635-2600. Daily 6 a.m. to 8:30. Prehistoric Park admission $5; MC/VISA. Adjacent RV park with showers, pull-throughs, groceries, game room and volleyball court; sites $12 to $16.* ◻ Started as an RV park with a Flintstones theme, Bedrock City has grown into a small amusement center. You're greeted by a *Flintstones* soundtrack as you step into the large gift shop and café. For $5 each, you and the kids can enter the somewhat barren—but growing—Prehistoric Park. Well, yabba dabba doo! It's good old Bedrock City of cartoon fame, complete with a green Dino, simulated rock slab structures and stone-wheeled vehicles. The admission price includes a dinosaur slide, a photo with Fred and Barney, train ride and all the *Flintstones* cartoons you'd care to watch.

☺ **Planes of Fame Air Museum** ● *HCR 34, Box B, Williams (Valle), AZ 86046; (520) 635-1000. Daily 9 to 6. Adults $5, seniors $4, kids $1.95; Constellation tour $3. MC/VISA.* ◻ This small operation, an extension of the larger Chino Air Museum in California, occupies a hangar and part of the tarmac at the Grand Canyon Valle Airport. Sixteen aircraft, mostly World War II through Korea, are parked outside or stuffed into the hanger. Star of the show is a nicely restored Lockheed C-121A transport that served as General Douglas MacArthur's personal plane during his role as boss of the Japanese occupation and the Korean War. It was this craft that carried him to that fateful meeting with President Harry S Truman on Wake Island, where he was fired for questioning the way Harry wanted to fight the war. Another interesting exhibit, rather macabre, is a jet-powered "human bomb," a Fuji Ohka suicide rocket used by the desperate Japanese in the closing days of the war. It was flown over its target strapped to the belly of a bomber and then released; an on-board pilot steered it to his final destination.

From Valle, continue south on Highway 64 to Interstate 40 and follow it past Williams, Ash Fork and Seligman (which we cover in Chapter five, heading west from Flagstaff). Just above Seligman, pick up historic Highway 66 and follow it northeast. You'll shortly encounter an interesting limestone cave in the desert:

Grand Canyon Caverns ● *P.O. Box 180, Peach Springs, AZ 86434; (520) 422-3223 or 422-3224. Cave tour $7.50 for adults and $4.75 for kids 4 to 12. Tours 8 to 6 daily in summer and 10 to 5 the rest of the year.* ◻ This owned complex includes a motel, restaurant, gift shop and RV park (see below), in addition to the caverns. An elevator takes visitors the equivalent of 21 stories into the earth, where they're conducted on a one-mile, 45-minute stroll past interesting stalactites, stalagmites and sundry other cave formations. The **Restaurant/motel/RV park** is open 7:30 a.m. to 6:30 p.m. in summer and 9:30 to 5:30 in the off-season. It features breakfast fare, fast foods, light lunches and barbecued beef rib dinners; served in a rustic knotty pine dining room. Motel rooms are $21.50 to $50.50 for couples and $18.50 to $37 for singles. RV parking with no hookups is $5 per night. Self-contained RVs only.

Hualapai country

Just beyond the caverns, Highway 66 enters the Hualapai Reservation. From here, State Route 18 heads about 70 miles northeast, terminating at Hualapai Hilltop. This is the trailhead for hikes and mule or horseback rides down into Havasu Canyon and the isolated village of Supai. It's one of the few towns in America not served by a road.

If you like solitude, you'll enjoy exploring the wilds of the Hualapai Indian Reservation. Occupied by fewer than a thousand people, the million-acre reserve offers vast, lonely sweeps of high desert, Ponderosa forests and Grand Canyon views. Rough roads lead to remote corners of the reservation. You'll need a vehicle with good ground clearance for most of them; a four-wheel drive is best. A 21-mile gravel and dirt road will take you to Diamond Creek, one of the rare spots in the canyon where you can drive right to the river's edge. This was the site of the first Grand Canyon tourist facility, a now-departed hotel built in 1884. Other roads, even rougher, lead to other canyon viewpoints.

Back on Highway 66, you'll encounter **Peach Springs**, the only town on the reservation and home to the Hualapai Tribal Council. It consists of a few service stations—mostly dead—an abandoned motel, a live market, a small museum that's essentially an Indian crafts center, and the tribal office. Just beyond town, a right turn onto Buck and Doe Road will put you on track for the new **Hualapai Casino,** perched on the edge of the Grand Canyon.

RV ADVISORY ● Most of the rough roads on Hualapai Reservation aren't recommended for RVs and trailer rigs, although the 57-mile road to Hualapai Casino can be negotiated with patience.

Reservation Activities ● *Fees are $4 for day use, $7 for camping (in the boonies; there are no formal campgrounds) and $8 for fishing. One-day and two-day motorized river trips from Diamond Creek to Pearce Ferry are offered by Hualapai River Runners. Prices are $245 to $366, including all meals; the firm accepts MC/VISA and DISC. For information, contact: Hualapai River Trips, P.O. Box 246, Peach Springs, AZ 86434; (520) 769-2210, 769-2219; outside Arizona, call (800) 622-4409.* ❑

Hualapai Casino ● *P.O. Box 761, Meadview, AZ 86444; (520) 699-4161. Details are in Chapter four, page 89.*

The Havasupai Hike

Beyond the reach of any highway, Supai and the beautiful Havasu Canyon have become popular destinations for Arizona visitors. An easy eight-mile trail reaches the village from Hualapai Hilltop; it has no services, but plenty of trailhead parking. Instead of hiking, you can rent horses or mules to carry you and/or your cargo. The trail begins with several switchbacks, then it follows a gentle downslope into Havasu Canyon.

The *AAA Arizona-New Mexico TourBook* calls the trail precipitous, but it's hardly that. The switchbacks are wide enough for a golf cart (although too bumpy), and the rest of the trail is an easy path where you're liable to see a resident chugging along in an all-terrain vehicle. It can get hot in summer, so carry plenty of water.

Havasu Falls, one of Arizona's beauty spots, is your reward for hiking down to the Supai village

The route is pleasant, but not awesome as Grand Canyon trails go. The scenery is impressive, although you never see the main gorge. The trail is a busy thoroughfare of horses and mules, as mounted tribal members haul tourists and cargo back and forth. So watch where you step. It doesn't always smell so great, either.

On my hike down, I counted fifty passing horses and mules, some with mongrel dogs yapping at their heels. So this is hardly a wilderness experience. One of the dogs abandoned his outbound pack string and dutifully escorted me all the way to the village. Perhaps I smelled better than the mules.

Lest you get the wrong impression, this is a fascinating and meaningful experience. Arriving at Supai, you discover a neat and tidy village of small pre-fab cottages, a museum, café, post office, grocery and a remarkably modern lodge for such a remote spot. With dusty paths for streets, Supai is probably the only community in America with a five-mile-an-hour speed limit.

Supai Lodge is nicely done of wood and stone; each room has two comfortable double beds and complete baths. The Havasupai Tribal Café serves light meals (see below) and the Havasupai Museum has exhibits of tribal crafts, including some for sale.

The village is populated by about 500 people and probably an equal number of horses, mules and free-roaming dogs. Nearly every house has a horse or mule tethered in front. Folks here live in the saddle, much as their ancestors did after rounding up Spanish strays a couple of centuries ago.

No highway could possibly reach this village, tucked into a dramatic red-wall enclave a few miles above the Colorado River. And one gets the impression that the Havasupai like their isolation. They've been living here since prehistoric times. Spanish Padre Francisco Tomás Garcés visited in 1776 and found the Indians to be quite content with their lot. They still are, since they're among the few Native Americans still occupying their ancestral village site.

☺ The region's prime tourist attraction is the beautiful **Havasu Canyon** area below the village, and the hike along Havasu Creek is one of the prettiest in the Grand Canyon. Two waterfalls, Havasu and Mooney, take spectacular plunges over lava ledges. Black, gnarled stone fingers reach out from cliff faces, like creatures from the spooky forest scenes in *Snow White*. Along the cottonwood-shaded creek, water spills over pretty little travertine terraces, like miniature Niagara Falls. The terraces are created when limestone from the mineral-rich water combines with floating leaves and twigs to form curved spill-overs. Some of the larger ones are wonderful swimming holes.

Havasu Campground starts just below Havasu Falls and extends along the creek for nearly a mile to the crest of Mooney Falls. It has picnic tables, barbecues and pit toilets. Refreshing mineral-rich water issues from a spigot in the side of the canyon. This may be the most appealing campsite in the Southwest.

The trail along Havasu Creek is an easy stroll until you reach the top of Mooney Falls. Here, a sign invites only the brave to venture down the rough lava cliff. It can be done, if you're careful and not afraid of heights. Hacked out by early miners, the trail passes through two holes in the cliff face, then ends with a near-vertical, chain-assisted incline. We made it with only a little heavy breathing. But it was a bit disconcerting to see a trail sign pointing to a hole in the ground.

From here, the trail leads on to the Colorado River, eight miles below Mooney Falls. It's alternately easy and rough as it descends into the main gorge.

Supai Village essentials • Contact Havasupai Tourist Enterprise, Supai, AZ 86435; call (520) 448-2121 for camping permits, horseback or mule transit and other information. You also can arrange chopper flights in and out of the canyon by contacting Grand Canyon Helicopters, P.O. Box 455, Grand Canyon, AZ 86023; phone (520) 638-2419 in Arizona and (800) 528-2418 outside. For lodge reservations, contact Havasupai Lodge, Supai, AZ 86345; (520) 448-2111. All who enter the canyon must pay a $12 entry fee and must be carrying at least a gallon of water. Lodge rooms are $50 for a double and $45 for a single; the hostel is $10 per person. Camping is $9, horse or mule transit is $70 from Hualapai Hilltop to Supai and $90 from the hilltop to the campground. Upon arriving at the village, you must register at the Havasu Tourist Enterprise office and pay the entry fee. Those with motel reservations can continue to the lodge, since the fee is added to the room rate.

Havasupai Tribal Café • *Open 7:30 to 5.* ☐ It serves breakfast fare, hamburgers, sandwiches, stew, chili, homemade desserts and the legendary Indian Taco; no alcohol.

HOOVER DAM

Chapter four

THE WESTERN EDGE

A mighty river; a thirsty land

THE STORY OF THE WEST is the story of water. Range wars were fought over water rights. Rich placer mines lay idle for lack of water to separate gold from gravel. Farms shriveled and died when droughts struck or worse, when cities diverted their irrigation streams.

"Whiskey is for drinking; water is for fighting," Mark Twain once observed.

Nowhere is the role of water more evident than along Arizona's western edge. Here, the mighty Colorado River forms a squiggly border between Arizona, California and the southern tip of Nevada. Walk a hundred feet from the shoreline, and you're in a thirsty desert. Annual rainfall—as little as three inches—supports creosote bush and a few critters with the good sense to keep out of the noonday sun, and not much else.

The Colorado River once ran untamed through this desert. After scouring the Grand Canyon ever deeper, it slowed its flow in this shallow basin, dropping much of its load of silt. Thousands of years ago, Native Americans farmed along the river's rich shoreline. White settlers did the same thing, as early as the mid-1800s. As settlements grew, small paddlewheel steamboats chugged upstream from the Gulf of California, serving mining camps and bottomland farms along the sun-baked shoreline. They journeyed as far as

TRIP PLANNER

BEST TIME TO GO ● The Colorado River corridor is a fall-winter-spring playground. Numerous reservoirs attract legions of Snowbirds; they hit their peak just after Christmas. Some RV parks may fill with seasonal renters, so reservations are advised. It can be hotter than the hinges of hades in summer, with daytime temperatures routinely averaging more than 100 degrees. However, a surprising number of people come then to play in the chain of lakes formed behind the many dams of the Colorado River.

WHAT TO SEE ● Boulder Dam Hotel and Boulder City/Hoover Dam Museum; contemporary rock paintings of Chloride; Mohave Museum of History and Arts in Kingman; Hualapai Mountain County Park above Kingman; the London Bridge in Lake Havasu City; Buckskin Mountain State Park north of Parker.

WHAT TO DO ● Float the Black Canyon below Hoover Dam; tour Hoover Dam and the new visitor center; play on one or more of the Colorado River corridor's chain of lakes; explore remote South Cove and Pierce Ferry on Lake Mead; sip a phosphate in Mr. D's Route 66 Diner in Kingman; drive Historic Route 66 over Sitgreaves Pass; feed carrots to the burros in Oatman; join the crowd at the Quartzsite Gemboree.

☺ *Indicates an attraction, restaurant or lodging with special appeal.*

USEFUL CONTACTS

Boulder City Chamber of Commerce, 1497 Nevada Highway, Boulder City, NV 89005; (702) 293-2034

Bullhead Area Chamber of Commerce, 1251 Highway 95, Bullhead City, AZ 86430; (520) 754-4121.

Kingman Area Chamber of Commerce, P.O. Box 1150 (333 W. Andy Devine Ave.), Kingman, AZ 86402; (520) 753-6106.

Lake Havasu City Chamber of Commerce, 1930 Mesquite Ave., Suite Three, Lake Havasu City, AZ 86403; (800) 242-8278 or (520) 453-3444.

Laughlin Visitor Bureau, Box 29849, Laughlin, NV 89028; (702) 298-3321.

Oatman Chamber of Commerce, P.O. Box 423, Oatman, AZ 86433.

Superintendent, Lake Mead National Recreation Area, 601 Nevada Highway, Boulder City, NV 89005-2426; (702) 293-8906.

Parker Area Chamber of Commerce, P.O. Box 627 (1217 California Ave.), Parker, AZ 85344; (520) 669-2174.

Quartzsite Chamber of Commerce, P.O. Box 85, Quartzsite, AZ 85346; (520) 927-5600.

AREA RADIO STATIONS

KFLG-FM, 102.7, Havasu-Bullhead-Kingman—Country.
KLUK-FM, 107.9, Laughlin-Lake Havasu—Assertive rock.
KVBC-FM, 101.1, Lake Havasu City—Rock.
KRZY-FM, 105.9, Bullhead City—Rock and roll and pops oldies.
KJUL-FM, 104.3, Las Vegas—Light rock and pop.
KNPR-FM, 89.5, Las Vegas—National public radio; classic, news
KSLX-FM, 98.3, Kingman—Rock.
KJZZ-FM, 99.1, Kingman—PBS with news and jazz.
KUNB-FM, 91.5, Las Vegas—Jazz.
KWAZ-FM, 97.9, Needles, Calif.—Top 40, tilted toward light rock.
KZUL-FM, 105.1, Lake Havasu City—Light rock; easy listening.
KZZZ-FM, 94.7, Kingman—Light rock, pop.
KSWJ-AM, 980, —Oldies.
KORK-AM, 920, Las Vegas—Nostalgia, big band and pops.
KAAA-AM, 1230, Kingman—News and talk.
KLPZ-AM, 1380, Parker—Country.

300 miles upstream, to the now defunct Mormon settlement of Callville, near present day Hoover Dam.

Without the river, there could have been no settlement. But Rio Colorado was unpredictable. Dropping more than 12,000 feet from its Rocky Mountain heights and draining 12 percent of America's land area, it often raged across this lowland, flooding farms and beaching boats. In dry years, it would shrink to a trickle by autumn.

For fifty years, riverside farmers gambled with the Colorado's finicky flow. Then in 1901, water was diverted into the Imperial Canal near present-day Yuma to irrigate the dry but rich soils of California's Imperial Valley. But the Colorado was reluctant to be domesticated. A flood roared through the canal in 1905 and the wild river changed course. For 16 months, it flowed unchecked into the Salton Basin, 235 feet below sea level. By the time the breach was finally closed in 1907, the runaway river had created the 40-mile-long Salton Sea, which still exists.

Men were more determined than ever to control the big Red. In 1909, the Laguna Dam was completed just north of Yuma. It provided desert irrigation and put the river steamers out of business. However, it was too far south for effective flood control. To finally subdue the river, the U.S. Bureau of Reclamation launched one of the largest public works programs in history—the construction of a 762-foot high concrete dam in the narrow, steep-walled Black Canyon. The completin of Hoover Dam in 1935 marked the end of the free flowing Colorado and the beginning of major development along its shorelines.

The river is now completely domesticated—thrust into harness to provide water, power and flood control in the arid Southwest. So many dams now straddle the stream that they've formed a chain of lakes for hundreds of miles, from Colorado to Mexico's Gulf of California.

The Nile of the Southwest

No other river in the world—except perhaps Egypt's Nile—is so essential to the survival of so many million people. Without Rio Colorado, the Los Angeles, Las Vegas and Phoenix of today wouldn't exist. There would be no Imperial Valley farmlands; no inexpensive iceberg lettuce in February.

Men no longer fight water wars with guns, but political feuds still rage over who should get how much of the Colorado's water and hydroelectric output. While politician poke holes in the air with their fingers, Snowbirds flock to the river like geese on a hot day. Its shoreline offers the greatest concentration of reservoirs and rec vehicle parks in the world.

The advent of air conditioning has spawned a string of skinny little towns that hug reservoir shorelines, stretching from Hoover Dam south to Parker. At night, these slender cities sparkle across the desert like a milky way. It's an impressive sight as you fly over the area or approach the river by highway.

By day, it's evident that most of the riverside towns are unplanned and not very pretty. The subtle beauty of the desert suffers under the weight of asphalt and the glare of neon. They are lively places, however, where glossy speedboats skim over placid reservoirs and senior citizens live out their American dream of a winter place in the sun. One community *is* a model of urban planning, because it was built as the company town of Hoover Dam, the key element of the Lower Colorado River Project.

Boulder City

Elevation: 1,232 feet   **Population: 2,500**

Although Boulder City is in Nevada, it deserves mention in this book because it provides the closest lodging and dining to Hoover Dam. Except for elements of Lake Mead National Recreation Area, there are no facilities on the Arizona side.

This former construction camp is an attractive community, occupying a knoll seven miles from the dam, fronted by a park that adds a rich splash of green to this tawny desert. Like the dam, Boulder City was built with esthetics in mind. The old arcaded business district along Arizona Street is a well preserved Art Deco Main Street USA. Downtown's centerpiece is the gleaming white Dutch colonial Boulder Dam Hotel, with a handsome turn of the century lobby.

The Art Deco downtown area has earned a spot on the National Register of Historic Places. Its suburbs are more modern, typical of any middle class community. Years ago, its citizens voted to ban gambling, and it is thus the only city in Nevada with nary a slot machine or spinning roulette wheel. If you need the feel of dice in your hands, you can stop at Gold Strike Inn. It's a typical Nevada casino occupying a swatch of unincorporated asphalt midway between the town and the dam.

Approaching Boulder City from the Las Vegas area, you'll enter town on the Nevada Highway (U.S. 93). Watch on your right for the **Chamber of Commerce** in a rather ugly brown shingled geodesic dome. It's at 1497 Nevada Highway, open Monday-Friday 9 to 6; (702) 293-2034. A couple of blocks farther at 1297 Nevada Highway, the **Expedition Center** of Black Canyon River Raft Tours serves as a secondary visitor center, and it's open weekends. In addition to selling rafting tours (below, under "Activities,") it provides area brochures and booking services for Grand Canyon flights and show tickets.

Several blocks beyond, you'll enter the historic downtown area, just beyond the Lake Mead National Recreation Area administrative offices, at Nevada Highway and Wyoming Street. Old Boulder City is an attractive area, dressed up in green parklands that surround its primly kept buildings. **Bicentennial Park,** crowning a hill just beyond the historic district, is particularly appealing. After passing the Lake Mead NRA office, make a half right onto Arizona Street and you're in the heart of the historic district. The **Boulder Dam Hotel** is on the right, and the **Boulder City/Hoover Dam Museum** is just across the plaza.

RV advisory ● Most of the parking here is diagonal, so RVs won't fit. RVers will find ample parking by driving just beyond the museum on Nevada and turning right on Colorado Street into Bicentennial Park.

East of town, the highway makes a jarring transition, passing from the lush green of Bicentennial Park to dusty desert beige. A turnout allows you to pause and view the arid landscape, the turquoise blue of Lake Mead and the great wedge of concrete that holds it in place. Pressing toward The Dam, you'll pass the **Alan Bible Visitor Center** of Lake Mead National Recreation Area (listed below). Although it appears to front on Highway 93, you must turn left onto State Route 166 to reach the parking lot. Just beyond is **Gold Strike Casino** with its multi-colored Western façade. It's your last chance to pull a Nevada slot machine handle before entering Arizona.

A RIVER BE DAMMED

The Colorado is the most harnessed river in America. Dams of the lower Colorado River Reclamation Project provide water for 21 million people in Arizona, California and Nevada and generate more than six billion kilowatt-hours of electricity each year. Reading from north to south, these are the dams of the lower Colorado and their functions:

Hoover Dam ● Completed in 1935, it's the keystone to the project, providing flood control, water storage and hydroelectric power. It's a concrete arch dam, holding back Lake Mead, America's largest reservoir, capable of storing 30 million acre-feet of water.

Davis Dam ● This earth and rock-fill dam was completed in 1953 and is used primarily to store water for delivery—via lower dams—to Mexico under the Mexican Water Treaty. It also generates electricity. Its reservoir, Lake Mohave, can store 1.8 million acre-feet of water.

Parker Dam ● A curved concrete structure, Parker was completed in 1938 to provide water storage and hydroelectric power. This also is the diversion dam for the Colorado River Aqueduct that sends water to southern California, and the Granite Reef Aqueduct that delivers it to Phoenix and Tucson.

Palo Verde Diversion Dam ● This earth and rock-fill structure was completed in 1957 to divert water to the Palo Verde Valley in California.

Senator Wash Dam ● It's an earthfill embankment dam designed to store excess water in a small, 12,250 acre-foot reservoir for later use. After release, the water passes through hydroelectric turbines.

Imperial Dam ● Two miles below Senator Wash, this concrete dam was completed in 1938. It provides water for southwestern Arizona through the Yuma Project and to southern California through the All-American Canal.

Laguna Dam ● The senior citizen of the project, Laguna was completed in 1909 and now augments water deliveries of Imperial Dam, five miles upstream.

The highway twists down through craggy riverside peaks into narrow Black Canyon, then crosses the spade-shaped chunk of concrete that is Hoover Dam. This incredible wedge, still the Western Hemisphere's highest concrete dam, provides dramatic entry into Arizona from Nevada. First, of course, you'll want to tour the dam and its new visitor center, opened in 1995. The four-tiered parking structure, a curious mix of Art Deco and Egyptian, is on the Nevada side. Park and walk to the visitor center and get in line for the tour.

RV ADVISORY ● RV spaces are available on the ground floor of the parking structure, although trailers or fifth-wheel rigs will have a problem. Some of the older lots on the Arizona side can accommodate them.

HOOVER DAM

The Colorado River's mightiest dam came about as the happy result of unfortunate timing. Early in this century, the Bureau of Reclamation proposed damming the Colorado and began its site selection process. Choices were narrowed to Boulder Canyon and Black Canyon. Boulder was the initial selection, then engineers decided that downstream Black Canyon was a better site. However, the plan was still called the Boulder Canyon Project.

Several years passed before the Southwestern states could agree on how the water and hydroelectric power should be divided. By the time final plans were drawn, America was deep in the Depression. However, instead of hampering the dam project, it provided a ready flow of men, willing to work in the hot sun for fifty cents an hour. Since the area was then a remote wasteland, a complete town—Boulder City—was built.

More than 5,000 men, working in shifts around the clock, finished the massive concrete dam two years ahead of schedule and under budget. When it was completed in 1935, it was the world's highest dam, holding back the world's largest man-made reservoir. It has been declared one of America's seven civil engineering marvels. Originally called Boulder Dam, it was renamed in 1947 to honor Herbert Hoover. He was largely responsible for its creation—first as secretary of commerce and later as President.

BOULDER CITY & HOOVER DAM ATTRACTIONS
In order of appearance

Boulder City/Hoover Dam Museum • *444 Hotel Plaza (P.O. Box 60516), Boulder City, NV 89005-0516; (702) 294-1988. Daily 10 to 4; admission $1 for adults; 50 cents for seniors and children under 12. MC/VISA accepted in the gift shop.* ☐ This small museum in the Boulder City historic district exhibits photos, documents and artifacts concerning Hoover Dam's construction. A gift shop sells souvenirs and a film relates the story of the dam project. Nearby, along Arizona Street and Hotel Plaza, you can stroll beneath the sidewalk overhangs of the Art Deco shops and stores of old Boulder City.

☺ **Boulder Dam Hotel** • *1305 Arizona St., Boulder City, NV 89005; (702) 293-1808.* ☐ Rooms in this fine old hotel are being restored to their 1930s Art Deco look. The lobby and Tiffany's restaurant (listed below) are open, both decorated with pictures of the dam and early Boulder City. The lobby is particularly appealing with its oak paneling, period furnishings and brick fireplace. Boulder City Art Guild Gallery in the hotel is open daily noon to 5, displaying and selling works of local and regional artists. Most of the art has Southwest themes.

☺ **Hoover Dam** • *C/o Hoover Dam Visitor Services, P.O. Box 60400, Boulder City, NV 89006; (702) 293-8321. Thirty-five minute guided tours $5 for adults, $2.50 for seniors and kids. Daily 8:30 a.m. to 6:30 p.m.; closed Thanksgiving and Christmas Day. (All times are Pacific.) The three-level facility includes a rotating theater, exhibits and a rooftop overlook.* ☐

Wedged dramatically between the ruddy walls of Black Canyon and the dam, the new multi-million dollar visitor center is designed to harmonize with both. Its ruddy color complements the rough texture of Black Canyon and its curving Art Deco design agrees nicely with the dam's sweeping lines. A new viewing terrace offers vistas of the dam and spillway that were impossible before—at least without a helicopter.

Folks on tour no longer have to queue up in the hot sun; they wait in the visitor center, then ride swift elevators 500 feet down into the dam's innards. ("During summer, we used to average about 35 faintings a day," our guide said.) The new operation can handle twice the volume of visitors as before, which is fortunate, since nearly a million people a year take the dam tour.

Once inside the dam, the tour is essentially the same as before. People follow their guide through rock-ribbed tunnels blasted through solid rock, stare at ranks of humming turbines and step out onto a lower deck to peer up at the incredible mass of the dam and down into the depths of Black Canyon. And the guides still love to regale their visitors with statistics:

"The dam's face is 726 feet high and 1,244 feet wide at the crest. Nearly four million cubic yards of concrete were poured into interlocking forms to create it. And no, there's nobody buried in the dam. Those buckets could hold tons of wet concrete, but each pour raised the height only six inches."

I asked our guide how much the new visitor complex cost.

"About twenty-three million, according to the papers." Then he gave me a furtive glance. "Truth is, it was closer to thirty..."

Lake Mead National Recreation Area

Surrounding Hoover Dam and created as a result of it, Lake Mead NRA is a desert aquatic playland. It encompasses the huge 110-mile-long Lake Mead to the north and 67-mile-long Lake Mohave below the dam. Twice the size of Rhode Island, with a 550-mile shoreline, Lake Mead is America's largest reservoir and one of the largest in the world. Lake Mohave, occupying a rugged and often steep-walled canyon, is formed by Davis Dam, about 65 miles below Hoover Dam, near Bullhead City.

Between the two reservoirs, the aquatic set can explore hundreds of miles of shoreline. Nine developed sites have lengthy lists of recreational facilities. Swimming beaches and picnic areas are scattered along the banks as well. Trailer villages at the marinas are popular with Snowbirds and a few year-around residents. They've learned that summer desert survival is easy if you have plenty of Coors in the refrigerator and keep the air conditioner cranked up.

Fishing is excellent on the two reservoirs, according to the people who like that sort of thing. Most marinas have serious tackle shops. Fisherpersons often catch their limits of striped and largemouth bass and rainbow trout. Willow Beach Fish Hatchery on the Arizona side is in business to keep the fake lakes stocked.

(**Spelling note:** Readers—particularly from California—may accuse us of misspelling Mohave. It's written as *Mojave* in the Golden State, as in Mojave Desert, but it's *Mohave* in most Arizona and Nevada applications.)

Alan Bible Visitor Center, Lake Mead NRA ● *Near the junction of U.S. Highway 93 and State Highway 166, on the Nevada side, three miles from the dam; (702) 293-8990. Open daily 8:30 to 4:30.* ❑ Offerings at the center include films on Lake Mead and Hoover Dam construction, small wildlife exhibits, a botanical garden, gift shop and bookstore. Visitor center brochures list the recreation area's nine marinas—six on Lake Mead and three on Lake Mohave. If you're frustrated at being land-bound, you can rent boats at most of them, or book boat tours from Boulder Beach. For a complete list of marinas and their facilities, contact: Lake Mead National Recreation Area, 601 Nevada Highway, Boulder City, NV 89005-2426; (702) 293-8907

These are the four Arizona-side marinas and their facilities:

Willow Beach ● *On Lake Mohave, 15 miles southeast of Hoover Dam on U.S. 93, then four miles west.* ❑ It has a ranger station, motel, trailer village, marina, restaurant, grocery store, gasoline, picnic area, laundry and houseboat rentals. Nearby is Willow Beach National Fish Hatchery (listed below).

Temple Bar ● *On Lake Mead, 19 miles southeast of Hoover Dam on U.S. 93, then 28 miles northeast.* ☐ Facilities include a ranger station, motel, trailer village and campground, marina, restaurant, grocery store, gasoline, picnic area and laundry. Note the impressive "Mormon Temple," a great butte rising from Lake Mead. It was named by Daniel Bonelli, an 1875 pioneer who established a ferry crossing upstream.

South Cove & Pearce Ferry ● *On Lake Mead, 41 miles southeast of Hoover Dam on U.S. 93, then 48 miles northeast.* ☐ Both are in remote and scenic areas on Lake Mead's Arizona shoreline, with boat launches but no developed facilities. There's a ranger station in the community of Meadview on the national recreation area border and primitive no-fee camping at Pearce Ferry.

Willow Beach National Fish Hatchery ● *Lake Mohave; P.O. Box 757, Boulder City, NV 89005; (520) 767-3456. Daily 7 a.m. to sunset; free.* ☐ Despite the address, the fish hatchery is on the Arizona side. Visitors can take self-guided strolls past the hatching room and raceways. Here, hundreds of thousands of rainbow and brook trout are being reared for Lake Mohave and Lake Mead anglers. You'll learn a bit about the history of the Colorado River in an exhibit room, and you'll see enough fish to drive Garfield or Sylvester out of their feline minds. About 1.2 million trout are set free each year, mostly in the two reservoirs.

LAKE MEAD NRA ACTIVITIES

Boat and water sports rentals ● Ski boats, fishing boats, jet skis, patio boats and other watercraft rentals are available on Lake Mead at Temple Bar Resort (520-767-3211) in Arizona and the resorts of Lake Mead (702-293-3484) and Echo Bay (702-394-4000) on the Nevada side. Or contact Seven Crown Resorts, P.O. Box 16247, Irvine, CA 92713; (800) 752-9669.

Houseboat rentals ● Rentals are available on the lake at Echo Bay, Temple Bar and Lake Mead resorts. Contact Seven Crowns Resorts, P.O. Box 16247, Irvine, CA 92713-0068; (800) 752-9669. Houseboat rentals also are available from Forever Resorts at Calville Bay Resort and Marina; (800) 255-5561 or (702) 565-4813.

Lake Mead Cruises ● The sternwheeler *Desert Princess* has sightseeing, breakfast buffet and dinner cruises, departing Lake Mead Resort Marina; contact Lake Mead Cruises, (702) 293-6180.

River trips ● Day-long float trips on the Colorado River below Hoover Dam are offered by Black Canyon River Raft Tours, 1297 Nevada Hwy., Boulder City, NV 89005; (800) 696-RAFT or (702) 293-3776.

WHERE TO DINE
Boulder City and Lake Mead resorts in Arizona
Captain's Table ● ☆☆ **$$**

☐ *Temple Bar Resort, Lake Mead; (520) 767-3211. American; full bar service. Daily 8 a.m. to 7 p.m. MC/VISA.* ☐ Aquatically styled restaurant with a menu tilted toward seafood; lake view from the dining room.

☺ **Happy Days Diner** ● ☆☆ **$**

☐ *512 Nevada Highway (Avenue B), Boulder City; (702) 294-4637. American graffiti. Sunday-Thursday 7 a.m. to 8 p.m., Friday-Saturday 7 to 9. MC/VISA.* ☐ Cleverly done Fifties style diner with black and white vinyl floors, ceramic tile and chrome trim, old Coke signs and other nostalgic touches. The menu matches the look, with chicken fingers, chicken fried steak, baked ham and such, served with mashed potatoes. Umbrella tables out front.

Oasis Restaurant ● ☆☆ $$

❑ *Highway 93, 27 miles southeast of Hoover Dam; (520) 767-3222. American; full bar service. Daily 7 a.m. to 10 p.m. MC/VISA.* ❑ Boasting that it's not in the middle of nowhere, but in the middle of everywhere, the Oasis is a rustic café and RV park between the Temple Bar and South Cove turnoffs. Menu features are steak, chicken, chops and seafood.

Shannon's Pasta Pub ● ☆☆ $$

❑ *1129 Arizona St. (Nevada Highway), Boulder City; (702) 293-5166. Italian-American; full bar service. Monday-Saturday 4 to 10 p.m.; Sunday 4 to 9. MC/VISA.* ❑ Cute little place in the historic district, with burgundy tablecloths, white nappery and ceiling fans. The fare is a mix of Italian standards and a few American entrées; outdoor tables.

☺ Tiffany's ● ☆☆☆ $$

❑ *In the Boulder Dam Hotel at 1305 Arizona St., Boulder City; (702) 294-1666. Italian-American; full bar service. Dinner nightly 4 to 11; lounge open 4 to 1 a.m. Major credit cards.* ❑ Elegantly attired restaurant with floral wall panels, tulip chandeliers and lots of warm woods. Menu offerings range from pastas and Italian chicken and veal to steaks, chops and seafood.

Willow Beach Resort Restaurant ● ☆☆ $$

❑ *Willow Beach Road, Willow Beach Marina, Lake Mead; (520) 767-3311 or 767-3331. American; full bar service. Daily 8 a.m. to 6 p.m. MC/VISA.* ❑ The dining room features views of Lake Mohave; menu is the usual mix of steak, fish and chicken, with the emphasis on beef.

WHERE TO RECLINE

Prices reflect high season rates and may be lower at other times. (In Sunbelt areas, prices can drop by more than half in summer.) Most were provided by the management and are subject to change; use them only as a guide.

Boulder Dam Hotel ● ☆☆☆ $$

❑ *1305 Arizona St., Boulder City, NV 89005; (702) 293-1808.* ❑ Room portion closed for remodeling; call for re-opening dates. **Tiffany's** restaurant open; listed above.

Gold Strike Inn ● ☆☆☆ $$

❑ *Highway 93, Boulder City, NV 89005; (702) 293-5000 or (800) 245-6380. Couples and singles $34 to $46 ($10 higher on weekends). Major credit cards.* ❑ Part of the Gold Strike Casino; rooms have TV, phones and oversized beds. **Restaurant**, cocktail lounges, gaming, gift shop and live entertainment.

Temple Bar Resort ● ☆☆ $$$

❑ *Temple Bar, AZ 86443-0545; (800) 752-9669 or (520) 767-3211. Couples and singles $59 to $69; housekeeping units $43 to $89. MC/VISA.* ❑ Color TV in some units; marina, boat and water ski rentals, restaurant (see listing above).

Willow Beach Resort ● ☆☆ $$$

❑ *Willow Beach Road, Willow Beach, AZ 86445; (520) 767-3311 or 767-3331. Couples and singles $48. MC/VISA.* ❑ Color TV; marina, boat rentals, restaurant (listed above).

WHERE TO CAMP

Hemenway Harbor • *Lake Mead National Recreation Area; (702) 293-8907. RV and tent sites; no hookups, $6. No reservations or credit cards.* ☐ Pleasant oleander-shaded campground is on the Nevada side of Lake Mead, a mile north of the Alan Bible Visitor Center on State Highway 166. Flush potties, water, picnic tables and barbecues; boat launch and swimming areas nearby.

Oasis RV Park • *Highway 93, Oasis (c/o P.O. Box 980, HC 37, Kingman, AZ 86401); 27 miles southeast of Hoover Dam; (520) 767-3222. RV sites, full hookups, $12.50. MC/VISA.* ☐ Showers, coin laundry, groceries, Propane, snack bar, dump station, pool, hot tub and clubhouse. Located behind the Oasis Restaurant (listed above).

Lakeshore Trailer Village • *268 Lakeshore Rd., Boulder City, NV 89005; (702) 293-2540. RVs only, full hookups $14. Reservations accepted; no credit cards.* ☐ An 80-space trailer park with some pull-throughs, showers, picnic tables; fishing and swimming in adjacent Lake Mead.

Pierce Ferry • *Lake Mead National Recreation Area; (702) 293-8907. Primitive camping with no hookups or water; free.* ☐ On the Arizona shore of Lake Mead at Pearce Ferry boat launch. Pit potties; no designated campsites but campers must stay at least 100 feet from the water's edge.

Temple Bar Trailer Park • *Temple Bar, AZ 86443; (520) 767-3211. Full hookups, $18. Reservations, MC/VISA.* ☐ There's also a Lake Mead NRA campground here, no hookups, $8. No reservations or credit cards. Adjacent Temple Bar Resort facilities include a marina, restaurant, laundry, groceries and fuel are nearby. Barbecues and picnic tables at the NRA campground, along with flush potties and water.

Willow Beach Resort • *Willow Beach, AZ 86445; (520) 767-3311 or 767-3331. Full hookups, $8.50. Reservations, MC/VISA.* ☐ On the Arizona shore of Lake Mohave. RVs only; no camping. Marina facilities nearby, including restaurant, laundry, groceries and fuel.

SOUTH TO CHLORIDE AND KINGMAN

There is no highway south along the Colorado River through this part of Arizona. Our route thus becomes somewhat erratic, designed to touch most of the points of interest on or near Arizona's western edge. Begin by following U.S. 93 southeast into dusty desert, through the Detrital Valley.

☺ Although facilities there are limited, we recommend the 48-mile detour northeast from Highway 93 to **South Cove**. Venture beyond the cove and you'll encounter a rarity—a casino perched on the edge of the Grand Canyon. The turnoff is about 40 miles south of Hoover Dam. After passing the scattered and scruffy community of **Dolan Springs**, you'll enter a virtual forest of Joshua trees. These hairy-armed desert plants resemble trees and many are certainly tall enough, but they're members of the lily family. Just short of Lake Mead, you enter **Meadview**, a low-budget resort and retirement community. It's comprised mostly of double-wide trailers on desert lots. Groceries and gasoline are available.

From here, you catch striking views of Lake Mead, rimmed on both sides by barren, craggy peaks. A paved road winds down through a shallow canyon toward South Cove. The desert flora, following some biological dictate, shifts from Joshua trees to cactus, yucca and mesquite. South Cove itself has

The Western Edge

LAKE MEAD NATIONAL RECREATION AREA

Lake Mead

Hoover Dam

Boulder City

Temple Bar

LAKE MEAD NATIONAL RECREATION AREA

165

Colorado

93

Meadview

Dolan Springs

Cottonwood Cove

Searchlight

Lake Mohave

Chloride

River

Katherine

Davis Dam

Katherine

163

68

Kingman

CALIFORNIA

Laughlin

Bullhead City

Bullhead Co. Park

95

Oatman

40

Searchlight Junction

Fort Mohave Indian Reservation

40

Needles

Golden Shores

Topock

Havasu National Wildlife Refuge

N

CALIFORNIA

Chemehuevi Indian Reservation

Lake Havasu City

Lake Havasu State Park

Lake Havasu

95

Parker Dam

Vidal Junction

Parker

62

COLORADO RIVER INDIAN RESERVATION

95

95

Quartzsite

95

10

Blythe

Ehrenberg

only a boat launch and bisexual pit pottie. But the setting of the blue reservoir against wrinkled brown butcher-paper mountains is impressive.

Even more eye-catching is the backdrop for **Pearce Ferry**, reached by a four-mile dirt road. The route down—easily handled by an ordinary sedan—takes you into serious canyon country with red and tawny stratified walls and wedding cake buttes. You're near the uppermost reach of Lake Mead and the Grand Canyon is just around the next rocky bend. The park's western boundary, in fact, is about a mile away.

If you're driving an RV or have a tent in the trunk of your car, consider spending a night here. Facilities are primitive, with only a pit toilet, but the setting is grand and peaceful. The only sound you're likely to hear is the campground host's generator, and he turns that off at night.

Branching to the right from the Joshua tree forest, a 16-mile road (originally dirt but it may be paved) will deliver you to into the Hualapai Indian Reservation and a new Native American gaming parlor with a rather splendid view:

☺ *Hualapai Casino* ● P.O. Box 761, Meadview, AZ 86444; (520) 699-4161. ☐ Whazzis? Slot machines with a Grand Canyon view? The new Hualapai Casino is perched at the edge of the canyon, near Quartermaster Viewpoint. The facility has slots, a snack bar and even a small landing strip. Other activities include canyon rim barbecues and west rim tours, including a "bat's eye view of guano cave," led by Native American guides.

RV ADVISORY ● *Tie down the coffee pot and expect some bumps; a slowly driven RV will have no problem on the four-mile road to Pearce Ferry. Expect more bumps if you drive out to Quartermaster Viewpoint and the Hualapai Casino, although the road may have been improved by the time you arrive, since the opening of the casino likely is generating more visitor traffic.*

Back on Highway 93, the Cerbat Mountains form a rocky, rough-hewn curtain as you continue south. The lure of silver brought prospectors into these mean hills in the 1860s. They stayed around to establish one of Arizona's longest surviving mining camps, and the first one in this part of the state. To get there, turn left onto Chloride Road, about eleven miles south of the Dolan Springs junction.

Chloride

Our first impression was that scruffy old Chloride was about as pretty as its name, which comes from silver-chloride deposits in the nearby hills. The town is a dusty gathering of dog-eared buildings, a couple of stray dogs and a few junk cars.

However, it does a rather good job of playing funky tourist spot, and the folks are friendly. Many of its hundred or so residents are retired, attracted by the small town atmosphere and cheap lodging. Visitors can prowl through a few galleries and antique stores and peek into a restored miner's shack at Shep's store, a block and a half south of the post office. Citizens sometimes stage mock gunfights on Saturdays and they sponsor Friday night street dances with live music and a fish fry.

Old timey melodramas are presented on the first and third Saturdays from March through May and September through November. There's no admission charge; the players pass the hat after the show. These are delightfully amateurish skits that are rife with silly puns. The performers are brightly costumed and seem to be having as much fun as the audience. And no, they'll never make it on Broadway. Or even off.

☺ **Rock paintings,** not Indian but quite contemporary, are the town's main attraction. Continue out the main street (Tennessee Avenue), which becomes a bumpy dirt road leading into old tailing dumps. After a mile and a third, you'll see artist Roy Purcell's large murals, painted on the stone faces of a dry wash canyon. "Journey: Images from an inward search for self" is what Purcell calls his strange offerings. They were painted in 1966 and enhanced in 1975. They're a surrealistic-impressionistic mix—sort of a blend of Picasso, Mexican art and petroglyphs.

RV advisory ● Rigs 21 feet or less can negotiate the steep rough road to the murals, although there are a couple of dry (sometimes wet) stream bed crossings. Anything larger, particularly trailer rigs, will have problems turning around at the limited parking area by the murals.

Back in town, couple of restaurants provide simple fare. **Tennessee Saloon Social Club** in the 1928 Chloride General Store is a basic formica place with an American menu and full bar service; open daily 7 a.m. to 9 p.m. **The Broken Spoke Café** adjacent to the Wheeler Inn serves light meals, and the inn has a bar. The café is open weekdays 11 to 8 and weekends 7 to 8. Camping is available for $12 a night with water and electric at Chloride RV and Trailer Park; (520) 565-4492.

Rock paintings by Roy Purcell brighten the rough-hewn terrain near Chloride.

Continuing southeast from Chloride on Highway 93, you'll climb into some rough-hewn mountains and top 3,759-foot Coyote Pass. The route then drops into a sturdy old town that recalls the days when people got their kicks on an historic highway; see box on next page.

Kingman

Elevation: 3,320 feet   **Population: 12,345**

Cradled in a rugged desert valley of eroded cliffs and buttes at the junction of Interstate 40 and U.S. 93, Kingman traces its roots to 1882. It was named for surveyor Lewis Kingman, who was plotting a rail route between Needles, California, and Albuquerque, New Mexico. However, it was the discovery of silver and copper in the surrounding hills that kept the town on the map. Local history buffs say Kingman became the seat of Mohave County in a rather curious manner. Residents of nearby Mineral Park refused to surrender county records, even though they'd lost the seat to Kingman in an election. So folks from the new county seat simply slipped over to the rival community and snatched away the records under cover of darkness.

Mining declined during the 1930s and was virtually shut down by World War II. The surrounding countryside is dotted with ghost towns and semighost towns worthy of exploring. They include the aforementioned Chloride and Oatman, Cerbat, Mineral Park, Goldroad and Old Trails. While those towns withered, Kingman survived as a provisioning center for travelers on the Santa Fe railway and historic Route 66.

The first path through here dates back to 1859, when Army Lieutenant Edward Fitzgerald Beale's construction crew hacked a wagon route that eventually led from Arkansas to Los Angeles. It was the first federally-funded road in the Southwest; old U.S. 66 roughly follows its course here. Two years earlier, the lieutenant had passed through with a rather curious procession—a herd of camels. He'd convinced the U.S. Army that they'd be useful for southwestern transport, and he made this crossing to demonstrate his point.

GETTING YOUR HISTORICAL KICKS

There was a time, in the 1960s, when we were humming Bobby Troup's *Get your kicks on Route 66*. We watched the weekly adventures of two young men who traveled that historic highway in their Corvette, getting into all sorts of trouble with people they met along the way. (I never did figure out where they put their luggage.)

Like the Santa Fe Railway before, U.S. Highway 66 tied Chicago to Los Angeles. It provided a pathway for generations of tourists and migrants who flocked to the sunny Southwest. During the Dust Bowl days of the great Depression, hundreds of thousands of displaced families struggled over the route, their possessions stuffed into dilapidated old cars.

Most of the old highway has disappeared under the multi-lane asphalt of I-40; many towns along its route have been bypassed. The last section was decommissioned as a federal highway when the freeway link between Kingman and Flagstaff was completed in the 1980s. A weepy little ceremony was held in Williams, with Troup in attendance. Many of the bypassed towns, like Topock, Oatman, Hackberry, Truxton and Peach Springs, went to sleep. Those near I-40 interchanges, such as Kingman, Seligman, Ash Fork, Williams and Flagstaff, survive in varying degrees of prosperity.

Some folks didn't want to see the old highway die. They formed the **Historic Route 66 Association** to call attention to the highway and encourage preservation of towns along its remaining routes. The group is based in Kingman, which calls itself the "heart of historic highway 66." For a map and brochure about the remaining sections of the old highway, contact the group at P.O. Box 66, Kingman, AZ 86402; (520) 753-5001.

The most scenic surviving segment is between Kingman and Oatman, which twists and turns through the rugged Black Mountains and writhes over Sitgreaves Pass. It was so intimidating for some Dust Bowl refugees that they hired locals to drive or tow their wheezing Model-Ts and Model-As over the steep climb.

The cranky critters proved their worth but the government, preoccupied with the coming Civil War, abandoned the project. Kingman is still an important crossroad and a popular pausing place for motorists hurrying along I-40.

Incidentally, the town's favorite personality isn't surveyor Kingman or Lieutenant Beale. It's a rotund character actor with a gravelly voice named Andy Devine, who was born in nearby Flagstaff and grew up here. The main street is named for the late actor, and he's featured in a special exhibit at the local museum (see below).

Driving Kingman

The turn-of-the-century downtown looks a bit sleepy these days, since most of the business has shifted to suburban shopping centers. Efforts are afoot to preserve some of Kingman's yesterday buildings and our suggested driving tour takes you past the more interesting ones.

Approaching on U.S. 93, you'll cross under Interstate 40 and travel along Beale Street, which is the town's motel row. The route then forks to become parallel main streets—Beale and Andy Devine Avenue. At the point where they split, you'll see the fine **Mohave Museum of History and Arts** on your right. Just beyond is the **Visitor Information Center** of the Kingman Chamber of Commerce. In addition to the usual brochures, it has an extensive collection of Historic Route 66 memorabilia, from license plate frames to milepost guides. The center is open weekdays 8 to 5, Saturday 9 to 4 and Sunday 10-3; (520) 753-6106.

From the chamber, head east on Andy Devine Avenue past **Railroad Park,** an appealing swatch of green with a vintage Atchison, Topeka and Santa Fe steam engine and caboose on display. Just below, you encounter what's left of the old historic district; unfortunately, it's comprised mostly of empty storefronts. Preservation efforts are afoot. State, city and private historic groups are working to restore the block long Beale Hotel and its several storefront shops, between Third and Fourth streets. Opposite is the Spanish colonial **Santa Fe Depot**, which has been restored.

Continue east on Andy Devine and turn left onto Seventh Street, then go left again onto Beale. A turn-of-the century bungalow called the **Kayser House** appears on the left, between Seventh and Sixth; it's now a specialty foods boutique. Turn right onto Fifth Street, noting the mission revival 1915 **IOOF building** on your right; it now houses a carpet and fabrics store called the Palace. Continue a block up to Fifth to Spring and you'll see the **Bonelli House Museum** on your left. Across Fifth is the 1917 **St. John's United Methodist Church,** now housing Mohave County offices. Go left onto Spring and you shortly encounter the classic Greek tufa stone, glass domed **Mohave County Courthouse**. Continue on Spring to First Street, go uphill to Lead Street and turn right. It becomes White Cliff Road and takes you about half a mile through an attractive rocky canyon and out to the **White Cliffs Wagon Trail Historic Site.** This preserves several wagon grooves from one of the town's early freight roads.

If you'd like to visit the county's fine mountain park and smell some pine needles, retrace your route down First to Beale Street and head east about a mile and a half to Hualapai Mountain Road. Turn right (southeast) and follow it a dozen miles to **Hualapai Mountain County Park.**

ATTRACTIONS
In order of appearance

☺ *Mohave Museum of History and Arts* • *400 W. Beale St. (Grandview), Kingman, AZ 86401; (520) 753-3195. Monday-Friday 9 to 5 and weekends 1 to 5; closed major holidays. Adults $2, kids 50 cents. Gift shop accepts MC/VISA, DISC.* ❑ A cut above the typical small-town museum, it tells the story of this valley's settlement, from Native Americans through the silver and copper rush to the present. It also features a complete set of painter Lawrence Williams' portraits of U.S. Presidents and their ladies, and a rather extensive book shop.

The sizable Andy Devine exhibit is titled "The good guys wore white hats." Filled with photos and other memorabilia, it traces the portly performer's life from his boyhood through his movie career to his passing in 1977. His larynx was damaged when he fell on a stick as a child, leaving him with a gravelly voice that became famous in dozens of Western movies. He was the captain in TV's *Flipper* series and was the voice of Friar Tuck in Disney's *Robin Hood.*

Railroad Park • *Between Andy Devine Avenue and Beale Street, just east of the museum.* ☐ A 1927 Baldwin steam engine with a bright red caboose is the centerpiece in this pretty downtown park. It once paused here to take on water during its Santa Fe run between Los Angeles and Chicago. The park also has benches and grassy picnic areas.

The Kayser House • *616 E. Beale St. (between Sixth and Seventh). Monday-Thursday 7 to 5;30, Friday 7 to 8, Saturday 8 to 4, closed Sunday. Major credit cards.* ☐ This cute little turn-of-the- century bungalow is now a gourmet food, coffee and gift shop and tearoom. Adjacent is Old Town Square, with several boutiques and offices in tiny row-house cottages.

Bonelli House • *430 E. Spring St. (Fifth), Kingman, AZ 86401. Free; donations requested. Thursday-Monday 1 to 5 p.m.; closed major holidays.* ☐ The Bonellis were Swiss Mormons who made a modest fortune as jewelers and merchants in Kingman and nearby Chloride. Their impressive tufa stone, balconied mansion, built in 1915, has become a museum of turn-of-the century elegance. Rooms contain period furnishings such as music boxes, antique wall clocks, brass beds and an unusual water jacketed stove. Docents conduct tours of the sturdy two-story structure, whose architecture is described as "Anglo-territorial."

White Cliffs Wagon Trail Historic Site • *Off White Cliff Road about half a mile from downtown.* ☐ Deep ruts cut into tufa bedrock are all that remain of an 1863 wagon road used to haul ore from the Stockton Hill Mines north of Flagstaff. When you get to the site, look for a rock shelter, then walk across a bridge and you'll encounter the tracks. Alongside the ruts you'll note curious—and historically unexplained—depressions, as if people were trying to pole the ore wagons along.

☺**Hualapai Mountain Park** • *Thirteen miles from Kingman on Hualapai Mountain Road; (520) 757-3859.* ☐ This Mohave County park spreads over the forested slopes of the Hualapai Mountains, offering a refreshing alpine retreat from Kingman's high desert. A visitor center has exhibits of the geology, plants and critters of the area. With altitudes ranging from 5,000 to 8,500 feet, the park has hiking trails, picnicking, camping and a play field. Overlooks provide striking views of the desert below. Rustic cabins and campsites (see camping section below) can be reserved through the Mohave County Parks Department, P.O. Box 390, Kingman, AZ 86402.

TRANSPORTATION

Amtrak serves Kingman on the old Atchison, Topeka and Santa Fe route, with service west to Los Angeles and east to Albuquerque and beyond; call (800) USA-RAIL. **Greyhound** has bus service east and west on I-40; the stop is behind MacDonald's at 3264 Andy Devine; (800) 231-2222 or (520) 757-8400. Local **taxi service** is provided by Kingman Cab, (520) 753-3624.

ANNUAL EVENTS

For details on these and other events, contact the Chamber of Commerce at (520) 753-6106.

Route 66 Classic Car Rally and Show, in April.

Downtown Antique Fair, first Saturday of June.

Festival of Arts, Chili Cookoff and **Country Showdown** music festival, during Mothers Day weekend in May.

Mohave County Fair, second week of September.

Andy Devine Days, late September to early October.

WHERE TO SHOP

Most of Kingman's downtown business—what little survives—is scattered along the parallel streets of Andy Devine Avenue and Beale Street. The two merge at the eastern end, where you'll find some regional shopping centers.

WHERE TO DINE

Calico's Restaurant ● ☆☆ $$

◻ *418 Beale St. (near the museum, next to Motel 6); (520) 753-5005. American; full bar service. Daily 6 a.m. to 10 p.m. MC/VISA.* ◻ This attractive high-ceiling restaurant features prime rib, chicken fried steak, pork chops, sautéd calves liver and other essential American fare; salad bar.

House of Chan ● ☆☆ $$

◻ *960 W. Beale St. (near I-40 exit 48), Kingman; (520) 753-3232. Chinese and American; full bar service. Monday-Saturday 11 a.m. to 10 p.m. MC/VISA, AMEX.* ◻ It specializes in Cantonese dishes and American fare, including prime rib, steaks, seafood and chicken. Separate cocktail lounge.

The Kingman Deli ● ☆ $

◻ *419 Beale St. (between Fourth and Fifth), Kingman; (520) 753-4151. American; no alcohol. Monday Friday 10 to 3:30, Saturday 10 to 2:30. No credit cards.* ◻ More of a small café than a deli, it has 36 varieties of sandwiches, salads, soups, chili and other light meals.

☺ Mr. D's Route 66 Diner ● ☆☆ $

◻ *106 Andy Devine Ave.; (520) 718-0066. American; no alcohol. Monday-Thursday 11 to 9, Friday-Saturday 11 to 11, closed Sunday. MC/VISA.* ◻ Exceptionally cute Fifties style green, pink and chrome diner, decorated with memorabilia of Route 66 and film stars of that era. The fare is what it ought to be—hamburgers, malteds and phosphates. Sip a soda, lean against its old fashioned Wurlitzer jukebox and hum that Bobby Troup song.

WHERE TO RECLINE

Prices reflect high season rates and may be lower at other times. Most were provided by the management and are subject to change; use them only as a guide.

Best Western Kings Inn ● ☆☆ $$$ Ø

◻ *2930 E. Andy Devine (I-40 exit 53 then right), Kingman, AZ 86401; (520) 753-6101 or (800) 528-1234. Couples $65 to $68, singles $58 to $63. Major credit cards.* ◻ A 53-room motel with TV movies, phones and refrigerators; tennis courts, pool, spa and sauna, coin laundry. A **Bakery** serves pastries and light fare from 6 a.m. to 2 p.m.

Hualapai Mountain Lodge ● ☆☆ $$$

◻ *4525 Hualapai Mountain Road (Andy Devine), Kingman, AZ 86401; (520) 757-3545. Couples and singles $50 to $75. AMEX.* ◻ A six-unit lodge in a wooded setting with TV, and in-room coffee; game room, cocktail lounge, hiking trails. **Restaurant** serves weekdays 11 to 10 and weekends 9 to 10; dinners $9 to $19; full bar service.

Mohave Inn ● ☆ $ Ø

◻ *3016 E. Andy Devine, Kingman, AZ 86401; (520) 753-9555. Couples and singles $19 to $39. MC/VISA.* ◻ Simple 40-unit motel with TV, phones.

Quality Inn ● ☆☆ $$$ Ø

◻ *1400 E. Andy Devine, Kingman, AZ 86401; (520) 753-4747 or (800) 221-5151. Couples $49 to $59, singles $44 to $54, kitchenettes $49 to $59.*

Major credit cards. ☐ A 98-unit motel with TV movies, phones and in-room coffee; some refrigerators. Whirlpool and sauna, beauty salon, fitness room, pool, coin laundry. Continental breakfast at Route 66 Distillery, a virtual museum of historic Route 66, with memorabilia from the 50s and 60s.

Rodeway Inn ● ☆☆ $$$ ∅

☐ *411 W. Beale St. (across from Mohave Museum), Kingman, AZ 86401; (520) 228-2000. Couples $44 to $55, singles $38 to $45. Major credit cards.* ☐ A-38 unit motel with TV movies, and phones; pool. **Coffee shop** open 6 a.m. to 9 p.m.; American-Mexican; dinners $4 to $9; wine and beer.

The Sunny Inn ● ☆☆ $$ ∅

☐ *3275 E. Andy Devine (I-40 exit 53, then one block east), Kingman, AZ 86401; (520) 757-1188. Couples and singles $35 to $45. MC/VISA, AMEX.* ☐ A 65-unit motel with TV movies, room phones; coin laundry and pool.

WHERE TO CAMP

Blake Ranch RV Park ● *Blake Ranch Road (12 miles east at I-40 exit 66), Kingman, AZ 86401; (800) 270-1332 or (520) 757-3336. RV sites, full hookups $16. Reservations accepted; MC/VISA.* ☐ Some pull-throughs, showers, coin laundry, restaurants, fuel and Propane, rec room. Well-kep park in a quiet country setting.

Hualapai Mountain Park ● *County Park 13 miles from Kingman on Hualapai Mountain Road; (520) 757-3859. Tent and RV sites; no hookups; $6 to $12. Reservations through Mohave County Parks, P.O. Box 390, Kingman, AZ 86402; no credit cards.* ☐ Flush potties, barbecues, picnic tables, play field, nature trails.

Kingman KOA ● *3820 N. Roosevelt Ave. (I-40 exit 53 then a mile west on Airway Avenue), Kingman, AZ 86401; (800) 232- 4397 or (520) 757-4397. RV and tent sites, $15 to $21; Reservations accepted; MC/VISA.* ☐ Some pull-throughs; disposal station, showers, coin laundry, pool, groceries and Propane; miniature golf.

Quality Stars RV Park ● *3131 McDonald Ave. (I-40 exit 53), Kingman, AZ 86401; (520) 753-2277. RV sites, $14 to $18. Reservations accepted; MC/VISA.* ☐ Some pull-throughs, some shade; showers, coin laundry, minimart, pool and spa.

WEST TO LAUGHLIN AND BULLHEAD

☺ The most direct path back to the Colorado River is west from Kingman on State Route 68 to Bullhead City. However, Historic Route 66 (Oatman Highway) is much more interesting. From Kingman, head southwest on I-40, then after five miles, take exit 44, following signs to Oatman. Historic Route 66 travels through brushy, undulating desert. After several miles, it begins a winding climb into the ramparts of the Black Mountains—dramatic spires and ridges that look like dark, storm-tossed waves on a petrified ocean.

This portion of the highway, both in size and contour, has changed little since the days when hopeful souls followed its course west toward the promise of California. This section is now a Bureau of Land Management Scenic Byway and a BLM display at a turnout tells of the highway's early days. Look for it on your right, shortly after you begin the uphill climb. You learn that Highway 66 extended 2,200 miles from Chicago to Los Angeles. It was completed in 1926 and remained in use until 1984 when the coming freeways, particularly I-40, made it obsolete. (See box on page 92.)

Oatman, a weathered survivor on Historic Route 66, basks at the base of the craggy Black Mountains

As you top 3,350-foot Sitgreaves Pass, pause at turnouts on either side to admire this wildly rugged country of terraced buttes, conical spires and wave upon wave of ridges. Then, spiral downhill to an old mining town that's on the verge of spoiling itself.

RV ADVISORY ● The steep, winding climb up the Black Mountains and over Sitgreaves Pass is not recommended for vehicles or trailer combinations over 40 feet. In fact, trucks over 40 feet are prohibited. Smaller rigs can make it with care, but expect a few bumps in the asphalt and some hairpin turns.

Oatman

Like Chloride, Oatman went to sleep after the ore ran out and then managed to struggle along without quite becoming a ghost town. Gold was discovered around Elephant's Tooth pinnacle above town at the turn of the century and a post office was established in 1909. More than 1.8 million ounces of ore were taken by the mid-1930s and the town's population approached 12,000. It had its own stock exchange and at least 20 saloons. Then the inevitable decline began. After producing more than $30 million in ore, the mines were shut down in 1942.

The town managed to survive as a stopover on Highway 66, then the road was re-routed in 1952 and death seemed eminent. In the 1980s, it started a modest reemergence with the historification of Highway 66. Incidentally, the town was named in honor of Olive Oatman, who in 1851 was captured by Apaches in central Arizona and later traded to Mohave Indians who brought her west. She was rescued five years later and lived in Fort Yuma.

Unlike Chloride, Oatman is overdoing its struggle to stay alive. With growing ranks of curio shops and souvenir stores—some of them in doublewides and tent shelters—this once funky hamlet is well on its way to becoming a genuine tourist trap. It even has a tour bus parking lot. Still, it's fun to poke about the shops, most of which are housed in weathered old wooden shacks, and perhaps have a beer and stomp the cowboy two-step at the Oatman Hotel saloon.

Take time to pet the wild burros that—encouraged by locals—wander the streets and beg for handouts. They're descendants of miners' pack animals, turned loose decades ago after the ore gave out. To encourage this quadruped panhandling, some shops sell carrots for 25 cents apiece. In keeping with its new role as a tourist town, shootouts are staged on weekends and holidays at 1:30 and 2:30 by the Oatman Ghostriders.

The rickety 1902 Oatman Hotel has an interesting collection of early 20th century memorabilia, including old movie posters, theater costumes and rusty mining equipment. Room 15 has a curious claim to fame. Clark Gable and Carol Lombard spent their wedding night here after getting hitched in Kingman on March 18, 1939. The hotel was closed for refurbishing and probably gentrifaction when we last visited, although the adjacent restaurant and saloon were very much alive.

WHERE TO DINE

☺ *Oatman Hotel Café and Saloon* ● ☆ *$$*

◻ *Main Street; (520) 768-8308. American-Mexican; full bar service. Daily 7 a.m. to 11 p.m. MC/VISA.* ◻ Lively, funky old joint with barnboard walls and pioneer artifacts hung thereon. The menu is appropriate—steaks, chops, Indian fry bread and other frontier fare. Live music and cowboy dancing most weekends.

Oatman Mining Company Food and Spirits ● ☆ *$*

◻ *Main Street; (520) 768-8308. Italian; full bar service. Daily 10 a.m. to 8 p.m. MC/VISA.* ◻ That's Italian? The building has the look of a weathered frontier saloon and there's a proper Western bar in back. Yet the food is from Italia—chicken marsala, assorted spaghettis and even fettuccini alfredo. You also can get Gringo T-bone steak or charbroiled chicken.

A few miles beyond Oatman, fork right onto Boundary Cone Road and head toward Bullhead City. (The bold promontory for which the road is named is just to your left.) This takes you off Highway 66, which continues south to the Colorado River at Golden Shores. However, that community offers little of interest, other than a string of shoreside motels and RV parks. Bullhead City is popular as a winter haven for Snowbirds and boaters on the Colorado River. Its Nevada neighbor Laughlin is much more interesting—so much so that we've conspired to take you there first.

Fourteen miles downhill from Oatman, you'll hit a traffic signal where Boundary Cone Road intersects State Highway 95. Continue across the highway, following signs toward Avi Hotel and Casino. No, you aren't in Laughlin yet, although it has a Laughlin address. This is the largest of the region's new Native American casinos, operated by the Fort Mohave tribe. You'll encounter it about six miles into the Mohave reservation, just across the Colorado River on the Nevada side:

Avi Hotel-Casino ● 10000 Aha Macav Parkway, Laughlin, NV 89029-7011; (800) 284-2946. Rooms from $49 on weekends, less weekdays, as little as $19 in summer. ◻ This ambitious multi-million dollar project rivals

SOME LIKE IT HOT, BUT *THIS* HOT?

We heard it on the radio as we drove our motorhome *Ickybod* across California's Mojave desert, headed for Arizona to begin updating this book. Rooms at the Edgewater Hotel in Laughlin, Nevada, were going for $14 a night.

"Heck, that's cheaper than an RV park!" I said. "Let's do it! We want to do something on Laughlin in the new edition anyway."

"Now?" Betty stared if my sanity had melted in the heat. "We're supposed to go there this winter, not in August! Do you have any idea how hot it'll be?"

"Oh, probably no more than a hundred and twenty. Let's see if it's possible to survive in Laughlin in the summer."

It's not only possible; it's almost comfortable. Obviously everything is air conditioned and the Citizens Area Transit (CAT) runs air-cooled buses between the casinos every few minutes. The worst visitors may suffer—clutching their buckets of coins—is a quick sprint from bus to casino, over sizzling sidewalks hot enough to do eggs sunnyside up. An even better way to casino-hop is aboard the shuttle boats on the river. One-way fare is $2, round trip is $3 and frequent fliers can buy multi- ride discount books. We rode the boats at midday and felt quite comfortable, leaning over the rail to catch the water-cooled breezes. Further, the temperature chilled down nicely that evening; the thermometer plummeted to 91 degrees.

Two of the casinos, Harrah's and the Pioneer, have sandy beaches and several hardy souls were catching a few rays as we boated past. Of course, they alternated their basting with dips in the river. Most shoreside casinos rent water play equipment and jet skis were particularly popular during our hot summer visit. Laughlin was surprisingly busy on that sizzling August day, although not at all crowded. Room bargains were abundant—nearly all of the nine casinos had rates in the middle teens. Ramada Express offered two nights' free lodging just for promising to play the dollar slots for two hours. Throughout Laughlin, discount dining, inexpensive pig-out buffets and two-for-one dinner deals were common.

Incidentally, we didn't take advantage of the room bargains. Since poor Ick would have fried in the heat, we drove into the Riverside Resort's RV park, plugged him in and let the coach air conditioner run during our visit. Riverside's RV rate is $14 (the same as some of Laughlin's hotel rooms), and it's not discounted in summer. Several Laughlin casinos provide free RV parking on their lots, but we wouldn't advise it in summer without a plug-in to run the air conditioner. In this heat, interior vehicle temperatures can top 150 degrees.

some Las Vegas resorts. Offerings include 302 rooms, five cafés or snack stands, a pool and riverside beach, a 25,000-square foot casino with hundreds of slots, table games, live entertainment, bingo and keno. Completed in 1995, it's all done up with an appealing Southwestern décor. This is a rather a bold experiment by the Mohave tribe, since it sits by itself on the reservation, competing against the growing Laughlin casino center, 13 miles to the north. The experiment appears to be working; even on a hot August day, the place was jumping. Many patrons obviously were drawn by bargain summer room rates.

From the Avi, follow signs west, then north on the Needles Highway to a remarkable success story in Nevada gaming. After five miles, turn right onto Casino Drive and follow it three miles to Nevada's new riverfront casino hub:

Laughlin, Nevada

Elevation: 540 feet   **Population: 3,000**

A few years ago, entrepreneur Don Laughlin guessed that Bullhead's thousands of winter vacationers might like to pass the time by pulling a few slot machine handles. He bought a bankrupt bait shop and six acres of riverfront in 1966, then gradually built up his Riverside Hotel and Casino. After a slow start, the place caught on and soon more casino hotels followed. Laughlin named the new town for himself and spent millions of dollars on street improvements and a even a bridge across the Colorado for a more direct link with Bullhead City.

Nearly a dozen casinos now line the Nevada side, beguiling Bullhead residents and visitors with the seductive glitter of neon. To lure more visitors, Laughlin created a large parking lot on the Bullhead City side, adjacent to the airport. Free shuttles run from there to his casino. Shuttle boats also ferry visitors among the other riverfront casinos for a small fee.

Laughlin has become more than a diversion for winter visitors to Bullhead City. With its appealing riverside location, it's now a major destination resort. It recently passed Lake Tahoe to become Nevada's third largest gaming center, after Las Vegas and Reno.

Driving through town on Casino Way, you'll see the **Laughlin Visitors Bureau,** across from the Don Laughlin's Riverside Hotel and Casino. It's open daily 8 to 5; until 7 on Fridays; (702) 298-3321. The Riverside, incidentally, unveiled a new Classic Car Exhibit Hall in the summer of 1995; it's free and open 9 to 10 weekdays and 9 to 11 weekends. Exhibits include the *Back to the Future* Delorean, Don Laughlin's personal 1931 Model A roadster, a 1942 Jeep and a first-year Ford Thunderbird.

From Laughlin's Casino Drive, follow signs north toward Davis Dam. Beyond the dam, you'll get back into Arizona, where you and this book belong. En route, you'll pass by more of those rugged mountains that look like storm-tossed ocean waves.

Davis Dam ● *Free self-guiding tours daily 7:30 to 3:30.* ☐ Sixty-five miles downstream from Hoover Dam, Davis forms craggy, steep-walled Lake Mohave. It provides flood control and sends hydroelectric power into the Southwest. Tours take you by elevator into the concrete and earthfill structure, where you can look down the line of huge humming turbines. On the dam's lower deck, you can watch the water boiling up from their penstocks. From here, it flows briefly downstream before bumping into Lake Havasu, the reservoir formed by Parker Dam. A merciful feature for summer visitors to Davis Dam—the parking area is shaded, with a roof tall enough for RVs.

Just east of the dam, a left turn will take you three miles north to **Katherine Landing** of Lake Mead National Recreation Area. It has a ranger station, NRA-operated campground, commercial RV park (below, under "Where to camp") and marina with boat launch, restaurant, mini-mart and tackle shop. Beyond the Katherine Landing turnoff, swing south onto State Route

95, headed toward Bullhead City. Within a mile, before you reach the town, you'll encounter **Davis Camp,** a Mohave County Park with camping and picnicking; see below. Just beyond is Bullhead City's small archive:

Colorado River Museum • *355 Highway 95, Bullhead City; (520) 754-3399. Closed during July and August. Donations appreciated.* ☐ Exhibits at this modest museum, housed in a tin-roof cottage, focus on the Colorado River, the building of Davis Dam and the resultant birth of Bullhead City.

Bullhead City

Elevation: 540 feet   **Population: 13,600**

Continue southward through the scattered downtown area of Bullhead City. You'll pass the Don Laughlin-financed bridge across the Colorado, the airport and Riverside Resort parking lots. After a couple of miles, you'll see the **Bullhead Area Chamber of Commerce** visitor center on your right, just beyond the city park and public launching ramp. It's open weekdays 9 to 5; (209) 754-4121.

Named for a rock promontory now submerged into Lake Mohave, Bullhead City is a low-rise scatter of housing tracts, modular homes and mobile home parks. This sun-warmed jumble of hasty settlement is the northernmost of a skinny string of towns stretching along the Colorado River's desert shoreline. South from here on State Route 95, unincorporated communities of Riviera, Fort Mohave and Golden Shores stretch this streamside settlement for more than 20 miles to Interstate 40. Much of the area is encompassed in the Fort Mohave Indian Reservation.

Bullhead City wasn't incorporated until 1984, but its roots go back to the 1945, when it was the construction camp for Davis Dam. A mere 540 feet above sea level, it often earns the dubious honor of being the nation's hottest spot in summer. In winter, thousands of folks fleeing America's—and Canada's—coldest spots triple Bullhead's population. A couple of dozen RV and mobile home parks line the river's shores. Aquatically-inclined visitors can rent speedboats, water-ski gear and houseboats. The area also lures fisherpeople to the adjacent reservoir, which is the world's largest inland fishing grounds for striped bass.

ACTIVITIES
Including Laughlin

Bus and boat tours • Tours to Oatman, Lake Mead and the Grand Canyon and Black Canyon rafting trips are offered by Blue River Safaris, P.O. Box 31998, Laughlin, NV 89028; (800) 345-8990 or (702) 298-0910.

Golf • These golf courses rim Bullhead City and Laughlin—Chaparral Country Club, nine holes with a practice green, snack bar and cart rentals, 1260 E. Mohave Drive, Bullhead City; (520) 758-6330. Desert Lakes Golf Course, 18 holes with a driving range and putting green, pro shop, golf lessons and snack bar. East on Joy Lane from Highway 95, four miles south of Bullhead City; (520) 768-1000. Emerald River Golf Course, 18 holes with a driving range, cart and club rentals, golf lessons and pro shop, 1155 S. Casino Dr., Laughlin; (702) 298-0061. River View Golf Course, 9 holes with rental carts, pro shop and snack bar; (520) 763-1818. Willow Spring Golf Course, 9 holes with a driving range, cart and club rentals, (520) 768-4414.

River cruises • In addition to the boat shuttles, five daily cruises are offered by the Riverside Resort and Casino in Laughlin; (800) 277-3849 or

(702) 298-2535, extension 5770. Paddlewheeler river cruises are available aboard the *Fiesta Queen* at Gold River Casino and the *Little Belle* at the Edgewater Casino by Laughlin River tours, P.O. Box 29279, Laughlin, NV 89029; (800) 228-9825 or (702) 298-1047.

Water sports rentals ● Jet ski and other boat rentals at these outfits: Lake Mohave Resort Boat Rentals, Katherine Landing, (520) 754-3245; Riverfront Water Sports, 1631 Highway 95, Bullhead City, AZ 86430, (800) 342-3667 or (520) 763-3245; River Raddness, 2124 Highway 95, Bullhead City, AZ 86430, (520) 763-1554. Sea-Doo Rentals, 1631 Highway 95, Bullhead City, AZ 86420; (800) 342-3667 or (520) 763-5333. Several riverfront casinos in Laughlin also rent water sports gear.

ANNUAL EVENTS

For more on these and other events, contact chamber at (520) 754-4121.
Lake Mohave Boat Show, first weekend of April.
Chili Cook-off, last weekend of April.
Laughlin River Days, second weekend of May.
Western Craft Fair, second weekend of October.
Bullhead-Laughlin Rodeo, fourth weekend of November.
Boat Parade of Lights, mid-December.

WHERE TO DINE

Most of the dining is on the Nevada side, where Laughlin casinos lower their prices to lure visitors to the gaming tables. These restaurants in Bullhead are worthy of note:

Lake Mohave Resort Restaurant ● ☆☆ $$

❏ *Katherine Landing (just above Davis Dam), in Lake Mead National Recreation Area; (520) 754-3245. American; full bar service. Sunday-Thursday 8 a.m. to 8 p.m., Friday-Saturday 7 a.m. to 8 p.m. MC/VISA.* ❏ The menu tilts toward seafood in this marina resort restaurant on Lake Mohave.

Nicki's Restaurant ● ☆☆ $$

❏ *1070 Highway 95 (Fifth Street); (520) 754-7557. Italian; full bar service. Daily 5 to 11 p.m. MC/VISA.* ❏ Pleasantly dim and cozy café with ceiling fans and linen nappery. The mostly- Italian menu includes such standards as veal piccata, chicken cacciatore, plus American dishes such as steak and seafood. Try the cross-over steak Sicilian with peppers, tomatoes and onions.

Rick's Restaurant ● ☆☆ $$

❏ *1081 Highway 95 (in Arizona Clearwater Resort, 1.5 miles south of Davis Dam bridge); (520) 754-2201. American; full bar service. Daily 6 a.m. to 11 p.m. MC/VISA, AMEX.* ❏ Ribs and steaks are featured in this river-view restaurant.

WHERE TO RECLINE

Arizona Clearwater Resort Hotel ● ☆☆ $$ Ø

❏ *P.O. Box 207 (1081 Highway 95), Bullhead City, AZ 86430; (520) 754-2201. Couples and singles from $50, kitchenettes from $60. MC/VISA, AMEX.* ❏ An 82-unit motel with TV movies, VCRs and refrigerators; pool, spa, launch ramp and boat dock. **Rick's Restaurant** listed above.

Desert Rancho Motel ● ☆☆ $$$

❏ *1041 Highway 95 (a mile south of the bridge), Bullhead City, AZ 86430; (520) 754-2578. Couples and singles from $55, family units from $70.*

MC/VISA. ☐ A 74-unit motel with TV, room phones and refrigerators; pool, near boat docks.

Grand Vista Hotel ● ☆☆☆ $$$ Ø
☐ *1817 Arcadia Plaza (on Highway 95), Bullhead City, AZ 86430; (520) 763-3300 or (800) 528-1234. Couples and singles $39 to $75. Major credit cards.* ☐ TV movies, room phones, pool, spa; free dinners at nearby casinos.

Lake Mohave Resort ● ☆☆ $$$
☐ *Katherine Landing, Bullhead City, AZ 86430-4016; (800) 752-9669 or (520) 754-3245. Couples $60 to $83, singles $60 to $69. MC/VISA.* ☐ A 51-unit resort with full marina facilities including boating, boat and houseboat rentals, fishing, swimming and waterskiing. On attractively landscaped grounds. **Restaurant** listed above.

River Queen Resort ● ☆☆ $$
☐ *Seventh and Long, off Highway 95 (P.O. Box 218), Bullhead City, AZ 86430; (520) 754- 3214. Couples and singles $43 to $53, kitchenettes $48 to $58, suites $60 to $100. Major credit cards.* ☐ A 98-unit inn with TV, phones; pool, some suites and family units on the river.

Silver Creek Inn ● ☆☆ $$$
☐ *1670 Highway 95 (1.5 miles south of town), Bullhead City, AZ 86442; (520) 763-8400. Couples and singles $54 to $59. MC/VISA, AMEX.* ☐ A 68-unit inn with TV, phones and refrigerators; pool and restaurant.

Laughlin casino hotels
Toll-free reservation numbers for Laughlin casino resorts are: Colorado Belle, (800) 458-9500; Pioneer Hotel and Gambling Hall, (800) 634-3469; Golden Nugget, (800) 237-1739; Harrah's Casino Hotel Laughlin, (800) 447-8700; Edgewater Hotel and Casino, (800) 67-RIVER; Ramada Express Hotel and Casino, (800) 2-RAMADA; Flamingo Hilton Laughlin, (800) FLAMINGO; Don Laughlin's Riverside Resort Hotel and Casino, (800) 227-3849; Gold River Resort and Casino, (800) 835-7904.

WHERE TO CAMP
About 20 RV parks are crowded around Bullhead City; most are set up for long-term stays. For a complete list, contact the Bullhead City Chamber of Commerce. These are among the places that accept overnighters:

Davis Camp ● *A Mohave County park at the north end of town, below Davis Dam; (520) 754-4606. Full hookups $15, dry camping $8, day use $3; no credit cards or reservations.* ☐ Campsites just below Davis Dam, with flush potties, visitor center, boat ramp, water sports.

Katherine Landing ● *Just above Davis Dam, Lake Mead National Recreation Area, (702) 293-8907. Tent and RV sites, no hookups, $8 per night, half for Golden Age and Access passes. No reservations or credit cards.* ☐ Flush potties, showers, ranger station; adjacent Lake Mohave Resort (below) has additional facilities.

Lake Mohave Resort ● *c/o Katherine Landing, Bullhead City, AZ 86430-4016; (520) 754-3245 or (800) 752-9669. RVs only (tents at Katherine Landing above), full hookups, $18. Reservations accepted.* ☐ Showers, ranger station, boat ramp, marina, palm-shaded landscaping, restaurant, groceries.

Riverside Resort RV Park ● *P.O. Box 500, Laughlin, NV 89029; (800) 227-3849 or (702) 298-2535. RVs only, full hookups $14. Reservations accepted; major credit cards.* ☐ Across Casino Drive from Riverside Resort; full hookups, showers, coin laundry, dump station. Free shuttle service within the park to bus stop and walkway to Riverside Casino.

SOUTH TO HAVASU

The route south offers choices and both are relatively direct. From Bull-head City, follow State Highway 95 south until it intersects with I-40 at Topock. From Laughlin, take the Needles Highway south through Nevada and California to Needles, where it links with I-40. The Needles route is faster since it avoids the string of riverside communities below Bullhead City, with their speed zones. Neither route is particularly awesome, although the Mohave Mountains that rim the river exhibit some contour.

Once you've found I-40, head east to exit 9 and take Highway 95 south for 23 miles through more of the Mohave Mountains' dramatic rumples. You won't see the river until you enter another scatter of a town—this one made famous by a misplaced bridge.

Lake Havasu City

Elevation: 575 feet   **Population 17,300**

You've likely heard the story by now. The London Bridge, while not fall-ing down, was too old and narrow to handle modern traffic, so city officials put it up for sale in 1968. They didn't really expect any buyers, but entrepre-neur Robert P. McCulloch offered $2,460,000. He said he wanted to move it to the Arizona desert, where he'd purchased a piece of Lake Havasu shore-line.

The Arizona desert? The London Bridge?

About $9 million later, McCulloch had accomplished the ridiculous. The bridge was dismantled stone by stone, hauled over by barge and recon-structed over a strip of sand linking Pittsburg Peninsula to the mainland. Then the sand was scooped out; the peninsula became an island with the venerable bridge linking it to the shore.

Voile! McCulloch had the centerpiece for his planned city in the desert. Incidentally, there were some pieces left over, and you can buy them at local souvenir shops.

Lake Havasu City is the largest of the new resort communities along Rio Colorado, pushing 25,000 residents. Local officials say The Bridge is Ari-zona's second-most-visited attraction. The McCulloch folks decided to pro-vide a bit of British atmosphere for the bridge's desert locale, so they built an "authentic" English village at its base. It features a London cab, double-decker bus and a proper pub—the City of London Arms.

The problem was—and still is—that they didn't know when to stop. Ye olde English Village has become schlock city with fast food stands and curio shops selling souvenirs of doubtful usefulness. Not much of it is very British. What you will find is the world's largest candle shop, assorted other tourist marts and a couple of restaurants. Out on the pond, watercycles and paddle-boats paddle about and the *Dixie Belle,* an "authentic replica" of a paddle-wheeler, takes visitors on narrated tours.

Authentic replica?

This is a fun playground for the younger set, and a visit can be rewarding even for fussy folks like ourselves. The bridge *is* impressive and even beauti-ful when it's bathed in night lighting. A faithful replica of Britain's gold coro-nation coach sits in a recess in the lobby of the London Bridge Resort.

Furthermore, the folks splashing about in the lake with their rental water toys are having a ball, so who are we to criticize?

Coming into town on State Highway 95, you'll see a sign at a stoplight on Industrial Boulevard, indicating **Windsor Beach State Park** to the right. It has camping (see below), beach access and picnic areas. After passing the park, swing south onto London Bridge Road, which takes you through the town's main motel row. After two miles, the street does a 90-degree left and passes the English Village parking lot, which has a $2 fee. (You can bypass Windsor State Beach and motel row by continuing south on Highway 95. Turn right at the tourist information sign onto London Bridge Road and left into the parking lot.)

RV PARKING ADVISORY ● Free RV parking is available on a sandy area opposite the English Village lot.

The city's **Tourist Information Office** is just to the right as you walk into the village. It's open daily 9 to 5; summer 9 to 4; (520) 855-5655. From here, you can explore the shops, rent water play equipment and regard that noble old bridge. You can walk about its abutments and climb stone stairs to stroll across the reassembled span. To drive across the bridge, leave the parking area and cross Highway 95 (which passes beneath the span), turn right onto Lake Havasu Avenue and right again onto McCulloch Boulevard. There's not much to see on the brushy, low-lying island beyond. It does have a biking-walking trail, three RV parks (see below), beach access and several boat launching ramps.

ACTIVITIES

Golf ● London Bridge Golf Course, 18 holes with pro shop, driving range, restaurant and night lighting, 2400 Clubhouse Road; (520) 855-2719. London Bridge Resort, 9-hole executive course near the bridge and English Village. Nautical Inn Resort, 18 holes with a putting green, pro shop and coffee shop, near London Bridge, 1000 McCulloch Blvd.; (520) 855-2131. Queens Bay Golf Course, 18 holes, with a pro shop; (520) 855-4777. Stonebridge Golf Course, 18 holes with a pro shop and restaurant, 2400 Clubhouse Dr.; (520) 855-2719.

Four wheel drive tours ● Outback Off-Road Adventures, 2178 McCulloch Blvd., Suite 12-G, Lake Havasu City, AZ 86403; (520) 680-6151.

Jet boat tours ● Blue Water Charters, P.O. Box 2032, Lake Havasu City, AZ 86405; (520) 855-7171.

Jet ski tours ● London Bridge Watercraft Tours, 1519 Queens Bay Road, Lake Havasu City, AZ 86405; (800) 453-8883 or (520) 453-8883.

Lake cruises ● *Dixie Belle* at the English Village; (520) 855-0888 or (520) 453-6776. *Miss Havasupai* at Island Fashion Mall; (520) 855-7979.

Parasailing ● Nautical Inn, 1000 McCulloch Blvd., Lake Havasu City, AZ 86405; (520) 855-2141, ext. 429.

Water sports rentals ● Arizona Aquatics, 1535 El Camino Way, Lake Havasu City, AZ 86405; (520) 680-4151. Arizona Jet Ski Rental, 635 Kiowa Blvd., Lake Havasu City, AZ 86405; (520) 453-5558. Havaski, 600 W. Acoma Blvd., Room 53, Lake Havasu City, AZ 86405; (520) 855-8028. Lake Havasu Marina, 1100 McCulloch Blvd., Lake Havasu City, AZ 86405; (520) 855-2159. London Bridge Watercraft Tours, 1519 Queens Bay Road, Lake Havasu City, AZ 86405; (520) 453-8883. London Bridge Watersports & Tours, Adler Marine Center, Lake Havasu City, AZ 86405; (520) 855-9220. Palm Oasis

Rentals, 1550 Industrial Blvd., Lake Havasu City, AZ 86405; (520) 680-1131. Resort Boat Rentals, London Bridge Resort, P.O. Box 2932, Lake Havasu City, AZ 86405-2032; (520) 453-9613. Scotteezz Jet Ski and Seadoo Rentals, P.O. Box 397, Lake Havasu City, AZ 86405; (520) 680-7541. River Rat Rentals, 475 London Bridge Rd., Room 2, Lake Havasu City, AZ 86405; (800) 824-LAKE or (520) 855-4600. Water Sports Center, Nautical Inn, 1000 McCulloch Blvd., Lake Havasu City, AZ 86405; (520) 855-2141, ext. 429.

ANNUAL EVENTS

For information on these and other events, contact the Lake Havasu Area Chamber of Commerce at (800) 242-8278 or (520) 453- 3444.

Snowbird Jamboree, mid-February.
Bluewater Invitational Regatta, first weekend of March.
Square Dance Jubilee, first weekend of April.
Lake Havasu Pro-Am golf tourney, third week of April.
Lake Havasu Striper Derby, third weekend of May.
London Bridge Days, late October.
London Bridge Invitational Regatta, fourth weekend of November.
Lighted boat parade, first weekend of December.

WHERE TO SHOP

Lake Havasu City's downtown is uptown—on a low bluff overlooking London Bridge. Most of its shops are along McCulloch Boulevard, Mesquite Avenue and Swanson Avenue, three parallel streets perpendicular to Highway 95. To get there, drive northeast from London Bridge on McCulloch Boulevard. Island Fashion Mall is a covered shopping complex on the island side of the bridge, opposite English Village.

WHERE TO DINE

Casa de Miguel ● ☆☆ $$

❑ *1150 S. Palo Verde; (520) 453-1550. Mexican; full bar service. Daily 11 to 10, Sunday brunch 10 to 2. Major credit cards.* ❑ Look for the large two story building with the Mexican murals, then step inside to absorb more Latin décor, along with such staples as enchiladas chile verde and chimichangas. Specials include red snapper with green olives and capers and charbroiled chicken with rice, beans and tomatoes. Hussongs Bar on the ground floor is a popular local hangout.

London Arms Pub and Restaurant ● ☆☆ $$

❑ *In English Village; (520) 855-8782. Mostly British; full bar service. Sunday-Thursday 11:30 to 9, Friday-Saturday 11:30 to 10. Major credit cards.* ❑ This Tudor style restaurant features English specialties such as steak and mushroom pie, bangers and mash and baked cod, plus some American sandwiches and other gringo fare; outdoor deck.

London Bridge Chinese Restaurant ● ☆☆ $$

❑ *1971 McCulloch Blvd. (Riviera); (520) 453-5002. Chinese; full bar service. Daily 11 a.m. to 10 p.m. MC/VISA.* ❑ Despite the name, this modern, roomy restaurant does not serve English style Chinese food. The menu tilts toward spicy Szechuan and Hunan fare.

Max and Ma's Restaurant ● ☆☆☆ $

❑ *90 Swanson Ave. (near the London Bridge); (520) 855-2524. American; full bar service. Breakfast, lunch and dinner daily. MC/VISA, AMEX.* ❑ The

Transplanted London Bridge is hardly falling down; it has become the tourist focal point of Lake Havasu City.

busy menu in this handsome early American style restaurant ranges from fresh fish to chicken, spaghetti and steak. Salad bar with more than 60 items.

Shakespeare Inn Restaurant ● ☆☆ $$

☐ 2191 McCulloch Blvd.; (520) 855-4157 or 855-4313. German-American; full bar service. Wednesday-Sunday 4 to 1 a.m., breakfast weekends from 8 to 1. MC/VISA. ☐ Like most things with English names in Lake Havasu City, this restaurant isn't English. It's a cozy little German place serving schnitzels and such; it also features inexpensive American dinner specials such as chicken fried steak or meatloaf.

Shugru's Restaurant ● ☆☆☆ $$

☐ 1425 McCulloch Blvd. (near Island Fashion Mall across London Bridge); (520) 453-1400. American-continental; full bar service. Daily 11 a.m. to 1 a.m. MC/VISA. ☐ Fresh seafood, steak and wok specialties are featured on Shugru's health-conscious menu. This attractive restaurant sits opposite London Bridge with views of bridge and lake.

WHERE TO RECLINE

Blue Danube Inn ● ☆☆ $$$ Ø

☐ 2176 Birch Square (McCulloch and Acoma), Lake Havasu City, AZ 86403; (520) 855-5566. Couples and singles $45 to $75, kitchenettes $60 to $90, suites $110 to $140. MC/VISA. ☐ TV, phones, refrigerators; pool, spa.

Hidden Palms All Suite Inn ● ☆☆ $$$ Ø

☐ 2100 Swanson (Acoma Boulevard), Lake Havasu City, AZ 86403; (800) 254-5611 or (520) 855-7144. Suites $50 to $80; also weekly rates. MC/VISA. ☐ A 22-unit all-suite resort with TV, phones, full kitchens including microwaves; pool, barbecue area, coin laundry.

Holiday Inn ● ☆☆☆ $$$ Ø

☐ 245 London Bridge Road (Highway 95 and Mesquite), Lake Havasu City, AZ 86403; (520) 855-4071 or (800) HOLIDAY. Couples and singles $55 to $70, suites $95 to $130. Major credit cards. ☐ A 162-unit inn with TV movies, phones and refrigerators; pool, spa, laundry. **Bridge Room Restaurant** serves from 6 a.m. to 2 p.m. and 5 to 10 p.m., American; dinners $6 to $16; cocktail lounge with nightly entertainment.

Lake Havasu City Super 8 Motel ● ☆☆ $$ ∅

◻ *305 London Bridge Rd. (two blocks from bridge), Lake Havasu City, AZ 86403; (800) 843-1991 or (520) 855-8844. Couples and singles $28.88 to $46.88. Major credit cards.* ◻ A 60-room motel with TV movies and phones; some lake views. Pool and spa.

The London Bridge Resort ● ☆☆☆☆ $$$$ ∅

◻ *1477 Queens Bay (just above the bridge and English Village), Lake Havasu City, AZ 86403; (520) 855-0888 or (800) 225-2879 in Arizona and (800) 624-7939 outside. Recently refurbished waterfront resort hotel. Couples and singles $59 to $200, suites $139 to $269. Major credit cards.* ◻ Resort complex next to the bridge with two pools, spa, tennis courts and gift shop; boat slips. Nice rooms with TV movies and phones, many with lake and bridge views. **The Crazy Coyote Restaurant** serves Southwest and American fare; dinners $15 to $20; full bar service.

Nautical Inn Resort ● ☆☆☆ $$$$

◻ *1000 McCulloch Blvd., Lake Havasu City, AZ 86403; (800) 892-2141 or (520) 855-2141. Couples and singles $90 to $149, kitchenettes $97 to $149, suites $150 to $225. Major credit cards.* ◻ A 120-room lakeside resort with TV and phones, some refrigerators and microwaves; pool, spa, tennis courts, beach boutique, coin laundry, barbecue area, golf course and water ski area. **Captain's Table** serves continental and American fare; 7 a.m. to 10 p.m.; dinners $10 to $19; nautical décor; full bar service.

Sands Vacation Resort ● ☆☆☆ $$$

◻ *2040 Mesquite Ave., Lake Havasu City, AZ 86403; (800) 521-0360 or (520) 855-1388. An all suite hotel; units from $69 to $189. Major credit cards.* ◻ Nicely furnished suites with TV, phones and kitchens with refrigerators and microwaves; pool, tennis courts, barbecue area, coin laundry.

Travelodge ● ☆☆ $$$ ∅

◻ *480 London Bridge Rd., Lake Havasu City, AZ 86403; (800) 578-7878 or (520) 680-9202. Couples $50 to $65, singles $45 to $60 (microwaves and refrigerators $5 extra), suites $90 to $125; rates include continental breakfast. Major credit cards.* ◻ A 41-unit motel with TV movies and phones, some microwaves and refrigerators; boat parking, boat launch ramp nearby.

WHERE TO CAMP

Crazy Horse Campground ● *1534 Beachcomber Blvd. (on the peninsula, across London Bridge), Lake Havasu City, AZ 86403; (520) 855-4033. RV sites, full hookups $22 to $38, no hookups $10. Reservations accepted; MC/VISA.* ◻ Showers, some lakeside sites, disposal station, coin laundry, groceries and gifts at Western theme store, Propane, spa, pool and swimming beach, boat dock and launch, recreation room.

Islander RV Resort ● *751 Beachcomber Blvd. (on the peninsula, across London Bridge), Lake Havasu City, AZ 86403; (520) 680-2000. RVs only; full hookups, $22 to $35. Reservations accepted; MC/VISA.* ◻ Large park with 500 RV sites, clubhouse, showers, laundromat, library, billiard and cardroom, TV lounge. Also shuffleboard and horseshoe pits, pools, spas, barbecue area, boat ramp, docks swimming beaches and nature trail.

Sandpoint Marina and RV Park ● *P.O. Box 1469, Lake Havasu City, AZ 86405; (520) 855-0549. RV sites, full hookups, $22; also tent sites; trailer rentals $50 to $125. Reservations accepted; MC/VISA.* ◻ Showers, store, service station, café, marina with boat launch, boat and houseboat rentals. Ten miles south off Highway 95, near Cat Tail Cove of Lake Havasu State Park

Lake Havasu State Park • *Two state beaches, Cat Tail Cove and Windsor Beach, have camping sites and a $5 day use fee; with flush potties, boat ramps and swimming areas. No reservations or credit cards.* ☐ Windsor Beach at the north end of Lake Havasu City (1350 McCulloch Blvd.) has tent and RV sites, no hookups, $10. Cat Tail Cove (17 miles south on Highway 95) has RV sites only, $15 with hookups and $10 without; with a disposal station, flush potties, coin laundry, Propane and rental boats.

SOUTH TO PARKER AND QUARTZSITE

Heading south from Lake Havasu City, Highway 95 swings away from the river for about a dozen miles, and then returns near Cat Tail Cove and Sandpoint Marina. Just south of there, you can pause at a turnout adjacent to milepost 162 and read about the **Lake Havasu National Wildlife Refuge.** It extends inland along the Bill Williams River, which joins the Colorado here. The mouth, which is curiously marshy and green in this dusty desert, is a good place to spot marsh birds and migrating water birds. A bit farther south is yet another dam, set among rugged hills. The sign says "Parker Dam takeoff point," referring not to a flying dam but to launch ramps above and below. You can tour the dam by crossing it to the California side.

Parker Dam • *Free self-guided tours daily 7:30 to 4 on the California side (Pacific time).* ☐ This curved concrete dam appears to be small, with the crest rising only 85 feet. However, most of it us underground; workers bored 235 feet into the riverbed to set the foundation. The dam creates Lake Havasu and sends Colorado River water to southern California and the Arizona cities of Phoenix and Tucson. The self-guiding tour is rather limited, consisting of an elevator ride down into the dam and a stroll past four turbines in the generator room. Earlier, visitors could step inside a huge turbine pit and watch the shaft spin, but this was barred when we last visited.

Lake Moovalya is another of Rio Colorado's chain of lakes, starting just below Parker Dam. It's one of the more appealing reservoirs along this border—a slender, jade-colored lake cradled between rugged, russet hills and terraced buttes. People have trouble pronouncing *Moovalya*, so this 11-mile stretch of water recreation area is called the Parker Strip. And it *is* busy. Shorelines in both states are lined with beach resorts and RV parks. Even in summer, the reservoir is aswarm with power boats, jet skis and water skiers.

☺ **Buckskin Mountain State Park** is a couple of miles below Parker Dam, just beyond mile marker 155. It has streamside camping (see "Where to camp" below), grassy picnic areas and boat launch facilities. Immediately south of the park, take Riverside Drive through the heart of the Parker Strip water recreation area. Marked "business route," it parallels Highway 95, tucked between ruddy bluffs and the slender reservoir.

If you're young and rowdy or would like to feel that way, pause for lunch, dinner or general hell-raising at the Western style **Rivers Edge Restaurant** and **Sundance Saloon,** a mile or so south of the state park. A popular river folk hangout, the saloon offers bikini and "macho-man" contests, wet T-shirt competitions and live musical entertainment. The restaurant serves American and Mexican fare from its river-view dining room, along with a lot of camaraderie and loud jukebox music. The complex has a "floating cocktail lounge" and a dock for boaters; (520) 667-3036.

Just over two miles below, you'll see **La Paz County Park** on your right, with camping and water access (see "Where to camp" below); and Emerald Canyon Golf Course on the left. And yes, golfers are insane. When we last passed, several were playing in the August heat, with the mercury approaching 110. After seven miles of Riverside Drive, turn right at a signal, which puts you back onto Highway 95. Follow it into a well-kept community that's the commercial heart of the Colorado River Indian Reservation.

Parker

Elevation: 417 feet   **Population: 3,035**

As you enter Parker, look to your left for a curious combination of commercialism—the Moovalya Plaza shopping center with a side-by-side Safeway supermarket and the **Blue Water Casino.** This prosperous looking shopping complex is operated by the Colorado River tribes, and includes several smaller shops. The casino has the usual ranks of slots, plus a poker parlor, bingo and keno, and a 24-hour restaurant serving bargain-priced meals; see below, under "Where to dine." (Note: A larger hotel, casino and RV park complex is planned northeast of Moovalya Plaza off Highway 95; it may be in place by the time you pass through.)

A few blocks beyond the casino, turn south onto California Avenue to stay with Highway 95. After a couple of blocks, you'll see the **Parker Chamber of Commerce** visitor center on your left, in front of the Arizona-California trainyard. It's open weekdays 9 to 5; (520) 669-2174. About eight blocks south of the visitor center, turn west onto Mohave Road and follow it to the tribal archive:

Colorado River Indian Tribes Museum ● *Agency and Mohave roads, Parker; (520) 669-9211. Open weekdays 8 to 5 and Saturday 10 to 4 (closed during the lunch hour); free admission.* ☐ Exhibits feature tribal lore of the Mohave, Chemehuevi, Navajo and Hopi Indians and their prehistoric predecessors. Indian crafts and publications are sold at a small gift shop.

ACTIVITIES

Golf ● Emerald Canyon Golf Course, 18 holes with a driving range, putting green, pro shop and snack shop, seven miles north of Parker; (520) 667-3366. Havasu Springs Resort, nine holes with a restaurant nearby, half mile north of Parker Dam; (520) 667-3361.

Jet ski rentals ● Steve's Jet Ski Rental, The Roadrunner, Business Route 95 (Parker Strip; P.O. Box 705), (520) 667-2845.

Boat rentals ● Havasu Springs Resort, Route 2, Box 624 (on the Parker Strip), Parker, AZ 85344; (520) 667-3361.

ANNUAL EVENTS

The Score Parker 400, off-road race in late January.
Balloon Fest, first weekend of March.
Parker Enduro Classic Boat Races, last weekend of March.
Parker Innertube Float in late June.
Christmas Lighted Boat Parade, second Saturday in December.

WHERE TO DINE

Blue Water Casino Restaurant ● ☆☆ **$**

☐ *Moovalya Plaza at 119 W. Riverside Dr.; (520) 669-7777. American-Mexican; full bar service. Open 24 hours. MC/VISA, DISC.* ☐ Large café in the midst of Blue Water's 300 slot machines serves chicken, meat loaf, steaks, pasta and sandwiches. The casino's restaurant probably has Parker's best food prices, although patrons have to be 18 or older to enter the casino.

Los Arcos Restaurant ● ☆☆ $$

☐ *1200 California Ave. (across from the Chamber of Commerce); (520) 669-2375. Mexican-American; full bar service. Monday-Thursday 11 to 9, Friday- Saturday 11 to 10, closed Sunday. MC/VISA.* ☐ Homemade Mexican fare, such as chili Colorado, carne asada and an interesting ground beef and potato taco, plus American barbecued ribs, chicken and steaks. Cozily dim place with typical Mexican décor.

Paradise Café ● ☆☆ $

☐ *Highway 95 at Casa del Rio (Parker Dam turnoff), Parker; (520) 667-2404. American barbecue; wine and beer. Sunday-Thursday 5:30 to 10 and Friday-Saturday 5:30 to 11. MC/VISA.* ☐ Calling itself "a fun place with a serious kitchen," this homey little café specializes in barbecue ribs and chicken and homemade pies and desserts.

WHERE TO RECLINE

Casa del Rio Resort ● ☆☆ $$$ Ø

☐ *Route 2, Box 269 (Highway 95 at Parker Dam turnoff), Parker, AZ 85344; (520) 667-2727. Kitchenette units $50 to $75 for up to four people; monthly rentals in winter. MC/VISA, AMEX.* ☐ Riverside duplex apartment resort with room TV; spa. **Paradise Café** serves American grill weekdays 11 a.m. to 1 a.m. and weekends 8 a.m. to 1 a.m.; dinners $4 to $20; full bar.

El Rancho Motel ● ☆☆ $$ Ø

☐ *709 California Ave. (north end of town), Parker, AZ 85344. Couples and kitchenettes $32 to $50, singles $28 to $40. Small motel near the river with TV movies, refrigerators, phones; pool.*

Holiday Kasbah Motel ● ☆☆ $$ Ø

☐ *604 California Ave. (Riverside Drive), Parker, AZ 85344; (520) 669-2133. Couples $40 to $50, singles $30 to $37, suites $53 to $71. Major credit cards.* ☐ A 41-room motel with TV movies, room phones, refrigerators; continental breakfast.

Kofa Inn ● ☆☆ $$

☐ *1700 California Ave. (Highway 95), Parker, AZ 85344; (800) 742-6072 or (520) 669-2101. Couples $40, singles $35. Major credit cards.* ☐ TV, room phones, pool. Coffee Ern's café adjacent (listed above).

Stardust Motel ● ☆☆ $$

☐ *700 California Ave. (Seventh), Parker, AZ 85344-5042; (520) 669-2278. Couples $35 to $95, singles $30 to $60, suites $45 to $130. MC/VISA, AMEX.* ☐ TV movies, phones; many refrigerators and microwaves; pool.

WHERE TO CAMP

Parker is practically wall-to-wall RV parks. There are five in town, plus 23 on the Arizona side of Parker Strip and 20 on the California side. For a list of the many commercial parks in the area, contact the chamber of commerce. Here are three state or county operated ones that accept overnighters:

Buckskin Mountain River Island Unit ● *P.O. Box BA (12 miles north on the river), Parker, AZ 85344; (520) 667-3386. RV and camp sites, no hookups, $10, day use $5. No credit cards or reservations.* ☐ Smaller satellite to Buckskin Mountain (below) with a boat launch ramp, flush potties, lawn areas, barbecues and picnic tables.

Buckskin Mountain State Park ● *P.O. Box BA (11 miles north on the river), Parker, AZ 85344; (520) 667-3231. Tent and RV sites; shade cabanas with hookups, $20; regular hookups, $15, day use $5. No credit cards or reservations.* ☐ Attractive park on Lake Moovalya with a boat launch ramp, flush potties; grassy lawn area, barbecues and picnic tables.

La Paz County Park ● *Route 2, Box 706 (eight miles north on the river), Parker, AZ 85344; (520) 667-2069. RV and tent sites, $6 to $9. No credit cards or reservations.* ☐ Flush potties, disposal station, boat ramp, swimming beach, tennis, nature trails, playground, bike paths; golf course adjacent.

There's not much to see south of Parker. Highway 95 swings away from the river and travels through uninteresting beige desert at the foot of the Plomosa Mountains. After 35 miles, you'll encounter a scruffy collection of mobile home and RV parks whose main claim to fame appears to be cheap rent:

Quartzsite

Elevation: 875 feet   **Population: 900**

It might be the strangest town in Arizona, and possibly on the planet. Actually, it isn't exactly a town, but more of a scraped away piece of desert covered with RV parks and a few permanent buildings.

Quartzsite dates back to 1856 when one Charles Tyson built a civilian fort and stage stop. Today, the town resembles a huge traveling show that's about to pull up stakes. As a matter of fact, most of its residents do just that, since they're Snowbirds who flee back north to beat the summer heat. This annual spring exodus shrinks the population from 200,000 to a handful. A few of the town's structures are anchored to the desert dirt, but most winter business is conducted out of tents and shade ramadas.

This dusty desert village has no town government, schools, police department or zoning regulations. What it has is a mobile population whose median age is somewhere between Social Security and infinity. They're having the time of their lives at barbecues, potluck dinners and dances. Some merely unfold camp chairs on a swatch of Astroturf beside their RVs and breathe the clean desert air. At Stardusty Ballroom, which has only a floor—no walls or ceiling—oldsters fox-trot to music of the swinging years. "Dance at your own risk," a sign warns.

With dozens of RV parks competing for customers, space rent is the lowest in Arizona—perhaps in America. Further, the Bureau of Land Management will let you park at La Posa Recreation Area for just $25 for six months. Located south of I-10, La Posa has no utilities, not even water, but you can't beat the rates. The town's transient 200,000 swells to nearly a million during the Quartzsite Gemboree, a monster gem and mineral show, flea market and RV rendezvous held each winter. During the show, folks say you can walk from one end of town to the other over the roof tops of RVs.

Exploring Quartzsite is a simple matter. Coming south on State Route 95, turn west onto Main Street at the four-way stop, before you reach the freeway interchange. The **Quartzsite Museum** appears within a few dozen feet, in a crumbling adobe building on the left. Drive a few more blocks toward the western end of town and you'll see a pair of side-by-side gem, mineral and curio shops that operate the year around—**The Main Event** and **Hardies.** Just beyond, a sign points south to the **Hi Jolly grave site** in the town cemetery. Hi Jolly was a Syrian camel herder hired to assist Lieutenant Beale's southwest desert camel caravan experiment. When it was disbanded, he stayed in Quartzsite.

ATTRACTIONS AND ACTIVITIES

☺ **Quartzsite Gemboree** ● *Late January through early February in three overlapping shows: The Main Event, Quartzsite PowWow and Tyson Wells Sell-A-Rama. For details, contact the Quartzsite Chamber of Commerce, P.O. Box 85, Quartzsite, AZ 85346; (520) 927-5600.* ⊔ This series of gem shows, flea markets and desert festivals was started in 1964 by a few rock-swappers tailgating out of their pickups. Combined, they have become the world's largest gem show and swap meet. About 6,000 booths peddle everything from 7,000-pound quartz boulders and petrified dinosaur poop to snow cones and hot dogs. During the two-week run, the festivals feature antiques and collectibles exhibits, flea markets, an auto show, a professional rodeo, country and Western music jamboree, camel and ostrich races and—good grief!— even a history of Quartzsite pageant. For details, contact the Quartzsite Chamber of Commerce, P.O. Box 85, Quartzsite, AZ 85346; (520) 927-5600.

Quartzsite Museum ● *In an adobe brick building downtown, (north side of the freeway); open Wednesday through Saturday 10 to 3; usually closed in summer. Free; donations are appreciated.* ⊔ Occupying the former Tyson Wells stage stop that ran between Ehrenberg and Wickenburg, the museum exhibits old bottles, mineral specimens, pioneer artifacts and a mock-up school room and assay office.

Hi Jolly grave site ● *In the local cemetery, west end of town, south of Main Street.* ⊔ When Lieutenant Edward Beale marched his camel corps through the Southwest in 1857, he was assisted by a Syrian camel herder named Haiji Ali. That's as difficult to pronounced as Moovalya, so he became "Hi Jolly." After the camel program was disbanded, Hi Jolly remained in Quartzsite until his death in 1902. His grave is marked with a pyramid and a camel silhouette that looks like it was copied from a cigarette pack.

WHERE TO DINE AND RECLINE

Ted's Bullpen ● ☆ **$$**

⊔ *Main Street; (520) 927-6625. American; wine and beer. Daily 5 a.m. to 10 p.m. No credit cards.* ⊔ A basic truck stop café offering the usual steaks, chickens, chops and several Mexican dishes. Hefty breakfasts are a specialty.

Don's Stagestop Restaurant & Motel ● ☆ **$ Ø**

⊔ *P.O. Box 4854 (904 W. Main St.); Quartzsite, AZ 85359; (520) 927-4334. Couples $30, singles $25. No credit cards.* ⊔ Simple ten-unit motel with TV. The **restaurant** is a bit more prim and than the Bullpen, serving American essentials such as ground round, fried chicken, pork chops and such; dinners $5 to $7; no alcohol.

WHERE TO CAMP

Good grief, practically anywhere! There are too many RV parks in Quartzsite to even think about listing them. A few are rather nice places with landscaping, palms and pools. Most are merely dirt patches, where the fragile desert has been rudely scraped away. You can "dry camp" with no hookups in some for as little as $3 a night, or merely go outside of town and park beside a creosote bush. For a list of RV parks, contact the Quartzsite Chamber of Commerce, P.O. Box 85, Quartzsite, AZ 85346; (520) 927-5600.

TRIP PLANNER

WHEN TO GO ● The Colorado Plateau and San Francisco Peaks offer an all-year playground. This is forest country, not cactus country. Summers are pleasantly warm and occasional winter snows dust Flagstaff, the area's commercial center. Arizona Snowbowl is a popular winter sports resort.

WHAT TO SEE ● Riordan State Historic Park, Museum of Northern Arizona and Lowell Observatory in Flagstaff; Grand Canyon Deer Park near Williams; Sunset Crater, Wupatki and Walnut Canyon national monuments; Meteor Crater, Homol'ovi Ruins State Park and Little Painted Desert County Park near Windslow.

WHAT TO DO ● Poke about the shops and boutiques of historic downtown Flagstaff; hike to the top of Mount Humphreys; quaff a cool one in Flagstaff's Museum Club (particularly if you've hiked to the top of Mount Humphreys); schedule an evening stargaze at Lowell Observatory; ski the slopes of the Arizona Snowbowl in winter or ride the tram in summer; ride the Grand Canyon Railway from Williams to Grand Canyon National Park; stroll the rim of the Meteor Crater.

☺ *Indicates an attraction, restaurant or lodging with special appeal.*

USEFUL CONTACTS

Coconino National Forest, 2323 Greenlaw Way, Flagstaff, AZ 86001; (520) 527-7400.

Flagstaff Visitors Center, 101 W. Route 66 (Amtrak Depot), Flagstaff, AZ 86001; (800) 842-7293 or (520) 774-9541.

Kaibab National Forest, 800 S. Sixth St., Williams, AZ 86046; (520) 635-2681.

Williams-Grand Canyon Chamber of Commerce, 200 Railroad Ave., Williams, AZ 86046; (520) 635-4061.

Winslow Chamber of Commerce, P.O. Box 460 (300 W. North Road), Winslow, AZ 86047; (520) 289-2434.

FLAGSTAFF RADIO STATIONS

KAFF-FM, 92.9—Country.
KDBK-FM, 92—Rock.
KSLX-FM, 105.1—Light rock
KMGN-FM, 93.9—Classic light rock.
KQNA-AM, 1130—Talk radio, news.

KNAU-FM, 88.7—NPR
KOLT-FM, 107.5—Country.
KVNA-FM, 97.5—Easy listening.
KAFF-AM, 930—Country.

WUPATKI RUIN

Chapter five
THE NORTHERN MIDDLE
Flagstaff and its surrounds

ALTHOUGH THIS IS ARIZONA, you may think you've taken a wrong turn and wound up in the Pacific Northwest. Great stands of Ponderosa pines carpet Coconino National Forest, and the serrated San Francisco Peaks thrust more than 12,000 feet into the sky.

North central Arizona occupies the southern reaches of the Colorado Plateau. This tableland—4,000 to 8,000 feet high—extends down from the Grand Canyon and drops off abruptly at the 200-mile-long Mogollon Rim. It's a wonderfully mixed land of alpine lakes, volcanic peaks and red rock canyons, offering Arizona's greatest variety of lures.

The area's first settlers were drawn to these high, cool pine forests around 15 to 20 thousand years ago. They shared the land with antelope, bison and camels, migrating with the seasons to hunt and forage. About four thousand years ago, they began rudimentary agriculture, getting their balanced protein diet from a blend of corn, squash and beans.

From these early tribes evolved the Sinagua *(si-NAU-wa)*, who settled around present-day Flagstaff and south through Oak Creek Canyon around 1000 A.D. Although they occupied much of the green Colorado Plateau, their name in Spanish means "without water." It was a reference to the porous, leaky volcanic soil in the eastern region of the plateau, where their aban-

115

doned pueblos were first noted by Spanish explorers. An advanced society, the Sinagua farmed, built irrigation canals and constructed elaborate adobe pueblos above ground and in the niches of protective cliffs.

Then curiously, by the time those Spanish travelers passed through here in the 16th century, the Sinagua had gone. Were they driven out by drought, disease or the arrival of warlike Athabaskans from the north? Archaeologists can only speculate. Hundreds of ruins have been found to prove they were here; nothing has been found to confirm why they left. It's possible that the Hopi of northeastern Arizona are their descendants, although they're more commonly linked to another prehistoric group, the Anasazi.

Flagstaff

Elevation: 6,906 feet   **Population: 46,000**

At the center of all this, Flagstaff is the seat of government for huge Coconino County. It's Arizona's second largest, covering 18,629 square miles. Within a day's drive of Flagstaff are seven national parks and monuments, including several intriguing Indian ruins. Flagstaff and Williams each claim to be the southern gateway to the Grand Canyon. Williams is closer; Flagstaff has more accommodations.

White settlement of the region didn't begin until the 1870s, after the Apaches had been cornered—but still not defeated—in southeastern Arizona. Judge Samuel Cozzens spent three years exploring the area, then went back East and returned with a group of colonizers in 1876. They started a settlement called Agassiz near San Francisco Peaks. But they, too, left, deciding the area wasn't good for farming or mining.

Finally, sheepherder Thomas Forsythe McMillan arrived, concluded that it was good sheep country and stayed. By 1880, the area's population had swelled to 67. The railroad came through two years later and Flagstaff's future was assured.

The town's curious name came from a flagpole that may or may not have existed. Some historians say that limbs were stripped from a tall Ponderosa and a flag was hoisted on July 4, 1876, to honor the centennial of America's independence. Others insist that the pole was a marker to guide travelers headed west. Some attribute the pole to that ubiquitous camel-herder, Army Lt. Edward Beale. Later, the tree was chopped down and used as firewood at Sandy Donahue's Saloon. So much for historic preservation.

The name Flagstaff was selected by a group of citizens in 1881, meeting in P.J. Brennen's tent store. Twice in three years, the new settlement was burned and rebuilt. Fortunately, there was plenty of lumber in the area. The city was incorporated in 1894.

Lumbering is still an important industry and the county is home to more than half of Arizona's domestic sheep. However, tourism is Flagstaff's major enterprise. Interestingly, Northern Arizona University is its largest employer, with a staff of 1,600.

Flagstaff is the most versatile small city in Arizona, both for visitors and residents. The university provides cultural opportunities, while excellent museums and historic buildings preserve the area's past. The nearby San Francisco Peaks offer alpine lures. Climb a steep street from downtown Flagstaff and you're at Lowell Observatory, where the existence of the planet Pluto was confirmed in 1930. A short drive east takes you to Indian cliff dwellings at Walnut Canyon. Swing north and you're in the scenic volcanic wilds of

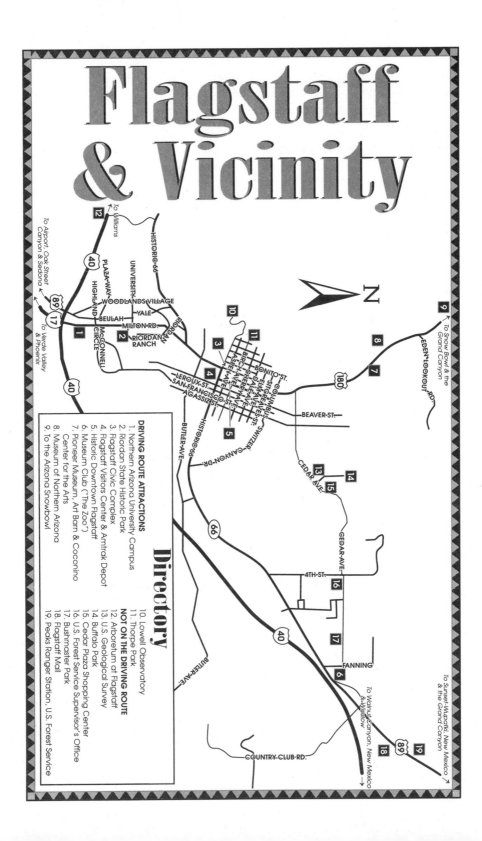

Flagstaff & Vicinity

Directory

DRIVING ROUTE ATTRACTIONS
1. Northern Arizona University Campus
2. Riordan State Historic Park
3. Flagstaff Civic Complex
4. Flagstaff Visitors Center & Amtrak Depot
5. Historic Downtown Flagstaff
6. Museum Club ("The Zoo")
7. Pioneer Museum, Art Barn & Coconino Center for the Arts
8. Museum of Northern Arizona
9. To the Arizona Snowbowl

10. Lowell Observatory
11. Thorpe Park

NOT ON THE DRIVING ROUTE
12. Arboretum at Flagstaff
13. U.S. Geological Survey
14. Buffalo Park
15. Cedar Plaza Shopping Center
16. U.S. Forest Service Supervisor's Office
17. Bushmaster Park
18. Flagstaff Mall
19. Peaks Ranger Station, U.S. Forest Service

Sunset Crater Volcano National Monument and the scattered Sinagua pueblos of Wupatki National Monument. Head south and you descend the red-walled depths of Oak Creek Canyon.

Coconino County has an abundance of open space. More than 92 percent of its land area is within a national forest, park, monument or other preserve. By contrast, Flagstaff is a mini-metropolitan center; more than half county's 83,000 residents live there. It's a four season vacation land with balmy summers and pockets of stunning fall color in cottonwood and sycamore groves. Nearly 7,000 feet in elevation, Flagstaff receives about 80 inches of snow each winter but it stays on the ground only on the higher peaks.

Naturally, such a tourist oriented area offers plenty of places to stay. Motels line east Santa Fe Avenue—now called Historic Route 66—and others are clustered around freeway offramps. Several RV parks are within minutes of downtown.

As in most older Arizona communities, Flagstaff's downtown is a mix of turn-of-the-century and modern buildings. Most of the town's shopping has moved to the suburbs, while cafés, specialty shops and antique stores occupy many of the well-tended old structures in the historic district along Santa Fe Avenue. There is little of the scruffiness seen in other towns that suffer suburban scatter.

Driving Flagstaff

Approaching from either direction on Interstate 40, hop off at exit 195B and head north into town on Milton Road. The campus of **Northern Arizona University** arrives shortly. To pay it a visit, turn right onto University Drive and follow it to the University Union, where you can pick up a campus map. Ask directions to the Parking Office at Lumberjack Stadium, where you can obtain a parking permit.

Continuing north into town, through a spread of new shopping centers, watch for a sign to **Riordan State Historic Park,** also on the right. You will, in fact, turn into one of those shopping centers and do a left and a right to get into the park. It's rimmed by split-rail fences and sheltered by ancient pines—a quiet sanctuary amidst Flagstaff's spreading commercialism.

Return to Milton Avenue and press northward. The route passes through several stoplights then swings to the right onto Historic Route 66 (Santa Fe Avenue) in the heart of the old town area. Note the handsomely modern brick **Flagstaff civic complex** on your left as you make the turn. The Flagstaff Chamber of Commerce is on your right, at Route 66 and Beaver Street. The large and well stocked **Flagstaff Visitors Center** is across Beaver, sharing space with Amtrak in the town's 1926 railroad depot. The Visitor Center is open Monday-Saturday 8 to 9 and Sunday 8 to 5 from mid-March through mid-October, and Monday-Saturday 8 to 6 and Sunday 8 to 5 the rest of the year; (520) 774-9541.

RV AND PARKING ADVISORY ● Parking is limited for cars and impossible for RVs at the Amtrak station. Signs guide visitors to a pair of nearby lots. The first, across the tracks and to the right off Beaver, is for cars; the second, around the corner to the right on Phoenix Avenue, has RV spaces ample for big rigs and trailers. A short walk along the railroad tracks delivers you to the visitor center.

☺ Once parked, you may want to stroll among the cowboy and Indian shops, antique stores, specialty shops and galleries in **Historic Downtown**

Flagstaff, which is undergoing a serious resurgence. Elderly buildings are being renovated, arcades are being shaped from alleys and trendy cafés are spilling onto newly bricked sidewalks. Many of the old structures bear signs detailing their ancestry. A half-block-long building at Larue and Birch as been converted into specialty shops, galleries and eateries. The district extends east for several blocks along Route 66 and the parallel streets of Aspen and Birch.

From Old Flagstaff, we suggest a detour east on Route 66 to visit a legendary cowboy bar called the **Museum Club.** (If you plan a later trip northeast to Sunset Crater and Wupatki national monuments, you can catch the club then.) Drive about four miles from old town and you'll see the club on your left at 3404 E. Route 66, just beyond a HoJo Howard Johnson motel. Look for the club's free-standing guitar sign. Now, return to old town and turn north onto U.S. 180 (Humphreys Street). After nine blocks, Highway 180 swings left and then right to become Fort Valley Road. This takes you to most of the rest of Flagstaff's attractions and—if you stay aboard long enough—to the Grand Canyon.

After about a mile, turn right into a pine tree-shaded complex that houses the **Pioneer Museum, Coconino Center for the Arts** and the **Art Barn.** Drive another mile or so to the excellent **Museum of Northern Arizona,** in an old fieldstone complex on the left. Pressing northward on Highway 180, you'll encounter the turnoff to the **Arizona Snowbowl** after about 4.5 miles. Its lures aren't limited to winter; aerial tram rides are available in summer and the seven-mile drive into the foothills of the San Francisco Mountains offers fine views back down to wooded valleys and distant peaks.

RV ADVISORY ● This is an easy climb with a few tight turns but no hairpins. In summer, parking and RV turnaround space is ample; in winter, it can be rather congested, particularly on weekends. Consider using the skiers' shuttle back at the Highway 180 junction, if it's operating.

Follow Highway 180 back into Flagstaff until it T-bones into Historic 66. Turn right (this section is still called Santa Fe Avenue) and follow signs uphill to **Lowell Observatory.** The drive provides pleasing aerial views of Flagstaff, particularly from a turnout about mid-way. (**RV note:** parking for long vehicles is available the observatory.) On the way back down, you might like to pause to explore the large **Thorpe Park,** with lawns, picnic and play areas and hiking/biking trails that extend far up a wooded hillside. To reach it, turn left onto Toltec Street, which runs along the front of the park. Continue driving a block or so, and you can pick up the **Flagstaff Urban Trail System,** open to walkers and bikers.

If you head back down Santa Fe Avenue from the Lowell Observatory or the park, your only choice is to turn right onto Milton Road, which completes a driving loop and heads you back to through town to the freeway.

ATTRACTIONS
In order of appearance

Northern Arizona University ● *P.O. Box 1842 (southwest of downtown) Flagstaff, AZ 86011; (520) 523-9011. Visitor parking pass and campus maps available at the Parking Office outside Lumberjack Stadium.* ◻ *For a complete rundown of activities both on and off campus, get a copy of the free newsletter, Un-tv, the Northern Arizona Arts and Entertainment Guide. University in-*

Riordan State Historic Park, while looking rather rural, is completely surrounded by growing Flagstaff.

spired arts and crafts exhibits, live entertainment, Flagstaff Symphony concerts and activities ranging from *tai chi* to tennis tournaments abound on campus and off. On-campus lures include the NAU Observatory, open for public viewing on clear Thursday evenings from 7:30 to 10, the NAU Art Gallery (523-3471), the Skydome and Lumberjack Stadium for sports events and an indoor swimming pool.

A free shuttle bus, running at 15-minute intervals, takes visitors around campus during the school year on weekdays from about 7:30 a.m. to 10 p.m.

☺ **Riordan State Historic Park** ● *Riordan Ranch Road (off Milton and Riordan roads in the downtown area); P.O. Box 217, Flagstaff, AZ 86002; (520) 779-4395. Daily 8 to 5 in summer; hours may be shorter the rest of the year. Mansion tours hourly 9 to 4; $3. Tour reservations advised in summer.* ☐ Flagstaff has swelled outward and surrounded this large ranch style estate, once the home of a pioneer lumbering and merchant family. State park rangers conduct tours of the bold fieldstone, shingle-sided structure. It's actually two homes, once occupied by the Riordan brothers and their families, joined in the middle by a communal meeting and recreation room.

Furnishings are appropriate to the turn-of-the-century period when Michael and Timothy Riordan built this Carpenter style, 13,000 square foot structure. A visitor center, occupying the carriage house, has historical exhibits and a touch table, where you can pick up stuff and peer through a stereooptigan. The extensive pine-shaded grounds, framed by split-rail fences, has a picnic area.

☺ **Museum Club of Flagstaff** ● *3404 E. Route 66, Flagstaff, AZ 86004; (520) 526-9434. MC/VISA.* ☐ Created in 1931 to house thousands of taxidermied specimens, the Museum Club has evolved into a wonderfully funky cowboy bar. It has hosted generations of country music performers, including Waylon Jennings, Willie Nelson, Bob Wills and Wanda Jackson. *Car and*

Driver magazine once voted it one of America's top ten roadhouses and locals affectionately call it "The Zoo" because of its large collection of stuffed animals (no longer thousands, of course). Patrons pass through an inverted tree-fork entrance to reach the barn like log cabin interior, held up by polished tree trunks. Most nights, an aspiring Western band or vocalist will be twanging away at a corner stage, tempting the Levi and Stetson set for a bit of cowboy two-step or line dancing. Between dancing and sipping suds, patrons can browse through a Route 66 gift shop, or simply look at all the stuff hanging from the walls. A very nice touch—owners Martin and Stacie Zanzucchi have an "operation safe ride program," providing free transportation for patrons to and from the bar. It's great to hang out in a pub that provides its own designated drivers.

Pioneer Museum • *2340 Fort Valley Road, Flagstaff, AZ 86001; (520) 774-6272. Free admission; donations appreciated. Monday-Saturday 9 to 5, closed Sundays and major holidays.* ☐ Operated by the Arizona Historical Society, the museum offers an extensive collection of Flagstaff area lore. Exhibits include memorabilia from astronomer Percival Lowell and Grand Canyon photographer Emery Kolb, plus the usual array of high-button shoes, branding irons and yesterday photos. Some exhibits are changed periodically. A 1929 Baldwin logging train and Santa Fe caboose are parked out front, alongside the highway. The building itself is a museum piece. Built in 1907-08 of volcanic tufa, it originally served as the Coconino County Hospital for the Indigent.

Coconino Center for the Arts and the Art Barn • *Fort Valley Road (P.O. Box 296, Flagstaff, AZ 86002). Center for the Arts open Tuesday-Sunday 10 to 5 April through September and Tuesday-Saturday 10 to 5 the rest of the year; (520) 779-6921. Art Barn hours are Tuesday-Sunday 10 to 5; (520) 774-0822. Admission to both is free.* ☐ Occupying a modern building beneath the pines, the Coconino Center for the Arts is a focal point for local artists and other things cultural, with galleries, a bookstore, art shop and an auditorium for special events. The next-door Art Barn exhibits and sells works of local and professional artists, and it has a good selection Indian arts and crafts, including new and old turquoise and silver jewelry. A yearly Native American exhibit, running from late June through August, features Southwestern Indian arts, crafts, music, dance and cultural workshops.

☺ **Museum of Northern Arizona** • *Fort Valley Road; mailing address is Route 4, Box 720, Flagstaff, AZ 86001; (520) 774-5213. Adults $5, seniors $4, students $3, children $2. Daily 9 to 5.* ☐ Housed in an attractive complex of fieldstone and timber in a shady Ponderosa grove, this—along with the Heard in Phoenix—is one of Arizona's two great museums. It's "dedicated to the anthropology, biology, geology and fine arts of the Colorado Plateau." Although the museum is old—dating back to 1935—its exhibits are innovative and modern. A recent remodeling and expansion has brightened and lightened the facility while retaining the rustic look of stonework and log beam ceilings. Native American ethnological and archaeological exhibits are outstanding, focusing on the shelters, settlement patterns, social organizations, crafts and food sources of northern Arizona's first inhabitants. A complete skeletal reconstruction of a *dilophosaurus*, a carnivorous cousin to T-Rex that inhabited the Colorado Plateau, is the centerpiece of the prehistoric exhibit. Other displays feature early and modern Navajo and Hopi silver and turquoise jewelry, basketry and assorted other arts and crafts. The museum shop has a good assortment of books and giftwares, and a second gift shop sells old and new Native American artwork, including some rare—and expensive—Navajo and Hopi jewelry.

Galleries are arrayed around a central courtyard, where visitors can relax and converse with a couple of resident Abert squirrels. This world-class museum has tens of thousands of biological, fossil rock and mineral specimens and more than 2,000 paintings and sculptures in its collections. It earns international recognition for its annual Hopi, Navajo and Zuni shows.

☺ **Arizona Snowbowl** ● *P.O. Box 40, Flagstaff, AZ 86002; (800) 842-7293 or (520) 779-1951. Skyrides daily 10 to 4, mid- June to Labor Day; Friday-Sunday through mid-October (weather permitting).* ⧠ Although primarily a winter ski area, the Snowbowl is certainly worth a snowless visit. The 14-mile drive from downtown Flagstaff will take you into the handsome alpine slopes of Coconino National Forest.

Hop on a sky ride for a journey from the 9,500-foot base to the dizzying heights of the San Francisco Peaks at 11,500. Or hike from base camp into the Kachina Wilderness Area (see "Hiking" below). Fall color can be awesome along the twisting, aspen-lined road to the ski area. Call the Flagstaff Visitors Bureau at (800) 842-7293 or (520) 774-9541, or the forest service at (520) 527-7400 to find out when the leaves are turning.

☺ **Lowell Observatory** ● *1400 West Mars Hill Road (follow Santa Fe Avenue west and uphill), Flagstaff, AZ 86001; (520) 774-2096. Daily 9 to 5; tours at 10, 11, 1 and 3 daily. Night sky shows Monday, Tuesday, Wednesday and Saturday at 8, 8:45 and 9:30. (Shorter hours and fewer activities in the off-season.) Daytime and evening admissions $2.50 for adults and $1 for children. Many special events throughout the year.* ⧠ Privately endowed Lowell Observatory sits atop a pine-covered mesa less than a mile from downtown. Its primary focus is the study of the solar system. Boston businessman and author Percival Lowell founded the institution in 1894 and it's still one of America's leading astronomical centers. It was this wealthy amateur astronomer who first determined—in 1902—that a ninth planet existed beyond Uranus and Neptune. Nearly three decades later, the observatory's Clyde Tombaugh pinpointed and named Pluto.

Studies at Lowell also led to the theory of the expanding universe. Although a skilled observer, Lowell sometimes let his imagination work overtime. He titillated other astronomers—and science fiction writers—by discovering "canals" on Mars. This led to his conclusion that Martians were scampering about up there. Subsequent Mars landings, of course, have found no canals and no little green men.

The new Steele Visitor Center is the public's gateway to this campus of astronomy. It has interactive "Tools of the Astronomer" exhibits, a multimedia presentation room and a bookstore. Evening visits are particularly intriguing, when you can see star shows and peer through one of the observatory's telescopes. Two are available for daytime viewing and a new 16- inch reflector was added in 1996 for evening star-gazing. Our favorite exhibit is an outdoor "Pluto Walk," where you can stroll through a sidewalk solar system. The sun and planets are sized proportionately, although the walk has been condensed 20 times to save space and shoe-leather. If the block-long path were on a normal scale, a sign advises, you'd have to hike to Boise, Idaho, to reach *Proxima Centauri,* our nearest star.

Attractions off the tour route

The Arboretum at Flagstaff • *Woody Mountain Road (west on old Route 66, then south 3.8 miles on Woody Mountain Road), P.O. Box 670, Flagstaff, AZ 86001; (520) 774-1441. Free; donations appreciated. Monday-Friday 10 to 3; guided tours at 11 a.m. and 1 p.m.* ⊡ Plants of northern Arizona's high desert, forest and alpine climate zones flourish at this botanical garden, which occupies a 200-acre meadow surrounded by Ponderosa forest. Visit a humid, solar-heated "production house" and stroll the winding paths to communicate with local flora. If you're a real plant enthusiast, you can attend exciting events such as a bulb-forcing class.

U.S. Geological Survey • *McMillan Mesa (off Cedar Avenue, a mile and a half northeast), Flagstaff, AZ 86001; (520) 527-7000. Weekdays 8 to 4:30; free.* ⊡ This isn't a museum either, but a geological survey field office specializing in astro-geology. Scientists study and interpret space photos and "Landsat" (land-satellite) images of the earth, taken from space. There are no tours or exhibit rooms, but visitors can stroll the hallways to admire the giant color wall maps and photos of the moon and planets, including impressive photos of Planet Earth. Many of these, with computer-enhanced color and detail, are spectacular. Most are in Building 1, along with a science library.

THE OUTDOOR THING

National forest lands spill down from the San Francisco Peaks, skirt Flagstaff and continue south through Oak Creek Canyon and Sedona—which we'll discuss in he next chapter. Obviously, this wilderness largess provides sightseeing, hiking, backpacking, camping, fishing and hunting, all within minutes of Flagstaff. **Coconino National Forest** headquarters at 2323 E. Greenlaw Way (east end of town, off Fourth Street behind Knowles Village Shopping Center) has assorted hiking maps, campground lists and such; (520) 527-7400.

Hiking • Miles of trails traverse Coconino National Forest, particularly in the Kachina Wilderness and San Francisco Volcanic Field just north of Flagstaff. Maps are available at national forest offices. Summer is hiking season for the high country, since snow closes trails most of the rest of the year. Be wary of lightning storms during July and August.

☺ One of the most challenging trails leads to the top of **Humphreys Peak,** the highest point in Arizona at 12,633 feet. Although this isn't a technical climb that requires rock scaling and cliff hanging, it's a tough all- day outing. You'll need considerable endurance. Elevation gain is more than 3,000 feet; plan on eight or nine hours for the nine- mile trudge to the summit and back. The trailhead is at the Arizona Snowbowl. Check with the forest service to determine when the trail is clear of snow.

Other interesting hikes are up 9,299-foot **Mount Elden,** with trailheads off U.S. 89 north of Flagstaff and off Schulz Pass Road; the **Weatherford** and **Inner Basin** trails that wind through Kachina Peaks Wilderness and the **Kendrick Peak** trails northwest of Flagstaff, which offer awesome views of the area.

Crater Climbing • Want to scramble down into the jaws of a crater? Several cinder cones in the San Francisco Volcanic Field are climbable. Two easily reached by dirt roads are **SP** and **Colton** craters. Drive 27 miles north of Flagstaff on U.S. 89, then turn west just below Hanks Trading Post at milepost 446. You'll see SP Crater directly ahead. Get a national forest map for specific directions. "SP" is a tactful abbreviation for "S— Pot, a description of the crater's spattered rim applied by early ranchers. Actually, it's more appealing than that, with a nearly symmetrical cone. An 800-foot scramble gets you to the top. The climb up Colton Crater is easier—around 300 feet.

☺ **Red Mountain** • This is a large, low-rise cindercone with a huge, fantastically-eroded crater that invites exploration. Drive 33 miles north on U.S. 180, then turn west onto a dirt road for a mile and a half. You can drive right to the base and enter the crater through an eroded cleft in the rim.

Schulz Pass scenic drive • Many roads extending into the national forest offer pleasant alpine vistas. Particularly pretty is Schulz Pass Road, a graded thoroughfare that branches to the east from U.S. 180 just above the Museum of Northern Arizona. It tucks in through the foothills of the San Francisco Peaks and joins U.S. 89 south of the Sunset Crater Volcano National Monument turnoff.

WINTER SPORTS

DOWNHILL—Arizona Snowbowl • *P.O. Box 40, Flagstaff, AZ 86002; (800) 828-7285 or (520) 779-1951 for ski and lodging information, (520) 779-4577 for snow reports. All-day adult lift tickets $30, ski-boot-pole rental package $16.* ⊡ The Arizona Snowbowl's four chairs and one surface lift take skiers to more than 30 trails, with a 2,300-foot vertical drop. Facilities include ski school for all levels, equipment rental and repair, two day lodges with cafeterias and lounges and sport shops. To ease parking, skiers can catch a round-trip shuttle from the junction of Highway 180 and Snowbowl Road. (Call the Snowbowl to see if the shuttle is operating.) Nearest lodging is at Ski Lift Lodge at the junction; see listing below under "Where to Stay."

CROSS-COUNTRY • *Flagstaff Nordic Center, on Highway 180, nine miles past the turnoff to the Snowbowl; c/o Arizona Snowbowl, P.O. Box 40, Flagstaff, AZ 86002; (520) 779-1951. All-day trail passes $7.50* ⊡ Operated by the Snowbowl, the Nordic Center has 40 kilometers of groomed trails, plus a warming hut with rentals, vending machine snacks and lessons. During the summer, 12 miles of two-track mountain bike trails are available.

ACTIVITIES

Bike tours • Mountain hike, hiking and camping gear can be rented from Mountain Sports, 1800 S. Milton Rd., Flagstaff, AZ 86001; (800) 286-5156 or (520) 779-5156. Conducted bike trips are offered by Arizona Mountain Bike Tours, P.O. Box 816, Flagstaff, AZ 86002; (800) 277-7985 or (520) 779-4161. Cycling tours in Arizona, Colorado and Utah are available from Southwest Cycling Expeditions, P.O. Box 30731, Flagstaff, AZ 86003; (520) 526-4882. California-based Backroads offers six-day bike tours from Flagstaff through Sedona's red rock country. Contact the firm at 1516 Fifth St., Berkeley, CA 94710-1740; (800) 462-2848 or (510) 527-1555.

Scenic flights • Hops over the Grand Canyon, Sedona-Oak Creek Canyon, Monument Valley, the Meteor Crater and San Francisco peaks are offered by Flagstaff Safe Fliers, (520) 774-7858.

Scenic tours • Gray Line operator for the area is Nava- Hopi Tours, with trips throughout northern Arizona; 114 W. Route 66, Flagstaff, AZ 86004; (800) 892-8687 or (520) 774-5003. Outings to Sunset Crater, Wupatki and Walnut Canyon national monuments, the Arizona Snowbowl and Mount Elden are available from by Flagstaff Jeep Tours, 3200 E. Route 66, Flagstaff, AZ 86004; (520) 522-0592. Tours over northern Arizona's backroads, including nearby national monuments, the Navajo Reservation and Canyon de Chelly, San Francisco Peaks, Sycamore Canyon near Williams and Schnebly Hill Road are featured by Northern Arizona Scenic Tours, 1251 W. Shullenbarger Dr., Flagstaff, AZ 86001; (520) 773-7788. Van excursions to various scenic areas of northern Arizona are offered by Seven Wonders Scenic Tours, (520) 526-2501. Tours through Oak Creek Canyon, Montezuma's Castle and other spots are available from Blue Goose Budget Tours and Shuttle, (520) 774-6731.

Shuttle service ● Shuttles to the Grand Canyon are provided by Budget Tours and Shuttle, (520) 774-6731.

TRANSPORTATION

America West has several flights daily from Flagstaff to Phoenix, with connections from there to assorted other points; (520) 774-4830 or (800) 872-7245. Most major **rental car** agencies operate out of the airport, including Avis, (800) 331-1212; Budget, (800) 527-0700; Enterprise, (800) 325-8007; and Hertz, (800) 654-3131. **Taxi service** is provided by Alpine Taxi Cab, (520) 526-4123; Flagstaff Taxi, (520) 774-1374; Friendly Cab, (520) 774-4444 and Northland Taxi and Tours, (520) 556-0041.

Amtrak travels west to Los Angeles and east to Chicago with connections east and south. The depot is in old town at One W. Santa Fe Ave. (520) 774-8679; for reservations, call (800) USA-RAIL.

Greyhound has cross-country service west to Los Angeles, Las Vegas and San Francisco, and to various eastern points. The depot is at 399 S. Malpais Lane, juste south of downtown; (520) 774-4573 or (800) 231-2222. **Nava-Hopi Tours** serves the Grand Canyon and Phoenix areas. The terminal is at 114 W. Route 66; (800) 892-8687 or (520) 774-5003. **Pine Country Transit** serves Flagstaff and suburbs; (520) 779-6624 or 779-6635.

ANNUAL EVENTS

For more details on these and other events, call the numbers listed below, or the Flagstaff Visitors Bureau at (800) 842-7293 or (520) 774-9541.

Flagstaff Winter Festival, February with skiing, dog sled races and entertainment, at the Snowbowl and elsewhere.

Arizona High School Rodeo, early June at Fort Tuthill County Park fairgrounds; (520) 527-2162 or 774-0614.

Route 66 Flagstaff Celebration, early June in Wheeler Park; (520) 774-1330.

Arizona Jazz, Rhythm & Blues Festival, early July in Wheeler and Foxglenn parks; (800) 520-1646.

Coconino County Horse Races, late June through early July at the fairgrounds.

Outdoor Indian Market, early July at Coconino Center for the Arts; (520) 779-6921.

Festival of Native American Arts, July through mid-August at the Coconino Center for the Arts; (520) 779-6921.

Arizona Cowpunchers Rodeo, late July at the fairgrounds; (520) 632-7730 or 442-3483.

Flagstaff Festival in the Pines, early August, art exhibits, food and live entertainment at Fort Tuthill County Park; (520) 967-4877.

Coconino County Fair, late August through Labor Day weekend at the fairgrounds.

WHERE TO SHOP

Business I-40 takes you through the heart of Flagstaff's shopping areas. Coming from the west, you'll be on Milton Road, then swing right onto Santa Fe Avenue, (Historic Route 66). Most of the city's shopping centers are around the freeway interchange at Milton and east on Route 66. Old downtown Flagstaff is the best place for curio, Western wear Indian crafts shops, antique shops and galleries. Fourth Street, north of Santa Fe Avenue in eastern Flagstaff, leads to a neighborhood shopping area. Flagstaff Mall, the town's large enclosed shopping center, is at the east end, off Santa Fe.

WHERE TO DINE

Alpine Spaghetti Station ● ☆☆ $

◻ 2400 E. Route 66 (Fourth Street); (520) 779-4138. Italian; full bar service. Monday-Saturday 11:30 to 9:30; Sunday 4:30 to 9:30. MC/VISA, AMEX. ◻ A cozy cottage style café offering an abundance of Italian atmosphere with its pizzas, lasagna, manicotti and fettucini.

☺ Black Bart's Steakhouse ● ☆☆☆ $$

◻ 2760 E. Butler (I-40 exit 198; across from Little America); (520) 779-3142. American; full bar service. Sunday-Thursday 5 to 9 p.m., Friday-Saturday 5 to 10. Reservations recommended; MC/VISA, AMEX. ◻ This busy Western-theme complex includes a restaurant, dinner theater, saloon with bat-wing doors, RV park (listed below) and adjacent antique shop. Singing waiters entertain diners in the rustic barnwood interior; dinner-theater variety shows are scheduled in summer. The menu wears a cowboy brand—steaks, prime rib and barbecued ribs and chicken.

Brix Grill & Wine Bar ● ☆☆☆ $$$

◻ 801 S. Milton; (520) 779-5117. American nouveau; wine and beer. Monday-Saturday 11 to 3 and 5 to 10, Sunday 5 to 10. Major credit cards. ◻ Stylishly moderne bistro with a daily changing menu tilted toward innovative Southwestern fare, with an extensive wine list. Entrées may include eggplant Napoleon or ribeye steaks stuffed with scallops and gorgonzola cheese.

☺ Chez Marc Bistro ● ☆☆☆☆ $$$

◻ 503 Humphreys (at Elm); (520) 774-1343. French country cuisine; wine and beer. Lunch 11:30 to 2:30, dinner 5:30 to 9. Major credit cards. ◻ Casually elegant bistro style café occupying a grand turn-of-the-century fieldstone house. The menu is a mix of rural French and some creative lighter entrées. Extensive wine list; patio dining.

Charly's Restaurant and Pub ● ☆☆ $$

◻ 23 N. Leroux (downtown, a block north of the train station); (520) 779-1919. American/Southwestern; full bar service. Daily 11 to 10. Major credit cards. ◻ Located in the 1897 Weatherford Hotel, Charly's has Old World décor and a menu featuring posolé (green chili pork), chicken fajitas, Navajo tacos and other Southwestern specialties. Lunch patrons can adjourn to a sidewalk café, part of the growing ambiance of historic downtown Flagstaff. Nightly entertainment

Cottage Place ● ☆☆☆ $$$

◻ 126 W. Cottage Ave. (downtown, near Beaver Street); (520) 774-8431. American- continental; wine and beer. Dinner Tuesday-Sunday 5 to 9:30. Reservations advised; MC/VISA, AMEX. ◻ Housed in a refurbished 1909 cottage, this charming restaurant features a versatile menu that dances from tenderloin *au poivre* to lamb chops, bouillabaisse and vegetarian *spanikopita*. It's casual, yet quietly elegant; good wine list.

☺ *Crazy Bill's Steakhouse* ● ☆☆☆ $

◻ *3130 E. Santa Fe Ave. (near Pony Soldier Motel, east end); (520) 526-3935. Western; full bar service. Monday-Saturday 11 a.m. to 1 a.m., Sunday noon to 1. Reservations advised on weekends; MC/VISA.* ◻ This funky, lively Western style café features steak, seafood and barbecued ribs and chicken. It's one of Flagstaff's better restaurant bargains and it produces an excellent, spicy beef jerky. The adjoining saloon is a popular sports bar.

El Chilito Restaurant ● ☆☆ $

◻ *1551 Milton Road (half mile north of I-17/I-40 interchange); (520) 774-4666. Mexican; full bar service. Daily 11:30 a.m. to 11 p.m. Reservations suggested; MC/VISA, AMEX.* ◻ Mexican restaurant with a modern look, dishing up Mexican and Southwest fare.

Downtown Diner ● ☆ $

◻ *Seven Aspen Street (at Leroux); (520) 774-3492. Light American fare. Monday-Saturday 5:30 a.m. to 3 p.m., Sunday 8 to 2. MC/VISA.* ◻ A 1950 style diner with Naugahyde booths and a menu to match—Philly cheese sandwiches, chicken fried steak and assorted breakfast fare.

Fiddlers Restaurant, Bar & Grill ● ☆☆ $$

◻ *702 S. Milton (at Route 66 downtown); (520) 774-6689. American; full bar service. Dinner 5 to 10. Reservations advised; MC/VISA, AMEX.* ◻ Fiddlers features modern, upscale décor and serves prime rib, charbroiled steak, seafood, chops and pasta.

☺ *Horsemen Lodge* ● ☆☆☆ $$

◻ *North Highway 89 (three miles north of Flagstaff Mall); (520) 526-2655. American rural; full bar service. Daily from 5 p.m. Reservations advised; MC/VISA.* ◻ This ranch style log and stone restaurant trimmed with knotty pine, Navajo blankets and hunting trophies, is a popular local favorite. The American country menu focuses on fresh trout, steak and oak pit barbecued chicken and ribs. Heavily-laden dinners include a salad bar, bread, spuds and desert. A huge fieldstone fireplace is a nice spot for before dinner drinks.

☺ *Kelly's Christmas Tree Restaurant* ● ☆☆☆ $$

◻ *1903 Second Street (Second Avenue, near downtown); (520) 779-5888. American; full bar service. Lunch Tuesday-Friday 11:30 to 2, dinner Tuesday-Sunday from 5:30 (closed Monday). Reservations advised; MC/VISA.* ◻ This comely restaurant with an early American look and a light touch of Christmas trim features an "Americana" menu. Offerings include sautéed chicken livers, baby back ribs, chicken and dumplings and assorted steaks. Live entertainment in the cocktail lounge.

Mandarin Gardens Restaurant ● ☆☆ $$

◻ *3518 E. Santa Fe (east end, in the Park Santa Fe Shopping Center); (520) 526-5033. Northern Chinese; wine and beer. Monday-Saturday 11 a.m. to 9 p.m., Sunday 4 to 9 p.m. MC/VISA.* ◻ This simply decorated restaurant serves tasty examples of the spicy fare of Hunan, Szechuan, Mongolia and other Mandarin foods.

Mason Jar Restaurant ● ☆☆ $$

◻ *2610 E. Santa Fe Avenue (Five Flags Inn, listed below); (520) 526-1399. American; full bar service. Daily 6 a.m. to 10 p.m.; shorter hours in winter.*

MC/VISA, DISC. ☐ Early American décor provides a homey atmosphere of print wallpaper, tulip chandeliers and—a cute touch—mason jars filled with colored beans as table decorations. The menu matches the theme, with homestyle regional American dishes.

The Quaff & Nosh ● ☆☆ $$

☐ *16 E. Route 66 (Leroux); (520) 556-1512. American-Mexican; wine and beer, Daily 11 to 9. MC/VISA.* ☐ Trendy and lively café done in light woods, occupying a refurbished 1893 storefront in historic downtown. Inexpensive dinner fare ranges from honey dijon chicken to burritos and fajitas. Adjacent **Flagstaff Brewing Company** has local brews and light snacks; open Monday-Thursday 11 to 10, Friday-Saturday 11 to 2 a.m. Both have outdoor patios.

WHERE TO RECLINE

Prices reflect high season rates and may be lower at other times. Most were provided by the management and are subject to change; use them only as a guide.

Flagstaff Central Reservations has a free hotel and motel bookings; (800) 527-8388 or (520) 527-8333.

Best Western Kings House ● ☆☆ $$$ Ø

☐ *1560 E. Santa Fe Ave. (I-40 exit 198, east of downtown), Flagstaff, AZ 86001; (520) 774-7186 or (800) 528-1234. Couples $60 to $70, singles $55 to $65. Major credit cards.* ☐ A 59-unit motel with TV movies, room phones, pool, free continental breakfast.

Best Western Pony Soldier ● ☆☆☆ $$$ Ø

☐ *3030 E. Santa Fe (near Kachina Square Shopping Center), Flagstaff, AZ 86004; (520) 526-2388 or (800) 528-1234. Couples $68, singles $55, suites $85 to $95. Major credit cards.* ☐ A 90-room inn with TV movies, room phones, pool, fireside lounge. **Afton House Restaurant** serves American and Chinese fare 6 a.m. to 10 p.m.; dinner $10 to $15; full bar service.

Best Western Woodlands Plaza Hotel ● ☆☆☆ $$$$$ Ø

☐ *1175 W. Route 66, Flagstaff, AZ 86001; (800) 528-1234 or (520) 773-8888. Couples $109 to $199, singles $99 to $109, kitchenettes and suites $175 to $275.* ☐ Well appointed 183-unit lodge with TV, phones; pool, spa and sauna, gift shop and coin laundry. Two **restaurants** serve American and Japanese fare; 6 a.m. to 10 p.m.; dinners $10 to $30; full bar service.

Comfort Inn ● ☆☆ $$$ Ø

☐ *914 S. Milton Road (I-40 exit 195B, then a mile north), Flagstaff, AZ 86001; (520) 774-7326 or (800) 221-2222. Singles and couples $54 to $59. Major credit cards.* ☐ A 67-room inn with TV movies, phones, pool; free use of adjacent fitness center.

Five Flags Inn ● ☆☆ $$ Ø

☐ *2610 E. Santa Fe Ave. (Country Club Drive off-ramp from I-40); Flagstaff, AZ 86004; (520) 526-1399. Couples $45 to $66, MC/VISA, DISC.* ☐ TV movies, room phones, pool; winter ski packages. **Mason Jar Restaurant** listed above.

Holiday Inn Flagstaff/Grand Canyon ● ☆☆☆ $$$$ Ø

☐ *2320 E. Lucky Lane (Butler exit from I-40), Flagstaff, AZ 86004; (800) 533-2754 or (520) 526-1150. Couples and singles $89 to $109 Major credit cards.* ☐ Nicely appointed 157-room inn with TV movies and phones; pool, spa, coin laundry, video game room. Airport, bus and train shuttles. **Humphreys Restaurant** serves 6 to 10 a.m. and 5 to 10 p.m.; meals $5 to $13.

InnSuites Hotel Flagstaff ● ☆☆☆ $$$ Ø

⌂ *1008 E. Route 66 (downtown) Flagstaff, AZ 86001; (800) 898-9124 or (520) 774-7356. Studios and two-room suites, $69 to $79* ⌂ Newly refurbished suite hotel with TV movies and phones; pool, exercise room, laundry. Room rates include buffet breakfast, afternoon social hour and newspapers.

Ski Lift Lodge ● ☆ $$

⌂ *Highway 180 and Snow Bowl Road (Route 4, Box 957) Flagstaff, AZ 86001; (520) 774-0729. Couples $48 to $56; singles $44 to $52. MC/VISA, AMEX.* ⌂ Special ski packages with lodging and all-day lift tickets. This small complex includes a restaurant, lounge, ski rental shop and liquor store. **Restaurant** serves 6 a.m. to 9 p.m.; homestyle fare; dinners $5 to $12.

TraveLodge I-40 ● ☆☆☆ $$$ Ø

⌂ *2520 E. Lucky Lane (Butler Avenue exit from I-40), Flagstaff, AZ 86004; (800) 255-3050 or (520) 779-5121. Couples $54 to $59, singles $45 to $49, kitchenettes $57 to $62. Major credit cards.* ⌂ TV movies and phones; some refrigerators and microwaves; pool and spa.

University Inn ● ☆☆ $$ Ø

⌂ *602 Mikes Pike (off Milton Road, opposite university campus), Flagstaff, AZ 86001; (800) 654-4667 or (520) 774-4581. Couples $35 to $40, singles $25 to $30, kitchenettes and suites $65 to $85. MC/VISA, AMEX.* ⌂ TV movies, room phones, spa, lounge. **Coffee shop** serves 6:30 a.m. to 9 p.m.; dinners $4 to $10.

Bed & breakfast inns

Dierker House Bed & Breakfast ● ☆☆ $$ Ø

⌂ *423 W. Cherry (Park), Flagstaff, AZ 86001; (520) 774-3249. Couples $50; full breakfast.* ⌂ European style comforts in a restored early 20th century home; furnished with antiques. Guest kitchen, sitting room with TV.

Birch Tree Inn ● ☆☆☆ $$$ Ø

⌂ *824 W. Birch (Toltec, off Santa Fe), Flagstaff, AZ 86001; (520) 774-1042. Couples $60 to $75; full breakfast.* ⌂ Period furnishings in a restored 1917 home with a colonnade porch. Billiard room; off-street parking; afternoon wine or tea.

Red's Bed & Breakfast ● ☆☆ $$ Ø

⌂ *2217 N. Talkington Dr. (off Fort Valley Road near Museum of Northern Arizona), Flagstaff, AZ 86001; (520) 774-7851. Couples $30 to $45; full breakfast.* ⌂ All private baths, outside deck (breakfast served there in summer), afternoon wine.

WHERE TO CAMP

Black Bart's RV Park ● *2760 E. Butler (Butler exit off I-40), Flagstaff, AZ 86004; (800) 774-1912 or (520) 774-1912. RV and tent sites, full hookups $16, tents $10. Reservations accepted; MC/VISA.* ⌂ Coin laundry, groceries; restaurant (listed above) and antique shop nearby.

Flagstaff Grand Canyon KOA ● *5803 N. Highway 89 (exit 201 off I-40, then three stoplights north on U.S. 89), Flagstaff, AZ 86004; (800) KOA-FLAG or (520) 526-9926. RV and tent sites, full hookups $23, no hookups $17. Reservations accepted; MC/VISA and DISC.* ⌂ Coin laundry, showers, groceries, Propane, dump station; planned summer recreational activities, playground, cook-outs, hiking trails.

Fort Tuthill County Park ● *U.S. 89A (Fort Tuthill exit from I-17 south of Flagstaff); (520) 774-5139. RV and tent sites, no hookups $6. No reservations or credit cards.* ☐ Barbecues and picnic tables, play area, nature trails, racquetball courts. Open from May 15 to September 15.

J&H RV Park ● *7901 N. Highway 89 (three miles north), Flagstaff, AZ 86004; (800) 243-5264 or (520) 526-1829. RVs only, full hookups $22. Reservations accepted; MC/VISA.* ☐ Nicely appointed park with showers, minimart, other amenities; grills and picnic tables in a barbecue area. Off Munds Park exit from I-17, 18 miles south of Flagstaff

Munds Park RV Campground ● *P.O. Box J , Munds Park, AZ 86017; (520) 286-1309. RV and tent sites, full hookups $16, tents $13. Reservations accepted; MC/VISA.* ☐ Showers, coin laundry, groceries, pool, spa, recreation room, playground.

NORTH TOWARD THE GRAND CANYON

Heading north of Flagstaff on U.S. 89, you'll climb quickly into the foothills of the San Francisco Peaks, continue past them and travel across the semi-arid expanses of the Colorado Plateau. However, the peaks seem to stay with you, lurking in your rearview mirror. Wherever you travel in north central Arizona, you see this mighty mountain cluster, like a mystery ship floating on the horizon. The main peaks—Humphreys, Fremont, Doyle and Agassiz—are craggy remnants of a million-year-old volcano that may have jutted 15,000 feet skyward. Scattered about their flanks are more recent cinder cones and lava flows.

A few miles north of Flagstaff, you'll encounter two national monuments on this semi-arid downslope. Although each has its own identity and visitor center, they're jointly administered by the National Park Service, with an office at 2717 N. Steves Blvd., Suite 3, Flagstaff, AZ 86004.

☺ **Sunset Crater Volcano National Monument** ● *Twelve miles north on U.S. 89, then east; (520) 556-7042. Visitor center open daily 8 to 5; $4 per car (includes admission to Wupatki). Bonito Campground near the visitor center operated by the U.S. Forest service; water, no hookups, $8; open late spring through early fall.* ☐ You have to look for it, but in the right light, the bold brown cindercone of Sunset Crater has an orange-red cast to it, and thus the name. Tinged by iron oxide, it's the centerpiece of a starkly beautiful volcanic area. Although Sunset Crater last erupted more than 700 years ago, the klinkery, jagged lava fields look as if they were deposited just last week. Scrub Ponderosas share the lava landscape with assorted desert flora. A few aspens contribute brilliant fall yellow to the stark moon-like landscape.

Sinagua, Anasazi and Cohoniña Indians once occupied these arid lands, building hilltop pueblos and pit houses and tilling the rough soil. Sunset Crater's eruption obviously sent them scurrying for shelter. Hundreds of ruins have been found in the area, mostly in present-day Wupatki National Monument to the north. The visitor center features exhibits on volcanism in general and Sunset Crater's formation about eight centuries ago. Films of Hawaii's Kilauea eruption convey the drama that the startled Indians might have experienced. Ranger programs and hikes are scheduled, mostly in summer. Beyond the visitor center, a one-mile loop trail near the base of Sunset Crater offers a first-hand study of volcanism at work. You can't climb the crater itself, but hiking is permitted on Lenox Crater, a smaller cinder cone about a mile east of the visitor center.

Wukoki ruin is the main visitor attraction at Wupatki National Monument.

Outside the park, you can drive almost to the top of **O'Leary Peak**, then hike the rest of the way. A lava dome nearly 9,000 feet high, it has impressive views of the surrounding landscape. If the climb intimidates your vehicle, you can park and hike the last mile. Views of the peaks and lava fields are worth the effort. As you motor northeast through the monument, heading for Wupatki, pause at the Painted Desert Overlook for a view of the color banded mesas and badlands on the distant horizon. Picnic tables may entice you to take a lunch break.

☺ **Wupatki National Monument** ● *Fourteen miles north of Sunset Crater; (520) 527-7040. Visitor center open daily 8 to 5; $4 per car (fee paid at Sunset Crater).* ☐ Wupatki is home to one of the Southwest's largest and most intriguing Indian ruins. Wupatki Pueblo, a short walk from the visitor center, is a four-story, 100-room village created from Moencopi sandstone building blocks. Nearby is an oval "ball court" and an amphitheater whose functions still puzzle scientists. The ball court resembles those of Mexico's Mayan and Toltec cultures, but did they play road games this far north?

Although Wupatki is the monument's largest ruin, hundreds more are scattered about this lava plain. This is one of the intrigues of the area. If you first register at the visitor center, you can get off by yourself and explore several unexplored ruins, perhaps pretending you're an archaeologist who's just tripped over a rare find. Of course, you are expected to mind your archaeological manners and disturb nothing you see.

Wupatki Pueblo's rooms can't be entered because of its heavy visitor traffic, but you may explore the less popular sites. You can poke around the roofless rooms of **Wukoki Pueblo**, just beyond the visitor center. **The Citadel** is a toppled-over ruin occupying a low butte. Vertical rows of slate-thin sandstone indicate where walls have collapsed. **Lomaki** is our favorite discovery in the monument. Remarkably well-preserved, it's tucked into the protective walls of a small canyon. Some homes were built on the canyon rim, complete with view balconies. Rangers conduct talks daily in summer.

Leaving Wupatki and continuing north on U.S. 89, you enter the Navajo Reservation that occupies a husky chunk of northeastern Arizona. The communities of **Gray Mountain** and **Cameron** have gasoline, modest-priced motels, restaurants and gift shops featuring souvenirs and local Indian crafts. Particularly interesting is the Cameron Trading Post.

A left turn onto State Route 64 just below Cameron takes you on a slow climb from desert to the piñons and junipers of Kaibab National Forest and into the back gate of Grand Canyon National Park at Desert View. For specifics on this route, along which we passed in Chapter three; see page 73.

WEST TO WILLIAMS AND SELIGMAN

Interstate 40 hurries through roadside stands of Ponderosas as it heads west toward Williams, Ash Fork and Seligman. All were early stops along the original Highway 66 and the Santa Fe Railway. Historic 66 parallels I-40 for a few miles out of Flagstaff, then it disappears under the new freeway and re- appears at Ash Fork. The first town of any consequence on this route is a community which, in setting and temperament, is sort of a mini-Flagstaff.

Williams

Elevation: 6,762 feet   **Population: 2,500**

Like Flagstaff, Williams is rimmed by a national forest—Kaibab, in this instance and it's nearly as high, surrounded by stands of Ponderosas. Williams is the closest town to the Grand Canyon's South Rim—58 miles—and the chamber likes to boast about that. In fact, it calls itself the Williams-Grand Canyon Chamber of Commerce.

Because of this canyon proximity, the town is top-heavy with motels. There were about 25 at last count, lining the parallel one-way thoroughfares—Bill Williams Avenue and Railroad Avenue. The small business district is caught in a pleasant early 20th century time warp. Other than the new motels, it has changed little from the days when it was an important pause on the Santa Fe Railway and old Route 66. Several of its brick front and false front stores are occupied by antique and curio shops.

Like most communities along this route, Williams was put on the map by the early railroad. Cattle ranching began in the late 1870s, then the coming of the rails in the 1880s spurred the local timber industry and the town began growing. The settlement takes its name from a randy old mountain man and guide, Bill Williams, who prowled these parts for a quarter of a century until Ute Indians got to him in 1849. To honor his spirit, townsfolk dress up as Bill Williams Mountain Men and Shady Ladies. They stage frontier style celebrations over Memorial Day and Labor Day weekends and they conduct a 200-mile horseback ride to Phoenix each spring. They've even been invited to several Presidential inaugural parades in Washington, D.C.

If you're approaching from the east and you'd like to pet some deer, take I-40 exit 171 to the **Grand Canyon Deer Farm.** Then continue east to exit 165 and follow a frontage road two miles into downtown Williams. Once there, turn right onto Grand Canyon Boulevard for the town's main attractions, the historic depot that houses the **Grand Canyon Railway** ticket office and the **Fray Marcos** hotels, old and new. All three have a kind of Romanesque turn of the century look with Roman columns and vintage American décor; all are painted a matching gray. The railroad depot has a gift shop, café and railway museum. Visitors can inspect—but not board—

some of the railway's vintage rolling stock nearby. The elegant **Fray Marcos Hotel** was completed in late 1995. Step inside its splendid lobby to admire ornate beamed ceilings, a massive chandelier, Grand Canyon paintings and a collection of Frederick Remington bronzes. The original hotel, built in 1908, now houses offices.

To learn all about Williams and its surrounds, step into the **Williams-Grand Canyon Chamber of Commerce** at Railroad and Grand Canyon Boulevard, just up from the depot; (520) 635-4061. Occupying a renovated former freight depot, it shares office space with a **Kaibab National Forest** ranger station; they're open daily 8 to 6; shorter hours in the off-season. A second ranger district office is on the western edge of town; follow signs on the I-40 frontage road. It's open weekdays 7:30 to 4; (520) 635-2633.

At either office, ask about **Sycamore Canyon**, little known when compared with Sedona's Oak Creek Canyon, yet nearly as attractive. To get there, drive south from town on Fourth Street; after eight miles, turn left onto Forestry Road 110 and follow it 15 miles to its end. From Sycamore Canyon Point, you'll get an awesome view of the canyon and the alpine countryside. The 11-mile Sycamore Trail provides a more intimate exploration of this area.

ATTRACTIONS

Grand Canyon Deer Farm • *100 Deer Farm Road (eight miles east, just off I-40), Williams, AZ 86046; (520) 635-4073. Daily from 9 a.m. to dusk in spring and fall, 8 a.m. to dusk in summer, 10 to 5 in winter (subject to weather conditions). Adults $3.95, kids 3 to 12 $2; MC/VISA.* ☐ Who can resist all those doe-eyed deer strolling about their pine-shaded enclosure? You can pet and feed a regiment of spotted fallow deer and axis deer, along with assorted antelope, sheep and goats (stay downwind of the latter). A few volunteer Abert squirrels, an emu from Australia and a bored-looking buffalo complete the menagerie. It's a clean, well run operation, fronted by a large souvenir shop and snack bar in a big red barn. Naturally, you can buy critter food.

☺ *Grand Canyon Railway* • *Historic steam train rides between Williams and Grand Canyon Village. Ticket office at Grand Canyon Boulevard and Railroad Avenue, Williams, AZ 86046; (800) THE-TRAIN or (520) 635-4000. Main office and mailing address: 123 N, San Francisco, Suite 210, Flagstaff, AZ 86001; (520) 773-1976. Adult round-trip $49; kids 3 to 16, $23. Upgrades to "Club Class" $12 per person; to "Chief Class" $50 per person. Canyon rim tours available at additional cost. Major credit cards.* ☐

The Grand Canyon Railway has resumed the historic run from Williams to the park that began in 1901, using vintage steam trains in summer and 1950s diesel locomotives the rest of the year. Passengers ride in restored 1920s coaches, entertained en route by strolling musicians and descriptive narratives as the train climbs from desert to the Ponderosa forests of the South Rim. Club Class and Chief Class feature complimentary snacks and a cocktail bar; Chief passengers ride in a luxury parlor car that originally ran with the Wabash Cannonball.

Trains run daily except December 24 and 25, departing Williams Depot at 9:30 a.m., arriving at the Grand Canyon at 11:45. They depart the canyon at 3:15, returning to Williams at 5:30. AMTRAK's cross-country service stops at Flagstaff, with a connecting bus to the Grand Canyon Railway in Williams; call (800) USA-RAIL for schedules.

Fray Marcos Hotel and Williams Depot ● *Grand Canyon Boulevard at Railroad Avenue.* ☐ The firm that reactivated historic steam train rides between Williams and the Grand Canyon (see above) renovated the venerable Fray Marcos Hotel, which now houses offices and the Grand Canyon Railway Museum. One of the original Harvey Houses, the Fray Marcos was the first poured concrete building in Arizona. The museum, which is free, displays artifacts and photos of early railroading, mining, ranching and logging, plus a display about the Fred Harvey Company. It has rather curious hours—daily from 7 a.m. to 10 a.m. Why? Because that's when passengers gather to catch the train to the Grand Canyon.

ANNUAL EVENTS

For specifics on these and other events, contact the Williams-Grand Canyon Chamber of Commerce at (520) 635-4061.

Bill Williams Rendezvous Days, Memorial Day Weekend, with Western shootouts, steam train rides, silent films, parades, food booths and other activities.

Arizona Cowpunchers Reunion and Rodeo, first weekend in August, with wrangling competitions by working cowboys, parade and barn dances.

Williams Rodeo, Labor Day weekend.

WHERE TO SHOP

Downtown Williams is rather compact, focused along Bill Williams Avenue and Railroad Avenue, which parallel I-40. Most commercial growth, what little there is, will be found in the eastern end. Several antique and curio shops are in the heart of downtown. With its fine old brick front and false front stores, it recently was declared a national historic district. Check out the Dusty Bunch Gallery at the east end of town, with Western arts and crafts and life-sized carved wooden cowboy figures.

WHERE TO DINE

Parker House Restaurant ● ☆☆ *$*

☐ *525 W. Bill Williams Ave. (west end I-40 interchange); (520) 635-4590. American; no alcohol. Daily 6 a.m. to 9:30 p.m. MC/VISA, AMEX.* ☐ Simple family diner with a few Mexican dishes mixed with the American menu. Try some of the inexpensive lunch specials.

Fireside Italian Restaurant ● ☆☆ *$$*

☐ *106 S. Ninth St. (at Bill Williams Avenue); (520) 635-4130. Italian; wine and beer. Daily 11 to 9. MC/VISA.* ☐ Think of it as a spaghetti Western café, with knotty pine, cowboy décor and an Italian menu. Several chicken dishes, plus veal parmagiana, assorted pastas and an array of pizzas.

☺ *Old Smoky's Restaurant* ● ☆ *$*

☐ *624 W. Bill Williams (near west end interchange); (520) 635-2091. American. Breakfast and lunch only, 6 to 1:30 and Saturday. MC/VISA.* ☐ It's Williams' most funkily charming café. The interior is frontier West and the waitstaff scampers about in coonskin caps. Breakfasts have a spicy Mexican accent; there's also a large assortment of waffles. Lunches include assorted hamburgers and other sandwiches. Popular with locals are the homemade bakery goods, such as cinnamon raisin, banana nut, zucchini and pumpkin raisin breads.

Pancho McGillicuddy's ● ☆☆ *$$*

☐ *141 Railroad Ave. (at Grand Canyon Blvd.); (520) 635-4150. Mexican-American; wine, beer and margaritas. Daily noon to 10. MC/VISA.* ☐ Lively cantina occupying a century-old saloon with pressed tin ceilings and bright *Latino* décor. Typical Mexican fare, plus Gringo grub such as honey chicken and New York strip steak. Outdoor dining.

Rod's Steak House ● ☆☆ *$$*

☐ *301 E. Bill Williams Ave. (Slagle); (520) 635-2671. American; full bar service. Daily 11 a.m. to 10 p.m. MC/VISA, DISC.* ☐ Featuring a cozy, warm-wood dining room with flagstone tile, this appealing restaurant serves mesquite-broiled steak and prime rib, plus chickens, chops and seafood.

WHERE TO RECLINE

Prices reflect high season rates and may be lower at other times. Most were provided by the management and are subject to change; use them only as a guide.

Days Inn of Williams ● ☆☆☆ *$$$$* Ø

☐ *2488 W. Bill Williams Ave. (at west interchange), Williams, AZ 86046; (520) 635-4051 or (800) 325-2525. Couples $86 to $96, singles $66 to $76, suites $95 to $135. Major credit cards.* ☐ A 73-room motel with TV movies, free in-room coffee, room phones, indoor pool and spa. **Denny's Restaurant** is adjacent; dinners $4 to $10; open 24 hours; full bar service.

☺ *Fray Marcos Hotel* ● ☆☆☆☆ *$$$$$*

☐ *One Fray Marcos Blvd., Williams, AZ 86046; (800) THE-TRAIN or (520) 635-4000. Couples and singles from $119. Major credit cards.* ☐ Elegant new turn-of-the-century style hotel with 88 rooms featuring period décor and modern amenities. Appealing **restaurant** serves 7:30 a.m. to 9:30 p.m. Cocktail lounge, gift shop, meeting rooms and fashionable lobby with ornate beam ceilings, massive fireplace and an impressive collection of Frederick Remington bronzes and oil paintings of the Grand Canyon.

Grand Canyon Red Lake Hostel & Campground ● ☆ *$*

☐ *C/o Red Lake Campground, Highway 64, Williams, AZ 86046; (800) 581-4753 or (520) 635-4753. April-September $15 per person, October-March $12 per person. MC/VISA, DISC.* ☐ Hostel facilities including some family units at Red Lake Campground, about eight miles north of Williams on State Route 64.

Mountain Side Inn ● ☆☆☆ *$$$*

☐ *642 E. Bill Williams Ave. (east interchange, just north of freeway); Williams, AZ 86046; (520) 635-4431. Couples and singles $63 to $75. Major credit cards.* ☐ Attractive inn occupying a pleasant foothills setting; TV, room phones, pool. **Dining Car Restaurant** serves 6 a.m. to 10 p.m.; dinners $7 to $15; full bar service.

Norris Motel ● ☆☆☆ *$$* Ø

☐ *1001 W. Bill Williams Ave. (P.O. Box 388), Williams, AZ 86046; (520) 635-2202. Couples $62 to $74, singles $62. Major credit cards.* ☐ A 33-room motel with TV movies, phones and refrigerators; indoor pool and spa.

Red Garter Bed & Bakery ● ☆☆ *$$*

☐ *137 W. Railroad Ave., Williams, AZ 86046; (520) 635-1484. Rooms $45 to $85. MC/VISA, AMEX.* ☐ Nicely appointed rooms with period décor, in a former 1897 bordello; private baths. Rooms upstairs, bakery downstairs, serving light fare 6:30 a.m. to 9 p.m. daily.

WHERE TO CAMP

Circle Pines KOA • *1000 Circle Pines Rd. (I-10 exit 167); Williams, AZ 86046; (800) 732-0537 or (520) 635-4545. Tent and RV sites, full hookups $21; "Kamping Kabins" $28.50. Reservations accepted; MC/VISA, DISC.* ☐ Pine shaded pull-through sites, showers, disposal station, coin laundry and groceries. Indoor pool and spa, recreation room, playground. Hay rides, horseback riding and outdoor café open May 15 through September 15.

Grand Canyon KOA • *North Highway 64, Williams, AZ 86046; 635-2307. Tent and RV sites, full hookups, $13.50; also "Kamping Kabins" $20. Reservations accepted; VISA/MC.* ☐ Coin laundry, groceries, Propane. Situated on State Highway 64, seven miles northeast of Williams and 52 miles south of Grand Canyon National Park. Free movies, hay rides and "cowboy steak dinners" in summer; an indoor pool and spa, grocery and gift shop.

Grand Canyon Red Lake Hostel & Campground • ☐ *Highway 64, Williams, AZ 86046; (800) 581-4753, (520) 635-4753 or (520) 635-9122. Full hookups $16, no hookups $12, tent sites $10. Reservations accepted. MC/VISA, DISC.* ☐ Campground and hostel about eight miles north of Williams, with pull-throughs, picnic tables and barbecues, dump station, coin showers and laundry; groceries, gift shop, hunting and fishing supplies, gasoline and Propane.

Railside RV Ranch • ☐ *877 Rodeo Rd., Williams, AZ 86046; (520) 635-4077. Full hookups $18, no hookups and tents $15. Reservations accepted; MC/VISA.* ☐ Some pull-throughs, showers, picnic tables and barbecues, TV hookups; laundry, mini-mart, dump station, rec hall, playground, horseshoes and basketball court.

Ash Fork

Elevation: 5,140 feet   **Population: 650**

From Williams, I-40 drops from pine forests to a high prairie and skirts the hamlet of Ash Fork. A large flagstone tile company is this burg's primary industry. It also catches a few tourists for meals, gas and overnight stops. Most motels along the main street are rather scruffy. Here's two that aren't:

Stage Coach Motel • ☆ $$ ∅

☐ *823 Park Avenue (west end), Ash Fork, AZ 86320; (520) 637-2278. Couples from $30 to $45, singles from $22 to $30. MC/VISA, AMEX.* ☐ Modest motel with TV movies.

Ash Fork Inn • ☆☆ $$

☐ *Ash Fork, AZ 86320 (west end, I-40 exits 144 or 146); (520) 637-2511. Couples and singles from $27. MC/VISA.* ☐ Old, well-tended inn with TV movies, room phones.

For dining, try **Ted's Bullpen Restaurant** at the east end of town. It's a big trucker's hangout with hearty American fare, open 24 hours. There's also a service station (with diesel, obviously) and general store. **Little Fat Lady Restaurant** next to the Ash Fork Inn, serves inexpensive American and Mexican food, with wine and beer; MC/VISA.

Ash Fork Grand Canyon KOA • *P.O. Box 357 (Ninth and Pine, at freeway exits 144 or 146), Ash Fork, AZ 86320; (520) 637-2521. Tent and RV sites, full hookups $15.50, water and electric $14, tents $10, "Kamper Kabins" $20. Reservations accepted, MC/VISA.* ☐ Shaded sites; coin laundry, groceries, snack bar, Propane, dump station, playground.

Seligman

Elevation: 5,250 feet   **Population: 600**

Continuing west (either on I-40 or old Route 66), you'll breeze into the little pretend Western town of Seligman, which has been around since 1886. A mock-up of false front stores stands beside a good old boy bar called the **OK Saloon**. The saloon is real; the fake storefronts cleverly disguise a corral. Beside it is an old jail that supposedly contained Three-Fingered Jack, Jim Younger and—good grief!—even Seligman Slim.

Who?

Seligman doesn't offer much cause to pause, although it does have a couple of inexpensive motels, should you need a driving break:

Navajo Motel ● ☆ $$

☐ *500 W. Chino, Seligman, AZ 86337; (520) 422-3204. Couples $32 to $37, singles $24 to $32. MC/VISA, AMEX.* ☐ Small motel with TV movies, room phones.

Romney Motel ● ☆ $$

☐ *155 W. Chino, Seligman, AZ 86337; (520) 422-3394. Couples $25 to $40, singles $21 to $25; MC/VISA.* ☐ TV and room phones.

Catch a meal at the **Copper Cart** on the east end of town, open 6 a.m. to 10 p.m., serving the usual steaks, chicken and chops for $5 to $12; wine and beer; MC/VISA. Near the west end is **Mr. J's Coffee Shop**, similar hours, similar menu but a bit cheaper than the Cart; no alcohol; MC/VISA.

You can camp at the **Northern Arizona Campground** near the OK Saloon and Corral. It's scruffy but clean, with showers, coin laundry and a store with groceries, a fast-food counter and Indian curios. It's $11.55 with full hookups, $8 for dry camping.

EAST TOWARD A BIG HOLE IN THE GROUND

Two important lures draw tourists east of Flagstaff on I-40. Not far from town is one of our favorite Arizona Indian ruins, Walnut Canyon National Monument. About 40 miles beyond is Meteor Crater, where a stony visitor slammed into the earth 49,500 years ago. Another ten miles gets us to that "takin' it easy" town of pop music fame—Winslow, Arizona.

Heading east, you'll soon put Coconino's forests behind, and you won't see another serious stand of timber along I-40—at least not in Arizona. Nor is there much of anything else to see as you breeze from the Indian ruin to the crater to Winslow.

☺ *Walnut Canyon National Monument* ● *Walnut Canyon Road (seven miles east on I-40, then three miles south), Flagstaff, AZ 86004; (520) 526-3367. Daily 8 to 5; the Island Trail closes at 4; $4 per vehicle.* ☐ About 800 years ago, a band of Sinagua Indians found an idyllic home, deep in the sheltering recesses of Walnut Canyon. They departed around 1250, leaving behind a fine set of cliff condos. Tucked into overhangs between the rim and floor of the canyon, they can be reached by a 251-step trail from the visitor center. Keep that number in mind as you start back up. The path, which takes you past two dozen ruins, is called the Island trail, since many of the relics are on a free-standing ridge in the middle of the canyon.

We like to visit the ravine late in the day, when most of the others have gone and slanting light bathes the ruddy adobe niches. We can retreat to the shade of one of the dwellings and ponder how the Sinagua passed their days half a millennium ago. The interpretive center, perched dramatically on the rim, offers a picture-window view of the rock-ribbed, forested canyon. It also provides a quick study of the Sinagua and the geology of the area. There's a good selection of natural history books available as well. Rangers conduct walks and talks daily in the summer. A half-mile rim trail provides impressive views of the narrow chasm from above.

Meteor Crater ● *Forty miles east of Flagstaff to Meteor Crater exit, then six miles south. Meteor Crater Enterprises, 603 N. Beaver, Suite C, Flagstaff, AZ 86001; (520) 774-8350. Daily 6 to 6 in summer, 7 to 5 mid-September to mid- November, 8 to 5 mid-November to mid-March and 7 to 5 mid-March to mid-May. (You get all that?) Adults $7; seniors and kids, $6* ☐

Imagine this: A monster chunk of nickel and iron weighing millions of tons streaks earthward at 40,000 miles an hour. It slams into the earth with a force that buries fragments hundreds of feet deep. Most of the mass explodes into a gaseous cloud that flattens trees and kills every living thing for miles around. When the dust settles, an impact crater 550 feet deep and three-quarters of a mile across steams silently on the broad plain.

Operators of the privately-owned Meteor Crater have done an outstanding job preserving and interpreting this awesome hole in the ground. A large visitor center perched on the rim houses a fine astro-geology museum, where graphic illustrations portray the meteor's lethal impact. Studying the exhibits brings to mind the dust cloud theory of dinosaur extinction. The museum also provides a quick study of space exploration, exhibiting a space capsule, suits, photos, badges and other regalia of every American space flight. Videos teach visitors about the mysteries of the world beyond. One particularly moving film is dedicated to the lost crew of the Challenger space shuttle.

In order to protect the site, visitors aren't allowed to hike down into the depression. But you tour the rim. Get to the visitor center at least an hour before closing time if you want to do the loop, and allow another hour to study exhibits in the museum.

The best preserved impact crater in the world, it has been used by astronauts to get a feel of outer-world terrain. When the great depression was first discovered in 1871, folks thought it was of volcanic origin. Philadelphia mining engineer Daniel Moreau Barringer spent the last 25 years of his life in an obsessive quest to prove that the crater had been caused by a meteor impact. It was finally accepted by the scientific community when he died in 1929.

Meteor Crater RV Park ● *Meteor Crater turnoff from I-40 (c/o 603 N. Beaver St., Suite C, Flagstaff, AZ 86001); (520) 282-4002. RV and tent sites, full hookups $18, water and electric $18, no hookups $10.* ☐ Showers, laundry, individual bathrooms, mini-golf, horse shoes and a service station.

Winslow

Elevation: 4,856 feet   **Population: 8,500**

From a 49,500-year-old hole in the ground, we move to lures of somewhat more recent vintage. Winslow is an old-fashioned town with a sturdy brick business district rimmed by tree-lined residential areas. Nearby are considerably older villages—the Homol'ovi ruins of the Anasazi. The railroad gave birth to the town in 1882 and it thrived as a cattle and freight center. Although Winslow itself has no tourist lures other than a small museum, the Chamber of Commerce touts its position in the center of things touristy, from the Meteor Crater to the west to the new Homol'ovi Ruins State Park and Little Painted Desert County Park to the northeast and the Navajo-Hopi nation beyond. It thus offers a good selection of motels.

Approaching from the west on I-40, you can reach the chamber by taking exit 253 and crossing under the freeway. It's at 300 W. North Road, open Monday-Friday 8 to 5; (520) 289-2434. In addition to tourist information, it has a small museum with a diorama depicting area Indians, white settlers and Arizona points of interest. Look for a totem and railway caboose outside.

The small Old Trails Museum is downtown on Kinsley Avenue. To get there from the visitor center, go south under the freeway, following North Park to one-way Second Street, go left three blocks and turn left onto Kinsley; it's between Second and Third. To reach Homol'ovi Ruins State Park, take Second Street east to the I-40 interchange, turn left under the freeway onto State Route 87 and follow it north for than a mile. The park entrance is on the left, although some AAA maps show it on the right. Little Painted Desert County Park is about a dozen miles beyond, also on Highway 87.

ATTRACTIONS

Old Trails Museum ● *212 Kinsley Ave. (between Second and Third), Winslow, AZ 86047; (520) 289-5861. Tuesday-Saturday 1 to 5 March through October; Tuesday, Thursday and Saturday 1 to 5 the rest of the year. Free admission, donations accepted.* ☐ This small museum in a 1916 bank building in downtown Winslow features exhibits concerning the Santa Fe Railroad, early Native Americans, ranching, mining and other things historical. It's operated by the Navajo County Historical Society.

☺ **Homol'ovi Ruins State Park** ● *HC63-Box 5, Winslow, AZ 86047; (520) 289-4106. Day use 6 a.m. to 7 p.m.; visitor center open daily 9 to 5; $3 per car. Camping $13 with hookups, $8 without; flush potties.* ☐ If you enjoy exploring untouched archaeological sites, far from tourist crowds, you'll like Homol'ovi ruins, where Anasazi clans lived during the 13th to 16th centuries. Several mounds along the Little Colorado River, known to locals for decades and unfortunately raided by pot thieves, have not been restored. Two are

Little Painted Desert above Winslow is an often-overlooked jewel.

easily reached by park roads, simply called Homol'ovi I and Homol'ovi II. Walking about, you can still see pot shards on the ground (and they're to be left untouched, of course) and fragments of stone walls. Limited excavation has started at these sites and will be expanded in the future.

Although the park was owned by the state for several years, development didn't start until the early 1990s. It now has a handsome new visitor center crafted of rough stone to resemble the walls of the Anasazi dwellings, new roads leading to the two ruins and a campground. Homol'ovi I is about a mile beyond the campground, alongside the Little Colorado River. No excavation had been done when we last visited, although stakes outlined some of the walls. Homol'ovi II, about 2.5 miles beyond the visitor center, is showing some signs of work, with a few walls exposed.

☺ **Little Painted Desert County Park** ● *Just off State Highway 87, 13 miles north of Winslow; gates open 8 a.m. to 9 p.m. Flush potties and picnic ramada.* ☐ This is a surprising jewel of a park—a mini-badlands of softly contoured, pastel-hued sandstone. From a parking area, you can drive or walk along rim roads in either direction for varied vistas of this fluted amphitheater of erosion. A trail from the north rim road takes you into this sensuously rounded landscape. Railroad ties help you keep your footing as you descend from a shallow cliff edge.

WHERE TO DINE

El Papagayo Restaurant ● ☆☆ $

☐ *1942 W. Third St., Winslow; (520) 289-3379. Mexican-American; full bar service. Daily 10 a.m. to 11 p.m. MC/VISA.* ☐ Mexican specialties including fajitas and *pollo asada*, American steaks, chops, seafood.

The Falcon ● ☆☆ $

☐ *1113 E. Third St. (east end), Winslow; (520) 289-2342. American, full bar service. Daily 5:30 a.m. to 9:30 p.m. MC/VISA.* ☐ A popular local restaurant since 1955, the Falcon features homestyle steaks, seafood, chops and such. Soups and pies are created on the premises.

WHERE TO RECLINE

Best Western Adobe Inn ● ☆☆☆ $$$ Ø

☐ *1701 N. Park Dr. (I-40 exit 253), Winslow, AZ 86047; (520) 289-4638. Couples $48 to $54, singles $38 to $48. Major credit cards.* ☐ TV movies, phones; indoor pool and spa. **Restaurant** serves from 6 a.m. to 2 p.m. and 4 to 10 p.m., American, full bar service.

Best Western Town House Lodge ● ☆☆ $$

☐ *1914 W. Third St. (I-40 exit 252, then half mile east), Winslow, AZ 86407; (520) 289- 4611. Couples $44 to $54, singles $38 to $48. Major credit cards.* ☐ A 68-room inn with TV movies, phones; pool, coin laundry, playground. **Restaurant** serves 6 a.m. to 9:30 p.m.; full bar service.

EconoLodge ● ☆ $$

☐ *I-40 at Northpark Dr. (exit 2530), Winslow, AZ 86407; (520) 289-4687. Couples $33 to $44, singles $29 to $44. Major credit cards.* ☐ A 72-room motel with TV movies and phones; pool and spa.

Super 8 Motel ● ☆☆ $$ Ø

☐ *1916 W. Third St. (I-40 exit 252, then half mile east); Winslow, AZ 86407; (520) 289-4606. Couples $41 to $45, singles $37 to $41.* ☐ A 46-room motel with TV movies and phones; pool.

CATHEDRAL ROCK

Chapter six

THE RED ROCK MIDDLE
From scenic Sedona to cowboy Prescott

THE LAND BELOW Flagstaff is a mosaic of natural beauty, from the stunning rose-colored monoliths of Oak Creek Canyon to the thick forests embracing Prescott.

The northern area around Oak Creek Canyon is particularly imposing. Picture a narrow chasm, walls cloaked with pines, a sun-sparkled stream wandering about its floor, with fairy castle shapes of red rock cliffs at the lower end. Place an art colony among those rocks and give it a nice feminine name, like Sedona.

Most chasms are admired from the rim. Oak Creek, however, is a lived-in canyon. You can explore its depths from winding roads and admire its ramparts from picture-window restaurants and resort patios. Sedona and Oak Creek Canyon are Arizona's most popular in-house retreats. Natives come by the thousands, seeking solace from the summer sun of Phoenix and Tucson. They return in the fall to admire the saffron leaves of sycamore, aspen and cottonwood along Oak Creek and the Verde River.

The region is rich in history as well. Visitors can explore ancient pueblos of the Sinagua, the old mining district of Jerome and Arizona's territorial capital of Prescott. The area contains a fourth of the state's working and worked-out mining claims. This diverse landscape is packaged in Yavapai

County, except for upper Oak Creek Canyon and Sedona, which occupy a corner of Coconino.

If you've just left the previous chapter and you're headed in this direction from Flagstaff, drive south on Interstate 17 for a couple of miles, then take exit 337 and follow U.S. 89A west toward Oak Creek Canyon and Sedona. As you leave I-17, you'll hit a stop sign at Flagstaff's Fort Tuthill County park. Go left and travel south through gently rolling Ponderosa country. After several miles, turn left into a view area for your first look at Oak Creek Canyon. This popular stopping place has a seasonal ranger station and a "Native American Vendor Project," where Navajos and others sell their hand-crafted jewelry and artwork.

The view is impressive—several hundred feet down into a rock-ribbed ravine, thickly cloaked with Ponderosa pines and hardwoods. Modest little Oak Creek has carved its way through five layers of the earth's surface—basalt, Kaibab limestone, Toroweap sandstone, Kokino sandstone and supai sandstone. The strata peering through the trees is mostly beige. The canyon's famous red rock country is farther south. From this high vantage point, the highway you are about to follow is a small gray ribbon far below with a yellow thread running down its center.

RV ADVISORY ● The highway down into Oak Creek Canyon is a twisting spiral, easily manageable by big rigs. Since it's very steep, it's better—on a hot day—to be going down than coming up.

Oak Creek Canyon and Sedona

Sedona elevation: 4,500 feet   **Population: 15,250**

When Frank Lloyd Wright first saw Oak Creek Canyon, he said simply: "Nothing should ever be built here."

Obviously, his advise was ignored. The canyon is dotted with campgrounds and small resorts; Sedona is busy with art galleries, gift shops and posh retreats. It's been estimated that as many as seven million people a year pass through Oak Creek Canyon and Sedona each year. Good grief, that's more than the number of visitors to the Grand Canyon!

One can hardly blame folks for almost swamping the area. This is one of America's most beautiful community settings. Sunlight and shadows play off the red sandstone buttes, spires and fluted cliffs that surround Sedona. Every daylight hour and every season brings new form and color to this crimson backdrop. We find it hard to believe that all 15,250 inhabitants don't drop whatever they're doing each evening to admire the sunset. The region can be particularly striking in summer, which residents jokingly call their monsoon season. Occasional thunder showers drench the area, then the clouds part and the sun scatters stunning rainbows about the red rocks.

Despite its tempting beauty, the area didn't attract permanent white settlement until 1876 when one James Thompson began farming here. A Pennsylvania Dutch couple, Carl and Sedona Schnebly, arrived in 1901 and built a boarding house. The following year, they petitioned for a post office, which they offered to operate from their lodge. Carl had two suggestions for the town's name—Schnebly's Station and Oak Creek Crossing. The post office department rejected them, saying they were too long to fit on a cancellation stamp.

"Keep it simple," his brother Ellsworth said. "Let's just name it after your wife."

TRIP PLANNER

WHEN TO GO ● This is spring-summer-fall country. Sedona, Prescott and the Verde Valley are havens for Arizona desert- dwellers fleeing the heat, so make lodging reservations early. Sedona attracts millions of visitors a year; it's very crowded on summer weekends. Oak Creek Canyon and the Verde River feature striking fall color, generally from late October to mid-November.

WHAT TO SEE ● Oak Creek Canyon from the overlook south of Flagstaff; Chapel of the Holy Cross and Red Rock State Park near Sedona; Fort Verde State Park; Montezuma Castle and Tuzigoot national monuments; Jerome Historic State Park and Gold King Mine Museum in Jerome; Phippen Museum of Western Art, Smoki Museum and Sharlot Hall Museum in Prescott; Arcosanti en route to Phoenix; and Shrine of St. Joseph of the Mountains in Yarnell, en route to California.

WHAT TO DO ● Drive beneath the ramparts of Oak Creek Canyon and then drive and hike the red rock country around Sedona; skid down the natural water slide at Slide Rock State Park; browse the boutiques of Sedona's Tlaquepaque; luxuriate beneath the red rocks at nearby resorts; ride the Verde Canyon Railroad from Clarkdale; explore the Mingus Mountain Recreation Area above Prescott; take a tour of curious Arcosanti.

☺ *Indicates an attraction, restaurant or lodging with special appeal.*

USEFUL CONTACTS

Camp Verde Chamber of Commerce, P.O. Box 1665 (435 S. Main St.) Camp Verde, AZ 86322; (520) 567-9294.

Coconino National Forest, 225 Brewer Road (P.O. Box 300), Sedona, AZ 86336; (520) 282-4119.

Cottonwood-Verde Valley Chamber of Commerce, 1010 S. Main St., Cottonwood, AZ 86326; (520) 864-7593.

Jerome Chamber of Commerce, P.O. Box K, Jerome, AZ 86331; (520) 634-2900.

Prescott Chamber of Commerce, P.O. Box 1147 (117 W. Goodwin St.), Prescott, AZ 86302; (800) 266-7534 or (520) 445-2000.

Prescott National Forest, 344 S. Cortez, Prescott, AZ 86303; (520) 445-1762.

Sedona-Oak Creek Canyon Chamber of Commerce, P.O. Box 478 (89A & Forest Rd.), Sedona, AZ 86336; (800) 228-7336 or (520) 282- 7722.

AREA RADIO STATIONS

KAHM-FM, 102.1, Prescott—Easy listening.

KNOT-FM, 99.1, Prescott—Country.

KSLX-FM, 105.1, Flagstaff—Light rock, easy listening.

KZTL-FM, 95.9, Flagstaff, Sedona—Light rock, easy listening.

KVBB-FM, 96,7, Prescott—Old and new top 40.

KGZZ-FM, 91.5, Phoenix—Jazz and PBS (strong in this area).

KNOT-FM, 98.3, Prescott—Country and news.

KQST-FM, 100.1 & 104.9, Sedona—Adult contemporary, jazz, "New Age."

KLKY-AM, 1130, Prescott—Popular music and news.

KNOT-AM, 1450, Prescott—Country and news.

KYCA-AM, 1490, Prescott—News and talk.

KAZM-AM, 780, Sedona—Old and new popular music, talk, news.

KVRD-AM, 1600, Cottonwood—News and talk.

A fortunate suggestion, for it's difficult to picture an art colony called Schnebly's Station. Schnebly Hill Road bears the family name, however. Carl had it built to haul produce to Flagstaff, in exchange for lumber. It's now a popular scenic drive. Early in this century, Hollywood movie makers were attracted by the area's handsome rock formations. The first film was a silent version of Zane Gray's *Call of the Canyon*. Artists began settling in, drawn by the isolation and beauty. Then resort builders arrived. They put a end to the isolation but more or less protected the setting.

Sedona has grown considerably in recent years, more than doubling its population since 1976. Surprisingly, it wasn't incorporated until 1987. While not a model of urban planning, the town still retains much of its early-day charm. There are no highrises to block those orange-hued rocks and no neon to compete with the canyon's light-and-shadow shows. The community is divided into three sections by a mid-town "Y" at the junction of U.S. 89A and State Highway 179. It's also split between Coconino and Yavapai counties. The original site in Coconino county (which locals call "Uptown Sedona") hasn't changed much in the 25 years since we first visited there.

Most of the growth is concentrated south on 179 (still in Coconino) and southwest along 89A on the Yavapai County side. Although these new areas are a bit sprawled, developers have taken a cue from Uptown and resisted neon and highrises. Route 89A through "new" Sedona is lined with spur streets leading to planned residential areas with predictable names like Shadows Estates, Settlers Rest, the Palisades, Western Hills, Rolling Hills and Mystic Hills.

..but it's upscale tourism

The town is unabashedly tourist-oriented and it is upscale tourism, for the most part. More than two dozen galleries display fine examples of Western and other contemporary art. About 300 artists live here, including Joe Wheeler, founder of the Cowboy Artists Association. In a reader survey by *Southwest Art* magazine, Sedona was rated as the sixth best place in America to buy art; it even finished ahead of New York City. Performing arts thrive as well. Musicales and plays are presented at the Sedona Arts Center. Each summer, the community sponsors the Jazz on the Rocks Festival and the Sedona Chamber Music Festival.

Some of Arizona's finest resorts are tucked against the red rock cliffs and the town has a deserved reputation as a dining center. It also has the usual curio shops with their real and imagined turquoise and other native crafts. Most stop short of being tacky. A jolly little trolley dingalings through Uptown, taking visitors between there and Tlaquepaque, a very attractive arts and crafts village off Highway 179. It also runs south along 89A through new Sedona.

The primary tourist pastime is staring at all those rock formations, from every conceivable angle. Visitors can take jeep tours through them or hot air balloon flights above them. Several scenic drives are on the chamber of commerce must-see list. National forest trails offer some of the prettiest hiking you'll find anywhere.

As you explore the area, you'll learn to recognize such promontories as the Coffee Pot, Sugar Loaf, Capital Butte, Courthouse Rock, Chimney Rock and the majestic Cathedral Rock, which seems to be in nearly every photo of Sedona. Look to the west of Highway 179 and you might recognize a more contemporary shape—Snoopy Rock with Woodstock sitting on his tummy.

Sedona enjoys one of the most imposing setting of any city in America, nestled at the base of lower Oak Creek Canyon's red rock ramparts.

Driving Oak Creek and Sedona

The forested floor of Oak Creek Canyon, most of which is within Coconino National Forest, is busy with campgrounds, picnic areas and turnouts for creek access. A fortunate few residents occupy inholdings along the creek and a few lodges have accommodations. Most of the more elegant resorts, however, are among the red rocks farther south.

Dropping down from the rim, you'll first encounter **Pine Flat Campground** with sites arrayed on either side of the highway. Just below, the west fork of Oak Creek flows into the main stream. A hike along this aspen-lined slickrock creek bed is one of the most popular in the area. In fact, it is so favored that forestry officials are considering limiting access with a permit program. No sign marks the beginning of the West Fork trail. It starts just north of a small resort called Don Hoel's Cabins.

A bit farther down the highway, the turnoff to **Cave Spring Campground** appears on the right. It's one of our favorites, since it's off the road on the far side of the creek. Next, strung out along the highway, is **Bootlegger Campground** and then **Halfway Picnic area.** Just beyond is one of the most popular places in the canyon—a natural waterslide:

☺ *Slide Rock State Park* • *Daily 8 to 6; $5 per vehicle, $1 for pedestrians and bikes; (520) 282-3034.* ☐ Long before man built the first water park, nature created a waterslide in this slickrock section of Oak Creek. Thousands come each summer and get in line to slide, splash and hollar down this long incline. Don't wear your teeny-weenie bikini or Australian beach briefs; they don't provide enough fanny protection as you bounce down this shallow cataract. Take a pair of old jeans that don't mind getting wet. Slide Rock gets jammed on summer weekends and parking is at a premium. Do your water-sliding on weekdays if possible. The park has picnic and barbecue facilities and a snack bar, an old and a half-mile hiking trail along the creek bank.

Below Slide Rock, the first of those grand red rock shapes appears, and the Ponderosa forest begins yielding to cactus, century plants and other desert flora. **Manzanita Campground** arrives next, and then a mile or so below is a popular Forest Service swimming access, **Grasshopper Point Recreation Site.** It's open 9 to 8; $2 per vehicle and 50 cents for walkers and bikers. (**RV advisory:** Parking is limited to vehicles under 20 feet.)

Just below Grasshopper, you enter Sedona, with its galleries, tourist shops, restaurants and motels posing handsomely before red rock backdrops. The well staffed and well stocked **Sedona-Oak Creek Canyon Chamber of Commerce** is downtown—sorry, Uptown—at the corner of Forest Road and Highway 89A. It's on the right, just north of the "Y"; open weekdays 8 to 5 and weekends 9 to 5; (520) 282-7722. (**RV parking advisory:** RV and trailer parking is available at a lot behind the chamber, off Forest Road.)

The first thing you'll be handed, upon stepping into the chamber office, is a map of the many scenic drives around Sedona. Since it's almost surrounded by sculpted rock formations, virtually every road is a scenic drive.

Sedona scenic routes

We'll steer you through the most popular drives in a logical sequence, with our little ☺ to indicate our favorites. Begin by turning south at the "Y" onto Highway 179, just beyond the visitor center. On your right is **Tlaquepaque,** Sedona's best shopping complex (listed below). Continue across an Oak Creek bridge, then immediately turn left and uphill.

☺ *Schnebly Hill Road* ● It isn't in much better shape than it was when Carl Schnebly paid men a dollar a day to hack out a wagon road, but the vistas are worth the bumps. You'll leave pavement after the first few blocks. The road remains bumpy and incredibly scenic for the next several miles as you climb out of the canyon. At several inviting turnouts, you can park and hike among the red rock formations. Schnebly Hill Vista, five miles up, is a particularly impressive viewpoint. From here, you can continue another six miles to I-17 at Munds Park then head south and loop back to your starting point on Highway 179. However, the scenery isn't as inviting on that side, so we'd suggest retracing your route down Schnebly Hill; you can enjoy those grand vistas both coming and going. Don't try this route in winter without a road check (282-4119); it's often closed by snow or bogged by mud.

This, incidentally, is a favorite route for jeep tours, although they go off the road and climb about the formations in several forest service permit areas. We've taken these trips and while they're fun and scenic, we were bothered by the black tire tracks and other scarring of this beautiful landscape.

RV ADVISORY ● Despite some tight turns and almost constant bumps, RVs can survive Schnebly Hill if driven slowly and carefully. Plan on thumping along at about five miles an hour or less, unless you don't mind having your dishes and possibly your furniture rearranged. Check with a local Forest Service office on road conditions if it has rained recently.

Back in Sedona, head south on Highway 179 for a couple of miles, and turn east onto Chapel Road. It takes you through an upscale subdivision to Sedona's most striking human-made landmark, the **Chapel of the Holy Cross**, dramatically fused into a red rock perch above the valley; it's listed below under "Other attractions." There's no sign on the highway indicating the chapel, so watch carefully for the small Chapel Road marker. Then return to Highway 179 and follow it south about 15 miles to the village of Oak Creek, a satellite art colony to Sedona. Turn west for yet another red rock encounter:

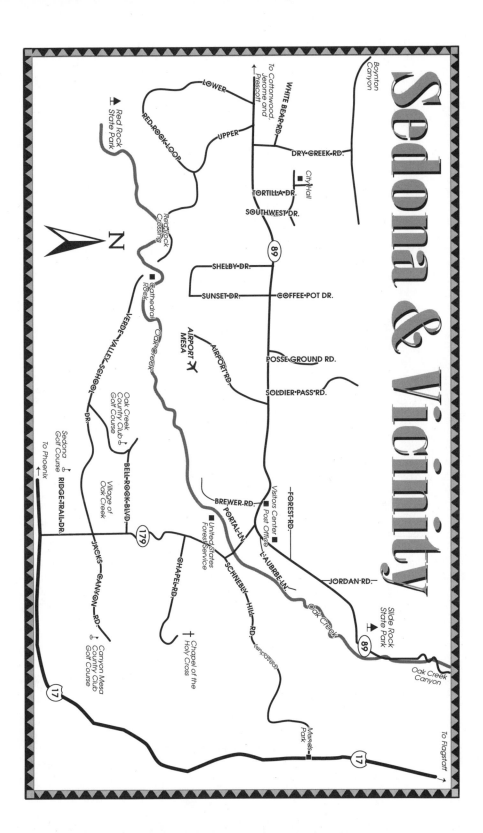

Verde Valley School Road ● This route heads toward Cathedral Rock, one of the area's most famous formations. It dead ends at a point called Red Rock Crossing, once a ford across Oak Creek. No longer a crossing point, it's a fine place from which to view Cathedral Rock, towering above. On the way back, cross Highway 179 onto Jacks Canyon Road for more red rock views.

Return to Sedona and head west on 89A. About a mile out of town, turn left onto Airport Road for a short scenic drive missed by most, unless they're catching a plane. Sedona Airport occupies a flat ridge above the valley; views of Uptown and new Sedona with their red rock backdrops are quite grand. You'll find a scenic overlook just inside the airport fence. Continue west out 89A through new Sedona for about three miles and turn right for your next fine set of rocks:

☺ *Dry Creek Road* ● This is one of the more pleasing drives in the area. It travels about five miles into the red rocks and then forks, with one branch going to Long Canyon and the other to Boynton Canyon. Take both. The left branch takes you to Boynton Canyon trailhead and to the elegant John Gardiner's Enchantment resort (both discussed below). The other route leads you past beautiful rock formations before it dead ends into one of them. Back on the main highway, you'll soon reach the turnoff to Sedona's most famous red rock drive, although it has been chopped up of late by developers:

Red Rock Loop ● This scenic drive curls through about 15 miles of red rock country. It's partly paved and partly not, with a bumpy three-mile stretch in the middle. Turn left onto Red Rock Loop Road from U.S. 89A, then go left again onto Chavez Ranch Road after a couple of miles and follow it to Red Rock Crossing (across the creek from the Verde Valley School Road). This is the most popular photo spot in Sedona, with Cathedral Rock across the way reflected in the shallow waters of Oak Creek. It can become very congestion in summer. The Forest Service has established a fee parking area ($2 per vehicle) at adjacent Crescent Moon Ranch. This can fill up busy summer days so you may have to find a spot on the shoulder and walk in.

Back on the loop drive, you'll soon hit that three miles of bumpy dirt. Just beyond, after you've recaptured pavement, take a break at a fine new state preserve:

☺ *Red Rock State Park* ● *HC-Box 886, Sedona, AZ 86336; (520) 282-6907. Daily 8 to 6; visitor center open 9 to 5. Vehicles $5; pedestrians and bikes, $1. Nature walks, talks and other ranger programs.* ☐ This 286-acre park originally was a vacation retreat owned in the 1940s by Jack Frye, then president of Trans-World Airlines. Through various land swaps, it became state park property in 1986 and was opened to the public in 1991. Red Rock is a state-of-the-environmental-art park, with a major focus on the ecosystems along Oak Creek, and a pack-in-pack-out policy for all visitors. Swimming and wading are prohibited in the creek and visitors are asked to stay on trails and roads to avoid disturbing the vegetation. And leave you your doggie outside; he's not considered native wildlife.

One learns about the geology, plant and animal life and history of the area in the excellent Center for Environmental Education, a stately native stone structure bunkered into a slope of the terrain. It has hands-on displays, plant and animal community exhibits, a gift shop and theater where *Scenic Sedona* and other films are shown on request. Several hiking trails take visitors creekside and along ridges for red rock views.

From the park, the Red Rock Loop shortly returns you to 89A.

Chapel of the Holy Cross appears to emerge from the red rocks near Sedona.

THE OUTDOOR THING

The **Coconino National Forest** office is at 225 Brewer Road. Go right at the "Y" on 89A, then turn left opposite the post office. It's open weekdays 7:30 to 4:30; (520) 282-4119. Hiking into surrounding forest lands will bring you into close contact with the area's red rock formations. Here are some of our favorite trails:

☺ ***West Fork of Oak Creek*** • *Easy hike, mostly level; varying lengths.* ☐ This is probably Oak Creek Canyon's worst-kept secret. Thousands of tourists come and go without knowing this pretty hiking trail through Oak Creek's west fork exists, for there is no marked trailhead. However, thousands of others obviously know where it is, because it's so heavily impacted that forest service officials may decide to limit access to this fragile stream-side environment. The trail starts just north of Don Hoel's Cabins and leads into the higher reaches of the canyon. Most people content themselves with a scenic mile or three, then return to the highway. For the more adventurous, the trail goes far up this side canyon, becoming more steep and difficult. Incidentally, this is not a hike into solitude. During the summer, and on fall color weekends, you'll have more than enough company on the trail.

Sterling Pass Trail • *Moderate to difficult; 2.4 miles.* ☐ Less crowded than the over-used West Fork trail, this route starts at Manzanita Campground in Oak Creek Canyon and climbs switchbacks through a pretty, heavily-wooded ravine to Sterling Pass. From there, it drops down into Sterling Canyon and meets Vultee Arch Trail (described below).

☺ ***Boynton Canyon*** • *Five miles, easy to moderate.* ☐ Like the West Fork of Oak Creek, this also is heavily used, so you might want to avoid it on weekends. To get there, take our earlier-described scenic drive up Dry Creek

Road to Boynton Canyon. You'll find the trailhead on the right, just short of the John Gardiner resort. The trail skirts the edge of the resort, then winds up into a narrow red rock canyon.

After about an hour of moderate elevation gain, the route enters a dramatic box canyon, with red rock formations rising all about you. Sit down, catch your breath and have lunch. This is one of the most dramatically beautiful spots you'll ever find.

Vultee Arch Trail ● *Easy to moderate; 3.5 miles round-trip.* ☐ This is a relatively mild hike up Sterling Canyon, reached from a trailhead off Dry Creek Road. To reach it, turn right onto Dry Creek, go two miles to Forest Road 152, then go right five miles. This gently inclined trail leads to a natural arch, named for Gerard and Sylvia Vultee. The noted aircraft designer and his wife died when their plane crashed nearby in 1938. **RV advisory:** The trail isn't difficult, although RVs may have a problem on the dirt road to the trailhead. It's rough and can become badly eroded after storms. Check with the local Forest Service office about its condition. If you don't want to drive it, you can walk five miles along the approach road. It's a nice all-day outing and the total round-trip is 13.5 miles.

Devil's Bridge Trail ● *Moderately steep, two-mile round-trip.* ☐ This is a shorter version of the Vultee trail, leading to another natural arch. Take Dry Creek Road to the same bumpy Forest Road 152. Then walk, or drive if you can, 1.2 miles to the Devil's Bridge trailhead. If you walk all the way from the Dry Creek road turnoff, the round trip is about 4.5 miles.

OTHER ATTRACTIONS

☺ **Chapel of the Holy Cross** ● *Chapel Road off Highway 179 (two miles south of town); (520) 282-4069. Daily 9 to 5; free.* ☐ Some call it the most striking religious structure in America. Rising from the red rocks with a bold cross for a façade, the chapel rivals the rocks themselves as Sedona's best-known landmark. Within this quietly grand setting, soft music and soft lights mellow you out for a spiritual experience. Unfortunately, this experience is being disturbed somewhat by encroaching suburbia. Expensive houses are creeping up the surrounding hills. Rising between two redstone pinnacles, the chapel looks to be a creation of the late Frank Lloyd Wright. Actually it was designed by one of his disciples, Marguerite Brunswig Staude. This is not a church with regular services but a chapel for quiet retreat. **RV parking:** There isn't any in the small chapel parking lot or even sufficient turnaround space. It's best to stop at a wide spot in the road below and hike up.

Creekside Scenic Theater ● *In Tlaquepaque shopping center; (520) 282-6611. Scenic Sedona film shown on the half hour, daily 10 to 5; $4 for adults and $2.50 for kids. Western classics Friday and Saturday evenings, 7:45; $4. Live music and other shows periodically; various prices.* ☐ This small upstairs showplace is fashioned like an informal dinner theater, where visitors can sit at tables, sip drinks and watch assorted entertainments. The main feature is *Beauty of Sedona*, presenting a scenic overview of the area. It's nicely filmed with lots of red rocks and some cute wildlife shots. We felt the narrative was a bit gushy, although it may have been toned down since our visit. (A wise photographer once said: "Let your pictures do the talking.") The lobby is a mini-museum with photos of old Sedona and black and white studio shots of longtime Western film stars. Other activities at the theater range from Karaoke and jazz sessions to magic shows.

Sedona Arts Center • *Art Barn road, north end of town; (520) 282-3809. Tuesday-Saturday 10:30 to 4:30, Sunday 1:30 to 4:30, closed December 24 to January 5; free admission.* ◻ This is a center for both creative and performing arts. The "Art Barn" hosts plays, music recitals and readings, as well as exhibiting the works of local artists. Paintings, batiks, sculptures, ceramics and other things artistic are on sale in the gallery shop.

☺ *Tlaquepaque* • *Just south of Uptown on Highway 179; most shops open daily 10 to 6 (shorter hours in the off-season).* ◻ This Spanish colonial style shopping complex was named for an arts and crafts colony in the suburbs of Guadalajara, Mexico. However, Sedona's Tlaquepaque is much more elegant than the rather scruffy original. It's built around tiled, nicely landscaped courtyards, shaded by giant sycamores. Dozens of shops, galleries and cafés are tucked into arcaded buildings. *RV parking:* Rigs up to 21 feet can find spaces by turning in at the first entrance and going right into the north parking area.

ACTIVITIES

Balloon Flights • Aerozona Balloon Company, P.O. Box 10081, Sedona, AZ 86339; (520) 282-1499. Inflated Ego, 3230 Valley Vista Drive, Sedona, AZ 86336; (520) 284-9483. Northern Light Balloon Expeditions, P.O. Box 1695, Sedona, AZ 86336; (800) 230-6222 or (520) 282-2274. Sky High Balloon Adventures, 165 Zane Grey Dr., Sedona, AC 86336, (800) 551-7597 or (520) 204-1395.

Bike rentals • Mountain Bike Heaven, 1695 W. Highway 89A, Sedona, AZ 86336; (520) 282-1312. Sedona Sports, 245 N. Highway 89A, Sedona, AZ 85336; (520) 282-6956.

Bike tours • *Backroads, 1516 Fifth St., Berkeley, CA 94710-1740; (800) 462-2848 or (510) 527-1555.* ◻ This firm, specializing in active vacations, offers bike tours through Sedona's red rock country, starting and ending in Flagstaff. Guests sleep in resorts and accompanying vans carry their gear.

Golf • Canyon Mesa Country Club, nine-hole executive course, 500 Jacks Canyon Road in Oak Creek Village; (520) 284-0036. Oak Creek Country Club, 18-holes, 690 Bell Rock Blvd., Village of Oak Creek; (520) 284-1660. Poco Diablo Resort, nine-hole executive, Highway 179, two miles south of Sedona; (520) 282-7333. Sedona Gold Resort, 18 holes, 7260 Highway 179 Oak Creek Village; (520) 284-9355.

Jeep Tours • This is the most popular way to get next to the red rock landscape. Those garish vehicles of Sedona Pink Jeep Tours have been at it the longest, operating out of an office across from the Chamber of Commerce at 204 N. Highway 89A; the address is P.O. Box 1447, Sedona, AZ 86336; (800) 8-SEDONA or (520) 282-5000.

Other jeep trip firms are Sedona Adventures, 273 N. Highway 89A (Box 1476), Sedona, AZ 86336, (800) 888-9494 or (520) 282-3500; Sedona Red Rock Jeep Tours, 270 N. Highway 89A (P.O. Box 10305), Sedona, AZ 86336, (800) 848-7728 or (520) 282-6826; and Time Expeditions, 276 N. Highway 89A, (Box 2936), Sedona, AZ 86336; (800) 999-2137 or (520) 282-2137.

Horseback rides • El Rojo Grande Ranch, P.O. Box 4143, Sedona, AZ 86340; (520) 282-1898. Kachina Stables of Sedona, Lower Loop Road (P.O. Box 3616), Sedona, AZ 86340; (800) 723-3538 or (520) 282-7252.

Jeep rentals • Sedona Jeep Rentals, Sedona Airport (P.O. Box 902), Sedona, AZ 86339; (520) 282-2227.

Nature hikes for kids • 252 N. Highway 89A, Sedona, AZ 86336; (520) 282-4320.

Scenic Flights • Most of these operate out of Sedona Airport. Action Helicopters of Arizona, P.O. Box 2699, Sedona, AZ 85336; (520) 282-7884. Air Safari, Inc., 1225 Airport Rd., Sedona, AZ 86336; (520) 282-3485. Arizona Helicopter Adventures, P.O. Box 1729, Sedona, AZ 86336; (800) 282-5141 or (520) 282-0904. Scenic Airlines Sedona, 235 Air Terminal Dr., Sedona, AZ 86336; (800) 634-6801 or (520) 282-7935. Sedona Sky Treks, 30 Cedar Court, Sedona, AZ 86336; (520) 284-2998. Skydance Helicopters, 1225 Airport Rd. Sedona, AZ 86336; (800) 882-1651 or (520) 282-1651.

Van, bus and limo tours • Earth Wisdom Tours, 293 N. Highway 89A, Sedona, AZ 86336; (800) 482-4714 or (520) 282-4714. Red Rock Limousine Co., 1615 W. Highway 89A, Sedona, AZ 86336; (800) 279-1945 or (520) 282-0175. Roadrunner Tours, 841 Highway 179 (P.O. Box 498), Sedona, AZ 86336; (520) 282-4696. Sedona Art Tours, P.O. Box 10578, Sedona, AZ 86336; (520) 282-7686. Sedona Photo Tours, 252 N. Highway 89A, Sedona, AZ 86336; (800) 973-3662 or (520) 282-4320. Sedona Trolley Tours, 201 N. Highway 89A (P.O. Box 1635), Sedona, AZ 86336; (520) 282-5400. Time Expeditions Archaeological-Culture Tours, 276 N. Highway 89A (P.O. Box 2936), Sedona, AZ 86336; (800) 999-2137 or (520) 282-2137. Town and Country Limousine Service, 2550 Blue Horizon Rd., Sedona, AZ 86336; (800) 775-6739 or (520) 204-1383.

Forces afloat? • Do you feel any strange vibes? Some say there are mystical forces loose in this area, with focal points for magnetic feminine and electric masculine vortex fields. Masculine vortex vibes are best at Bell Rock, while feminine energies are focused at Cathedral rock. Need some of both? Boynton Canyon offers an "electromagnetic masculine-feminine combination." Companies that will point your Nikes in the proper metaphysical and spiritual directions include Dorian Tours Spirit Steps, P.O. Box 3151, Sedona, AZ 86340, (800) 728-4562 or (520) 282-4562; and Sedona Nature Excursions, 10 Traumeri Lane, Sedona, AZ 86336, (520) 282-6735. Outings such as these are designed to "put you in touch with the dynamic energies of your inner self."

Fasten your seat belts.

ANNUAL EVENTS

For information on these and other events, contact the Sedona-Oak Creek Canyon Chamber of Commerce at (800) 228-7336 or (520) 282-7722.

Hopi Show with dances, arts and crafts, mid-May; (520) 282-6428.

Sedona Chamber Music Festival at various locations, first half of June; (520) 204-2801 or (520) 204-2415.

Western Americana Festival in late June; (520) 282-9441.

Sedona Jazz on the Rocks, June through September; 282-1985.

Sedona Heritage Days, late September to early October; 282-2186

Sedona Arts Festival, mid-October; (520) 282-8949.

Festival of Lights, *luminarias* at Tlaquepaque, starts in early December; (520) 282-4838.

WHERE TO SHOP

For shoppers, Sedona comes in three pieces. Most of the crafts and curio shops, motels and some galleries are Uptown. The fine Tlaquepaque complex and several other galleries are along State Highway 179 south of Uptown.

For practical supplies and such, regional shopping centers line Highway 89A in West Sedona, on the Yavapai County side.

WHERE TO DINE

Atrium Restaurant ● ☆☆ $$$

☐ *In Tlaquepaque on Highway 179; (520) 282-5060. American-continental; wine and beer. Daily from 8 a.m. MC/VISA.* ☐ One dines under glass in this aptly-named place with a greenhouse roof; it also has an outdoor patio. The versatile menu features grilled chicken breast, sautéed calves liver, steaks and several European dishes.

☺ Cowboy Club ● ☆☆☆ $$

☐ *241 Highway 89A (Uptown); (520) 282-4200. Southwestern cuisine; full bar service. Daily 11 to 10. Major credit cards.* ☐ Brightly attired Southwestern style bistro with Navajo rug-draped booths, a stone fireplace and cowboy regalia on the walls. Entrées—rather fancy for cowboys—include chicken adobe on Gouda cream and trout with chili-fried cactus strips.

El Rincon ● ☆☆ $$

☐ *In Tlaquepaque; (520) 282-4648. Mexican; full bar service. Tuesday-Saturday 11 to 9, Sunday noon to 5, closed Monday. MC/VISA.* ☐ Navajo accents such as Indian fry bread influences the Mexican fare at this pretty garden restaurant, which labels its cuisine "Arizona Style." You can dine indoors or on a patio beside Oak Creek.

Hitching Post Restaurant ● ☆ $

☐ *269 W. Highway 89A (across from Canyon Portal Motel); (520) 282-7761. American; no alcohol. Daily 7 a.m. to 8 p.m.; no credit cards.* ☐ This cozy little café features basic, inexpensive fare, including luncheon specials.

Humphreys ● ☆☆☆ $$

☐ *1405 W. Highway 89A (across from the Flicker Shack); (520) 282-7748. American; full bar service. Daily 3:30 to 9 p.m. Reservations suggested; MC/VISA.* ☐ This nautical theme place specializes in fresh seafood, prime rib and mesquite grilled steaks. Entertainment in the lounge.

☺ L'Auberge de Sedona Restaurant ● ☆☆☆☆ $$$$

☐ *301 Little Lane (Uptown, in L'Auberge resort); (520) 282-7131. French; full bar service. Daily 7 to 10, noon to 3 and 5:30 to 10. Reservations essential; major credit cards.* ☐ This small, opulent restaurant with picture window views of Oak Creek offers a six-course *prix-fixe* dinner with a selection of several appetizers, soup and salad, a choice of seven or eight entrées and dessert. The food and service are worth the price.

☺ Oaxaca Restaurante ● ☆☆☆ $$

☐ *231 N. Highway 89A (Uptown); (520) 282-7149. Mexican- American; full bar service. Daily 8 a.m. to 9 p.m. MC/VISA, DISC.* ☐ Very appealing Southwest style café, with polished tile floors and thick ceiling beams hung with things *Latino*; outdoor dining deck with red rock views. The health-conscious menu (no animal fats or preservatives) tilts toward the Southwest, with fare such as Sedona chicken (with goat cheese, tomatoes and chilies), steaks and fish with spicy sauces, plus a good range of Mexican fare.

The Orchards ● ☆☆☆ $$$

☐ *254 N. Highway 89A (Uptown); (520) 282-7200. American regional; full bar service. Daily 7 a.m. to 10 p.m. Major credit cards.* ☐ An interesting menu mix ranges from Greek pasta to chicken Santa Fe (with citrus, cilantro and black beans) to grilled vegetable brochette. The look is a mix of Southwest outside and early American inside.

☺ René at Tlaquepaque ● ☆☆☆ $$

☐ *In Tlaquepaque on Highway 179; (520) 282-9225. Mostly French; full bar service. Thursday-Monday 11:30 to 2:30 and 5:30 to 9 (until 9:30 weekends). Reservations suggested; major credit cards.* ☐ The décor is Spanish outside and French provincial within. The menu in this elegant place tilts toward *La belle France,* with some American and continental accents.

Shugru's Restaurant, Bakery & Bar ● ☆☆☆ $$$

☐ *2250 W. Highway 89A (opposite First Interstate Bank); (520) 282-2943. Continental and Mexican; full bar service. Monday-Thursday 11 to 9, Friday-Saturday 8 to 10, Sunday 8 to 9. MC/VISA, AMEX.* ☐ The eclectic menu at this stylish place includes steaks, seafoods, wok dishes and Mexican specialties, backed up by baked beans. Omelets and homemade cinnamon rolls are a breakfast specialty.

WHERE TO RECLINE

Prices reflect high season rates and may be lower at other times. Most were provided by the management and are subject to change; use them only as a guide.

Bell Rock Inn ● ☆☆☆ $$$$

☐ *6246 Highway 179 (near Oak Creek Village), Sedona, AZ 86336; (800) 881-ROCK or (520) 282-4161. Couples $79 to $115, singles $59 to $65, suites $109 to $125. MC/VISA, AMEX.* ☐ A 96-room lodge with TV, room phones, some fireplaces; pool, spa, tennis, golf packages. **Restaurant** open 7 a.m. to 9 p.m.; American-continental; dinners $11 to $18; Southwest décor, full bar.

Black Forest House ● ☆ $$$ Ø

☐ *50 Willow Way (just off 89A in west Sedona), Sedona, AZ 86336; (520) 282-2835 or 282-9416. Couples $50 to $80, singles $45 to $70. MC/VISA.* ☐ A 12-room motel with TV, VCRs, microwaves and refrigerators.

Cedars Resort ● ☆☆ $$ Ø

☐ *Highway 89A and 179 (P.O. Box 292), Sedona, AZ 86339; (520) 282-7010. Couples and singles $40 to $70. MC/VISA, AMEX.* ☐ A 39-room lodge on Oak Creek with TV movies, phones, refrigerators; pool, spa. Red rock views, Spanish courtyard; all rooms non-smoking.

Cimarron Inn ● ☆☆ $$ Ø

☐ *2991 W. Highway 89A (P.O. Box 1589), Sedona, AZ 86336; (520) 282-9166. Couples and suites $58 to $64, singles $54. MC/VISA.* ☐ A 66-unit motel with TV, phones, refrigerators, balconies or patios; pool and spa.

Don Hoel's Cabins ● ☆☆ $$$$

☐ *9440 N. Highway 89A (in Oak Creek Canyon), Sedona, AZ 86336-9623; (800) 292-HOEL or (520) 282-3560. Couples and singles $78 to $100.* ☐ Eighteen rustic cottages in Oak Creek Canyon, sized to fit two to six people; some kitchenettes. Mini-mart; fishing, swimming and hiking trails nearby.

☺ Enchantment Resort ● ☆☆☆☆☆ $$$$$ Ø

☐ *525 Boynton Canyon Road (Dry Creek road off 89A in west Sedona), Sedona, AZ 86336; (800) 826-4180 or (520) 282-2900. Couples and singles $165 to $225, suites $275 to $355, two-bedroom casitas with kitchenettes $425 to $595. Major credit cards.* ☐ Set in a secluded canyon against red rock cliffs, John Gardiner's Enchantment is perhaps the most elegant and beautifully situated resort in Arizona. Full amenities in all rooms; tennis, cro-quiet, pools, full health spa, six-hole golf course. **Enchantment Dining Room** serves breakfast 7:30 to 10, 11:30 to 2, dinner 6 to 9; Southwest cuisine; dinners from $35, full bar service.

Junipine Resort ● ☆☆☆ $$$$$ Ø

◻ *8351 N. Highway 89A (eight miles north in Oak Creek Canyon); Sedona, AZ 86336; (800) 742-7463 or (520) 282-3375. All condo units with full kitchens; couples and singles $160 to $250. Major credit cards.* ◻ Handsome "creekhouse" suites in a hideaway Oak Creek setting; TV movies, room phones, some fireplaces; spa, grocery store. **Junipine Café** serves daily 8:30 to 3 and 5 to 9; dinners $13 to $21; wine and beer.

☺ L'Auberge de Sedona Resort ● ☆☆☆☆ $$$$$ Ø

◻ *301 Little Lane (P.O. Box B); Sedona, AZ 86336; (800) 272-6777 or (520) 282-1661. Couples and singles $140, cottages $275 to $385. Major credit cards.* ◻ Posh 57-unit resort in a secluded creekside setting in the heart of Uptown Sedona; TV movies, phones; pool, spa. **L'Auberge Restaurant** listed above.

☺ Los Abrigados ● ☆☆☆☆ $$$$$ Ø

◻ *160 Portal Lane (adjacent to Tlaquepaque), Sedona, AZ 86336; (800) 521-3131 or (520) 282-1777. All suites; $210 to $395. Major credit cards.* ◻ Opulent new Spanish style resort with 172 suites, all with TV movies, wet bars and view balconies; some with fireplaces and spa tubs. Health spa, saunas, swimming pools and tennis courts. **Dining** at three restaurants,—Joey Bistro, Steaks & Sticks and the posh Celebrity Room; breakfast, lunch and dinner; full bar service.

Oak Creek Terrace Resort ● ☆☆☆ $$$

◻ *4548 N. Highway 89A (in Oak Creek Canyon, four miles north), Sedona, AZ 86336; (800) 224-2229 or (520) 3567. Couples and singles $69 to $160. MC/VISA, DISC.* ◻ Woodsy resort with TV movies, fireplaces, spa tubs, kitchenettes. Some units have private decks. Hammocks, double swing, picnic tables and barbecues by the creek. Jeep rentals available.

☺ Poco Diablo Resort ● ☆☆☆☆ $$$$$ Ø

◻ *Highway 179 two miles south (P.O. Box 1709) Sedona, AZ 86336; (520) 282-7333. Couples and singles $135 to $185. Major credit cards.* ◻ Luxury resort on 25 acres at the foot of red rock cliffs near Oak Creek; some suites; room fireplaces, phones, TV movies, refrigerators, whirlpool tubs. Par three golf, tennis, pools, spas, racquetball, fitness center. **Restaurant** open Sunday- Thursday 7 a.m. to 9 p.m. and Friday-Saturday 7 to 10; Southwest cuisine; dinners $9 to $21; full bar service.

Star Motel ● ☆ $$

◻ *295 Jordan Road (Uptown, just off 89A), Sedona, AZ 86336; (800) 896-7301 or (520) 282-7301. Couples $45 to $85, singles $35 to $70. Major credit cards.* ◻ Small motel with TV and refrigerators; some fireplace units and kitchenettes. Second location with same rates and phone numbers at 500 N. Highway 89A, Sedona, AZ 86339-2294.

Bed & breakfast inns

Cathedral Rock Lodge Bed & Breakfast ● ☆☆☆ $$$ Ø

◻ *61 Los Amigos Lane (Off Highway 89A, downstream from Red Rock Crossing), Sedona, AZ 86336; (520) 282-7608. Couples $70 to $110; private baths; full breakfasts; MC/VISA.* ◻ Rambling country home with gardens and spacious wooded grounds; barbecue and picnic areas; red rock views. Living room with fireplace; videotape collection of movies filmed in the area. Rooms furnished with antiques.

☺ *The Graham Bed & Breakfast Inn* ● ☆☆☆☆ *$$$$$* Ø

⧠ *150 Canyon Circle Drive (two blocks from intersection of Highway 179 and Bell Rock Boulevard), Sedona, AZ 86336; (520) 284-1425. Couples $109 to $219, $15 less for singles. Six rooms with TV/VCRs and private baths; full breakfasts; MC/VISA, DISC.* ⧠ An appealing Southwest style B&B inn with a mix of antique, Art Deco and Southwest furnishings, and works by local artists; red rock views. Some units with spa tubs, all with balconies. Pool and spa, bicycles; fireplace in the dining room; large video collection.

Lantern Light Inn ● ☆☆☆ *$$$$* Ø

⧠ *3085 Highway 89A (near Dry Creek Road), Sedona, AZ 86336-5056; (520) 282-3419. Three units with room TV and private baths; full breakfast. Couples and singles $85 to $110, three people $125. Country French style B&B with antique furnishings, in red rock setting; private entrances and views of Cathedral Rock; one room has a kitchenette. European style lounge with library and video collection; three outdoor patios.*

Territorial House Bed & Breakfast ● ☆☆☆ *$$$$* Ø

⧠ *65 Pike Dr. (near Kachina Dr.), Sedona, AZ 86336; (800) 801-2737 or (520) 204-2737. Four units with private baths; full breakfast. Couples $95 to $155, two-bedroom suite $185. MC/VISA, AMEX.* ⧠ Western style early Sedona home with rural décor. Some rooms have spa tubs, decks, balconies and fireplaces. Great room with stone fireplace; veranda, hot tub and landscaped grounds. Bicycles and exercycle.

WHERE TO CAMP

Oak Creek Canyon ● *Five Coconino National Forest campgrounds are in the canyon; (520) 282-4119. RV and tent sites, no hookups, $10; half price for Golden Age and Golden Access passes. Sites at Pine Flat and Cave Spring may be reserved by calling (800) 280-CAMP, using MC/VISA (or call to request a mail-in reservations form). Pine Flat, 12 miles north of Sedona on 89A is open all year. Some of the others—Manzanita, Banjo Bill, Bootlegger and Cave Spring—may close in the off-season. All are on or near Highway 89A and all have pit toilets, picnic tables and barbecues; most offer nature trails and swimming and fishing in Oak Creek. All but Bootlegger (which costs $6) have drinking water. Cave Spring has a small convenience store.*

Hawkeye/Red Rock RV Park ● *40 Art Barn Road (off 89A, near Uptown) Sedona, AZ 86336; (520) 282-2222 or (800) 229-2822. RV and tent sites; full hookups $27.50, water and electric $22.50, no hookups $17. Reservations accepted.* ⧠ Showers, coin laundry, groceries, snack bar, Propane, dump station ($5 fee). Swimming and fishing in nearby Oak Creek. Within walking distance of town.

Rancho Sedona RV Park ● *135 Bear Wallow Road, just off Schnebly Hill Road near Uptown (P.O. Box 450), Sedona, AZ 86336; (520) 282-7255. RV and tent sites; $20 to $25. Reservations accepted.* ⧠ Some pull-throughs, showers, coin laundry, dump station. Along Oak Creek; short walk to Tlaquepaque and Uptown Sedona.

Sedona RV Resort ● *6701 W. Highway 89A (two miles south of town), Sedona, AZ 86336; (800) 547-8727 or (520) 282-6640. RV and tent sites; $18.50 to $24.50. Reservations accepted; MC/VISA.* ⧠ Many pull-throughs, some shaded sites; pool, spa, restaurant, coin laundry, mini-mart, hair salon, miniature golf, playground, basketball, badminton and shuffleboard, horse-shoe pits. Two-room camping cabins available.

SOUTH TOWARD COTTONWOOD

Oak Creek Canyon fans out into the semi-arid Verde Valley to the south, where the ancient Sinagua once tilled their beans, squash and corn. *Verde* is Spanish for green, and the name may have come from the emerald swath of the Verde River or from malachite, a green copper mineral that's abundant in the lower valley. The Verde River is fed by creeks draining the Colorado Plateau, including Oak, Sycamore and a couple called Wet and Dry Beaver creeks. The valley glitters with blazing bits of fall color in late October through mid-November, particularly along the course of the Verde and its tributaries. Otherwise, it's a rather ordinary looking agricultural basin offering several interesting tourist lures.

Two Indians ruins in the area are preserved in national monuments—Tuzigoot to the southwest and Montezuma Castle, the well-known cliff dwelling directly south. The name came from early settlers' fanciful notion that the Aztec ruler took refuge here in the 16th century, fleeing from the soldiers of Cortez. Men and women of a more recent vintage came looking for gold, silver and copper. They left behind a cliff dwelling of quite another sort—the scruffy copper mining town of Jerome. It's steeply terraced into the brushy, rocky face of Mingus Mountain above the Verde Valley. Yet another attraction in the area preserves a troubling link between Native Americans and the new Americans. At Fort Verde State Historic Park, you can learn about the troops sent to protect white settlers from the Yavapai and Tonto Apaches. It's no wonder the settlers needed protection; they were stealing the Indians' land.

The Verde Valley is a thousand or more feet lower than Sedona and Oak Creek Canyon, so expect it to be hot in summer. Temperatures beyond the hundred mark are not uncommon. However, as we keep rationalizing, it's a dry heat. Do your exploring in the morning, and then head for the shade or even better, the cooling waters of the Verde River.

Driving the Verde Valley

Moving south on U.S. 89A, you'll leave red rock country, probably with some reluctance, and enter the valley's juniper and sage desert. We've assembled a driving route that ties together the area's assorted lures without too much overlap.

About 16 miles below Sedona, turn left onto county road 30 at the sign indicating **Cornville**. This takes you past that aptly named farm hamlet, 13 miles through low hill country to Interstate 17 for your first Verde Valley attraction. Montezuma Castle National Monument comes in two pieces—the main ruin a few miles south of here and a sinkhole called Montezuma's well. We'll send you first to the well, reached by crossing over I-17 and driving a couple of miles east. (If you're coming here on I-17, take exit 293.)

☺ **Montezuma Well** ● *Daily 8 to 7 in summer, 8 to 5 the rest of the year; no admission charge.* ☐ Since Montezuma Castle supposedly was the lair of the famous Aztec ruler, he needed a sacrificial well in which to toss an occasional virgin, right?

Wrong, of course.

Sinagua Indians—not a fugitive Montezuma—once occupied this imposing cliff dwelling.

Montezuma Well is a limestone sinkhole rimmed by several pueblo ruins. A trail down to the sink, 55 feet from the rim, provides a close-up of several ruins near the water's edge. If the water wasn't so green and scummy and if a sign didn't warn of leeches, this might be a tempting swimming hole. Another trail leads to a vent outside the rim, where warm, clean water flows into nearby Wet Beaver Creek. Both Hohokam and later arriving Sinagua used the well for irrigation, and traces of their limestone lined ditches are still visible.

This is a wonderful little spot, shaded by a giant leaning sycamore. We prefer it to the more crowded Montezuma Castle. On a sign here, we found one of our favorite passages, penned by retired National Park Service employee Jean Henderer:

> *Take time to see the sky*
> *Find shapes in the clouds*
> *Hear the murmur of the wind*
> *And touch the cool water.*
> *Walk softly—*
> *We are the intruders*
> *Tolerated briefly*
> *In an infinite universe.*

From the well, return to the freeway, head south three miles to exit 289 and follow signs to the main monument:

☺ ***Montezuma Castle National Monument*** • *P.O. Box 219, Camp Verde, AZ 86322; (520) 567-3322. Daily 8 to 7 in summer, 8 to 5 the rest of the year. Adults $2, kids 16 and under free.* ☐ Montezuma Castle is small as ruins go. However, the drama of its perch high in a cliff face and its Aztec ruler legend have caught the fancy of visitors. We know that it wasn't Montezuma's lair and certainly not his revenge; it's an ordinary Sinagua cliff dwelling in an extraordinary setting, framed by giant sycamores. The only Aztecs to have come this far north are green-carders and tourists. The structure is a five-story apartment containing 20 rooms, probably built in the 12th century. Nearby Castle "A" was even larger—six stories with perhaps 45 rooms, although it's badly deteriorated.

Visitors can't climb up to the fragile castles, but the view from a self-guiding nature path is impressive. A diorama nearby features a cutaway of Montezuma Castle, with a recording about a day in the life of those who occupied it. The visitor center does its usual excellent job of interpreting the geology of the area and the sociology of the Sinagua and Hohokam Indians who once occupied the Verde Valley.

Returning to the Montezuma Castle interchange, you'll see a considerably more contemporary structure—a Native American casino, along with an inn attractively done in Southwest décor. So if you have some loose change seeking holes in your pocket:

Cliff Castle Casino ● *P.O. Box 3430, (I-17 exit 289) Camp Verde, AZ 86322; (520) 567-6611.* ❒ Opened in 1995, the casino is stuffed with ranks of slot and video poker machines, with the usual bells, whistles, chimes and intercom announcements of big winners typical of a Las Vegas game room. There are no table games here; only the machines. It also has a small café, a larger restaurant and rooms. For specifics on these, see below, under "Where to recline."

Camp Verde

Elevation: 3,160 feet   **Population: 6,000**

From the castle, head south to Camp Verde, either by following Montezuma Castle Highway or returning to the freeway and taking exit 287. Once there, signs will direct you to its main—and possibly only—attraction, Fort Verde State Park.

Settlement here dates from 1863 when a minor gold rush drew prospectors to the Hassayampa River and Lynx Creek. They didn't find much gold, but farmers and ranchers later settled here and began unsettling the Indians. The Army arrived in 1865, after several skirmishes between the newcomers and the original residents.

The town is scruffily appealing in a Western sort of way, with a few false front stores lining Main Street. Some house antique shops and cafés and you might find a gallery or Western shop or two. The **Chamber of Commerce Visitor Center** is at 435 S. Main, open weekdays 8 to 5; (520) 567-9294.

☺ ***Fort Verde State Historic Park*** ● *P.O. Box 397 (off Lane Street downtown), Camp Verde, AZ 86322; (520) 567-3275. Daily 8 to 4:30; adults $2, kids $1.* ❒ As its original name implies, "Camp" Verde was not a walled fort, but an encampment from which U.S. Army troops sallied forth to quell Apache and Yavapai uprisings. Camp Verde was built in the early 1870s, then re-named Fort Verde in 1879 to imply a permanent Army presence. Three years later, the local Apaches were defeated although the fort was not abandoned until 1891. Local settlers helped themselves to most of the lumber. By the time citizens began preserving the relic in 1956, only four buildings remained.

Visitors today can take a self-guiding tour through the furnished commanding officer's quarters, surgeons' house and bachelor officers' quarters. The administration building is now a museum with relics of the period. The commanding officer's house, with its fireplace, piano and fine Victorian furnishings, suggests that life wasn't terribly tough in frontier Arizona if you were the boss.

ANNUAL EVENTS

For specifics on these and other events, call the chamber at 567-9294.

Southwestern Day, late April, with pioneer crafts, military reenactments, food and music.

Armed Forces Day salute with early-day activities at Fort Verde State Park, first weekend of May; (520) 567-3275.

Arts and Crafts Festival, mid-June.

Fort Verde Days, second weekend in October; (520) 567-3275.

WHERE TO DINE

Ming House ● ☆☆ $

☐ *Fort Verde Plaza Shopping Center; (520) 567-9488. Chinese; full bar service. Daily 11 to 9. MC/VISA.* ☐ Health conscious Chinese restaurant serving low fat, low cholesterol and MSG-free fare. Typical Cantonese and spicier Mandarin entrées range from sesame chicken and chow mein to Szechuan pork and Mongolian beef.

Olde Adobe Grille ● ☆☆ $$

☐ *Main Street (in Sutler's Stores); (520) 567-5229. American, Southwestern; full bar service. Daily 11:30 to 10; MC/VISA.* ☐ Southwestern fare, ribs, seafood and chops are served amidst Santa Fe décor in an 1871 adobe building. Jazz and guitar music in adjoining cocktail lounge.

Rio Verde ● ☆☆ $$

☐ *Highway 260 (General Crook Trail) at the "Y" downtown; (520) 567-9966 or (520) 567-2435. Southwest; full bar service. Lunch and dinner. MC/VISA.* ☐ Southwestern style café with a menu to match, featuring spicy Spanish chicken, steak *picaro* (with wine glazed in onions, mushrooms, bell peppers and tomatoes), plus American chili, steak and burgers.

Valley View Copper Room Restaurant ● ☆☆ $$

☐ *Arnold and Main streets; (520) 567-3592. American- Mexican; full bar service. Daily 6 a.m. to 9 p.m. MC/VISA.* ☐ An attractive Western style restaurant and lounge with valley views; outdoor patio. Steaks, chops and seafood menu with several Mexican dishes. Piano bar in the lounge.

WHERE TO RECLINE

Best Western Cliff Castle Lodge and Casino ● ☆☆☆ $$$$ ∅

☐ *P.O. Box 3430, (I-17 exit 289) Camp Verde, AZ 86322; (520) 567-6611. Couples and singles $74 to $80. Major credit cards.* ☐ An 82-room lodge with TV movies, phones and refrigerators; some microwaves. Pool and spa; **Dining room** serves Southwest fare 7 to 9; dinners $8 to $18; full bar service. **Casino** details above.

Super 8 Motel ● ☆☆ $$$ ∅

☐ *1550 W. Highway 260 (P.O. Box 2838), Camp Verde, AZ 86322; (520) 567-2622. Couples $51 to $55, singles $46. Major credit cards.* ☐ Well-kept 44-room motel with TV movies, room phones; pool and spa.

From Camp Verde, cross I-17 and follow State Route 260 a dozen miles northeast to the valley's largest town:

Cottonwood

Elevation: 3,320 feet   **Population: 5,000**

Once a small farming community, Cottonwood is now the Verde Valley's commercial center. In an important secondary role, it provides affordable housing for employees of Sedona's smart shops and restaurants. Its collection of motels provide a good base for exploring the Verde Valley. Predictably, the lodgings are less expensive than those in Sedona. Beyond the shopping centers, motels and service stations of the newer community is Old Cottonwood, with a handful of false front stores housing Indian crafts shops, antique stores and a couple of souvenir places.

Approaching town, you'll enter new Cottonwood and discover the **Cottonwood-Verde Valley Chamber of Commerce.** It's at the junction of State Highway 260 and U.S. 89A, in front of a large Walmart; open daily 9 to 5; phone (520) 634-7593. After loading up on brochures, follow Main Street, labeled Historic 89A, north toward the old town section. To visit the town's museum, installed in a venerable school building, turn left onto Mingus Avenue (at the blue "Hospital" sign) and follow it several blocks:

Clemenceau Heritage Museum ● *Willard at Mingus; (520) 634-2868. Wednesday 9 to noon, Friday-Sunday 11 to 3.* ☐ The museum occupies several classrooms in a wing of the large, low-rise stucco 1924 Clemenceau School. Displays include a model railroad, period classroom and the usual pioneer photos and artifacts, plus changing exhibits.

If you'd like to picnic, hike, swim or camp at a state park, turn north either from Mingus or Main onto Tenth Street. Follow signs past the city's Riverfront Park; the state park is just beyond:

Dead Horse Ranch State Park ● *P.O. Box 144, Cottonwood, AZ 86326; (520) 634-5283. Day use $5 per vehicle or $1 for walk-ins and bikes. Camping $15 with hookups, $10 without; see details below, under "Where to camp."* ☐ On the site of a former working ranch, the state park offers swimming in the Verde River, trout fishing in a stocked lagoon, picnic tables and barbecues. Hiking trails lure visitors along the river's riparian shoreline (which may be redundant).

Return to Main Street and continue into original Cottonwood. Its small collection of false front and brick front stores contains several curio and antique shops. Some of the old buildings are brightly painted, and garlands of peppers dangle from sidewalk overhangs, giving the place a cheerful Mexican bordertown look.

As you press northwest from Cottonwood, note the huge brushy hill filling the horizon. That's Mingus Mountain, with the bawdy old mining town of Jerome clearly visible on its steep slopes. A fortune in copper was discovered there in the 1880s and mining thrived for than sixty years. You'll visit that town shortly, along with its satellite community of Clarkdale. First, however, turn right at a sign indicating the Verde Valley's other major Indian ruin:

☺ *Tuzigoot National Monument* ● *P.O. Box 68, Clarkdale, AZ 86324; (520) 634-5564. Daily to 5 (until 7 p.m. in summer); $2 per person.* ☐ These extensive ruins, once housing about 250 Sinaguas, crown a low ridge. "Tuzigoot" is an Apache word meaning "Crooked Water," referring to the Verde River that meanders nearby. Built in the latter stages of Sinagua society, Tuzigoot may have hosted families driven from other areas by a drought in the 13th century. Ultimately, it, too, was abandoned—perhaps due to the same persistent famine. Archaeologists excavating the ruin in the 1930s found 450 burial sites. From this they drew some interesting conclusions about a typical Sinagua's life on earth. Life expectancy was in the mid-forties and two-thirds of Tuzigoot's residents never saw their 21st birthday. A strapping male was about five feet, six inches tall.

The complex was restored as a Depression-era WPA project and the visitor center, also a WPA undertaking, is nearly as interesting as the ruin. It's fashioned of river stone with a pole and twig ceiling similar to the original pueblos. Exhibits provide a quick study of the Sinagua lifestyle—tool-making, pottery-shaping, weaving and such. Should you wonder, those odd patterns that look like dead rice paddies fanning out from Tuzigoot are tailing dumps from the Jerome mines.

Back on the highway, you'll shortly enter **Clarkdale,** an early 20th century town with brickfront stores and a city park boasting an old fashioned gazebo. The community was born in 1912 because Jerome copper mining tycoon William Andrews Clark needed a flat place to build a large smelter. Clarkdale got the smelter and nearby Tuzigoot got the slurry from its operation. When the smelter shut down in 1950, most of Clarkdale shut down as well. Dozing contentedly today, it isn't a tourist town, although it has one tourist lure—a train ride along the Verde River:

☺ *Verde Canyon Railroad* ● *300 N. Broadway, Clarkdale. Mailing address: Railroad Inn, 2545 W. Highway 89A, Sedona, AZ 86336; (800) 858-RAIL, (800) 293-7245 or (520) 639-0010. Departures daily at 11 a.m.; adults $34.95, seniors $30.95, first class $52.95; kids under 12, $19.95. Room, ride and meal packages available with the Railroad Inn.* ☐ An old freight locomotive pulls several 1940s Pullman cars, a fancy first class coach and open-air gondolas on a 20-mile, four- hour trek along the Verde River to the ghost town of Perkinsville. Along the way, it passes through a tunnel, skirts a few redrock cliffs and flushes an occasional deer and blue heron. The train originally hauled cargo and passengers between Jerome and Prescott. In addition to daily trips, it makes several moonlight runs during the summer.

To catch the train (reservations should be made in advance), fork to the right at the "train depot" sign as you enter Clarkdale. If you haven't booked the train, you may like to check out some of the old rolling stock parked there. Otherwise, veer to the left onto Main Street for the small downtown area. It's little more than a collection of old brick buildings and a few tree-shaded homes. At a stop sign just beyond the business district, turn left, drive a long block and turn right onto Highway 89A to start uphill toward Jerome. (There were no directional signs when we passed through, but we guessed right and didn't get lost.)

VERDE VALLEY ACTIVITIES

Chuck wagon supper ● Blazin' M Ranch, Cottonwood; (800) WEST-243 or (520) 634-0334. Cowboy suppers, plus live music, petting arena and old west town with specialty shops and shooting gallery.

Float trips ● Worldwide Explorations, P.O. Box 686, Flagstaff, AZ 86022-0686; (520) 774-6462 or (800) 2-PADDLE. The outfit takes visitors on half-day float trips through the riparian environment of the Verde River in inflatable kayaks, departing from Cliff Castle Lodge.

Golf • Beaver Creek Golf Resort, Lake Montezuma; (520) 567-4487. Resort with restaurant and 18-hole golf course near Montezuma's Well; take exit 293 from I-17 and drive three miles southeast.

Tours • Montezuma Outback Tours, P.O. Box 2074, Camp Verde, AZ 86322; (520) 567-9519. This firm takes visitors in air- conditioned jeeps to caves once occupied by man in the remote desert, and to the high country of the Mogollon Rim. Other offerings include hikes to Indian petroglyphs and Camp Verde area historical tours.

Trail rides • Assorted rides are available from Blazing Trails Stable at Cliff Castle Lodge, (520) 567-6611. Mailing address: P.O. Box 973, Sedona, AZ 86336. Among offerings are one to three hour rides, breakfast and steak dinner rides, all day rides with lunch and extended pack trips.

COTTONWOOD-CLARKDALE ANNUAL EVENTS

For details on these and other events, contact the Cottonwood-Verde Valley Chamber of Commere at (520) 864-7593.

Verde Valley Gem & Mineral Show in March.

Verde Valley Fair, last weekend in April.

Arizona Garlic Festival, mid-June at the fairgrounds.

Verde River Days, environmentally conscious festival the last Saturday in September.

WHERE TO DINE

Michael D's Restaurant • ☆ $

❑ *891 S. Main St. (Vlotti Village), Cottonwood; (520) 634-0043. Breakfast and lunch daily.* ❑ Small Southwest style diner featuring all-day breakfasts including an assortment of Belgian waffles, plus luncheon soups, salads and sandwiches.

☺ Parlor Company • ☆☆ $

❑ *202 N. Main Street, Cottonwood; (520) 634-7835. Lunch Tuesday-Saturday 11 to 2, dinner Tuesday-Saturday 4:30 to 8, open Sunday 11 to 8.* ❑ This nice little country style café and gift shop is housed in a 1913 school house, with homestyle fare backed up with fresh baked breads. Dinner entrées include soup, salad and mashed potatoes. For lunch try the chicken pita or the roast beef sandwich with chilies, onions and tomato.

Rosalie's Bluewater Inn • ☆☆ $$

❑ *12th and Main, Cottonwood; (520) 634-8702. American; full bar service. Tuesday-Sunday 7 a.m. to 8:45 p.m. No credit cards.* ❑ Cozy little inn between new and old town Cottonwood serving durable American fare such as liver and onions, prime rib, fried chicken, steaks and assorted seafoods.

WHERE TO RECLINE

Prices reflect high season rates and may be lower at other times. Most were provided by the management and are subject to change; use them only as a guide.

Best Western Cottonwood Inn • ☆☆☆ $$ ∅

❑ *993 S. Main St., Cottonwood, AZ 86326; (520) 634-5575 or (800) 528-1234. Couples $44 to $53, singles $36 to $49, suites $64 to $79. Major credit cards.* ❑ A 77-unit motel with TV and room phones; some suites with refrigerators and private patios; pool, spa, coin laundry. **Restaurant** serves 7 a.m. to 9 p.m.; dinners $7 to $14; full bar service.

The View Motel ● ☆ $$

☐ *818 S. Main St., Cottonwood, AZ 86326; (520) 634-7851. Couples $36 to $48, singles $34 to $42. MC/VISA.* ☐ A 34-unit motel with TV; some kitchenettes; pool and spa; hillside location with Verde Valley views.

Willow Tree Inn ● ☆ $$ ∅

☐ *1089 Highway 279 (across from Walmart shopping center), Cottonwood, AZ 86326; (520) 634-3678. Couples $38 to $58, singles $36 to $48. Major credit cards.* ☐ A 30-unit motel with TV and hones; some kitchens.

WHERE TO CAMP

Camelot RV Center ● 651 N. Main St. (two miles south of Highway 89A-260 junction), Cottonwood, AZ 86326; (520) 634-3011. RV sites; full hookups $15. MC/VISA. ☐ An adult RV park with showers and coin laundry.

Dead Horse Ranch State Park ● P.O. Box 144, Cottonwood, AZ 86326; (520) 634-5283. RV and tent sites; hookups $15, no hookups $10, day use $3 per vehicle. ☐ Some pull- throughs and shaded sites; picnic tables and barbecue grills, flush potties and showers. Picnicking, river access and hiking.

Rio Verde RV Park ● 3420 Highway 89A, Cottonwood, AZ 86326; (520) 634-5990. RVs and tents; full hookups $18. Reservations accepted. ☐ On the Verde River, some shaded sites; showers, coin laundry, disposal station.

Jerome

Elevation: 5,246 feet   **Population: 500**

Scruffy can be beautiful if you're a member of the Jerome Historical Society, trying to convince tourists to follow a twisting highway up the side of a dry, brushy mountain. Historians say Jerome never was pretty. Cantilevered into the slopes of Cleopatra Hill, halfway up Mingus Mountain, it was one of Arizona's largest and raunchiest mining camps. In 1903, a visiting *New York Sun* reporter called it "the wickedest town in America."

Its terraced streets were lined with saloons and bawdy houses. Sloping yards sprouted tailing dumps and mining gear instead of rose bushes. Homes were so steeply terraced, claim old-timers, that you could look down your neighbor's chimney. Slides were common and the town jail skidded several dozen feet downhill, where it remains to this day. Smelters belched pollution. Nearly a mile underground, men stood in boot-deep water, groveling for copper ore in humid 100-degree heat. Dozens died from falls, blasts and other miscalculations.

The bawdy houses and smelters are gone, along with the miners and most of the littered mining machinery. Jerome survives today as an attraction for visitors fascinated by its wicked past. It has lured a rather youthful population of artists and shopkeepers, as well. Instead of old miners dozing in the sun, one is more likely to see pretty young entrepreneurs who would look more at home in a bikini on Malibu Beach. The weathered business district is terraced on three levels as the highway switchbacks through town. Galleries, curio shops and antique shops occupy many of its old buildings. Red and green scars are still evident in the hillsides, where miners dug for gold, silver and copper.

The first claim was filed on Mingus Mountain in 1876. Prospectors found a little gold and silver and a lot of copper. In 1883 the United Verde Copper Company built a smelter and the boom began; at its peak, Jerome bustled with 15,000 citizens. In less than 80 years, a billion dollars worth of copper, gold, silver, lead and zinc was rooted from 80 miles of tunnels beneath the town. Alternately leveled by fire and rebuilt, tough old Jerome thrived until 1953, when the last copper mine was shut down. Some folks decided they were history, so they formed the Jerome Historical Society. They hoped visitors and new residents might be attracted by the town's naughty past. Population dwindled to 150, then slowly climbed to its present 500 or so.

Touring Jerome is simple, since there isn't much left to the town. As you climb the hill, you'll see the **Jerome Art Center** on the left, housed in the large red brick former Jerome school complex. Various artists create and sell their wares here, and their shops keep various hours. Just beyond is the turn-off to **Jerome State Historic Park,** preserving the palatial home of copper tycoon James S. Douglas. Beyond that, you'll hit the business district, terraced into the town's switchback streets. Find a place to park and start walking—which in Jerome entails some modest hiking. The **Jerome Historical Society Mine Museum** is on the upper level of Main, and the wonderfully funky **Gold King Mine** is farther up, at the end of a one-mile dirt road. That will require retrieving your vehicle.

RV ADVISORY ● Despite Jerome's tilted condition, RV parking is abundant and the switchback climb to get there is no problem for any size rig.

ATTRACTIONS

☺ *Jerome State Historic Park* ● *P.O. Box D, Jerome AZ 86331; (520) 634-5381.* ☐ *Daily 8 to 5; adults $2, kids $1.* ☐ The park embraces the estate of "Rawhide Jimmy" Douglas, owner of the Little Daisy Mine. It became an historic park in 1965, after it was donated to the state by his sons.

Occupying a ridge with views of Jerome above and the Verde Valley below, the large, square shouldered mansion is now a museum to the town's yesterdays. Some of the oversized rooms contain period furniture; others display mining memorabilia and mineral exhibits. One of the more interesting displays is a three-dimensional model of Jerome with its complex webwork of mine shafts. A cleverly-done video recounts the history of the rowdy mining camp through the eyes of a "ghost." He recalls that an 1880 fire burned 24 saloons and 14 Chinese restaurants.

Jerome Historical Society Mine Museum and Gift Shop ● *200 Main Street, Jerome, AZ 86331; (520) 634-5477. Daily 9 to 5 (museum closes at 4:30); fifty cents. The gift shop offers a good selection of crafts and curios, particularly copperware; it accepts MC/VISA.* ☐ Although not professionally done, the museum is nicely arrayed, with simple exhibits of the history of Jerome and its copper boom days. You'll learn that William A. Clark made $60 million from his United Verde Copper Company, and that Rawhide Jimmy did even better. After investing nearly half a million in exploration, he hit a 45 percent copper pocket and eventually pocketed $125 million.

☺ *Gold King Mine Museum* ● *P.O. Box 125, Jerome, AZ 86331. Adults $3, seniors $2.50, kids $2. Daily 9 to 5:30. Gift shop can be visited without paying the museum admission.* ☐ Located among the tailing dumps of the old Hayes mining camp a mile east of Jerome, the Gold King is a cluttered scatter of early-day memories. "Where the pavement ends, the Old West begins," reads a sign at the entrance.

This place walks a fine line between museum and junkyard, and the owners make it interesting. They'll fire up a 1914 sawmill powered by a burping, coughing kerosene engine, or other ancient contraptions. A blacksmith hammers out souvenirs; peacocks and goats wander about a petting zoo. Outdoor exhibits range from stamp mills to cast-off toilet seats. Inside the gift shop, you can buy souvenirs and rural scenes painted on saws and hinges.

ANNUAL EVENTS

For details on these and other events, contact chamber at 634-9090.
Liars' Festival and chili cookoff, early April.
Historic home tours, the third full weekend of May.
Jerome Music Festival, third Saturday of September.

WHERE TO DINE

English Kitchen ● ☆ $

◻ *119 Jerome Ave.; (520) (520) 634-3123. American; no alcohol. Daily 8 a.m. to 3:30 p.m.* ◻ Claiming to be Arizona's oldest restaurant, this small café dates back to 1899, It serves hefty breakfasts, plus assorted salads, burgers (including a rather good veggie burger) and other sandwiches for lunch. Patio dining with valley views.

Flatiron Café ● ☆ $

◻ *Main and Hull; (520) 634-2733. American; breakfast and lunch only.* ◻ This tiny wedge of a place is handy for a quick bite, and it has views of sorts. The décor is funky old Jerome and the menu includes specialty coffees, scrambled eggs, bagels and other light fare.

☺ House of Joy ● ☆☆☆☆ $$$

◻ *Hull Avenue (just off the lower tier of Main Street); (520) 643-5339. American-continental; wine and beer. Saturday and Sunday only, 3 to 9 p.m.; reservations required, sometimes weeks in advance. No credit cards.* ◻ Housed in an old red brick bordello, it's one of central Arizona's in-vogue restaurants with a stylish old dining room. The frequently changing menu offers an interesting mix of seafood, veal, lamb and fowl dishes, innovatively prepared and seasoned. *Condé Nast* readers voted the House of Joy one of America's 100 best restaurants in 1994 and yes, it once was a bordello.

☺ Jerome Grill ● ☆☆☆ $$$

◻ *315 Main Street; (520) 634-5095. American-Southwest; full bar service. Daily 7 a.m. to 9 p.m. Major credit cards.* ◻ Sharing the old Clinksdale building with the recently refurbished Inn at Jerome (see below), it's an attractive place with oak furniture, ceiling fans, wainscotting and mining implements. Entrées include filet mignon, Blue Mesa trout, Mingus Mountain meatloaf and Southwest specialties.

WHERE TO RECLINE

☺ The Inn at Jerome ● ☆☆☆ $$$$ ∅

◻ *P.O. Box 901 (309 Main St.), Jerome, AZ 86331; (800) 634-5094 or (520) 634-5095. Couples or singles $55 to $75. Major credit cards.* ◻ Opulent Victorian style inn recently installed in the 1899 Clinksdale building, originally used for a hardware store and offices. The inn features a cozy fireplace parlor and individually decorated rooms with TV and ceiling fans. Furnishings range from Victorian to Art Deco. **Jerome Grill** listed above.

WHERE TO CAMP

Mingus Mountain and **Potato Patch campgrounds** ● *Two Prescott National Forest campgrounds, six miles southwest of Jerome on Highway 89A; (520) 567-4121. No fee; no credit cards or reservations.* ◻ Pit toilets, water;

hiking trails, picnic tables and barbecues. Groceries available at Potato Patch.

Gold King Mine ● *P.O. Box 125, Jerome, AZ 86331. No hookups, $5. No credit cards or reservations.* ◻ Rudimentary camping on an old mine tailing dump next to the museum.

SIDE TRIP: JEROME TO WILLIAMS

One of our readers accidentally stumbled upon this scenic route and recommended it to us. (Actually, she was going from Williams to Jerome, although the best scenery is probably in the mountains just above Jerome.)

From the Gold King Mine road, continue northward into Prescott National Forest on a dirt and gravel forestry road. It twists and climbs up the flanks of Mingus and surrounding mountains and passes the semi-ghost hamlet of Perkinsville. About 22 miles from Jerome, the route becomes paved Perkinsville Road; it crimps around the flanks of Bill Williams Mountain before entering the back door of Williams. The scenery is spectacular, although the road has some cliff-hanging edges, with no guard rail in areas.

"It reminded me of a Bright Angel Trail for cars!" said reader Kristin Friend, a visitor from Florida.

RV ADVISORY ● Because of its narrow lanes, tight turns and general bumpiness, the Jerome-Williams route isn't recommended for RVs—particularly large rigs or trailers. Also, the route can become impassable for any vehicle in wet weather.

JEROME TO PRESCOTT

Jerome is only halfway up the hill, so you have a long climb ahead before topping a pass over Mingus Mountain and tilting down toward Prescott. The climb, which takes you quickly into the pines of Prescott National Forest, has been labeled Mingus Mountain Scenic Road, and it certainly is that. You'll catch vistas down to the Verde Valley as you climb, although there are no turnouts permitting you to pause and enjoy the view. You will, however, get to a spectacular panorama if you're willing to bump over three miles of dirt forestry road near the top of the pass:

☺ **Mingus Mountain Recreation Area** ● Arrayed over the crests of Mingus Mountain, this area has camping, hiking trails and spectacular views of the Verde Valley, the San Francisco Peaks and the red rock rim of the Colorado Plateau. To reach it, follow a sign to the right about a dozen miles above Jerome, where the highway tops out after the long climb.

After two miles of a steep, bumpy incline, you'll pass through Camp Mingus, a Methodist retreat. The state recreation area is just beyond, with primitive camping, hiking trails and one of Arizona's most impressive picnic viewpoints. From your picnic table, you can see every community in the Verde Valley, those fan-shaped copper tailing dumps near Tuzigoot and even the ancient adobe dwellings. You'll get great radio reception as well, since the mountain's crown is a steel forest of transmitters.

For an even more imposing view, requiring an easy half-mile hike, drive from the picnic area to the campground, fork to the right and pass the radio towers. You'll reach a parking area where hang gliders gather to launch themselves over the valley. With luck, you may see some of them at play. Park and follow a trail to the left into the forest, past the hang glider launching pad. After perhaps a quarter of a mile, take a right fork in the trail where it ducks beneath some oak saplings and you'll shortly be delivered to a rocky outcropping. (If you reach an area where the trail has been filled in with rocks, you missed the right fork; go back a few hundred feet and try again.)

This vista point permits an even wider panorama than the picnic area, as if you're staring through a fisheye lens. Look to your left and you'll see a sloping profile of Jerome far below.

RV ADVISORY ● There are no tight hairpin turns or deep ruts on the road to the recreation area, so most RVs and trailer rigs can make the climb. Drive at a crawl and expect a lot of bumps.

Back on the highway, you'll drop quickly from the heights of Mingus, soon shedding Prescott National forest and its attendant trees. On the floor of a dry, brushy basin, you'll pass the scattered town of **Prescott Valley.** Just beyond, you approach the edges of Prescott, nestled into the foothills of the Bradshaw Mountains. The terrain attains more green as you draw near, for it occupies an appealing transition zone between high prairie and forest.

Prescott

Elevation: 5,346 feet   **Population: 21,500**

Isolated from the rumble of freeways, Prescott is one of the best-balanced and most self-contained towns in the state. Friendly natives may gently correct you when you say "Pres-kott." It's "PRESS-kit," with the last syllable bitten off quickly. Even local radio announcers, alleged guardians of proper pronunciation, say it that way.

Once you've learned the language, townsfolk will boast of PRESS-kit's idyllic location, between the dry high desert and the cool pines of PRESS-kit National Forest. It's cooler in summer than Sedona, they'll tell you, and not nearly so crowded. PRESS-kit has its art galleries, they point out, and an active performing arts center. Two colleges and an aeronautical university provide an academic base. The town has a several museums and the whole of the Bradshaw Mountains for a playground. History? Why, PRESS-kit was where Arizona began! Territorial capital, it was. Hadn't you heard?

When Arizona was sliced free from New Mexico to become its own territory in 1863, the new governor—John N. Goodwin—began casting about for a capital site. The mineral-rich central highland seemed most logical, so a temporary capital was set up at Fort Whipple near Del Rio Springs, in the nearby Chino Valley. Later, a permanent site was selected about 22 miles south on Granite Creek. Well, it was *supposed* to be permanent.

A town was laid out in a neat grid and a sturdy log and whipsaw-board governor's mansion was constructed. The fort was moved here to protect the new capital. But in 1867, before something fancier than an oversized log cabin could be built, the government was shifted to Tucson. Prescott citizens lured it back briefly in 1877 before it settled for good in Phoenix. No matter, the people said. Who wanted all that political ruckus and traffic, anyhow?

They were left with an attractive community in a pretty location at the foot of the Bradshaws. After fighting off Indians late in the 19th century, the town grew up as a mining, lumbering and farming center. A 1900 fire destroyed most of it, but the citizens put it back together again.

Prescott today looks more like a vintage New England village than a Southwestern community. The bold, Doric-columned Yavapai County Courthouse occupies a large town square. Early American homes and occasional Victorians line streets shaded by mature trees. Many business buildings are of sturdy brick. The downtown area appears prosperous despite a commercial exodus to suburban shopping centers. An abundance of motels, restaurants and a few curio shops serve the thousands of tourist drawn to this contented, tree-shaded community.

Don't be fooled by Prescott's Eastern look, however. The town is decidedly Western, with several cowboy shops and galleries. Locals claim that their annual Frontier Days is America's oldest rodeo, dating back to 1888.

Driving Prescott

The first thing you should do as you approach Prescott on Highway 89A is to turn away from it. At the junction of 89A and 89, turn right toward the airport at Love Field. This will take you—within a mile—to Prescott's first attraction, the **Phippen Museum of Western Art.** Now, reverse yourself and follow Highway 89 into town. It becomes Gurley Avenue, the main business street. Turn right onto Arizona Street, just short of an athletic field, and drive a block to the **Smoki Museum,** in an appealing stone structure on

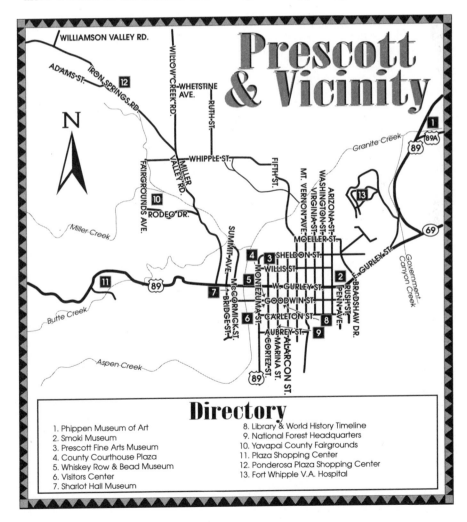

Directory

1. Phippen Museum of Art
2. Smoki Museum
3. Prescott Fine Arts Museum
4. County Courthouse Plaza
5. Whiskey Row & Bead Museum
6. Visitors Center
7. Sharlot Hall Museum
8. Library & World History Timeline
9. National Forest Headquarters
10. Yavapai County Fairgrounds
11. Plaza Shopping Center
12. Ponderosa Plaza Shopping Center
13. Fort Whipple V.A. Hospital

the right. Arizona Street is one way, so drop down a block to return to Gurley and continue toward the downtown area. The promontory you see ahead is Thumb Butte; a park and recreation area is arrayed around its base. (See "Things outdoors" below.)

A few blocks down Gurley, turn right onto Marina Street in front of the brick Hassayampa Hotel and travel a block to the **Prescott Fine Arts Theatre and Gallery,** housed in an old brick church building at Marina and Willis. Turn left onto Willis, drive down two blocks, turn left onto Montezuma Street, cross Gurley and start looking for a place to park. You're among several other attractions. The four-block-square **Yavapai County Courthouse Plaza** is on your left and **Whiskey Row** where randy cowboys once came to play is on the right. The interesting little **Bead Museum** is on Whiskey Row at 140 S. Montezuma.

The **Prescott Chamber of Commerce** occupies an old cut stone building behind Courthouse Plaza at 117 W. Goodwin Street, near Montezuma. Housed in the former jail and firehouse, it's open Monday-Saturday 9 to 5 and Sunday 10 to 5; (520) 445-2000. From the chamber, go west on Goodwin for two blocks, turn right onto south McCormick Street (in front of the Park Plaza shopping center), drive a block back to Gurley, and the extensive **Sharlot Hall** museum complex appears on your left.

RV PARKING ADVISORY ● Despite its wide streets, downtown Prescott is not convenient for RV parking. Most of the parking is angular, so anything over 20 feet juts into traffic lanes. The best RV area is behind the old Prescott railroad depot on Gurley near Montezuma, adjacent to Depot Shopping Center. If you're following our driving route, after you've left the art center, turn right instead of left onto Montezuma, drive a block and turn left. You'll see an open area between the shopping center and the depot; it's an easy walk from here to the rest of the downtown attractions.

ATTRACTIONS
In order of appearance

☺ *Phippen Museum of Western Art* ● *4701 Highway 89 North, Prescott, AZ 86302; (520) 778-1385. Wednesday-Monday 10 to 4, Sunday 1 to 4, closed Tuesday. Adults $3, seniors $2, kids under 12 free. Gift shop with good selection of Native American crafts and Western art; MC/VISA.* ☐ This fine museum, housed in a modern bungalow seven miles north of town, is named in honor of the late George Phippen, a noted local painter and sculptor. He was co-founder and first president of the Cowboy Artists of America. Paintings, prints, bronzes, sculptures and ceramics of past and contemporary Western artists are displayed in this attractive structure, which resembles an upscale ranch house. Exhibits, which change frequently, are drawn from the museum's own extensive collection that includes many of Phippen's works, and art on loan from other museums and collectors. A visitor may find a complete retrospective of Charles Russell or Frederick Remington, or works of contemporary Native American artists.

☺ *Smoki Museum* ● *100 N. Arizona St. (P.O. Box 123), Prescott, AZ 86302; (520) 445-1230. Admission $2. Tuesday-Saturday 10 to 4 and Sunday 1 to 4, closed Wednesday* ☐ Never assume a pronunciation in PRESS-kit. The "Smoke-Eye" Museum offers a significant collection of artifacts of Southwest Indians and other American tribes, including stone tools, baskets and pottery excavated from local sites. The collection is huge—everything from bead-

Mannequin soldiers talk about yesterday at the Sharlot Hall Museum.

work and cradleboards to paintings, photographs and a fine exhibit of plains Indians headdresses. A mock-up kiva occupies the middle of the large exhibit room. The structure is an imposing thing, built of rough fieldstone with a log and limb roof, suggestive of—although considerably larger than—ancient Indian dwellings. A local tribe, in fact, had a hand in its construction. The unusual name comes from a non-Indian group organized in the 1920s to stage mock tribal dances for tourists. The present group, all volunteer, was incorporated in 1991 to operate the museum as a non-profit entity.

Prescott Fine Arts Center ● *208 N. Marina (Willis), Prescott, AZ 86302; (520) 445-3286 or (520) 778-7888. Gallery-gift shop open Wednesday-Saturday 11 to 4 and Sunday noon to 4; MC/VISA.* ❑ When a local congregation outgrew the town's 19th century Sacred Heart Church, a citizen bought it—lock, stock and Bible racks—and donated it to the Prescott Fine Arts Association. The former nave has become the group's 200-seat theater, where it hosts a season of dramas, concerts and children's plays. The rectory on Marina Street is now a gallery, where one can buy the works of local artists.

Yavapai County Courthouse Plaza ● *Gurley and Montezuma.* ❑ After admiring the classic Greco-Roman lines of the courthouse, spend a few moments exploring the Plaza surrounding it. On the north side is a bronze statue of a mounted Bucky O'Neill, former sheriff, mayor and newspaperman. He died in Teddy Roosevelt's Rough Rider charge up Cuba's San Juan Hill. The sculptor was Solon Borglum, the lesser-known but perhaps equally talented brother of Gutzon Borglum, flamboyant creator of the Mount Rushmore Memorial. Extending out from the statue is an intriguing Yavapai "time-line," with the county's history carved and painted chronologically in concrete. Nearby is a gazebo and a bronze sculpture entitled Medivac, which is a memorial to Yavapai County residents who died in America's conflicts, from World War I to Vietnam. Another bronze, of a cowboy and his horse taking a break, occupies the south side, opposite the Chamber of Commerce.

Whiskey Row ● *Montezuma Street between Gurley and Goodwin.* ☐ Once the bawdy district, Whiskey Row burned with most of the rest of downtown Prescott in 1900. This solid rank of storefronts was quickly rebuilt. Of course, the bawdy ladies have faded into the night, although several saloons survive to recall those bad old days. Have a Corona Extra w/lime at Matt's Saloon, Big Mike's Palace Bar, Sundance's Place or the Western Bar. Most try to retain their Old West ambiance, despite the boutiques next door.

The Bead Museum ● *140 S. Montezuma (Gurley), Prescott, AZ 86303; (520) 445-2431. Monday-Saturday 9:30 to 4:30. Free.* ☐ This little museum features beadwork and trade beads from all over the world. It's more interesting than the name may imply. We spent more than an hour there, peering curiously at ancient Indian tribal beads, huge beads from West Africa, a beaded alligator, beaded tapestry that looks as fine as embroidery, and beaded sashes. The place also sells every conceivable kind and shape of bead—strung and unstrung, along with art books and sundry giftwares.

☺ **Sharlot Hall Museum** ● *415 W. Gurley St., Prescott, AZ 86302; (520) 445-3122. Monday-Saturday 10 to 5 and Sunday 1 to 5 from April through October; Tuesday-Saturday 10 to 4 and Sunday 1 to 5 from November through March. Adults $2.* ☐ The Sharlot Hall is actually a three-acre collection of museums, containing several historic buildings, either original or re-constructed. They include the Governor's Mansion built for Prescott's brief tenure as the territorial capital. Plan a couple of hours to stroll about the landscaped grounds and poke into these memories of Prescott's past.

The "mansion" has been faithfully reconstructed from old photos. Inside, you'll see period furnishings ranging from elegant to rudimentary—from a Victorian settee to packing crate tables. The cut log structure seems rather inelegant for a governor's mansion. However, since most of the townspeople were living in ragtag tents or wagon boxes at the time, Mr. Goodwin's lodgings were classy indeed. Another hand-hewn building was occupied by another territorial governor, the much traveled John C. Frémont. The Victorian-era Bashford House contains a stylish little gift shop, and a transportation building displays a stagecoach, prairie schooner and Model-A Ford.

The modern Museum Center offers permanent and changing art and historic exhibits while the Sharlot Hall building features a retrospective of the founder's busy life. Ms. Hall was a remarkable woman who came to Arizona in 1882. Fascinated with the frontier, she began collecting artifacts and writing history as it happened. She served as Arizona's historian for several years, then opened a museum in the old Governor's Mansion in 1928.

"I couldn't be a tame house cat woman," the energetic lady once said.

Lures not on the driving tour

Prescott Animal Park ● *Heritage Drive at Willow Creek Road, Prescott, AZ 86302; (520) 778-4242. Daily 10 to 5 in summer; weekdays 11 to 4 and weekends 10 to 5 the rest of the year. Adults $3, kids 14 and under, $1.50.* ☐ This small animal compound is devoted to protection of endangered species and conservation education. Critters include a goodly collection of reptiles, animals of the Southwest and friendly farm beasts.

World history time-line ● *In front of the city library on Goodwin Street between Alarcon and Marina, two blocks up from Courthouse Plaza.* ⬜ It's similar to the Plaza timeline, but on a global scale. Sidewalk etchings and paintings trace the history of our weary old world from 3300 B.C. Optimistically, it continues to 2050 A.D. It was conceived in 1984 by Francis Widman III, a retired geography teacher. Unfortunately, it was in serious need of restoration when we last visited.

THINGS OUTDOORS

Prescott National Forest offices are at 344 S. Cortez St. downtown, (520) 445-1762, open weekdays 7:30 to 4:30; and 2230 E. Highway 69 (east of town), (520) 445-7253. It's open Monday-Saturday 8 to 4:30. The town sits in the middle of this 1.25 million acre national forest, with campgrounds, fishing lakes and reservoirs, picnic sites, hiking trails and the like. These are some of the more appealing recreation areas and hikes around Prescott:

Granite Dells ● *Watson Lake Park, four miles north on U.S. 89.* ⬜ Day-hikers, rock-climbers and picnickers are attracted to this strange land of huge boulders jutting from a brushy hillside. Now a county park, this was a resort during the middle of this century.

Granite Mountain Wilderness ● *About three miles northwest of Prescott on State Highway 255, then north on Forest Road 375.* ⬜ Several trails branch into the wilderness from Granite Basin Lake Campground. They range in difficulty from moderate to wearying; check with a ranger for suggested routes.

Thumb Butte Park ● *On Thumb Butte Road (an extension of Gurley Street). Hiking trails, picnic areas; free.* ⬜ This basaltic monolith four miles south of town is the area's most prominent landmark. Should you get turned around in Prescott, it will help you get oriented. Several trails from the picnic area wind in and about this rock-ribbed butte. Only skilled rock climbers should attempt to reach the top, however.

ACTIVITIES

Golf ● Antelope Hills Golf Course near the airport, 36 holes, 445-0583; and Prescott Country Club, 14 miles east on Route 69, 18 holes, 772-8984.

Horse racing ● Prescott Downs thoroughbred and quarter horse racing season is held on weekends at the Yavapai County Fairgrounds May through Labor Day; (520) 445-1700.

Horseback riding ● Granite Mountain Stables, Williamson Valley Road; (520) 771-9551.

Performing arts ● A variety of plays, musicales and other cultural functions are held at the Yavapai College Performance Hall. The box office and adjacent art gallery are open Monday-Saturday 10 to 3; (520) 776-2031. Also culturally active is the Prescott Fine Arts Association, which presents a variety of productions and musicales at its theater in a former church at 208 N. Marina at Willis; (520) 445-3286 or (520) 778-7888.

Tours ● Bradshaw Mountain Backcountry Tours features jeep trips into the surrounding wilds and treks to area ghost towns, plus cookouts and guided hikes; (520) 445-3032. Prescott Historical Tours are offered by Melissa Ruffner, (520) 445-4567.

TRANSPORTATION

America West Express flies from Prescott's Love Field to Phoenix; (800) 235-9292 or locally (520) 4445-7701. The **Rural Connection** has daily van service to the Greyhound station at Camp Verde; (520) 445-5470. Shuttle-U has airport transportation and service between Prescott and Phoenix; (520) 772-6114. **Taxis** are provided by Ace City Cab, (520) 445-1616 and Reliable Taxi, (520) 772-6618. For **auto rentals**, call Alamo, (800) 327-9633; Enterprise, (800) 325-8007 or (520) 778-6506; Hertz (800) 654-3131 or (520) 776-1399; and Budget, (800) 527-0700 or (520) 778-3806.

ANNUAL EVENTS

Sharlot Hall Museum sponsors many activities; call (520) 445-3122. For details on other annual events, call the Prescott chamber at (520) 445-2000.

Spring Arts Festival, second weekend of March.

Prescott Valley Days parade and fiddlers' contest, early June.

Territorial Days, second weekend in June.

Yavapai Inter-Tribal Pow Wow, fourth weekend in June.

Frontier Days Rodeo, five days over Fourth of July,

Blue Grass Festival, third weekend of July.

Smoki Ceremonials, mid-August at the Smoki Museum.

Arizona Cowboy Poets Gathering, Sharlot Hall, mid-August.

Faire on the Square, arts and crafts exhibits, Labor Day Weekend.

Yavapai County Fair, fourth weekend of September.

Governor's Cup Antique Car Display and Rally, early October.

WHERE TO SHOP

Western shops and galleries, Indian crafts and curio shops are centered downtown, along east-to-west Gurley Street, then south along Montezuma Street. Continuing west on Gurley, you'll encounter the Plaza West regional shopping area. If you turn north off Gurley onto Grove Avenue (which becomes Miller Valley Road), then fork left onto Iron Springs Road, you'll hit another regional shopping district. One of our recommended restaurants, Dry Gulch Steakhouse is out this way.

WHERE TO DINE

☺ *Casey Jones Sportseatery* ● ☆☆☆ *$$$*

☐ *Montezuma at Sheldon; (520) 771-1995. American-Mexican; full bar service. Daily 11 to midnight. Major credit cards.* ☐ This could be the ultimate sports bar, in a stylish new building tucked into an aspen grove, with indoor and outdoor dining and several dozen satellite-fed TV sets. Autographed jerseys and photos of pro stars are scattered about. The fare bounces from steaks to Cajun chicken to several Mexican dishes.

Clancy's Pub ● ☆☆ *$$*

☐ *124 N. Montezuma St. (Gurley); (520) 445-1904. Mexican-Irish; full bar service. Daily 11 to 10. MC/VISA.* ☐ Try to think of it as an Irish Cantina, with a stucco *Latino* look and a curious menu that ranges from Clancy's chili and American sandwiches to fish and chips. Outdoor tables; live music Friday and Saturday.

Dry Gulch Steakhouse ● ☆ *$$*

☐ *1630 Adams St. (off Iron Springs Road northwest of town); (520) 778-9693. American; full bar service. Tuesday-Friday 11:30 to 9:30, Saturday-Sun-*

day 4 to 9:30. MC/VISA. ◻ A popular local hangout, this Western style restaurant specializes in beef, with chicken-chop-fish items and some spicy *Latino* fare. Margaritas are a house specialty.

El Charro Restaurant ● ☆☆ $

◻ *120 N. Montezuma (Gurley); (520) 445-7130. Mexican; margaritas, wine and beer. Monday-Thursday 11 a.m. to 8 p.m., Friday-Saturday 11 to 8:30, Sunday 11 to 89. MC/VISA.* ◻ This is one of several good, inexpensive Mexican cafés in Prescott. The menu features the typical smashed beans and rice items.

Golden Gate Restaurant ● ☆☆ $

◻ *620 E. Gurley (Washington; (520) 778-0042. Chinese; full bar service. Monday-Saturday 11 to 2 and 5 to 9. MC/VISA.* ◻ This well-appointed establishment runs the Chinese gamut from Cantonese to spicy Hunan and Szechuan. The interior is brightly Asian and rather elegant.

Gurley Street Grill ● ☆☆ $$

◻ *230 W. Gurley St. (Montezuma); (520) 445-3388. Eclectic menu; wine and beer. Daily 11 to 10. MC/VISA.* ◻ Attractive old style café housed in a former brothel, with the requisite high ceilings, fans and warm woods. The busy menu ranges from various pastas and pizzas to spit roasted chicken and Sonoran black bean turkey chili.

Los Amigos Casita ● ☆ $

◻ *150 S. Montezuma (on Whiskey Row); (520) 445-3683. Mexican-American; wine and beer. Lunch and dinner daily. MC/VISA, AMEX.* ◻ Basic Mexican café serving the usual beans and rice creations, plus a few American dishes. Handy lunch stop while exploring Whiskey Row.

Mario's ● ☆☆ $

◻ *1505 E. Gurley (opposite Prescott Resort); (520) 445-1122. Italian-American; full bar service. Monday-Saturday 11 to 11, Sunday noon to 10. Major credit cards.* ◻ This lively place with all-you-can eat specials, pizza and some American dishes. A jumping cocktail lounge features dancing, wide screen TV and a fireplace. Patio dining.

☺ Murphy's ● ☆☆☆☆ $$

◻ *201 N. Cortez St. (Willis), (520) 445-4044. American; full bar service. Sunday-Thursday 11 to 3 and 4:30 to 10, Friday-Saturday 11 to 3 and 4:30 to 11. Reservations advised; MC/VISA, AMEX.* ◻ Housed in a beautifully restored 1890 mercantile building, Murphy's is one of Arizona's more appealing restaurants, and it's relatively inexpensive, with most entrées in the middle teens. Prime rib, mesquite broiled steaks and seafood are served in an elegant setting of antiques, ceiling fans and high-backed booths.

Peacock Room ● ☆☆☆ $$

◻ *112 E. Gurley (in Hassayampa Inn at Marina); (520) 778-9434. American; full bar service. Daily 6:30 to 2 and 5 to 10. Reservations advised; major credit cards.* ◻ Centerpiece of the Hassayampa Inn, the restaurant features steak, fish and chop specialties, served amidst 1920s ambiance.

☺ Prescott Brewing Company ● ☆☆ $$

◻ *130 W. Gurley St. (Montezuma); (520) 771-2795. Light brewpub fare; full bar service. Sunday-Thursday 11 to midnight; Friday-Saturday 11 to 1 a.m. MC/VISA, AMEX.* ◻ Pleasant brewpub with light woods, ceiling fans and the requisite brewing tanks from which emerge Lodgepole Light,

Prescott Pale Ale and Petrified Porter. Family dining area up front; adults bar in the rear. Full dinner entrées, plus typical brewpub snacks.

WHERE TO RECLINE

Prices reflect high season rates and may be lower at other times. Most were provided by the management and are subject to change; use them only as a guide.

Best Western Prescottonian ● ☆☆ $$$ ∅

◻ *1317 E. Gurley (Highway 69 and 89 junction), Prescott, AZ 86301; (520) 445-3096 or (800) 528-1234. Couples $60 to $75, singles $45 to $60, suites $115 to $150. Major credit cards.* ◻ A 212-unit hotel with TV, rental movies, phones, some refrigerators; pool and spa. **Restaurant** serves 5 a.m. to 10 p.m.; dinners $5 to $12; full bar service.

Comfort Inn ● ☆☆ $$$ ∅

◻ *1290 White Spar Rd., Prescott, AZ 86301; (520) 778-5770. Couples $57 to $68, singles $48 to $68, kitchenettes and family units $70 to $77; rates include continental breakfast. Major credit cards.* ◻ A 61-unit motel with TV and phones, some refrigerators; spa.

Days Inn ● ☆☆ $$$ ∅

◻ *7875 E. Highway 69, Prescott, AZ 86301; (800) 329-7466 or (520) 772-8600. Couples $65 to $120, singles $57 to $95, suites and family units $99 to $175; rates include continental breakfast. Major credit cards.* ◻ A 59-unit motel with TV movies and phones, some microwaves and refrigerators; pool and spa.

Hassayampa Inn ● ☆☆☆ $$$$$ ∅

◻ *122 E. Gurley St. (Marina), Prescott, AZ 86301; (800) 322-1927 or (520) 778-9434. Couples and singles $99 to $119, suites $150 to $175. Major credit cards.* ◻ Attractive luxury lodging in downtown Prescott; 67 rooms with TV movies, phones and turn-of-the-century décor; free coffee and snacks in the lobby. **Peacock Restaurant** and lounge listed above.

Hotel St. Michael ● ☆☆ $$

◻ *205 W. Gurley St. (Montezuma), Prescott, AZ 86301; (800) 678-3757 or (520) 776-1999. Couples and singles $36 to $52, family units $52 to $72. MC/VISA.* ◻ Restored 1900 hotel with cable TV and room phones. On Whiskey Row in the heart of downtown, with specialty shops and cappuccino café on its ground floor.

Hotel Vendome ● ☆☆☆ $$$

◻ *230 S. Cortez St. (Carleton), Prescott, AZ 86301; (520) 776-0900. Couples and singles $65 to $130; rates include continental breakfast. Major credit cards.* ◻ A refurbished 1917 lodging house in downtown Prescott. Period furnishings in the lobby and cozy lobby bar; contemporary-early American mix in the rooms. Phones, TV, brass ceiling fans.

Pine View Motel ● ☆☆ $$ ∅

◻ *500 Copper Basin Rd. (U.S. 89, a mile south of the courthouse), Prescott, AZ 86301; (520) 445-4660 or 445-4030. Couples from $40; kitchenettes and family units $65 to $95. MC/VISA, AMEX.* ◻ A nine-unit motel with TV/stereo and room phones; some refrigerators and microwaves.

Prescott Resort & Conference Center ● ☆☆☆ $$$$$ ∅

◻ *1500 Highway 69 (east side, near Highway 89 junction), Prescott, AZ 86301; (800) 967-4637 or (520) 776-1666. Couples and singles $140 to $170. Major credit cards.* ◻ Crowning a hill in east Prescott, this stylish 160-

unit facility offers a pool, spa, sauna, tennis and racquetball courts and massage. Room phones, TV/stereo, movies. **Restaurant** serves 6 a.m. to 10 p.m.; dinners $8 to $25; cocktail lounge, entertainment.

Sierra Inn ● ☆☆ *$$$*

❑ *809 White Spar Road (1.5 miles south on Highway 89), Prescott, AZ 86301; (520) 445-1250. Couples $49, singles $40, kitchenettes and family units $75 to $95. Major credit cards.* ❑ TV movies, room phones, some fireplaces; guest laundry, pool, spa; free coffee, tea and snacks.

Bed & breakfast inns

The Marks House Inn ● ☆☆☆ *$$$$* Ø

❑ *203 E. Union St. (Marina), Prescott, AZ 86303; (520) 778-4632. Couples and singles $75 to $120. Four units with private baths; full breakfast. MC/VISA, DISC.* ❑ Nicely restored 1894 Victorian home listed on the register of historic places. Comfortable rooms with Victorian and early American décor.

☺ *Prescott Country Inn Bed & Breakfast* ● ☆☆☆ *$$$$* Ø

❑ *503 S. Montezuma (downtown, three blocks from plaza), Prescott, AZ 86301; (520) 445-7991. Twelve units, $95 to $129 per couple including full breakfast. MC/VISA, DISC.* ❑ Private cottages with baths, kitchens, TV; some with canopy beds, fireplaces and porches or patio decks. Furnished with antiques, live plants and artwork. Landscaped grounds with outdoor barbecues.

Prescott Pines Bed & Breakfast ● ☆☆ *$$$* Ø

❑ *901 White Spar Rd. (Highway 89 south), Prescott, AZ 86301; (800) 541-5374 or (520) 445-7270. Couples $55 to $95; chalet $179 for up to eight people; optional breakfast $5 per person. MC/VISA.* ❑ Refurbished 1902 country home on elaborately landscaped grounds. Country furnishings; some fireplaces and kitchens; TV and phones in all rooms.

WHERE TO CAMP

Point of Rocks RV Park ● *Route 5, Box 636 (four miles south on U.S. 89), Prescott, AZ 86301; (520) 445-9018. RV sites, full hookups $15.25. Reservations accepted; MC/VISA.* ❑ Pleasant hillside location; some shaded sites. Phone and TV hookups, showers, coin laundry, groceries and Propane.

White Spar Campground ● *U.S. 89 (2.5 miles south) c/o Prescott National Forest; (520) 445-7253. No hookups, $6; half price for Golden Age and Access cardholders. For phone reservations using a MC/VISA or to request a mail-in reservation form, call (800) 280-CAMP.* ❑ Water, pit toilets, no showers; some shaded spots; nature trails.

Willow Lake RV & Camping Park ● *1617 Heritage Park Rd. (five miles northeast), Prescott, AZ 86301-6010; (520) 445-6311. RV and tent sites; $13 to $17. MC/VISA.* ❑ Nicely situated campsites in Granite Dells on Willow Lake; full hookups, some pull-throughs; showers, pool, country store, playground, rec room, coin laundry.

HEADING FOR PHOENIX?

Driving southeast from Prescott on State Highway 69, you'll drop quickly from pines to cactus. At the interchange with I-17 at Cordes Junction, you can follow signs to a most curious development.

☺ *Arcosanti* ● *HC 74, Box 4136, Mayer, AZ 86333; (520) 632-7135. Daily 9 to 5; tours on the hour 10 to 4; four people minimum, $5 per person.*

Arcosanti bakery serves whole-grain pastries and light meals from 10 to 4; brunch at 10:30. Accommodations available for $20 to $25 for couples and $15 to $20 for singles. ☐ Arcosanti is the curious creation of Italian architect and visionary Paolo Soleri. Seeking to solve most of the world's problems in one architectural swoop, he conceived an idyllic, energy-efficient, space-saving community. Here, energized yet mellowed out people would live blissfully together in a smoke-free, drug-free, stress-free environment.

In reality, Arcosanti looks like a space station that crash- landed in the desert. Or perhaps a low-budget EPCOT Center. Its geometric pre-cast concrete shapes have begun to weather since Soleri's disciples started building it in 1970, although new construction and sprucing up continues. The creator himself doesn't live here. He's in Scottsdale, where he operates an arts center and bell-making shop that helps finance the project. The famous free-form Soleri bells—both bronze and clay—are made here, too. They can be purchased in the gift shop. The bellworks is part of a tour, conducted by Soleri's workers.

This is not a sect or cult. Soleri waves no political or religious banner. His message is simple: Mankind must learn to live and work in close harmony, taking up less space and consuming less. He calls his discipline "arcology"—a blend of architecture and ecology. When he really starts dreaming, he envisions a megalopolis triple the height of the Empire State Building, a mile and a half wide, with living and working space for a million people. You will find no vertical Los Angeles at Arcosanti, but a rather squat collection of odd shapes. You can get a better feel for the place from afar. After the tour, follow a bumpy road south to the base of a shallow cliff, across a ravine from the complex, for an overview. You can get a map at the reception center.

From Arcosanti, return to I-17 for a quick run south to Phoenix and the next chapter. There is little of interest along this freeway through the desert, although the New River Mountains add some contour to the east.

HEADING THE OTHER WAY?

If your destination is California—particularly southern—head west from downtown Prescott on Montezuma Street (State Route 89). You'll travel through the foothills of Prescott National Forest's Sierra Prieta, and then begin a long and winding descent into Peeples Valley, a high desert basin. Heading down toward **Wilhoit,** you pass through some handsomely rugged terrain of rounded and fractured metamorphic rock. In the small ranching community of **Yarnell,** turn north and drive half a mile to an impressive Christian shrine built among those rocks:

☺ ***The Shrine of St. Joseph of the Mountains*** ● *Shrine Road (P.O. Box 267), Yarnell, AZ 85362; free.* ☐ A group called the Catholic Action League of Arizona sponsored construction of this rather moving monument to world peace in 1939. A tree-shaded path takes visitors up to a rocky, oak-shaded grotto, where they see a statue of St. Joseph holding the Christ Child. From here, a path leads past a vivid portrayal of the Stations of the Cross, done in *bas relief* plaques set on large wooden crosses. Detailed descriptions of each of the episodes paint a graphic picture of the terrible cruelty of the crucifixion. Even non- Christians may come away from this place deeply moved.

Just below Yarnell, the highway splits and spirals steeply downward, falling carefully off the edge of the Creek Mountains, headed for Arizona's lower deserts. You'll pass through assorted flora as the elevation undulates, from

Joshua trees to saguaro to brushy Mojave Desert creosote bush. At tiny **Congress,** shift to Highway 71, which crosses U.S. 93 and then dissolves into U.S. 60 just east of the ranching town of **Aguila.** You're now traveling through a wide basin between the rocky and dry Harcuvar and Harquahala Mountains. A succession of nondescript towns come and go, offering little more than service stations and mini-marts.

Salome is no different than the rest, other than the fact that the lady of seven veils supposedly danced here, and ranchers named the town in her honor. It gained further note some years ago by the tall tales of one Dick Wick Hall, who operated the Laughing Gas service station. He'd regale his visitors with funny stories of this hot, dusty desert, and some were picked up by the press. This place is so dry, he said, that he had a seven-year- old frog who had never learned to swim. There's a small monument to Hall on the north side of the highway at the western end of town.

Dry humor also flourishes in the hamlet of **Hope** a few miles southwest of Salome. After you've passed through town—an act that requires about fifteen seconds—a sign reads: *You're now beyond hope.*

You're nearly beyond Arizona as well. Highway 60 blends into Interstate 10, which carries you quickly through Quartzsite (see Chapter two) and on to California. Ragged peaks of the Dome Rock Mountains dominate the horizon here. They cradle the Colorado River and the final Arizona town of **Ehrenberg.**

TRIP PLANNER

WHEN TO GO ● Fall through spring are the Valley of the Sun's idyllic days. Tourism reaches its peak between January and March, so make reservations early if you're going then. It's no secret that the summer sun sizzles, although it's not as hot as the Colorado River corridor. During summer months, Phoenix offers good room bargains and plenty of air conditioning.

WHAT TO SEE ● Of the valley's many museums, our favorites are the new Arizona Mining and Mineral Museum, State Capitol Museum, the Heard, Hall of Flame and the Pueblo Grand in Phoenix; the Fleischer Museum in Scottsdale; the new Arizona Historical Society Museum in Tempe; and the Mesa Southwest Museum and Champlin Fighter Museum in Mesa. Other worthy Valley of the Sun lures are the Desert Botanical Garden, Heritage Square and Phoenix Zoo in Phoenix; Taliesin West and Rawhide frontier town in Scottsdale; Out of Africa in Fountain Hills and the ASU campus in Tempe.

WHAT TO DO ● Stroll among the downtown highrises and admire the view from the 23rd floor of the Compass Room; explore the rocky ramparts of Papago Park; hike to the top of Squaw Peak for aerial views of the valley; shop among the wind bells at Cosanti in Scottsdale; sink your teeth into cowboy steak and enjoy Western entertainment at Rawhide, Pinnacle Peak Patio or Reata Pass steak house; browse the shops of old town Scottsdale; catch a Cactus League baseball game.

☺ *Indicates an attraction, restaurant or lodging with special appeal.*

USEFUL CONTACTS

Phoenix & Valley of the Sun Convention and Visitors Bureau, 400 E. Van Buren St., Suite 600, Phoenix, AZ 85004-2290; (602) 254-6500.

Visitor Information Hotline (24 hours): (602) 252-5588.

Visitor Centers are located at the main office in the Arizona Center (400 E. Van Buren) and at the northwest corner of the Hyatt Regency hotel block, Adams and Second streets downtown.

Phoenix Transit System: (602) 253-5000.

Local art events (recording): (602) 257-1222.

Fountain Hills Chamber of Commerce, P.O. Box 17598, Fountain Hills, AZ 85269; (602) 837-1654.

Greater Paradise Valley Chamber of Commerce, 16042 N. 32nd St., C-2, Phoenix, AZ 85032; (602) 482-3344.

Mesa Convention and Visitors Bureau, 120 N. Center St., Mesa, AZ 85201; (602) 969-1307.

Scottsdale Chamber of Commerce, 7343 Scottsdale Mall, Scottsdale, AZ 85251-4498; (602) 945-8481.

Tempe Chamber of Commerce, 60 E. Fifth St., Tempe 85281; 894-8158.

Tonto National Forest, 2324 E. McDowell Rd., Phoenix 85010; 225-5200.

PHOENIX RADIO STATIONS

KEZE-FM, 99.9—Light rock.
KYOG-FM, 95.5—Easy listening.
KJGZ-FM, 96.9—Rock, top forty.
KJZZ-FM, 99.5—PBS, news, jazz.
KJLT-FM, 98.7—Oldies rock.
KSLX-FM, 100.7—Classic rock.
KNIX-FM, 102.5—Country, news.

KCWT-FM, 103.5—Soft hits, light rock.
KVRY-FM, 104.7—Pops and light rock.
KNIX-FM, 102.5—Country.
KTAR-AM, 620—News and talk.
KFYI-AM, 910—News and talk.
KGME-AM, 1360—All sports.

PHOENIX SKYLINE

Chapter seven

THE COSMOPOLITAN MIDDLE
Phoenix and the Valley of the Sun

MORE THAN SIXTY percent of Arizona's population lives in a mountain-rimmed desert basin called the Valley of the Sun. Phoenix and its neighboring cities form a megalopolis covering more land area than Los Angeles. For purposes of geography, we'll discuss Phoenix and its next-door neighbors of Scottsdale, Tempe and Mesa in this chapter, then catch the more outlying towns in the next.

The Valley of the Sun is a delightfully curious mix of Old West and New Wave. You can pull on your Levi's and eat cowboy steaks or wrap yourself in society's most sophisticated trappings. Some Scottsdale shops rival those of Rodeo Drive in Beverly Hills. Resorts like the Arizona Biltmore, Marriott's Camelback Inn and the Scottsdale Princess have no equals. Without question, this area is the resorting, dining and shopping mecca of Arizona.

Starting life simply as small farming communities, Phoenix, Scottsdale, Tempe and Mesa have merged into a major metropolitan sprawl with attendant congestion and even an occasional tinge of smog. In less than 50 years, the Valley of the Sun has made the transition from cow ponies to helicopter traffic spotters, and Phoenix is now the seventh largest city in the nation.

Incidentally, that "Valley of the Sun" label is the creation of tourism promoters, not map makers. Officially, it's the Salt River Valley, but that sounds a bit astringent for a vacation paradise. And with more than 300 days of sunshine a year, promoters have a right to brag.

181

Phoenix

Elevation: 1,083 feet   **Population: 1,036,000**
Valley of the Sun population: 2,300,000

Even with a few growing pains, Phoenix remains one of the cleanest, safest and most appealing large cities in America. It was rated second in the nation for visitor services, accommodations and dining by the New York-based *Zagat Guide* survey. It has more *Mobil Travel Guide* five-star resorts than any other city in the country. The American Automobile Association also gives the Phoenix-Scottsdale area high marks, awarding its prestigious five-diamond rating to a pair of resorts and four diamonds to a dozen more. Even with all these amenities, it's is one of the least expensive major cities in America. A survey several years ago indicated that it was the third cheapest in the country for lodging and meals. Finally, the Carl Bertrelsmann Foundation rated Phoenix as the "Best-run City in the World" in 1993.

It's also a major league city, home to the National Basketball Association's Phoenix Suns, the National Football League's Arizona Cardinals and the new baseball expansion team, the Arizona Diamondbacks. The Cardinals hosted Superbowl XXX at next door Tempe's Sun Devil Stadium in 1996. The annual Phoenix Open set a 1995 PGA record for attendance when 400,000 spectators came to watch the pros.

In a state rich with Spanish, Mexican and cowboy lore, Phoenix had a rather conventional beginning. Indians farmed the area for several centuries, diverting water from the Salt River. Judging from archaeological sites, their population may have reached 100,000. Then they mysteriously vanished around 1400 A.D., abandoning their irrigation canals. Later Pima Indians noted the ditches and called their builders "Hohokam," which means "gone away" or "used up."

This desert basin dozed in the sun until a fellow with the memorable name of John Smith started a hay camp in 1864. Ex- Confederate soldier Jack Swilling arrived three years later and formed a company of unemployed miners to dig out the abandoned Hohokam canals. The group soon had a fine wheat and barley crop growing. One of the settlers, a sophisticated Englishman named Darrel Duppa, predicted that a great city would rise from the site of the former Indian camp, as the Phoenix bird rises from its own ashes every 500 years.

This Phoenix didn't take that long.

Off like a roadrunner

A town was surveyed in 1870 and a few adobe houses went up. The railroad arrived in 1887, bringing new settlers anxious to get a look at the Wild West. Many stayed, replacing those mud huts with Victorian houses and brick bungalows that gave the place a prosperous New England-in-the-desert look. Just 19 years after its founding, Phoenix snatched the state capitol from Prescott. In 1911, the Roosevelt Dam was completed on the Salt River, encouraging major agricultural expansion. Then Arizona got a share of Colorado River water and the Phoenix bird took off—like the roadrunner with Wile E. Coyote on its tail. It has never looked back. World War II brought the military, looking for year-around weather for flight and combat training. At the war's end, many GIs returned, forming a nucleus for a rapid post-war population explosion.

By every measure, Phoenix is the economic, agricultural, manufacturing and certainly political capital of the state. Its growth has been staggering. From 1980 to 1987, it ranked first in population gain among major U.S. cities, swelling by 30 percent. Growth has slowed a bit in the decade of the 90s, although it certainly hasn't stopped. It surpassed Los Angeles in late 1995, not in population but in total land area. A small annexation boosted the city to 469 square miles, two squares larger than L.A.

Phoenix is the core of a glop of 20 fused-together communities in the Valley of the Sun. These peripheral towns have grown even faster than their leader. During the boom years of the eighties, places like Mesa, Glendale, Tempe and Scottsdale doubled or tripled their populations.

The slowdown of the 1990s has given these communities a chance to catch their municipal breaths. While they're doing that, Phoenix is nearing completion on the largest city improvement project in America's history. In 1988, citizens voted a $1.1 billion bond issue for a total revamping of the downtown area. Before the turn of the century, the town will have a new convention center, art center, professional baseball stadium, history museum, science and technology museum, theater for the performing arts, aquatic center and several new public parks. Many of these already have been completed. The focal point is the new Phoenix Civic Plaza, a huge convention center rimmed by parklands and patios. It covers about eight city blocks between Third and Fifth Streets and Monroe and Jefferson.

Meanwhile, out at Sky Harbor—a great name for an airport—a new 48-gate terminal has been added. And yes, Sky Harbor International is the fastest growing airport in the country.

GETTING THERE

Interstate 10 approaches Phoenix from the west and merges with north-south I-17 just northeast of the downtown core. It does an abrupt 90-degree turn, heads east toward Tempe, then swings south. The Superstition Freeway, U.S. 60, branches off I-10 in Tempe and goes through Mesa and well beyond. A new north-south freeway (State Route 51) links downtown with the resort areas of Scottsdale and Paradise Valley. Most major airlines serve the Phoenix Sky Harbor Airport, and Amtrak and Greyhound also serve the city; see "Transportation" below.

If you're motel shopping, many are clustered along Van Buren, including some of the less expensive ones. Others hover around I-10 and I-17 off-ramps. Several first class hotels are in downtown Phoenix and most of the luxury resorts are northeast of downtown, tucked into the foothills of rugged desert mountains in and about Scottsdale and Paradise Valley. The area's attractions are divided between Phoenix and Scottsdale. Most of the museums are in Phoenix while the Scottsdale area tilts toward Western lures. Downtown Phoenix has two highrise clusters—the main core northeast of the state capitol and a secondary "mid-town" area to the north along Central Avenue. Redevelopment is focused in the main core, around the attractively landscaped Phoenix Civic Plaza.

Getting about

Phoenix is an easy city to learn. Although its sheer sprawl can be intimidating, most of it is laid out in a precise grid. Most streets are one-way, with east-west ones named for U.S. Presidents; Washington is the axis street. Cen-

Squaw Peak offers a dramatic backdrop to the desert landscaped grounds of the Arizona Biltmore, a noted Phoenix resort.

tral Avenue is the dividing north-south thoroughfare. Numbered avenues parallel it to the west and numbered streets are to the east. Addresses coincide with numbered streets and avenues for the most part. (For instance, the 300 block of west Van Buren starts at Van Buren and Third Avenue.)

What you will see, as you explore downtown Phoenix, is a remarkably clean and spacious city, despite its cluster of highrises. You will see buildings in various levels of construction and parks in various stages of planting. And incredibly, in the heart of the seventh largest city in America, you probably can find a place to park.

RV ADVISORY ● Although passenger vehicles have no parking problems in the downtown area, RVs have been neglected in the parking scheme of things. If you have a tow-along, trailer or fifth wheel, set up at a suburban RV park (there are none downtown; see "Where to camp" below) and drive the smaller vehicle into the city. Another choice is to leave your rig near the state capital complex, where you'll find street parking (see "Driving and walking Phoenix" below) and take DASH (Downtown Area Shuttle) into the city center. It runs every few minutes and costs only thirty cents. If you like to hike, the distance between the capital/museum complex and downtown is fewer than a dozen blocks.

VISITOR SERVICES

The Phoenix-Valley of the Sun Convention and Visitors Bureau is located at One Arizona Center, Suite 600, at the corner of Van Buren and Third Street. Hours are 8 to 5 weekdays; A street level **Visitor Center** is at Adams and Second Street in the southeast corner of the Hyatt Regency block; the entrance is on the street, not inside the hotel. It's open weekdays 8 to 4:30; (602) 254-6500. The *Phoenix Official Visitors Guide* is available free at either location, or by phone.

DRIVING AND WALKING PHOENIX

Since this is an area of substantial sprawl, we've made this driving and walking tour rather complex in order to knit together all of its attractions. It's best to get a city map and trace our route with a marking pencil. Detailed ones are available at a modest price at visitor centers. (Bold faced items marked with a ■ are listed with more detail below, under "Attractions".)

Approaching Phoenix on southbound Interstate 17, take exit 199B at the State capitol/Jefferson street sign and go left over the freeway on Jefferson. You'll see the cluster of state offices on your left after about five blocks. The handsome if rather squat original capitol building with its copper dome is almost hidden behind newer structures. This historic building has been turned into the ■ **State Capitol Museum.**

RV PARKING ADVISORY ● To plant your rig, turn left from Jefferson onto 19th Avenue just short of the capital complex, and then go left again onto Washington Street, where you'll find unmarked street parking.

For conventional vehicles, there's ample visitor parking in a lot on the northeast corner of Jefferson and 19th, with an entrance on Jefferson. From here, walk eastward through the lobby of the tall beige State Capitol Executive Tower and you'll wind up in the original capitol with its museum exhibits. A brochure rack on your left as you enter the capitol foyer is stuffed with leaflets of Phoenix area attractions.

From the capitol, continue east through two-block-long **Capitol Park**, peopled with statues and other exhibits. They include an impressive Vietnam War memorial and a monument to the crew of the ill-fated *U.S.S Arizona* that was sunk during the Pearl Harbor attack. One of the its anchors and the signal mast are displayed, along with an honor roll of the men who died. At the end of the park, where Washington swings north and then west around the capital complex, you'll see the new home of the ■ **Arizona Mining and Mineral Museum** on your left at 1502 West Washington. It's housed in an old Shriner's Temple, easy to spot with its blue Moorish façade.

Return to your car and drive several blocks east on Jefferson, turn left onto Tenth and left again onto Washington to the ■ **Arizona Hall of Fame** Museum, housed in the old Carnegie Public Library on your left. Next, go north three blocks on Tenth to West Van Buren and you may see the ■ **Phoenix Museum of History** (formerly the Arizona Museum) in an adobe structure in University Park. On the other hand, you may not, since it was scheduled at press time to move into the new downtown Heritage and Science Park at Washington and Fifth. Next, drive east on Van Buren toward the highrises of downtown Phoenix. After several blocks, turn left onto Central and follow it north to the new ■ **Phoenix Art Museum** at Central and McDowell. Continue a few more blocks and then turn right onto Monte Vista for the ■ **Heard Museum.**

Now, retrace your route on Central, cross Van Buren, turn left onto Adams and start looking for a place to park. As we mentioned above, the Phoenix-Valley of the Sun **Visitor Center** is at Adams and Second Street, on the southeast corner of the Hyatt Regency block. It's open weekdays 8 to 4:30. Pick up a free copy of the *Phoenix Official Visitors Guide,* which is even more comprehensive than what we're presenting here, although it's rather dry reading. Also pick up a downtown Phoenix walking map because that's what we're about to do.

Downtown walkabout

The central core of Phoenix is compact enough to be seen afoot, and really too small to bother starting and stopping your vehicle. Our starting point is the Hyatt Regency. Begin your walk by stepping inside the lobby and riding an elevator to the 23rd floor Compass Room revolving restaurant. There, over lunch or a drink, you can get your bearings as the city revolves below.

Step outside and walk to the corner of Second and Adams; the **Phoenix Symphony Hall** is on your left across Second, with the **Phoenix Civic Plaza** a block beyond. Cross Adams and you may or may not see the ■ **Arizona Museum of Science and Technology** just to your right. Like the Phoenix Museum of History, it's slated to undergo a name change—-Arizona Science Center—-and move to the Heritage and Science Park. Walk a block down Second to Washington; you'll see the **America West Arena**, home of the Phoenix Suns, a block beyond. Now, turn right onto Washington Street, and walk two blocks past the city bus terminal to **Patriots' Park.** It's an attractive square of red brick, glass bricks, lawns and fountains. The focal point is a modernistic gazebo with a ship's sail roof that shelters an outdoor stage.

Across First Avenue on Washington, you'll see the ornate old sandstone **Maricopa County Courthouse,** which is still in use. Just beyond is **Cesar Chavez Memorial Plaza** with tributes to the United Farmworkers' founder, and beside it, the 1929 **Historic City Hall** with a stately copper door and bas relief eagles over the entry. Some of its offices are still occupied, although most of the town's business has moved to the new city hall at Washington and Third Avenue. Before visiting this structure, look southward through Cesar Chavez Plaza and you'll see a great windowless box of granite, housing the **Central Court Building.** It's windowless because it's also the jail and why should the bad guys have nice views?

Now, walk back through Chavez Plaza and cross Washington Street to the new **Phoenix City Hall**, a curious structure of glass and stainless steel. It's more impressive from within than without, with a lofty barrel-arch glass atrium ceiling. From the here, walk north through a landscaped plaza past the elaborately trimmed Spanish Colonial **Orpheum Theatre,** which is being restored to its 1920s elegance. Note particularly the octagonal tower over the theater's entrance on Adams Street.

Go right on Adams and then left onto first Avenue in front of the 12-story brick faced **First Interstate Bank** building, one of the few old fashioned skyscrapers left in this section of downtown. Continue past the **Federal Building and Courthouse** on your left, and turn right onto Van Buren Street. Ahead on the right is the towering mirror-glass **Bank One Center,** the tallest building in Arizona, with 38 floors. Next, set your sights on the slightly shorter stack of smoked glass that is the **First Interstate** bank tower. It's at Van Buren and Third Street, with the **Arizona Center** shopping complex at its base. The Phoenix & Valley of the Sun Convention and Visitors Bureau is in the tower, providing services similar to those at the visitor center at the Hyatt; open weekdays 8 to 5. If you're foot weary, pause at Hooters in the Arizona Center, noted for its shapely and skimpily clad waitresses and its good selection of cold beers. (See "Where to dine" below.)

From the center, go south down the west side of Third Street, along a park strip beside the **Herberger Theater.** It's lined with modern bronze statues, mostly of nubile ladies. (Some of the waitresses at Hooters could

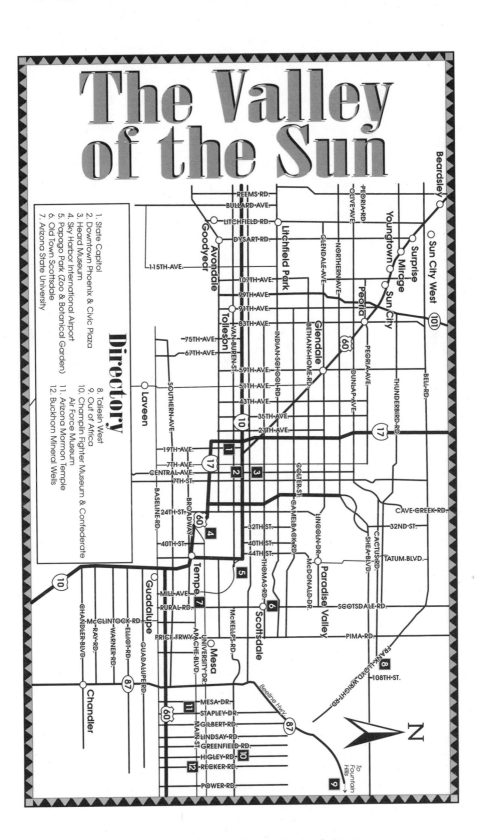

Brass lamps with etched glass adorn an 1889 hand pumper at the Hall of Flame Firefighting Museum.

have been models, but this is only speculation.) Turn left onto Monroe Street, passing in front of the beautiful Spanish style **St. Mary's Basilica,** standing in vivid architectural contrast to the surrounding glass and steel. Continue another block on Monroe to ■ **Heritage Square,** a collection of early day Phoenix homes—mostly Victorian—now housing smart shops and a tearoom or two. Across Monroe, which may be in place by the time you arrive, is the new Heritage and Science Park housing the **Arizona Science Center** and the **Phoenix Museum of History.**

Finally, to return to your starting point, drop down to Washington Street and cut through the landscaped patios of Phoenix Civic Plaza. Washington becomes an underpass between the north and south wings of the plaza, with elevated sidewalks leading up to its buildings and gardens.

East Phoenix driving tour

Retrieve your vehicle and head east on Van Buren for several miles, counting up the cross streets until you hit 44th. Turn right toward the airport, drive a short distance to Washington Street, turn left (east) and then do a quick right into ■ **Pueblo Grande Museum and Cultural Park,** a Hohokam archeological island surrounded by growing Phoenix. Continue east on Washington a mile to 52nd Street, turn left and go another mile to Mc-Dowell Road. Turn left onto McDowell and then make a quick right (just beyond the federal credit union building) to the ■ **Arizona Military Museum.** Head back down 52nd, turn left onto Van Buren and follow it through the edge of **Papago Park.** Instead of going into the park, swerve to the right and then turn right again onto Project Drive for two close-together attractions—the ■ **Hall of Flame** firefighting museum and the **Salt River Project History Center.**

Backtrack briefly and turn right at a traffic signal onto Galvin Parkway, taking you into Papago Park. You'll encounter in short order the ■ **Phoenix Zoo** and **Desert Botanical Garden,** both on your right. In a city surrounded by parklands, Papago Park is the crown jewel, with rocky ramparts, shaded picnic areas, hiking trails and grand gardens of desert flora (both within the botanical garden and without). You'll be struck—as you turn into the park—with the startlingly abrupt transition from suburban sprawl to a desert retreat.

Scottdale, which in recent years has become another suburban sprawl, lies just beyond and we'll visit it later in this chapter.

ATTRACTIONS
In alphabetical order

Arizona Hall of Fame Museum ● *1101 W. Washington St. (near 11th Street, in the former Carnegie Public Library), Phoenix, AZ 85007; (602) 255-4675. Weekdays 8 to 5; free.* ⊓ The museum features photos and memorabilia of Arizona's "famous, not yet famous and perhaps infamous," including Arizona's leading women and the state's Medal of Honor winners. A special exhibit honors the Navajo Code-Talkers, who used their native language as the basis for a communications code in the Pacific during World War II. Since Navajo is little known outside Arizona, the code was never broken and it was used again by Navajo Marines and soldiers during the Korean and Vietnam conflicts. Equally interesting is the building itself. The old cut stone Carnegie Public Library was completed in 1908, one of four such structures in the state. Rehabilitated in 1984 at a cost of $1.3 million (compared with the original cost of $25,000!) and now houses the offices of the Arizona Department of Library, Archives and Public Records, as well as the museum.

Arizona Military Museum ● *5636 E. McDowell Rd.; (602) 267-2676. Tuesday and Thursday 9 to 2, weekends 1 to 4. Free; donations appreciated.* ⊓ This unprofessional but nicely done museum is housed in the Depression era Arizona National Guard arsenal completed by the WPA in 1937. Exhibits trace the history of the military as it relates to Arizona, starting with Francisco Vásquez de Coronado, who came here in 1540 in his quest for the fictitious golden cities of Cibola. Displays of uniformed mannequins and military gear recall the westernmost battle of the Civil War at Arizona's Pacheco Pass in 1862, conflicts with Mexico along the border, battles with Geronimo and Cochise, and Arizona's involvement in the world wars, Korean Conflict and Vietnam War. In interesting juxtaposition are a 1902 horse-drawn artillery piece and a Vietnam era Arizona National Guard Apache attack helicopter.

☺ *Arizona Mining and Mineral Museum* ● *1502 W. Washington St. (Fifteenth Avenue), (602) 255-3791. Weekdays 8 to 5, Saturday 1-5; free.* ⊓ Appropriate to Arizona, this museum focuses on the mining end of minerals, with core samples, tools and mine models, plus an extensive collection of minerals. No ordinary rock house, it features unusual exhibits such as "pseudo fossils," minerals that have fooled even experts into thinking they were of fossil origin. It also offers displays of turquoise, both raw and shaped into the popular Navajo jewelry. Other mineral specimens include radiant examples of copper ore, gemstones and things that glow under ultraviolet light. It's the state's most comprehensive mineral museum, with lapidary exhibits, rock specimens from around the state and around the world and a gift shop selling everything from minerals to mining books to gold pans.

☺ **Arizona Science Center** ● *Washington and Fifth in the new Heritage and Science Park; or at 147 Adams Street near Second; (602) 256-9388. Monday-Saturday 9 to 5, Sunday noon to 5. Adults $4.50, kids 4 to 12 and seniors $3.50.* ☐ By the time you scan this, the former Arizona Science and Technology Museum may be a state-of-the-art facility in new quarters opposite Heritage Square. It was slated to move to its home in the new Heritage and Science Park in early 1997 as part of the $1.1 billion downtown renovation project. Otherwise, you can visit a small yet appealing facility with hands-on exhibits at Third and Adams. Wherever you find it, you'll find a busy museum with interactive displays where kids and adults can learn about energy, physics and the human body. Docents give rock talks and conduct lab experiments. A new computer exhibit, added to the downtown museum in 1995, likely will make the move to the new site.

☺ **Arizona State Capitol Museum** ● *1700 W. Washington (17th Avenue), Phoenix, AZ 85007; (602) 255-4675. Weekdays 8 to 5; tours at 10 a.m. and 2 p.m.; free.* ☐ Arizona outgrew its copper-domed state capitol in 1972 and moved to an adjacent highrise. Sitting in the shadow of its replacement, the old Grecian style tufa and granite relic has become a museum of the state's early government. It was built in 1900 as the territorial capital, 12 years before statehood. Senate and house chambers and several other offices have been returned to their 1912 look, with wooden desks, tulip chandeliers and spittoons. Other rooms serve as museums to the state's political past. Special exhibits honor Arizona's Supreme Court justice, Sandra Day O'Connor, and the Battleship Arizona. In the governor's office, a waxen George W.P. Hunt, Arizona's first head of state, sits behind his cluttered desk.

The old and new capitol are an unlovely combination, with the squared highrise towering over the distinguished copper dome. Frank Lloyd Wright had a better idea. In 1957, he submitted plans and a model for a sweeping, open-air, honeycombed structure called "Oasis." It was a grand design with a skeletal canopy and open breezeways to take advantage of the sunny climate. It's a pity the state didn't take him up on his offer.

☺ **Desert Botanical Garden** ● *1201 N. Galvin Parkway (in Papago Park), Phoenix, AZ 85008; (602) 941-1225. September-May 9 a.m. to sunset, June-August 8 a.m. to sunset; gift shop open 9 to 5. Adults $6, seniors $5, and kids 5 to 12, $1.* ☐ In Arizona's finest botanical garden, you'll see desert plants from around the globe, including more than half of the world's cactus varieties. You'll even learn the difference between a *stenocereus griseus* and a *stenocereus thurberi*. March to May is the desert garden's peak blooming season. A special exhibit shows how the Hohokam and other Indians used plants to survive and thrive in this dry environment. Winding paths take you past a Tohono O'odham saguaro-harvesting ramada, an Apache wickiup and other desert structures. Docents station themselves about this beautifully-maintained garden to discuss things botanical. Guided tours are conducted periodically. You can buy botanical books, souvenirs and your own personal "dish garden" in the gift shop. Serious cactus shoppers can get all sorts of prickly plants in the large sales greenhouse.

☺ **Hall of Flame Museum of Firefighting** ● *6101 E. Van Buren St. (in Papago Park), Phoenix, AZ 85008; (602) 275- 3473. Monday-Saturday 9 to 5 and Sunday noon to 5; guided tours daily at 2. Adults $5, seniors $4 and kids 6-17, $2.* ☐ Every kid of every age whose pulse is quickened by the shriek of a siren and the red flash of a fire engine will love this place. It's the world's

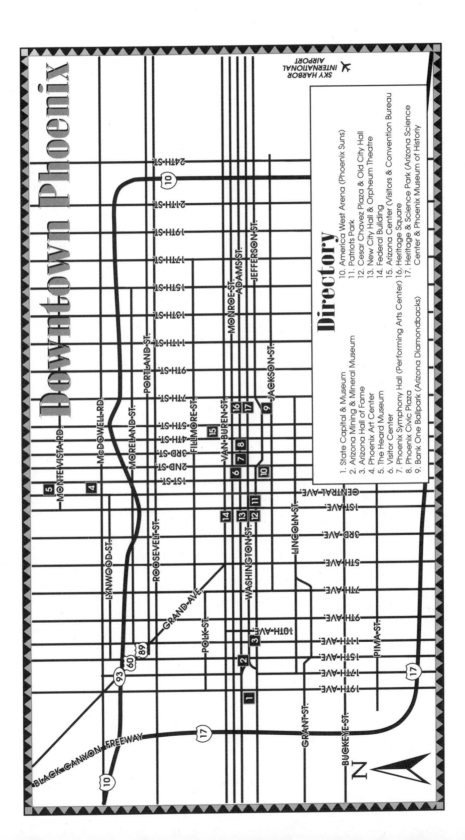

Downtown Phoenix

Directory

1. State Capital & Museum
2. Arizona Mining & Mineral Museum
3. Arizona Hall of Fame
4. Phoenix Art Center
5. The Heard Museum
6. Visitor Center
7. Phoenix Symphony Hall (Performing Arts Center)
8. Phoenix Civic Plaza
9. Bank One Ballpark (Arizona Diamondbacks)
10. America West Arena (Phoenix Suns)
11. Patriots Park
12. Cesar Chavez Plaza & Old City Hall
13. New City Hall & Orpheum Theatre
14. Federal Building
15. Arizona Center (Visitors & Convention Bureau
16. Heritage Square
17. Heritage & Science Park (Arizona Science Center & Phoenix Museum of History)

SKY HARBOR INTERNATIONAL AIRPORT

N

largest museum of firefighting equipment, exhibiting glittering ranks of hand-drawn pumpers, early hook-and-ladder rigs and other smoke-chasing classics.

More than 100 restored fire engines are on display, from a 1725 English hand pumper to 1920s ladder and chemical trucks. Most interesting are the pre-20th century pumpers; some are pieces of art with scroll work, rosettes and dainty brass lanterns with cut glass lenses. The extensive collection also includes badges, helmets and uniforms, plus lithographs, drawings and photos of firemen in action. Exhibits trace the history of "America's most dangerous profession" from Benjamin Franklin's Philadelphia volunteers to modern fire control techniques.

☺ **The Heard Museum** ● *22 E. Monte Vista (Central Avenue), Phoenix, AZ 85004; (602) 252-8840 or 252-8848 (taped information). Monday-Saturday 9:30 to 5 (until 9 Wednesday) and Sunday noon to 5. Adults $5, seniors and college students $4, teenagers $3 and children 4 to 12, $2. Wednesday evenings are free from 5 to 9 p.m.* ☐ Quite simply, the Heard is the finest museum in Arizona and probably the world's greatest monument to Native Americans. Although it dates back to 1929, this treasury of American Indian cultures is a state of the art facility. With more than 30,000 objects to draw from, its staff exercises artistic discipline in keeping displays both simple and topical. Every exhibit is designed to interpret and inform. This is a living museum as well as a repository of the past. Entering the Southwest style courtyard, you're likely to see a Hopi working on a kachina doll or a Navajo weaving on an ancient loom. A herd of happy school children might be pulverizing corn on primitive grinding stones.

Major exhibits provide a simple and enlightening study of Arizona's ancient and modern Indian cultures, with artifacts, graphics and mock-ups. You first encounter an audio-visual show with slides of Arizona's Indian country and its residents. They discuss their heritage and their efforts to embrace a society thrust upon them. Entering a mock-up mud-roofed Navajo hogan, you see a blending of past and present with traditional utensils and blankets—and a Propane tank. Special exhibits focus on native peoples in other parts of the world who have been impacted by conquest, colonization and tourism. An excellent museum shop has a fine assortment of Indian arts and artifacts and one of the state's largest selections of books on Arizona and Native American lore.

☺ **Heritage Square** ● *Sixth Street and Monroe (a block east of Civic Plaza); (602) 262-5071.* ☐ This is a scene from Phoenix yesterday—eight structures dating from the late 19th and early 20th centuries. They're gathered around an attractive patio garden, shaded by a curved-wood lath house. Surprisingly, all but one are in their original locations. These are some of the more interesting buildings and their present functions:

Rosson House, built in 1886 and handsomely restored, is open for guided tours 10 to 3:30 Wednesday through Saturday and noon to 3:30 Sunday. Tour price is $3 for adults and $2 for kids; (602) 262-5029.

The Teeter House, an 1899 Midwestern style bungalow, contains a cute little Victorian tearoom, serving sandwiches and other light fare, beer and wine and tea, of course. Hours are Monday- Saturday 10 to 4 and Sunday noon to 4.

The Silva House is a classic "revival bungalow" built in 1900. The Salt River Project maintains a turn-of-the-century lifestyle museum, focusing on the development of the domestic use of water and electricity. Hours are Tuesday-Saturday 10 to 4 and Sunday noon to 4; (602) 236-5451.

The Stevens-Haustgen House is a 1911 brick bungalow occupied by the Craftsmen's Cooperative Gallery. It sells garments, ceramics, sculptures and costume jewelry crafted by local artists. Hours are Monday-Saturday 10 to 4 and Sunday noon to 4; (602) 253-7770.

The Stevens House, a 1901 bungalow, is home to the Arizona Doll and Toy Museum. Exhibits include American, English and Japanese dolls, advertising symbols such as the Campbell Soup kids and Crackerjack sailor and 25 years of G.I. Joe. It's open Tuesday-Saturday 10 to 4 and Sunday noon to 4; (602) 253-9337.

☺ *Phoenix Art Museum* ● *1625 N. Central Ave. (McDowell Road), Phoenix, AZ 85004; (602) 257-1222. Tuesday- Saturday 10 to 5 (Wednesday to 9), Sunday 1 to 5. Tours Tuesday-Sunday at 1 p.m., plus 6 p.m. Adults $4, seniors $3 and students $1.50.* ☐ The American West, contemporary art and old world classics are featured in Phoenix' large, versatile art museum. A major renovation and expansion program was completed in mid-1996, nearly doubling its exhibit space. Permanent collections include a gallery of Western Art, galleries of early European and American art, an Asian gallery, costume displays and decorative arts. The museum sponsors study programs, art classes, concerts, lectures and tours. Its changing exhibits range from Frank Lloyd Wright drawings to Rodin sculptures to Ansel Adams photos. Founded in the 1950s, it has become the largest art museum in the Southwest, with more than 160,000 square feet of exhibit space. New facilities include a lecture hall, restaurant, an inter-active hands-on children's gallery and two art reference libraries.

☺ *Phoenix Museum of History* ● *105 N. Fifth Street at Washington or at 1002 W. Van Buren at Tenth Avenue; (602) 253-2734. Monday-Saturday 10 to 5 and Sunday noon to 5; modest admission charge.* ☐ Originally called the Arizona Museum, the newly-named Phoenix Museum of History was slated to move into the Heritage and Science Park in the mid-1990s. The gallery focuses on Phoenix area history from the territorial era to the "Romantic Movement" of the 1920s. Exhibits include Hohokam artifacts, battleship Arizona mementos, an egg from a former Phoenix ostrich farm, a rifle collection, modern Kachina dolls, the first Phoenix newspaper press, early Arizona paintings, old maps and minerals. The new structure will have an atrium with printing press and railroading displays and a special gallery featuring rotating exhibits that change every few months.

☺ *Phoenix Zoo* ● *455 N. Galvin Parkway (in Papago Park), Phoenix, AZ 85072; (602) 273-1341. Daily 9 to 5 (7 to 4 in summer). Adults $7, seniors $6 and kids 4 to 12, $3.50; Safari Train trip $1.50.* ☐ This would be a pleasant place to stroll even if it weren't stocked with 1,300 animals. Occupying 125 acres of Papago Park, the zoo encloses a fine slice of desert terrain. It's landscaped with giant eucalyptus trees, pools, trickling streams and shady patios. It reflects the current zoo trend of providing open-air enclosures and focusing on procreation of endangered species. Among recent additions are the Baboon Kingdom and Tropical Flights rainforest.

The zoo is organized into five trail systems that wind through simulated natural habitats. The Arizona Trail features plants and animals of the American Southwest; the Africa Trail presents meerkats, lions, a warthog and other denizens of that continent; the Children's Trail brings kids close to animals and includes a petting zoo; the Tropics Trail provides encounters with rain-forest critters; and the Desert Trail features international desert creatures, from American bighorn sheep to the Nubian ibex.

☺ *Pueblo Grande Museum* ● *4619 E. Washington St. (44th Street), Phoenix, AZ 85034; (602) 945-0901. Monday-Saturday 9 to 4:45, Sunday 1 to 4:45. Adults $2, seniors $1.50 and kids $1.* ☐ Surrounded by the expanding city, this site preserves a large Hohokam settlement described by anthropologists as a "mound platform." There's little left of the village, which can be viewed from an overlook. Ridges and depressions suggest the shapes of an ancient ball court and canal banks. The museum does a fine job of presenting slices of life from the early days. Exhibits include a scale-model Hohokam home and artifacts taken from the site. Excavations, which have been continuing since 1887, indicate that this was a major village served by at least 18 canals. It was occupied from about 700 to 1450 A.D.

Salt River Project History Center ● *1521 Project Dr. (at the "Y" between Washington and Van Buren), Tempe, AZ 85281; (602) 236-2208. Weekdays 9 to 4; free.* ☐ Located in the Salt River administration building, this small museum centers on the reclamation project that provides much of the Valley of the Sun's water. Exhibits, artifacts and videos trace the history of the project from the Hohokam canals through the construction of Roosevelt Dam to modern water delivery methods.

Attractions not on the driving-walking tours

☺ *Deer Valley Rock Art Center* ● *3711 Deer Valley Rd.; mailing address: P.O. Box 41998, Phoenix, AZ 85080; (602) 582-8007. Thursday-Friday 8 to noon, Saturday 8 to 4 and Sunday noon to 5. Adults $3, seniors and teens $2, kids 6 to 12, $1.* ☐ Operated by Arizona State University's Department of Anthropology, this 47-acre desert site preserves more than 1,500 petroglyphs in the Hedgpeth Hills. A quarter-mile wheelchair accessible interpretive trail takes visitors to the site, or one can arrange for a guide tour. Exhibits at the center focus on area plant and animal life as well. Interesting graphics at the site attempt to interpret these ancient rock writings and link Arizona's first dwellers to the present. It's the largest petroglyph collection in the valley.

Duppa-Montgomery Homestead ● *116 W. Sherman (First Street), Phoenix, AZ 85003; (602) 253-5557 or 255-4470. Sundays 2 to 5, November through May; free.* ☐ This weathered adobe may be the oldest home in Phoenix, situated on land homesteaded by city- namer Darrel Duppa. He didn't occupy the structure itself, however; it was built later by the pioneering Montgomery family. It's now surrounded by growing neighborhoods and an industrial area. Inside—when it's open to the public—you'll find period furnishings and artifacts.

Mystery Castle ● *800 E. Mineral Rd. (at the end of Seventh Street, near South Mountain Park), Phoenix, AZ 85040; (602) 268-1581. Open October 1 to July 4, Tuesday-Sunday 11-5. Adults $4, kids 4 to 14, 1.50.* ☐ Mary Lou Gulley, daughter of eccentric builder Boyce Luther Gulley, conducts short tours through this curious conglomeration. It's more of a complicated multi-gabled house than a castle. Her father built it in erratic stages from 1927 until his death in 1945. The structure is an assemblage of native stone and odd bits and pieces that Gulley scavenged through the years. To reach it, drive south on Seventh Street, jogging slightly to the right on Baseline Road, then continuing on Seventh up toward South Mountain.

☺ **Pioneer Arizona Living History Museum** • *c/o Black Canyon Stage, Phoenix, AZ 85027; (602) 993-0212. Wednesday- Friday 9 to 3, weekends 9 to 4, shorter hours during the summer. Adults $5.75; seniors and students 16 and older, $5.25.* ☐ Since 1956, a non-profit group has been assembling an historic Arizona town on a chunk of desert 30 miles north of Phoenix. About 20 buildings—either originals or reconstructions—occupy the site. It's a sampler town of Arizona from its earliest Spanish days to statehood. Although the site seems a bit disconnected and some of the graphics need a good preparator's touch, the exhibits are worth the drive north. Some, such as a turn-of-the century brick bank and a wood frame Victorian, are nicely furnished. The adobe sheriff's office and jail looks right out of *Rio Bravo*. You expect John Wayne to step outside and confront the bad guys. Other worthy structures are a log and mud-chink "northern cabin," an opera house where live melodramas are performed, and the Whiskey-Road-to-Ruin Saloon. Its wooden bar and back bar came around the Horn to San Francisco and somehow found its way to Gila Bend and finally to the pioneer village.

The Whiskey-Road-to-Ruin Saloon serves home style meals and it can be patronized without paying admission to the park.

To reach the complex, drive about 30 miles north of Phoenix on I-17 and take Pioneer Road (exit 225) west. From the Cave Creek-Carefree area, you can take the Carefree Highway west to I-17 and then go north to the Pioneer Road offramp.

Plotkin Judaica Museum • *3310 N. Tenth Ave. (at Osborn Road in Temple Beth Israel), Phoenix, AZ 85013; (602) 264-4428. September through May—Tuesday-Thursday 10 to 3 and Sunday noon to 3; closed in summer; free.* ☐ This small museum displays artifacts and documents from the Holy Land concerning the history of Judaism and Jewish holidays. In addition to its permanent exhibits, it hosts occasional touring shows.

Wildlife World Zoo • *16501 W. Northern Avenue, Lichfield Park, AZ 85340; (602) 935-WILD. Open mid-September to mid-June, daily 9 to 5. Adults $6.75, seniors $5.75 and kids $4.* ☐ Several endangered species are members of this small zoo, including the African oryx, Saharan addax and a monkey that can whip along at more than 30 miles an hour. Its collection of birds—many of them in a walk-in aviary—includes sundry ostriches, rare New Guinea pigeons and Philippine Palawan pheasants. The zoo started as an endangered species breeding farm. To reach it, go north on I-17 about eight miles to Northern Avenue (exit 206) and go west about 18 miles to Litchfield Park. It's just past Luke Air Force Base.

THE OUTDOOR THING: REGIONAL PARKS

Although Phoenix is a major city, the wilds are never far away. The metropolis is surrounded by desert and mountain parks and some are within the city itself. Most are administered by the city or Maricopa County. The 2.9 million acre Tonto National Forest lies just to the northeast. Here, you can hike the trails, camp the campgrounds and swim and boat in the Verde River and Salt River reservoirs.

The **Tonto National Forest** main office is in Phoenix at 2324 E. McDowell Road, open weekdays 7:45 to 4:30; (602) 225-5200 or (602) 225-5296 (recording). There's another between Cave Creek and Carefree at 7171 E. Carefree Rd., Cave Creek. Hours are the same as the main Phoenix office; (602) 488-3441.

Echo Canyon Recreation Area • *East MacDonald Drive at Tatum Boulevard; (602) 256-3220. Open 6 a.m. to sunset.* ☐ This is a hikers' and climbers' park on Camelback Mountain. Steep 200-foot cliffs challenge climbers, and hikers can follow a variety of trails, including a trek to the top of Camelback. At 2,704 feet above sea level, it's the highest point in the Phoenix Mountains.

Encanto Park • *North 15th Avenue and West Encanto Boulevard. Open daily 5:30 a.m. to 12:30 a.m.* ☐ Lagoons, lakes, a swimming pool, two golf courses, tennis courts and picnic areas dot this 222-acre park two miles north of downtown. Water play and other sports equipment can be checked out from the recreation building.

Estrella Mountain Regional Park • *Twenty miles west of Phoenix on State Highway 85, then three miles south of Avondale on Bullard Avenue; (602) 932-3811.* ☐ A golf course adds a bit of civilized green to this 18,600-acre park, although most of it is rugged desert terrain that lures hikers and equestrians. Undeveloped campsites are available. Other facilities include an archery range, golf pro shop and snack bar.

Lake Pleasant Regional Park • *Thirty miles north; take I-17 to State Highway 74 (exit 223), then go west; (602) 566-0405. Admission $4 per car, $2 per motorcycle.* ☐ This is a 14,400-acre desert garden with two lakes and stands of saguaro cactus. Dirty Shirt Campgrounds offers undeveloped sites. The lakes are centers for sailing, bass fishing, wind-surfing and swimming. Rowboats, wind-sails and small sailboats can be rented.

North Mountain Recreation Area • *Off Seventh Street and Peoria Avenue; (602) 276-2221. Open 5:30 a.m. to 12:30 a.m.* ☐ North Mountain park is a true urban wilderness, with few developed facilities other than picnic areas. Trails take hikers to some spectacular city viewpoints.

☺ **Papago Park** • *Between Phoenix and Scottsdale; (602) 256-3220; open 6:30 a.m. to midnight.* ☐ The hilly desert terrain of Papago is host to the Phoenix Zoo, Botanical Garden and Hall of Flame; Phoenix Municipal Stadium is on the edge. (Details in "East Phoenix driving tour" above.) Other facilities include picnic areas, an 18-hole golf course, quiet lagoons, game fields and hiking and biking trails.

Saguaro Lake • *East on Freeway 60, then north on Power Road, which becomes Bush Highway; follow signs to the reservoir; (602) 986-0969.* ☐ The Salt River Project has turned the stream into a chain of lakes; Saguaro is closest to Phoenix—about 25 miles east. It's a popular spot that fills up quickly on summer weekends, so arrive early to claim your picnic or camping site. Call ahead for boat rentals at (602) 986- 0969. The 10-mile-long reservoir has a marina and boat ramp, with boat rentals (fish or ski), a snack bar and boating supplies. Bagley Flat Campgrounds offers primitive sites for no fee; boat camping along the reservoir is permitted.

☺ **South Mountain Park** • *Eight miles south on Central Avenue; (602) 276-2221. Daily 5:30 a.m. to midnight; free.* ☐ Billed as the world's largest city park, this 16,000-acre wilderness contains jagged canyons, pinnacle peaks, extensive cactus gardens and awesome city vistas. You can hike or follow a paved road to the top for impressive Valley of the Sun views from 2,330-foot Dobbins Lookout. Facilities include a children's playground, picnic areas, and 40 miles of hiking trails. Riding stables are outside the entrance.

☺ **Squaw Peak Park** • *West of Paradise Valley, nine miles from downtown Phoenix; take 24th Street to Lincoln Drive, go left, then turn right onto*

Squaw Peak Drive; (602) 276-2221. Daily 5:30 a.m. to 12:30 a.m. ☐ Jutting skyward between the populated suburbs of north Phoenix and Paradise Valley, this park has been left in its natural state, with few developed facilities. A steep trail winds through terraced desert gardens to the 2,068-foot Squaw Peak, one of the area's most noted landmarks. The view from this rocky aerie is spectacular.

White Tank Mountain Regional Park • *Thirteen miles west of Peoria on Olive Avenue; P.O. Box 91, Waddell, AZ 85355; (602) 935-2505. Day use $2; camping $8, with water and showers; no hookups. To reach it, take Grand Avenue (Highway 60) about 15 miles northwest from Phoenix and then make a half left onto Olive Avenue in Peoria.* ☐ This Maricopa County park embraces 26,337 acres of mountain desert wilderness, with elevations ranging from 1,402 to 4,083 feet. It has several miles of trails reaching into desert canyons, including 15 miles for mountain bikes. Some trails lead to back country camp sites (permits required and available at park headquarters.)

ACTIVITIES
Including all of the Valley of the Sun

Air tours • Fixed-wing air tours are provided by Scenic Airlines, 15000 N. Airport Dr., Suite 107, Scottsdale, AZ 85260, (602) 991-8252. Helicopter flights are conducted by Superstition Mountains Helicopters, 4650 N. Mammoth Mine Rd., Goldfield, AZ 85219, (602) 830-9410.

Aquatic parks • Two parks prove that it's fun to get all wet. Big Surf is at 1500 N. Hayden Rd. (McClintock Dr.), Tempe, AZ 85281; (602) 946-SURF. This Polynesian-theme water park brings the ocean to Arizona with a large wave-making machines. It offers swimming, surfing and boogie-boarding. Waterworld U.S.A. is at 4243 W. Pinnacle Peak Rd., Phoenix, AZ 85027; (602) 581-1947. This 20-acre water play park features slides, swimming pools and a wave machine.

Auto race training • The Bob Bondurant School of High Performance Driving teaches people techniques and tactics of auto racing and high performance driving—handy in case you need to elude the bad guys; 20000 S. Maricopa Rd., Chandler, AZ 85226; (800) 842-7223.

Auto tape tours • Trailblazing Tape Tours features self- guiding tours of the Valley of the Sun; packages include a cassette tape and map; 3627 E. Indian School Rd., Suite 108, Phoenix, AZ 85018; (602) 553-0226.

Cowboy entertainment and dining • Several operators bring the Old West back to life with cookouts, cowboy outings and country saloons. Most are in or about Scottsdale, northeast of Phoenix. Here's a sampler: Blackhawk Adventures, 11111 N. Seventh St., Phoenix (993-1356), features cowboy cookouts, Western theme parties, horseback riding and hayrides. Corona Ranch and Rodeo Grounds, 29th Avenue and Baseline Road in Phoenix (253-7297) has Mexican and Western style rodeos, steaks and Mexican food and country and Western dancing. Goldfield Ghost Town, four miles east of Apache Junction on Highway 88 (983-0333), is an old mining camp with museums, gold panning, historic buildings and Western dining. Pinnacle Peak Patio, 10426 E. Jomax Rd., Scottsdale (585-1599), features a cowboy steak house, country music, false-front stores, dramatic valley view. (More details below, under "Where to dine" in Scottsdale.) Rawhide, 23023 Scottsdale Road, Scottsdale (502-5600), is an 1880s reconstructed Western town with theme shops, cowboy steak house, shootouts and Western entertainment (reviewed below, under Scottsdale). Reata Pass Steakhouse, 27500 N. Alma School Parkway in the mountains above Scottsdale (585-7277), is a cowboy café and bar stop, with gunfights, country music and dancing. (Listed below, under "Where to dine" in Scottsdale.)

Red River Opry presents Western musical and comedy productions at its theater at 730 N. Mill Ave., Tempe (829-OPRY). Rockin' R Ranch, 6136 E. Baseline Rd., Mesa, AZ 85206 (832-1539) is a Wild West town with chuck wagon suppers, gunfights, wagon rides, Indian dancers and gunfighters. (See "Where to dine" under Mesa/Tempe.) Rustler's Rooste at the Pointe Hilton Resort at 7777 S. Pointe Parkway in Phoenix (431-6474), features "beef and brew with a view" from atop South Mountain, plus country music and dancing. Tortilla Flat on Highway 88 east of Apache Junction (984-1776) is a former construction camp shaped into a Western town with theme shopping, restaurant and saloon. Waterin' Hole Chuckwagon 'N Saloon at Pointe Hilton Resort at Tapatio Cliffs, 11111 N. Seventh (944-4451) features Western fare, poolside dining and country music.

Desert jeep excursions • Several companies have tours into the surrounding Sonoran desert, Superstition Mountains, along the Apache Trail and to nearby ghost towns and gold panning areas. Among the operators are Absolutely Arizona Adventure Tours, P.O. Box 4961, Scottsdale, AZ 85261-4961, (602) 905-1055; Ancient Trails Photo Tours, 5265 E. Karen Dr., Scottsdale, AZ 85254, (602) 953-1296; Apache Trail Tours, Goldfield Ghost Town, Apache Junction, AZ 85219, (602) 982-7661; Arizona Awareness Tours, 835 E. Brown St., Phoenix, AZ 85020, (602) 947-7852; Arizona Bound Tours, 5638 E. Thomas Rd., Phoenix, AZ 85018, (602) 994-0580; Arizona Desert Mountain Jeep Tours, 10110 E. Jenan Dr., Scottsdale, AZ 85260, (602) 860-1777; Arizona Unique Buggy Adventures, 13221 N. 19th Place, Phoenix, AZ 85022, (602) 971-2469; Old West Trails Jeep Tours, P.O. Box 4486, Cave Creek, AZ 85331, (602) 488-9541; and Wild West Jeep Tours, 7127 E, Becker Lane, Room 74, Scottsdale, AZ 85254, (602) 941-8355.

Golf • More than 30 courses add cool patches of green to the Valley of the Sun, most of them at various resorts. Many are listed in the *Golf Arizona* brochure, available at Phoenix-Valley of the Sun visitor centers and other tourist information centers in the state, or contact Golf-Market, 15704 Cholla, Fountain Hills, AZ 85268; (602) 837-2184. Resort Tee Time has a toll free number to confirm tee times at several courses in the Valley of the Sun, as well as those in other areas of the Southwest; (800) 468-7918.

Horseback riding • All Western Stables, 10220 S. Central Ave., Phoenix, AZ 85040, (602) 276-5862; Blackhawk Adventures, 11111 N. Seventh St., Phoenix, AZ 85020, (602) 993-1356; Cowboy Adventures, P.O. Box 17052, Fountain Hills, AZ 85269, (602) 837-8585; Outdoor Adventures Unlimited, P.O. Box 33582, Phoenix, AZ 85067-3582, (800) 678-3929 or (602) 253-2789; Ponderosa Stables, 10215 S. Central Ave., Phoenix, AZ 85050, (602) 268-1261 or (602) 276-8131; and Rio Verde Riding Stable, 152nd Street and Dynamite Road, Scottsdale, AZ 85225, (602) 471-7281.

Hot Air Ballooning • These firms market balloon flights over the Valley of the Sun: A Balloon Experience, 7119 E. Shea Blvd., Room 363, Scottsdale, AZ 85252; (800) 866-3866 or (602) 820-3866; Cloud Chasers Balloon Co., 1716 W. Butler Ave., Phoenix, AZ 85021, (602) 944-4080; Get Carried Away, 7254 E. Camino del Monte, Scottsdale, AZ 85225, (602) 502-1757; Hot Air Balloon Company, (800) 843-59876 or (602) 461-8689; Hot Air Expeditions, 15115 N. Airport Dr., Scottsdale, AZ 85260, (800) 831-7610 or (602) 788-5555; Sky Climber Balloon Adventure, 5822 E. Larkspur Dr., Scottsdale, AZ 85254; (602) 483-8208; and Unicorn Balloon Company, 15001 N. 74th St., Suite F, Scottsdale, AZ 85260, (800) 468-2478 or (602) 991-3666.

River rafting ● Two firms specialize in white-water rafting on the upper Salt and the Verde rivers. Salt River Recreation, P.O. Box 6568, Mesa 85216-6568, offers rental tubes and shuttle service on the Lower Salt River; (602) 984-3305. There are several shuttle stops, so you can float for a couple of hours or all day. The lower Salt River turns into a giant pool party on summer weekends, so you might want to schedule a weekday float. Sun Country Rafting, P.O. Box 9429, Phoenix 85068-9429, has raft trips down the upper Salt, Verde and Gila rivers; (800) 2-PADDLE or (602) 493-9011.

Soaring ● Arizona Soaring, P.O. Box 858, Maricopa, AZ 85239, (602) 267-2318; and Turf Soaring School, 8700 W. Carefree Hwy., Peoria, AZ 85382, (602) 439-3621.

Specialty tours ● Gray Line Tours offers a variety of local and statewide motorcoach tours; P.O. Box 21126, Phoenix, AZ 85036, (602) 495-9100. Dozens of other van and bus tours, photo tours, shopping tours and other specialized outings are listed in the *Phoenix Official Visitors Guide.*

Performing arts

Dillard's Box Office sells tickets to many performing arts and sporting events in the Valley of the Sun; call (800) 638-4253 or (602) 678-2222. Among other ticket agencies are Curtain Call at (602) 997-6409 (mostly theater); Danny's Tickets, (800) 825-8497 or (602) 840-2340 (all cultural and sports events); Jack's Ticket Agency, (800) 825-3773 or (602) 968-3939 (all events); Select Ticket Service, (602) 254-3387 (specializing in hard to get sports and concert tickets); and Team One Tickets, (800) 800-9494 or (602) 894-9494 (sports, theater and concerts).

Assorted performing arts ● Gammage Center for the Performing Arts on the ASU campus presents concerts, theater and variety shows; (602) 965-3434. Other cultural events are presented at ASU's Kerr Cultural Center at 6110 Scottsdale Rd., in Scottsdale; (602) 965-KERR. Sundome Center, 19403 Johnson Blvd., Sun City West, has a busy performing arts program for the west Phoenix area; (602) 975-1900. Chandler Center for the Arts at 250 N. Arizona Avenue in Chandler, presents a variety of musicales and other shows; (602) 786-3954. Scottsdale Center for the Arts presents assorted entertainments at 7383 Scottsdale Mall; (602) 994-ARTS.

Opera ● The Arizona Opera presents five productions in Symphony Hall each year from October through March; (602) 226-SING.

Symphony ● Phoenix Symphony presents concerts ranging from pops to classics, including world-noted guest stars. Most are held in Symphony Hall; (800) AT-CIVIC or (602) 264-6363.

Theater ● The professional Arizona Theatre Company presents classic and contemporary plays at the old Herberger Theater Center, 222 E. Monroe, Phoenix, (602) 252-TIXS or 256-6899. Phoenix Little Theatre presents popular productions in its facility behind the Phoenix Art Museum; (602) 254-2151). Mesa Little Theatre presents plays and conducts classes in various arts at the Mesa Arts Center, 155 N. Center; (602) 834-9500. Actors Lab Arizona has productions, road shows and acting classes; (602) 990-1731.

Spectator sports

Several baseball teams conduct spring training and play out their Cactus League schedule in and about the Valley of the Sun. (Complete details on opposite page.) Now the valley has a major league club of its own, the expansion Arizona Diamondbacks, starting with the 1998 season.

Baseball ● The Arizona Diamondbacks expansion team will play at the new Bank One Ballpark at Jefferson and Fourth Streets, southeast of Civic Plaza. For information contact the team office at 400 N. Fifth, Suite 1100, (P.O. Box 2095), Phoenix, AZ 85001; ticket office (602) 514-8400, administration (602) 514-8500. The minor league Phoenix Firebirds now play at Scottsdale Stadium at 7408 E. Osborn Road, but will move to a new city when the Diamondbacks begin play, probably to Austin, Texas. For information, call (602) 275-0500.

Basketball ● The National Basketball Association's Phoenix Suns play at Arizona Veterans Memorial Coliseum at 1826 W. McDowell Rd.; call (602) 379-SUNS.

Football ● The Arizona Cardinals of the National Football League play at ASU's Sun Devil Stadium; for tickets, call (602) 379-0102.

Hockey ● The Phoenix Roadrunners of the International Hockey League play at Veterans Memorial Coliseum from October to April; (602) 340-0001.

Auto racing ● Several events are held each year at Manzanita Speedway, 35th Avenue at West Broadway, (602) 276-7575; and Phoenix International Raceway, South 115th Avenue and Baseline Road; (602) 252-3833.

Greyhound racing ● It's dogs, not buses. The canines canter at Phoenix Greyhound Park, East Washington and 40th streets, (602) 273-7181; and at Apache Greyhound Park, 2551 W. Apache Trail in Apache Junction, (602) 982-2371.

Thoroughbred racing ● The ponies gallop at Turf Paradise, 1501 W. Bell Road near 19th Avenue from October through May; (602) 942-1101.

University sports ● ASU's Sun Devils play intercollegiate football, baseball, basketball and assorted other sports at various sites on the ASU campus in Tempe; for tickets call (602) 965-2381. Sun Devil Stadium is the site for the New Year's Day Fiesta Bowl college football classic.

TRANSPORTATION

Sky Harbor International Airport, three miles southeast of downtown, is served by 23 U.S. and foreign carriers with more than a thousand arrivals and departures each day; (602) 273-3321. It's home base to America West Airlines, with service throughout the United States and flights to Mexico and Canada; (800) 235-9292. Other majors include Alaska, (800) 426-0333; American, (800) 433-7300; Continental, (800) 525-0280; Delta, (800) 221-1212; Southwest, (800) 435-9792; TWA, (800); and United, (800) 241-6522.

Among major **rental car** agencies serving the airport are A-1, (800) 899-4320; Alamo, (800) 327-9633; Avis, (800) 831-3847; Dollar, (800) 800-4000; Enterprise; (800) 829-1853; Hertz, (800) 654-3131; National, (800) 227-7368; and Thrifty, (800) 367-2277.

SuperShuttle offers airport transfers to downtown, (800) 258-3826; and service is also provided by Phoenix Transit, with departures every 30 minutes; (602) 253-5000. Among Phoenix **taxi companies** are Yellow Cab, (602) 252-5252; Ace Taxi, (602) 254-1999; AAA Cab, (602) 253-8294;

CACTUS LEAGUE: SUN COUNTRY BASEBALL

Every March, shouts of "play ball!" echo among the Southwest's sunny deserts as several members of the majors launch their spring training. The Valley of the Sun is the focal point, hosting the California Angels, Chicago Cubs, Milwaukee Brewers, Oakland A's, San Diego Padres, San Francisco Giants and Seattle Mariners. The Colorado Rockies work out in Tucson, and the new Arizona Diamondbacks of Phoenix also may take the short trip south to play their Cactus League games in Tucson.

Fans like the informality and vigor of Cactus League baseball, and the intimacy of the small stadiums. It's baseball played with enthusiasm, gusto and mistakes; the way we played as kids on America's sandlots. They like the ticket prices, too: $5 to $10 for the best seats in the stands. The communities like spring training, too; one survey indicated that Cactus League play generates as much as $150 million to host communities each year.

Many people come to Arizona specifically to watch these exhibition games, particularly the "Snowbirds"—long-term retired winter-spring visitors. A recent survey showed that three-fourths of the spring training ticket-buyers are from out of state and two-thirds of these hotdog clutchers come specifically to witness spring baseball action.

If you're one of these baseball junkies, here's where you can catch the action. Tickets for the Angels, Athletics, Brewers and Cubs Cactus League games are available through Dillard's Box Office, (800) 638-4253 or (602) 678-2222. For others, contact the individual teams at the numbers below. All games start at 1 p.m.

The new **Arizona Diamondbacks** of Phoenix likely will host their Cactus League games at Tucson's Hi Corbett Field in Reid Park, East Broadway and Randolph Way; (602) 514-8400.

California Angels play at Tempe's Diablo Stadium, 48th Street and Broadway; (602) 438-9300. They work out at Gene Autry Park, 4125 E. McKellips in Mesa.

Chicago Cubs play at HoHoKam Park, 1235 Center St. (near Brown Road) in Mesa; (602) 964-4467.

Colorado Rockies play at Tucson's Hi Corbett Field in Reid Park, East Broadway and Randolph Way; (520) 327-9467.

Milwaukee Brewers play at Compadre Stadium, 1425 W. Ocotillo Rd. (off Arizona Avenue), in Chandler; (602) 895-1200.

Oakland A's play at Phoenix Municipal Stadium, 5999 E. Van Buren (near Galvin Parkway in Papago Park), Phoenix; (602) 392-0217. They practice at Scottsdale Community College, 9000 E. Chaparral Road, Scottsdale.

San Diego Padres play at Peoria Stadium, 10601 N. 83rd Dr.; (602) 486-2011.

San Francisco Giants play at Scottsdale Stadium, 7408 E. Osborn Rd., Scottsdale; (602) 990-7972. They work out at Indian Bend Park, 4289 N. Hayden Road in Scottsdale, and in Scottsdale Stadium.

Seattle Mariners play at Peoria Stadium, 10601 N. 83rd Drive; (602) 878-4337.

Checker Cab, (602) 257-1818; and Discount Cab, (602) 253-5500.

Amtrak serves Phoenix from a terminal at 401 W. Harrison, with trains west to Yuma and Los Angeles and east to Tucson, Chicago and New Orleans, (800) USA-RAIL.

Greyhound provides service from its station at 525 E. Washington, just east of downtown; (800) 231-2222 or (602) 271-7429. The bus also serves northwest Phoenix (246-4341) and Valley of the Sun communities of Mesa (834-3360), Sun City (933-5716); and Tempe (967-4030). Bus service to Payson, Show Low and the White Mountain Reservation is offered by **White Mountain Passenger Lines,** (602) 275-4245; and **Nava-Hopi Express** has runs north from Sky Harbor and Phoenix to Flagstaff and the Grand Canyon; (800) 892-8687.

Local bus service is provided by Phoenix Transit. Its downtown area shuttle (DASH) runs every six to 12 minutes between several city center stops and the state capital complex for just 30 cents; weekdays from 6:30 a.m. to 6 p.m. For long term visitors, monthly bus cards and discounted DASH tokens are available; call (602) 495-5795. The transit information numbers is (602) 253-5000.

ANNUAL EVENTS
Includes nearby communities

For details on these and other events, contact the Phoenix-Valley of the Sun Convention and Visitors Bureau at (602) 254-6500 or the Visitors Hotline at (602) 252-5588.

Fiesta Bowl Football Classic, Sun Devil Stadium, ASU, January 1; (602) 350-0911.

Carefree Art and Wine Festival, late January to early November; (602) 837-5637.

Phoenix Open, PGA golf tournament, last week of January.

Parada del Sol rodeo in Scottsdale, late January; (602) 990-3179.

Heard Museum Guild Indian Fair, early March; (602) 252-8840.

Best of Scottsdale Art Festival, March; (602) 990-3939.

Scottsdale Art Festival, March; (602) 994-ARTS.

Phoenix 500 Air Races in Mesa; (602) 990-1822.

Ostrich Festival, mid-March in Chandler; (602) 963-4571.

National Festival of the West, mid-March at Rawhide; 996-4387.

The Tradition Classic golf tournament, early April; (602) 443- 1597.

Maricopa County Fair, late April to early May in Phoenix; 252-0717.

Phoenix Jaycees Rodeo, May; (602) 263-8671.

Arizona State Fair, mid-October-early November, Phoenix; 268-FAIR.

Air Fair/Hot Air Balloon Festival, October, Scottsdale; 994-2321.

Annual Cowboy Artists of America Exhibit, October through mid-November at the Phoenix Art Museum; (602) 257-1880.

Carefree Wine and Art Festival, early November; (602) 837- 5637.

Thunderbird Invitational Balloon Race, first weekend of November in Scottsdale; (602) 978-7208.

Fiesta Bowl Duck Race, early November in Scottsdale; 350-0911.

Scottsdale Stampede in mid-November; (602) 860-5721.

Fiesta of Lights in late November, Christmas lighting festival and parade in downtown Phoenix; (602) 534-FEST.

Annual Indian Market, mid-December in Phoenix; (602) 495-0901.

WHERE TO SHOP
Also see Scottsdale, below

As in most Western cities, the major shopping malls are in the 'burbs. However, downtown remains a lively shopping venue, with several department stores and specialty shops. Two shopping centers function here—the modern **Arizona Center,** an indoor- outdoor facility at Van Buren and Third Streets, with several restaurants, food courts and specialty shops; and the Spanish-Moorish **Mercado** at Van Buren and streets.

Suburban shopping complexes include the **Metrocenter** at 9617 Metro Parkway (northwest of downtown; take Peoria Avenue west off I-17); **Paradise Valley Mall** at 4568 E. Cactus Rd. (northeast of downtown, near Paradise Village Parkway, west off Tatum); **Park Central Mall** at Central Avenue and Earll Drive (just north of downtown) and **Westridge Mall** at 7611 W. Thomas Rd. (west of downtown, near 75th Avenue). Three malls are northeast, on Camelback Road between 19th and 25th streets: **The Colonnade** at 1919 E. Camelback, **Town and Country Mall** at 2101 E. Camelback and **Biltmore Fashion Mall** at 2470 E. Camelback.

For Indian crafts, try the **Heard Museum** gift shop at 22 E. Monte Vista Rd. (just north of downtown, between Central and Third Street); and **Gilbert Ortega's**, with stores at 122 N. Second St. (downtown, near Phoenix Civic Plaza) and 1803 E. Camelback Rd. (18th Street). Ortega's has four other locations in Scottsdale.

WHERE TO DINE
American

Another Pointe in Tyme ● ☆☆☆☆ $$$

□ *7777 S. Pointe Parkway (The Pointe Hilton Resort on South Mountain); (602) 431-6472. "New American cuisine," full bar service. Daily 5 to 10 p.m. (Friday-Saturday to 11). Reservations advised; major credit cards.* □ Seafood, lamb, beef and pastas are specialties in this handsome restaurant with warm mahogany décor. Cocktail lounge featuring more than 50 microbrews and imported beers; live jazz on Friday and Saturday nights.

☺ **Compass Restaurant** ● ☆☆☆ $$$

□ *Atop the Hyatt Regency on Second between Monroe and Adams; (602) 252-1234. American-continental; full bar service. Lunch Monday-Saturday 11:30 to 2, dinner nightly 5:30 to 10, Sunday brunch 10 to 2. Major credit cards.* □ Stylish revolving restaurant top the 23rd floor of the Hyatt Regency, providing a fine panorama of the city and surrounding hills. Menu offerings include medallions of beef, Northwestern halibut, chicken with wine and shallots, roast pork tenderloin and grilled lamb chops. An adjacent cocktail lounge provides the same view for non-diners.

Ed Debevic's ● ☆☆ $

□ *2102 E. Highland Ave. (Town and Country Shopping Center at Highland); (602) 956-2760. American diner; full bar service. Sunday-Thursday 11 to 10, Friday-Saturday 11 to midnight. MC/VISA.* □ Busy family style 1950s diner with nostalgic décor and old fashioned "juiceboxes."

☺ **Hooters** ● ☆☆ $$

□ *Arizona Center at Van Buren and Third streets, street level, downtown; (602) 257-0000. Monday-Thursday 11 to midnight, Friday-Saturday 11 to 1 a.m., Sunday 11 to 10. Major credit cards.* □ Presumably, your service person at Hooters will be a nubile young lady wearing hot orange briefs and an equally brief T-shirt top, and not a pouting male in gym shorts and tank top. At this writing, the National Organization for Women and assorted courts were trying to force this lively sports bar into hiring men, in equal numbers with the sexy ladies that have given the restaurant chain national publicity. The place is harmlessly outrageous, boasting that it is "delightfully tacky yet unrefined." The fare is typical sports bar—Philly cheese steak, buffalo wings and other light fare, supported by a long list of beers and wines by the glass. The décor consists mostly of the girls and their pin-ups and logo items, plus TV sets tuned to the latest games.

☺ *Wright's at the Arizona Biltmore* ● ☆☆☆☆ *$$$$*

❑ *Missouri and 24th Street; (602) 954-2507. "New American" fare; full bar service. Lunch Monday-Friday 11:30 to 2:30, dinner Monday-Saturday 6 to 10. Reservations required; major credit cards.* ❑ Contemporary award-winning dining room in the Arizona Biltmore. Innovative menu features fare such as pepper seared ahi tuna, smoked venison loin, grilled lamb chops and pastas; excellent wine list.

Oscar Taylor ● ☆☆☆ *$$$*

❑ *2420 E. Camelback Rd. (in Biltmore Fashion Park); (602) 956-5705. American steak house; full bar service. Monday- Saturday 11 to 10, Sunday brunch 11 to 2:30. Reservations advised; major credit cards.* ❑ A Roaring 20s Chicago style bistro with ceiling fans, globe chandeliers and brick walls. It serves prime steak, ribs and homemade desserts and breads; some fresh fish.

Oyster Grill ● ☆☆☆ *$$$*

❑ *Arizona Center at Van Buren and Third streets, second level, downtown; (602) 252-6767. Mostly seafood; wine and beer. Major credit cards.* ❑ A serious seafood house with modern multi-colored geometric décor. The menu features several fresh fishies grilled over alderwood, a serious shell fish selection, plus pasta and pizza for those who don't care for things slippery. Window walls open to create a breezy effect on warm days.

Steve's Greenhouse Grill ● ☆☆ *$$*

❑ *139 E. Adams St.; (602) 252-2742. Full bar service. Monday-Saturday 6 a.m. to 10 p.m., closed Sunday. Major credit cards.* ❑ You can dine beside blow-up dummies of Reagan and Nixon at this downtown indoor-outdoor restaurant. The menu features hamburgers, pastas, salads and assorted American entrées; white chili is a specialty.

Tom's Tavern ● ☆☆ *$*

❑ *Two N. Central (Washington); (602) 257-1688. Full bar service. Weekdays 7 a.m. to 8 p.m. Major credit cards.* ❑ Lively old-fashioned pool hall atmosphere, with patio seating and a bakery. Menu specialties include creative breakfast omelettes, "pool room chili," spaghetti red with chili over angel hair pasta, and chicken stir fry.

European

☺ *Christopher's* ● ☆☆☆☆ *$$$$$*

❑ *2398 E. Camelback Rd.; (602) 957-3214. French; full bar service. Dinner Tuesday-Sunday 6 to 10. Reservations essential; major credit cards.* ❑ Chef-owned award winning restaurant with elegantly prepared *haut cuisine* served in intimate surroundings. *Conde Naste* rates it as one of America's top 50 restaurants and the *Wine Spectator* raves about its selection of more than 700 wines. It is pricey; the *prix fix* dinner is $75, with another $40 for wines matched to each course. One can order from the menu, where prices start around $30. If this still rumples your credit cards, adjourn next door to Christopher's Bistro, less expensive and more casual.

☺ *Goldie's 1895 House Restaurant* ● ☆☆☆ *$$$*

☐ *362 N. Second Ave. (Van Buren, downtown); (602) 254-0338. Continental-American menu; full bar service. Monday-Friday 11 to 2 and 5 to 9, Saturday 5 to 9 and Sunday 4 to 8:30. Reservations advised; major credit cards.* ☐ Nicely appointed restaurant in Phoenix' oldest Victorian. The atmosphere is intimate yet casual, with steaks, seafood, chicken and pasta on the menu. Live theater in adjoining cocktail lounge.

Pronto Ristorante ● ☆☆ *$$$*

☐ *3950 E. Campbell Ave. (40th Street); (602) 956-4049. Regional Italian; full bar service. Weekdays 11:30 to 11 2 and 5:30 to 10:30, weekends 5:30 to 10:30. Major credit cards.* ☐ Cozy, locally popular family owned neighborhood restaurant featuring traditional Italian fare, from *gnocchi de palate* to *risotto alla pescatora*.

Mexican

La Parilla Suiza ● ☆☆ *$$*

☐ *3508 W. Peoria; (602) 978-8334. Full bar service. Sunday 1 to 10 p.m., Monday-Thursday 11 to 10, Friday-Saturday 11 to 11. Major credit cards.* ☐ This Mexico City based restaurant serves excellent charcoal-broiled specialties, plus unusual dishes such as a chicken melt, and beef-bell pepper taco.

Macayo ● ☆☆ *$$*

☐ *7829 W. Thomas Road (near Westridge Mall); (602) 873-0313. Full bar service. Open daily 11 a.m. to 10 p.m., to midnight Friday-Saturday. Major credit cards.* ☐ Cheerful restaurant serving Sonoran and other Mexican fare, from basic burritos and chimichangas to interesting fajita treatments.

Marilyn's First Mexican Restaurant ☆☆ *$$*

☐ *12631 Tatum Blvd. (Paradise Valley Mall); (602) 953-2121. Full bar service. Open daily 11 a.m. to 10 p.m. Major credit cards.* ☐ Charming and cheerful little place noted for its margaritas, fajitas, chimichangas and chili rellenos; generous portions. Marilyn now has a second restaurant at 7001 Scottsdale Road in Scottsdale; (602) 443-1399.

Matador Restaurant ● ☆☆☆ *$$*

☐ *125 E. Adams (First Street) downtown; (602) 254-7563. Mexican-American; full bar service. Daily 7 a.m. to 11 p.m. Major credit cards.* ☐ Appealing restaurant with a Mexican-Tiffany look—leaded glass lamps, subtle Latin decorator touches and art on the walls. Entrées, often creative, include shrimp fajitas, chili Colorado and verde and Spanish steak with green salsa.

Asian

Ayako of Tokyo ● ☆☆ *$$$*

☐ *2564 E. Camelback Rd. (Biltmore Fashion Park); 955-0777. Japanese; full bar service. Lunch 11:30 to 2, dinner Sunday-Thursday 5:30 to 10, Friday-Saturday 5:30 to 10:30. Major credit cards.* ☐ Chefs chop and cook at tableside in this upscale Americanized Japanese restaurant; also a sushi bar and cocktail lounge.

Golden Phoenix ● ☆☆ *$*

☐ *6048 N. 16th St. (263-8049) and 1534 W. Camelback Rd. (279-4447). Chinese; wine and beer. Monday-Friday 11:30 to 10, Saturday 4 to 10. Major* credit cards. ☐ Extensive menu features Szechuan, Hunan and other spicy northern China dishes; large portions at modest prices.

Sing High Chop Suey House ● ☆☆ $

☐ 27 W. Madison (between First Avenue and Central); (602) 253-7848. Chinese; wine and beer. MC/VISA. ☐ Confucius probably didn't say "A mouthful is worth a thousand worlds," since one isn't supposed to say anything with a mouthful of food, although that's the claim to fame of one of Phoenix's oldest Cantonese restaurants, dating back to 1928. The fare is typical and well-prepared.

WHERE TO RECLINE

Prices reflect high season rates and may be lower at other times. (In Sunbelt areas, prices can drop by more than half in summer.) Most were provided by the management and are subject to change; use them only as a guide.

Ambassador Inn ● ☆☆ $$$ ∅

☐ 4727 E. Thomas Rd. (44th Street), Phoenix, AZ 85018; (800) 624-6759 or (602) 840-7500. All kitchenette units with refrigerators and stoves; couples $50 to $67. Major credit cards. ☐ TV, room phones; pool. **Café Ambassador** serves 7 a.m. to 10 p.m.; American and Mexican; dinners $5 to $11; full bar service.

American Lodge Motel ● ☆☆ $$ ∅

☐ 965 E. Van Buren (Civic Plaza near Convention Center), Phoenix, AZ 85006; (602) 252-6823. Couples $32 to $38, singles $24 to $28. MC/VISA, AMEX. ☐ Some new and refurbished rooms; TV movies, room phones; pool.

Best Western Bell Motel ● ☆☆ $$$ ∅

☐ 17211 N. Black Canyon Hwy. (Bell Road East exit off I-17), Phoenix, AZ 85023; (800) 528-1234 or (602) 993-8300. Couples $64 to $74, singles $59 to $69. Major credit cards. ☐ A 103-room motel with TV movies and phones; pool, spa, in-room coffee.

Courtyard by Marriott ● ☆☆☆ $$$$$ ∅

☐ 2101 E. Camelback Road (Town & Country Shopping Center), Phoenix, AZ 85016; (800) 321-2211 or 955-5200. Couples $126, singles $116. Major credit cards. ☐ Attractive 155-room patio style hotel with TV movies, refrigerators, phones and coffee makers; pool, spa and sauna, exercise room, tennis courts and coin laundry. **Restaurant** serves 6:30 a.m. to 11 p.m.; dinners $10 to $20; full bar service.

Doubletree Suites at Phoenix Gateway ● ☆☆☆ $$$$ ∅

☐ 320 N. 44th St. (Van Buren), Phoenix, AZ 85008; (602) 225-0500 or (800) 528-0444. All suites; couples $79 to $285, singles $69 to $275; prices include buffet breakfast. Major credit cards. ☐ Stylish 242-room hotel with TV movies, phones, coffee, refrigerators and wet bars and honor bars. Pool, spa and sauna, exercise room, two tennis courts. **Toppers Restaurant** serves 6:30 a.m. to 10 p.m.; dinners $12 to $20; full bar service.

Embassy Suites Thomas Road ● ☆☆☆ $$$$ ∅

☐ 2333 E. Thomas Rd. (1/4 mile from Squaw Peak Parkway), Phoenix, AZ 85016; (602) 957-1910 or (800) EMBASSY. All suites; $89 to $179. Major credit cards. ☐ Nicely appointed 183-unit hotel with TV movies, phones and refrigerators; pool, spa, gift shop, free cooked-to-order breakfast. **Squaw Peak Café** serves American and continental fare; dinners $10 to $20; full bar service.

Hampton Inn I-17 ● ☆☆☆ $$$$ Ø

❑ *8101 N. Black Canyon Hwy. (Northern Avenue, east of I-17), Phoenix, AZ 85021; (602) 864-6233. Couples $86, singles $89; rates include continental breakfast. Major credit cards.* ❑ Attractive 149-room lodge with TV movies, room phones; pool and spa.

Hotel Desert Sun ● ☆☆ $$$ Ø

❑ *1325 Grand Ave. (15th Avenue), Phoenix, AZ 85007; (602) 258-8971 or (800) 227-0301 outside Arizona. Couples and singles $69 to $79. Major credit cards.* ❑ Downtown location, spacious grounds; TV movies, room phones; coin laundry, exercise room. **Desert Sun Restaurant** open 24 hours; home-made soups and other American fare; full bar service.

☺ Hyatt Regency Phoenix ● ☆☆☆☆ $$$$$ Ø

❑ *122 N. Second St. (Monroe), Phoenix, AZ 85004; (602) 252-1234 or (800) 233-1234. Couples $170, singles $145, suites $250 to $750. Major credit cards.* ❑ Striking 712-room atrium hotel in the heart of downtown phoenix with pool, spa, exercise room and other resort amenities. Stereo/TV movies, room phones and refrigerators. **Compass** revolving rooftop restaurant listed above. Informal **Terrace Theatre Café** serves 6 a.m. to midnight. Both have full bar service.

La Mancha Hotel and Athletic Club ● ☆☆☆ $$$ Ø

❑ *100 W. Clarendon Ave. (two blocks north of Park Central Mall), Phoenix, AZ 85013; (800) 422-6444 or (602) 279-9811. Couples and singles $65 to $85, kitchenettes and suites $95 to $125. Major credit cards.* ❑ TV movies, room phones; pool, spa; adjacent athletic club free to guests. **Brass Helmet Restaurant** and Lounge, open 24 hours with "social gambling"; dinners $4 to $11; full bar service.

Radisson Hotel Midtown ● ☆☆☆ $$$$ Ø

❑ *401 W. Clarendon, Phoenix, AZ 85013; (602) 234-2464 or (800) JARDINS. Couples and singles $85 to $135, suites $105 to $135. Major credit cards.* ❑ Downtown hotel with TV and phones in appealing, oversized rooms. **Les Jardins Restaurant** serves 6 a.m. to 10 p.m. (from 7 a.m. Sundays); dinners $14 to $19; full bar service.

Ramada Downtown Phoenix ● ☆☆☆ $$$$$ Ø

❑ *401 N. First (Polk), Phoenix, AZ 85004; (602) 258-3411. Couples, singles and suites $99 to $109. Major credit cards.* ❑ Handsome 160-room city center hotel with TV, phones, in-room coffee; pool and gift shop. **Kricket's Restaurant** serves American and Mexican fare; 6:30 a.m. to 2 p.m. and 5 to 10; dinners $10 to $15; full bar service.

☺ The Ritz-Carlton Phoenix ● ☆☆☆☆ $$$$$ Ø

❑ *2401 Camelback Rd. (24th Street), Phoenix, AZ 85016; (602) 468-0700 or (800) 241-3333. Couples and singles $150 to $225, suites $325 to $550. Major credit cards.* ❑ European elegance in a new cosmopolitan resort with opulently-furnished oversized rooms. TV/stereo, several phones in rooms, honor bars and safes; pool, sauna, spa, fitness center, tennis courts. Two **restaurants** feature continental and American fare; 6 a.m. to 11 p.m.; dinners $22 to $35; full bar service.

Royal Palms Inn ● ☆☆☆ $$$$ Ø

❑ *5200 E. Camelback Rd. (44th Street), Phoenix, AZ 85018; (800) 672-6011 or (602) 840-3610. Rooms $109 to $220. MC/VISA, AMEX.* ❑ A 116-

unit inn with spacious rooms; TV, phones, refrigerators. Landscaped grounds with tennis courts, two swimming pools, sauna and coin laundry. Two **restaurants** serve American and Mediterranean fare; 7 a.m. to 10:30 p.m.; dinners $10 to $20; full bar service.

San Carlos Hotel ● ☆☆☆ $$$$

⌂ *202 N. Central Ave. (Monroe), Phoenix, AZ 85004; (800) 528-5446 or (602) 253-4121. Couples $89 to $109, singles $79 to $99, suites $129 to $150. Major credit cards.* ⌂ Small, attractive hotel in historic downtown building; TV and room phones; outdoor pool and fitness room. Three **restaurants** serve breakfast, lunch and dinner.

RESORTS

☺ Arizona Biltmore ● ☆☆☆☆☆ $$$$$ Ø

⌂ *24th Street and Missouri, Phoenix, AZ 85016; (602) 955-6600 or (800) 228-3000. Couples $210 to $290, suites $550 to $1,300. Major credit cards.* ⌂ Arizona's historic, award-winning "jewel of the desert," designed in collaboration with Frank Lloyd Wright more than 50 years ago. Now surrounded by Phoenix but still secluded on lushly landscaped acres. TV movies, room phones, elegant furnishings. Three swimming pools, eight tennis courts, fitness center, cabanas, boutiques, hair salon, massage salons; bicycling, jogging paths, two 18-hole golf courses and putting courses, lawn games, fitness programs. Southwestern architecture with textured block walls, artwork in rooms and public areas. Several **restaurants**; see Wright's listing under "Where to Dine" above.

The Pointe Hilton Resort on South Mountain ● ☆☆☆☆ $$$$$ Ø

⌂ *7777 S. Pointe Parkway (west off I-10 at Baseline Road), Phoenix, AZ 85044; (602) 438-9000 or (800) 528-0428. All suites; couples $120 to $265, singles $110 to $265. Major credit cards.* ⌂ Luxurious, handsomely landscaped resort in South Mountain foothills; six pools, spas, saunas, putting green, 18- hole golf course, lighted tennis courts, racquetball, health club. Units have living room, den and bedroom; two TVs, VCR with rentals, desks phones, wet bars, refrigerators, balconies. Many rooms have city views. Four **restaurants**—Another Pointe in Tyme (American, listed above), Aunt Chilada's (Mexican), Sport Club (Mexican) and Rustler's Rooste (Western); dinners $11 to $29; full bar service.

The Pointe Hilton Resort at Squaw Peak ● ☆☆☆☆ $$$$$ Ø

⌂ *7677 N. 16th St. (half mile east of Northern Avenue), Phoenix, AZ 85020; (800) 528-0428 or (602) 997-2626. Double and single studios and suites $229 to $259, larger suites to $1,000. Major credit cards.* ⌂ Opulent Spanish colonial style resort in the Squaw Peak foothills; six pools, spas, saunas, 18-hole golf course, lighted tennis courts, racquetball, fitness center, equestrian center. Rooms and suites have stocked refrigerators, honor bars, TVs with VCR rentals, desks with dual-line phones, private balconies—some with city views. Three **restaurants**—Avanti Trattoria serving Italian fare; Aunt Chiladas serving Mexican and Beside the Pointe serving American and Southwest cuisine, with an adjacent sports lounge; food service 6 a.m. to 11 p.m. All restaurants have full bar service.

☺ The Wigwam Resort ● ☆☆☆☆ $$$$

⌂ *300 Indian School Road (Lichfield Road), Lichfield Park, AZ 85340; (800) 327-0396 or (602) 935-3811. Couples $280 to $310, singles $260 to $290, suites $380 to $430. Major credit cards.* ⌂ Luxury desert garden resort

El Pedrigal Market near Carefree is a curious architectural study.

17 miles west of downtown Phoenix and three miles north of I-10, with 331 casitas and suites. Historic property dating from 1929, refurbished with modern amenities. Guest rooms have leather and distressed wood furniture, walk-in closets, TV movies, phones, honor bars and safe deposit boxes. Expansive grounds with three golf courses, tennis courts, fitness center, swimming pools, jogging paths, volleyball, badminton, croquet and shuffleboard. Six **restaurants** serve breakfast, lunch and dinner; American, continental and Southwest cuisine; full bar service.

WHERE TO CAMP

Covered Wagon RV Park ● 6540 N. Black Canyon Hwy. (Glendale Avenue exit 205 from I-17, then half mile south on service road), Phoenix, AZ 87017-1891; (602) 2442-2500. RV and tent sites, $15 to $25. Reservations accepted; MC/VISA. ⊓ Shaded, grassy sites with showers, coin laundry, pool and patio; near shopping areas.

Desert's Edge RV Park ● 22623 N. Black Canyon Hwy. (East Deer Valley Road exit from I-10, then half mile north on frontage road), Phoenix, AZ 85027; (602) 869-7021. RV sites, from $15. No credit cards. ⊓ Full hookups, showers, coin laundry, Propane, dump station. Pull-throughs, shaded sites, swimming pool and spa, recreation hall with planned activities.

North Phoenix Campground ● 2550 W. Louise Drive (northwest side of Deer Valley Road I-10 exit), Phoenix, AZ 85027; (602) 869-8189. RV and tent sites; full hookups $20, tents $17, cabins $25. Reservations accepted; major credit cards. ⊓ Level sites with cable TV; showers, convenience store and gift shop, recreation room with planned activities, playground, pool and spa, outdoor games. Camping cabins and trailers for rent.

Phoenix West Citrus Grove KOA ● 1440 N. Citrus (15 miles west of Phoenix, off I-10 Cotton Lane exit 124 and left), Buckeye, AZ 85326; (800) KOA-1225 or (602) 853-0537. RV and tent sites; full hookups $20.50, no hookups $15.50, tents $14.50. Reservations accepted; MC/VISA. ⊓ Tidy park with pull-throughs and picnic tables; showers, coin laundry, groceries, Propane and gasoline, dump station, snack bar, recreation room with planned activities, pool and spa, playground.

Pioneer RV Park • *36408 Black Canyon Hwy. (Pioneer Road exit 225 from I-17, 30 miles north), Phoenix, AZ 85027; (800) 658-5895 or (602) 465-7465. RV sites, full hookups $13. Reservations accepted.* ◻ Large park with showers, coin laundry, pool and spa, rec center with planned activities, billiards, shuffleboard, horseshoes, TV hookups. Located adjacent to (but not affiliated with) the Arizona Pioneer Living History Museum.

White Tank Mountain Regional Park • *Thirteen miles west of Peoria on Olive Avenue; P.O. Box 91, Waddell, AZ 85355; (602) 935-2505. RV and tent sites $8; no hookups. Day use $2.* ◻ White Tank (listed above, under "The outdoor thing,") has campsites in a mountainous desert wilderness; picnic tables and barbecue pits, with water, flush potties and showers nearby. To reach it, take Grand Avenue (Highway 60) about 15 miles northwest from Phoenix and then make a half left onto Olive Avenue in Peoria.

THE COMMUNITIES NEXT DOOR
Scottsdale, Carefree & Cave Creek

Scottsdale elevation: 1,260 feet　　　　　　**Population: 134,000**

This appealing and upscale area has caught the Arizona growth bug. When we first visited this mountainous desert region 25 years ago, Scottsdale was a quiet cowboy style hamlet. As we explored its Western wear stores, art galleries and curio shops, words like "quaint" and "charming" came to mind. Those shops still exist, but they're surrounded by a burgeoning suburbia.

In the past two decades, Phoenix has spilled northward and threatened to engulf Scottsdale. In self defense, the little town went on an annexation binge and promptly covered the pretty desert landscape with its own suburban scatter. However, it is still the Valley of the Sun's most inviting city, and it hosts some of the area's most opulent resorts. Scottsdale's growth, although rapid, has been more controlled than most other cities. It thus remains an enticing community, with the same Southwest and Santa Fe style architecture that visitors remember from the smaller town. And since it's on the outer edge of the Phoenix megalopolis, a brief drive north takes you into a desert that is still free of subdivisions and service stations.

The craggy Camelback Mountain, so named because it resembles a kneeling camel, offers a dramatic backdrop. Most of the posh resorts are tucked into its foothills. Others share cactus country with luxurious Southwestern style homes in the rock-rimmed Paradise Valley, north of Scottsdale.

All of this sprawl had rather humble beginnings. In 1894, Rhode Island Banker Albert G. Utley came to this spot, subdivided 40 acres of desert and sold off lots. Utleydale or Utleyburg didn't sound right, so he named the new town for former Army chaplain Winfield Scott, an early resident who did much to encourage settlement. Through the years, it became famous as a charming little Western town, way out in the desert beyond Phoenix. Horses had the right-of-way and hitchin' rails stood before false-front stores. Scottsdale prided itself in being one of America's most Western towns.

Today, with its fashionable shopping centers and expensive desert homes, it more resembles Palm Springs with a Stetson, which isn't necessarily bad. The Old West still lurks nearby—in Rawhide, Pinnacle Peak and Cave Creek.

Carefree and Cave Creek are a joined pair of desert hamlets about 20 miles north of Scottsdale. Although neighbors, they come from different backgrounds. Carefree is a planned community, begun in 1959 as a vacation retreat. Cave Creek is a deliberately funky Western town—some would say a little scruffy. Populated with false-front stores, cowboy saloons and steak houses, it dates back to the 1870s, when gold was discovered in the rough surrounding hills. Both communities enjoy imposing settings, nestled among desert gardens, giant boulders and red rock ramparts. They're more than a thousand feet higher than Phoenix and thus somewhat cooler.

If you like country cooking in a Western atmosphere, plan to invest a dinner hour in Cave Creek. Its rustic main street is lined with cowboy steak houses. Choose from among these—Jackalope Café, Cave Creek Corral, Horny Toad Restaurant, Crazy Ed's Satisfied Frog and the Original Wild West Saloon. They're all pretty much the same in rustic atmosphere and steak-chops-ribs menus. Other Western restaurants, some with cowboy entertainment, are Rawhide Steakhouse at Scottsdale and Pinnacle Peak roads, and Pinnacle Peak Patio and Riata Pass, in the craggy hills east of Paradise Valley (see listings below.)

Carefree consists mostly of boutique shopping centers with Southwesterny names like Spanish Village, Sundial Plaza and Carefree Plaza. Make it a point to check out El Pedrigal shopping complex and The Boulders luxury resort on the southern edge of town (listed below).

Driving Scottsdale-Cave Creek

This drive, covering about 70 miles round-trip, will provide a good sampler of the area, from the shops of Old Town Scottsdale to the fancy homes and resorts of Paradise Valley. The route is garnished with rugged desert-mountain scenery and slices of the Old West. (Items marked with a ■ are described in more detail below, under "Attractions.")

Begin where we left off in the "Driving East Phoenix" section. Continue north on Galvin Parkway, which becomes 64th Street as it leaves Papago Park and enters Scottsdale. Sixty-fourth ends at Thomas Road; turn right and follow Thomas a mile to Scottsdale Road and turn left. Drive several blocks north and, as you cross Second, First and Main streets, start looking for a place to park. You're in **Old Town Scottsdale.**

RV PARKING ADVISORY ● As in downtown Phoenix, RVs weren't taken into account when parking was planned. Several lots have been cleared for parking, although anything longer than 21 feet won't fit. The Scottsdale Mall garage won't accommodate high profile vehicles. The only option is to drive about neighboring streets, off the main thoroughfares.

What little survives of the original Scottsdale has been turned into a Western theme shopping complex with boutiques, galleries and cafés tucked behind false front stores and beneath sidewalk awnings. Most of this is concentrated along Main Street and Brown Avenue. Although the Western look survives, much of the original Scottsdale charm is lost in the transition from tack shop to tacky tourism. Shops have names like "Hair it Is", "Life's a Juice" and "Flagg's T-Shirt Factory."

To be more fair, Old Town has some fine little shops and galleries and the area west along First Avenue is a serious art and antique row. Two particularly fine Western art galleries share a building at Main and Scottsdale Road—Troy's Western Heritage Gallery and Legacy Gallery; both have excellent examples of Western theme oils, bronzes and other artwork. Art walks through Scottsdale are conducted Thursday evenings from 7 to 9. Call for details—Heritage at (602) 941-9041 or Legacy at (602) 945-1113.

To learn more than you could ever possibly need to know about the town, pick up the *Scottsdale Destination Guide*—nearly as thick as the *Phoenix Official Visitors Guide* at the **Scottsdale Chamber of Commerce.** It's located on a landscaped pedestrian walk between Old Town and Scottsdale Mall, open 8:30 to 5 weekdays; (602) 945-8481. *To reach it, walk east on Main Street, which becomes the pedestrian path.*

Next door is the ■ **Scottsdale Historical Museum,** housed in "The Little Red Schoolhouse," one of the town's oldest surviving structures. Built in 1909, it was the town's first elementary school, then it served as the city hall, justice court and library. Also within the mall is the attractive ■ **Scottsdale Center for the Arts.**

From Old Town, drive north about half a mile on Scottsdale Road, then sweep left onto Camelback Road in front of Scottsdale Fashion Square. You'll travel for about 2.5 miles along the foothills of Camelback Mountain, haven for upscale desert living. Posh homes and elegant resorts sit among the rocks and cactus on the slopes above. At 44th Street, turn right (north) and follow it a mile around the edge of Camelback Mountain. Sweep right onto McDonald Drive, then shortly swoop left (north) onto Tatum Boulevard and follow this into the town of Paradise Valley.

Stay on Tatum for about three miles, then turn right at a traffic signal onto Doubletree Ranch Road and follow it east two miles to a four-way stop at Invergordon Road. Immediately beyond Invergordon, on the right, is ■ **Cosanti,** the curiously contoured studios of architectural visionary Paolo Soleri. Continue about a mile on Doubletree to Scottsdale Road. If you like old trains, head south on Scottsdale for three miles to ■ **McCormick Railroad Park.** Otherwise, go north on Scottsdale for three miles and turn right onto Cactus Road. After about four miles, you'll cross Frank Lloyd Wright Boulevard. Continue across and climb up a desert slope to Wright's ■ **Taliesin West**.

Returning from Taliesin, turn right onto Frank Lloyd Wright Boulevard, which angles northwest along the foothills, past new desert subdivisions. After about three miles, go north (right) onto Pima Road, follow it a short distance to Bell Road, turn left and follow signs to the ■ **Fleischer Museum.** Return to Pima and continue north about two miles to Pinnacle Peak Road, turn left and follow it to Scottsdale Road. Immediately south is the cowboy complex of ■ **Rawhide.**

Press northward on Scottsdale Road and you'll finally break free of suburbs and travel through handsome, hilly and boulder strewn desert. After about four miles, note the curious Spanish-postmodern architecture of ■ **El Pedrigal Marketplace** on your right, near the junction of the Carefree Highway. Just beyond, Scottsdale Road becomes Tom Darlington Road as it enters the desert suburb of **Carefree.** At a four-way stop, a left turn will deliver you to **Cave Creek.** The Cave Creek Ranger Station of Tonto National Forest comes up immediately on the left, at 7171 E. Carefree Rd., Cave Creek. Hours are weekdays 7:45 to 4:30; (602) 488-3441. When you reach deliberately rustic Cave Creek, a right turn onto Basin Road will fetch you to the small ■ **Cave Creek Museum.**

The long way home

When you've finished exploring Carefree and Cave Creek, head back toward Scottsdale. If you'd like to take a different route home, turn east onto

Dynamite Boulevard about four miles south of Carefree. This route offers aerial views of the valley, a wild animal park and a town with a giant fountain as a centerpiece. The road climbs into the rocky heights of Pinnacle Peak with some nice views back over your shoulder of the Valley of the Sun.

After about four miles, a right turn onto Alma School Parkway will take you to a pair of view restaurants with cowboy themes—**Reata Pass Steakhouse** and **Pinnacle Peak Patio**. They're both good places for watching the sunset. Beyond Alma School Parkway, Dynamite becomes Rio Verde Drive, passing through rocky desert lands behind **McDowell Mountain Park** and the Southwest style community of Rio Verde. A short distance beyond Rio Verde, head south on McDowell Mountain Park Road.

As you approach **Fountain Hills**, a planned desert community of about 10,000 souls, you'll see its namesake fountain spewing a towering column of water into the heavens. This imposing liquid landmark, like the great water jet on Switzerland's Lucerne Lake, is visible for miles. It was in fact designed by the Swiss and it's the world's tallest fountain, shooting water 560 feet into the air. As you enter the town's northern outskirts, your route becomes Fountain Hills Boulevard. Watch for Saguaro Boulevard, turn left and you'll pass that spouting spigot, spouting skyward from a park-rimmed lake.

A few blocks beyond, turn left from Saguaro onto Shea Boulevard and—if you want to visit the wildlife park—go left again onto the Beeline Highway. Two miles later, turn right onto Fort McDowell Road and you'll see ■ **Out of Africa** immediately on your right. From here, the southbound Beeline Highway (not really a beeline because it curves through the desert) will take you back toward Phoenix.

ATTRACTIONS
In order of appearance

Scottsdale Historical Museum • *7333 Scottsdale Mall; (602) 945-4499. Wednesday-Saturday 10 to 5, Sunday noon to 4. Free; donations appreciated.* ⊡ Small and nicely done, the historical society museum exhibits original furniture of town founders Winfield and Helen Scott, along with artifacts and photos of the early days. Featured displays include an early American kitchen and a mock-up of a turn of the century school room. It's appropriate since the museum is housed in Scottsdale's first grammar school.

Scottsdale Center for the Arts • *Scottsdale Mall; (602) 995-8481 or 944-ARTS. Monday-Saturday 10 to 5, Sunday noon to 5. Free; fees for stage shows, concerts and films.* ⊡ Scottsdale's cultural mecca, the city-owned center hosts performing arts in its 830-seat theater, art exhibits and sales, classic movies and other things cultural. Statuary decorates an outdoor sculpture garden. Works of local artists can be purchased in the gift shop.

☺ *Cosanti* • *6433 Doubletree Ranch Road (Invergorden), Scottsdale, AZ 85253; (602) 948-6145. Daily 9 to 5; $1 donation. Tours Monday 9 to 3; $5, students and seniors $4.* ⊡ From late in Chapter six, you know that Paolo Soleri is an architectural visionary working on an environmental city called Arcosanti, 68 miles north of Phoenix. Cosanti is his home, workshop and art studio in Paradise Valley, north of Scottsdale. Here, he and his students create the famous Soleri bronze and ceramic bells and wind chimes and other decorator items. Like Arcosanti, his Cosanti studio has an extra-terrestrial look with pre-cast concrete free-form shapes. It suggests melted geometry, with a kind of doughy primitive look. Yoda would feel right at home here.

The complex includes a gallery of sculptures and other artwork by Soleri and his students, a sales shop and a small foundry. On weekdays, you can watch the artists at work.

McCormick Railroad Park ● *7301 E. Indian Bend Rd. (Scottsdale Rd.) Scottsdale, AZ 85253; (602) 994-2312. Daily 10 to 5:30. Park admission is free; train rides and carousel rides are a dollar.* ☐ Half-pints and adults can ride a half-scale train around this 30-acre park devoted to railroad buffs, and operated by the city of Scottsdale. Exhibits include a full-size Mogul Baldwin steam engine and several historic cars. Visitors can ride a 1929 carousel and browse through a railway antiques store and model railroad hobby shop. If you're a model train nut, drop by on Sunday afternoons, when local clubs set up and run their mini-railroading layouts. The Maricopa Live Steamers group offers free train rides on Sunday afternoon; folks visiting then also can see several elaborate model train layouts.

☺ **Taliesin West** ● *114th Street at Cactus, Scottsdale, AZ 85261; (602) 860-2700. Tours daily, on the hour 9 to 4 (at 8 and 11 in summer); adults $10, students and seniors $8 and kids 4 to 12, $2.50. Desert walks Monday-Saturday at 9 and 11 a.m., $12; or $18 combined with the Taliesin tour. Bookstore open daily 8:30 to 5.* ☐ The former winter home and studio of America's foremost architect, Taliesin West is an intriguing mix of concrete and stone that seems fused into the desert instead of rising from it. Frank Lloyd Wright came here from Wisconsin in the 1930s to create a teaching center for his concept of "organic architecture." The complex sits on a 600-acre alluvial fan, sweeping down from the McDowell Mountains.

Wright's designs involved the repeated play of geometric forms. Natural materials were used to embody nature, man and architecture. Taliesin West is mostly triangular, with red sandstone and concrete wedges and desert stone sculpted into the sloping hill. The 45-minute tours begin hourly—more often if crowds warrant. They take visitors over landscaped terraces and courtyards and past a drafting studio where students are learning the Wright stuff. In the "Kiva" conference center, you see architectural drawings and models by Wright and his followers.

After the master's death in 1959, the Frank Lloyd Wright Foundation was created to continue his architectural school. It also sponsors public programs, including seminars on art, architecture and Wright's philosophy, plus half-day tours, evenings of music and dancing, and buffet suppers. Nights are beautiful here, with the lights of the Valley of the Sun sparkling like scattered diamonds. But the master didn't like this intrusion. He once told his wife, long before Phoenix-Scottsdale had spread this far: "It's time to move Taliesin. I can see a light in the valley."

☺ **Fleischer Museum** ● *17207 N. Perimeter Dr., Scottsdale; (602) 585-3108. Daily 10 to 4; tours by appointment. Free; contributions accepted.* ☐ The grand atrium lobby and second floor of the Perimeter Center office building have been given over to a fine museum of American impressionistic art. Exhibits—mostly oils—focus primarily on California and the west, although special shows are sometimes featured. Several bronze sculptures occupy a glass domed rotunda courtyard beyond the foyer. This is the first museum of its kind to feature the California School of impressionistic art, which spanned the first half of this century. Artists combined European impressionistic styles with the vivid colors of the typical American artist, focusing primarily on the West's expansive scenery and seascapes. The

Southwest-modern building was completed in 1990 as the corporate headquarters of the Franchise Corporation of America. Its leaders wanted to create a "corposphere" to integrate a work environment with an artistic setting. The result is one of the Valley of the Sun's most inviting museums.

☺ **Rawhide** ● *23023 N. Scottsdale Rd. (Pinnacle Peak Rd.), Scottsdale, AZ 85261; (602) 563-5600. Monday-Thursday 5 to 10 and Friday-Sunday 11 to 10 from October through May; daily 5 to 10 the rest of the year. Adults $2, kids $1; train ride, theater, burro, camel and stage coach rides $2 each; museum $1.* ☐ "How the West was fun," says the sign out front. Rawhide is the largest and best of several wanna-be cowboy towns in the area, with a couple of dozen false-front stores standing along its main street. They house boutiques, curio shops, saloons and restaurants. Visitors can catch a stagecoach, witness a shoot-out, feed goats in a petting zoo and watch a "mellerdrammer" in the Moonshine Theatre. An Old West museum boasts 5,000 items—from high-button shoes to antiques. You can have a friend arrested for a few dollars, and hung for few dollars more. Or you can just clump along the boardwalks, feeling like a son or daughter of the Old West. The Rawhide Steakhouse has country cooking and live country music. (See "Where to Dine" listing.)

The last time we were there, the streets were busy with Japanese visitors looking a little silly in cowboy hats and red neckerchiefs. Rawhide obviously is the darling of the tour bus set.

El Pedrigal Festival Marketplace ● *Cave Creek Road near Carefree Highway, Carefree; (602) 488-1072.* ☐ Built into the base of an impressive mountain of boulders, El Pedrigal looks like a cross between Frank Lloyd Wright architecture and Tune Town. The building material might have been multicolored play dough. Most of the shops in this gaudy complex are upscale boutiques, Western art galleries and jewelry stores. The quality and prices obviously are designed for guests at the posh Boulders resort, just up Darlington Road. We hope they have an architectural sense of humor.

Cave Creek Museum ● *Basin and Skyline, Cave Creek, AZ 85331; (602) 488-2764 or 488-3183. Wednesday-Sunday 1 to 4:30; closed in summer. Free; donations appreciated.* ☐ This typically small-town historical museum displays relics of Cave Creek's past as a mining and ranching center. A model pit house and Indian artifacts trace early Native American cultures in the area.

☺ **Out of Africa** ● *Two S. Fort McDowell Rd. (near Beeline Highway), Fountain Hills, AZ 85269; (602) 837-7779 or 837-7677. Tuesday-Sunday 9:30 to 5. Adults $10.95, seniors $9.95, kids $4.95. Major credit cards.* ☐ Two animal enthusiasts intrigued with people/big cat relationships have turned their research project into a public attraction. Visitors can see lions, tigers and panthers and an assortment of other critters and watch animal handlers work with the big felines. These aren't training sessions, they say, but animal-human encounters. Meals and snacks are available at the Kalahari Café, and the Mombassa Trading Company sells gifts with an animal angle. There's also a kid's playground. Visitors can swim with tigers every day at 1:15 p.m. at the Tiger Splash.

WHERE TO SHOP

Scottsdale is a-brim with shops featuring cowboy art, Western wear and Indian crafts. Most are in old town near Civic Center Plaza, along Brown Avenue between Main and Second streets. Several modern malls lure shoppers as well. **Scottsdale Mall** is immediately east of Old Town; the upscale **Scottsdale Fashion Square** is at Scottsdale Road and Camelback. The posh **Borgata of Scottsdale,** fashioned after Italy's San Gimignano towers, is on Scottsdale Road, a quarter mile south of Lincoln Drive. **Scottsdale Focus** is the area's largest concentration of galleries and specialty shops, in a landscaped setting with a Southwestern theme, at 4175 N. Goldwater Boulevard. Several malls are along Indian School Road, west of Old Town. Then there's **El Pedrigal Marketplace** in Carefree, more interesting for its architecture than its shops (listed above).

WHERE TO DINE
American-continental

☺ *Chaparral Room* ● ☆☆☆☆ *$$$*

❒ *At Marriott's Camelback Resort, 402 E. Lincoln Dr. (off Scottsdale Road), Scottsdale; (602) 948-1700. Continental; full bar service. 6 p.m. to 10 p.m. (to 11 Friday-Saturday). Reservations essential; major credit cards.* ❒ Stylishly casual award-winning restaurant in one of Arizona's premiere desert resorts (see listing below). Fare is classic European, from beef Wellington to sautéed veal medallions in a seafood sauce.

☺ *8700* ● ☆☆☆☆ *$$$*

❒ *8700 E. Pinnacle Peak Rd. (In the Citadel Resort), Scottsdale; (602) 994-8700. Southwestern; full bar service. Daily 6 to 10 p.m. Reservations advised; major credit cards.* ❒ One of three restaurants at the Inn at the Citadel Resort complex (listed below); luxurious Southwestern setting with antiques, fireplaces and valley views. Menu features mesquite grilled steaks, chops and seafood. Live entertainment Tuesday through Sunday in the Marquee Bar & Grill.

El Chorro Lodge ● ☆☆☆☆ *$$$*

❒ *5550 E. Lincoln Dr. (across from Mountain Shadows), Scottsdale; (602) 948-5170. American-continental; full bar service. Lunch Monday-Friday 11 to 3 and Saturday-Sunday 9 to 3, dinner nightly 5:30 to 11. Reservations advised; major credit cards.* ❒ Historic lodge on 22 acres in Paradise Valley; Western style dining room with original art. American-continental menu with chateaubriand, rack of lamb, French fried lobster tails and steaks.

The Grapevine ● ☆☆ *$$*

❒ *4013 N. Brown at First in Old Town Scottsdale; (602) 994-1792. Eclectic menu; full bar service. MC/VISA.* ❒ This place with an indecisive menu specializes in *al fresco* dining, open to the weather on two levels. The menu is all over the map, from American hamburgers and salads to Mexican burritos, Greek specialties, spaghetti, fondue and catfish.

☺ *Oaxaca Restaurant* ● ☆☆☆ *$$$*

❒ *8711 E. Pinnacle Peak Rd. (Pinnacle Peak Village), Scottsdale; (602) 998-2222. American; full bar service. Daily from 5 p.m. Reservations advised; major credit cards.* ❒ Southwest style restaurant with an "all-American" menu featuring prime rib, baby-back ribs, fresh seafood and pasta. It sits a thousand feet above the valley, with grand views.

Schlotzky's Deli ● ☆ *$*

❒ *4017 Scottsdale Road in Old Town Scottsdale; (602) 949-1122. Italian deli; wine and beer. Daily 11 to 9. MC/VISA.* ❒ Handy place for sandwiches, pizzas, salads and other quick bites. Tables indoors and out.

Asian
Emperor's Garden ● ☆☆ $$

❑ 7228 First Avenue in Old Town Scottsdale; (602) 946- 6565. *Chinese; wine and beer. Sunday-Thursday 11 to 10, Friday- Saturday 11 to 11. MC/VISA.* ❑ Simply decorated, dimly lit café running the full gamut from Cantonese through Mandarin to Hunan and Szechuan cuisine. Several inexpensive lunch combos make this a handy midday stop.

European
Italian Grotto ● ☆☆ $$

❑ *Main and Scottsdale Road in Old Town Scottsdale; (602) 994-1489. Italian; wine and beer. Lunch and dinner daily. Major credit cards.* ❑ Maybe we can call it a spaghetti western; this small café in old town specializes in Italian accented seafood, plus chicken cacciatore, chicken marsala and pastas. It's a trim little place with white nappery and window-walls that open to the sidewalk.

Mancuso's ● ☆☆☆ $$$

❑ *6166 N. Scottsdale Rd. (in Borgata Center), Scottsdale; (602) 948-9988. Italian-French; full bar service. Daily 5 p.m. to 10:30. Reservations advised; major credit cards.* ❑ A local favorite featuring veal, pasta, fowl and seafood.

Marché Gourmet ● ☆☆ $$

❑ *4121 N. Marshall Way, Scottsdale; (602) 994-4568. French-continental; full bar service. Daily 7:30 a.m. to 10 p.m. Reservations advised; major credit cards.* ❑ The only European style restaurant in the valley open daily for breakfast, the Marché is quite popular with locals. The eclectic menu is a continental-Mediterranean mix, including some vegetarian dishes.

Mexican
El Paraiso y Mucho Mas ● ☆ $$

❑ *7220 First Avenue in Old Town Scottsdale; (602) 423- 1707. Mexican-American; full bar service. Daily 11 to 10. MC/VISA.* ❑ Patio café tucked between specialty shops in Old Scottsdale. Fare ranges smashed beans and rice to American 'burgers and salads; cocktail lounge adjacent.

Los Olivos Mexican Patio ● ☆☆ $$

❑ *7328 Second St. (at Wells Fargo Avenue), Scottsdale. Full bar service. Sunday-Thursday 11 to 10, Friday-Saturday 11 to 1 a.m. Reservations advised; major credit cards.* ❑ Long-time local favorite, dating from 1919. The ethnic menu features sour cream enchiladas, chimichangas and fajitas. Try the *Camerones al Mojo*—garlic and butter sautéed shrimp.

Marilyn's Mexican Restaurant ☆☆ $$

❑ *7001 Scottsdale Rd., Scottsdale; (602) 443-1399. Full bar service. Daily 11 a.m. to 10 p.m. Major credit cards.* ❑ A charming and cheerful little place noted for its margaritas, fajitas, chimichangas and chili rellenos.

Western
☺ Crazy Ed's Satisfied Frog ● ☆☆ $$

❑ *6245 E. Cave Creek Rd. (in Frontier Town), Cave Creek; (602) 253-6293. Full bar service. Monday-Thursday 11 to 10, Friday-Saturday 11 to 11, Sunday buffet 9 to 4 in the cantina and regular service 11 to 10 in the frog. MC/VISA, AMEX.* ❑ Rustic, fun and lively dining room featuring "giant portions" of country American, Mexican and barbecue. Cantina adjacent with music on weekends.

☺ *Pinnacle Peak Patio* ● ☆☆ *$$*

◻ *10426 E. Jomax Rd. (Pinnacle Peak), Scottsdale; (602) 585-1599. Full bar service. Monday-Thursday 4 to 10, Friday- Saturday 4 to 11, Sunday noon to 10. Major credit cards.* ◻ Well, dang my britches if this ain't the cutest and corniest western style café around! It's seriously casual and patrons who wear neckties get them snipped off and hung from the rafters (the neckties, not the patrons). There are more than a million up there. The fare is what you'd expect—mesquite broiled steaks, chicken and things barbecued. Live country music, dancing, hayrides and shoot-outs; outdoor dining.

Rawhide Steakhouse ● ☆☆☆ *$$*

◻ *23023 N. Scottsdale (in Rawhide theme park), Scottsdale; (602) 502-5600. Full bar service. Weekdays 5 to 10, weekends 11 to 10 (shorter hours in summer). MC/VISA, AMEX.* ◻ Rustic old West restaurant with country and Western band in the restaurant and live entertainment in adjoining saloon. Mesquite broiled steaks, ribs and chicken.

Reata Pass Steakhouse ● ☆☆ *$$*

◻ *27500 N. Alma School Parkway (Pinnacle Peak), Scottsdale; (602) 585-7277. Full bar service. Dinner nightly from 5, sometimes earlier on weekends. Major credit cards.* ◻ Similar to its neighbor Pinnacle Peak Patio but without the necktie parties, Reata Pass serves Western food and entertainment indoors or under the stars. Live country music, dancing, shootouts and other Western shenanigans are part of the scene. Its root go back to 1882 when an adobe stage stop occupied this spot; a portion of it survives.

☺ *Rusty Spur Saloon* ● ☆ *$*

◻ *Main Street between Scottsdale Road and Brown in Old Town Scottsdale; (602) 941-2628. Full bar service. Food served from 11 to 3; bar open until 1 a.m. Major credit cards.* ◻ Housed in a former 1921 bank building, the Spur looks convincingly like an old Western saloon and then some, with a bale of hay and a wagon wheel chandelier. The menu, hand-written on brown paper bags, is limited to hamburgers and other light fare; the place is noted more for Western entertainment and cowboy camaraderie.

WHERE TO RECLINE

Prices reflect high season rates and may be lower at other times. (In Sunbelt areas, prices can drop by more than half in summer.) Most were provided by the management and are subject to change; use them only as a guide.

Cave Creek Tumbleweed Hotel ● ☆☆ *$$$*

◻ *6333 E. Cave Creek Rd. (at Schoolhouse Road), Cave Creek, AZ 85331; (602) 488-3668. Couples and singles $69, kitchenettes $74. MC/VISA.* ◻ TV, room phones, pool. **Longbranch Saloon** serves 10 a.m. to 1 a.m., Western style (mesquite grilled steaks, fish, pork, chicken); dinners $9 to $18; full bar service.

Best Western Papago Inn ● ☆☆☆ *$$$$* Ø

◻ *7017 E. McDowell Rd. (70th Street), Scottsdale, AZ 85257; (602) 947-7335 or (800) 528-1234. Couples and singles $78 to $135. Major credit cards.* ◻ A 120-room inn with TV, room phones, room refrigerators; pool, exercise room. **Dining room** serves 7 to 2 and 5 to 9; dinners $7 to $16; full bar.

Days Inn Scottsdale ● ☆☆ *$$$$* Ø

◻ *4710 N. Scottsdale Rd. (Camelback), Scottsdale, AZ 85251; (602) 947-5411 or (800) 325-2525. Couples $85 to $122, singles $75 to $110. Major* *credit cards.* ⊡ A 168-room inn on landscaped grounds with TV movies, phones; some microwaves and refrigerators. Pool, spa and tennis and volleyball courts, coin laundry.

Embassy Suites Scottsdale ● ☆☆☆ $$$$$ Ø

⊡ *5001 N. Scottsdale Rd. (Chaparral), Scottsdale, AZ 85250; (800) 528-1456 or (602) 949-1414. Couples $130 to $170, singles $120 to $160; prices include full breakfast. Major credit cards.* ⊡ Attractive all-suite facility with two pools and spas, two tennis courts, gift shop, coin laundry. The 310 rooms have TV movies, phones, refrigerators, microwaves and in-room coffee. **Fourth Floor Grille** serves lunch from 11 to 2:30 and dinner from 5 to 10; dinners $10 to $19; full bar service.

Howard Johnson Inn Scottsdale ● ☆☆☆ $$$$ Ø

⊡ *5101 N. Scottsdale Rd. (Chaparral Road), Scottsdale, AZ 85250; (602) 945-4392 or (800) 446-HOJO. Couples and singles $88 to $118; rates include continental breakfast. Major credit cards.* ⊡ A 216-room inn with TV movies, room phones. Pleasant grounds with heated pool and spa.

Marriott Suites-Scottsdale ● ☆☆☆ $$$$$ Ø

⊡ *7325 E. Third Ave. (near Indian School and Scottsdale Road intersection), Scottsdale, AZ 85251; (602) 945-1550 or (800) 228-9290. All suites; couples $199 to $235, singles $189 to $235. Major credit cards.* ⊡ Attractive 251-room suite hotel with TV movies, phones, refrigerators, wet bars. Pool, spa and health club; sundry shop, meeting facilities. **Allie's American Grille** serves 6:30 a.m. to 11 p.m.; dinners $13 to $19; full bar service.

The Safari Resort ● ☆☆☆ $$$$ Ø

⊡ *4611 N. Scottsdale Rd. (north of Camelback, opposite Scottsdale Fashion Square), Scottsdale, AZ 85251; (800) 845-4356 or (602) 945-0721. Couples $52 to $114, singles $42 to $104, kitchenettes $60 to $140, suites $75 to $160; rates include continental breakfast. Major credit cards.* ⊡ A 198-unit lodge with TV movies, room phones, refrigerators; two swimming pools. The **Brown Derby** restaurant serves 11 a.m. to 10 p.m.; coffee shop open 24 hours; dinners $6 to $19; full bar service.

Shangrila Resort ● ☆☆ $$$

⊡ *6237 N. 59th Place (Lincoln Drive), Scottsdale, AZ 85253; (602) 948-5930. Couples $70 to $75, singles $65 to $75. Major credit cards.* ⊡ A 10-unit apartment motel with TV, room phones; some efficiency units. In desert setting with private patios; pool, citrus trees on landscaped grounds.

RESORTS

☺ *The Boulders* ● ☆☆☆☆☆ $$$$$

⊡ *P.O. Box 2090 (34631 N. Tom Darlington Rd.), Carefree, AZ 85377; (602) 488-9009. Couples $580 and singles $480 with two meals; couples $465, singles $230 without meals. Major credit cards.* ⊡ Posh adobe style resort with over-sized rooms in a stunning boulder-desert setting with dramatic architecture to match. Rooms have fireplaces, patios, TV movies, phones, refrigerators and other amenities. Swimming pools, spa, tennis courts, exercise room, 27 holes of golf. **Dining room** serves 6:30 to 10 a.m., 11:30 to 2:30 and 6 to 9:30; full bar service.

Hyatt Regency Scottsdale ● ☆☆☆☆ $$$$$ Ø

⊡ *7500 E. Doubletree Ranch Rd. (Paradise Valley), Scottsdale, AZ 85258; (602) 991-3388. Couples and singles $145 to $390, suites and casitas $215 to*

$2,300. Major credit cards. ☐ Expansive, palm shaded desert garden resort with 27 holes of golf, two-and-a-half-acre "water playground" with beach and water slide, fitness center, art collection. Stylish rooms with TV movies, phones and all amenities. Three **restaurants**—Squash Blossom (Southwestern), Golden Swan (regional American) and Sandolo (Italian); dinners $9 to $48; full bar service.

☺ *Inn at the Citadel* ☆☆☆☆ *$$$$$* ∅

☐ *8700 E. Pinnacle Peak Rd. (Pima Road), Scottsdale, AZ 85255; (800) 927-8367 or (602) 585-6133. Couples and singles $225 to $295; rates include continental breakfast. Major credit cards.* ☐ Opulent small resort in a desert-mountain setting with eleven individually decorated suites; TV, phones, refrigerators and other amenities. Landscaped courtyard, art gallery and boutiques. Three **restaurants**—8700 (listed above), the Market Room (American, Mexican and Southwestern); and the Marquee Bar (American) with view outdoor seating. Food service 7 a.m. to 10 p.m.; full bar service.

☺ *Marriott's Camelback Inn* ● ☆☆☆☆☆ *$$$$$*

☐ *5402 E. Lincoln Dr. (off Scottsdale Road), Scottsdale, AZ 85253; (602) 948-1700 or (800) 242-2635. Couples and singles $180 to $225, suites $250 to $1,200. Major credit cards.* ☐ Historic resort on lushly landscaped grounds; 36 holes of golf, putting green, indoor and outdoor pools, elaborate 27,000 square foot spa, lighted tennis courts, playground, rental bicycles, health club with massage studio, coin laundry. Casita style rooms with full amenities including TV/stereo, movies, balconies or patios, refrigerators; some fireplaces and private pools; mountain views. **Restaurants** include the Chaparral Room (see listing above) and the Navajo Room, serving 6:30 a.m. to 10 p.m.; dinners $8 to $15; full bar service.

Marriott's Mountain Shadows ● ☆☆☆☆ *$$$$$* ∅

☐ *5641 E. Lincoln Dr. (east of Tatum), Scottsdale, AZ 85253; (800) 228-9290 or (602) 948-7111. Couples and singles $280 to $325. Major credit cards.* ☐ A 336-unit resort in a desert setting with elegantly furnished rooms; TV movies, room phones, refrigerators, mini bars and other amenities. Extensive grounds with 18-hole golf course, three swimming pools, spas, eight lighted tennis courts, pro shops, fitness center, game room, activities program, guided hikes up Camelback Mountain; youth program. Four **restaurants**—Shells Oyster Bar (seafood); Nectarines (light poolside fare); Country Club Dining Room (breakfast and lunch) and Cactus Flower Café (American); plus a sandwich shop at the country club. Food service 6 a.m. to 10 p.m.; dinners $13 to $25; full bar service.

Orange Tree Golf Resort ● ☆☆☆☆ *$$$$$* ∅

☐ *10601 N. 56th St. (Shea), Scottsdale, AZ 85254; (602) 948-6100 or (800) 228-03886. All mini-suites; couples $100 to $210, singles $90 to $190. MC/VISA, AMEX.* ☐ Elegant resort with 18-hole golf course, pool, sauna, health club with massage studios. Rooms with wet bars, oversized TV/stereo/VCRs, spa tubs. **Orange Tree Restaurant** serves 7 a.m. to 10:30 p.m.; American-continental cuisine; dinners $12 to $23; nicely appointed dining room overlooking 18th fairway; full bar service.

☺ *The Phoenician Resort* ● ☆☆☆☆ *$$$$$* ∅

☐ *6000 East Camelback Rd. (60th Street), Scottsdale, AZ 85251; (800) 888-8234 or (602) 941-8200. Couples and singles $170 to $465; suites $450 to $1,650. Major credit cards.* ☐ Luxurious resort set into the foothills of

Camelback Mountain; expansive desert garden grounds with city views. The 580 rooms have three phones, remote-control TV/stereo, Italian marble bathrooms and other amenities. Tennis courts, 18-hole golf course, seven swimming pools, spas, elaborate health clubs; supervised children's activities. Five **restaurants**—Mary Elaine's, the Terrace Dining Room, Windows on the Green, the Oasis and the Café & Ice Cream Parlor—serve Mediterranean, Italian, Southwestern and American fare; dinners $4 to $39; full bar service; lounge with entertainment.

☺ *Scottsdale Princess Resort* ● ☆☆☆☆☆ *$$$$$*

◻ *7575 Princess Dr. (near Bell Road and Scottsdale Road), Scottsdale, AZ 85255; (602) 585-4848. Couples and singles $135 to $380, suites $175 to $2,300. Major credit cards.* ◻ Posh resort with Mexican colonial architecture, on 450 acres in the McDowell foothills. Six hundred luxury rooms, suites and casitas with TV movies, phones, wet bars, refrigerators, terraces; some with fireplaces. Two 18-hole golf courses, seven tennis courts, one-mile fitness trail, racquetball and squash courts, large health club, spa with saunas, steam bath and beauty salon; "Westworld" adjacent with polo field and stables. **Several restaurants**, including La Hacienda (upscale Mexican), Marquesa (Spanish), Las Ventanas (Southwestern), Cabana Café (casual poolside dining) and The Grill (steaks, seafood and oyster bar); full bar service; several indoor and patio lounges.

THE SOUTHEASTERN SUBURBS

Tempe, Mesa and Chandler, the Phoenix neighbors to the southeast, comprise much of the Valley of the Sun's population, with a combined total of more than half a million. Mesa, with 288,000 residents, is Arizona's third largest city, after Phoenix and Tucson. Mostly residential communities, these aren't major tourist destinations. However, Tempe boasts the fine Arizona State University, with several on-campus attractions. Tempe and Mesa have a few other lures that are worth a peek.

Tempe

Elevation: 1,105 feet　　　　　　　　**Population: 150,000**

ASU dominates both the cultural and economic life of this fast-growing suburb. More than 70 percent of Tempe's residents are college-educated, and the large campus functions as the area's cultural center.

The town began life in 1872 when Charles Trumbull Hayden opened a general store and flour mill on the banks of the Salt River. He called the place Hayden's Ferry. Darrel Duppa—who had named Phoenix—commented in 1878 that this area resembled the Vale of Tempe in Thessaly, Greece, and the name took hold. Many of the town's early buildings, including Hayden's home, have been preserved in the Old Town section near the ASU campus. The look is a pleasant mix of contemporary and Western rustic, with palm-lined streets and shaded sidewalks.

Mesa

Mesa elevation: 1,225 feet　　　　　　**Population: 288,000**

A group of Mormons settled on a bluff above the Salt River in 1877 and named their village for the Spanish word for plateau—*mesa*. Like the pioneers of neighboring Phoenix, they cleaned out old Hohokam canals and soon had a thriving farming community. However, they had no idea how much it would thrive. During the Valley of the Sun's feverish surge from 1983 to 1987, it was one of the fastest growing cities in America. It's an attractive residential community with Spanish colonnade sidewalks and brick crosswalks downtown. Orange trees and palms line its streets.

Tucked under Tempe and Mesa is **Chandler,** with a population of 90,000-plus and climbing. The town was founded in 1887, shortly after Canadian-born Dr. Alexander Chandler arrived to serve as Arizona's territorial veterinarian. He became more interested land development and had the first irrigation canal dug from the Salt River through present-day Mesa. He went on to establish a resort, bank and other properties. The town today has an historical museum (listed below), but no other tourist lures of note.

DRIVING TEMPE-MESA

Tempe shares Papago Park with Phoenix and Scottsdale, so it's a logical place to begin a driving tour. (Items marked with a ■ are described in more detail below, under "Attractions.") If you're heading south on the Beeline Highway from Fountain Hills, turn west onto McDowell Road, follow it to Galvin Parkway, go south through the park and then go southeast on Van Buren, which becomes Tempe's North Mill Avenue. Coming from Phoenix, head east on Van Buren until it curves southeast into Mill Avenue.

Follow Mill southward and then go left on Curry Road. You'll shortly see, on your left, the new brick ■ **Arizona Historical Society Museum,** at Curry and College. Return to Mill Avenue and continue south, crossing the dry bed of the Salt River. You'll see—within half a mile—Tempe Beach Park on your left, which houses the ■ **Tempe Arts Center.** Just beyond, you pass through attractive and prim downtown Tempe with tree lined streets, sidewalk cafés and prim shops. You may want to park and stroll about this prosperous, nicely manicured city center.

As Mill Avenue crosses University Drive, it skims the western edge of the large ■ **Arizona State University** campus. Stay to the left and curve around onto Apache Boulevard, passing the dramatic Frank Lloyd Wright designed Grady Gammage Auditorium. Several blocks beyond, at the juncture of Apache and Rural Road, you'll see the **ASU Visitor Information Center** in a squat geodesic dome on your left. Here you can pick up campus maps and information on what's happening at Arizona's largest university.

Now, head a mile and a half miles south on Rural Road to Southern Avenue for the ■ **Tempe Historical Museum.** Swing west and follow Southern two miles to Priest Drive and the Victorian ■ **Niels Peterson House.** (Note: Its hours are limited so you may not want to make the drive if it's closed; see listing below.) Return to Apache Boulevard and continue east. At some point (we missed the sign), you enter **Mesa** and the route becomes Main Street. While this is a long stretch, it's fairly fast since signals are widely spaced—about half a mile apart—and timed to traffic. Mesa, while not at all shabby, is a low rise scatter that doesn't quite have the prosperous look of neighbor Tempe.

After about five miles, you'll cross a major intersection at Country Club Road. Two blocks later, turn left onto Robson Drive and you'll see the ■ **Arizona Museum for Youth.** Go another block, turn right onto West First Street and you'll immediately spy the excellent ■ **Mesa Southwest Museum** at First and MacDonald. Should you want to learn more about these Phoenix suburbs, go another block to Center, turn left for the **Mesa Con-**

vention and Visitors Bureau at 120 Center. It's open weekdays 8 to 5; (602) 969-1307.

Press eastward on Mesa's Main Street, shortly passing the ■ **Arizona Temple and Visitor Center** of the Mormon Church; it sits below a large swatch of green on your right, just beyond the Mesa Drive intersection. Backtrack to Mesa and go north 2.5 miles to McKellips Road. Go left on McKellips for half a mile, and then take North Horne Road three blocks north to the ■ **Mesa Historical Museum** on the old Crismon Farm. Return to McKellips and head east. Mesa's outskirts finally begin to thin, giving way to orange groves—although some of the new subdivisions have been chopped into the groves, saving a few trees for landscaping. After about four miles, you'll reach the southwest corner of Falcon airfield at McKellips and Greenfield Road. Turn left onto Greenfield and then take a quick right turn into the first of two aviation museums.

The ■ **Confederate Air Force Museum** preserves several World War II military aircraft. After checking them out, return to McKellips, go east briefly and turn left into the airport for the ■ **Champlin Fighter Museum** on Fighter Aces Drive. From here, go east briefly on McKellips and then take Higley Road south, back to Main Street. Press eastward briefly, watching on your right for ■ **Buckhorn Mineral Wells,** just short of Rucker Road.

And so this long trek through Tempe-Mesa suburbia finally ends. From here, you can backtrack to Higley, go south to the Superstition Freeway for a quick return to Phoenix, or press eastward into the Apache Junction-Roosevelt Dam tour in the next chapter.

ATTRACTIONS
Tempe and Mesa, in order of appearance

☺ *Arizona Historical Society Museum* ● *1300 N. College Ave., Tempe, AZ 85281; (602) 929-0292. Weekdays 9 to 4, Saturday 10 to 4 and Sunday noon to 4; free.* ☐ Opened in 1996, this elegant facility captures Arizona's yesterdays, from the coming of the Spanish, the Mexican era, cowboys and bad guys to the 20th century irrigation projects that blossomed the desert. The structure is built around a sunny courtyard and gurgling stream, with exhibits featuring "The Apache Trail" and "Water—Lifeline of the Desert." Inside, the initial exhibits concern the Theodore Roosevelt dam that first brought water to Phoenix, the physical and cultural geography of central Arizona with a three-screen multimedia show, the transformation of the Salt River Valley from desert to urban oasis, and a look at the agricultural communities of the valley. Upcoming displays, which may be in place by the time you arrive, feature "healthseekers, tourists and retirees," the wartime years with pilot training and Japanese relocation camps, mining and manufacturing boomtowns, and a "Futures Lab" concerning planning for tomorrow.

Tempe Arts Center ● *Tempe Beach Park (Mill Avenue and First Street), Tempe, AZ 85282; (602) 968-0888. Tuesday-Sunday, noon to 5; free.* ☐ Works of local artists are displayed here. Modernistic shapes inhabit a sculpture garden. Most of the paintings, ceramics, sculptures, photographs and other artwork are for sale. You also can buy creative snacks.

☺ *Arizona State University Campus* ● *Visitor Center at the southeast corner of the campus, Apache and Rural Road. open weekdays 8 to 4:45; (602) 965-0100. Campus tours weekdays at 10:30 and 2; (602) 965-2604.* ☐ Green lawns and palms create a park-like setting for ASU's imposing gathering of brick buildings. The centerpiece is Wright's Gammage Center for the Performing Arts, a dramatic sandstone pink structure of circles within circles. The effect is a bit like a masonry circus tent. Start your visit by getting a campus map at the visitor center; it will direct you to parking areas as well as attractions. The open air University Tram will scoot you around. Four information booths are spotted about the campus. These attractions are worthy of a visit:

ANTHROPOLOGY MUSEUM, *north side of Tyler Mall; (602) 965-6213; weekdays 8 to 5; free.* Prehistoric and modern Indian cultures are the focus.

ARIZONA UNIVERSITY ART MUSEUM, *second floor of Matthews Center; (602) 965-2874; Wednesday-Saturday 10 to 5, Sunday 1 to 5.* The ASU art museum displays paintings, ceramics, statuary and other artwork from the Americas and Europe.

GALLERY OF DESIGN, *in the College of Architecture and Environmental Design building; (602) 965-3216; weekdays 8 to 5; free.* The gallery offers drawings and scale models of current architectural trends.

GEOLOGY MUSEUM, *south of University Drive; (602) 965-5081; 10 to 1 during the school year; closed in summer; free.* Exhibits include sundry rocks and minerals, a seismograph and six-story Foucault Pendulum.

GAMMAGE CENTER FOR THE PERFORMING ARTS, *southwest corner of the campus; (602) 965-3434 for concert schedule and (602) 965-4050 for tour information.* Tours of the dramatic structure are conducted weekdays from 1 to 4 during the school year; less frequently in summer; call for times.

HARRY WOOD GALLERY, *in the School of Arts building; (602) 965-3468; weekdays 8 to 5; free.* Student artists display their work in this small gallery.

MEMORIAL UNION, *at the west end of Orange Street; (602) 965-5728. Hours vary; early morning through the evening during classes; shorter in summer.* This focal point of campus activity has an information desk where you can learn about upcoming activities, several places to eat, a campus shop, lounge and even a bowling alley and movie theater. The **MEMORIAL UNION ART GALLERY** in the building's north end is open weekdays from 8 to 8.

NORTHLIGHT GALLERY, *in Matthews Hall; (602) 965-5667. Monday-Thursday 10:30 to 4:30 and Sunday 12:30 to 4:30; closed in summer; free.* This gallery behind Matthews Center, it features changing photo exhibits.

PLANETARIUM, *in the Physical Science Center just south of University Drive; (602) 965-6891; shows $2.* Public star shows are held Tuesday and Thursday at 7:30 p.m. the school year; it's in the Physical Sciences Center. The **CENTER FOR METEORITE STUDIES** here displays rocky visitors from outer space; (602) 965-6511; weekdays 8 to 4:30; free.

Tempe Historical Museum ● *Tempe Community Center (3500 S. Rural Road at Southern Avenue), Tempe, AZ 85282; (602) 731-8842. Tuesday-Saturday 10 to 4:30; free.* ☐ Tempe's early days are preserved in this collection of farm implements, historical photos, Utensils, toys, furniture and clothing. Exhibits include a Model-T fire truck, post office and a prairie schooner.

Niels Peterson House ● *1414 W. Southern Ave. (Priest Drive), Tempe, AZ 85282; (602) 350-5151 or 350-1500. Tuesday through Thursday and Saturday 10 to 2; free.* ☐ This red brick Queen Anne Victorian with a distinctive eyebrow cupola was built in 1892, although the interior is furnished in a 1930s style. Niels Peterson was a Danish immigrant who homesteaded land here in 1872.

Arizona Museum for Youth • *35 N. Robson St. (Main Street), Mesa, AZ 85201; (602) 644-2647. Tuesday-Friday 9 to 5; Saturday 10 to 5 and Sunday 1 to 5 in summer; Tuesday-Friday and Sunday 1 to 5 and Saturday 10 to 5 the rest of the year.* ☐ Aimed at the grade school set, this museum is a hands on center that stirs children's interest in the fine arts. Displays are changed several times a year. (It's sometimes temporarily closed for new exhibit installation, so call first.) It also features child-oriented art displays and craft classes.

☺ *Mesa Southwest Museum* • *53 N. MacDonald St. (First Street), Mesa, AZ 85201 (602) 644-2230 or 644-2169. Tuesday-Saturday 10 to 5, Sunday 1 to 5. Adults $4, seniors $3.50 and kids under 3 to 12, $2.* ☐ This fine City of Mesa museum effectively captures the area's history, from the mysteries of the vanished Hohokam Indians to the legend of the Lost Dutchman Mine. It's housed in an attractive Spanish style structure surrounded by landscaped gardens

Among the professionally done exhibits are "Dinosaurs of the Southwest" with an animated *triceratops* and other models and fossil specimens; Indian artifacts and reconstructions of their dwellings using native materials; and elements from Mesa's past. The garden shelters several outdoor exhibits, including an adobe schoolhouse, 1890s territorial jail, covered wagon and a stagecoach. You can pan for gold outside and shop for books and souvenirs in the gift shop. Kids have fun trying to break the code and find the Lost Dutchman mine.

Arizona Temple and Visitor Center • *525 E. Main St. (near Mesa Drive), Tempe, AZ 85203; (602) 964-7164. Daily 9 to 9; one-hour tours on the hour and half-hour. Free.* ☐ Mesa's Mormon founders built this striking temple in a landscaped park in 1927. It's still the town's most noted landmark— a low-rise granite structure that more resembles a government center than a religious bastion. Visitors can tour the well-tended grounds and the visitor center with its biblical murals and five-ton marble Christ statue. A frankly religious pitch is delivered through movies and displays. If you want to learn more, the good brothers and sisters will haul out more information. Only the faithful can enter the temple itself.

Mesa Historical Museum • *2345 N. Horne St. (Lehi Road), Mesa, AZ 85201; (602) 835-7358. Thursday-Saturday 10 to 4; closed in summer. Adults $3, seniors $2 and kids $1.* ☐ Housed in a large 1913 schoolhouse, this busy museum exhibits antique farm machinery, a country store, grist mill, turn of the century wedding gowns and other Mesa memorabilia. Murals in the old school auditorium portray the valley's settlement from Native American societies to the coming of the Mormons, Asians, African Americans and others.

☺ *Confederate Air Force Museum* • *2017 McKellips Road; (602) 924-1940 or (602) 981-1945. Daily 10 to 4. Adults $5, kids $2.* ☐ Arizona's Confederate Air Force, made up of World War II pilots and younger men with an interest in flying, is devoted to collecting, restoring and flying military aircraft of that war. Their collection, while not large, is impressive. Star of the show is the airworthy *Sentimental Journey,* a Flying Fortress with a leggy Betty Grable adorning its fuselage. You can crawl through its tight tin-can innards and wonder what it must have been like to be strapped into one of these things in an air raid over Germany. Equally interesting is a rare German Heinkel HE-111 two-engine medium bomber. It also can be toured. Other members of the collection are a couple of C-47 Skymaster transports, a Grumman AF-2S submarine killer and a pair of training planes.

☺ **Champlin Fighter Museum** ● 4636 Fighter Aces Dr. (Falcon Field, off McKellips Road), Mesa, AZ 85205; (602) 830-4540. Daily 10 to 5. Adults $6.50, kids 5 to 12, $3. ☐ Snoopy would love this place. You can fantasize dogfights with the Red Baron and other aces at this impressive gathering of fighter planes from both world wars, Korea, Vietnam and Desert Storm. Thirty-three planes, either restored originals or airworthy replicas, seem ready to take off into the wild blue yonder. Our favorite is the world's first combat aircraft—a 1914 German Rumpler Taube fabric-winged observation plane. It streaked along at 74 miles an hour and carried only four hours of fuel. The pilot's only weapons were hand-lobbed grenades.

Others in the collection are a Fokker tri-plane, Sopwith Camel, Russian MIG-21, Focke Wulf 190D and one of those legendary Nationalist Chinese P-40 Flying Tigers with shark's teeth painted on its cowling. The museum has thousands of other bits of aviation memorabilia—weapons, flight gear, medals and oil paintings of fighters in action. More than 700 autographed photos paper the "Hall of Aces," honoring the world's top fighter pilots. Combat films recall those dangerously romantic days when men with flying scarves and nerves of steel fought to the death in the heavens.

Buckhorn Mineral Wells ● 5900 E. Main St. (Recker Road), Mesa, AZ 85205; (602) 832-1111. Museum and baths open Tuesday-Saturday 9 to 5. Museum admission $4 for adults and $2 for kids; mineral baths, $15; Swedish massage $25. ☐ You can soak your cares away in hot mineral pools, then wander through a museum of 400 stuffed animals in this health spa, seven miles east of downtown Mesa. Also, you can spend the night in rustic housekeeping units for $45.

Not on the tour route

Chandler Museum ● 178 E. Commonwealth Avenue in downtown Chandler (off Arizona Place, between Buffalo and Boston streets); (602) 786-2842. Monday-Saturday 11 to 4; closed in summer; free. ☐ This museum recalls the days when Dr. Chandler came here late in the last century to establish this fast growing community. Exhibits include a scale model of Chandler's downtown plaza, farming and ranching regalia and mockups of historic buildings.

WHERE TO DINE
Mesa
☺ **The Landmark Restaurant** ● ☆☆☆ $$

☐ 809 W. Main St. (Extension Street); (602) 962-4652. Midwestern American; full bar service. Lunch Monday-Friday 11 to 2, dinner Monday-Saturday 4 to 9 and Sunday noon to 7. Major credit cards. ☐ Old fashioned restaurant in a former Mormon church, furnished with Victorian antiques. It serves such home style fare as meatloaf, chicken pot pie, roast turkey and—good grief!—even chicken fried steak. Tasty homemade desserts.

The Olive Garden ● ☆☆ $$

☐ 1261 W. Southern (west of Alma School Road, near Fiesta Mall); (602) 890-0440. Italian; full bar service. Sunday-Thursday 11 a.m. to 10 p.m., Friday-Saturday 11 to 11. ☐ Typical Italian entrées plus combination platters; free refills on soup, salad and beverages.

Rockin' R Ranch ● ☆☆ $$

☐ 6136 E. Baseline Rd. (half mile west of Power Rd.); (602) 832-1539. "Chuck wagon" supper with Western stage show; no alcohol. Scheduled dinner *and show; call for times. Major credit cards.* ❏ Western style chuckwagon dinner with barbecued beef or chicken, baked potato, beans, biscuits and dessert; cowboy music and entertainment follows. Also, a "frontier town" with gift and Western shops.

☺ *Romeo's Euro Café* ● ☆☆ $$

❏ *1111 S. Longmore, Mesa; (602) 962-4224. Mediterranean- international; wine and beer. Monday-Thursday 11 to 11, Friday-Saturday 11 to midnight, Sunday 11 to 10. Major credit cards.* ❏ Lively art-filled bistro, with adjoining Undici-Undici art gallery, coffee house and collectibles shop. The eclectic menu is European with spicy Mediterranean accents, with seafood, eggplant and lamb dishes, plus creative pizza and calzone. Live rock, blues, jazz or folk music Friday-Saturday nights; changing exhibits in the gallery.

Tempe

Garcia's ● ☆☆ $

❏ *1604 S. Southern Ave. (McClintock); (602) 820-0400. Mexican; full bar service. Sunday-Thursday 11 to 10, Friday- Saturday 11 to 11. Major credit cards.* ❏ Cheerful Latin place with strolling mariachis; typical Mexican menu.

Manuel's Mexican Food ☆☆ $

❏ *1123 W. Broadway; (602) 968-4437. Mexican; wine and beer. Daily 11 a.m. to 11 p.m. Major credit cards.* ❏ Family-owned business serving Mexican food for 30 years; typical *Latino* menu and a couple of American dishes.

Ming's Restaurant ☆☆ $

❏ *3300 S. Mill Ave. (Southern Avenue); (602) 966-6464. Chinese; wine and beer. Daily 11:30 a.m. to 10 p.m. Major credit cards.* ❏ A mix of Cantonese and Mandarin styles; specials include Peking duck, lemon chicken and garlic shrimp.

WHERE TO RECLINE

Prices reflect high season rates and may be lower at other times. (In Sunbelt areas, prices can drop by more than half in summer.) Most were provided by the management and are subject to change; use them only as a guide.

Mesa-Chandler

Arizona Golf Resort ● ☆☆☆☆ $$$$$ ∅

❏ *425 S. Power Rd. (a mile north of Freeway 360), Mesa, AZ 85206; (800) 528-8282 or (602) 832-3202. Couples $175 to $205, singles $155 to $185. Major credit cards.* ❏ Appealing 186-room resort with TV, phones, refrigerators, microwaves and coffee makers; private patios. Golf course, fitness center, pool, spa, tennis courts, gift shop, coin laundry, bicycles, basketball, volleyball, croquet and bicycles. Three **restaurants**—Sunrise Café, Annabelle's and Anna's Grill; food service 7 a.m. to 10 p.m.; prime rib, seafood and Southwest cuisine; dinners $11 to $16; full bar service.

Mesa Pavilion Hilton ● ☆☆☆ $$$$ ∅

1011 W. Holmes Ave. (off Highway 60, exit Alma School Road), Mesa, AZ 85202; (602) 833-5555 or (800) 445-8667. Couples and singles $75 to $122; suites $89 to $139. Major credit cards. ❏ Imposing atrium style resort hotel; 262 rooms with TV movies, phones and refrigerators; pool, gift shop, styling salon; golf adjacent. **Zuni Grill** serves 6:30 a.m. to 10 p.m., continental and Southwestern fare, fresh seafood; full bar service.

Holiday Inn Mesa ● ☆☆☆ $$$$ Ø

□ *1600 S. Country Club Dr. (Off Freeway 360), Mesa, AZ 85210; (602) 964-7000 or (800) 999-MESA. Couples $79 to $99, singles $69 to $89. Major credit cards.* □ A 246-room inn with TV movies, phones, wet bars and mini bars, refrigerators; indoor-outdoor pool, sauna, spa, lounge with entertainment. **Restaurant** serves 6 a.m. to 10 p.m.; dinners $9 to $17; full bar.

Wyndham Garden Hotel-Chandler ● ☆☆☆ $$$$ Ø

□ *7475 W. Chandler Blvd. (exit 160 off I-10), Chandler, AZ 85226; (602) 961-4444 or (800) WYNDHAM. Couples $84 to $139, singles $74 to $129; rates include buffet breakfast. Major credit cards.* □ A 159-room courtyard hotel with TV, phones and in-room coffee; pool, spa, fitness room, coin laundry, hearthside lounge. **Garden Café** serves 6:30 to 2 and 5 to 10; American-continental; dinners $8 to $25; full bar service.

Sheraton Mesa Hotel ● ☆☆☆ $$$$ Ø

□ *200 N. Centennial Way (downtown area), Mesa, AZ 85201; (800) 456-6372 or (602) 898-8300. Couples and singles $90 to $140, suites $110 to $250. Major credit cards.* □ Luxuriant 271-room hotel with a landscaped courtyard; TV movies, mini bars and phones. Pool and spa in courtyard; concierge floor. Two **restaurants**––Quail Run (American-continental) and Dos Lobos Cantina (Mexican); dinners $7 to $20; food service 6 to 10; breakfast buffet and Sunday brunch; full bar service.

Sheraton San Marcos Golf Resort ● ☆☆☆☆ $$$$$ Ø

□ *One San Marcos Place (7 miles south of I-10 on State Highway 87), Chandler, AZ 85224; (602) 963-6655 or (800) 325-3535. Couples and singles $120 to $215. Major credit cards.* □ Nicely restored 1912 resort on 123 acres with an 18-hole golf course, tennis courts, swimming pools and spas and workout rooms. Three **restaurants** and two lounges. Dinners $6 to $35 at A.J.'s Café, Nineteen Twelve and Mulligan's; 6 a.m. to 10 p.m.; full bar.

Tempe

☺ The Buttes ● ☆☆☆☆ $$$$$ Ø

□ *2000 Westcourt Way (south of 48th and Broadway), Tempe, AZ 85281; (602) 225-9000 or (800) 843-1986. Couples and singles $215, suites $300 to $475. Major credit cards.* □ Strikingly modern resort built onto a 25-acre mountaintop site; some rooms and dining rooms have panoramic views of the Valley of the Sun. TV movies, VCRs, stocked refrigerators, hair dryers and other amenities. Pool, spa, saunas, health club, tennis courts, hiking trails; golf nearby. Concierge level with added amenities. Two **restaurants**––Top of the Rock and the Market Café; food service 6 a.m. to 11 p.m.; dinners $15 to $22; indoor pond with rock waterfall; full bar service.

Comfort Inn Tempe ● ☆☆ $$$ Ø

□ *5300 S. 56th St. (Baseline Road), Tempe, AZ 85283; (602) 820-7500 or (800) 221-2222. Couples $55 to $80, singles $50 to $65. Major credit cards.* □ A 160-room motel with TV movies and phones, some refrigerators; pool, spa and lounge.

Fiesta Inn ● ☆☆☆ $$$$ Ø

□ *2100 S. Priest Dr. (Broadway exit from I-10), Tempe, AZ 85282; (602) 967-1441 or (800) 528-6481. Couples and singles $75 to $150, suites $150 to $275. Major credit cards.* □ TV movies, phones, refrigerators and hair dryers; pool, spa, sauna, tennis, lighted golf practice range, exercise room. **Dale An-**

derson's Other Place serves 6:30 a.m. to 10 p.m.; dinners $10 to $26; Southwestern décor; full bar service.

Holiday Inn ● ☆☆☆ $$$$ Ø

◻ *915 E. Apache Blvd. (Scottsdale Road), Tempe, AZ 85281; (602) 968-3451 or (800) HOLIDAY. Couples and singles $94 to $124, suites $186. Major credit cards.* ◻ A 190-room inn with TV movies, phones, stocked refrigerators; many balconies or patios. Pool, fitness center, hot tub. **Ducks Sports Lounge & Grill** serves 6 a.m. to 10 p.m.; dinners $6 to $13; full bar.

Ramada Plaza Hotel Sky Harbor ● ☆☆☆ $$$$$ Ø

◻ *1600 S. 52nd St. (Broadway exit off I-10), Tempe, AZ 85283; (602) 967-6600. Couples and singles $120 to $159. Major credit cards.* ◻ A 213-room hotel with TV movies, multiple phones and in-room coffee, some refrigerators; pool. **Restaurant** serves 6 a.m. to 10 p.m.; dinners $9 to $15; full bar service.

Tempe Motel ● ☆☆ $$$

◻ *947 E. Apache Blvd. (near ASU), Tempe, AZ 85381; (602) 894-0909. Couples $45 to $125; singles $40 to $115. Major credit cards.* ◻ A 38-unit motel with TV movies and phones; coin laundry.

WHERE TO CAMP
Tempe-Mesa

Apache Palms RV Park ● *1836 E. Apache Blvd. (McClintock), Mesa, AZ 85281; (602) 966-7399. RV sites, full hookups $20. Reservations accepted; MC/VISA, DISC.* ◻ A 72-site park with showers, coin laundry, dump station. Pool and spa; RV supply and repair nearby.

Green Acres RV Park I ● *2055 W. Main St. (Dobson), Mesa, AZ 85201; (602) 964-5058. RV sites, full hookups $16.20; no credit cards.* ◻ Showers, coin laundry, dump station. Family and adult sections available; pool and spa. RV supply and repair nearby.

Green Acres RV Park III ● *1890 E. Apache Blvd. (two miles north on McClintock from Highway 360), Tempe, AZ 85281; (602) 829-0106. RV sites, full hookups $16.20; no credit cards.* ◻ Pull-throughs; showers, coin laundry, dump station; RV supply and repair nearby.

THE LOST DUTCHMAN

Chapter eight

PHOENIX NEIGHBORS
Out Wickenburg Way; into the Superstitions

THE PHOENIX SUBURBS stretch to the edges of the Salt River Valley, then give way to open desert and rocky, low hills. In sharp contrast to the Phoenix megalopolis, surrounding communities are small and scattered. This chapter takes you in three directions from the Valley of the Sun to visit these neighboring communities.

First, if you take Horace Greeley's advice and go west—well, northwest from Phoenix—you'll encounter that most Western town of all, Wickenburg. Driving east of Mesa, you climb into the rough lowlands of the Superstition Mountains, home to the legendary Lost Dutchman Mine. A loop through Apache Junction, rugged Salt River Canyon and back through the copper towns of Globe, Miami and Superior is a popular scenic drive—although bumpy through the canyon.

Heading south on State Route 79, you'll encounter one of Arizona's oldest communities at Florence, take brief side trips to Casa Grande National Monument and the Gila Indian community, and then continue south through the desert gardens of the Pinal Pioneer Parkway. Just short of Tucson, we'll suggest a stop at a place that's anchored to the earth but, in a sense, is out of this world—Biosphere 2.

TRIP PLANNER

WHEN TO GO ● Like Phoenix, most nearby communities are primarily spring-winter-fall destinations. Wickenburg to the northwest is famous for its dude ranches. To the east, Apache Junction attracts around 35,000 Snow-birds each winter. Get reservations early during peak season for both areas. Florence is an appealing historic center and Casa Grande, named for a huge pueblo that's closer to Coolidge, is a handy provisioning stop between Phoe-nix and Tucson and a growing retirement community.

WHAT TO SEE ● Desert Caballeros Western Museum in Wickenburg, Goldfield ghost town near Apache Junction, Tonto National Monument above Roosevelt Lake, McFarland State Historic Park in Florence, Casa Grande Ru-ins National Monument near Coolidge, Gila River Arts and Crafts Center near Sacaton and Biosphere 2 north of Catalina.

WHAT TO DO ● Go west on a dude ranch near Wickenburg and walk the riparian trails of Hassayampa River Preserve, hike into the wilderness of leg-endary Superstition Mountain, drive the beautiful if bumpy Salt River Canyon from Tortilla Flat to Roosevelt Dam, explore old town Florence, walk the de-sert garden trails of Boyce Thompson Arboretum State Park, hike to the top of Picacho Peak and enjoy the desert vistas along Pinal Pioneer Parkway.

☺ ***Indicates an attraction, restaurant or lodging with special appeal.***

USEFUL CONTACTS

Apache Junction Chamber of Commerce, P.O. Box 1747 (1001 N. Idaho Rd.), Apache Junction, AZ 85217; (602) 982-3141.

Greater Florence Chamber of Commerce, P.O. Box 929, Florence, AZ 85232; (520) 868-9433.

Gila River Indian Community, P.O. Box 457, Sacaton, AZ 85247; (520) 836-8178.

Greater Casa Grande Chamber of Commerce, 575 N. Marshall, Casa Grande, AZ 85222; (520) 836-2125.

Pinal County Visitor Center, 135 N. Pinal St., Florence, AZ 85232; (520) 868-9433.

Tonto National Forest, 2324 E. McDowell Rd., Phoenix, AZ 85010; (520) 225-5200.

Tonto National Monument, HC02, Box 4602, Roosevelt, AZ 85545; (520) 467-2241.

Wickenburg Chamber of Commerce, P.O. Drawer CC (Sante Fe depot at 215 Old Railroad St.), Wickenburg, AZ 85358; (520) 684-5479.

AREA RADIO STATIONS

KTIM-AM, 1250, Wickenburg—Big band sounds, old favorites
KTIM-FM, 105.3, Wickenburg—Big band sounds, old favorites
Also see Phoenix listings in previous chapter and Globe-Miami listings in Chapter twelve.

OUT WICKENBURG WAY

U.S. 60 runs northwest out of Phoenix at an odd angle. It brushes past the growing communities of Glendale, Peoria, Sun City and Youngtown, and then heads into the desert. Expect to hit a lot of suburbs and stop lights, al-though the route is reasonably fast, with the lights timed to through traffic.

In Peoria, Olive Avenue leads 13 west miles to **White Tank Regional Park,** a striking desert-mountain wilderness area which we covered under "The outdoor thing" in the previous chapter on page 197. If you haven't been there yet, this is as close as you'll get. Otherwise, continue northeast through a string of suburban communities, occupied mostly by contented retirees.

Some people think Del Webb invented the retirement community with the creation of Sun City in 1948. But Youngtown came first, opening in October, 1954. Sun City is now the largest, however, with a population topping 54,000; nearby Sun City West has about 14,500. A third Webb pension farm, Sun City Vistoso near Tucson, opened in 1987.

Beyond Sun City West, the final metro Phoenix suburbs surrender to creosote bush desert. The highway then gains altitude as it climbs into the rugged and saguaro-studded Vulture Mountains. As you approach Wickenburg, you'll see the entrance to the **Hassayampa River Preserve.** Three miles beyond that, you're greeted by a sign exclaiming: "Howdy! You're Out Wickenburg Way!"

Wickenburg

Elevation: 2,093 feet   **Population: 4,500**

I'll be danged if this ain't the cutest little cowboy town in Arizona. Wickenburg works at being Western, with balconied store fronts, boardwalks and a friendly down-home attitude. "Tie up, come in and swap stories," invites a sign outside Ben's Saddlery. The town calls itself the dude ranch capital of the world, and real cowboys still ride herd in the surrounding high desert.

Gold, not beef, put the town on the map. In 1862, an Austrian named Henry Wickenburg hitched his hopes to an ornery burro and began prospecting in the nearby hills. He struck it rich with the Vulture Mine. Some say he picked up a rock to throw at a vulture, or at his stubborn mule—and the rock was veined with gold. Either version of the story sounds like campfire talk. But one truth is undeniable: Gold mines in the area yielded $30 million between the 1860s and 1900. Miners needed water to wash their diggin's, so they settled along the Hassayampa River and Wickenburg was born.

Ore from 80 mines poured into town, along with the usual ration of drifters, rascals and fallen angels. At its prime, Wickenburg was the third largest city in Arizona, and one of the wildest. Folks were too busy seeking gold to build a jail, so they simply chained the bad guys to a large mesquite tree. During visiting hours, prisoners' relatives would come out and have a picnic. The tree still stands, at Tegner Street and Wickenburg Way.

As the mines played out, cattlemen began running their herds in the brushy desert. Easterners, reading newspaper reports and dime novels about the Wild West, came out to see what all the excitement was about. Dude ranching, born in Montana, quickly spread to Arizona. Wickenburg and Tucson were early dude ranch centers, and they still are. Nowadays, of course, folks call them guest ranches.

Wickenburg's downtown area is small, covering only a few blocks and it's all cutely Western. False-front stores tempt visitors with cowboy clothing, Indian crafts and curios. The town also has a few antique stores and several galleries sell paintings, sculptures and ceramics; most have Western themes. Tourism has replaced gold and cattle as the town's reason for being. Indeed, 80 percent of Wickenburg's jobs are directly tied to visitor services. Thus, you will find a surprisingly large assortment of restaurants and motels for such a small community.

Coming into town on Highway 60, which becomes Wickenburg Way, you'll hit a stop light opposite an underpass, where Route 60 goes left and U.S. 83 goes to the right. (The cross street is Tegner.) Veer slightly to the right, avoiding the underpass, and you'll wind up beside the excellent **De-**

Phoenix Neighbors

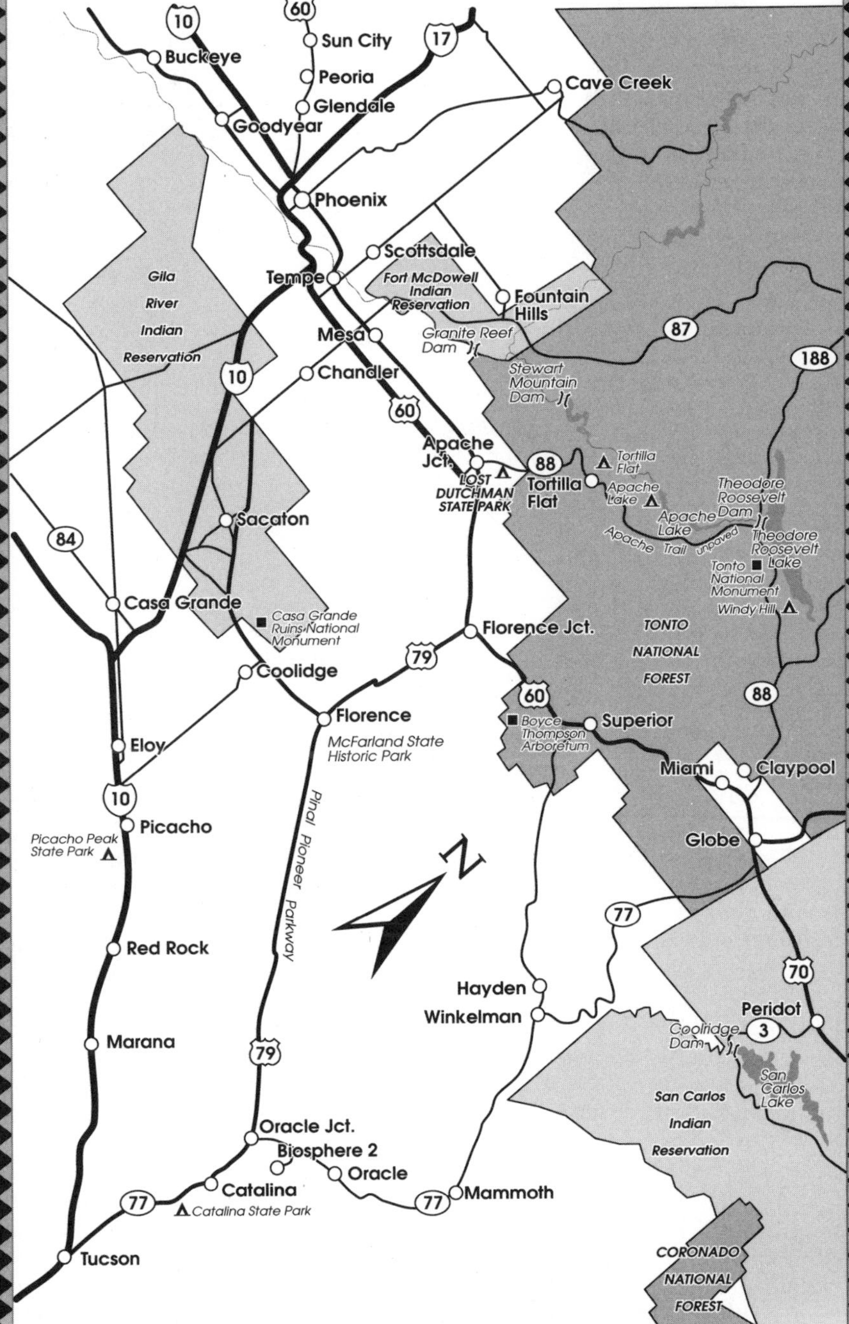

sert **Caballeros Western Museum**. From the museum, turn right onto Old Railroad Street (formerly Frontier Street), go two blocks and you'll encounter the **Wickenburg Chamber of Commerce**. It occupies the restored 1895 Santa Fe Railway depot at 215 Old Railroad Street. In addition to numerous brochures, you can pick up a walking tour map and stroll past an assortment of turn-of-the-century homes and stores. The chamber is open weekdays 9 to 5, and on weekends from October to May; (520) 684-5479

The depot itself is worth a look. Note the old Railway Express baggage cart on the loading dock, now carrying a cargo of potted plants. Another point of interest in town is the **Old Wishing Well** near the highway bridge crossing the Hassayampa River. The funny name is Apache for "up-side down river," since most of the flow through here is beneath its dry sands. A sign warns that anyone drinking from the well will never be able to tell the truth. Why? During Wickenburg's wicked mining era when fiction flew thick and fast, a tall story was called a "Hassayamper."

ATTRACTIONS AND ACTIVITIES

Hassayampa River Preserve ● *West side of Highway 60/93, three miles southeast town (P.O. Box 1162), Wickenburg, AZ 85358; (520) 684-2772. Wednesday-Sunday 8 to 5 from mid-September to mid-May and 6 to noon the rest of the year. Suggested donation $5.* ☐ This is a fine example of a riparian woodland along the course of the Hassayampa, which flows above ground in this area. Once a stage stop and guest ranch, it was opened as a preserve in 1987 by the Nature Conservancy. The old ranch house is now a natural history museum, library and bookstore. Self-guided nature trails take you along the lush river bottom, where the Hassayampa supports a rich plant and animal habitat. It's a great place for bird-watching, and a fine place to picnic; there are several tables along the stream. Free guided nature walks are conducted periodically; call for dates and times.

☺ **Desert Caballeros Western Museum** ● *21 Old Railroad St. (at Wickenburg Way), Wickenburg, AZ 85358; (520) 684-2272. Monday-Saturday 10 to 4, Sunday 1 to 4. Adults $4, seniors $3.50, kids $1.* ☐ The local branch of the Maricopa County Historical Society has done an outstanding job of preserving Wickenburg's lively past. Instead of a clutter of high-button shoes and butter churns, the Desert Caballeros Western Museum features a full-scale turn-of-the-century street scene to capture that yesterday feeling. In the museum's Hall of History, dioramas and artifacts recall the area's development from the Paleozoic to the present. Other exhibits include a mineral collection, Indian arts and crafts, and rooms with period furnishings. An adjoining gallery, with Western art by such notables as Russell, Remington and Catlin, would be the envy of a major metropolitan museum.

There's more to see outside. A stagecoach sits on the porch of this handsome adobe-sandstone structure. Bits of Arizona history are captured in ceramic wall plaques. A large bronze statue of a kneeling cowboy and his horse, entitled "Thanks for the rain," occupies a landscaped cactus garden.

Hiking ● *See "Guide to Hiking in the Wickenburg Area" brochure, available at the Chamber of Commerce.* ☐ This brochure, prepared by a naturalist, directs you to four hikes in the area. You can walk the extensive grounds of the venerable Wickenburg Inn and visit its nature center, explore the Hassayampa River Preserve, trek into Box Canyon northwest of town and walk about the Vulture Peak area where old Henry struck it rich.

WHAT IN TARNATION IS A COWBOY, ANYHOW?

Nothing has captured the world's fancy quite so much as the American cowboy. Folks from around the country—and the globe—are lured to Arizona guest ranches to stuff themselves into blue denims, sit tall in the saddle and eat beef and beans around a campfire. Of course, most ranches offer swimming pools and other amenities, so greenhorns can play cowboy in comfort.

Although he's considered an American institution, the cowboy has his roots in Mexico. And the "cowboy era"—which endures in books, movies, TV shows and in romantic hearts—lasted less than 25 years.

Gold, not cattle, lured the first flood of settlers to the American West. When California's Forty-niners and Arizona's argonauts arrived in the mid-1800s, they'd never heard of ten- gallon hats, lassos or blue denims.

As gold played out in the 1870s, some pioneers began running cattle and sheep. Those early ranchers marveled at the skill of Mexico's *vaqueros*, who could catch a running steer with a length of braided rawhide called a *riata*. Their saddles had high backs to help them keep their seats, and snubbing horns for their rawhide ropes. The *vaqueros* wore broad-brimmed *sombreros* for sun shelter and leather leggings—or "chaps"—as protection from scratchy *chap*arral. These outfits made sense, so the gringos adopted them.

To reach Eastern markets, livestock had to be herded to northern railheads, and the romance of the great cattle drives was born. Yes, cowboys *did* sing to calm the spooky critters at night—and they were probably terribly off-key.

Spreading railroads soon eliminated the need for cattle drives, and straight-shooting marshals eliminated most of the bad guys in rowdy Western towns. Settlers fenced in much of the open range. By the 1890s, the era of cattle drives and range wars was over. The beef you barbecue today probably came from a feedlot.

What about those blue denims, which are *de rigueur* for every cowboy from Tucson to Tinseltown? Well, dang my britches, they weren't even produced until 1874, well after the "cowboy period" had begun. Levi Strauss made his first jeans from gray tent canvas, and they were for California gold miners, not Arizona cowpokes. When he did begin producing his famous blue "Levi's," he obtained the fabric from Nimes, France, and it became known as *serge de Nimes,* eventually shorted to *denim*.

Ghost town prowling ● *See "Out Wickenburg Way" booklet published by the Chamber of Commerce.* ☐ Remnants of four ghost towns survive in the rough hills around Wickenburg. A chamber of commerce booklet tells you about them: **Weaver**, first a mining camp and then a hangout for bad guys; **Stanton**, now a privately owned town, once run by a notorious defrocked priest; **Octave**, which yielded $8 million from its deep pit quartz vein; and **Congress**, with only a tailing dump surviving from its glory years, when it yielded $1 million in gold. **Wickenburg Desert Jeep Tours** books outings to some of these ghost towns, plus other trips into the surrounding wilds; (800) 596-JEEP or (520) 684-0438. The Vulture Mine headframe and outbuildings still stand outside of Wickenburg, but it's privately owned and off limits to visitors.

Geologists say only 10 percent of the area's gold has been mined; the rest lies hidden underground. Recreational panning is still popular. The best place to find gold is in an alluvial fan at the base of a hillside ravine. Like the miners of old, you'll have to carry your diggin's to water to separate the gold.

Robson's Mining World ● *P.O. Box M2, Wickenburg, AZ 85358; (520) 685-2609. To reach it, drive 14 miles northwest of Wickenburg on U.S. 93 and then go about 12 miles southwest on State Route 71; look for the turnoff near Milepost 90, at the Maricopa-Yavapai county line.* ☐ Several old buildings and tons of antique mining equipment have been assembled at a former mining camp to create a "typical" ghost town and mining exhibit. A working blacksmith shop, generating plant, print shop, post office, livery stable and general store stand along Main Street. Several homes of early miners are being restored and furnished to the turn of the century, when mining was active in the area. A restaurant and bed and breakfast inn are available by reservation; call before you go, since it may be closed in summer.

Joshua Forest Parkway ● *Twenty-four miles northwest on U.S. 93.* ☐ Great stands of Joshua trees, those strange fuzzy-armed desert plants, line the highway above Wickenburg. Details below, on page 239.

ANNUAL EVENTS

For information on these and other events, contact the Wickenburg Chamber of Commerce at (520) 684-5479.

Gold Rush Days, second weekend of February.

Desert Sports Festival, first weekend of August.

Four-Corner States Bluegrass Festival and Fiddle Championship, second weekend in November.

Cowboy Christmas Poets' Gathering, first weekend in December.

WHERE TO DINE

Anita's Cocina ● ☆ **$**

☐ *57 N. Valentine (off Wickenburg Way); (520) 684-5777. Mexican; wine, beer and margaritas. Daily 11 to 9.* ☐ Busy, locally popular café with simple décor and the usual beans and rice fare. Among its specialties are quesadillas, giant tostadas and a Mexican vegetarian plate.

B.A.'s Restaurant ● ☆ **$**

☐ *Downtown, on Wickenburg Way; (520) 684-5331. Eclectic menu; wine and beer. Lunch and dinner Tuesday-Friday from 11 a.m.; breakfast, lunch and dinner weekends from 8 a.m.; closed Monday. MC/VISA.* ☐ Curious looking place with simulated brick walls, pretend pressed tin ceilings and modern brass and smoked glass chandeliers. From the kitchen emerges "chicken *coq au vin*," beef papagallo and other continental and American dishes.

Charlie's Steakhouse ● ☆☆ **$$**

☐ *1187 W. Wickenburg Way (California Highway); (520) 684-2413. American; full bar service, Daily 5 to 10 p.m. MC/VISA.* ☐ Pleasantly rustic family diner featuring assorted charbroiled steaks, chicken and seafood.

Frontier Inn ● ☆☆ **$$**

☐ *430 E. Wickenburg Way; (520) 684-4419. Western style fare. Monday-Thursday 4:30 a.m. to 11 and 5 p.m. to 11, Friday-Saturday 4:30 to 11 and 5*

*to 2 a.m., Sunday 5 to noon and 5 to 11. Reservations accepted; MC/VISA,
DISC.* ☐ Knotty pine Western café featuring mesquite-cooked meats; homemade soups, sauces and pies. Popular for early-riser breakfasts.

Gold Nugget Restaurant ● ☆☆ $$

☐ *222 E. Wickenburg Way (adjacent to Best Western Rancho Grande);
(520) 684-2858. American-continental; full bar service. Daily 6 a.m. to 10
p.m. Reservations accepted; major credit cards.* ☐ Bright and cheerful place
with white wrought iron and Gay Nineties décor and live entertainment. The
busy menu features American, Italian and other European dishes.

☺ Rancho Seven Restaurant ● ☆☆ $$

☐ *Wickenburg Way at Tegner; (520) 684-2492. American-Mexican; full
bar service. Major credit cards.* ☐ Cozy and cleverly done early American
style restaurant trimmed with farm implements. The American side of the
menu is quite rural—pepper steak, beef ribs, beef liver, grilled pork chops. A
few basic Mexican entrées occupy the *Latino* side.

Wickenburg Inn ● ☆☆☆☆ $$$

☐ *Prescott Highway between Wickenburg and Congress; (520) 684-7811.
American; full bar service. Open daily; breakfast 7 to 9, lunch noon to 2, dinner
6 to 8:30. Reservations required. Major credit cards.* ☐ This Western style dining room at Wickenburg Inn guest ranch is open to the public by reservation.
American menu, with theme night variations such as Mexican buffets.

WHERE TO RECLINE

*Prices reflect high season rates and may be lower at other times. Most were
provided by the management and are subject to change; use them only as a guide.*

AmericInn Motel ● ☆☆ $$$ Ø

☐ *850 E. Wickenburg Way (just east of downtown), Wickenburg, AZ
85358; (520) 684-5461. Couples $43 to $66, singles $43 to $54. Major credit
cards.* ☐ A 29-room motel with TV, fee movies and phones, some refrigerators; pool, spa. **Willows Restaurant** is open Monday-Saturday 7 to 1:30
and 5 to 8:30, Sunday 7 to 1:30; dinners $5 to $20; full bar service.

Best Western Rancho Grande ● ☆☆ $$ Ø

☐ *293 E. Wickenburg Way (P.O. Box 1328), Wickenburg, AZ 85358;
(800) 854-7235 or (520) 684-5445. Couples $59 to $89, singles $54 to $75,
efficiencies $57 to $90, family units and suites $70 to $95. Major credit cards.*
☐ An 80-room motel with TV movies, phones and refrigerator; pool, spa,
tennis courts and playground. **Gold Nugget Restaurant** listed above.

Garden City Resort ● ☆ $$

☐ *Highway 60 at Garden City Road (P.O. Box 70), Wickenburg, AZ 85358;
(520) 684-2334. Couples and singles $35 to $40. No credit cards.* ☐ TV; some
fully-furnished units with complete kitchens; weekly and monthly rates.

J Bar J Ranch ● ☆☆ $$$ Ø

☐ *P.O. Box 524 (Rincon Road), Wickenburg, AZ 85358; (520) 684-9142.
Couples $65, singles $50; rates include full breakfast. MC/VISA, AMEX.* ☐
Cozy five-unit resort with TV in rooms; fireplace, wet bar, refrigerator and
microwave in the "great room"; spa, barbecue area and patio lounge.

Mecca Motel ● ☆ $$

☐ *163 E. Wickenburg Way (downtown), Wickenburg, AZ 85358; (520)
684-2753. Couples $29.50, singles $26.50. Major credit cards.* ☐ Small motel
with TV and room refrigerators.

Westerner Motel ● ☆ $$

⧠ 680 W. Wickenburg Way (P.O. Box 1682), Wickenburg, AZ 85358; (520) 684-2493. Couples $40 to $50, singles $40. MC/VISA, DISC. ⧠ Small motel with TV and phones; some in-room coffee makers and refrigerators.

WHERE TO PLAY COWBOY

These guest ranches are within a short drive of Wickenburg, earning it the title of "the dude ranch capital of the world." Most are open from October through May; call for precise times.

Flying E Ranch ● P.O. Box EEE (four miles west at 28-1 W. Wickenburg Way), Wickenburg, AZ 85358; (520) 684-2690. From $185 to $250 per couple and $110 to $140 for singles, including all meals. No credit cards; checks OK. ⧠ Small, family-run ranch with 17 guest units, on a 2,400-foot mesa near Vulture Peak. Breakfast and lunch rides, chuck wagon cookouts, hay rides, square-dancing, swimming pool, spa, sauna, shuffleboard, ping pong, horseshoes, tennis; golf nearby.

Kay El Bar Ranch ● P.O. Box 2480 (Rincon Road, off N. Highway 89/93), Wickenburg, AZ 85358; (520) 684-7593. From $225 to $240 per couple, including all meals. ⧠ An 80-year-old historic landmark ranch. Lodge rooms and cottages; pool, full bar service, hiking, outdoor games and—of course—lots of horseback riding. Golf courses nearby.

Rancho Casitas ● P.O. Drawer A-3 (five miles north, off State Route 89), Wickenburg, AZ 85358; (520) 684-2628. From $400 to $525 per week, without meals. No credit cards. ⧠ A small national historic site guest ranch with old adobe buildings; casual and cozy. Fine desert views from its hilltop site. Riding, horseshoes, pool and laundry. Units are one and two-bedroom casita style with full kitchens, TVs, phones and fireplaces; Spanish décor.

Rancho de los Caballeros ● P.O. Box 1148 (two miles west on U.S. 60, then two miles south to 1551 Vulture Mine Road), Wickenburg, AZ 85358; (520) 684-5484. From $254 to $399 per couple, including all meals. No credit cards. ⧠ A large, resort style guest ranch surrounded by 20,000 acres of desert. Four tennis courts, 18-hole golf course, putting green, pool, trap and skeet range.

Wickenburg Inn Guest and Tennis Ranch ● P.O. Box P (Highway 89 between Wickenburg and Congress), Wickenburg, AZ 85358; (800) 528-4227, (520) 942-5362 or (520) 684-7811. From $209 to $389 per couple, including all meals. Major credit cards. ⧠ Historic guest ranch on a 4,700- acre desert nature preserve. TV, room phones; most rooms have fireplaces, refrigerators and other amenities. Swimming pool and spa, arts and crafts studio, tennis (with clinics), trail rides and other ranch activities, archery, wildlife study and nature walks with a resident naturalist. **Restaurant** listed above.

WHERE TO CAMP

Desert Cypress RV Park ● 610 Jack Burden Rd. (just southeast of town, off U.S. 60), Wickenburg, AZ 85358; (520) 684-2153. RV sites, full hookups $15. Reservations accepted. ⧠ Good graveled sites, some shaded, in a mobile home park. Pool, putting green, showers, laundry, rec hall.

Horspitality RV Park ● 51802 Highway 60 (P.O. Box 2525), Wickenburg, AZ 85358; (520) 684-2519. RV sites, full hookups $15. Reservations accepted; MC/VISA. ⧠ Well-kept park on the southern edge of town. Some pull-throughs; showers, coin laundry, snack bar, rec hall with planned activities. That's right, it's *Hors*-pitality, and it has a boarding stable to prove it.

This Joshua tree along the Joshua Forest Parkway doesn't look much like a lily.

Side trip: Joshua Forest Parkway

After you've done with Wickenburg, if you're going to Las Vegas or California, or if you simply like to explore, head northwest on U.S. 93. After about 16 miles, just beyond the State Route 17 junction, the highway becomes the Joshua Forest Parkway of Arizona, passing through thick stands of these strange, spiny armed, tree-like plants. Joshua trees earned their odd name because Mormon settlers said they resembled Joshua praying to Heaven. (Joshua must have had very hairy arms). They can reach heights of 30 feet or more. But they aren't trees; they're members of the lily family.

Shortly after passing a tiny hamlet consisting of a service station, mini-mart and a great name—Nothing—you'll leave the Joshua forest and enter attractively stony terrain, accented by thin stands of saguaro cactus. If you'd like to spend more time in this area and you have a tent in the trunk or a small RV (big ones won't fit), watch on the left for a sign to the Bureau of Land Management's **Burro Creek Campground.** It's down among the rocks near a rugged, steep-walled canyon carved by the creek; water, no hookups, $5 per night. A bit beyond on Highway 93, you'll cross the Burro Creek Canyon on a high concrete arch bridge. A scenic viewpoint at the bridge's southern anchorage invites you to pause and admire this 200-foot rock-ribbed gorge. Beyond Burro Creek, you'll travel through more hilly desert dotted with saguaro, pass the town of **Wickiup** (basic provisions available) and then pick up Interstate 40, about 20 miles east of Kingman.

THE MYSTERY OF THE DUTCHMAN'S GOLD

And in death he still is laughing,
For the grave his secret holds,
And the mighty Superstition
Keeps the Dutchman's yellow gold
— from *The Dutchman's Gold*

The story of the Lost Dutchman Mine is an intriguing chapter in the treasure trove of Western folklore. It's the kind of tale old-timers like to spin as they sit around a pot-bellied stove, pausing now and then to spit into the ash box. Some dismiss the story as hogwash, yet many people who have entered the Superstitions in search of the mine have been found dead—sometimes beheaded. The most recent mystery death occurred in 1979 when the skeletal remains of a missing hiker were discovered in a rugged canyon. What started all of this?

Jacob Waltz, gold-seeker and chicken farmer, was born around 1810 in Oberschwandorf, Germany. He came to America in 1841 and was lured west by the 1849 California Gold Rush. Failing to find a strike, he drifted to Arizona, seeking gold in the Prescott mining regions. Golden wealth still eluded him, so he settled on 160 acres near Phoenix in 1868 and began chicken farming. But he still wandered in the nearby mountains, seeking that elusive treasure trove. He did find small amounts of gold—he wouldn't say where—and sold it to augment his meager chicken income. In 1878, sick and aging, he signed his homestead and possessions over to a German friend, Andrew Starar, with the agreement that Starar would care for him until he died.

Waltz continued prospecting when he felt able, and he began spinning tales of a rich mine he'd found in the Superstitions. Some say it was the mine of a Mexican family named Peralta that was massacred by Apaches in 1848. Supposedly, one of the Peraltas escaped with a map, and that document fell into Waltz' hands. Stories began circulating about the mystery mine of the "Dutchman" (a common mispronunciation of *Deutschman,* or German).

Jacob's death was rather bizarre. He caught pneumonia after being chased up a tree by a flood in early 1891. He never fully recovered and expired seven months later—broke and homeless—at the house of a neighbor, Mrs. Julia Thomas. Shortly after his death, the story of the Lost Dutchman gained momentum. A Phoenix newspaper reported in 1892 that a "Mrs. Julia Thomas has traveled by wagon to the western end of Superstition Mountains in search of a gold mine and she has returned unsuccessfully." Had Jacob given her his map?

Julia never did find gold, nor have the thousands who followed her into the Superstitions. For a few years, con men did a brisk business peddling "authentic" maps, but the quest for the Dutchman's gold has lost its luster in recent years. Today, these mystic mountains are part of the Superstition Wilderness. Thousands of hikers tramp its trails in search of solitude—and perhaps gold. For the past several decades, they have emerged unscathed.

Maybe geologists and Tonto National Forest officials have the final chuckle. They say the Superstitions are composed mostly of igneous dacite and andacite, an unlikely repository for gold. But what about those killings? Perhaps it *is* the ghosts of the Peraltas and Jacob Waltz who are laughing last.

APACHE TRAIL-HIGHWAY 60 LOOP

If you're willing to subject your vehicle to some dusty bumps, we recommend one of the state's most interesting and varied loop trips. It takes you along the Apache Trail, up the Salt River Canyon, past Tortilla Flat to the old copper town of Globe, and then back to Florence Junction on Highway 60.

The route basically wraps around the Superstition Mountains, or Superstition *Mountain*, the reference preferred by old-timers. Glowering on the skyline, looking appropriately sinister—particularly during a storm—this range provided the proper setting for the strange saga of the Lost Dutchman Mine (see box). This mystery mine, which probably doesn't exist, has been heralded in book, film and TV documentary.

RV ADVISORY ● Twenty-two miles of dirt road lie between Tortilla Flat and Roosevelt Dam. It's washboardy in spots, although easily negotiable by RVs. A road sign above Tortilla Flat advises that vehicles over 40 feet shouldn't attempt it, however. If you'd rather not run the dirt road through the canyon, you can still see a good slice of desert scenery and the bold Superstitions by driving from Apache Junction to Tortilla Flat and back.

Beyond Tempe and Mesa, the seemingly endless metropolitan sprawl of the Valley of the Sun dissolves into desert gardens, steep river canyons and starkly rugged mountains. If you're pressing on from the previous chapter, we left you on Mesa's Main Street. Head east through ten miles of strip malls and you'll encounter Apache Junction, a fast-growing community on the outer rim of the megalopolis.

If you're starting from downtown Phoenix, go east on U.S. 60 freeway and take the Apache Junction exit. That imposing presence filling the horizon as you approach the town is the ruggedly stark profile of the legendary Superstitions.

Apache Junction

Elevation: 1,715 feet   **Population: 17,500**

This scattered community has come of age in the last decade as a Snowbird retreat, as well as a bedroom community for the Valley of the Sun. Sitting at the junction of the Apache Trail (State Highway 88) and U.S. 60, it's the gateway to the Salt River Canyon and Tonto National Forest.

The "Trail" was carved through the rough canyon early in this century as a construction road for the Theodore Roosevelt Dam. Completed in 1911, the dam is the cornerstone of the Salt River Project, which provides water to the valley. In the 1920s, Highway 60 was cut through the Pinal Mountains to the south, linking Phoenix with the silver and copper mines of Globe. Apache Junction was born in 1922 when entrepreneur George Cleveland Curtis put up a tent and started peddling sandwiches and water to travelers along the two routes.

Curtis must have sold a lot of sandwiches, because he later began developing a town. Sitting on the outer fringe of the Valley of the Sun, Apache Junction has more of a rural look than neighboring Mesa and Tempe.

The **Apache Junction Chamber of Commerce** at the Civic Center, 1001 N. Idaho Road (near the Highway 88-60 junction), can provide data on eating and sleeping places and material on the Superstitions. It's open weekdays 9 to 5; (602) 982-3141. The town itself offers no tourist lures, although it's a handy provisioning stop en route to the Salt River Canyon.

ANNUAL EVENTS
Arizona Renaissance Festival, mid-February to mid-March.
Lost Dutchman Days, early March; (602) 982-3141.

WHERE TO DINE AND RECLINE
Mining Camp Restaurant • ☆☆ $$
☐ 6100 E. Mining Camp Rd. (four miles north on Highway 88); (602) 982-3181. American; no alcohol. Tuesday-Saturday 4 to 9:30, Sunday noon to 9:30. Reservations accepted; MC/VISA. ☐ Western style all-you-can-eat restaurant with cowboy singers and comedy Western shoot-outs.

Apache Junction Motel • ☆ $$$
☐ 1680 W. Apache Trail, Gold Canyon, AZ 85219; (602) 982-7702. Couples $57 to $69, singles $52 to $57. Major credit cards. ☐ A 15-room motel with TV, microwaves and refrigerators.

Gold Canyon Resort • ☆☆☆ $$$$$
☐ 6100 Kings Ranch Rd. (off Highway 60), Gold Canyon, AZ 85219; (800) 624-6445 or (602) 982-9090. Couples and singles $150 to $230; rates include continental breakfast. Major credit cards. ☐ An attractive resort in the Superstition foothills with impressive mountain views. Fifty-seven units with TV, rental movies, phones and refrigerators; some in-room spas and private patios. Eighteen-hole golf course, horseback riding, pool, spa, tennis courts, barbecue area and gift shop. Two **restaurants**—Kokopellis and 19th Hole Bar & Grill; American and Southwestern fare; food service 6:30 a.m. to 10 p.m.; dinners $10 to $25; full bar service.

Palm Springs Motel • ☆☆ $$
☐ 950 S. Royal Palm Rd., Apache Junction, AZ 85219; (602) 982-7055. Couples $35 to $42, singles $30 to $32, kitchenettes $48 to $82. MC/VISA. ☐ Small motel with TV, refrigerators and free coffee.

Superstition Grand Hotel • ☆☆☆ $$$ Ø
☐ 201 W. Apache Trail (Idaho Road), Apache Junction, AZ 85220; (602) 982-3500. Couples $65 to $72, singles $59 to $66, kitchenettes and family units $95 to $110. Major credit cards. ☐ Old Spanish style resort hotel where luminaries such as Ronald Reagan, Elvis Presley and Audie Murphy stayed. Tennis courts, pool, spa, shuffleboard and gift shop; golf and shopping nearby. The 130 rooms have TV, phones and free morning coffee. The Western style **Grand steakhouse** serves 6 a.m. to 10 p.m.; dinners $7 to $12.

WHERE TO CAMP
Lost Dutchman State Park • 6109 N. Apache Trail (five miles north) Apache Junction, AZ 85219; (602) 982-4485. RV and tent sites $8, no hookups. ☐ Set amidst thick desert foliage, the campground has barbecues, tables, pit toilets and a dump station. The views are worth much more than the modest fee and the place fills up early. (Details on other facilities below.)

Mesa-Apache Junction KOA • 1540 S. Tomahawk Rd. (Freeway 60 exit 197), Apache Junction, AZ 85219; (602) 982-4015. RV and tent sites; full hookups $22.50, water and electric $20.50, tents and no hookups $15.50, "Kamping Kabins" $28. Reservations accepted; MC/VISA. ☐ A 148-space campground with some pull-through sites; showers, coin laundry, mini-mart, Propane, dump station, snack bar. Heated pool, recreation building with organized activities, TV lounge, pool table, shuffleboard and horseshoes.

The Superstition Mountains, the stuff of which legends are made, rise above Lost Dutchman State Park near Apache Junction.

Rock Shadows Travel Trailer Resort ● *600 S. Idaho (U.S. 60), Apache Junction, AZ 85219; (800) 521-7096 or (602) 982-0450. RV sites; full hookups $25. Reservations accepted; MC/VISA, DISC.* ❑ A seniors park with showers, coin laundry, pool, spas, coin laundry, shuffleboard and horseshoes.

Tortilla Flat and the Salt River Canyon

As you drive east through Apache Junction, fork left onto North Apache Trail, which becomes State Route 88, heading into rough-hewn Salt River Canyon. (If you miss the turn, take a left onto Idaho Street at the Highway 88 junction.) Driving along the foothills of the Superstition, which resemble a rough hewn Roman temple, you finally get into some serious desert wilderness. Well, almost wilderness. You soon encounter a ghost town that—having failed as a mining center—is succeeding as a rustic tourist attraction.

☺ **Goldfield Ghost Town** ● *About four miles north of Apache Junction; (602) 983-0333. Daily 10 a.m. to 6 p.m. Free admission to the grounds. Museum open 10 to 5; adults $2, kids $1.* ❑ Goldfield was established in 1892 when a sizable vein was found at the base of the nearby Superstitions. It soon played out and the town went to sleep. Today, its weathered old buildings attract tourists, who eat cowboy grub, tour an underground mine, ride a train and browse through assorted shops. The grounds are scattered with a rusting museum of old mining and railroad equipment. An indoor museum offers interesting exhibits on the geology, mining history and folklore of the area, including a good gathering of artifacts and an historic audio-visual presentation on the Superstitions.

Just beyond Goldfield is a state park named in honor of the man who made the Superstition Mountains a legend:

☺ **Lost Dutchman State Park** ● *6109 N. Apache Trail (five miles north) Apache Junction, AZ 85219; (602) 982-4485. Day use $3, camping $8, no hookups; picnic areas.* ❑ This state park preserves 292 acres of foothill desert gardens at the base of the mountains. Ranger hikes and talks are conducted from October to April. Nature trails wind about the gardens of saguaro, paloverde and other desert flora, and longer trails lead into the Superstitions themselves. For a nice day hike, take the **Siphon Draw Trail** from a trailhead above the campground and follow it toward the rugged escarpment of the mountains. The area presents a particularly striking setting in spring when poppies bloom among the cactus and paloverde. The campground is set amidst thick desert foliage, with barbecues, tables and pit toilets.

Continuing eastward, the Apache Trail enters Tonto National Forest and picks its way through tumbled foothills that suggest gray-green waves of a petrified sea. A turnout provides a view of Weaver's Needle in the distance; it's a huge, tapered monolith named for trail-blazer Pauline Weaver. Along the route, trailheads offer hiking access into the Superstition Wilderness. After a few miles, the Apache Trail thick saguaro forests and enters steep-walled Salt River Canyon, a favorite playground for heat-fleeing Phoenicians. Mostly they seek the cooling waters of three reservoirs that serve as holding basins for the Salt River Project—Saguaro, Canyon and Apache Lakes.

Canyon Lake Marina ● Held in place by Mormon Flat Dam, Canyon Lake is popular for fishing, swimming and boating. The marina has boat moorage, a launch ramp, picnic areas and swimming beaches. Day-use is $7 per vehicle. A pretend steamboat, *Dolly II,* has 90-minute cruises around the shoreline daily at noon and 2 p.m.; $9.50 per adult and $7.40 per child. Two-hour dinner cruises are $23.25 and $15.95.

Continuing into sheer-walled Salt River Canyon, you'll pass trailheads, picnic areas and a national forest camping area:

Tortilla Flat Campground ● *Two miles beyond Canyon Lake Marina; RV and tent sites; no hookups $8. For phone reservations using a MC/VISA or to request a mail-in reservation form, call (800) 280-CAMP.* ☐ Mesquite-shaded sites are terraced above the canyon, with barbecues, tables, flush potties and a dump station.

A short distance beyond is another weathered Western town devoted essentially to tourism. It's not nearly as old as it looks, nor is it a former mining camp, although it's kind of funky and fun.

Tortilla Flat ● *Restaurant and shops open weekdays 9 to 6 and weekends 8 to 7; (602) 377-5638 or (602) 984-1776. MC/VISA accepted in restaurant and gift shop.* ☐ Boasting a population of six, Tortilla Flat is a deliberately rustic collection of buildings that appear to be leaning against one another for support. They house a post office, grocery store, gift shop, a properly weathered restaurant serving rural American fare, and a saloon. A sign makes joking references about the "Dutchman" Jacob Waltz enjoying Tortilla Flat's home cookin', but of course his soul departed long before the hamlet was founded. Tortilla Flat started as a road camp for work crews on the Salt River Project in 1904. It has since survived as a watering hole and tourist stop for travelers along the Apache Trail.

That trail's pavement ends just beyond Tortilla Flat as it begins a twisting climb up Fish Creek Hill, deep into the heart of Salt River Canyon. It's one of Arizona's more ruggedly appealing drives, with vistas rivaling—in brief sections, at least—some of the canyonlands of southern Utah. It's also a virtual desert garden of saguaro and assorted other cacti, agave and ocotillo.

The view is particularly impressive just after you top Fish Creek Hill. From there, the road snakes down to the canyon floor. It's notched into sheer

Tonto National Monument shelters several cliff dwellings amidst lush cactus gardens.

cliffs in areas although it's wide and safely fenced. At the bottom, you enter a pleasant riparian zone; there isn't much of a stream because most of it has been captured in reservoirs on either side. Midway through the canyon, you'll encounter another reservoir with attendant marina:

Apache Lake Marina ● *Box 15627, Tortilla Flat, AZ 85290; (602) 467-2511. Day use $3; RV park $15 with full hookups and showers; motel units $49 per couple and $62 for kitchenettes. Restaurant open Sunday-Thursday 7 a.m. to 8 p.m., Friday-Saturday 7 to 9. MC/VISA.* ☐ Occupying an impressive setting beneath sheer cliffs several hundred feet high, Apache is popular with fisherfolk, who catch sunfish, trout and assorted bass. Facilities include fuel, boat rentals, moorage and storage, groceries, RV park, fishing supplies and a restaurant. In addition to the RV park, primitive camping is available at a forest service site.

Beyond Apache Lake, the dusty road slips through a narrowing, russet colored, steep-walled chasm, with a slim blue ribbon of Roosevelt Lake far below. Finally, after a long and certainly bumpy ride, you'll see ahead the great curved wedge of concrete that is the keystone of the Salt River Project:

Theodore Roosevelt Dam and Lake ● If a dam can look rustic, it's the Theodore Roosevelt. This unusual cut-stone structure is the largest masonry dam in the world, a 280-foot high wedge in Salt River Canyon. The superlatives were even greater when it was completed in 1911. It was the world's highest dam of any sort, and it created the globe's largest manmade lake, covering 17,335 acres. Since every scrap of material had to be hauled by high-wheeled wagon over the bumpy, corkscrew Apache Trail, it was a remarkable engineering accomplishment. And it gave thirsty Phoenix a much-needed drink, launching its future as the Southwest's largest city.

Although the dam is old, many of its facilities are not. A new steel arch bridge—the longest such two-lane span in North America—leaps across the reservoir just up from the dam. The surrounding lands are part of a Tonto National Forest recreation area and a visitor center—jointly operated by the Forest Service and Bureau of Reclamation—opened in late 1994:

☺ **Roosevelt Lake Visitor Center** • *At Roosevelt Marina; HC02, Box 4800, Roosevelt, AZ 85545; (520) 467-3200. Daily 7:45 to 4:30* ☐ This attractive blue roofed facility has exhibits on the dam's construction, stuffed critters indigenous to the area and fine regional photos. Several displays focus on the importance of water to mankind. You learn that 1.5 million gallons is needed to produce the food that an average American consumes in a year. It takes 300 gallons to produce a loaf of bread and 3,000 gallons to produce a pound of hamburger, so hold the meat and just give me the bun.

Roosevelt Lake Marina • *Below the visitor center; (520) 467-2245.* Roosevelt Lake's sloping shorelines are popular with swimmers, sunners and boaters. The marina below the visitor center offers moorage, a boat launch, groceries, a snack shop, plus boat, jet ski and water ski rentals, groceries, a snack shop and other essentials.

Camping • Two new campgrounds have been opened by the Forest Service—Windy Hill, east of the Tonto National Monument turnoff, and Cholla, north of the dam on State Route 188. Both have RV and tent sites for $10 (flush potties and showers; no hookups). The sites are too new to be tree-shaded although each has a shade ramada for the picnic table and barbecue. Several other campgrounds and informal lakeside camping are available around the reservoir.

Just beyond the visitor center is a small and very appealing Indian ruin:

☺ **Tonto National Monument** • *HC02, P.O. Box 4603 (a mile off Highway 88), Roosevelt, AZ 85545; (520) 467-2241. Daily 8 to 5; Lower Ruins trail closes at 4; $4 per car or $2 for walkers and bikers.* ☐ A small tribe called the Salado ("salt" in Spanish) built elaborate cave-sheltered masonry adobes in cliffs above the Salt River in the 13th and 14th centuries. These cliff dwellings are now protected within this pocket-sized national monument. Although not well known, this is a jewel of a preserve. Its steep slopes are gardens of saguaro, cholla, palo verde and other desert flora; and its high perch offers fine views of Roosevelt Lake. This would be a pleasant place even without the Indian ruins. A half-mile trail takes you to the first of these pueblos, simply called the Lower Ruin. It's a steep uphill climb with a 350-foot elevation gain, so it's best planned for early morning if you're visiting in the summer. The more extensive Upper Ruin, a 40-room complex, can be reached only by ranger-led hikes, from November through April. Advance reservations are needed for these three-hour treks. A small museum displays fragments of cotton cloth, tools, polychrome pottery and other implements found at the sites. The Salado were among the more advanced of Arizona's early tribes. Farmers, hunters and gatherers, they diverted water from the Salt River to irrigate their food and cotton patches. They were excellent potters and weavers. They abandoned these dwellings around 1450 A.D.

About seven miles beyond Tonto, you'll pass a small resort:

Roosevelt Lake Resort • *c/o HC-02, Box 901, Roosevelt, AZ 85545; (520) 467-2276. Couples and singles $35; kitchenette cabins $36.* ☐ This complex also has a steak house, cocktail lounge and mobile home park.

Beyond the resort, the highway climbs over a ridge and then drops out of the national forest into **Globe** and **Miami**, two copper mining towns that we explore in detail in Chapter twelve. Between the two, pick up Highway 60 and head west, back toward Phoenix. The road, designated as the Gila-Pima Scenic Route, curves gently through Devil's Canyon, which becomes rather dramatically steep walled and rugged as it penetrates the Dripping Springs Mountains. Toward the western end where the canyon closes in, the highway was bored through Queen Creek Tunnel. From there, it swerves swiftly down to another of Arizona's once booming copper mining towns.

Superior

Elevation: 2,730 feet   **Population: 3,500**

Named for a town on the banks of Lake Superior in Michigan, the community was platted in 1900 and it boomed for several years as a major copper center. Then as happens with many mining towns, the boom went bust and Superior went to sleep. Most of the masonry and brick front stores along Main Street are closed. However, it's hardly a ghost town, since more than three thousand people live here—a mix of retirees and commuters. This is a grand setting for a town, between the Dripping Springs Mountains and the fluted buttes of Picketpost Mountain, which bears a strong resemblance to the Superstitions. For a quick look at the town, fork to the right at the green exit sign as you approach Superior's eastern edge, then go left onto Main Street. This leads you through town and back to the highway. Just below is one of Arizona's finest botanical gardens, a gift a Superior copper king:

☺ ***Boyce Thompson Arboretum State Park*** ● *P.O. Box AB, Superior, AZ 85273; (520) 689-2811. Daily 8 to 5; adults $4, kids 5 to 17, $1.* ☐ Say hello to a boojum tree and listen to a cactus wren in this large desert arboretum. It's operated jointly by a foundation set up by the late copper baron William Boyce Thompson, Arizona State Parks and the University of Arizona.

More than 1,500 species of desert plants from around the world are crowded into this "Noah's Ark" of a semi-arid garden. The Smith Interpretive Center museum occupies a 1920s cut-stone mansion listed on the National Register of Historic Places. A nearby visitor center houses an orientation room and a gift shop selling books, cacti and sundry other succulents. Adjacent greenhouses display hundreds of varieties of semi-arid plants, and nature trails wind through 35 acres of landscaped grounds.

SOUTH TO TUCSON VIA CASA GRANDE

From the arboretum, the route drops from rough-hewn foothills into a low desert basin. At Florence Junction, you can complete your loop back to Apache Junction by continuing straight ahead on four-lane U.S. 60, or you can aim south on State Route 79 toward Florence and Tucson.

For southbound travelers, we recommend little-used Highway 79 over busy Interstate 10, which is noted mostly for semi-monotonous desert. It's also noted for dust storms, so try to avoid it on windy days.

Florence

Elevation: 1,493 feet   **Population: 6,300**

One of Arizona's first American settlements, Florence dates from 1866, when one Levi Ruggles laid out a townsite near a ford in the Gila River. It was named for the sister of Territorial Governor Richard McCormick. Although it's smaller than nearby Casa Grande, it is the seat of Pinal County.

This is a handsome old town, with several 19th century homes in the Florence Townsite National Historic District. More than 100 of these structures are listed on the National Register of Historic Places. Styles range from Sonoran to Victorian to Arizona territorial. The Western flavor downtown with false front stores and sidewalk overhangs looks right out of a cowboy movie set. In fact, it's often used by Hollywood film makers. For visitors, it offers a few gift, curio and antique shops.

As you enter the outskirts of Florence, you'll see a section of **Arizona State Prison** with its grim looking concertina wire-topped fence. It was moved here in 1909 when the Yuma Territorial Prison was closed. With more than 3,000 inmates (half the town's population), it's the largest facility in the state prison system. Opposite the prison, turn right onto Ruggles Street and follow it a few blocks to Main Street and **McFarland State Historic Park.** Opposite is the abandoned two-story brick **Silver King Florence Hotel** built in 1876. Just below on Main Street is the crumbling two-story adobe 1884 **William Clark House** which—if funds can be found—will be restored. This is the same Clark copper king of Jerome and Clarkdale fame (Chapter six). Before it fell to ruin, it boasted an elegant Victorian interior, sheathed in adobe brick.

Also on Main, at 715 South, is the **Pinal County Historical Museum,** reached by driving about a dozen blocks south from McFarland State Park. Retrace your route on Main and turn east onto 12th Street and you'll run into the town's architectural gem, the 1891 **Pinal County Courthouse** at 12th and Butte. It's an ornate brick structure with gingerbread trim and a hexagonal clock tower topped by a witch's hat peak. The **Pinal County Visitor Center** is a few blocks away, at 135 N. Pinal Street; open weekdays 9 to noon and 1 to 4; (520) 868-9433. Pick up a walking map of historic homes and other buildings. (When you arrive, the chamber may have returned to its original site at 912 N. Pinal in the restored Jacob Suter house.)

ATTRACTIONS

☺ **McFarland State Historic Park** ● *Main and Ruggles streets (P.O. Box 109), Florence, AZ 85232; (520) 868-5216. Thursday-Monday 8 to 5. Adults $2, kids 12 to 17, $1, under 12 free.* ⛶ Pinal County got its start here; this adobe functioned as the courthouse, sheriff's office and jail from 1878 to 1891. It spent another half century as a county hospital. One side of the structure houses the old courtroom with its jury box, wooden pews and judge's bench, while the other contains early 20th century hospital exhibits. A special display focuses on local boy-makes-good Ernest W. McFarland, author of the G.I. Bill of Rights and chief justice of the Arizona Supreme Court. Arriving in the state in 1919 with $10 in his pocket, he climbed the political staircase from a local irrigation district counsel to county attorney to state governor. He was sent to Washington as a U.S. Senator, became Senate Majority Leader and finally wound up on the state's high court. McFarland never lived in this structure; he purchased it as a gift to the state in 1974, thus earning the right to have his name attached.

Pinal County Historical Museum ● *715 S. Main St., Florence, AZ 85631; (520) 868-4382. Wednesday-Sunday 1 to 5; closed July 15 to September 1; free.* ⛶ A typical county history center, it has some untypical exhibits. They include a hundred varieties of barbed wire, a large bullet display, an-

Birds of a feather—pigeons in this case—flock about the distinctive clock tower of the Pinal County Courthouse in Florence.

tique woodworking tools, cactus furniture and some gruesome photos of hanging victims, a gas chamber chair and hang nooses from Arizona prisons. Exhibits of Southwest Indians are quite extensive. Newspaper clippings report the sad news of the death of cowboy star Tom Mix. He rolled his high-speed Cord sports car into a ditch south of here on October 12, 1940.

From downtown, head west on Highway 287, which delivers you to the area's other primary attractions. You first encounter, nine miles from Florence, one of the America's largest free standing adobe ruins:

☺ *Casa Grande Ruins National Monument* ● *1100 Ruins Dr., Coolidge, AZ 85228; (520) 723-3172. Daily 7 to 6; $4 per family, $2 per person.* ☐ It looks odd, standing there with its sheltering metal roof supported by tall pylons, like a blend of adobe ruin and Chinese pagoda. But the roof over Casa Grande is necessary to keep this massive, multi-storied structure from melting back into the earth. This is the tallest and perhaps the most mysterious of Arizona's pueblos. It's four stories high with four-foot thick walls at the base to support its 2,800-ton mass. Six hundred wooden beams were needed to hold up its ceilings. The structure was the centerpiece of a Hohokam village, occupied for about a century, until 1450 A.D. Archaeologists don't know why Casa Grande was built, nor why it was abandoned.

The towering structure may have been used for ceremonies or astronomical observations. Visitors can observe it only from the ground, for it is too fragile to be entered. Rangers conduct frequent tours around its perimeter, discussing its construction methods and its long vanished inhabitants. Fragments of the village wall and smaller buildings rim the great structure. The visitor center contains fine example of large, fully intact pots and exhibits concerning irrigation, tool-making and other crafts of the Hohokam.

Continue northeast past the ruin on State Route 87 and you'll encounter a much more contemporary Native American settlement:

Gila Indian Community

Unnoticed by many Phoenix-Tucson travelers on I-10, the 337,000 acre Pima-Maricopa Reservation is one of Arizona's most progressive Native American communities, with 32 industries, a 15,000-acre cooperative farm and a modern hospital. The main community is **Sacaton,** about a dozen miles northeast of the national monument. The reservation's primary visitor attraction is an excellent arts and crafts center. To reach it from Sacaton, go eight miles northwest, cross under I-10 and drive half a mile west on Casa Blanca Road. (If you're traveling down I-10, take exit 175 onto Casa Blanca.)

☺ *Gila River Arts and Crafts Center* • *Casa Blanca Road, P.O. Box 457, Sacaton, AZ 85247; (520) 315-3411. Daily 8 to 5; free.* ☐ More than 30 different tribes and 2,000 years of Native American history are represented in this modern cultural center. It's actually a blend of four facilities—the Gila River Museum, with historical exhibits; the Arts and Crafts Center; Heritage Park, with reconstructions of Indian dwellings; and a restaurant serving fry bread and other typical Indian fare.

Museum displays include old photos and examples of Pima and Maricopa basketry, pottery, weapons and other artifacts. In Heritage Park, you can poke through traditional dwellings of Pima, Maricopa, Tohono O'odham and Apache tribes. The handiwork of more than a dozen Southwestern tribes is on display in the Arts and Crafts Center; much of it is for sale in the gift shop. Craft demonstrations, traditional dances and other activities are held periodically—particularly during the fall-winter-spring tourist season. Casa Blanca RV park is adjacent to the center; see below.

ANNUAL EVENTS

The Gila Indian Community sponsors a variety of annual events, permitting visitors to witness both traditional and contemporary festivities.

St. John's Indian School Festival, first Sunday in March.

Native American Festivities and Crafts Sale, mid-March.

"Gathering of the People" tribal fair, the second weekend of April.

Pima-Maricopa Arts Festival, the second weekend of November.

Native American Dance Festival, the fourth weekend of November.

From Sacaton, you can take the fast way to Tucson on I-10, or the scenic route by returning to Highway 79 and heading down the Pinal Pioneer Parkway. If you chose the former, you'll hit the area's largest community.

Casa Grande

Elevation: 1,398 feet   **Population: 19,000**

Once a wide spot in the road, Casa Grande has grown into a fair-sized residential community in recent decades. It provides visitors with a provisioning pause between Phoenix and Tucson. Although it is named for the Casa Grande pueblo ruin, that structure actually is closer to the farm town of

Coolidge. The community of Casa Grande offers one item of visitor interest:

Casa Grande Valley Historical Museum ● *110 W. Florence Blvd., Casa Grande, AZ 85222-4033; (520) 836-2223. Tuesday-Sunday 1 to 5 mid-September through Memorial Day weekend; adults $1, kids free.* ☐ Furnished rooms of the town's early days and a 1928 American LaFrance pumper are the focal points of this museum. Other exhibits feature the area's Indian cultures, mining, railroading and agricultural development.

Pressing down I-10 from Casa Grande, you'll see a rather dramatic monolith that looks like a giant tiger's fang. From some angles, it resembles a mountain trying to thumb a ride. It was the site of one of the strangest battles of the Civil War:

Picacho Peak State Park ● *P.O. Box 275, Picacho, AZ 85241; (520) 466-3183. Day use $3, RV and tent sites with hookups for $10. No reservations or credit cards.* ☐ The park has picnic areas and hiking trails, including a path to the 1,400-foot summit of this stone upcropping. The campground has flush potties, showers, picnic tables and barbecue facilities. Confederate and Union forces clashed near here on April 15, 1862, in the westernmost battle of the Civil War. These weren't regular troops, but members of the Confederacy's Texas Volunteers and the Union-supporting California Volunteers. Although the Texans won the first skirmish, killing four Californians, they realized that reinforcements would soon arrive in this pro-Union territory, so they hightailed it back to Texas.

WHERE TO RECLINE AND CAMP

Francisco Grande Resort & Golf Club ● ☆☆☆ *$$$$*

☐ *26000 Gila Bend Hwy. (five miles west), Casa Grande, AZ 85222; (520) 836-6444 or (800) 237-4238. Couples and singles $59 to $139, kitchenettes $99 to $169, suites $175 to $250. MC/VISA, AMEX and DC.* ☐ Full-service resort with 18-hole golf course, tennis courts, croquet, volleyball, horseshoes and conference facilities. TV movies, phones, pool and spa. **Palo Verde Dining Room** serves 6:30 a.m. to 10 p.m.; indoor and outdoor dining; dinners $9 to $16; full bar service.

Casa Blanca RV Park ● *Adjacent to the Gila Arts and Crafts Center (P.O. Box 176), Sacaton, AZ 85247; (520) 315-3534. RV and tent sites, full hookups $12 (discounts by the week and month), no hookups $7. Reservations accepted; no credit cards.* ☐ Showers, laundromat, convenience store nearby, Propane, dump station, TV cable. New park with all pull-throughs.

Picacho KOA ● *I-19 exit 212, north of Picacho Peak State Park (P.O. Box 368), Picacho, AZ 85241; (520) 466-7401. RV and tent sites; $15.50 to $22.45. Reservations accepted; MC/VISA.* ☐ Some pull-throughs; showers, coin laundry, pool, spa, rec room, groceries and Propane, disposal station.

SOUTH VIA PINAL PIONEER PARKWAY

If you take Highway 79 south from Florence, it soon becomes Pinal Pioneer Parkway, passing through a broad basin lush with desert plants. Signs along the route identify the flora—cat claw, prickly pear, paloverde, saguaro and such. Think of it as a 55-mile-an-hour nature trail. There are occasional turn-outs and picnic tables.

Tom Mix Monument, 17 miles south of Florence, has been erected near the site where the 1930s movie cowboy met his Maker in October, 1940. He crashed his Cord sports car in a shallow ravine just beyond. A stone

BEAM US OUTA HERE, SCOTTY!

After a rather tumultuous beginning and some bad press, the brave new world experiment of Biosphere 2 has settled down as a serious science project. Columbia University signed a five-year agreement to manage the space age facility, starting in 1996. Immense in scope and certainly noble of concept, Biosphere 2 is an attempt to create a self-sustaining ecosystem under glass. Experiments will be useful in planning a space station, colonizing the moon or a planet beyond earth, and testing the greenhouse theory that excess carbon dioxide may be pollution our atmosphere.

The three-acre mass of triangular glass is the work of Texas oil billionaire Edward Bass, who spent more than $200 million of his own fortune on the construction of this airtight "space station" on earth. Mini-ecosystems of a tropical rainforest, savannah, desert, marsh, baby ocean and an intensified food production facility were created to make life livable within. All necessary food would be produced for resident "bionauts," and all water and waste would be recycled. Plants would produce oxygen for humans who would—in turn—exhale carbon dioxide for the flora.

It all seemed like a nifty idea. Four women and four men entered this self-sustaining environment in September, 1991, intending to stay for two years. They did so, but not without problems. Excess levels of carbon dioxide had to be artificially removed and pigs that were intended to provide pork got picky about their diets and started eating the baby chicks.

"It upset the animal psychology," our guide pointed out.

Other problems plagued the group. The winter of 1993 was the wettest on record in Arizona—too cool to create enough of a greenhouse effect to raise sufficient food. Although the volunteers didn't starve, they all lost several pounds and started looking rather emaciated. There were reports of squabbles, although one couple was married shortly after emergence.

Another group entered in 1994, but remained only six months. Technically, the experiment worked, claim Biosphere officials, although with a Catch 22. Eight people were too few to perform all the tasks necessary to sustain themselves, and there wasn't enough space to produce sufficient food for larger numbers. The unit is still sealed through a triple airlock, and scientists continue to conduct experiments, although they don't stay for extended periods.

So if this is Biosphere 2, where is Biosphere 1? You're standing on it—the planet Earth.

marker with a riderless, sad-looking horse is inscribed: *In memory of Tom Mix, whose spirit left his body on this spot, and whose characterization and portrayals in life served to better fix memories of the Old West in the minds of living men.* There's a parking area and picnic tables here, if you want to spend a few moments with the famous star's memory. Expect your kids to ask: "Tom who?"

The desert garden parkway ends at the junction of state highways 79 and

77, about 25 miles below the Tom Mix monument. Turn left onto Route 77 toward Oracle and—after six miles—you'll reach the turnoff to a desert garden of quite a different stripe. This one's under glass.

☺ ***Biosphere 2*** • *P.O. Box 689 (Highway 77), Oracle, AZ 85623; (520) 825-6200; inn (520) 825-6222. Daily 9 to 5. Tours on the half hour; last one departs at 3:30. Adults $12.95, seniors $10.95, children $6. Tour and room packages at the Biosphere Inn, $68 per person double occupancy, including lodging, tour, dinner and breakfast and $5 gift shop credit; $54 per person in summer. Room only $80 single or double and $49 single or double in summer. Biosphere Café serves breakfast, lunch and dinner.* ◻

Started in 1990, Biosphere 2 is an attempt to create a completely self-sustaining, sealed environment on earth. A massive glass greenhouse, supposedly more airtight than a space shuttle, sprawls over three acres of hilly desert. Volunteer scientists lived inside with self-sustaining plants and animals in an attempt to prove that life could be maintained within a man-made facility. One group stayed for two years, another for six months. Scientific experiments are continuing, although for shorter periods. To spur public interest—and help pay the bills—Biosphere was opened to tourists a few years ago, complete with a café, motel and even a logo shop, where you can buy your own personal Biosphere 2 T-shirt or coffee mug.

Tours begin with a trip through a greenhouse and enclosed animal compound outside the Biosphere, where ongoing experiments are conducted with vegetables, chickens and goats to maximize food production. The livestock facility is called the Domestic Animal System, although it sounds like a chicken coop and smells like a goat pen. Visitors then adjourn to a small theater where they see an idealistic video about Biosphere 2, then they tour the perimeter of the great glass greenhouse. Unfortunately, unclean mortals such as ourselves aren't allowed inside, although—peering through the skin of triangular glass—one might see scientists working inside.

From Biosphere, head south on State Route 77, skimming the edge of the fluted, rock ribbed Santa Catalina Mountains. These desert foothills shelter several upscale subdivisions. Near the small town of Catalina, a state park offers access to their heights:

Catalina State Park • *P.O. Box 36986, Tucson, AZ 85740; (520) 628-5798. Day use $3, camping $13 with electric hookups, $8 without.* ◻ More than 5,500 acres of Santa Catalina Mountain foothills have been set aside in this ruggedly attractive state park in the upper reaches of the Sonoran Desert. It has picnicking, hiking and horseback riding. A trailhead provides access to adjacent Coronado National Forest hiking trails.

South of Catalina, the highway becomes four-lane Oracle Road, which takes you into the heart of Tucson and our next chapter.

TRIP PLANNER

WHEN TO GO ● Tucson's best weather is fall and spring; lodgings get crowded just after Christmas, when the snowbird crowds hit. Some hotels and RV parks book up by mid-January. Tucson has more days of sunshine than any other American city. Winters are cool to warm; summers warm to hot. Although farther south than Phoenix, it's is nearly 1,500 feet higher and therefore slightly cooler. If you like it hot, July has an average high of 101. Like Phoenix, Tucson has some great room bargains in summer.

WHAT TO SEE ● Flandrau Science Center, Arizona State Museum and Arizona Historical Society Museum on the University of Arizona campus; the International Wildlife Museum, Old Tucson Studios, Arizona-Sonora Desert Museum, Saguaro National Park, Tohono Chul Park, Pima Air and Space Museum and Mission San Xavier del Bac in Tucson; Titan Missile Museum in Green Valley, Tubac State Historic Park and Tumacacori National Historic Park south of Tucson.

WHAT TO DO ● Prowl the old streets of El Presidio Historic District, drive and hike the desert wilds of Tucson Mountain Park, hike the cactus ravines of Sabino and Bear canyons, drive to the dizzying heights of Mount Lemmon, go Western at Tanque Verde or other area dude ranches, talk to the birds in Madera Canyon and walk or drive from Nogales to Nogales to visit our friends south of the border.

☺ *Indicates an attraction, restaurant or lodging with special appeal.*

USEFUL CONTACTS

Metropolitan Tucson Convention & Visitor's Bureau, 130 S. Scott Ave., Tucson, AZ 85701; (520) 624-1889.

Sun Tran (Tucson bus system schedules): (520) 792-9222.

Tucson Airport Authority (airline schedules): (520) 573-8000.

City arts line (for cultural activities): (520) 642-0595.

Road and weather information: (520) 294-3113.

Coronado National Forest, 300 W. Congress, Tucson, AZ 85701; (520) 670-6483. Mount Lemmon information—(520) 576-1542; Sabino Canyon information—(520) 749-8700 or (520) 629-5101.

Nogales-Santa Cruz County Chamber of Commerce, 123 W. Kino Park Place, Nogales, AZ 85621; (520) 287-3685.

Tubac Chamber of Commerce, P.O. Box 1866, Tubac, AZ 85646; (520) 938-2704.

TUCSON RADIO STATIONS

KCUB-FM, 107.5—Country.
KIIN-FM, 99.5—Country.
KKLD-FM, 94.9—Adult contemporary.
KUIT-FM, 89.9—NPR
KLPX-FM, 96.1—Classic rock.
KRQQ-FM, 93.7—Rock and top 40.

KCUB-AM, 1290—Country.
KTKT-AM, 990—CNN news, talk.
KUAZ-AM, 1550—NPR
KTUC-AM, 1400—News and talk.
KSZA-AM, 580—Easy listening.

MISSION SAN XAVIER

Chapter nine

TUCSON & FRIENDS
Finding Arizona's Spanish roots

IT'S OUR FAVORITE city in the Southwest. Tucson is large enough to provide all the cosmopolitan essentials, yet small enough to be familiar and friendly. With a population just under half a million, it offers a great mix of indoor culture and outdoor recreation. Tucsonans—smiling smugly in the direction of Phoenix—boast that it's the only Arizona city with a major university, plus a professional symphony, theater company, ballet and opera. A *Wall Street Journal* article once called it "a mini-mecca for the arts." Modern highrises sprout from the heart of downtown, casting today's shadows over yesterday's El Presidio Historic District. Here, the "Old Pueblo" planted its Spanish roots while America was still a British colony.

Occupying the northeastern rim of the Sonoran Desert at 2,389 feet, Tucson sits in a virtual cactus garden, surrounded by five mountain ranges. In winter, you can work on your suntan at poolside, then drive to the Mount Lemmon ski area in about an hour and strap on the sticks.

If it weren't for the Mormons and the Gadsden Purchase, we might need a Mexican tourist card to visit Tucson. When the Mexican-American border

255

was set by the Treaty of Guadalupe Hidalgo in 1848, the southern third of Arizona—including Tucson—was on the Mexican side. However, Tucson was occupied by members of the Mormon Battalion. They had grabbed it two years earlier during the Mexican War, and they weren't about to give it up. Then in 1854, the 30,000-square-mile Gadsden Purchase was negotiated and the American flag remained over the Old Pueblo.

Tucson goes well beyond that period, of course. When mission- builder Eusebio Francisco Kino visited in 1687, he found Tohono O'odham Indians living in a village they called *Stjukshon* (Stook-shon). It means "blue water at the base of a black mountain," referring to springs in the now-dry Santa Cruz River and Sentinel Peak. The Spanish altered it to *Tucson*, which initially was pronounced "TUK-son." Local historians, possibly stretching a point, say St-jukshon-cum-Tucson is the oldest continuously inhabited settlement in America. (The same claim is made about Oraibi on the Hopi Reservation to the north and by New Mexico's Santa Fe.)

Father Kino returned in 1700 to build Mission San Xavier in the Indian village of Bac. Tucson itself was established in 1775 by a wandering Irishman who was scouting for the Spanish crown. Settlers began moving into the Tucson Basin and the original inhabitants naturally objected. They went on the warpath and a walled presidio was built to protect the intruders. This was the first walled city in America—-except that it was still part of Spain.

After the Gadsden Purchase put Tucson on our side of the border, it continued growing as a ranching and provisioning center. A Butterfield Stage stop was opened in 1857 and Tucson's cantinas became notorious hangouts for drifters, outlaws and randy cowpokes. Folks said the outpost was so primitive that stage passengers who spent the night had to sleep in a "Tucson bed"—using their stomach for a mattress and their back for a blanket.

The pueblo suffered the indignity of capture by rebel Texas troops during the Civil War. They were evicted by a pro-Union California battalion following the Battle of Picacho Pass in 1862—the war's westernmost conflict. Tucson lured the territorial capital from Prescott in 1867, only to have it taken away ten years later. By the turn of the century, this was a busy if still somewhat remote town of 10,000. World War II brought thousands of servicemen to Davis-Monthan Army Air Corps Base. Many of them liked the idea of January suntans and returned.

Galloping off in all directions

Tucson boomed after the war and—like its larger neighbor to the north—galloped off in all directions. The only fault we find with the city is that it's too spread out—a mini-Los Angeles with cactus. Indeed, this vast carpet of commerce covers 500 square miles—even larger than metropolitan L.A. However, much of this land is taken up in vast desert preserves, such as Tucson Mountain Park. Further, Tucson isn't surrounded by other suburban cities, as are Los Angeles and Phoenix. Once you hit the city limits, you're in open desert.

Wide thoroughfares get people from one end of town to the other with reasonable speed. Interstate 10 cuts a northwest- southeast diagonal, providing quick access to the town's opposite corners. I-19 whisks traffic south. Surprisingly, Tucson suffers little commuter congestion, except on some downtown surface streets; traffic watchers get excited over a ten-minute delay on I-10. Today's Tucson wears its Spanish heritage rather handsomely. Red-tile and flat-roofed pueblo architecture predominates. The town has more good Mexican restaurants than you can shake a tortilla at. Mexican arts and crafts add color to curio shops. Many signs are bilingual, since 26 percent of Pima County's citizens are Hispanic.

Tucson's attractions are widespread, so get a rental car with unlimited mileage if you've flown in. If you arrive by car, downtown is easy to reach; just take the Broadway-Congress exit from I-10 and go east. Broadway and Congress are parallel one-way streets cutting through the heart of the small downtown area. Motels are clustered around I-10 off-ramps. Others, including some budget ones, are strung along Broadway, just east of downtown.

DOING TUCSON

Begin your exploration by getting yourself to the **Visitor Center** of the Metropolitan Tucson Convention & Visitor's Bureau. It's in an old Spanish style building at 130 S. Scott Avenue, a block and a half south of Broadway. Hours are 8 to 5 weekdays and 9 to 4 weekends; (520) 624-1889.

Approaching on I-10, take the Broadway exit and signs will direct you to the visitor center. If you're emerging from the Florence-Tucson route outlined in the previous chapter, State Route 77 becomes Oracle Road. Press southward, following "City Center" signs (and avoiding Highway 77's swerve to the right.) Your route becomes, among other things, Business I-10 and U.S. 89. As you near downtown, veer right onto Main Avenue and you'll start picking up "Visitor Center" signs.

RV PARKING ADVISORY ● Temporary curbside RV parking is available just around the corner from the visitor center, on Ochoa Street. Otherwise, RVers will suffer the usual downtown parking problems, although some curbside parking is available on the fringes. Once you begin driving to outlying attractions, it's much easier to find places to plant your rig.

WALKING DOWNTOWN

Although most of Tucson's attractions are widespread, a few are focused within downtown and they're easy to reach on foot. Also, streets take some funny angles here, so you might go astray if you try to drive.

A downtown map is included in the *Tucson Official Visitors Guide,* which is the first thing you should ask for upon stepping up to the visitor center counter. (Plan-ahead travelers will call or write the bureau and request one in advance.) The downtown map pinpoints attractions but doesn't suggest specific routes, so we'll do so. (Bold faced items marked with a ■ are listed with more detail below, under "Attractions".)

Visitors Guide in hand, leave the center and wrap around the corner to your right onto Ochoa. Walk a block to Stone and cross to the attractive twin-towered **St. Augustine Cathedral.** Step inside to admire its lofty vaulted ceiling and stained glassed windows. Then pass through its landscaped grounds and cross Convent Avenue to the large **Tucson Convention Center** complex. Cross through a breezeway in the center and angle to the right toward Granada Avenue and the Sousa-Carillo-Frémont House, informally known as the ■ **Frémont Adobe.**

Return to the Convent Avenue side of the convention center and walk north through an olive tree shaded brick plaza. Guide on a modernistic brown sculpture that resembles the rusty conning tower of a skinny submarine. It will point you down to a lower plaza with a creek-fountain complex. By passing between the fountain and the **Leo Rich Theater,** you'll enter a

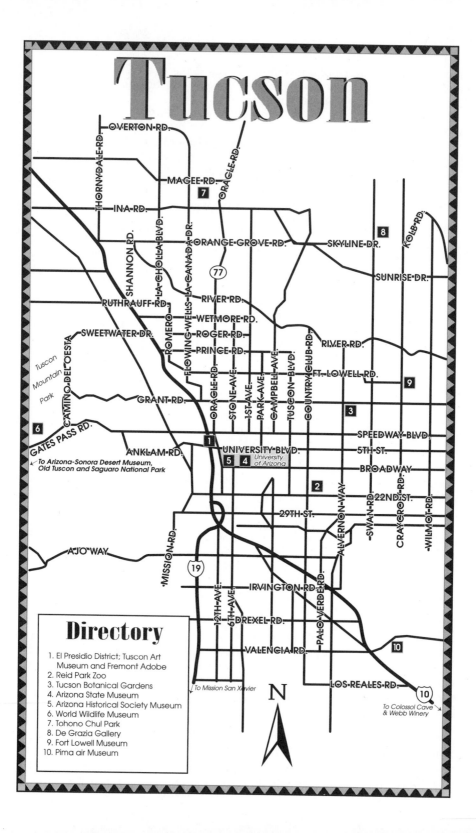

Tucson

Directory

1. El Presidio District; Tucson Art Museum and Fremont Adobe
2. Reid Park Zoo
3. Tucson Botanical Gardens
4. Arizona State Museum
5. Arizona Historical Society Museum
6. World Wildlife Museum
7. Tohono Chul Park
8. De Grazia Gallery
9. Fort Lowell Museum
10. Pima air Museum

N

sheltered corridor betwixt the back door of the Holiday Inn and **La Placita Village.** Styled as a Mexican market place, the village consists mostly of professional offices arrayed around a gazebo plaza. You can get some nice photos of the modern Tucson skyline from here, with the plaza in the foreground. Exit La Placita the way you came in, continue north and you'll cross a pair of pedestrian bridges, over Congress and Pennington streets. You next pass through **Plaza de las Armas** in El Presidio Park, at the rear of the curious Moorish domed **Pima County Courthouse.** Continue beyond the plaza and cross Alameda Avenue.

This gets you to ■ **El Presidio Historic District,** where a walled garrison was established in 1775. Patterns of the original walls are marked on the *Visitor Guide* map although little physical trace remains. The splendid ■ **Tucson Museum of Art,** not an historic building, is just to your left as you enter El Presidio. On your right, at Meyer and Tellis, is ■ **Old Town Artisans,** an extensive collection of handicraft galleries and shops. The old presidio area doesn't have a thick concentration of shops; many of the buildings are occupied by professional offices and some are still residences. However, Old Town Artisans and its adjacent Old Town Pot Shop provides an abundance of shopping. The popular **El Charro Restaurant** at 311 North Court Avenue (listed below, under "Where to dine") also has a shopping complex. Wander at will through El Presidio and you'll find a couple of other restaurants and several historic buildings with signs marking their vintage and significance. Most of the adobes are along Main Avenue and Meyer Avenue; most of the shops and restaurants are on Meyer and Court. The **Southwest Parks and Monuments Association Bookshop** at Court and Council is an excellent source for regional guidebooks.

Having done El Presidio, head east on Alameda and turn south (right) onto Church Street. You'll shortly cross in front of that Moorish domed **Pima County Courthouse.** Most of its offices open on a colonnade courtyard in front and the plaza in the rear. Continue south on Church to Congress, turn left and walk a block up to the **Bank One** building at Stone Avenue. This old brick front 10-story structure was Tucson's first highrise. Murals inside its lobby trace the area's history from dinosaurs to the territorial period.

Stroll now beneath newer skyscrapers, heading south on Stone. You'll leave the compact highrise district within a few blocks and enter the **Barrio Historic District** as you cross Cushing Street. Once a Mexican residential area, it's given over mostly to business and shops, some in adobe structures. Turn right onto Simpson, then right again onto Meyer and you'll encounter, on your left, the ■ **America West Gallery,** with an interesting collection of Southwestern and primitive art. Turn right onto Cushing, left onto Stone and follow it three blocks back to Ochoa and the visitor center.

DOWNTOWN ATTRACTIONS
In order of appearance

John C. Frémont House ● *Near the Convention Center downtown, off Granada (P.O. Box 2588), Tucson, AZ 85702; (520) 622-0956. Wednesday-Saturday 10 to 4; free.* ☐ John C. Frémont was one busy fellow. In a single lifetime he was a Western explorer and pathfinder, military commandant of California during the Mexican War, civil governor of California, U.S. senator from California, commander of the U.S. Army's Western Military Department and governor of the Arizona Territory.

During his stint as Arizona's governor, he occupied homes in Prescott and Tucson. This one is an 1858 adobe brick house, squatting almost timidly among the bold new structures of the Tucson Convention Center. Now a museum operated by the Arizona Historical Society, it's furnished with Victorian, American and Southwestern antiques.

☺ **El Presidio Historic District** • *Bounded by Pennington, Church, Washington and Main.* ❑ Although its adobe walls have long since melted back into the sand, El Presidio retains some of its yesterday flavor. Many of its 19th century adobes house galleries and restaurants. Signposts and plaques relate the history of homes dating back more than a century.

Tucson Museum of Art • *140 N. Main Ave. (Alameda, next to El Presidio Historic District), Tucson, AZ 85701; (520) 624-2333. Monday-Saturday 10 to 4 and Sunday noon to 4, Tuesday- Saturday 10 to 4. Adults $2, seniors and students $1, children free; Tuesday is free day for everyone. Gallery tours can be arranged through the museum office.* ❑ Galleries are arranged along downward spiraling ramps in this contemporary museum on the edge of Tucson's oldest district. The complex also has a sculpture garden and five houses built between 1850 and 1907. Galleries feature large collections of Western art, pre-Colombian artifacts and special changing exhibits. Original works and prints by Southwestern artisans are on sale in the museum gift shop.

Old Town Artisans • *186 N. Meyer (Telles); (520) 623-6024. Open daily; various hours.* ❑ The largest arts and crafts shopping complex in El Presidio, this 13-room marketplace features hand-crafted Southwestern art, Indian tribal arts, Latin American imports and sundry other giftwares and souvenirs. Hundreds of local artists are represented. Not merely a shop, Old Town Artisans is a collection of shops, including Navajo silver works, a general store and candle shop, Southwest art shop, jewelry and apparel store and the Old Town Pot Shop, with hundreds of pottery items and Southwest furnishings. The Old Town Grill serves mesquite broiled fare (listed below, under "Where to dine").

America West Art Gallery • *Meyer at Cushing; (520) 623-4091.* ❑ Housed in an 1860 ranch home, this gallery features Southwestern and primitive art. The home is furnished to the period and a patio exhibits several old Mexican grinding stones and other artifacts.

DRIVING TUCSON

Plan on more than a day for this lengthy tour, since it takes nearly 200 miles to stitch together greater Tucson's many lures. If we seem to be taking you in circles, it's because these attractions are scattered to the winds. (Bold faced items marked with a ■ are listed with more detail below, under "Attractions".)

Again using the visitor center as your launching point, head east on Broadway about 2.3 miles and turn right onto Country Club Road. Go south to **Reid Park** and turn left onto 22nd Street, wrapping around the corner of the Park. Drive toward the eastern edge and you'll see the entrance to ■ **Reid Park Zoo.** Reid Park also is home to Hi Corbett Field, home field for the minor league Tucson Toros and for the major league Colorado Rockies during Cactus League play. Continue out 22nd for less than a mile and turn left onto Alvernon Way, at the corner of Randolph Municipal Golf Course. Nearly three miles' worth of Alvernon will deliver you to the ■ **Tucson Botanical Gardens,** on your left. If you cross Grant Road, you just missed it.

Plaza de las Armas offers views of old and new Tucson—the Moorish domed Pima County Courthouse and modern downtown office buildings.

Retreat down Alvernon a mile, turn right onto Speedway Boulevard and follow it more than two miles until it crosses the top of the red brick campus of the ■ **University of Arizona.** Go left on Park Avenue and start looking for a place to—well—park.

RV PARKING ADVISORY ● The best advice is to visit on a weekend; the museums are open (check for individual hours) and students haven't taken all the parking places. Parking lots are too small for anything over 19 feet; the best bet is curbside parking on nearby streets, off University Boulevard just west of the campus.

University Boulevard, which crosses Park, is the keystone of this area. Follow it east into the campus and its imposing array of public attractions, including three major museums. Or walk west through a typical campus commercial area with its cafés, copy shops, poster shops, dry cleaner and other student essentials. A particularly lively spot for beer and a light lunch is the **Frog and Firkin** English style pub in a 1930s cottage at 874 E. University. As you head into the campus, the ■ **Arizona State Museum** is just inside the gate, with exhibit halls on either side of University Avenue. The ■ **Arizona Historical Society Museum** is just off campus at 949 E. Second and Park Avenue; and the ■ **Arizona University Museum of Art** is inside the campus, near Speedway between Park and Olive.

Most of the University's lures—■ **Flandrau Planetarium**, the Student Union, library, Centennial Hall and university ticket office—are along University Avenue, which is closed to traffic in the center of the campus. Walk past Old Main (on a landscaped island in the middle of University Avenue) and you'll shortly see the Community Service Center on your right, in front of Wildcat Stadium. This small building also serves as the **visitor information center**, and you can pick up a campus map.

From the university, get back on Speedway and drive west nearly ten miles until you clear the city, cross under the freeway and get into mountainous cactus country. The large castle like structure on your right houses the ■ **International Wildlife Museum.** Past the museum, the route becomes Gates Pass Road and climbs steeply into mountainous, cactus-dotted ■ **Tucson Mountain Park.** This remarkable swatch of desert wilderness—just minutes from the city—contains many of the area's major attractions. Top a steep rise, drop down into a desert basin, turn left onto Kinney Road and you soon encounter ■ **Old Tucson Studios.** Reverse your route and follow Kinney to the outstanding ■ **Arizona-Sonora Desert Museum** and beyond that—following directional signs, the western campus of **Saguaro National Park** (recently promoted from national monument status).

RV ADVISORY ● A sign advises that trailers shouldn't be driven over narrow, winding Gates Pass, and there are alternate routes around either edge of Tucson Mountain Park. It is a real twister, although large motorhomes—carefully driven—should have no problem.

From the western section of Saguaro National Park, continue past the Red Hills Information Center on Sandario Road and turn right onto Picture Rocks Road, following an I-10 sign. You'll pass through some rocky ridges, then re-enter the park briefly, where a sign directs you to **Picture Rocks,** a collection of petroglyphs. Beyond here, hit a stop sign and turn right onto Ina Road, which takes you under the freeway and back into Tucson.

You'll skim five miles across the top of Tucson—moving fairly rapidly because the signals are well spaced and timed. Just short of Oracle Road, turn left into ■ **Tohono Chul Park** botanical garden. From there, continue east on Ina, along the foothills of the Santa Catalina Mountains. About 1.5 miles past Tohono Chul, the route dips southeast to become Skyline Drive. Stay with it for three or four miles until it hits Swan Road. For a grand panorama of the city, better looking at night than in daylight, turn left and follow Swan into the foothills. Otherwise go right on Swan for a few hundred yards and turn left into ■ **De Grazia Gallery in the Sun.** Next, drive three miles down to Fort Lowell Road, go left for a mile, turn right onto Craycroft Road and take a quick left into Fort Lowell Park for the ■ **Fort Lowell Museum.** Continue about half a mile down Craycroft and turn left onto Grant Road.

Stay alert for a tricky turn here: After a mile and a quarter, Grant swerves to the right and you shortly make a left onto Tanque Verde Road. Go northeast for about a mile and turn left onto Sabino Canyon Road. Follow this four miles through rough hewn, cactus strewn foothills into ■ **Sabino Canyon** recreation area. Return to Tanque Verde Road, head east about 2.5 miles, and follow a double left turn lane up the Catalina Highway. You'll climb steeply and swiftly into the heart of the ■ **Mount Lemmon Recreation Area,** which offers evergreen escapes from the heat in summer and desert-to-alps skiing in winter. It's one of the most dramatic highway ascents in the West—a quick transition from narrow cactus lined canyons through oak woodlands into ponderosa forests. Vistas from here are absolutely splendid— again, particularly at night. Twenty-five miles up the road, the highway ends at the aptly named **Summerhaven,** where locals and summer visitors go to avoid simmering. Another road leads to the **Mount Lemmon Ski Area.**

Drop down from the mountain and, about two miles after you hit the flatlands, take a half left at a blinking amber signal onto Houghton Road. Follow it five mile south to a traffic light at Old Spanish Trail and turn left. After rambling through three miles of desert, you'll arrive at the eastern venue of

Fantastic rock formations line the Catalina Highway as it climbs to the Mount Lemmon resort area.

■ **Saguaro National Park** and eleven miles beyond that, ■ **Colossal Cave.** From the cave, turn south at an I-10 sign and drive a roller-coaster seven miles through desert dips to the freeway. You'll pass through the tiny town of **Vail** en route. If you want to sip some Arizona wine, take the freeway frontage road briefly east, following signs to ■ **R.W. Webb Winery.**

Now, head west on I-10 and jump off at Wilmot Road (exit 269) to follow signs to the ■ **Pima Air Museum** near the corner of Wilmot and Valencia. Take Valencia west from the museum, cross over I-10 and stay with Valencia about five miles to Interstate 19. Go south less than two miles to exit 92 and follow San Xavier Road west to your final stop in this marathon tour, ■ **Mission San Xavier del Bac.**

OUTLYING ATTRACTIONS
In order of appearance

☺ *Reid Park Zoo* ● *1100 S. Randolph Way (enter Lakeshore Drive off 22nd Street), Tucson, AZ 85716; (520) 791-4022. Daily 9:30 a.m. to 5 p.m. Adults $3.50, seniors $2.50, kids 5 to 14, 75 cents.* ⊡ This fine little zoo, landscaped with green lawns shaded by eucalyptus and palm trees, has a busy collection of giraffes, lions, tigers, hippos, primates and more. Some of its critters are housed in modern open-air enclosures; birds flit around a large aviary. About 400 critters occupy the zoo, which conducts ongoing conservation, educational and scientific research programs. It leads the zoological world in the successful breeding of the giant anteater––which might suggest that the zoo doesn't have any ant problems.

The zoo shares large Reid Park with a baseball and soccer field, rose garden, duck pond, fishing and paddleboat lake, swimming pools, golf course, playground and picnic areas. It's also home to Hi Corbett Field, a baseball park used by the minor league Tucson Toros, and for spring exhibition baseball by the Colorado Rockies, and quite possibly the new Arizona Diamondbacks baseball team from Phoenix; see below under "Spectator sports."

Tucson Botanical Gardens • *2150 N. Alvernon Way (Grant), Tucson, AZ 85712; (520) 326-9255. Daily 8:30 to 4:30 daily; gift shop open Monday-Saturday 9 to 4 and Sunday noon to 4. Adults $3, seniors $2 and kids under 12 free.* ☐ Once the estate of a local nurseryman, the garden rambles over 5.5 acres, with pleasant paths leading through lush plant life. Among its displays are an Australian garden, herb garden, historical garden with English ivy and such, and a Tohono O'odham garden with crops typical of early Native Americans. We were particularly interested in the Xeriscape Demonstration Garden which exhibits water-conservation methods essential to a desert environment. Solar energy is used to irrigate and illuminate this water- sipping garden. The Botanical Garden gift shop is particularly cute. In addition to gardening books, it has an assortment of gift items, many with gardening and chili-pepper themes.

University of Arizona campus • *The community Service Center at Cherry and University is open Monday-Friday 8 to 5 and Saturday 9 to 2; (520) 621-5130. One can pick up campus maps, brochures, activity lists, university catalogs and even a selection of brochures on Tucson's other attractions.*

Located in the heart of Tucson, the university's expansive campus is a major cultural resource as well as important learning center. Eight museums and galleries occupy its sturdy red brick buildings. You can grab a snack or a substantial meal at the Student Union. Visitor parking is available in the Second Street garage (corner of Highland) and in a lot next to the visitor center. Here's a list of on-campus attractions and activities. (Three major public attractions—Flandrau Science Center, Arizona State Museum and Arizona Historical Society Museum, are listed below the university roundup.)

CAMPUS TOURS, *call (520) 621-3641. During the academic year: weekdays at 10 a.m. and 2 p.m. and Saturday at 10; during the summer: Monday-Saturday at 10 a.m.* These tours are given by student volunteers. Meet in the lobby of the Nugent Building across from the student union.

CENTER FOR CREATIVE PHOTOGRAPHY, *across Olive Road from the art museum; (520) 621-7968. Weekdays 10 to 5 and Sunday noon to 5; free.* One of America's largest collections of Ansel Adams photos is displayed in the center's gallery, along with rotating exhibits.

MINERAL MUSEUM, *in the basement of the Flandrau Science Center; (520) 621-4227. Weekdays 9 a.m. to 5 p.m. and weekends 1 to 5; free.* Rocks and gems from the Southwest and around the world are on display.

☺ **UNIVERSITY OF ARIZONA MUSEUM OF ART,** *Speedway and North Park; (520) 621-7567. Monday-Friday 9 to 5 and Sunday noon to 4 during the school year; Monday-Friday 10 to 3:30 and Saturday noon to 4 in summer; free.* Rated as one of the finest university museums between Houston and Los Angeles, it has large collections of Middle Ages and 20th Century art.

WILDCAT HERITAGE GALLERY, *McKale Memorial Center; (520) 621-2411. Weekdays 8 to 5; free.* It's an essential stop for University of Arizona alumni, with photos and other memorabilia of U of A teams dating back to 1897.

☺ **Flandrau Science Center and Planetarium** • *Northwest corner of University and Cherry; (520) 621-4515 or (520) 621-STAR for recorded information. Museum and astronomy store open weekdays 10 to 5 and weekends noon to 5. Evening hours with public telescope viewing Wednesday-Thursday 7 to 9 and Friday-Saturday 7 to midnight. Museum admission and telescope viewing free; star and laser shows in the planetarium theater $3 to $5.* ☐ This is a science museum as well as a planetarium. Push assorted buttons and levers to learn about holography, radio waves and Light Amplification by Stimulated Emission Radiation. A holographic lady blows you a kiss as you walk by and a star projector in a mini-dome introduces you to the constellations. Shows in the planetarium theater change periodically, usually with the seasons. They range from laser light productions set to music to basic astronomy to Native American sky lore.

☺ **Arizona State Museum** ● *University Avenue at Park Avenue (c/o University of Arizona, Tucson, AZ 85721); (520) 621-6302. Monday-Saturday 10 to 4 and Sunday noon to 5; free.* ☐ Occupying two buildings just inside UA's main gate, this museum focuses on prehistoric and modern Indian cultures of the Southwest. A display in the main exhibit building (on the right as you enter the campus) offers an excellent view of the lifestyle of the Apache, past and present. Another intriguing exhibit discusses cave archaeology—how both prehistoric and modern societies have used earth recesses for shelter. A mezzanine is stuffed with stuffed animals indigenous to Arizona, along with a gemstone and Hohokam exhibit. The museum's administration building across the street is used primarily for changing exhibits.

☺ **Arizona Historical Society Museum** ● *949 E. Second St. (Park Avenue), Tucson, AZ 85719; (520) 628-5774. Monday-Saturday 10 to 4, Sunday noon to 4; free.* ☐ Located just outside the university campus, it picks up where the Indians left off, covering settlement from the arrival of the Spanish to the development of modern Arizona. Uncluttered, informative exhibits tell the state's story with cattle brands, Bull Durham pouches, high-wheeled bicycles and period costumes. In a full-sized mock- up mine, you learn about copper mining methods before the days of the open pit. Another exhibit traces Arizona's transportation from stagecoaches to Colorado River steamers to Lieutenant Beale's strange camel corps. A new exhibit aimed at children, "Exploring 1870s Tucson," features the daily lives of kids from three ethnic backgrounds—a Mexican-American ranch, a Tohono O'odham home and an Anglo American mercantile store. It has several touch and feel objects.

☺ **International Wildlife Museum** ● *4800 W. Gates Pass Rd. (Camino de Oeste), Tucson, AZ 85745; (520) 629-0100 or (520) 624-4024 (recording). Daily 9 to 5. Adults $5; seniors, students and military $3.50; kids 6 to 12, $1.50.* ☐ Talk about strange. The wildlife museum is enclosed in an architectural blend of feudal castle and French Foreign Legion fort. Exhibits, including more than 300 varieties of stuffed animals, are intended to "promote wildlife appreciation in a multitude of ways." Indeed, many displays do just that. Several videos focus on wildlife conservation; graphics tell of the threat to the world's rain forests.

However, one large room—Wildlife of the World Gallery—is filled with more than a hundred hunting trophies. Bodyless Cape buffalo, rhinos, elephants and assorted antelopes stare morosely from the walls in this room that suggests massive men's hunting lodge. Elsewhere, taxidermied exhibits—while excellently done—seem focused on violence: gray wolves beating up on a caribou, lions taking down an African buffalo and bears fighting over salmon. Despite these curiosities, the museum is *very* well done, and a good zoological teaching tool for kids. Exhibits discuss horns, hooves and hair and other mammalian characteristics. Particularly impressive is a 30-foot mountain occupied by stuffed wild goats and sheep. It's surrounded by 22 dioramas with critters of North America, Europe and Africa in natural settings.

☺ **Tucson Mountain Park** ● *Eight miles west of downtown; (520) 883-4200. Day use 7 a.m. to 10 p.m.; overnight camping (see listing under "Where to Camp").* ☐ This huge Pima County park sprawls over 17,000 acres of rough-hewn Tucson Mountain foothills. It provides instant desert wilderness to residents of the nearby city. Within the park's boundaries are three other attractions: the Tucson Mountain section of Saguaro National Park, Arizona-Sonora Desert Museum and Old Tucson Studios (all listed separately). Park facilities include picnic areas, hiking and riding trails and the Gilbert Ray Campground. A viewpoint at the top of Gates Pass is a great place to watch the sunset. Several hiking trails extend from there into the rugged, cactus-covered Tucson Mountains.

☺ **Old Tucson Studios** ● *201 S. Kinney Rd. (Tucson Mountain Park), Tucson, AZ 85746; (520) 883-6457 or 883-0100. Daily 9 to 9. Adults $12.95, kids 4 to 11 $8.95.* ☐ Old Tucson is Universal Studios with hay bales—a working memorial to all those shoot-outs that have blazed across the Arizona landscape. It began in 1939 when Columbia Pictures produced one of the

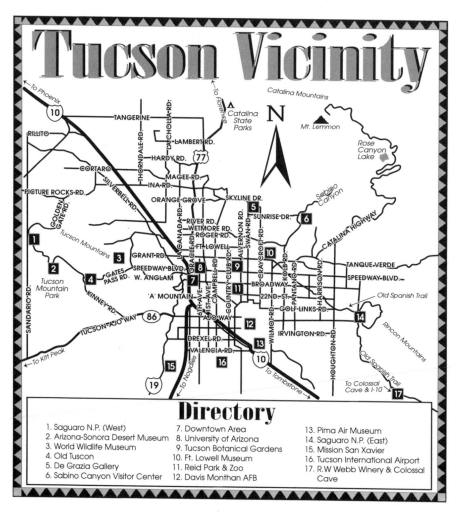

Tucson Vicinity

Directory

1. Saguaro N.P. (West)
2. Arizona-Sonora Desert Museum
3. World Wildlife Museum
4. Old Tucson
5. De Grazia Gallery
6. Sabino Canyon Visitor Center
7. Downtown Area
8. University of Arizona
9. Tucson Botanical Gardens
10. Ft. Lowell Museum
11. Reid Park & Zoo
12. Davis Monthan AFB
13. Pima Air Museum
14. Saguaro N.P. (East)
15. Mission San Xavier
16. Tucson International Airport
17. R.W Webb Winery & Colossal Cave

first big movie epics, *Arizona*. Seeking authenticity, producers built a life-sized model of early day Tucson, complete with adobe buildings, corrals and hitchin' rails. The star was a young actor named William Holden; Jean Arthur was his leading lady. When the shooting was completed (no pun intended), the company left Old Tucson to wither in the desert sun.

Twenty years later, entrepreneur Bob Sheldon bought the crumbling ruin, added more weather-worn buildings and created a permanent set for Western movies. Since then, more than 150 oat- baggers have been filmed here, including TV horse operas such as *The Young Riders*. Visitors can watch shoot-outs on Main Street, tour a giant sound stage and visit in the Royal Oak Saloon. Placards describing the films shot here read like a horse opera honor roll: *McClintock, Gunfight at the O.K. Corral* and *Rio Lobo,* along with television's *Little House on the Prairie* and *The High Chaparral*. Much of the park may be changed when you visit, since it suffered a major fire in 1995 and was being rebuilt at this writing.

☺ *The Arizona-Sonora Desert Museum* ● *2021 N. Kinney Rd. (in Tucson Mountain Park), Tucson, AZ 85743; (520) 883-2702. Daily 8:30 to 5 October through February and 7:30 to 6 the rest of the year. Ages 13 and older, $8.95; kids 6 through 12, $1.75.* ☐ Planners re-invented the museum when they created this indoor-outdoor complex. The *New York Times* once called it "the most distinctive zoo in the United States." Certainly, it is the finest such center in Arizona, and it's Tucson's most-visited attraction. The museum takes its name from the states of Arizona, U.S.A., and Sonora, Mexico. Its primary focus is ecological, telling the story of the plants, animals and geology of the Sonoran Desert that covers much of these two states. Plan most of a day to walk its paths, viewing desert creatures in typical habitats, learning about desert flora and strolling through bird-busy aviaries. Over-under exhibits allow you to watch beavers and river otters at play above and below the surface of streams

Our favorite exhibit is the Earth Sciences Center, an elaborate grotto featuring a realistic limestone cave, a jewel- like mineral display and a graphic explanation of the formation of our four-billion-year-old planet. You see the earth's transition from a meteor-impacted chunk of rock to the cloud- sworled globe so familiar to us from space photos. Among the museum's new displays are a walk-in hummingbird aviary with eight varieties of hummers flitting about, and a desert grassland that demonstrates the biodiversity of a community of plants and animals, right down to micro-organism. Also added recently are an art gallery, bird shop, coffee bar, terraced indoor-outdoor restaurant and a dining room.

☺ *Saguaro National Park* ● *Tucson Mountain section off Sandario Road in Tucson Mountain Park; (520) 883-6366; open 24 hours, Red Hills visitor center open daily 8 to 5; free. Rincon Mountain section off Old Spanish Trail east of Tucson; (520) 296-8576; 7 a.m. to 6 p.m., visitor center open 8 to 5; $3 per vehicle, $1 per hiker or biker. (Although the two regions occur at different points in our driving route, we've grouped them in this listing.) The two sections of Saguaro National Park serve the same function—to preserve and exhibit their giant cactus namesake. Yet the areas have different personalities.* ☐

SAGUARO WEST, the Tucson Mountain section covering 21,152 acres, has more bountiful cactus gardens than its eastern counterpart, although it doesn't have the elevation range. Its small visitor center has a fine natural sciences book shop. Wall graphics describe the geology, flora and fauna of

Sonoran Desert. A photo exhibit depicts a harvest of saguaro fruit, conducted annually in the park by local Indians. The six-mile Bajada Loop Drive will take you through a dense saguaro thicket, scattered over the rough surfaces of Tucson Mountain. Several 200-year-old giants line the road. Some are turning brown with age and drooping their arms, like tired old men. A rich cactus garden stands at their feet.

SAGUARO EAST, off Old Spanish Trail, is the larger of the two sections, covering 62,499 acres, and park headquarters is located here. This section climbs through five climate zones from the desert to conifer ramparts of the Rincon Mountains, offering a rich cross section of desert topography. Its saguaro forests are older and thinner than those of Saguaro West. At the visitor center, you learn more than you probably ever wanted to know about this strange plant. It grows only in the Sonoran Desert of Arizona and Mexico—lopping slightly into California. It can reach a height of 50 feet but it takes its time getting there. A seedling grows only a quarter of an inch the first year and it takes 15 years to reach a foot; those familiar arms don't appear until it's more than 50 years old.

A desert garden in front of the visitor center helps you tell a pincushion cactus from a prickly pear. The best way to experience the park is to purchase a driving guide and follow the eight-mile Cactus Forest Drive through the Rincon foothills. There are picnic areas and hiking trails along the way. If you're in good shape, get an early start and hike 17.5 miles to the top of 8,666-foot Mica Mountain.

☺ ***Tohono Chul Park*** • *7366 N. Paseo del Norte (northwest corner of Ina and Oracle), Tucson, AZ 85704; (520) 742-6455. Daily 7 a.m. to sunset; exhibit hall, gift gallery and Tea Room open Monday-Saturday 8 a.m. to 5 p.m. and Sunday 11 to 5. Free; contributions accepted.* □ Perhaps Arizona's finest privately endowed park, Tohono Chul preserves a patch of desert landscape in the middle of Tucson. Nature trails, patios, shade ramadas, two gift shops, and exhibit center and a wonderful Southwest style tea room provide refuge from the growing city. Fashioned from two estates, the park was created by Richard and Jean Wilson, former owners of the adjacent Haunted Bookshop. They purchased the land to rescue it from development, then formed a non-profit foundation to operate the park. The bookshop, named because people are "haunted by the books they haven't gotten around to reading," offers an excellent section on Arizona plus a good selection of general books. A park exhibit center has changing displays focusing on Arizona arts, crafts and life-styles. Two attractive gift shops—one in the exhibit center and another in the tea room—sell crafts, curios, artwork and Indian handicrafts. Tohono Chul Tea Room, set in a courtyard, is reviewed in the dining section below.

☺ ***De Grazia Gallery in the Sun*** • *6300 N. Swan Rd. (Skyline Drive), Tucson, AZ 85718; (520) 299-9191. Daily 10 to 4; free.* □ The late Ted De Grazia developed a large following for his impressionistic, whimsical style of painting. Simple, quick brush strokes created color-splashed Indians, Mexicans, roadrunners and other Southwestern subjects. An earthy individual, he used local adobe and other materials to build his studio and adjacent chapel called "Mission in the Sun." After his death, a foundation was created to continue operating his rustic gallery and gift shop. Exhibits are changed periodically, drawn from his extensive collection. De Grazia did not shy from commercialism. In the gift shop here, and throughout Arizona, you will see his style emblazoned on everything from greeting cards to refrigerator magnets. Ceramics, wind chimes, enamel work and reproductions of De Grazia's art can be purchased here.

Fort Lowell Museum • *Craycroft and Fort Lowell (mailing address: 949 E. Second St., Tucson, AZ 85719); (520) 885-3832. Wednesday-Saturday 10 to 4; free.* ☐ Part of a large city park and recreation center, Fort Lowell Museum is a reconstruction of a military camp established in 1873. Like most Arizona forts, it was not a stockade, but a garrison from which troops set forth to do battle with the Indians. When they weren't chasing Apaches, they were socializing with the citizens of Tucson, attending dances, fielding sports teams and raising a little Saturday night hell.

"The boys in blue raked over the dry embers of the town in pursuit of life and sport," the *Tucson Citizen* reported in a May, 1874, issue.

Museum structures include the commanding officers quarters with period furnishings and historical displays, and the "kitchen building," with exhibits concerning the fort's development and excavations of early Indian sites.

☺ **Sabino Canyon** • *Sabino Canyon Road; (520) 749-2327. From December through May, trams run every half hour, daily 9 to 4:30; the rest of the year, they run hourly 9 to 4 on weekdays and 9 to 4:30 weekends. Adults $5, kids 3 to 12, $2. Bear Canyon tram runs less frequently; adults $3, kids 3 to 12, $1.25. Sabino Canyon Visitor Center open 8 to 4:30 weekdays and 8:30 to 4:30 weekends.* ☐

Sabino Canyon is a prime example of Tucson's delightful contrast. Just minutes from downtown, this steep-walled chasm cuts deeply into the flanks of the Santa Catalina Mountains. Forests of saguaro cactus march from the banks of Sabino Creek up rugged canyon walls. Ultimately, they give way to forests of pines. Hiking trails lead into the more remote heights. Because of congestion on the narrow canyon road, vehicle access is limited to a tram. It takes visitors on a 45-minute round trip, with stops at picnic areas and trailheads along the way. The driver offers description of the canyon's geology, flora and fauna as the tram trundles along. On summer weekends, the canyon is wall-to-wall as residents come to splash in what's left of Sabino Creek, seeking relief from valley heat.

Bear Canyon is less crowded and equally rugged. Shuttles from the same tram station take visitors to Silver Falls Trailhead, from where they can hike just over two miles to the falls. A **Coronado National Forest** visitor center near the tram station has interpretive exhibits of the geology, plant life and critters of the Santa Catalina Mountains and their craggy canyons.

☺ **Mount Lemmon Recreation Area** • *Reached via the Catalina Highway from northeast Tucson. For information: Coronado National Forest, (520) 576-1542.* ☐ The Catalina Highway spirals quickly from the saguaro-thick foothills of the Catalina Mountains to the piney forests of Mount Lemmon. Along the way, you'll see fantastic roadside rock formations that look like misplaced Easter Island statues or broken columns of Greek temples. Several viewpoints provide impressive vistas of the Tucson Basin's vast carpet of civilization. Plan this drive in the afternoon, then return at night to watch Tucson twinkle like an upside-down universe.

In winter, you can hit the slopes at Mount Lemmon Ski Valley. The small facility offers two lifts and a dozen runs. One of the lift operates the year around for the benefit of sightseers; it runs weekdays 11 to 5 and weekends 10 to 5 in summer and daily 9 to 4 in winter. Nearby Summerhaven is an alpine community with shops, a couple of restaurants and a general store. A-

Titillating "nose art" decorates a World War II B-24 Consolidated at the Pima Air Museum.

frame homes tucked among the Ponderosas provide summer solace for desert dwellers. The region is part of Coronado National Forest, with the typical recreational opportunities of camping, picnicking, hiking, backpacking and fishing. And it's only an hour from poolside in downtown Tucson.

☺ **Saguaro National Park east** • *See listing on page 267.*

Colossal Cave • *Old Spanish Trail, P.O. Box D-7, Vail, AZ 85641; (520) 791-7677. Monday-Saturday 9 to 5, Sunday 9 to 6. Adults $6.50, youths 11 to 16, $5 and kids $3.50. MC/VISA.* ❑ Colossal Cave isn't quite. It might have been, but past decades of vandalizing ruined many of its formations. One early operator would break off stalactites and stalagmites and sell them to his customers for $2 apiece. The cave is still privately owned and of course the present operators are much more conscientious. Guides conduct one-hour tours past the formations of this dry limestone cavern. Actually, there's more here than meets the eye—literally. Colossal is thought to be the world's largest dry cave, with more than 40 miles of corridors. In fact, the end still hasn't been found. The public tour covers only about a mile.

R.W. Webb Winery • *13605 E. Benson Highway (14 miles southeast, I-10 exit 279), P.O. Box 130, Vail, AZ 85641; (520) 762-5777. Tours and tastings Monday-Saturday 10 to 5, Sunday noon to 5 (last tour starts at 4 each day). Admission $1, applied toward purchase.* ❑ Premium wine grapes among the cactus? The R.W. Webb Winery is the first in Arizona, producing and marketing an assortment of varietal wines. Tours cover the modern facility, followed by sips of the product. The winery is set against the Rincon mountains, with an inviting courtyard and fountain shaded by olive trees.

☺ **Pima Air and Space Museum** • *6000 E. Valencia Rd. (Wilmot), Tucson, AZ 85706; (520) 574-0462 or (520) 574-9658 (recorded message). Daily 9 to 5 (doors close at 4). Adults $6, seniors and military personnel $5, kids 10 to 17 $3.* ❑ If you've ever wanted to soar on fanciful wings of eagles, you'll love this place. More than 200 aircraft are on display, from a realistic full-scale model of the Wright brothers craft to a mach-3 Lockheed SR-71 Blackbird. Exhibits trace the development of aviation from pre-Wright brothers attempts to space flight. Five large buildings are filled with old planes, gliders, aircraft engines, flight suits and other airborne regalia. Out on the tarmac, about 150 planes glisten in the sun. Most are post World War II.

Of particular interest is a four-engine DC-6 that served as Air Force One for Presidents Kennedy and Johnson. You can tour the President's quarters, press and Secret Service compartments and full-sized kitchen. You'll see the desk and leather chair where our leaders contemplated the missiles of October and other frustrations as they flitted about the country.

☺ **Mission San Xavier del Bac** ● *San Xavier Road (9 miles south, off I-19); (520) 294-2624. Church, museum and gift shop open daily 9 to 6; Mass Saturday at 5:30 and Sunday at 8, 9:30, 11 and noon. Free; contributions appreciated.* ☐ The "White Dove of the Desert," with its Spanish-colonial architecture, gleaming white walls and brown façade, is perhaps Arizona's most beautiful structure. Its roots reach back to the earliest days, when Father Kino ministered to the people of the village of Bac. Located on the San Xavier Reservation, it still serves Native Americans. Its architecture is typical of the Southwest look. In the sanctuary, the elaborate alter contrasts the church's simple exterior, with busy columns and saintly niches. There is even whimsy in this hallowed place. Comical lions wearing wide grins guard the altar. Above the main door, a plaster-cast cat and mouse eye one another warily.

On weekends, members of the Tohono O'odham tribe set up a market on the mission grounds, selling crafts and tasty Indian fry bread. A gift shop occupies one end of the building and a nearby path leads to a hilltop cross with a fine view of the surrounding countryside.

The Tohono O'odham mission dates from Father Kino's arrival in 1700. The present church was constructed around 1778 by later Franciscans. Its architecture is a splendid curiosity. Lacking materials but wanting a church as elegant as those in Spain, the builders used Indian-made paints and dyes to simulate marble, tile and even chandeliers. These features have been faithfully preserved. Two mysteries surround the old church: Who designed it, and why was the second bell tower never finished? A fanciful story is that the Spanish Crown would tax a building only after it was completed, so the wily padres never finished the second tower. A less interesting but more logical theory is that they simply ran out of funds.

ACTIVITIES & ENTERTAINMENT

Air tours ● Spirit Aviation, 1921 E. Flight Line Dr., Tucson, AZ 85706, (520) 889-0593; fixed wing air tours. Tucson Aeroservice Center, 11700 W. Avra Valley Rd., Room 85, Marana, AZ 85653, (520) 682-2999; local, Grand Canyon, Sedona and Las Vegas sightseeing flights.

Golf ● Twenty golf courses are in and about Tucson. Many are listed in the *Golf Arizona* brochure, available at the Tucson visitor center and other tourist information centers in the state, or contact Golf-Market, 15704 Cholla, Fountain Hills, AZ 837-2184.

Jeep tours ● Mountain View Off-road Excursions, 3149 E. Prince Rd., Tucson, AZ 85716, (800) 594-9644 or (520) 622-4488. Sunshine Jeep Tours, 9040 N. Oracle Rd., Suite D, Tucson, AZ 85737, (520) 742-1943. Trail Dust Jeep Tours, 1665 S. Craycroft Rd., Tucson, AZ 85711, 747-0323.

Other land tours • Desert View Tour & Shuttle, 1011 E. Navajo Rd., Tucson, AZ 85719, (800) 227-5443 or (520) 887-2627; van tours to area attractions. Great Southwestern Tour Co., 5241 N. Bluebonnet, Tucson, AZ 85745, (800) 743-4833 or (520) 743-4833; tours to area attractions. Great Western Tours, P.O. Box 31831, Tucson, AZ 85751, (520) 721-0980; tours of area attractions and other Arizona communities. High Desert Convoys, Inc., 2242-A E. Spring St., Tucson, AZ 85719, (800) 93-TOURS or (520) 323-3386; desert and history tours in restored World War II military vehicles. Off the Beaten Path Tours, 5523 N. Crescent Ridge Dr., Tucson, AZ 85718, (520) 529-6090; daytime and overnight tours to area attractions, neighboring states and Mexico.

Walking tours • Backroads, 1516 Fifth St., Berkeley, CA 94710-1740, (800) 462-2848 or (510) 527-1555; six-day walking tours starting in Tucson with El Presidio Historic District, the Desert Museum and Saguaro National Park, followed by van transfers to southeastern Arizona for visits to several canyon preserves, Bisbee, Tombstone and Chiricahua National Monument.

Western cookout • CCC Chuckwagon Suppers, 8900 Bopp Rd. (eight miles west; Ajo Way to Kinney Road, then left on Bopp Road), Tucson, AZ 85746; (800) 446-1798 or (520) 883-2333. Cowboy grub and entertainment by a Western band singing trail-riding songs, plus a few modern country songs. Tuesday-Saturday late December through April.

Performing arts

Tucson Center for the Performing Arts • The center hosts a variety of performing arts and special events during the year; 408 S. Sixth Ave., Tucson, AZ 85701; (520) 884-8210.

Dance • Orts Theatre of Dance, 328 E. Seventh St., Tucson, AZ 85705; (520) 624-3799. This professional repertory dance company presents four programs each year.

Melodramas • Gaslight Theatre, 7010 E. Broadway Blvd., Tucson, AZ 85710; (520) 886-9428. Hiss the hero and boo the villain at these old fashioned melodramas and musical comedies.

Opera • Arizona Opera Company, 3501 N. Mountain Ave., Tucson, AZ 85719; (520) 293-4336; productions from October through March.

Symphony • Tucson Symphony Orchestra, 443 S. Stone Ave., Tucson, AZ 85701; box office (520) 792-9155, main office (520) 882-8585. Varied programs of classics, pops and chamber concerts October through April.

Theater • Arizona Theatre Company, Brady Court at 40 E. 14th St., Tucson, AZ 85701, (520) 622-2823; professional plays October through April at the Tucson Convention Center theater. Invisible Theatre, 1400 N. First Ave., Tucson, AZ 87919, (520) 882-9721; off-Broadway style productions.

University events • University of Arizona Office of Cultural Affairs. 800 E. University Blvd., Room 110, Tucson, AZ 85719, box office (520) 621-3341, main office (520) 621-3364. The office coordinates a broad range of cultural events ranging from Broadway shows and major star appearances to ethnic arts and dance in Centennial Hall on the campus.

Spectator sports

Auto racing • Stock car races are held Saturday nights March through October at Tucson Raceway Park, 12500 S. Houghton Rd., (520) 762-9200.

Cactus League baseball • The American League Colorado Rockies and possibly the new Arizona Diamondbacks of Phoenix will play their spring exhibition schedule at Hi Corbett Field; call (520) 327-9467 for the Rockies and (602) 514-8400 for the Diamondbacks. For more detail, see box in Chapter seven, page 200.

Greyhound racing ● Tucson Greyhound Park, 2601 S. Third Ave., (520) 884-7576. The mutts gallop the year around; parimutuel betting.

Minor league baseball ● The minor league Tucson Toros play at Hi Corbett Field, (520) 325-2621 or Dillard's box office at (800) 638-4253.

University sports ● The University of Arizona Wildcats field football, basketball, baseball and assorted other intercollegiate teams; (520) 621-2411 or check at the McKale Center on the campus.

ANNUAL EVENTS

For more information on these and other events, contact the Tucson Convention & Visitor's Bureau at (520) 624-1889.

Northern Telecom Tucson Open golf tournament, first weekend of January; (520) 571-0400.

Tucson Marathon and Relay, January; (520) 326-9383.

Indian Arts Benefit Fair, first weekend of February; (520) 623-6024.

La Fiesta de los Vaqueros professional rodeo third weekend of February; (520) 741-2233.

Ski Carnival at Mount Lemmon Sk Valley in March; (520) 576-1321.

Simon Peter Passion Play early April at the Tucson Convention Center Music Hall; (520) 327-5560.

Pima County Fair, early to mid-April; (520) 762-9100.

Tohono O'Odham Indian Arts Festival and **Fiesta del Presidio,** first weekend of April.

Mount Lemmon Music Festival, June at Ski Valley; 576-1321.

Music Under the Stars with the Tucson Pops Orchestra, September in Reid Park; (520) 791-4079.

Indian Arts Fair, mid-November at Old Town Artisans; 623-6024.

Copper Bowl New Year's football classic, late December at Arizona Stadium; (520) 790-5510.

WHERE TO SHOP

Tucson has a rich mix of Indian and Mexican handicraft shops and modern malls. One complex, El Mercado del Boutiques (Broadway and Wilmot, east of downtown) is a blend of both; it's a collection of ethnic Southwestern shops. Another good place to find Southwest arts and crafts is Old Town Artisans, 186 N. Meyer in El Presidio, which we mentioned above. The Mexican style Many Hands Courtyard, 3054 First Ave. (between Ft. Lowell and Grant), also features Southwestern boutiques. For a Western style shopping center, try Trail Dust Town at 6541 E. Tanque Verde Rd. (east of downtown near Wilmot).

Several enclosed shopping malls are worthy of a visit by your credit cards. They include large Tucson Mall at Oracle and Wetmore; El Con Mall, just east of downtown on Broadway (between Country Club and Alvernon); Park Mall, east of El Con on Broadway (between Craycroft and Wilmot); and Foothills Center, 7401 N. La Cholla Blvd. (northeast of town, near Ina Road). Among Tucson's boutique malls are The Plaza at Williams Center, 5420 E. Broadway (Craycroft); St. Philip's Plaza at 4330 N. Campbell Ave. (River Road); and Plaza Palomino at 2920 N. Swan Ave. (Ft. Lowell).

Downtown shopping is focused on Fourth Avenue between Fourth and

Seventh streets, with a mix of apparel shops, boutiques, antique shops and galleries. If you like used book stores, you'll love Bookman's at 1930 E. Grant Ave. (Campbell); phone 325-5767. It's a monster of a used book store—one of the largest in the Southwest.

TRANSPORTATION

Airlines serving Tucson International Airport include America West, (800) 548-8969; American, (800) 368-1955; Arizona Airways, (800) ARIZONA; Continental, (800) 525-0280; Delta, (800) 221-1212; and Southwest, (800) 935-9792. Information number for Tucson International is 573-8100.

Airport shuttle service is provided by Airline Transport, (800) 227-5443 or (520) 887-2627; Arizona Shuttle, (520) 889-1000; and Arizona Stagecoach, (520) 889-1000; Most major **car rental** companies serve the airport, including Alamo, (800) 327-9633; Avis, (800) 831-3847; Budget, (800) 279-3734; Dollar, (800) 800-4000; Enterprise; (800) 829-1853; Hertz, (800) 654-3131; National, (800) 227-7368; and Thrifty, (800) 367-2277.

Tucson's **cab companies** include Allstate, (520) 798-111; Caddy Cab, (520) 887-8744; Checker, (520) 623-1133 and Yellow, (520) 624-6611.

Greyhound gallops in and out of Tucson from its terminal at Two S. Fourth St., with service west toward Los Angeles, north to Phoenix, Flagstaff and beyond and east to Texas; (800) 231-2222 or (520) 882-4386. **Bridgewater Transport** serves Douglas, Fort Huachuca, Sierra Vista and Bisbee; (520) 628-8909.

Amtrak heads west to Yuma and Los Angeles and east to New Orleans and to Chicago from its station at 400 E. Toole Avenue; (800) USA-RAIL. **Local bus** service is provided by Sun Tran, which also serves the airport and operates the 25-cent Fourth Avenue Trolley Service between downtown and the University of Arizona campus; (520) 792-9222.

WHERE TO DINE
American
Alpine Inn Restaurant ● ☆☆ $$

☐ *In Summerhaven at the end of the Mount Lemmon Highway; (520) 576-1500. American-continental; full bar service. Monday noon to 8, Tuesday-Thursday 11 to 7, Friday 11 to 9, Saturday 8 to 9, Sunday 8 to 8. MC/VISA.* ☐ Woodsy café in the cool pines of Mount Lemmon. The mixed menu ranges from chicken sauté and veal Oscar to pan fried trout.

☺ Anthony's in the Catalinas ● ☆☆☆☆ $$$

☐ *6440 N. Campbell Ave. (Skyline); (520) 299-1771. Southwestern, continental, Italian; full bar. Lunch Monday-Saturday 11:30 to 2:30, dinner nightly 5:30 to 10. Reservations advised; major credit cards.* ☐ Elegantly appointed restaurant with indoor and outdoor dining, with striking views of Catalina Mountains and the city. Varied menu ranging from peppercorn steak to several continental entrées; extensive wine list.

Café Gazebo ● ☆ $

☐ *La Placita Plaza (downtown); (520) 622-7499. Light fare; no alcohol. Monday-Friday 7:30 a.m. to 3 p.m. MC/VISA.* ☐ Cute little lunch and breakfast stop featuring omelettes, quiche, salads, soups and 'burgers.

☺ Café Terra Cotta ● ☆☆☆☆ $$$

☐ *4310 N. Campbell Ave. (St. Philip's Plaza at River Road; (520) 577-8100. Southwestern; full bar. Daily 11 a.m. Reservations advised; major credit* cards. ☐ One of Arizona's leading contemporary Southwestern restaurants; menu specialties include prawns with goat cheese, lamb chops with sweet potato polenta and chili-marinated pork tenderloin with black beans and apricot preserve, plus creative pizzas. Extensive wine selection by the glass.

☺ *Janos* ● ☆☆☆☆ *$$$*

☐ *150 N. Main Ave. (in El Presidio Historic District); (520) 884-9426. American nouvelle; full bar service. Tuesday-Saturday from 5:30 p.m. (closed Monday from June to January). MC/VISA, AMEX.* ☐ Contemporary upscale restaurant featuring *nouvelle* menu with a Southwestern slant. Constantly changing menu may feature savories such as crispy skin salmon in maple glaze or sweetbread sauté. Janos occupies an historic landmark adobe.

Iron Mask Restaurant ● ☆☆ *$$*

☐ *2464 E. Grant Rd. (Tucson Boulevard); (520) 327-6649. American-continental; full bar service. Lunch Tuesday-Friday 11:30 to 2, dinner Tuesday-Saturday 5:30 to 9:30, closed Sunday-Monday. Major credit cards.* ☐ Chef-owned restaurant featuring Beef Wellington, Shrimp Wellington, roast duck, veal and fresh fish.

La Villa Restaurant ● ☆☆☆ *$$$*

☐ *In Westin La Paloma at 3800 E. Sunrise; (520) 577-5806. American; full bar. Daily 5 to 10:30 p.m. Reservations advised; major credit cards.* ☐ Casual dining in a Southwestern style restaurant with a fireplace; city views. Fresh fish, steaks and chops. Disco with deejay, nightly dancing in the adjoining Cactus Club.

☺ *Pinnacle Peak Steakhouse* ● ☆☆☆ *$$*

☐ *6541 E. Tanque Verde Rd. (Wilmot); (520) 886-5012. Western; full bar service. Daily 5 to 10 p.m. Major credit cards.* ☐ Tasty yet inexpensive mesquite-grilled steaks served in an Old West atmosphere, similar to Scottsdale's Pinnacle Peak. The open rafters are festooned with ties, snipped off by waitresses to insure the informality of this place. Located in Trail Dust Town, a Western style shopping complex with boutiques, galleries and other restaurants. Look for the full-sized prairie schooner sitting atop a stack of boulders.

PoFolks ● ☆☆ *$*

☐ *5632 E. Speedway Blvd. (Craycroft); (520) 748-2700. American; no alcohol. Sunday-Thursday 11 to 9, Friday-Saturday 11 to 10. MC/VISA, DISC.* ☐ Very inexpensive "down-home" cooking, including chicken and dumplings, catfish, pork chops and other rural fare. Voted "Tucson's Best Family Restaurant" by a local restaurant guide. Branches at 295 W. Valencia, (520) 294-3800 and 3867 N. Oracle, (520) 888-6800.

Solarium ● ☆☆☆ *$$*

☐ *6444 E. Tanque Verde; (520) 886-8186. American; full bar service. Lunch weekdays 11:30 to 2:30, dinner nightly from 5. Reservations advised; major credit cards.* ☐ Airy restaurant under glass, in architecturally-distinctive building. Culinary emphasis is on seafood, plus a couple of steaks and chickens. Try the oven roasted shrimp Solarium with garlic, oil and lemon, or flambéed tequila lime shrimp with tomatoes, scallions and lime juice.

☺ *Saguaro Corners Restaurant* ● ☆☆☆ *$$$*

☐ *3750 S. Old Spanish Trail (near Saguaro National Park entrance); (520) 886-5424. Southwestern; full bar service. Lunch Tuesday-Saturday noon to 2:30, Sunday service noon to 9:30, dinner Tuesday-Sunday 5 to 9:30. Reservations advised, MC/VISA, AMEX.* ☐ Charmingly rustic restaurant in the desert; windows look out on desert wildlife attracted by evening lights. Diners may spot a javelina or at least a covey of quail while dining on Southwestern and upscale Mexican fare.

☺ *The Tack Room* ● ☆☆☆☆ *$$$$*

☐ *2800 N. Sabino Canyon Rd. (half mile north of Tanque Verde Road), (520) 722-2800. Southwestern; full bar service. Daily from 6 p.m.. Reservations strongly advised; major credit cards.* ☐ Five-star Mobil and five-diamond AAA restaurant in a rustically elegant old adobe hacienda, with a stone fireplace and cozy living room atmosphere. Specialties include rack of lamb with mesquite honey, lime and garlic, and pepper steak with Zinfandel demiglase.

☺ *Tohono Chul Park Tea Room* ● ☆☆ *$*

☐ *7366 N. Paseo del Norte (in Tohono Chul Park, northwest corner of Ina and Oracle); (520) 797-1711. American; wine and beer. Daily 8 to 5, high tea 2:30 to 4:30. MC/VISA, AMEX.* ☐ Cute little café in a brick Southwest style home; outdoor dining in a central courtyard and serene landscaped patio. Light meals of sandwiches and soups, breakfast croissants. Tasty desserts; high tea with scones and pastries.

Asian

Lotus Garden ● ☆☆ *$$*

☐ *5975 E. Speedway Blvd. (between Wilmot and Craycroft); (520) 298-3351. Cantonese and Szechuan; full bar service. Sunday-Thursday 11:30 to 11, Friday-Saturday 11:30 to midnight. MC/VISA.* ☐ Chinese restaurant with a Polynesian look and some rum drinks to match. The large menu ranges from calm Cantonese including vegetarian dishes to spicy northern China fare such as *kung pao* shrimp and chicken in chili sauce.

Shogun ● ☆☆ *$$*

☐ *5036 N. Oracle Rd. (in River Village Center); (520) 888-6646. Japanese; full bar service. Lunch Monday-Friday 11:30 to 2:20 and Saturday noon to 2:30, dinner nightly from 5. Major credit cards.* ☐ Attractive restaurant attired in *shoji* screens, *bonsai* and Japanese floral arrangements. Regular or *tatami* tables plus a sushi bar. The menu offers typical teriyaki, tempura and sukiyaki dishes, plus lesser known entrées such as teppenyaki (broiled meats with rice wine, ginger and scallions).

European

Arizona Inn Restaurant ● ☆☆☆ *$$$*

☐ *2200 E. Elm St. (Campbell Avenue, near U of A); (520) 325-1541. Continental; full bar service. Breakfast 7 to 10, lunch 11:30 to 2, dinner 6 to 9, Sunday brunch 11 to 2. Reservations advised; major credit cards.* ☐ Located in an nicely landscaped resort complex (listed below), this European style dining room features fresh fish and rack of lamb. A pianist plays dinner music.

Charles Restaurant ● ☆☆☆ *$$$*

☐ *6400 E. Eldorado Circle (Speedway and Wilmot); (520) 296-7173. Continental; full bar service. Tuesday-Sunday from 4 p.m. Reservations advised; major credit cards.* ☐ An attractive restaurant in a stately stone mansion. Among menu features are veal, steak Diane, roast duckling and fresh fish. Piano bar Thursday, Friday and Saturday evenings starting at 7:30.

Daniel's Restaurant ● ☆☆☆ *$$$*

☐ *2930 N. Swan Road (in St. Phillip's Plaza, off Ft. Lowell); (520) 742-3200. Italian; full bar service. Daily 5 p.m. to 11 p.m. Reservations advised;*

major credit cards. ☐ This appealing restaurant features Northern Italian and some classic continental entrées on a weekly-changing menu. Offerings may include creative pastas or seafood with innovative sauces. Its large wine cellar has 160 varieties.

Le Rendez-Vous ● ☆☆☆ $$$

☐ *3844 E. Ft. Lowell Rd. (Alvernon); (520) 323-7373. French; full bar service. Tuesday-Sunday; lunch 11 to 2, dinner 6 to 10. Reservations advised; major credit cards.* ☐ Menu specials in this cozy French restaurant include duck l'orange, sweetbreads, mussels and peppercorn steak. Order the excellent Grand Mariner soufflé for dessert the moment you walk in.

☺ Mountain View Restaurant ● ☆☆☆ $$$

☐ *1220 E. Prince Rd. (Mountain Avenue); (520) 293-0375. European; full bar service. Daily 11 to 9, breakfast weekends starting at 7. MC/VISA.* ☐ Cozy and cheerful little chef-owned café specializing in Czechoslovakian, German and eastern European fare, plus some American dishes. A bit out of the way but worth seeking out for tasty entrées such as Cordon Bleu, Hungarian goulash and combinations like the Bohemian Farmers Dinner of roasted pork loin, smoked pork cutlet, meatloaf and sausage with dumplings. Also seafood and steaks.

Penelope's Restaurant Francais ● ☆☆☆☆ $$$$

☐ *3071 N, Swan Rd. (near Grant); (520) 325-5080. French; prix fixe dinners; wine and beer. Lunch Tuesday-Friday 11:30 to 2, dinner Tuesday-Sunday from 5:30. Reservations advised; MC/VISA.* ☐ An intimate French restaurant decorated by works of local artists. It serves both classic and country styles in a four-course or six-course *prix fixe* dinner. Changing menu has three to four entrées and excellent desserts.

Scordato's Restaurant ● ☆☆ $$

☐ *4405 W. Speedway Blvd.; (520) 792-3055. Italian-American; full bar service. Sunday from 4, Tuesday-Saturday from 5. Major credit cards.* ☐ Veal is a feature of the Italian menu in this attrqactive dinner house; the American side of the menu includes chicken, steaks, chops and seafood.

Mexican

El Adobe Café ● ☆ $

☐ *52 Congress (Church); (520) 624-6133. Wine and beer. Monday-Friday 10 a.m. to 9 p.m., Saturday 11 to 9. Major credit cards.* ☐ Simply attired little place with a few tables out front. A handy lunch stop during a downtown browse, featuring the usual Mexican fare, plus some vegetarian dishes and low fat "heart smart" entrées with fish or lean beef or pork. All non-smoking.

Old Town Grill ● ☆☆ $$

☐ *186 N. Meyer (Telles, in El Presidio Historic District); (520) 622-0351. Southwestern and Mexican; wine and beer. Open daily for lunch. A pleasant little café in the landscaped patio of Old Town Artisans. Menu features mesquite grilled beef, poultry and seafood and some creative Mexican dishes.*

☺ El Charro Café ● ☆☆ $

☐ *311 N. Court Street (Franklin, in El Presidio Historic District); (520) 622-1922. Full bar service. Sunday-Thursday 11:30 to 10 p.m., Friday-Saturday 11:30 to 11. MC/VISA, DISC.* ☐ In business since 1922, El Charro is Tucson's oldest Mexican restaurant. Present owners are seventh generation members of a pioneer Tucson family. *Carne seca,* a chewy, almost sweet sun-dried beef, is a specialty on the large menu. A gift shop occupies the cellar of the 1880 stone building and a lively cocktail lounge with an outdoor patio is adjacent. A branch opened recently at Tucson International Airport.

La Fuente Restaurant ● ☆ $

▢ 1749 N. Oracle Rd. (south of Grant Road); (520) 623-8659. Full bar service. Daily 11:30 to midnight. Reservations advised; major credit cards. ▢ Brightly decorated little place with nightly mariachi music, starting at 6:30. Menu items range from tortilla-wrapped things to beef, chicken and seafood.

La Parilla Suiza ● ☆☆☆ $$

▢ 5602 E. Speedway; (520) 747-4838. Full bar service. Sunday-Thursday 11 a.m. to 10 p.m., Friday-Saturday 11 to 11. Reservations advised; major credit cards. ▢ A cut above typical smashed beans and rice places, La Parilla Suiza specializes in Mexico City style fare. A menu feature is an open-faced "taco", with meat, fish or poultry stir-fried with chilies, onions and other veggies. The taco soup is excellent.

WHERE TO RECLINE

Prices reflect high season rates and may be lower at other times. (In Sunbelt areas, prices can drop by more than half in summer.) Most were provided by the management and are subject to change; use them only as a guide.

The Alpine Inn ● ☆☆ $$$$

▢ 12925 Sabino Canyon Parkway (in Summerhaven; P.O. Box 789), Mount Lemmon, AZ 85619; (520) 576-1544. Couples and singles $85 to $95. MC/VISA. ▢ Mountain style six-room inn tucked among the pines of Mount Lemmon above Tucson; near ski area. Free breakfast. **Restaurant** serves breakfast, lunch and dinner—until 6 p.m. Monday-Thursday, 8 p.m. Friday, 9 p.m. Saturday and 7 p.m. Sunday; continental-Southwestern; dinners $9 to $14; full bar service; weekend entertainment.

☺ Arizona Inn ● ☆☆☆ $$$$$ Ø

▢ 2200 E. Elm Street (off Campbell Avenue near U of A), Tucson, AZ 85719; (520) 315-1541. Couples $158 to $181, singles $110 to $141. MC/VISA, AMEX. ▢ Charming old world style resort hotel, sheltered from the surrounding city in a 14-acre garden setting. Eighty-three guest rooms feature fireplaces, antique furnishings, TV/stereo, phones; some have patios. Pool, tennis courts, cocktail lounge, gift shop, library-lounge. It offers typical resort amenities, yet it's close to downtown Tucson. **Arizona Inn Restaurant** (listed above).

Best Western Executive Inn ● ☆☆☆ $$$

▢ 333 W. Drachman (Speedway exit off I-10), Tucson, AZ 85705; (800) 255-3371 or (520) 791-7551. Couples $45 to $120, singles $40 to $115, suites $65 to $150. Major credit cards. ▢ A 127-unit motel with swimming pool, spa and wading pool. Large rooms with TV movies and phones. **La Fiesta Restaurant** serves breakfast, lunch and dinner daily; dinners $6 to $15; full bar service.

Best Western Tanque Verde Inn ● ☆☆☆ $$$$ Ø

▢ 7007 E. Tanque Verde Rd. (east of Kolb and Wilmot) Tucson, AZ 85715; (800) 882-8484 or (520) 298-2300. Couples and singles $90 to $100, kitchen units and suites $110 to $125. Major credit cards. ▢ A 90-unit hacienda-style inn with rooms open to a landscaped courtyard with Spanish fountains and tropical foliage. TV, phones and in-room coffee; pool, spa and coin laundry.

Chateau Apartment-Hotels • ☆☆ $$ to $$$ Ø

☐ *1402 N. Alvernon (Speedway), Tucson, AZ 85712; (800) 697-2789 or (520) 323-7121; and Chateau Sonata at 550 S. Camino Seco, Tucson, AZ 85710; (800) 597-8483 or (520) 886-2468.Couples and singles, $39 to $99. MC/VISA, AMEX.* ☐ Two apartment hotels with full kitchens; pools, spa and tennis courts.

Courtyard by Marriott • ☆☆☆ $$$$ Ø

☐ *2505 E. Executive Dr. (Tucson Boulevard and Valencia), Tucson, AZ 85706; (520) 573-0000 or (800) 321-2211. Couples $62 to $109, singles $49 to $99. Major credit cards.* ☐ A 149-unit hotel with TV movies, phones, in-room coffee service, desk; rooms have separate seating areas. Indoor and outdoor pool, hot tub, exercise room, laundry, lounge, enclosed courtyard. **Restaurant** serves weekdays 6 to 10 a.m. and 5 to 10 p.m., weekends 7 to 11 a.m.; dinners $8 to $15; full bar service; Southwestern décor.

Doubletree at Reid Park • ☆☆☆ $$$$$ Ø

☐ *445 S. Alvernon Way (between Broadway and 22nd), Tucson, AZ 85711; (800) 222-TREE or (520) 881-4200. Couples $122 to $180, singles $102 to $160. Major credit cards.* ☐ A 295-room hotel with nicely furnished rooms; TV movies, and phones. Pool, spa, exercise room, tennis courts. Adjacent to Reid Park with two golf courses, tennis, jogging track and zoo. **Cactus Rose** (continental) and **Javelina Cantina** (Mexican) restaurants; food service 6 a.m. to 11 p.m.; dinners $7 to $22; full bar service.

Embassy Suites • ☆☆☆ $$$$$ Ø

☐ *5335 E. Broadway (Craycroft, near downtown), Tucson, AZ 85711; (800) EMBASSY or (520) 745-2700. Couples $109 to $139, singles $99 to $129. Major credit cards.* ☐ All 204 units are two-room suites with two TVs and phones and sofa sleeper in the living room; wet bar, microwave, refrigerator and coffee maker. Atrium courtyard with landscaping and a fountain; pool and spa. **Jason's Deli** adjacent.

Holiday Inn Express • ☆☆☆ $$$$ Ø

☐ *750 W. Starr Pass (I-10 near 22nd St.), Tucson, AZ 85713; (800) HOLI-DAY or (520) 624-4455. Couples and singles $75 to $95, suites $95 to $135; prices include continental breakfast. Major credit cards.* ☐ Inviting 98-room lodging with TV, phones and refrigerators; pool, spa and sauna. **The Kettle** restaurant serves 24 hours; dinners $6 to $12; no alcohol.

Flamingo Travelodge • ☆☆ $$$ Ø

☐ *1300 N. Stone Ave., Tucson, AZ 85705; (800) 300-3533 or (520) 770-1910. Couples and singles $60 to $76, kitchenettes and family units $80 to $97; rates include continental breakfast. Major credit cards.* ☐ An 80-unit inn with TV movies, phones and in-room coffee; refrigerators and microwaves in some; pool, spa, exercise room and video games.

Hotel Congress • ☆ $$

☐ *311 E. Congress (downtown, near train station), Tucson, AZ 85701; (520) 622-8848. Couples $32 to $48, singles $29 to $38. Major credit cards.* ☐ Older refurbished hotel with TV, rental movies, pool. **Restaurant** and Club Congress lounge with full bar service.

Lexington Hotel • ☆☆☆ $$$$ Ø

☐ *7411 N. Oracle Rd. (Ina Road), Tucson, AZ 85704; (800) 537-8483 or (520) 279-9811. Couples and singles $89 to $129. Major credit cards.* ☐ TV movies, phones; pool, spa and free use of adjacent athletic club. **McKenna's** serves lunch and dinner Monday-Saturday; full bar service.

☺ *Lodge in the Desert* • ☆☆☆☆ *$$$$* ∅

◻ *306 N. Alvernon Way (P.O. Box 42500), Tucson, AZ 85733; (520) 325-3366. Couples $92 to $163, singles $80 to $151, kitchenettes $92 to $140, suites $112 to $140; rates include continental breakfast. Major credit cards.* ◻ A beautifully maintained 50-year-old garden lodge with adobe style casitas, pool, shuffleboard, croquet, ping pong, lounge and library. Large guest rooms with beam ceilings, ceramic tile accents, TV, phones and patios; many rooms with fireplaces, some with refrigerators. **Lodge Restaurant** serves daily 7 to 8:30; American-continental; full bar service.

Radisson Suite Hotel • ☆☆☆ *$$$$* ∅

◻ *6555 E. Speedway (Wilmot), Tucson, AZ 85710; (800) 333-3333 or (520) 721-7100. Couples and singles $75 to $135. Major credit cards.* ◻ All-suite hotel with 304 rooms, each with two TV sets, movies, phones, refrigerators, private balconies or patios overlooking central courtyard; free buffet breakfast and cocktails. **Restaurant** serves 6 a.m. to 11 p.m.; dinners $10 to $19; full bar service.

Ramada Inn Foothills • ☆☆☆ *$$$$* ∅

◻ *6944 E. Tanque Verde (near Sabino Canyon), Tucson, AZ 85715; (800) 228-2828 or (520) 886-9595. Couples $65 to $105, singles $55 to $95, suites $75 to $125; rates include breakfast buffet. Major credit cards.* ◻ A 114-unit inn; attractive rooms with TV movies, phones, some refrigerators; complimentary happy hour. Pool, spa, sauna; free passes to health club.

Residence Inn by Marriott • ☆☆☆ *$$$$$* ∅

◻ *6477 E. Speedway Blvd. (east side, a mile from Park Mall Shopping Center), Tucson, AZ 85710; (800) 331-3131 or (520) 721-0991. Couples $129 to $184, singles $109 to $160; rates include continental breakfast. Major credit cards.* ◻ An all suite hotel with full kitchens; 128 units with TV and phones, VCRs and movies available. Pool, spa, sports court; afternoon social hour.

Rodeway Inn • ☆☆ *$$$* ∅

◻ *810 E. Benson Hwy. (I-10 exit 262), Tucson, AZ 85713; (800) 228-2000 or (520) 884-5800. Couples $64 to $89, singles $50 to $83. Major credit cards.* ◻ TV movies, phones, free continental breakfast, some refrigerators; pool in landscaped courtyard.

RESORTS

☺ *The Lodge at Ventana Canyon* • ☆☆☆☆ *$$$$$*

◻ *6200 N. Clubhouse Lane (near Sunrise and Kolb), Tucson, AZ 85715; (800) 828-5701 or (520) 577-1400. All suites, from $295 to $410. Major credit cards.* ◻ Opulent resort in Santa Catalina foothills. One and two-bedroom suites have kitchen and living-dining areas; TV movies, phones and typical resort amenities. Extensive grounds with two golf courses, lighted tennis courts, pools, spas, sauna and complete health club facilities. **Clubhouse Dining Room** and **Terrance Lounge** serve 7 a.m. to 10 p.m.; continental, Southwestern and American fare; dinners $20 to $35; full bar.

☺ *Loews Ventana Canyon Resort* • ☆☆☆☆ *$$$$$*

◻ *7000 N. Resort Dr. (near Sunrise and Kolb), Tucson, AZ 85715; (520) 299-2020. Couples and singles $185 to $285. Major credit cards.* ◻ Elegant desert foothill resort. Rooms feature TV movies, phones, refrigerators, luxury furnishings. Two golf courses, pools, sauna, steam room, health club, expan-sive grounds. Four **restaurants**—Ventana Room (American nouvelle), Canyon Café (casual with luncheon buffets and Sunday brunch), Bill's Grill (poolside café) and Flying V Bar and Grill (steak house and disco).

☺ *Sheraton Tucson El Conquistador* ● ☆☆☆☆ *$$$$$* ∅

❑ *10,000 N. Oracle Rd. (north of Ina Road), Tucson, AZ 85737; (520) 742-7000 or (800) 325-3535. Couples and singles $150 to $225. Major credit cards.* ❑ Large full-service resort set against a backdrop of rugged desert mountains. Elegant guest rooms with Southwestern décor and private patios or balconies; TV movies, phones, some rooms with fireplaces. Tennis, 45 holes of golf, biking, hiking, horseback rides, racquetball, volleyball, swimming pools, spa, saunas, health club with masseur. Five **restaurants** serving Western, American, continental and Mexican fare; full bar service.

☺ *The Westin La Paloma* ● ☆☆☆☆ *$$$$$* ∅

❑ *3800 E. Sunrise, Tucson, AZ 85718; (800) 876-3683 or (800) 742-6000. Couples and singles $280 to $340, suites from $475. Major credit cards.* ❑ Luxurious recently renovated village style resort complex with Spanish Revival architecture; extensive grounds with 76 holes of golf, racquetball and tennis courts, fitness facilities, waterfall pool with swim-up bar, spas and saunas. The 487 rooms have Southwestern décor with TV movies, honor bars, refrigerators, coffee makers and other amenities. Three **restaurants** and a deli serve American and Southwest fare; full bar service.

Westward Look Resort ● ☆☆☆☆ *$$$$$* ∅

❑ *245 E. Ina Rd. (half mile east or Oracle), Tucson, AZ 85704; (800) 722-2500 or (520) 297-1151. Couples, singles and suites $95 to $269. Major credit cards.* ❑ In pleasant desert setting with three pools, spas, saunas, health club and fitness center, jogging track, tennis. Nicely furnished rooms with balconies or patios, TV movies, phones, in-room coffee, refrigerators, sitting areas. Two **restaurants**; food service 6:30 a.m. to 11:30 p.m.; American, Southwestern, continental fare; dinners $10 to $30, full bar service.

Bed & breakfast inns

El Presidio Bed & Breakfast Inn ● ☆☆☆ *$$$$* ∅

❑ *297 N. Main Ave. (in El Presidio Historic District), Tucson, AZ 85701; (800) 349-6151 or (520) 623-6151. Couples $90 to $115, singles $80 to $100. Three units with in-room TV, phones and private baths; full breakfast. No credit cards.* ❑ An 1870s American territorial Victorian with lush gardens, courtyards and fountains. Victorian and early American antiques in rooms. Complimentary wine and juices. Two suites and a guest house with kitchen.

La Posada del Valle ● ☆☆☆ *$$$$* ∅

❑ *1640 N. Campbell Ave. (Elm, near the university), Tucson, AZ 85719; (520) 795-3840. Couples and singles $85 to $105. Five units with private baths; full breakfast. MC/VISA.* ❑ A 1929 Southwest adobe surrounded by a garden and orange trees; rooms furnished with early 20th century and Victorian antiques. Afternoon tea served in courtyard patio.

The Peppertrees Bed & Breakfast ● ☆☆☆ *$$$$*

❑ *724 E. University Blvd. (near U of A between Euclid and First Avenue), Tucson, AZ 85719; (800) 348-5763 or (520) 622- 7167. Couples $88 to $160, singles $78 to $88. Five rooms, all with TV, phones and private baths; full breakfast. MC/VISA, DISC.* ❑ A turn-of-the-century territorial home elegantly furnished with English and early American antiques. Three guest rooms inside; two modern guest houses on grounds. Complimentary sherry, afternoon English tea, off-street parking; picnic baskets for day excursions.

Triangle L Ranch Bed & Breakfast ● ☆☆ $$$$ ∅
◻ *P.O. Box 900 (Oracle Ranch Road at Triangle L. Ranch Road, 35 miles north on Highway 77), Oracle, AZ 85623; (520) 623-6732 or (520) 896-2804. Couples $80 to $95, singles $65 to $75. Four private cottages with private baths; full breakfast.* ◻ An 1880s Southwest style adobe homestead on a former cattle ranch and guest ranch in the Santa Catalina foothills. All private cottages in desert gardens; farm animals; bird-watching, hikes.

WHERE TO PLAY COWBOY

Hacienda del Sol Guest Ranch ● *5601 Hacienda del Sol Rd. (in Santa Catalina foothills), Tucson, AZ 85718; (800) 728-6514 or (520) 299-1501. Couples and singles $99 to $175, without meals. MC/VISA, AMEX.* ◻ Trail rides, cookouts, swimming pool, spa, tennis, croquet, nature tours, cowboy barbecues, Mexican fiestas; lobby with library, bridge tables and fireplace. Housed in a 1929 pueblo style adobe that originally was a girls' prep school.

Lazy K Bar Guest Ranch ● *8401 N. Scenic Dr. (Silverbell Road and Pima Farm Road), Tucson, AZ 85743; (800) 321-7018 or (520) 744-3050. Couples $230 to $280, singles $140 to $170, including all meals. Major credit cards.* ◻ Modern guest ranch on 160 acres in the Tucson Mountain foothills. Trail rides, hay rides, cookouts, square dances, tennis, swimming pool and spa. Lounge, library, patio, barbecue area with ten-foot waterfall.

☺ **Tanque Verde Guest Ranch** ● *14301 E. Speedway (Route 8, Box 66), Tucson, AZ 85748; (800) 234-3833 or (520) 296-6275. Couples $280 to $350, singles $240 to $280, suites from $360, including all meals and ranch activities. Major credit cards.* ◻ One of America's oldest guest ranches on 640 acres between Coronado National Forest and Saguaro National Park. Casita style rooms with fireplaces, antiques and original art. Riding, breakfast rides, children's program, tennis with teaching pro. Nature rides, walks and talks. Indoor and outdoor pools, sauna, spa, five tennis courts, outdoor games, gym, gift shop, coin laundry and barbecue area.

White Stallion Ranch ● *9251 Twin Peaks Rd. (17 miles northwest, near Saguaro National Park), Tucson, AZ 85743; (520) 297-0252. From $192 to $318 per couple, including all meals. No credit cards.* ◻ A semi-working ranch with a few longhorns and quarter horses. Pool, spa, tennis, pool tables, ping-pong, shuffleboard, volleyball, basketball, horseshoes, breakfast rides, trail rides into the desert and mountains; hayride with cookout, bonfire and entertainment; steak barbecues and Indian oven dinners.

Wild Horse Ranch ● *6801 Camino Verde (I-10 exit at Ina Road, then 1.8 miles west), Tucson, AZ 85743; (520) 744-1012. Couples and singles $60 to $100; meals extra.* ◻ A 20-acre ranch resort near Tucson Mountain Park. Pool, tennis, horseback riding, hayrides, volleyball, ping-pong, cookouts, nature walks, horseshoes and volleyball. Well-stocked library, bar and breakfast room in the main ranch lodge.

WHERE TO CAMP

Cactus Country RV Park ● *10195 S. Houghton Rd. (I-10 exit 275), Tucson, AZ 85747; (800) 777-8799 or (520) 574-3000. RV and tent sites; from $12.60 to $19.50. Reservations accepted; MC/VISA.* ◻ Shaded pull-through sites; full hookups, showers, coin laundry, pool, whirlpool, recreation room, planned activities, horseshoes, shuffleboard; Propane, disposal station.

Catalina State Park • *P.O. Box 36986 (9 miles north on U.S. 89), Tucson, AZ 85470; (520) 628-5798. RV and tent sites; $13 with electric, no hookups $8, day use $3. No reservations or credit cards.* ☐ Picnic and barbecue areas, flush potties. Nature trails, hiking into adjacent Coronado National Forest. In desert foothills of Santa Catalina Mountains.

Crazy Horse Campground • *6660 S. Craycroft Rd. (seven miles east, off I-10), Tucson, AZ 85706; (520) 574-0157. RV sites only; full hookups, $18. MC/VISA.* ☐ Picnic tables, showers, swimming pool, coin laundry, small store, recreation center, dump station.

Desert Shores RV & Mobile Home Park • *1067 W. Miracle Mile (half mile east of I-10 Miracle Mile off-ramp), Tucson, AZ 85705; (520) 622-4332. RV sites; Full hookups $15. No credit cards.* ☐ Older but well-maintained RV park with rec hall, shuffleboard, horseshoes, swimming pool, lake and picnic area, showers, coin laundry.

Gilbert Ray Campground • *In Tucson Mountain Park (Route 13, Box 977), Tucson, AZ 85713; (520) 883-4200. RV sites with electrical hookups $9, tent camping $6. No reservations, no credit cards.* ☐ Picnic tables, barbecues, flush potties, dump station, nature trails. Inviting desert campsites in Tucson Mountain Park, close to Old Tucson, Arizona-Sonora Desert Museum and Saguaro National Park. Get there by noon during the busy winter season. Electric only available at RV sites although water sources are nearby.

Rincon Country West RV Resort • *4555 S. Mission Rd. (half mile south of Ajo Way exit 99 from I-19), Tucson, AZ 85714; (800) 782-7275 or (520) 294-5608. RV sites, full hookups $24; long-term rates available. No credit cards.* ☐ Senior park with showers, coin laundry, pool, spa and planned activities with a recreation director.

Mount Lemmon Recreation Area • *Several campgrounds are off the Mount Lemmon Highway in Coronado National Forest. RV and tent sites; no hookups $6 to $8. No reservations or credit cards.* ☐ Picnic and barbecue areas, water, pit potties. Fishing, nature trails.

Tratel Tucson RV Park • *2070 W. Fort Lowell Rd. (four miles west from I-10 Prince Road exit, then south on Ft. Lowell Road), Tucson, AZ 85705; (520) 888-5401. RV and tent sites; full hookups $16, no hookups and tents $13. Reservations accepted; MC/VISA.* ☐ Mid-sized park with all pull-throughs; showers, pool, coin laundry, recreation room, dump station.

Whispering Palms Travel Trailer Park • *3445 Romero Rd. (I-10 exit 254 onto Prince Road then south on Romero Road), Tucson, AZ 85705; (520) 888-2500. RV and tent sites; hookups $12.50. Reservations accepted.* ☐ Showers, coin laundry, pool, cable TV, recreation room.

SOUTH TO THE BORDER

Interstate 19 provides a fast link between Tucson and the twin border cities of Nogales, Arizona and the Mexican state of Sonora. Interestingly, the highway signs are in kilometers instead of miles.

The first community you'll encounter, other than dusty little Sahuarita, is Green Valley. Unkindly referred to as Wrinkle City by Tucsonans, it's a retirement town of 14,000. It started as an adult community in 1964 and has since blossomed into a full-scale community with shopping centers, four golf courses, heated swimming pools and other amenities that make the desert a

A Titan II missile poses ominously in its underground silo at the Titan Missile Museum near Green Valley.

pleasant place to live. It's also the site of a grimly fascinating reminder of the Cold War:

☺ **Titan Missile Museum** ● *Green Valley Road (Exit 69, then west), Green Valley, AZ 85614; (520) 625-7736. Open 9 to 5 Wednesday-Sunday from May through October and daily from November through April. One-hour tours; last tour at 4 p.m. Adults $6, seniors and military $5, kids 10 to 17 $3.* ▯ Standing in the command center, deep underground, you hear the deadly countdown as the crew prepares to launch a Titan II missile. In seconds, its 430,000 pounds of thrust will blast it from its silo. In less than an hour, its nuclear warhead will detonate above a computer-selected target thousands of miles away. As you listen to the countdown, your palms begin to sweat.

Fortunately, it's just a recording from a movie soundtrack, being played at an underground missile complex that's open to the public. When the SALT Treaty called for de-activation of the 18 Titan missile silos that ring Tucson, folks at the Pima Air Museum asked if one could be retained for public tours. After much negotiation, including additional talks with SALT officials, the Green Valley complex of the 390th Strategic Missile Wing was opened to the public. Of course, it was rendered inoperable.

This is one of the most fascinating tours in Arizona. After watching a video about the history of the Titan and its deadly nuclear delivery capability, you're taken deep into the "hardened" command center. Here, essential equipment—indeed the center itself—is mounted on springs to withstand anything but a direct hit. Then you pass through a couple of 6,000-pound blast doors and walk along a space-age corridor to the silo itself. The 110-foot-tall missile weighed 170 tons when it was fueled for flight. It's empty and harmless now, but it still looks deadly, crouched on its launch pad. Topside, you can peek down into the silo, half covered by its cemented-in-place lid. Nearby are the missile's jet engine and an empty nuclear warhead the size of a Mercury space capsule.

WHERE TO SLEEP AND CAMP

Quality Inn Green Valley ☆☆ *$$$$ Ø*

  ☐ *111 S. La Canada (west of Esperanza exit from I-19), Green Valley, AZ 85614; (800) 344-1441 or (520) 625-2250. Couples $75 to $85, singles $65 to $75. Major credit cards.* ☐ A 108- room motel with TV movies, phones, free morning coffee and paper; guest laundry; landscaped courtyard with pool and spa. **Palms Restaurant** serves 6 a.m. to 2 p.m. and 5 to 8 p.m.; continental-Southwestern; dinners $10 to $15; full bar service during restaurant hours.

  Green Valley RV Resort ● *Duval Mine Rd. (I-19 exit 69), Green Valley, AZ 85614; (800) 222-2969 or (520) 625-3900. RV sites with full hookups, $27.* ☐ Large, well-kept resort with showers, pool, spa, shuffleboard, horseshoes, rec rooms, coin laundry.

  Looking east from Green Valley, you'll see an island of mountains called the Santa Ritas, topped by 9,543-foot Mount Wrightson. They're an extension of Coronado National Forest, with miles of hiking trails and several campgrounds. The mountains also shelter a most appealing nature preserve:

  Madera Canyon ● *Thirteen miles southeast of I-19, via exit 63.* ☐ This pretty chasm in the Santa Ritas is a popular bird-watching venue, noted particularly for the brightly colored Mexican trogon, which spends its summers here. Bird- watchers have counted about 200 other winged species in Madera Canyon, as well. If you want to spend more time in this forested chasm, you can stay over at **Santa Rita Lodge** (HC 70, Box 5444, Sahuarita, AZ 85629; 625-8746), which has small kitchenette units for around $60. Nearby **Bog Springs** national forest campground has RV and tent sites for $7 per night, with barbecues, picnic tables, water and pit toilets; no hookups. Several hiking trails reach into the mountains from here, including a 4.5 mile round trip to Bog Springs.

  Continuing south on I-19, you'll pass hamlets of **Arivaca Junction** and **Amado,** and encounter a community that was here long before there ever was a Arizona:

Tubac

Elevation: Approx. 3,000 feet   **Population: 600**

  Established as a Spanish presidio in 1752, Tubac is Arizona's oldest non-Indian settlement. The year before, Pima Chief Oacpicagigua had led a revolt against missionaries and settlers because they had gained virtual control over the Indians' land—and their lives. The army was called to quell the uprising, then the troops stayed around to build a fort.

  Tubac commander Juan Bautista de Anza left here in 1776 on his historic overland trek to establish the pueblos of San Jose and San Francisco in California. After Mexico won its independence from Spain in 1821, troops left Tubac and the settlement—harassed by Apache raids—was abandoned. The

Gadsden Purchase brought the community under America's protection and it was resettled. In 1860, it was Arizona's largest town. But the Civil War pulled American troops away, and hostile Apaches again forced its abandonment. Resettlement came after the Apaches finally were subdued late in the 19th century.

Today, slightly scruffy little Tubac is a serious art colony, with more than 50 galleries housed in a mix of old and new adobe and brick buildings. This is where "art and history meet," proclaims a sign at the edge of town. A dozen or more boutiques, import and curio shops also line its quiet streets, selling Indian and Arizona crafts and assorted giftwares.

To get to the heart of the old town, take exit 40 (Chavez Siding Road/Tubac) from I-19, cross under the freeway and take a frontage road about two miles south. Turn left onto Plaza Road and follow signs toward Tubac Presidio State Park. The route will take you past most of the town's shops and galleries. You can park at the historic park and walk the few blocks that comprise the town.

If you like things spicy, check out the **Chili Pepper** on Tubac Road; it features a variety of chili-based products, along with Southwest cookbooks, herbs and spices, coffees and light snacks. **Tubac Center of the Arts** on Plaza Road exhibits works of local artisans; many can be purchased at its gift shop. **Mercado de Baca** on Tubac Road is a small shopping center with assorted boutiques, galleries and restaurants.

☺ *Tubac Presidio State Historic Park* ● *P.O. Box 1296, Tubac, AZ 85646; (520) 398-2252. Daily 8 to 5; adults $2, kids $1. Picnic area.* ☐ Little remains of the presidio, but an exhibit center effectively traces its history. Very nicely done displays take you from Tubac's days as a 17th century Pima Indian village through its Spanish, Mexican and American periods. Exhibits include a set of wrist irons tied to a post that served as the town's jail, plus period weapons, religious art and friars' frocks.

A volunteer docent might crank off a copy of the *Weekly Arizonan*, the state's first newspaper, on its original 1859 flatbed printing press. Outside the museum, paths lead through the presidio grounds where archaeological digs have been continuing on and off since 1974. Of particular interest is the "Stairway to the Past," which leads you down into an excavation. Artifacts found at different levels are displayed in place behind protective windows in this cut-away dig. At the schoolhouse, you can sit at an old style inkwell desk (assuming you can fit) and read rules of conduct for teachers. Among them: "Women teachers who marry or engage in other unseemly conduct will be dismissed."

From Tubac, return to the frontage road (not the freeway) and drive a few kilometers through the hamlet of **Carmen** to the area's other historic attraction:

☺ *Tumacacori National Historic Park* ● *P.O. Box 67, Tumacacori, AZ 85640; (520) 398-2341. Daily 8 to 5; $2 per person, kids free.* ☐ "At the rancheria of San Cayetano de Tumacacori, we found people so docile and so friendly. Such lovely and such fertile and delightful valleys inhabited by industrious Indians."

Thus, Father Kino described a small village he visited in 1691. He erected an earth-roofed adobe house and began preaching to the Indians. Half a century later, other missionaries built a small church, followed by a more elaborate structure in the 1790s. Today, Tumacacori Mission is a noble ruin, standing forlornly on a grassy field. The fine interpretive center features a diorama of the mission in its heyday, relics from the old church and an artistically-produced video of missionaries ministering to the Indians. The ruined church is short distance away—a time-stained shell of its former glory. Inside its darkened, weathered walls, you can still see traces of lime plaster and paint used to emulate the marble, carved woods and other fineries of Spain's great cathedrals.

WHERE TO DINE & RECLINE

Tosh's Hacienda de Tubac ● ☆☆ $$

❏ 14 Camino Otero, Tubac; (520) 398-3008 (at Burruel Street) Southwest-Mexican; full bar service. Lunch and dinner daily; MC/VISA. ❏ Attractive brick restaurant with Southwest style interior and patio out front. The menu ranges from creative Southwest cuisine to several essential Mexican dishes.

Tumacacori Mission Restaurant ● ☆☆ $$

❏ 1896 East Frontage Road, Tumacacori (across from the national monument; (520) 398-9038 ❏ Greek, Mexican and American; wine and beer. Tuesday-Sunday noon to 8. MC/VISA. ❏ Cute little café with blue-checked tablecloths. Small, versatile menu skips from Athenian baked chicken and lamb shanks to linguine and several Latin dishes.

Rio Rico Resort and Country Club ● ☆☆☆ $$$$$ Ø

❏ 1069 Camino Caralampiu (just south of Tumacacori, I-19 exit 17), Rio Rico, AZ 85648; (800) 288-4746 or (520) 281-1901. Couples $130, singles $120, suites $125 to $250. Major credit cards. ❏ Appealing resort in desert setting with Olympic-sized pool, spa, sauna, tennis and 18-hole golf course. The 180 units have TV movies, phones and other amenities. **San Cayetano Dining Room** serves 6:30 a.m. to 9:30 p.m.; Southwestern food and décor; full bar service.

Rancho Santa Cruz ● ☆☆☆ $$$ Ø

❏ P.O. Box 8 (off I-19 between exits 25 and 29), Tumacacori, AZ 85640; (800) 221-5592 (520) 281-8383. Casitas and suites $59 to $80. MC/VISA. ❏ Small resort style guest ranch with horseback riding, swimming pool, lawn games and walking trails. In original adobe ranch buildings with Southwestern décor. **Restaurant**, open to the public, serves 8 a.m. to 9 p.m.; American; dinners $8 to $15; full bar service.

South of Tumacacori, a sign directs you back to I-19. Several miles below, at exit 12 (Ruby Road), another sign points eleven miles west to **Pena Blanca Lake Recreation Area**. Pena Blanca is a 52-acre reservoir tucked among brushy hills in Coronado National Forest. The paved access road winds through oak woodlands rimmed by hills accented with rocky outcroppings. The lake is occupied mostly by ducks and planted fish—the latter being the main reason people come up here. Pena Blanca Resort has simple lodgings (rooms $30 to $42; kitchenettes $48 to $72), a lakeview restaurant and rowboat rentals; (520) 281-2800. Trails lead along the lakeshore to a fishing dock and boat launch. Nearby White Rock national forest campground has wooded sites for $5 with water and pit potties; no hookups. The recreation area also offers several picnic areas and hiking trails.

Back on I-19, you'll shortly encounter the twin towns of Nogales, or *Ambos Nogales*, as our Mexican neighbors ˙ ˌld say. Nogales, incidentally, means "walnuts."

Nogales

Elevation: 3,865 feet   **Population: 20,000**

Like the Walnuts they were named for, the two towns are scattered over the foothills of the Patagonia Mountains. It's a pretty setting for buildings that are often less than pretty.

Ethnically, there is little distinction between the two dusty communities, and only a border fence separates them. However, if you assume (as we did) that they were a single town sliced in half by the Gadsden Purchase, you are incorrect. They were established separately, long after the 1854 land deal that brought southern Arizona into the Union. A Mexican roadhouse was built on the Mexican side of Nogales Pass in 1880 by Juan José Vasquez. In the same year, Jacob Isaacson started a trading post on the Arizona territory side. The two towns grew up as good neighbors, even during the unsettling years when Pancho Villa was creating border havoc during this century's teens. Nogales, Mexico, grew much faster than its northern twin and now has ten times the population. The largest of the Arizona-Mexico border towns, it offers the best shopping—which we discuss in more detail in the next chapter.

DRIVING NOGALES

I-19's exit 8, which becomes Grand Avenue, gets you into downtown Nogales, Arizona, from where you can continue—by vehicle or afoot—to Nogales, Sonora. After a couple of miles on Grand Avenue, fork to your right onto West Kino Park Place at the blue "Arizona Tourist Information" sign for the **Nogales Chamber of Commerce.** It's just beyond the turnoff to State Highway 82, in Kino City Park. The office is open weekdays 9 to 5; (520) 287-3685.

Continue another mile or so on Grand Avenue into downtown Nogales and you'll see on your left—just two blocks short of the border—the town's historical museum. The structure, built in 1914 as the Nogales city hall, is easy to spot. Look for the Spanish colonial building with the conical-roofed clock tower.

Pimeria Alta Historical Society Museum ● *136 N. Grand Avenue and Crawford Street (P.O. Box 2281), Nogales, AZ 85621; (520) 287-4621. Tuesday-Friday 10 to 5, Saturday 10 to 4. Free; donations encouraged.* ☐ This museum personifies the close ties between *Los Nogales.* Photos, documents and pioneer artifacts trace the history of both communities. The graphics and museum brochure, like many signs in Nogales, are bilingual. Although not professionally done, it's quite interesting, with exhibits such as a hand-drawn fire pumper, a pictorial history of the town and archeological artifacts. The old iron-barred jail is still in place; gringos and their Mexican buddies slept off their hangovers in this grim looking lock-up until it was retired in 1978.

RV AND PARKING ADVISORY ● Several lots near the museum provide all-day parking ($3 to $5) for folks who want to walk the few blocks into Nogales, Mexico. One, adjacent to a McDonald's restaurant, has spaces large enough for RVs. To reach it, turn right from Grand onto West Crawford, right again onto North Terrace Avenue and then left into the lot. If you're driving into Mexico, simply continue on Grand Avenue. To reach I-19 and head back toward Tucson, take the right turn onto Crawford and follow the directional signs.

Unless you plan to drive beyond the border (requiring a Mexican tourist card available at the border and Mexican insurance), it's probably best to park your car and walk across. The vehicle crossing becomes quite congested during commute hours and on weekends.

ANNUAL EVENTS

For details on these and other area events, contact the Tubac Chamber of Commerce at (520) 398-2704 or the Nogales Chamber of Commerce at (520) 287-3685.

Tubac Arts Festival in Tubac, the first full week of February.

Bed Race in Nogales, Arizona, the last Saturday of March.

Cinco de Mayo, marking the Mexican victory over Napoleon III in 1862, is celebrated on both sides of the border in Nogales and elsewhere on May 5 and usually extending into the nearest weekend.

Santa Cruz County Fair, late September to early October in Nogales.

Intercultural Festival, Tumacacori National Historic Park, December.

Bullfights are held Sunday afternoons on the Mexican side of Nogales at Guadalupe Plaza de Toros; the American Nogales Chamber of Commerce can provide details.

WHERE TO DINE

Americana Courtyard Restaurant ● ☆☆ $$

□ 639 N. Grand Ave. (in Americana Motor Hotel, listed below); (520) 287-7211. Mexican-American; full bar service. Daily 6:30 a.m. to 10 p.m. Major credit cards. □ Interesting poolside restaurant featuring steak, daily seafood specials and assorted Mexican entrées.

Johnny's Coffee Shoppe ● ☆ $

□ 131 Grand Ave.; (520) 287-2082. American-Mexican; wine and beer. Monday-Saturday 8 to 4:45, Sunday 8 to 2:45. □ Simple café across from the museum; handy for a lunch stop, with steak, chops, sandwiches and several Mexican dishes.

Grand China ● ☆☆ $$

□ 1997 N. Grand Ave. (Mariposa); (520) 281-2888. Chinese; wine and beer. Weekdays 11:30 to 10, weekends noon to 10. MC/VISA. □ Shopping center restaurant the corner of Grand and Mariposa featuring spicy Mandarin and Szechuan entrées plus several seafood dishes.

Mr. C's Supper Club ● ☆☆☆ $$$

□ 282 W. View Point Dr. (three miles north of town); (520) 281-9000. American; full bar service. Monday-Saturday 11:30 a.m. to midnight. MC/VISA, AMEX. □ Crowning a hill north of town, this large, rather elegant restaurant features fresh seafood, steaks and other American specialties. Live music for dancing in an adjoining lounge.

Molina's PK Outpost ● ☆☆ $$

□ 555 E. Frontage Rd. (five miles north); (520) 281-1852. Mexican-Southwestern; full bar service. Daily 10 to 10. Major credit cards. □ The kitchen of the historic Pete Kitchen adobe ranch house produces tasty Sonoran and American Southwestern fare. To reach it, take I-19 exit 12 (Ruby Road) east and then go south on the frontage road.

Two restaurants in Sonora, Mexico, are worthy of mention. (See the next chapter about dining, shopping and traveling in Mexico.)

El Cid ● ☆☆ $$

□ *124 Avenida Obregon; (52) 2-64-00. Mexican- continental; Daily from noon. MC/VISA.* □ Seafoods are the specialty in this large tiled restaurant with an unusual domed ceiling; the menu focuses on classic Mexico City-style fare.

La Roca ● ☆☆☆ $$$

□ *91 Calle Elias; (52) 2-07-60. Mexican-continental; Daily from noon. Major credit cards.* □ This is where you dine if you're a wealthy Mexican or an American taking advantage of the favorable exchange rate. Candle-lit tables, formal waiters, a fireplace and courtyard fountain accent fine Mexican and European seafood and beef dishes.

WHERE TO RECLINE

Prices reflect high season rates and may be lower at other times. Most were provided by the management and are subject to change; use them only as a guide.

Americana Motor Hotel ● ☆☆ $$$ Ø

□ *639 Grand Ave., Nogales, AZ 85621; (520) 287-7211. Couples $49 to $57, singles $44 to $47. Major credit cards.* □ A 94-room motel with TV movies, some refrigerators, many rooms on courtyard pool; coin laundry. Poolside **restaurant** listed above.

Best Western Siesta Motel ● ☆☆ $$ Ø

□ *673 N. Grand Ave. (near highways 89 and 93), Nogales, AZ 85621; (800) 528-1234 or (520) 287-4671. Couples $42 to $52, singles $40 to $44. Major credit cards.* □ A 47-room motel with TV movies, phones, pool; coffee shop nearby.

Best Western Time Motel ● ☆☆ $$ Ø

□ *921 N. Grand Ave., Nogales, AZ 85621; (800) 528-1234 or (520) 287-4627. Couples $40 to $50, singles $34 to $44. Major credit cards.* □ A 43-unit motel with TV movies, phones, pool and spa; coffee shop adjacent.

WHERE TO CAMP

Patagonia Lake State Park ● *P.O. Box 274, Patagonia, AZ 85624; (520) 287-6965. Full hookups $15; no hookups $10. No reservations or credit cards.* □ Twelve miles north of Nogales, off State Route 82. Sites near the lake, with barbecues, picnic tables, flush potties, showers and dump station.

White Rock Campground ● *Near Pena Blanca Lake Recreation Area, 12 miles north of Nogales then 11 miles west at I-19 exit 12. Sites for tents and small RVs, $5; no hookups.* □ National Forest Campground with picnic tables and barbecues; flush potties, no hookups.

DOWN MEXICO WAY

Chapter ten

THE SOUTHWEST

Busy Yuma, organ pipes and dusty border towns

IF YOU'RE DRIVING to Arizona, you've got to come from somewhere, and if it's from southern California, you'll likely enter the state's southwestern corner, either on Interstate 8 or 10. Our preferred approach is I-8, since Yuma is considerably more interesting than Ehrenberg and Quartzsite.

The Sonoran Desert's great cactus garden extends along much of the border between southwestern Arizona and the Mexican state of Sonora. Much of it is untracked wilds, reachable only by four- wheel drive vehicle or possibly by parachute. A splendid and easy to reach slice of this desert has been set aside in Organ Pipe Cactus National Monument, southwestern Arizona's chief attraction. If you like desert wilderness, you'll love exploring the southwest, particularly from March to early May when the cacti offer their dazzling spring flower show.

We'll first cover the Arizona side of the border in this chapter, and then dip into Mexico to explore its friendly, pastel border towns. Incidentally, Mexico's Highway 2, running just south of the border from San Luis to Sonoita, travels through the heart of the Sonoran Desert. It passes between Cabesa Prieta National Wildlife Refuge on the Arizona side and De Gran Desierto Delpinacate National Park in Mexico, noted for its desert flora and lava formations. Access to the national park is via the Rocky Point Highway (Mexico 8) south of Organ Pipe.

Yuma

Elevation: 138 feet   **Population: 50,000**

If you've already experienced the mighty Colorado River upstream, you'll be startled by what's left of it at Yuma Crossing. Tamed and greatly reduced by water diversion, it flows meekly between desert bluffs marking the California-Arizona border. After it enters Mexico 25 miles south, additional water is captured, then what little is left dribbles into the Gulf of California.

The first attempts to harness the Colorado began near Yuma in 1901 with the diversion of water into California's Imperial Valley. Resisting man's tampering, the river washed the project away in 1905. In the 1930s, upstream Hoover Dam put an end to Rio Colorado's willfulness. What's left of the lower Colorado has turned the deserts around Yuma into thousands of acres of rich farmland.

Yuma earned its place in Arizona's historical sun early, since this was one of the few spots where westbound travelers could ford the Colorado. However, the first outside visitor may have come by water. In 1540, Spanish naval Captain Hernando de Alarcón sailed up the Gulf of California and into the mouth of the Colorado; he probably got this far north before turning back. Father Eusebio Kino, seeking a land route to California in 1699, found a suitable place to cross the Colorado at its junction with the Gila, in present-day Yuma. He is credited with naming the river for its reddish, silt laden waters. In his diary, he commented on the area's value as a river crossing, but decades passed before anyone followed his advise.

Finally, in 1779, Father Francisco Tomas Garcés established two missions along the river. A presidio was built to protect Mission la Purisima Concepcion on what is now the California side. The entire settlement—including the good padre—was wiped out in a bloody Quechan uprising two years later. That finished things for the Spanish at Yuma Crossing. In 1846, Colonel Stephen Watts Kearny and frontier scout Kit Carson forded the river here. They were headed west to snatch California lands from Mexico. The Mormon Battalion of Colonel Philip Cooke followed in Kearny's path, carving the first rough wagon road into California. When gold was discovered in northern California in 1848, many argonauts used Cooke's southern route through Yuma Crossing. They were reluctant to tackle the rugged east face of the Sierra Nevada range farther north. A few prospectors returned to this area, attracted by nearby gold strikes and the agricultural potential along the Colorado's bottomlands.

The army built an encampment on the California side in 1851 to keep an eye on the still restless Quechans. Small paddlewheel steamers churned upstream from the Gulf of California, supplying new riverside settlements. One of these was Colorado City, founded on the Arizona side in 1854. Historians tell us—with a sly grin—that the town's first permanent resident was a shady lady named Sarah Bowman, who ran a combined restaurant, bar and bawdy house. The river flexed its muscles in 1862, washing Colorado City into the Gulf of California, bordello and all. Another community, called Arizona City, was built on higher ground. Later, the name was changed to Yuma, after the local Indians, who were a blend of Quechans, Cocopahs and Mohaves.

In the 1870s, Governor Anson P. Safford sought construction of a territorial prison in Yuma to replace a scattering of local jails. "No provisions can be made for employing the prisoners (in county jails)," he complained. "Close

TRIP PLANNER

WHEN TO GO ● Southwestern Arizona, like the Colorado River corridor, is a fall-winter-spring place. Yuma's population is more than doubled by Snowbirds each winter. Great expanses of desert lie to the east, particularly on the Mexico side. Many tourist facilities shut down for the summer, generally reopening in early October. It's not cool to submit your car and yourselves to these remote areas during the summer. summers along the border are, in a word—HOT.

WHAT TO SEE ● Yuma Territorial Prison and Yuma Crossing Quartermaster Depot and Century House Museum in Yuma and Fort Yuma on the California side; the classic Spanish plaza of Ajo and its imposing New Cornelia open pit copper mine; Organ Pipe Cactus National Monument; Kitt Peak National Observatory.

WHAT TO DO ● Hike along Yuma's historic riverfront between Yuma Crossing and the territorial prison; hike the Desert View Trail and drive the cactus-rimmed roads at Organ Pipe Cactus National Monument; explore and shop the Mexican towns on the Arizona-Mexico border.

☺ *Indicates an attraction, restaurant or lodging with special appeal.*

USEFUL CONTACTS

Ajo Chamber of Commerce, 321 Taladro, Ajo, AZ 85321; (520) 387-7742.

Superintendent, Organ Pipe Cactus National Monument, Route 1, Box 100, Ajo, AZ 85321; (520) 387-6849.

Yuma Convention & Visitors Bureau, P.O. Box 10831 (377 S. Main at Giss Parkway), Yuma, AZ 85366-8831; (520) 783-0071.

YUMA RADIO STATIONS

KTLM-FM, 106.1—Country.
KJOK-FM, 93.1—Top 40, light rock.
KPTI-FM, 95.1—Country.
KYXI-FM, 100.9—Top 40, light rock.
KEZC-AM, 1400—Soft hits and news.
KBLU-AM, 1320—Public radio.

---

confinement and idleness often result injuriously to health, with scarcely a possibility for moral improvement."

Yuma Territorial Prison State Park, on a bluff overlooking Rio Colorado, is the main drawing card for passing tourists, along with the newly developing Yuma Crossing Quartermaster Depot Historic Site. For Snowbirds, however, Yuma's main draw is the climate. Its population doubles every winter as 40,000 retirees flock to mobile home parks on both sides of the stream.

The community continues its long role as a strategic provisioning center and rest stop for travelers. Motorists hopping off Interstate 8 have a good selection of motels and restaurants. Most are scattered along Business Route I-8. Coming from the west, it follows Fourth Avenue, passes through old downtown Yuma, executes an abrupt left turn called "The Big Curve" and follows 32nd Street east. Most of the town's shopping malls are along 32nd, east and west of downtown.

Approaching the city on I-8 through California, you'll pass through a sand dune area right out of *Lawerence of Arabia.* In fact, several films have been shot here, including desert scenes for *Star Wars.* From fall through spring, hundreds of RVers camp along a frontage road and run their dune buggies over this slice of California Sahara.

Incidentally, Yuma and its surrounding countryside have a street numbering system that can best be described as idiotic. Downtown, numbered streets run east and west, while numbered avenues run north and south.

That isn't too confusing if you can remember to designate street or avenue. However, rural sectional roads extending out from the city have their own numbering system that doesn't match the city's system. For instance, downtown 32nd Street becomes County 11th Street as it heads east. Further, some north-south streets and roads use letters instead of numbers. Patience, a good co-pilot and a copy of the Yuma map available from the visitors bureau should keep you on track.

DRIVING YUMA

The area's first attraction, closely linked to Yuma, is in California, so we'll suggest taking the last California offramp (Business Route 8) into **Winterhaven,** a small hamlet clustered on the western side of the Colorado River. Turn left at a stop sign and cross over the freeway, following a sign to **Fort Yuma** and the Quechan Nation Indian Reservation. This puts you on Picacho Road; cross a large canal and just short of a railroad underpass, fork right onto Quechan Road and follow it up to the old hilltop fort.

Pass in front of the handsome St. Thomas Mission Church with its two-bell tower, then turn left and enter the fort compound. In one of history's ironies, this former U.S. Army post now serves as tribal headquarters for the Quechan Nation (formerly called the Yuma tribe). Find a place to park, walk past tribal offices housed in a collonaded building and head toward a large Spanish colonial style bungalow. Behind that is a smaller cottage, housing the **Fort Yuma Quechan Museum.**

Retrace your path back over the freeway and then follow signs toward old downtown Yuma. The route becomes Fourth Avenue; cross the Colorado River and take an immediate left into **Yuma Crossing Quartermaster Depot Historic Site.** From there, go another block on Fourth and turn left at the first traffic light onto First Street. Follow it four blocks to Madison Avenue and turn right. A block and a half beyond, on the right is **Century House Museum.** Continue half a block to Giss Parkway, turn left and follow it two blocks to the **Yuma Convention and Visitors Bureau** in an old brick building between Main Street and Maiden Lane. It's open daily 9 to 5; (520) 783-0071.

This is a good place to pause—there's ample RV parking—and explore **old downtown Yuma.** Typically, much of the business has retreated to the suburbs and town planners are attempting to preserve what's left of the historic district. Many buildings have been demolished and replaced with parking areas, while others have been preserved. In deference to Yuma's toasty summer sun, most downtown sidewalks and some of the parking is shaded. A one-block section of Main Street between Second and Third has been converted into a landscaped mall. Although several storefronts are empty, you'll find some specialty shops and boutiques. A section called "224 Main Street Shops" is tightly packed with giftware and curio stores.

The area's other attractions are on Yuma's edges. From the visitor center, follow Giss Parkway under the freeway and turn left up Prison Hill Road to **Yuma Territorial Prison State Historic Park.** Then, take Giss back to Fourth Avenue, turn left, follow it five blocks to Eighth Street and turn right (west). Take Eighth about 1.5 miles to Avenue B and turn left. You'll see **Erlich's Date Garden** in a date palm grove on your right, within a few hundred feet. Drive another two miles south on Avenue B to an intersection marked County 11th Street to the right and 32nd Street to the left. (It's all part of Yuma's curious street numbering system.) Turn left (east) onto 32nd Street and follow it back into town, keeping to the right through a squiggle called "The Big Curve." At this point, 32nd blends back into Business I-8. Follow it past the edges of Yuma International Airport and the Marine Corps Air Station. Just opposite the air station runway, at the **Yuma County Fairgrounds,** you can browse through a small botanical garden and rusting farm equipment display. This also is a good place to watch swift Marine Corps jets and growling helicopter squadrons flit about as their pilots busily spend our tax dollars.

Turn right just beyond the fairgrounds, wrapping around the corner of the air station onto Avenue 3E. As you follow it south, note the three jet planes mounted on pedestals on your right, near the air station gate. After two miles on Avenue 3E, turn left onto County 13th Street and follow it a mile and a quarter to the **Peanut Patch** on the left. Continue about half a mile to a stop sign and turn left onto Avenue 5E, which takes you two miles north to Business I-8. From here, you can turn left to return to Yuma or take a right and—within a few miles—blend back onto the interstate.

ATTRACTIONS
In order of appearance

Fort Yuma Quechan Museum ● *Fort Yuma, c/o Quechan Tribal Council, P.O. Box 1352, Yuma, AZ 85364; (619) 572-0661 or (619) 572-0661. Weekdays 8 to 5, Saturday 10 to 4. Adults $1; kids under 12 free.* ⬜ Established in 1849 to protect settlers from the Indians, the fort was deeded to the Quechan tribe in 1884. This was one of eight Colorado River tribes sharing a common Yuman language. The small museum in an old pink adobe traces the history of the Quechan people with artifacts, crafts and photographs. It also covers the area's military history. Particularly interesting are clay figurines that suggest an ancestral tie between the Quechans and ancient Hohokam. More contemporary Indian crafts can be purchased at a gift shop. **St. Thomas Mission Church,** a classic of Spanish colonial architecture, is just below the museum. It was built in 1923 on the site of Mission La Purisima Concepcion, founded by Father Garcés and destroyed by the Quechans in 1781.

☺ *Yuma Crossing Quartermaster Depot Historic Site* ● *100 N. Fourth Avenue at the river, (P.O. Box 2768), Yuma AZ 85366-5735; (520) 329-0404. Daily 10 to 5; visitor center and gift shop 9:30 to 5:30. Adults $3, seniors $2.50, kids $2; family pass (two adults and five kids), $8.* ⬜ This site preserves two important elements in Western history—the ford across the Colorado River and a major Army supply center. Several buildings survive from the original depot, which operated from 1864 until 1883. Served by paddlewheel steamers, it kept six months worth of Army goods on hand to supply forts throughout the Southwest, along with 900 mules for pulling overland freight wagons to distant posts.

The original storehouse, office, commanding officers quarters and other structures have been refurbished and furnished. They're manned by costumed docents who present living history demonstrations from two periods: 1850, when California-bound gold seekers poured through Yuma; and 1876, the depot's peak activity year. Exhibits in the storehouse, mostly photographs and a few artifacts, recall the days when the lower Colorado teemed with sternwheelers. Just outside, costumed "emigrants" relax at a wagon train encampment, preparing to ford the Colorado and press on to the Golden State.

Yuma Territorial Prison wasn't as tough as Hollywood portrayed it. This is the watchtower, built over the old lockup's reservoir.

The facility is operated as a concession of the Arizona State Park system by Yuma Crossing Foundation, Inc., a non-profit group run mostly by volunteers. Eventually, they hope to create a 19th century village, with shops and restaurants covering 90 acres, extending along the river to Yuma Territorial Prison. A riverside trail, only partially completed when we last visited, will connect the two attractions.

☺ **Century House Museum** ● *240 Madison Ave. (Giss Parkway), Yuma, AZ 85364; (520) 782-1841. Tuesday-Saturday 10 to 4. Free; donations encouraged.* ☐ Italian pioneer E.F. Sanguinetti made his fortune as a Yuma merchant and developer, and he spent a lot of it on this spacious 19th century house and garden. Today, the 1870s adobe is a fine museum with exhibits concerning early Colorado River sternwheelers, mining, railroading, settlers and Indian cultures. The lush garden out back is alive with plants and birds, just as it was a century ago when Sanguinetti turned it into a virtual bird park. Caged cockatoos, peacocks, parrots, parakeets and mynah birds volunteer their comments as you explore the extensive grounds. The adjacent **Adobe Annex** at 2150 Madison houses a gift shop styled after a turn-of-the-century drygoods store. Some boutiques and the **Garden Café and Redondo Room Coffee House** are behind the annex, next to the museum's backyard aviary. (See restaurant listing below.)

☺ **Yuma Territorial Prison State Historic Park** ● *Prison Hill Road (P.O. Box 10792), Yuma, AZ 85366-8792; (520) 783-4771. Daily 8 to 5. Adults $3, teens $2, kids under 11 free.* ☐ Thick adobe walls and rusty bars over darkened cells are certainly grim enough to give the old prison its notorious reputation as "the hell-hole of Arizona." But that's merely the stuff of which Hollywood movies were made. In truth, it was regarded as a model prison for its day with a library, schooling for the convicts and—good grief!—even crafts classes. The men crocheted lace and sold their finery at a crafts mart. Some rather delicate examples are on display. The prison still wasn't a pleasant place to pass the time. Temperatures in the adobe cells hit 120 in the summer, and men who broke the rules wound up in a windowless dungeon—sometimes sharing it with scorpions and rattlesnakes. Although it hosted some hardened criminals, most of its guests were merely convicted burglars. Among offenses that would land you in the slammer were obstructing a railroad, seduction, polygamy and adultery. Most prisoners didn't serve out their terms; early paroles and pardons were easy to come by. No one was ever executed here, although eight were killed trying to escape.

The prison became overcrowded and was closed in 1909. It served as Yuma High School from 1910 until 1914, then it sheltered homeless families during the Depression. Through the years, residents helped themselves to most of the building materials. However, there's still much for the visitor to see. What remains are the cell block, the "new yard" where cells were dug into the hillside to relieve overcrowding, the main guard tower built atop a water tank, the main entrance gate and cemetery. A museum built over part of the mess hall foundation displays prison artifacts, scowling photos of inmates and graphics concerning prisoners and the men who guarded them. And yes, the bad guys did wear funny striped uniforms in those days.

Riverside path and Levee Trail ● *About two thirds of a mile.* ☐ A combination of trails leads from the prison to Yuma Crossing at the base of Madison Avenue, from where the Levee Trail continues to the Quartermaster Depot. Pick up the first segment of the route at the outer edge of the prison parking lot, where a rock-lined nature trail leads down to the river bank. A second trail loops through the thick rushes along the river. From here, you can follow a still undeveloped trail toward old town. It passes a picnic area under the I-8 overpass and blends into a sandy road at the base of Madison Avenue. Another section, the Levee Trail, leads to the Quartermaster Depot.

Erlich's Date Garden ● *868 Avenue B (Eighth Street), Yuma, AZ 85364; (520) 783-4778 or (520) 783-7327. Monday-Saturday 9 to 5. No credit cards; personal checks accepted.* ☐ Learn how the fruit of the desert grows in this date garden near downtown Yuma. You can nibble free samples of khadrawis, medjools, halawis and zahadis and buy gift packs to take home. The best time to buy is from late summer to winter, when you can get tasty fresh dates that are too fragile for commercial shipping and storage.

The Peanut Patch ● *4322 E. County 13th St. (Avenue 4E), Yuma, AZ 85365; (800) USA-PNUT or (520) 726-6292. Monday- Saturday 9 to 6; closed in summer.* ☐ The South hasn't cornered the market on peanuts. This farm produces an Arizona version of the goober. You can watch the harvest from October to December, and tour the processing facility from October through April or May. A gift shop sells all sorts of peanuts and peanutty things, plus citrus, dates, candies and specialty foods. When the gift shop is closed, you can find similar items at the Peanut Patch's downtown location in a shopping center (behind a Red Lobster Restaurant) at Fourth Avenue and 16th Street.

ACTIVITIES

Camel Farm tours ● Saihati Camel Farm, 15672 South Avenue 1E, Yuma, AZ 85366; (520) 627-2553. Tours of this camel farm and desert wildlife center are conducted Monday-Saturday at 10 and 2, October through

May; and at 10 a.m. only the rest of the year; $3. Call for directions and for an appointment, since the gate may be closed otherwise.

Colorado River cruises • Yuma River Tours has narrated jet boat tours along the lower Colorado, visiting old mining camps, petroglyphs, steamboat landings and pioneer sites; 1920 Arizona Ave., Yuma, AZ 85364; (520) 783-4400. *Colorado King I* paddlewheeler cruises about Martinez Lake from Fishers's Landing, 32 miles north of Yuma; (520) 782-2412.

Golf • Cocopah RV & Golf Resort, 6800 Strand Ave., (520) 343-9300; 36 holes, driving range, pro shop, weight room, pool and spa. Mesa Del Sol Golf Club, 10583 Camino del Sol (I-8 Foothills exit), (520) 342-1283; 54 holes, pro shop, driving range, restaurant and cocktail lounge.

Rail excursion • Yuma Valley Railway offers two-hour, 22-mile trips along the Colorado River to Mexico, in 1922 Pullman coaches pulled by vintage diesel engines. Weekend departures October through May (Saturday only in the shoulder seasons); Box 10305, Yuma, AZ 85366-8305; 783-3456.

TRANSPORTATION

Yuma International Airport shares runways with the Marine Corps Air Station. **America West** has daily flights to Phoenix and Los Angeles; (800) 247-5692 or (520) 344-2063. **Skywest Airlines** offers similar service; (800) 453-9417. **Amtrak** serves Yuma with east and westbound trains between Los Angeles and New Orleans; the station is at 291 Gila St.; (800) USA-RAIL. **Greyhound** provides service to Los Angeles, San Diego, Phoenix and Tucson with connections beyond; (800) 231-2222. It gallops from a terminal at 170 E. 17th Place behind Fed-Mart; (520) 783-4403.

Several major **rental car** agencies have offices at the airport, including Avis, (800) 331-1212 or (520) 726-5737; Budget, (800) 527-0700 or (520) 344-1822; Enterprise, (800) 325-8007 or (520) 344-5444; and Hertz, (800) 654-3131 or (520) 726-5160. Local **taxi** firms are AAA Taxi Co., (520) 782-4444; Friendly Taxi Service, (520) 783-1000; Yellow Taxi, (520) 783-4444; Yuma City Cab, (520) 782-0111; and Yuma One Taxi, (520) 783-1000. Yuma City Cab also has limousines.

ANNUAL EVENTS

Yuma Crossing Day in February, with pioneer and Native American crafts, demonstrations and such at the historic park.

Square and Round Dance Festival in March.

Yuma County Fair, late March or early April.

Armed Forces Day air show and displays in May at the Marine Corps Air Station.

Colorado River Crossing Balloon Festival in November.

Art and Jazz Festival in November.

WHERE TO DINE

Most of Yuma's restaurants and fast food places are along Fourth Avenue and 32nd Street, following the route of Business Route I-8. Two locally popular places, Chretins and Jack & Rosie's, are close together near 15th Avenue and Fifth Street, in a residential area ten blocks west of downtown.

☺ *Garden Café* • ☆☆ $

☐ *250 Madison Ave. (behind Century House Museum); (520) 783-1491. American; no alcohol. Tuesday-Friday 9 to 2:30, Saturday-Sunday 8 to 2:30. MC/VISA.* ☐ Indoor and outdoor dining in a pleasant garden setting beside the museum's landscaped aviary. Sundry soups, sandwiches, salads and an occasional quiche are served, along with specialty coffees and the usual breakfast fare.

Chretin's Mexican Food ● ☆☆ $

◻ 485 15th Ave. (corner of Fifth Street); (520) 782-1291. Mexican; full bar service. Monday-Saturday 11 to 10. MC/VISA. ◻ Longtime popular favorite, noted for its home cooking, nachos and margaritas. All ingredients are made from scratch. The place is rather scruffy outside, although the interior is cheerfully decorated.

Golden Corral ● ☆☆ $

◻ 2401 S. Fourth Ave. (24th Street); (520) 726-4428. American; no alcohol. Sunday-Thursday 7 a.m. to 10 p.m., Friday-Saturday 7 to 11. Country-style Cafeteria featuring inexpensive dinners, mostly under $10, plus assorted breakfasts and lunches. Large salad bar; booth and table seating.

El Charro Café ● ☆☆ $

◻ 601 W. Eighth St. (near Fourth Avenue); (520) 783-9790. Mexican-American; full bar service. Tuesday-Sunday 11 a.m. to 9 p.m. MC/VISA. ◻ Family-run café since 1949; traditional Mexican fare plus some American items; bright Latin decor.

Jack & Rosie's ● ☆☆ $$

◻ 1551 Fifth St. (16th Avenue); (520) 783-9172. American; full bar service. Tuesday- Sunday 4:30 to 10; MC/VISA. ◻ Family steak house with dark woods, cozy lighting and plush booths. A fixture since 1935, it specializes in steak and barbecued ribs, plus chicken, seafood and such.

La Casa Gutierrez ● ☆ $

◻ 520 S. Orange Ave. (Fifth Street); (520) 782-1402. Mexican; no alcohol. Daily 11 to 8. No credit cards. ◻ Basic but cute diner in a former house, trimmed with an occasional serapé. It's locally popular, featuring inexpensive rolled taco dinners, green and red enchiladas and similar fare.

Mandarin Palace ● ☆☆ $$

◻ 350 E. 32nd St. (Arizona Avenue); (520) 344-2805. Mandarin, Szechuan and American; full bar service. Weekdays 11 to 10, weekends 11 to 11. MC/VISA, AMEX. ◻ Large, attractive restaurant with sunken bar and elaborate Oriental decor; divided dining areas. Extensive Chinese menu plus a few American entrees, including prime rib; luncheon buffet.

WHERE TO RECLINE

Prices reflect high season rates and may be lower at other times. (In Sunbelt areas, prices can drop by more than half in summer.) Most were provided by the management and are subject to change; use them only as a guide.

Airport Travelodge ● ☆☆ $$$ Ø

◻ 711 E. 32nd St. (32nd Street), Yuma, AZ 85365; (800) 835-1132 or (520) 726-4721. Couples and singles $58 to $65, kitchenettes $75 to $85. Major credit cards. ◻ An 80-unit inn with TV movies and phones, some refrigerators and microwaves. Continental breakfast, pool, spa, tennis courts, coin laundry and barbecue area. **Panda Restaurant** serves daily from 11:30 to 9; Chinese; dinners $6 to $16; full bar service.

Best Western Chilton Inn ● ☆☆☆ $$$$ Ø

◻ 300 E. 32nd St. (Arizona Ave.), Yuma, AZ 85365; (800) 528-1234 or (520) 344-1050. Couples $89 to $99, singles $89 to $94; rates include break-

fast buffet. Major credit cards. ☐ A 121-motel with TV, phones and refrigerators; pool, spa, coin laundry, barbecue area, free newspaper; free use of fitness center. **Cactus Rose Café** serves 6 to 10 a.m. and 5 to 10 p.m,.; meals $6 to $14; full bar service.

Best Western Coronado Motor Hotel ● ☆☆☆ $$ Ø

☐ *233 Fourth Ave. (near Giss Parkway), Yuma, AZ 85364; (520) 783-4453 or (800) 528-1234. Couples and singles $46 to $75, kitchenettes and suites to $89. Major credit cards.* ☐ Well-kept 49-room motel with TV movies, phones, refrigerators, hair dryers, VCRs available, some in-room spas; free continental breakfast, swimming pool and spa. Adjacent **restaurant** serves 6 a.m. to 9 p.m.; dinners $5 to $25; full bar service.

Best Western InnSuites Yuma ● ☆☆☆ $$$$ Ø

☐ *1450 Castle Dome Rd., Yuma, AZ 85365; (800) 922-2034 or (520) 783-8341. Couples $89 to $149, singles $79 to $149, kitchenettes and suites $99 to $149; rates include buffet breakfast. Major credit cards.* ☐ Attractive 166-unit lodge with TV movies, phones, refrigerators and microwaves; pool and spa, tennis courts, coin laundry, barbecue area, exercise room and library. **Restaurant** serves 6 to 1 and 5 to 9; dinners $9 to $11; full bar.

Caravan Oasis Motel ● ☆☆ $$$

☐ *10574 Fortuna Rd., Yuma, AZ 85365; (520) 342-1292. Couples $40 to $45, singles $31 to $39, family units $43 to $49. MC/VISA, DISC.* ☐ A 20-unit motel with TV; most rooms with refrigerators and microwaves. Continental breakfast, pool, spa, coin laundry, barbecue area and beauty salon.

Desert Grove Motel ● ☆☆ $$

☐ *3500 S. Fourth Ave. (at 32nd Street), Yuma, AZ 85365; (520) 344-1921. All kitchen units, Couples and singles $41 to $58. Major credit cards.* ☐ Twenty-four rooms and several mobiles with TV and phones and refrigerators; pool, spa, barbecue area, coin laundry, horseshoes and shuffleboard at cabana by the pool; nicely landscaped grounds with grapefruit trees.

Interstate 8 Inn ● ☆☆ $$ Ø

☐ *2730 S. Fourth Ave., Yuma, AZ 85365; (800) 821-7465 or (520) 726-6110. Couples $33 to $50, singles $23 to $34. Major credit cards.* ☐ A 120-unit motel with TV, phones, microwaves and refrigerators; pool, spa, coin laundry and barbecue area.

Royal Motor Inn ● ☆☆ $$ Ø

☐ *2941 S. Fourth Ave. (Catalina Drive), Yuma, AZ 85364; (520) 344-0550 or (800) 729- 0550. Couples $35 to $55, singles $30 to $50. MC/VISA, AMEX.* ☐ A 62-unit motel with TV, phones, refrigerators, microwaves; pool and spa. **Jeanette's Country Kitchen** serves American fare daily 5 a.m. to 9 p.m.; dinners $4 to $7; no alcohol.

WHERE TO CAMP

Araby Acres Travel Trailer Park ● *6649 E. Highway 80 (I-8 exit 7, six miles east), Yuma, AZ 85365; (520) 344-8666. RV sites, full hookups $23. Reservations accepted; no credit cards.* ☐ Some pull-throughs, showers, coin laundry, Propane. A 55 and older park with recreation room, landscaped grounds, putting green, horseshoes, shuffleboard, gym, two swimming pools.

Bonita Mesa RV Resort ● *9400 N. Frontage Rd. (I-8 exit 12, eight miles east), Yuma, AZ 85365; (520) 342-2999. RV sites, full hookups $21.* ☐ Showers, coin laundry, Propane.

Mesa Verde RV Park ● *3649 S. Fourth Ave. (opposite Frontier Village), Yuma, AZ 85364; (520) 726-5814. RVs only; full hookups $14, plus weekly to yearly rates. Reservations accepted; no credit cards.* ⬜ Large park with showers, barbecues and TV cable; coin laundry, pool and spa, shuffleboard courts, pool rooms, library, exercise room and recreation hall; organized activities.

Roger's RV Resort, Golf & Country Club ● *9797 E. Highway 80, Yuma, AZ 85365; (520) 342-2992. RV sites, full hookups $20. Reservations accepted; MC/VISA.* ⬜ Full service resort with golf course and driving range, spa and pool, shuffleboard, volleyball, billiards, horseshoes, snack bar, exercise room, library and activity center with planned functions. RV sites have TV and phone hookups, showers, coin laundry, dump station.

YUMA TO ORGAN PIPE CACTUS

Most of Yuma's Snowbirds roost in a 14-mile-long string of RV parks east along Interstate 8. The route takes you past great fields of glistening RVs, then through green fields in a pretty little irrigated valley.

Shortly, these signs of civilization surrender to creosote bush, and you don't see much life again until you enter Gila Bend, 116 miles from Yuma. You will see some rough hewn scenery however, as the route passes through the rocky ridges of the Gila Mountains and then into Dome Valley. This isn't the cactus garden desert of the Sonoran, which is further south, but the less interesting creosote bush desert of the Mohave. Desert valleys and low mountains alternate between here at Gila Bend, and occasional tiny communities provide food and fuel. These who eschew freeways can hop off and follow a two-lane highway that parallels I-8 for 35 miles between Wellton and Mohawk. However, the scenery's the same and the speed limit is lower so it offers no real advantage.

At exit 67, the **Dateland** café, curio shop, mini-mart and RV park provides an excuse to stop and stretch your legs. The café serves excellent thick date shakes and date cream pies, plus basic American fare. It's open daily 6 a.m. to 10 p.m.; (520) 454-2772.

Gila Bend, a community of 2,000, started life as a Butterfield Stage stop back in the 1870s, and not much has happened here since. It's a provisioning center for surrounding ranches and a handy rest stop for travelers on this long strip of I-8. The town offers a few motels and cafés, and the small **Gila Bend Museum** with some pioneer artifacts on display. It's on the left, midway through town at 644 West Pima Street, sharing space with a tourist information center; open daily 8 to 4; (520) 683-2002.

From Gila Bend, pick up Highway 95 and head south toward Organ Pipe Cactus National Monument. The desert isn't terribly inspiring around Gila Bend, but as you drive south, you begin climbing into higher Sonoran cactus gardens. The route through craggy lava flows of the Crater Mountains just north of Ajo is particularly impressive.

Ajo

Elevation: 1,798 feet   **Population: 5,200**

Ajo occupies an appealing setting, surrounded by thick desert flora and the rough lava textures of the Little Ajo Mountains. The Spanish-Moorish style downtown plaza is quite attractive, although the suburbs consist mostly of old frame houses, doublewides and prefabs—many occupied by retirees. Ajo began as a company town in 1917, created to house workers at the nearby New Cornelia open pit mine. Now owned by the Phelps Dodge Corporation, the mine was shut down in 1985 because of falling copper prices. Retirees and tourists bound for Organ Pipe Cactus National Monument are the current contributors to the town's economy.

☺ As you enter downtown, note the **Plaza shopping complex** with Spanish colonnades, built around a central park. Part of the original company town, it contains most of Ajo's commercial activity. Directly across from the plaza, turn right onto La Mina Avenue and follow signs to Ajo's two visitor attractions, the copper pit lookout and a museum a few blocks farther uphill:

☺ *New Cornelia Mine* • *Lookout access and mining exhibit open Tuesday-Saturday 10 to 4; closed in summer; $1.* ⛶ It's an impressive sight—a terraced, multi-colored pit nearly a mile and a half across and 850 feet deep. The best view is from a lookout hut operated by the Ajo Chamber of Commerce. The structure also contains several exhibits concerning copper mining and smelting techniques. You can still see the pit when the chamber facility is closed, although a fence keeps you from getting close to the edge.

Ajo Historical Museum • Indian Village Road; (520) 387-7105. Daily 10 to 4; closed July through September; admission by donation. ⛶ Housed in the former St. Catherine's Indian mission and church, the museum presents a disorganized clutter of memorabilia. Some of it relates to Ajo's history, some does not; some doesn't seem to relate to anything. Displays in-

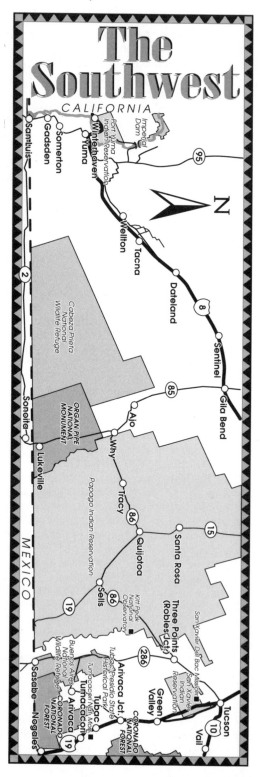

The Southwest

clude a large mineral exhibit, pioneer photos and assorted blacksmith tools.

Back downtown, you'll find the **Ajo Chamber of Commerce** on the left, just beyond the plaza. It's open weekdays 8:30 to 4:30, with weekend hours during the fall-winter-spring season; (520) 387-7742.

ACTIVITY

Bus tours ● Ajo Stage Line has one to four-day trips to Rocky Point and into the desert surrounding Ajo; 1041 Solana, Ajo, AZ 85321; (800) 942-1981 or (520) 387-6567.

WHERE TO DINE AND RECLINE

Copper Kettle Restaurant ● ☆ $$

☐ *Plaza Shopping Center; (520) 387-5555. American-Mexican; no alcohol. Monday-Saturday 7 a.m. to 8 p.m. No credit cards.* ☐ Roomy, rather stark restaurant serving American steaks, chickens and chops, plus several typical Mexican entrees.

Guest House Inn Bed & Breakfast ● ☆☆☆ $$$ Ø

☐ *Three Guest House Rd. (off La Mina Avenue), Ajo, AZ 85321; (520) 387-6133. Couples $69 to $79, singles $59 to $69. Four units with private baths; full breakfast. Major credit cards.* ☐ Built in 1925 by the Phelps Dodge Corporation for company officials, this plantation style structure is dressed up in a mix of Southwestern, Victorian and contemporary furnishings. Patio with desert views, large common room with fireplace and library.

Managers House Inn ● ☆☆☆ $$$ Ø

☐ *One Greenway Dr., Ajo, AZ 85321; (520) 387-6505. Couples $69 to $99. Four rooms with private baths; full breakfast. MC/VISA.* ☐ Ajo's second B&B also is mine- connected—a 1919 Craftsman bungalow built for the manager. Done in period decor, it's perched on a hilltop with views of the town and countryside. Spa and patio; afternoon wine and cheese.

South of Ajo, the highway passes the Phelps Dodge smelter, now undergoing demolition, then it skims multi-colored tailing dumps of the copper mine. A few miles below, it passes through a hamlet called **Why**, named for the "Y" junction where state highways 85 and 86 converge. Naturally, it has a service station and market called the Why Not Travel Store. Shortly, you'll begin climbing into rugged terrain, offering some of the richest botanical bounty of the Sonoran Desert. Here, you meet a cactus that earns its name from its long spiny arms, said to resemble pipes on an organ.

Organ Pipe Cactus National Monument ● *Route 1, Box 100, Ajo, AZ 85321; (520) 387-6849. Park open 24 hours; visitor center open daily 8 to 5; $4 per vehicle or $2 for bikers and hikers. RV and tent sites in campgrounds, no hookups, $8, or $4 with Golden Age or Access pass. Flush potties, water, picnic tables and barbecues. Appealing paved pull-through sites tucked among the desert flora; vehicle limit 35 feet.* ☐

Arizona's largest and most remote national monument preserves some of the world's most striking desert wilderness. It is named for a large cactus common in northern Mexico but rare in the United States. The organ pipe approaches the saguaro in size, but it's quite different, with multiple arms reaching upward from a common base. Of course, it is but one resident of this mountainous rock garden, which is busy with giant saguaro and hundreds of other desert plants. Far from civilization's pollution, Organ Pipe Cactus has been designated by the United Nations as an International Bio-

An organ pipe cactus casts a web-like shadow at sundown.

sphere Preserve. It's one of our favorite corners of Arizona—a peaceful place with unending panoramas of rock-strewn hills and a virtual showcase of desert flora. Twenty-nine species of cacti have been identified here. During springtime after a wet winter, the blooms of cactus, poppies, lupine and other flowers can be absolutely dazzling. Less conspicuous are the desert animals, most of whom prefer to come out at night. Take a flashlight hike and you're likely to encounter kangaroo rats with silly-looking pom-poms on their tails, along with jackrabbits and perhaps an owl or three. Rattlesnakes loves this desert, too, so step lightly.

Abrupt elevation changes create three distinct plant communities here. You can drive or hike into the hot and dry Lower Colorado division, with creosote bush and mixed scrub; the Arizona Upland section with its cactus and paloverde; and into rare pockets of the Central Gulf Coast division, where you'll see elephant trees and senita cactus, normally found only in Mexico. This remote corner can be a busy place, if you choose. Rangers conduct guided walks, talks and slide programs. The visitor center has fine exhibits on the flora, fauna, geology and history of the area. Several hiking trails take you into surrounding desert gardens. **Desert View Nature Trail**, which begins just inside the campground entrance, winds 1.2 miles through some excellent botanical displays, topping out on a ridge that offers grand views of the monument. The best way to discover this 330,690-acre haven is to take the two scenic drives. The 21-mile **Ajo Mountain Drive** winds through the foothills of the highest range in the area. The **Puerto Blanco Drive**, 53 miles long, circles the Puerto Blanco Mountains, with a variety of settings.

RV ADVISORY ● Both drives are over dirt roads that are generally well maintained although they can get a bit bumpy, so RVers need to exercise patience. Any small to mid-size RV or passenger car can make it.

The hamlet of **Lukeville** is wedged between the southern edge of the monument and the Mexican border. If you blink as you enter, you'll miss it and wind up in Mexico—except, of course, you'll be stopped for a border check. Lukeville's Gringo Pass complex comprises most of the tiny business district. Offerings include a trailer park, motel, service station, laundromat and Mexican insurance office, should you want to drive on into Mexico. **Gringo Pass Motel** has singles for $48 and couples for $52, with cable TV and a pool, plus RV sites with full hookups for $14, no hookups for $9; (520) 254-9284. The restaurant, across the street and adjacent to the general store, serves mostly Mexican fare; 7 a.m. to 8 p.m.

A couple of miles over the line is **Sonoita**, and about 60 miles beyond that is **Puerto Peñasco** or Rocky Point, a popular Mexican-American colony on the Gulf of California. We'll visit them in our South of the Border section at the end of this chapter.

EAST TO TUCSON OR NOGALES

From Organ Pipe National Monument, drive north to Why and head east across brushy desert on State Route 86. You'll shortly enter the **Tohono O'odham Reservation**. There's little to see through here—mostly brushy creosote bush and mesquite and broken volcanic hills, although you'll pass some nice saguaro and cholla gardens between Tracy and Quijotoa.

Tohono O'odham is America's second largest Indian reservation, after the huge Navajo-Hopi nation. The state of Connecticut would fit within its 2.8 million acres. Some maps still show this as the Papago Reservation, for that was the tribal name given to them by the Spanish. Seeking links to their past, tribe members adopted their ancestral name a few years ago; it means "desert dwellers who emerged from the earth." That's a considerable improvement over Papago, which means "bean people."

Better an earthly spirit than a bean counter.

Sells, the tribal headquarters, has basic services and fuel in a small business district south of the highway. You can buy Tohono O'odham baskets and assorted other Native American handiwork at Margaret's Indian Arts and Crafts Shop in a Southwest style shopping center.

East of Sells, you'll see—still more than 20 miles away—the glistening white domes of the world's largest astronomical observatory, crowning a rocky ridge of the Quinlan Mountains. Twenty-two miles from Sells, a right turn will take you to these lofty heights:

☺ *Kitt Peak National Observatory* ● *P.O. Box 26732, Tucson, AZ 85726-6732; (520) 620-5350. Daily 9 to 3:45; film and guided tours at 11, 1 and 2:30. Free.* ◻ This busy complex offers extensive visitor facilities, including a new reception center and theater. Self-guiding tours take you into structures housing three of the observatory's 13 telescopes. A highlight attraction is the monster McMath solar telescope, built into an angular shaft thrusting 300 feet into the earth. From a platform inside, you seem to be peering down the shaft of an ultra-modern mine. But there's a huge mirror, not an ore pocket, at the bottom. This giant telescope tracks the sun and projects its image onto a 30-inch surface. There, scientists can study its flares, spots and other quirks.

You can ride an elevator to the Mayall telescope observation deck for a panorama of the surrounding desert and Quinlan Mountains. The Burrell-Schmidt telescope, which takes wide-angle photographs of the heavens, also is open to visitors. These aren't the kinds of telescopes that one uses to peer at the moon, or into their neighbor's bedroom window. Some don't even have eyepieces, but feed their images into computers or fan them out as spectrographs. A complex instrument called the Very Long Baseline Array Radio Telescope studies the stars by gathering their radio waves. Funded by the National Science Foundation, Kitt Peak is operated by a consortium of 20 universities. Eager astronomers and astronomy students take turns at the instruments, which have produced some of America's most impressive galactic discoveries. Observers measured what had been the most distant galaxies ever seen, about 12 billion light years away—although the Hubbell space telescope has since peered further into the heavens.

The visitor center features heavenly exhibits and diagrams of several telescopes. The gift shop sells things astronomical (no pun intended), along with crafts of the Tohono O'odham Indians. A nearby picnic area provides a nice desert view. There's no food sold at the gift shop, so bring a lunch. Bring your jacket, too; the elevation here is 7,000 feet.

From Kitt Peak, we offer two choices. The most logical is to continue east on Highway 86 to Tucson. The less logical among you may be interested in visiting the scruffiest of all Mexican border towns. You can reach it by turning south onto State Route 286 at **Robles Junction**. This provisioning center on the far outskirts of Tucson also is known as Three Points. The only things south of here, neither of which is awesome, are the Buenos Aires National Wildlife Refuge and the border town of Sasabe. The only signs of life you'll encounter are a few desert ranches and an occasional roadrunner.

So why are we suggesting this route? Because Sasabe is intriguing—a true Mexican village that appears totally unaffected by its proximity with America. And besides, this is a Discovery Guide.

RV ADVISORY ● Highway 286 south is paved with only occasional rough spots, although the short road into the wildlife refuge headquarters is quite bumpy. Downtown Sasabe, Mexico, is a real challenge—twisted, lumpy and deeply rutted dirt streets. Also, the highway east from the wildlife refuge that gets you to Interstate 19 at Arivaca Junction is very twisty and bumpy, although it's paved.

The route south takes you through some nice stands of paloverdes, cholla and an occasional saguaro cactus. As you approach **Buenos Aires National Wildlife Refuge,** it changes to a less interesting blend of rabbit brush, bitterbush and creosote bush. The refuge itself occupies a brushy desert wetland where a few birds and deer hang out. Eight miles short of the border, you can follow a dusty, washboardy road a couple of miles to refuge headquarters. There, you can pick up a brochure and drive the Antelope Drive loop road to some bird-watching viewpoints. The most interesting feature in this area is the imposing granite dome of 7,730-foot Baboquivari Peak. This squared monolith is the dominant feature of the Baboquivari Mountains, about ten miles west.

Below the refuge, the terrain changes suddenly from a brushy desert basin to rocky hills that cradle the dual towns of Sasabe, Arizona and Mexico. The Arizona version consists of a few weathered houses and stores randomly scattered among these small, steep hills. The only modern structure is the large brick inspection facility for the U.S. Customs Office. Oddly elaborate for such a remote crossing, it stands in vivid contrast the buildings about it, like an over-dressed guest at a casual dinner. The small Mexican customs facility occupies a modest stucco edifice.

Across the border, the highway becomes a bumpy, rutted dirt street that wanders through a slice of old Mexico. A small ranching community, Sasabe is a collection of weathered adobe buildings and battered old pickups. The one cheerful structure is a gleaming white gazebo with mustard trim in the center of town. As we bumped along the main street, a small boy ran alongside, staring curiously, as if he'd never seen gringos before. Perhaps he'd never seen a Winnebago.

Back in the wildlife refuge, you can take a paved road east through the low Las Guijas Mountains and pick up Interstate 19 at **Arivaca Junction**. It's narrow and rough, not recommended for anyone in a hurry. Passenger cars can negotiate it easily, although RVers will feel the bumps. Unless your next stop is Nogales, you'll be more comfortable following Highway 286 back to Robles Junction.

EXPLORING SOUTH OF THE BORDER

Arizona shares a long border and many ethnic ties with Mexico. Indeed, Southwestern cooking, architecture and even cowboying are heavily influenced by our neighbors to the south. One out of six Arizonans trace their roots to Mexico.

Visiting the Mexican state of Sonora through any of the six border crossings is a simple matter. At most points, you can merely walk across the international boundary to nearby shopping areas, restaurants and cantinas. Bear in mind that these aren't typical Mexican cities, any more than Arizona border towns are typically American. Each is influenced by the presence of the other. With the exception of Sasabe, these towns cater heavily to tourists, with an inordinate number of curio shops and restaurants. While you won't experience a typical slice of Mexico, you'll enjoy browsing through these bordertown shops. They offer bewildering selections of leather goods, ceramics, costume jewelry, turquoise and silver, onyx and wood carvings, embroidered clothing and glassware. Some Mexican Indian handicrafts are quite nice.

Since most towns have shopping areas right next to the border, we recommend parking and walking across. U.S. Customs officials are more picky than their Mexican counterparts, and you might get stuck in a long line of cars, trying to get back into Arizona. Also, American car insurance policies aren't recognized in Mexico. Incidentally, it's best to avoid weekend visits, when most border crossings are extremely busy.

Entry formalities ● If you're an American or Canadian citizen, you need only to declare your citizenship for visits of 72 hours or less, if you aren't going beyond a border town. If you plan to stay longer and/or go deeper, you'll need a Mexican Tourist Card and an automobile permit. These can be obtained quickly at the border, or from the Mexico Tourist Office at 2744 E. Broadway in Tucson. You'll need proof of citizenship such as a birth certificate, passport, voter's registration certificate or military ID. A driver's license won't work. For a vehicle permit, you'll need proof of ownership, such as the registration slip. If you're driving someone else's car, *you may not permitted to enter Mexico.*

Auto insurance ● Don't drive anywhere in Mexico without Mexican auto insurance. Although insurance isn't mandated by law, your vehicle might be impounded if you're involved in an accident. Few American insurance policies extend coverage to Mexico and even if they do, Mexican officials won't recognize them. If you have a rental car, make sure your rental agreement permits driving into Mexico, and get proper insurance coverage.

Mexican auto insurance is available on both sides of the border. Rates are comparable with American premiums and don't bother shopping for the best prices because they're set by the government. We recommend **Sandborn's**, an American-owned company with offices at several border towns. In addition to insurance coverage, the firm provides a question-and-answer leaflet, Mexican milepost guides, camping directories and other helpful stuff. The firm has offices in Ajo, Douglas, Nogales and Yuma, or contact: Sandborn's, P.O. Box 310, McAllen, TX 78502.

Shopping ● American money is widely accepted in border towns, so don't bother with currency exchanges. Expect to haggle over prices in curio shops. The rule of thumb is to counter with a third what they ask, then meet somewhere in the middle. Don't embarrass the poor shopkeeper and take all the fun out of bargaining by paying full price. Because of lower labor costs and a favorable exchange rate, you'll find good buys. Booze is cheap because of the lack of tax, and Mexican-made liquor such as tequila and brandy are less than half the price that they are in the States. However, there are limits on what you can bring back; see below.

"Se habla Ingles?" ● You won't have to resort to your high school Spanish in the border towns; English is spoken at virtually every shop, motel and restaurant.

Health measures ● We've traveled extensively in Mexico without getting anything worse that diarrhea, but that's awfully unpleasant, so take precautions. Even in the finest restaurants, we routinely avoid drinking unbottled water or eating fresh vegetables that have been washed in tap water. Those nasty little bugs that commit Montezuma's revenge can be killed by heat, so eat only hot food while it's still hot. There's a simple solution to avoiding contaminated water, where these nasty critters often lurk. When in doubt, remember that our Mexican friends make great beer!

Driving the interior ● It's generally as safe as driving across Arizona, but there's a major difference. Once you get away from the border, service facilities are scarce and car parts even scarcer. For an extended trip into Mexico, take spare parts such as fan belts, water pumps and such—things that might likely conk out. And don't forget the tools needed to install them. Also, take plenty of bottled water in case you're stranded for a while. Paved Mexican roads are often narrower than ours. Watch out for potholes, tractors and cows who seem oblivious to the risk of colliding with a car. Because of open ranges in the state of Sonora and elsewhere, we make it a rule never to drive after dark. Unleaded gasoline is plentiful in border towns, less so as you travel south. You may want to filter your gasoline through a fine sieve or cloth, particularly if you have a fuel-injected vehicle.

Returning to Arizona ● You can bring back $400 worth of duty-free goods per family member, plus one quart of liquor per adult. Mexico enjoys favored nation status with the U.S., and certain handicrafts can be imported in excess of the $400 limit. Check with a U.S. Customs office to see what's currently on the list. Bear in mind that some items can't be imported from any country, including ivory and certain animal skins and sea turtle oil. Customs can advise you what not to buy when you shop across the border.

The Border Towns

While none of the border towns are cool in summer, Nogales and Agua Prieta—at nearly 4,000 feet elevation—are a bit more livable. San Luis, below Yuma, is near sea level; expect to sizzle if you plan a summertime visit.

Agua Prieta ● This is Mexico's twin to Douglas. The two towns rub shoulders at the border, and shops are less than a block from the boundary. With about 70,000 inhabitants—ten times as many as Douglas—Agua Prieta offers a fair variety of shops. They're not as abundant as those in Nogales or San Luis, however. Downtown here is more of a conventional mix of businesses, with gift shops tucked among department stores, *farmacias* and professional offices. Paved highways lead from here into the interior; it's the most direct driving route to Mexico City. (See Chapter eleven, page 330.)

Naco ● A hamlet south of Bisbee, Naco is one of our favorite border towns. If there's such a thing as scruffily cute, this is it. Naco is more like an interior village—uncrowded, with little Mexican shops behind dusty pastel store fronts. You won't find much of a shopping selection here, but there's one good-sized liquor store. The wide (although pot-holed) streets with center dividers give the place a nice colonial charm. (See Chapter eleven, page 326.)

Nogales ● Opposite Nogales, Arizona, it's the largest of the border towns, with a population exceeding 200,000. Predictably, it's also the best place to shop. Scores of curio and liquor stores are crowded into the Calle Obregon, a shopping area that starts just a block from the border. Narrow arcades are stuffed with stalls. Some carry a variety of crafts, curios and general junk, while others specialize in leather goods, fabric, glassware and such. (See Chapter nine, page 288)

San Luis ● South of Yuma, San Luis is an agricultural community of 50,000 or so. Its weathered old business district offers several shops within two blocks of the border. Selections are fairly good, although it's a distant second to Nogales for shopping variety. You can park free in Friendship Park on the American side; the lot closes at 9 p.m.

Sasabe ● At the bottom of Highway 286 southwest of Tucson, this is the smallest, least crowded and most typically Mexican of all the border towns. A handful of residents occupy its weathered buildings and its matching Arizona twin, and there are no tourist shops or other facilities. Only dirt roads lead south from here, so Sasabe obviously gets very little through traffic. Incidentally, the border station is closed between 8 p.m. and 8 a.m.

Sonoita ● Opposite Lukeville below Organ Pipe Cactus National Monument, Sonoita is about three miles from the border. A few shops are within walking distance of Lukeville but there isn't much of a selection. You might like to drive 63 miles south to **Rocky Point** (Puerto Peñasco), where you can swim, snorkel and fish in the clear waters of the Gulf of California. It has several tourist hotels and restaurants. Remember that you need a Mexican Tourist Card and vehicle permit to go south of Sonoita. The Sonoita-Lukeville border station is closed between midnight and 8 a.m.

TRIP PLANNER

WHEN TO GO ● Arizona's southeastern corner is all year territory. The desert basins cradling the towns of Tombstone, Sierra Vista, Bisbee and Willcox are nearly a mile high, easing summer temperatures. Winters are chilly with occasional light snowfall. Spring and fall are fine times to visit and you can catch a bit of autumn color in some of the mountain areas. Any time of year, you'll find the Cowboy Corner free of crowds, with the exception of Tombstone on summer weekends.

WHAT TO SEE ● Tombstone Courthouse, Boothill Cemetery, O.K. Corral and Bird Cage Theatre in Tombstone; Fort Huachuca Museum; Lavender Pit and Bisbee Mining Museum in Bisbee; Coronado National Memorial; Fort Bowie National Historic Site; Rex Allen Arizona Cowboy Museum in Willcox and Amerind Foundation Museum in Dragoon.

WHAT TO DO ● Prowl the shops of cute little Patagonia; watch for the birdies at Patagonia-Sonoita Creek Preserve and Ramsey Canyon and other nature reserves; have a Coors and dance the cowboy two-step at the Crystal Palace Saloon in Tombstone; take the Queen Mine tour in Bisbee; hike the forest trails of Coronado National Memorial and the rugged rocks of Chiricahua National Monument.

☺ *Indicates an attraction, restaurant or lodging with special appeal.*

USEFUL CONTACTS

Benson-San Pedro Valley Chamber of Commerce, P.O. Box 2255 (363 W. Fourth St.), Benson, AZ 85602; (520) 586-2842.

Bisbee Chamber of Commerce, P.O. Box BA, Bisbee, AZ 85603; (520) 432-5421.

Chiricahua National Monument, Dos Cabezas Route, Box 6500, Willcox, AZ 85643; (520) 824-3560.

Coronado National Forest, Sierra Vista Ranger District, 769 N. Highway 90, Sierra Vista, AZ 85635; (520) 455-5530; and Douglas Ranger District, Route 1, Box 228-R, Douglas, AZ 85607; (520) 364-3468.

Coronado National Memorial, 4101 E. Montezuma Canyon Rd., Hereford, AZ 85615; (520) 366-5515.

Douglas Chamber of Commerce, 1125 Pan American Ave., Douglas, AZ 85607; (520) 364-2477.

Fort Bowie National Historic Site, P.O. Box 158, Bowie, AZ 85605; (520) 847-2500.

Patagonia Visitors Center, P.O. Box 241, Patagonia, AZ 85624; 394-0060.

Sierra Vista Chamber of Commerce, 77 Calle Portal, Suite A- 140, Sierra Vista, AZ 85635; (800) 288-3861 or (520) 458-6940.

Tombstone Chamber of Commerce, P.O. Box 339 (Allan and Fourth streets), Tombstone, AZ 85638; (520) 457-9317 or (520) 457-3929.

Willcox Chamber of Commerce and Agriculture, 1500 N. Circle I Rd., Willcox, AZ 85643; (800) 200-2272 or (520) 384-2272.

AREA RADIO STATIONS

KWZB-FM, 92.3, Bisbee—Country
KIOI-FM, 100.9, Sierra Vista—Rock.
KKYZ-FM, 101.7, Sierra Vista—Top 40 oldies.
KDAP-FM, 96.5, Douglas—Country.
KJMC-AM, 1420, Sierra Vista/Bisbee—Easy listening, nostalgia.
KNXN-AM, 1470, Sierra Vista—Rock.
KHIL-AM, 1250, Willcox—Country.

BACK IN THE SADDLE

Chapter eleven

THE COWBOY CORNER
From tough old Tombstone to Apache country

WHAT WE'VE CHOSEN to call the Cowboy Corner is Cochise County, a history-laden rectangle—75 by 90 miles—occupying southeastern Arizona. It could as easily be called the Cochise Corner in honor of the Chiricahua Apache warrior chief, or the Copper Corner, for the great copper mines around Bisbee.

Some of Arizona's most intriguing historical pageants were played out here. Francisco Vásquez de Coronado passed through in 1540 during his search for the seven golden cities. Cochise made a futile stand against the intruding whites from 1858 to 1869, then Geronimo took up the lance of resistance. In a dusty ally in Tombstone, three men died on October 26, 1881, in the most celebrated gun battle of Western history. Then the dust settled and the southeastern corner dozed contentedly while Tucson, Phoenix and the Colorado River corridor lured hundreds of thousands of settlers and tourists.

In recent years, Cochise County has re-awaked as an important tourist destination and burgeoning new retirement haven. Its high altitude tempers the summer sun and its southern location moderates winter cold. Climatologists say it offers some of the most temperate climate in America. The county's mountain ranges—like ships on a desert sea—attract hikers and campers.

It's for the birds

Incidentally, several canyons of southeastern Arizona are noted for their bird watching, including some of the best humming bird spotting in America. Carr Canyon, Madera Canyon, the Patagonia Sonoita Creek Sanctuary, Ramsey Canyon Preserve and San Pedro Riparian Conservation Area are particularly noted for their birding. For a brochure on the best bird watching areas, contact the Sierra Vista Area Chamber of Commerce at 77 Calle Portal, Suite A-140, Sierra Vista, AZ 85365; (800) 288-3861 or (520) 458-6940.

Since Cochise County's lures are somewhat scattered, we've put together a scenic-historic drive that tourist promoters call the Cochise Trail. There are two approaches, and they converge in Tombstone. If you're coming from Tucson, head east on I-10 and take State Route 80 south from Benson. If you're in Nogales, drive northeast on State Route 82.

Tucson to Tombstone

After skimming the edge of the Rincon Mountains, Interstate 10 heads east into brushy desert. It offers little of interest until you hit **Benson**, a former cowboy town and Butterfield Stage stop. It has a few motels and restaurants, a small museum and historic train ride. To learn more about the area, stop at the **Benson Chamber of Commerce** in Oasis Court at 363 W. Fourth Street, open weekdays 9 to 4 and Saturday 10 to 3; (520) 586-2842.

San Pedro Valley Arts and Historical Museum ● 180 S. San Pedro St. (near Main), Benson, AZ 85602; (520) 586-3070. Tuesday-Friday 10 to 4, Saturday 10 to 2, shorter hours in summer. Free; donations accepted. ☐ The small museum has an art gallery and gift shop, along with displays of the usual pioneer and Indian artifacts. Exhibits focus on the Butterfield Stage and early railroading and ranching days.

San Pedro & Southwestern Railroad ● P.O. Box 1420 (793 E. Country Club Dr.), Benson, AZ 85602; (520) 586-2266. Excursion fares $15 one way and $24 round trip, seniors $12 and $21, students $9 and $6, parlor car upgrade (air conditioned cars with complimentary beverages) $5 or $8 per person. MC/VISA. ☐ The historic railroad runs trips through the San Pedro Riparian National Conservation Area between Benson and Charleston. Passengers ride in open cars or early 20th century parlor cars, pulled by a diesel locomotive. The train passes the ruins of several old mining towns, then turns around at Charleston, near Tombstone. Combined train and motor coach tours of southeastern Arizona also are available. Call the railroad or Cochise Tours at (520) 720-4900.

From Benson, pick up State Route 80 and head south through more brushy desert, rimmed here and there by low hills. This area was, appropriate to the title of this chapter, some of Arizona's earliest cattle country. Twenty-one miles south of Benson, just beyond the junction with State Route 82, you'll reach Tombstone.

Nogales to Tombstone

This approach is more appealing, not for the route itself—more brushy desert—but for several interesting stops along the way. It is, in fact, worth a deliberate side trip even if you hadn't intended to be in Nogales.

Assuming you're downtown, take Grand Avenue north a couple of miles, then follow the Highway 82 sign. The route goes left (west) and then swings east, looping over Grand Avenue. A couple of miles from town, you'll see something unexpected in Arizona—a winery:

Arizona Vineyards ● *1830 Patagonia Rd., Nogales; (520) 287-7972. Winetasting and sales. Daily 10 to 5.* ☐ This funky old winery and tasting room is probably more interesting for its collection of carved mythical animals and other odds and ends than it is for the wine. Owners have blended assorted heat resistant grapes and imported others to come up with Rainbo Rouge, Desert Dust, Coyote Red, Rattlesnake Red and Apache Red. While not awesome, they're well-made and quite drinkable.

After fifteen miles of brushy prairie country, you may find another reason to pause:

Patagonia Lake State Park ● *P.O. Box 274, Patagonia, AZ 85624; (520) 287-6965. Day use $5; camping $10 to $15 (camping details below). Boating, picnic areas and hiking trails; mini-mart open daily except Wednesday 8 to 6.* ☐ About four miles west of the highway, this park encloses a small reservoir created in 1968 by the damming of Sonoita Creek. Bass, crappie, catfish and

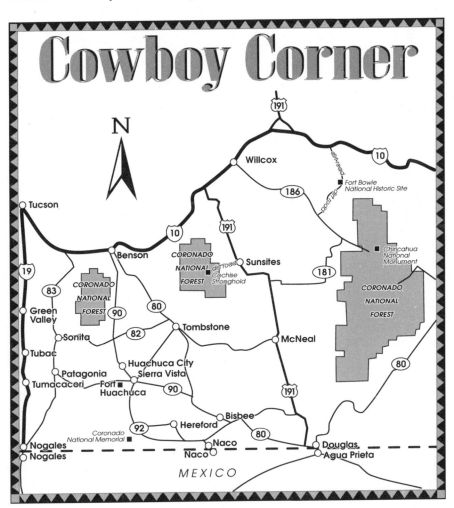

bluegill tempt anglers. Facilities include a boat launch, marina, swimming bay and short hiking trail.

Just beyond the state park, you'll find one of Arizona's more appealing small towns:

Patagonia

Elevation: 4,050 feet   **Population: 940**

Neatly arrayed on a high prairie between the low Patagonia and Santa Rita Mountains, prim little Patagonia has made a leisurely transition from cattle town to art colony. Its business district occupies two parallel streets separated by a park strip that once was a railroad right-of-way. The former depot, painted a traditional beige with mustard trim, now houses city offices. Galleries, boutiques and a couple of cafés occupy old false front buildings nearby.

Silver and lead were discovered in this area in the 1860s and several mining camps sprung up along Sonoita Creek and in the foothills. Wealthy miner and cattleman Colonel Rollin R. Richardson started Patagonia in 1896 when he moved his holdings from Crittenden, four miles northeast. A post office was established three years later and townsfolk—over the colonel's objections—changed its name from Rollin to Patagonia, after a nearby mine.

As you approach town, fork to the right onto McKeown Avenue (parallel Naugle Avenue is Highway 182) and find a place to park. The cluster of shops and boutiques extend only a couple of blocks—easy to explore on foot. **Mariposa Books, Etc.** on McKeown Avenue opposite the railroad depot, functions as an informal visitor center, with a rack of brochures. Pick up a copy of the *Patagonia Visitors Guide* booklet, which lists assorted businesses and a few turn-of-the-century homes. To check out a bit of local color, step into **McGraw's Cantina,** claiming to be Patagonia's original cowboy bar. It certainly looks the part—a dimly lit good old boy hangout with dark polished woods, Western regalia on the walls and pool tables.

☺ To reach the nearby **Patagonia-Sonoita Creek Preserve,** operated by the Nature Conservancy, take Fourth Avenue West to Pennsylvania, turn south and drive less than a mile. This riparian woodland preserves some of Arizona's finest stands of old-growth cottonwoods and it's a favorite haunt of birders, with more than 260 species flitting about—not all at once, of course. Guided walks are conducted on Saturdays at 9 a.m. For more information, contact Patagonia-Sonoita Creek Preserve, P.O. Box 815, Patagonia, AZ 85624; (520) 394-2400.

WHERE TO DINE AND RECLINE

Ovens of Patagonia ● ☆☆ *$*

❑ *Naugle Avenue near Third; (520) 394-2483. American; no alcohol. Wednesday-Saturday 10 to 3, Sunday 8 to 3.* ❑ Cheerful little bakery-café with blue and white décor; walls accented with watercolors by local artists. Breakfast fare, pastries, salads sandwiches and soups. A specialty is the *galette,* a meat or vegetable pie.

Stage Stop Inn ● ☆☆ *$$*

❑ *P.O. Box 777 (303 W. McKeown), Patagonia, AZ 85624; (520) 394-2211. Couples $56, singles $45, kitchenettes $67. MC/VISA.* ❑ Western-style hotel in downtown Patagonia with simple, comfortably furnished rooms. **Restaurant** serves American and Mexican fare; dinners $8 to $14.

Circle Z Ranch ● *P.O. Box 194-AG (off Highway 82), Patagonia, AZ 85624; (520) 287-2091. Adults $735 to $924 and kids $528 to $686 per week, including all meals. Also daily rates with three-day minimum. No credit cards.* ☐ A 6,000-acre guest ranch in the Patagonia and Santa Rita mountains, surrounded by federal and state lands. Rooms, suites and private cottages. Half-day, all-day, picnic and breakfast rides and overnight pack trips. Heated pool, tennis courts and bird watching.

WHERE TO CAMP

Patagonia Lake State Park ● *P.O. Box 274, Patagonia, AZ 85624; (520) 287-6965. Full hookups $15; no hookups $10. No credit cards.* ☐ Sites near the lake, with barbecues, picnic tables, flush potties, showers and dump station. (Park details above.)

Patagonia RV Park ● *566 Harshaw Rd. (P.O. Box 768), Patagonia, AZ 85624; (520) 394-2491. RV sites, $15 for full hookups; parked fifth-wheel rental for $45. Reservations accepted.* ☐ Small park with TV hookups, showers and coin laundry; just east of town.

ANNUAL EVENT

A Patagonia Affair, autumn art, craft and food festival and farmers market, late October; (520) 394-0060.

Twelve miles northeast, **Sonoita** is similar in size and shape but without Patagonia's charm. If you're in a shopping mood, poke about **La Pradera,** a theme shopping center on the east end of town, built into an old barn. The next door **Steak Out** restaurant and saloon serves open pit mesquite barbecued steaks, ribs, fish and chicken, weekdays 5 to 10, weekends noon to 10; MC/VISA. The **Kazzam Nature Center** at 3248 Highway 82 offers nature-oriented gifts, books and advice on exploring the Patagonia-Sonoita Creek Nature Preserve and the rest of the countryside. It's open Tuesday-Sunday 9:30 to 5; (520) 455-5895.

☺ After another thirty miles of prairie, you'll encounter a strip of startling contrast—**San Pedro Riparian National Conservation Area.** It's a lush woodland along the San Pedro River, reaching nearly 40 miles south toward the Mexican border. Although it shrinks to little more than a faucet drip in summer, the river supports an amazing variety of plants, animals and birds. The Bureau of Land Management maintains a series of trails and wildlife viewpoints. RVers and tenters can camp at primitive sites for a small fee. A BLM office sits beside the river in the townlet of Fairbank, open weekdays 7:45 to 4:15. For more specifics, contact: San Pedro Area Conservation Area, Bureau of Land Management, Box 9853, Route 1, Huachuca City, AZ 85616; (520) 457-2265.

A few miles beyond Fairbank, Highway 82 terminates at State Route 80. Turn south and, within minutes, you're in "the town too tough to die."

Tombstone

Elevation: 2,389 feet   **Population: 1,700**

Tombstone couldn't die even if it wanted to; Hollywood would never permit it. In recent years, two more films were added to the long list of movies portraying America's most famous gunfight, at Tombstone's O.K. Corral.

The town's roots can be traced to Ed Schieffelin, a prospector who decided to check out the rocky hills southeast of present-day Tucson in 1877, although he was warned that the Chiricahua Apaches were on the warpath. "All you'll find out there is your tombstone," a friend advised.

Ed found a big silver strike instead, and called it—appropriately—the Lucky Cuss. Word spread and other argonauts poured in. A town was staked out two years later, in Goose Flat, two miles from Schieffelin's hillside mine. Soon, it was one of the largest, wildest and wickedest mining camps in the Southwest. It attracted such characters as Doc Holliday, Johnny Ringo, Bat Masterson and—of course—the Earp brothers. Wyatt was co-owner of the Oriental Saloon, where gunslinger Luke Short was a faro dealer.

By 1881, Tombstone boasted 10,000 citizens and it became the seat of Cochise County. In that same year, the Earps shot it out with the Clantons and McLaurys (spelled McLowry by some sources) near the O.K. Corral. Actually, it was more of a blood feud than a police action. The Earps had accused the Clantons and McLaurys of cattle thievery and sheltering stage robbers at their ranches. The cowboys boasted openly that they would kill the Earps for besmirching their reputations.

"They tried to pick a fuss out of me," Wyatt testified at the hearing following the corral shootout. But he admitted that earlier on the day of the shooting, he and his brother Morgan had tried to goad Ike Clanton into a fight.

After the excitement from the West's most publicized gun battle faded, Tombstone faced other problems. Most of the downtown area burned in 1882. A few years later, water began seeping into its mines. Falling silver prices and labor problems closed the last of the mines early in this century. The county seat was moved to Bisbee in 1931 and the town too tough to die was on the verge of doing it. The population dropped to 150.

Then tourists began trickling in, lured by stories of the Earp brothers and the shootout. The town's old Western look, unchanged because nobody could afford to modernize, became an asset. That asset has been turned into to tourist excess. If you've ever been to Virginia City, Nevada, you'll feel a bit of *deja voux* in Tombstone. Visitors clunk along boardwalks shaded by overhangs from false front stores. They buy snow cones and John Wayne posters and visit museums that are mostly fronts for souvenir shops. They browse through boutiques called Big-Nose Kate's Gifts and Collectibles and Madame Mustache, Purveyor of Pleasure (and homemade fudge.) A sign above the O.K. Corral entrance invites tourists to "Walk where they fell." Other signs around town mark the spot where other unlucky cusses bit the dust. A stagecoach driver steers his horses about town, holding a microphone to describe historic features along the way.

Doing Tombstone

Approaching from the north on State Route 80, pause first at **Boothill Cemetery,** on your left about half a mile from Tombstone. Then continue into town, turn right at the blue "Allen Street" sign and look for a place to park. Everything except the Schieffelin Monument is within an easy boardwalk stroll. To reach the monument, head west on Allen Street; you'll find it out in the country, at the end of a dirt road.

RV ADVISORY • Curbside parking is plentiful, although spaces become scarce on weekends. The road to the Schieffelin Monument is rather rutted and bumpy but short; patience will get you there. Parking at the monument is limited, although it generally isn't that busy. Drivers of long rigs can park on the approach road and walk to the monument.

"DON'T SHOOT ANYMORE! YOU HAVE KILLED ME!"

It was like a scene from a low-budget Western movie, complete with stilted dialogue. But it was frighteningly real. Tombstone Police Chief Virgil Earp, his deputized brothers Wyatt and Morgan, and gunslinger Doc Holliday advanced upon five cowboys, who were standing in a narrow alley.

Word around town was that brothers Frank and Tom McLaury and Ike and Billy Clanton had threatened to kill the Earps. They'd been feuding for weeks, after the Earps accused them of cattle rustling and stealing six army mules. With the four was Billy "The Kid" Claiborne, a town tough who recently had killed a man over a drink.

Sheriff Johnny Behan failed to disarm the glowering cowboys, then he tried to stop the Earps and Holliday. "For God's sake don't go down there or you'll get murdered," he pleaded.

The four brushed past him and kept walking. They stopped within ten feet of the cowboys, who were between Camillus S. Fly's photo studio and the O.K. Corral. Frank McLaury stood beside his horse; his Winchester rifle was in a saddle scabbard.

"You sons of bitches, you've been looking for a fight, and now you have it!" Wyatt growled.

"Throw up your hands!" Virgil ordered.

Claiborne, not so tough when facing the Earps, ran for cover.

"Don't shoot me! I don't want to fight!" Billy Clanton pleaded, raising his hands.

In a split second, two shots were fired, followed by a wild volley. Frank McLaury fell first. Billy Clanton was hit in the chest; he lurched into a wall and slid to the ground. Tom McLaury clawed at the rifle scabbard on his brother's horse but the animal bolted. He started running and Morgan fired at him; McLaury pitched forward.

"I got him!" Morgan shouted. Then he spun and fell as a bullet smashed through both shoulders.

Ike Clanton grabbed Wyatt's left arm; the deputy gave him a rude shove. "Go to fighting or get away!" Earp yelled.

Clanton fled into Fly's studio. Virgil sagged to one knee as a bullet pierced his right calf. Billy Clanton struggled to sit up and fire, but he was too weak; the life was draining out of him. He slumped back against the wall.

"Don't shoot me anymore!" he begged. "You have killed me!"

Then, silence. The McLaurys and Billy Clanton lay dying. Doc Holliday winced from a bullet that had smashed into his holster and grazed his hip. Wyatt was unscathed. He and Doc and had stood and fired "as cool as cucumbers," an onlooker said. Virgil and Morgan would survive their wounds. A hearing was held to determine if the Earps and Holliday should be tried for murder. They were cleared, even though some witnesses—including the sheriff—said they had fired first.

Hundreds of gun battles echoed through the Old West, but none caught the public's fancy like the gunfight at the O.K. Corral. It has been played out thousands of times since, in movies and books, on TV and at the corral itself by actors before camera- clicking tourists. It seems ironic that, in the "town too tough to die," it was thirty seconds of death that put it on the map.

Most of the shops and quasi-museums are housed in century-old buildings along three blocks of Allen Street, a block south of—and parallel to—Highway 80 (Fremont Street). Some vacant lots have been cleared away to provide visitor parking. The **Tombstone Visitor Center** is at Allen and Fourth streets; (520) 457-9317 or (520) 457-3929. You can pick up a walking map that will guide you past such structures as the century-old St. Paul's Episcopal Church, Tombstone City Hall with its elaborate façade, the site of the Oriental Saloon and the 1888 Wells Fargo office. A more detailed *Tombstone Map and Guide* is available at museums and curio shops for 50 cents.

A mule-drawn surrey, stagecoach rides and Sunday afternoon gunplay—either in the O.K. Corral or on Allen Street—recall the days when newly-rich silver barons and steely-eyed gunfighters swaggered about. Downtown has been declared a national historic landmark and the courthouse is now an Arizona state historic park.

ATTRACTIONS

☺ *Boothill Cemetery and Gift Shop* • *Highway 80; (520) 457-3348. Daily 7:30 to 6; free.* ◻ You don't often find cemeteries that accept Visa and MasterCard. Of course, that's only in the gift shop, through which you pass to view the graves of Tombstone's fallen. As the sound of cash registers rings in your ears, you read the sign over the graveyard entrance:

This is a cemetery. Please treat it and the graves with respect. Thank you.

Frank and Tom McLaury and Billy Clanton lie side by side, near the parking lot fence. The marker says they were "murdered in the streets of Tombstone." More than 250 other citizens are buried here and grave markers remind you that life was often short and death was quick in the Wild West—Tom Waters. Shot, 1880; Dick Toby. Shot by Sheriff Behan; Two Cowboys. Drowned; Charley Storms. Shot by Luke Short, 1880; Teamster, 1881. Killed by Apaches; Della William, 1881. Suicide; Thos. Harper. Hanged, 1881; Geo. Johnson. Hanged by mistake.

Some mistake!

The original wooden markers, either weathered away or taken by souvenir hunters, have been replaced by steel nameplates mounted on pipes. This supposedly was the first cemetery to be called "boothill."

☺ *Tombstone Courthouse State Historic Park* • *219 E. Toughnut St. (Third Street), Tombstone, AZ 85638; (520) 457-3311. Daily 8 to 5; adults $2, kids $1.* ◻ This imposing brick structure with Greek pediments and a cupola served as the Cochise County Courthouse from 1882 until neighboring Bisbee snatched away the county seat in 1931. It's now a museum of Cochise County yesterdays with a restored sheriff's office, courtroom and various exhibits. A gift shop run by the Tombstone Restoration Commission has a good selection of books on local and Arizona history. Assorted versions of the O.K. Corral shootout hang on the courthouse walls. An exhibit case contains Wyatt Earp memorabilia, including his razor. Among other displays are photos of town founder Schieffelin, an assay office, mining paraphernalia, a mock-up saloon and cowboy gear. A reconstructed gallows is out back.

☺ *The O.K. Corral and Camillus Fly Photo Studio* • *Allen Street (between Third and Fourth); (520) 457-3456. Daily 8:30 to 5; shootout re-enactments first and third Sundays at 2 p.m. Admission $2.* ◻ The O.K. Corral has been corralled into a tourist attraction. Among its exhibits are Camillus S. Fly's photo studio, and 19th century rigs including a hearse that once toted

The bad guys bite the dust in this realistic re-enactment of the gunfight at the O.K. Corral.

unfortunate cowboys to Boothill. A movie poster reminds us that one version of *The Gunfight at the O.K. Corral* hit the big screen with Burt Lancaster as Wyatt and Kirk Douglas as Doc. It was filmed not at the original site but in the make-believe Western town of Old Tucson.

Near the scene of the shootout, beside Fly's studio, mannequins mark the position of the combatants when their guns started blazing. However, they're farther apart than newspaper accounts reported. The fight took place in a 15-foot-wide alley between two buildings, and the first shots were fired at nearly point-blank range. Fly's studio contains some fine example of his frontier photography, including photos taken at the surrender of Geronimo to the U.S. Army in 1886.

A group of volunteer actors called the Wild Bunch (a name borrowed from Utah's Butch Cassidy gang) re-enacts the shootout on the first and third Sundays of each month at 2 p.m. It takes place in another part of the corral, before a small grandstand. Obviously well researched, the shootout is startlingly realistic. You come away almost sensing that you just witnessed that violent 30 seconds of history when 34 shots were fired and three men died.

Bird Cage Theater ● *Sixth and Allen streets; (520) 457-3421. Daily 8 to 7 (shorter hours in the off-season); adults $3.50, seniors $3; kids $1.75.* ☐ This should be one of Tombstone's better attractions, for it's the town's only original, fully intact gambling hall-theater-saloon. However, the museum is cluttered with many items unrelated to the theater's lively history. You can see dusty four-by-six foot bird cage "cribs" suspended from upper walls, where fallen angels entertained their gents. During live stage performances, curtains were opened and the cribs functioned as box seats. The most interesting thing about the Bird Cage is the lively—if sometimes exaggerated—historical spiel that's delivered in the lobby before you enter the museum. You learn that Tombstone had 106 bars and 3,700 working girls who fattened the city's coffers with a $10 monthly tax. The lobby itself is nicely restored with an elaborately carved bar and back-bar with French mirrors. If you carefully examine a nine-foot portrait of a chubby, topless Lady Fatima, you'll see six patched bullet holes.

☺ **Crystal Palace Saloon** ● *Allen Street at Fifth; (520) 457-3611.* ☐ We like the Crystal Palace because it's not an "attraction" but a functioning saloon. It has been faithfully restored to its 1880's glitter, with American eagle wallpaper, hurricane lamp chandeliers and a handsome oversized back bar. You can get a schooner of Coors, listen to live Western music and watch wanna-be gunslingers and their ladies do the cowboy two-step.

Museum of the West • *109 S. Third (near Allen); (520) 457-9219. Daily 9:30 to 5. Adults $2, kids and seniors $1.* ⊡ This museum, with a gift shop adjacent, displays documents relating to the Earps and Clantons, firearms and a bullet dug up from the O.K. Corral fight, plus cowboy regalia and Native American pottery.

Tombstone Historama • *Allen Street near Third, adjacent to the O.K. Corral; (520) 457-3456. Admission $2; shows on the hour, 9 to 4.* ⊡ While not as awesome as its promotion suggests, Historama is a nicely-done 26-minute audio-visual presentation. Vincent Price narrates while five dioramas revolve. The animation is pretty simplistic, although you learn a lot about Tombstone. A screen drops occasionally to show films and slides.

World's Largest Rosebush Museum • *Fourth and Toughnut streets; (520) 457-3326. Daily 9 to 5; $2.* ⊡ What's a rose bush got to do with Arizona history? Nothing, but it's an impressive thing, crawling over 8,000 square feet of a lattice roofed patio. A white-blossoming *Lady Banksia,* it was planted as a cutting sent from Scotland in 1885. The adjoining Victorian style Rose Tree Inn houses a gift shop and one of Tombstone's nicer museums, with plush wallpaper and Victorian and early American antiques. It features an interesting lock exhibit, a cut-away of the Schieffelin's Lucky Cuss Mine and—of course—a diorama of The Shootout.

Schieffelin Hall • *Fourth and Fremont streets.* ⊡ Built by a Schieffelin relative, this imposing two-story structure is one of the largest adobe buildings in the West. It was the town's social and theatrical center where John Sullivan and traveling Shakespearean troupes performed. Although still intact, it was closed to the public at this writing.

Tombstone Epitaph • *Nine S. Fifth St. (P.O. Box 1880), Tombstone, AZ 85638 (520) 457-2211. Admission $1.* ⊡ The *Epitaph* was founded by Tombstone pioneer John P. Clum in 1880. A history-oriented version is still being published. You can order a year's subscription for $15, or buy souvenir editions containing accounts of the O.K. Corral shootout. The shop also sells books and pamphlets on local history. Displays include old type cases and the original hand-operated printing press on which Clum published his first edition. He commented in that issue that "no Tombstone is complete without an *Epitaph.*"

Schieffelin Monument • *Two miles west at the end of Allen Street.* ⊡ A 30-foot conical stone monument marks the final resting place of the father of Tombstone. Although he scored a major silver strike and founded one of the west's most famous mining towns, Schieffelin eventually lost his fortune. He left town after a few years and died in a simple cabin near Canyonville, Oregon, in 1897 at the age of 49.

ACTIVITIES

Western shootouts • The Wild Bunch reenacts the O.K. Corral shootout on the first and third Sundays of each month at 2 p.m. at the corral on Allen Street; admission $2; (520) 457-3456. Boothill Gunslingers blaze away Monday through Saturday at 2 p.m. at an outdoor theater at Fourth and Toughnut; adults $2.50, kids $1.50. Other shootouts occur periodically on Allen Street, particularly on summer weekends.

ANNUAL EVENTS

For details, contact the visitor center at (520) 457-9317 or 457-3929.
Territorial Days, first weekend in March.
Wyatt Earp Days, Memorial Day weekend.
Vigilante Days, third weekend of August.
Rendezvous of Gunfighters, Labor Day weekend.
Helldorado Days, Old West celebration the third weekend of October.

WHERE TO DINE

Nellie Cashman's Boarding House Restaurant ● ☆☆ $$

☐ *Fifth Street near Toughnut; (520) 457-3950. American-Mexican; wine and beer. Daily 7 a.m. to 9 p.m. MC/VISA, AMEX.* ☐ Housed in an 1879 Spanish style building with Western style wainscoting, lamps, historic posters and photos. Mexican and American lunch and dinner fare.

Bella Union Restaurant ● ☆☆ $$

☐ *401 E. Fremont (Highway 80, at Fourth Street); (520) 457-3656. American-Mexican; full bar service. Daily 6 a.m. to 9 p.m. Major credit cards.* ☐ Steaks, chops and seafood; prime rib a specialty. Housed in the old Tombstone post office; antique guns and other memorabilia on the walls.

Longhorn Restaurant ● ☆ $$

☐ *Allen at Fifth Street; (520) 457-3969. American and Mexican; wine and beer. Monday-Saturday 7 a.m. to 9 p.m., Sunday 8 to 9. MC/VISA.* ☐ Varied offerings from pasta to burritos, served amidst semi-cowboy décor in one of Tombstone's century-old buildings; nicely adorned Western saloon adjacent.

WHERE TO RECLINE

Prices reflect high season rates and may be lower at other times. Most were provided by the management and are subject to change; use them only as a guide.

Adobe Lodge Motel ● ☆ $$ Ø

☐ *505 E. Fremont St. (Fifth Street), Tombstone, AZ 85638; (520) 457-2241. Couples $55 to $65, singles $35 to $45. MC/VISA, AMEX* ☐ A 20-unit motel with TV and phones; downtown, near Tombstone attractions.

Best Western Lookout Lodge ● ☆☆☆ $$$ Ø

☐ *P.O. Box 787 (a mile northwest on Highway 80), Tombstone, AZ 85638; (800) 528-1234 or (520) 457-2223. Couples $60 to $70, singles $50 to $60; rates include continental breakfast. Major credit cards.* ☐ Well-kept 40-room inn with mountain views; TV, phones; heated pool, free coffee.

The Larian Motel ● ☆ $$ Ø

☐ *410 Fremont St. (Fourth Street) Tombstone, AZ 85638; (520) 457-2272. Couples and singles from $34. MC/VISA.* ☐ Small motel with TV and room phones; near Tombstone attractions.

Tombstone Motel ● ☆ $$ Ø

☐ *P.O. Box 837 (502 E. Fremont St.), Tombstone, AZ 85638-0837; (520) 457-3478. Couples $45 to $55, singles $50 to $50. Major credit cards.* ☐ An eleven-unit motel with TV and phones, some refrigerators; barbecue area.

Trail Riders' Motel ● ☆ $$ Ø

☐ *13 N. Seventh St. (Fremont), Tombstone, AZ 95638; (800) 574-0417 or (520) 457-3573. Couples $35 to $42, singles $29 to $35. Major credit cards.* ☐ A 13-unit motel with TV and phones, some refrigerators; gift shop and barbecue area; near downtown attractions.

Bed & breakfast inn

Tombstone Boarding House ● ☆☆ $$$ Ø

⊡ 108 N. Fourth St. (P.O. Box 906), Tombstone, AZ 85638; (520) 457-3716. Couples $60 to $80, singles $50 to $70. Eight units with private baths; full breakfast. ⊡ Two 1880s adobe homes have been converted into a comfortable bed & breakfast inn, furnished in country antiques and collectibles. Within a short walk of Tombstone attractions.

WHERE TO CAMP

Tombstone Hills KOA ● P.O. Box 99 (Highway 80, two miles northwest), Tombstone, AZ 85638; (520) 457-3829. RV and tent sites, full hookups $21.50, no hookups $18, "Kamping Kabins" $28. Reservations accepted; MC/VISA, DISC. ⊡ Large shaded sites with some pull-throughs. Playground, swimming pool, horseshoes and shuffleboard, coin laundry, groceries and souvenir shop, Propane, dump station; free shuttle to town.

Wells Fargo RV Park ● Fremont (Highway 80) and Third streets, P.O. Box 1076, Tombstone, AZ 85638; (520) 457-3966. RV and tent sites, full hookups $19.50, water and electric $18.50; cable TV $1.75. ⊡ Showers and coin laundry; downtown, close to Tombstone attractions.

Tombstone wasn't the only mining camp that flourished in and about the Dragoon Mountains, although it was the only one that survived. Several ghost towns dot the hills and hide in the ravines. You can visit Watervale, on a dirt road leading to the right from the west end of Allen Street; Charleston and Millville, nine miles southwest, toward Sierra Vista on Charleston Road; and Gleeson, 15 miles east on a dirt extension of Fremont Street.

Having had your moment with history, head southwest of Tombstone to a town that started only yesterday. To get there, turn south on Sumner Street and head out into the dusty prairie. It becomes Charleston Road which, after 16 miles, delivers you to Cochise County's newest and largest community.

Sierra Vista-Fort Huachuca

Elevation: 4,623 feet   **Sierra Vista population: 34,000**

Originally a bedroom town for Fort Huachuca, Sierra Vista was incorporated in 1956 as a retirement retreat. It has since become the largest city in Cochise County; more than one out of three residents live here. It's no wonder. Surrounding mountains provide an impressive backdrop and climate experts say its one of the most temperate regions in the nation. With an average maximum high of 75 and low of 50, this is a room temperature community. Rivaling neighbor Tucson in total land area, it looks more like a suburb than a town—an extensive spread of shopping centers, subdivisions and stoplights.

As you approach Sierra Vista from Tombstone, you'll hit a traffic light at State Route 90, opposite a Walmart center. Go left to the next signal and then right on Frye Boulevard (at the junction of highways 90 and 92). After half a mile (two traffic lights), turn left onto Calle Portal for the **Sierra Vista Chamber of Commerce,** in suite A-140 of the Southern Arizona Financial Center. It's open weekdays 8 to 5 and Saturday 9 to 1; (520) 458-6940. Although popular as a retirement community and handy as a provisioning center, Sierra Vista has no specific tourist lures. The area's main attraction is next-door Fort Huachuca, a still active 1877 army post with an excellent museum. To reach it, drive west about two miles on Fry Boulevard; it leads right into the fort. You must first stop at the Visitor Center to get a car pass and directions to the museum. Set against the dry, brushy Huachuca Mountains, the fort played a pivotal role in the settlement of the southwest. A drive around the extensive grounds and past austere wooden buildings lining the old parade field takes you back to the days of the Pony Soldiers. It's the only early Southwestern military post still active.

☺ **Fort Huachuca Museum** • *c/o U.S. Army Garrison, Fort Huachuca, AZ 85613-6000; (520) 533-5736. Weekdays 9 to 4, weekends 1 to 4; free.* ☐ This is one of Arizona's great surprises: an outstanding museum sitting among the barracks buildings of an old Army fort. It has a dual focus: the history of the Southwest and the history of the fort, which are frequently linked. The museum comes in two parts. The main building is an 1892 structure that housed the post chapel and later the officers' club. It has exhibits concerning the fort's role in various conflicts, from the Apache uprisings to Pancho Villa's border skirmishes to World War II. Among the displays are a fine collection of period uniforms, a special exhibit on the black "Buffalo Soldiers" who fought with the Army of the West and typically furnished rooms of military families, representing various historical periods.

The annex is our favorite part. The focal point is a large open exhibit portraying a patrol at evening's rest, somewhere on the desert. Tents are pitched, a campfire crackles and a soldier strums a guitar. Watching the dimly-lit scene, you can almost hear a coyote howling on a distant ridge. And that movement in the brush; is an Apache sneaking up on the camp?

This life-sized scene is surrounded by western storefront façades with tableaux set in window casings. They tell the story of the Army of the West as it wrestled Arizona, New Mexico and California from the Mexicans, then tried to keep the settlers and Indians out of one another's scalps.

WHERE TO DINE

Apache Pointe Ranch Steakhouse • ☆☆ $$

☐ *2528 Apache Point Rd., Hereford; (520) 378-6616. American; full bar service. Tuesday-Sunday 5 to 9. MC/VISA.* ☐ Ranch house style dining room just off the road to Ramsey Canyon (see below). It serves mesquite broiled bison steaks and other Western grub.

Golden China Restaurant • ☆☆ $$

☐ *325 W. Fry Blvd. (near Fort Huachuca main gate), Sierra Vista; (520) 458-8588. Chinese; full bar service. Lunch buffet Monday-Friday 11 to 2, dinner Monday-Friday 4 to 9:30; weekends noon to 9:30. Major credit cards.* ☐ Attractive café with an extensive Szechuan, Mandarin, Cantonese and Hunan menu. All-you-can-eat weekday luncheon buffet.

The Mesquite Tree • ☆☆ $$

☐ *South Highway 92 at Carr Canyon Rd., Sierra Vista; (520) 378-2758. American; full bar service. Tuesday-Saturday 11 to 2:30 and 5 to 9, Sunday 5 to 8. MC/VISA, DISC.* ☐ An appealing restaurant with southwestern décor, specializing in Southwest cuisine, plus steaks, barbecued ribs and seafood.

WHERE TO RECLINE

Bella Vista Motel • ☆ $$

☐ *1101 E. Fry Blvd., Sierra Vista, AZ 85635; (520) 458-6737. Couples $35, singles $27, kitchenettes $35 to $40. Major credit cards.* ☐ Small motel with TV, room phones; pool. The **Coffee Cup** restaurant serves 5 a.m. to 2 p.m.; American and Mexican; meals $5 to $6; no alcohol.

Ramada Inn ● ☆☆ $$$ Ø

◻ 2047 S. Highway 92, Sierra Vista, AZ 85635; (800) 825-4656 or (520) 459-5900. Couples and singles $58 to $86. Major credit cards. ◻ A well-kept 149-room inn with TV movies and phones; some refrigerators and microwaves. Pool, spa, coin laundry. **Dining room** serves 6 to 2 and 4:30 to 9; dinners $7 to $16; full bar service.

Sierra Suites ● ☆☆☆ $$$ Ø

◻ 391 E. Fry Blvd., Sierra Vista, AZ 95635; (520) 459-4221. Couples $50 to $70, singles $44 to $70; rates include continental breakfast. Major credit cards. ◻ Attractive 100-unit inn with TV, phones, microwaves and refrigerators in all rooms. Courtyard style with pool, spa and cocktail lounge; coin laundry.

Super 8 Motel ● ☆☆ $$ Ø

◻ 100 Fab Ave. (two blocks from Fort Huachuca entrance), Sierra Vista, AZ 85635; (800) 843-1991 or (520) 459-5380. Couples $48 to $50, singles $44. Major credit cards. ◻ A 52-unit motel with TV movies, phones and refrigerators; pool.

Thunder Mountain Inn ● ☆☆☆ $$$ Ø

◻ 1631 S. Highway 92 (a mile south of Highway 90 junction), Sierra Vista, AZ 85635; (520) 458-7900. Couples $50 to $70, singles $45. Major credit cards. ◻ A 105-unit resort with spacious rooms, some with Huachuca Mountain views; TV movies, phones and refrigerators. Pool and spa; golf and birding packages. **Coffee Shop** and **Baxters Restaurant** serve breakfast, lunch and dinner; entrées $5 to $11; full bar service.

Bed & breakfast inn

☺ Ramsey Canyon Inn ● ☆☆ $$$$ Ø

◻ 31 Ramsey Canyon Rd., Hereford, AZ 85615; (520) 378-3010. Inn rooms $90 to $95, one-bedroom housekeeping cottages $90 to $105; all with private baths. Full breakfasts for inn guests. No credit cards. ◻ A romantically rustic country inn located at creekside, adjacent to Ramsey Canyon Preserve (see below). Rooms furnished with antiques; homemade pies served in the afternoons. Kitchen facilities in housekeeping cabins.

WHERE TO CAMP

Ramsey Canyon Campground ● Ramsey Canyon Road (below entrance to Ramsey Canyon preserve); (520) 378-0549. RVs only; $14 to $17.50. Reservations accepted. ◻ Small campground with wooded sites; some full hookups, TV hookups; dump station.

TO CORONADO, BISBEE & DOUGLAS

From Fort Huachuca, take Fry Boulevard back to the highway 90-92 junction and turn right, following Route 92 south toward Bisbee. About six miles from Sierra Vista, turn right onto Ramsey Canyon Road and follow it four miles into a wooded ravine for a Nature Conservancy refuge. It is a refuge indeed, for this area is busy with country homes tucked among the trees.

Ramsey Canyon Preserve ● Ramsey Canyon Road; (520) 378-2785; trails open 8 to 5. ◻ This Nature Conservancy Preserve shelters 280 acres of a protected, wooded gorge in the Huachuca Mountains. Its a favorite haunt of hummingbirds; more than a dozen species have been counted here. The Mile Hi/Ramsey Canyon Bird Observation Station and a nature trail are free to the public. Folks who want to spend more time in this peaceful, pristine setting can rent rustic cabins at Mile Hi by the day or week. For lodging, contact Mile Hi Preserve: Route 1, Box 84, Hereford, AZ 85615; (520) 378-2785. Ramsey Canyon Inn Bed & Breakfast (listed above) also is near the preserve.

RV AND PARKING ADVISORY ● Vehicle space is limited, so you should call the above number for parking reservations on weekends and holidays; it can't accommodate trailers, or RVs over 21 feet.

If you'd like to explore more of these surrounding mountains, watch on your right for the **Sierra Vista Ranger Station** of Coronado National Forest, 5990 S. Highway 92; open weekdays 8 to 5; (520) 378-0311. It's about a mile south of the Ramsey Canyon turnoff. Pressing southward on Highway 92, look for a sign to the right, pointing you to a federal reserve honoring Francisco de Coronado's trek, although he didn't pass this way:

☺ ***Coronado National Memorial*** ● *4101 E. Montezuma Canyon Rd., Hereford, AZ 85615; (520) 366-5515. Visitor center open daily 8 to 5; free.* ▫ You've probably seen one of those gag signs that reads: "On April 22, 1934, nothing happened here." This could be said of Coronado National Memorial, a 4,750-acre preserve in the wooded flanks of the Huachuca Mountains. The memorial was established to mark Coronado's entry into present-day Arizona in 1540 to search for the Seven Cities of Cibola. However, he passed about ten miles to the east, wisely choosing the San Pedro River Valley instead of the rugged Huachuca Mountains. National parks officials had hoped to establish an international memorial at the Mexican border. But Coronado isn't exactly loved by our neighbors, so Mexico demurred. But American officials still wanted to honor him and—what the hey—this land in Montezuma Canyon happened to be available.

It's certainly a pretty site, tucked into a hillside oak and pine woodland. If you're willing to follow an awfully narrow and bumpy road a few miles beyond the small visitor center, you'll be rewarded by an awesome view of the surrounding desert and mountains. A short hike takes you even higher, to the top of Coronado Peak. Along the way, signposts with quotes from journals of the Coronado party give you an excuse to stop and catch your breath. The visitor center exhibits armor and weapons of Spanish soldiers of the era. Nicely done paintings and graphics detail Coronado's trek, which extended as far north as Kansas. We learn that he was only 30 years old at the time of his commission as "Captain General of the Provinces of Cibola." He left with a grand entourage of 339 soldiers, wives, servants and 1,500 head of horses, cows, goats and sheep. He staggered back two years later, footsore and dejected, having found nothing but a lot of open space and a few mud pueblos. The national memorial has no campground or services, although it has picnic areas and trails through the wooded slopes of Montezuma Canyon.

Moving with much more ease than Coronado's troupe, follow Highway 92 east and then Route 80 briefly north to one of early Arizona's great copper camps. You'll hit a Bisbee sign while still on Route 92, although that's a false alarm. The city limits have been extended well beyond its developed areas. Just outside of town, you'll see a sign indicating **Naco** to the south, should you wish to visit Old Mexico. Scruffily cute, it's one of the more ap-

The Lavender Pit near Bisbee once was one of the world's largest surface mines.

pealing small Arizona-Mexico border towns; see Chapter ten, page 309.

Farther along Highway 92, you begin to see what put Bisbee on the map—beige, yellow and magenta tailing dumps of copper mining operations. At the merger of routes 92 and 80, a traffic circle—which can be confusing if you're not alert—takes you a mile northwest into the historic district.

Bisbee

Elevation: 5,490 feet   **Population: 7,300**

Bisbee is a delightful Arizona surprise—a sturdy old mining town cantilevered into the steep flanks of Mule Pass Gulch. Like Jerome, this is the sort of place where your upper neighbor can look down your chimney. The post office department complains that it's too steep for mail delivery. Headframes and tailing dumps mark the slopes; corrugated buildings shelter smelters and stamp mills. Hillsides have been ripped away to expose orange, rust and gray-green wounds. You *know* this is mining country. Coming into Bisbee, you encounter something even more dramatic—the great terraced cavity of the Lavender Pit Mine. It's so close it appears ready to swallow the town.

Bisbee didn't burst into glory overnight, in the style of Tombstone. It grew steadily and sturdily as big corporations gouged deep into the earth for copper, gold, silver, lead and zinc. Army Scout Jack Dunn filed a claim in the area in 1877, then he brought in one George Warren as a partner. Warren cheated Dunn out of his share, found some investors, then eventually sold to a conglomerate headed by Judge DeWitt Bisbee of San Francisco. They formed the Copper Queen Mine Company and eventually merged with the large Phelps Dodge Corporation. In, around and under Bisbee, more than $2 billion worth of ore was pulled from miles of shafts and deep open pit mines. Reveling in this wealth, the town grew as a sort of vertical San Francisco, with plush Victorian homes, fine restaurants and—of course—bordellos. Brewery Gulch was Bisbee's version of San Francisco's Barbary Coast, with more than 50 drinking, gambling and whoring establishments. At its peak, Bisbee was the world's largest copper mining town, with 20,000 residents. Phelps Dodge operated the underground Queen Mine and the Lavender open pit mine until 1975 when diminishing returns and falling copper prices closed those operations.

Logic says Bisbee should have withered and died, but retirees and tourists began coming, drawn by the mild climate and sturdy charm of the old town. Boutiques, galleries and antique shops were opened in the red brick and tufa buildings. Bed and breakfast inns proliferated. The great Queen Mine, unable to process copper economically, is processing visitors by offering underground tours. The town even attracts a few movie companies, since the hillside buildings can become—with a little creative camera work—a bit of Old Spain, Greece or Mexico.

Your Bisbee exploration begins before you reach the historic district, with a pause at the huge **Lavender Pit,** one of the world's largest surface mines. After pausing at the pit, continue into town, forking to the right at the historic district sign.

RV PARKING ADVISORY • A downtown parking lot at Naco Road and Brewery Avenue has a section for RVs. It's a short walk from here to all of Bisbee's downtown attractions.

After parking whatever you're driving, walk two blocks west to the **Bisbee Chamber of Commerce** at 7 Main Street. It's open weekdays 9 to 5 and weekends 10 to 4; (520) 432-5421. Pick up a walking map (perhaps we should say hiking map) and begin exploring. When you've finished checking out downtown, you can either walk east of the parking lot and through an underpass or drive to the Queen Mine Tour.

ATTRACTIONS

☺ *Lavender Pit* • *Adjacent to Highway 80, immediately south of town.* ⌂ Tours aren't necessary to visit this gigantic rusty brown, yellow and pale green hole in the ground. You can simply park and walk to the fenced-off edge. A sign advises you that the great terraced pit is more than a mile long, three-fourths of a mile wide and 950 feet deep. More than 380 million *tons* of material came out of this hole, yielding 41 million tons of rich copper ore.

☺ *Queen Mine Tour* • *118 Arizona St., Bisbee, AZ 85603; (520) 432-2071. Mine tours daily at 9, 10:30, 2 and 3:30. Adults $8, kids $3.50, toddlers $2. Van tour of Lavender Pit, other area surface mines and historic district 10:30, noon, 2 and 4:30; $7.* ⌂ Tours, usually led by former miners, lead deep into the side of a mountain where participants learn about old and new mining techniques and the history of this particular operation. Tours last about and hour and a half. It's cool down there, so sweaters or jackets are recommended. See box for details on the tour.

☺ *Bisbee Mining & Historical Museum* • *Five Copper Queen Plaza, P.O. Box 14, Bisbee, AZ 85603; (520) 432-7071. Daily 10 to 4. Adults $3, seniors $2.50, kids free.* ⌂ This imposing brick building, once the Phelps Dodge headquarters, is probably the first thing to catch your eye as you enter old Bisbee. Inside, exhibits weave the story of the people and mines that transformed a frontier mining town into a sophisticated mini-city. An exhibit, "Urban Outpost on the Frontier," won a national award for its interpretation of

JOURNEY INTO THE SIDE OF THE EARTH

This was just plain fun! We were rigged up in slickers, hard-hats, lights and battery packs. Then we trundled deep into the heart of the Queen Mine, sitting astraddle a rattling, clunky shuttle called a miner's mule. Actually, we traveled horizontally into the face of the mountain, going slightly uphill.

Real mules were used deep in the mines before the days of electric ore carts. Some never saw daylight, living within the earth for as long as 17 years. Our guide, a former miner, told us that miners befriended rats by sharing their lunches because the varmints could sense the vibration of a coming cave-in. They'd be the first to give the alarm, and head for cover. And we learned that more than 2,500 miles of tunnels and shafts riddle the mountains around Bisbee.

Our lamps darted about like fat fireflies as we studied the walls, still marbled with veins of copper, lead, zinc and manganese. The guide explained drilling and blasting techniques—a process of setting rows of dynamite to loosen the stubborn rock.

"Our drills had no reverse and they could really get stuck in seven feet of rock," he said. "I used to wish the damned thing was alive so I could kill it."

local history. Various displays include photos of early mining days, equipment and a make-believe shaft with cutaways of mining methods as they evolved through the years. The founder's room, richly paneled in oak, with a coffered ceiling and period office furniture, is quite handsome. You can imagine cigar-chewing copper magnates talking million dollar deals.

Bisbee Restoration Association Museum ● *37 Main Street (Subway Street). Daily 10 to 3; free.* ◻ Located in the old Fair mercantile building, this museum looks more like an overstocked antique shop. Curators apparently tried to exhibit everything that was donated—and a lot of town attics obviously were cleared out. If you like clutter, you'll love this collection of old magazines, historic photos, spinning wheels, typewriters, period costumes, china, lace and the list goes on.

Brewery Gulch ● *Downtown, off Howell Avenue.* ◻ A stroll up a side canyon on elevated sidewalks takes you past century-old brick and stone buildings that once housed saloons and bawdy houses. They now contain restaurants, antique shops, boutiques and galleries.

Copper Queen Hotel ● *Howell Avenue near Brewery Gulch.* ◻ This opulent mix of Mediterranean and Spanish colonial architecture was one of the grandest hotels in the Southwest when it was built at the turn of the century. "Black Jack" Pershing and Teddy Roosevelt tested its beds and many wealthy miners came here to sleep off a night in Brewery Gulch around the corner. Even if you aren't staying here, stroll through the high ceiling lobby and visit the old fashioned saloon with its requisite nude portrait and elaborate bar. If the weather's warm, relax with a drink at an umbrella table on a patio elevated over Howell Avenue.

Muheim Heritage House ● *207 Youngblood Hill (a mile north of downtown); 432-7071 or 432-4461. Thursday-Monday 10 to 5. Tours by appointment, $2.* ◻ This elegant 1902 home above Bisbee is on the National

Register of Historic Places. Tours through its furnished rooms are conducted by the Bisbee Arts and Humanities Council.

WHERE TO DINE

☺ *Brewery Steakhouse* ● ☆☆☆ $$

☐ *Brewery Gulch (at Howell Avenue); (520) 432-3317. American; full bar service. Lunch daily 11 to 3, dinner nightly 5 to 9. No credit cards.* ☐ This attractive brick and dark wood steak house occupies the basement of the 1905 Muheim Block brewery building. The menu features steaks, baby back ribs, chicken and some Southwest dishes, such as Guaymas shrimp with onions, bell peppers, black olives and feta. The appealing Western style Stock Exchange bar sits above.

Café Cornucopia ● ☆☆☆ $

☐ *American; no alcohol. Tuesday-Saturday 6:30 a.m. to 4:30 p.m. No credit cards.* ☐ Cute café with an old fashioned ice cream parlor look—marble topped tables, wrought iron chairs and high ceilings. It serves light breakfast and lunch fare, plus fresh vegetable and fruit drinks.

☺ *Copper Queen Restaurant* ● ☆☆☆ $$

☐ *In the Copper Queen Hotel, 11 Howell Avenue; (520) 432-2216. American-continental; full bar service. Monday-Thursday 7 a.m. to 9 p.m, Friday-Saturday 7 to 10. MC/VISA, AMEX.* ☐ Mixed menu with American and continental fare, tilted toward Italian; veal, prime rib and lamb specialties; large wine list. Victorian décor with Tiffany style lamps.

El Zarape Café ● ☆☆ $

☐ *46 Main St.; (520) 432-5031. Mexican-American, no alcohol. Tuesday-Friday 8 to 6:45, Saturday 8 to 2:45. MC/VISA.* ☐ Cozy café with dark wood paneling and cheerful bits of Mexican trim. Assorted *Latino* entrées, plus chicken fried steak, fried chicken and seafood from the gringo side.

WHERE TO RECLINE

☺ *Copper Queen Hotel* ● ☆☆☆ $$$

☐ *11 Howell Avenue (P.O. Drawer CQ), Bisbee, AZ 85603; (520) 432-2216 or (800) 247-5829 (Arizona only). Couples and singles $65 to $115. MC/VISA.* ☐ Restoration is bringing this old hotel back to its former glory. Many of the rooms—all with private baths—have period furnishings. Attractive turn- of-the-century dining room (listed above).

Jonquil Motel ● ☆ $ ∅

☐ *317 Tombstone Canyon (downtown), Bisbee, AZ 85603; (520) 432-7371. Couples and singles $30 to $35. Major credit cards.* ☐ Small non-smoking motel with TV; free coffee in office.

Bed & breakfast inns

The Bisbee Inn ● ☆☆ $$$ ∅

☐ *45 OK St. (P.O. Box 1855), Bisbee, AZ 85603; (520) 432-5131. Couples $45 to $71, singles $35 to $71. Eighteen rooms, one with private bath; full breakfast. MC/VISA.* ☐ Restored 1917 copper miners boarding house within walking distance of historic downtown. Turn of the century décor with oak antiques, print wallpaper, metal bed frames and handmade quilts.

☺ *The Greenway House* ● ☆☆☆ $$$$

☐ *401 Cole Ave. (off Bisbee Road, south of town), Bisbee, AZ 85603; (800) 253-3325 or (520) 432-7170. Couples and singles $90 to $130. Seven units,* all with TV/VCRs, phones, kitchens and private baths; continental breakfast. MC/VISA, AMEX. ☐ Nicely restored 1906 Craftsman style home built for a mine superintendent. Individually decorated rooms, from Victorian to Southwest style. All rooms have refrigerators stocked with drinks and breakfast fixings. Robes, flowers, candy, complimentary wine and other amenities.

The Inn at Castle Rock ● ☆☆ $$$

☐ 112 Tombstone Canyon Rd. (P.O. Box 1161), Bisbee, AZ 85603; (520) 432-7195. Couples $50 to $80, singles $40 to $50. Sixteen rooms, all with private baths; full breakfast. MC/VISA. ☐ A restored 1890 miners boarding house near downtown, with Victorian and early American furnishings; three fireplaces and two comfortable parlors. Large garden with fish ponds and sitting areas.

Park Place Bed & Breakfast ● ☆☆ $$ Ø

☐ 200 E. Vista (near Congdon), Bisbee, AZ 85603; (520) 432-3054 or (520) 432-5516. Couples and singles $40 to $60. Four units; two with private and two with share baths; full breakfast. Major credit cards. ☐ A 5,000-square-foot, two-story 1920s Mediterranean style home with period furnishings, ceiling fans and print wallpaper. Large bedrooms with balconies or terraces; library and sun room.

WHERE TO CAMP

Queen Mine RV Park ● One Dart Ave. (above Queen Mine), P.O. Box 488, Bisbee, AZ 85603; (520) 432-5006. RV sites, full hookups $14, no hookups $12. Reservations accepted; MC/VISA. ☐ Gravel sites on a hill with impressive views of the city on one side and Lavender Pit Mine on the other. Showers, coin laundry, dump station.

Head southeast from Bisbee on State Route 80 through dry brushy hills toward Douglas, another copper town. Before reaching this community on the Mexican border, watch for a faded sign indicating the **Douglas Wildlife Zoo,** a mile and a half up a country road to your left (listed below).

Douglas

Elevation: 3990 feet   **Population: 14,135**

Douglas doesn't have the dramatic canyon setting of Bisbee; it's more of a working town than a tourist stop. It enjoys modest success as an "offshore manufacturing center" employing Mexican workers. Ranches and farms dot the surrounding Sulfur Springs Valley. The town began life in 1901 when a large smelter was built here by the Phelps Dodge Corporation to process copper from company mines in Mexico. It was named for company boss James Douglas. The Mexican revolution nearly disrupted the work-a-day life in Douglas when Pancho Villa and Mexican federal troops clashed just across the border in Agua Prieta in 1915.

As copper prices fell in recent years, civic leaders sought a way to keep Douglas afloat. Cheap labor across the border provided the solution. By the time the giant Phelps Dodge smelter belched its last puff of smoke in 1987, Douglas and Agua Prieta had about 40 manufacturing plants going. They use a "twin plant" concept, in which Mexican nationals assemble American products in factories on both sides of the border. While Douglas gained only about one percent population in the last decade, its Mexican neighbor boomed from 18,000 to 70,000. Life in Douglas is closely allied with Agua

Prieta. The **Douglas Chamber of Commerce** tourist maps and brochures tell you what to see on both sides of the border. The office is at 1125 Pan American Avenue, a few blocks from the boundary. It's open weekdays 9 to 5; (520) 364-2477. **Coronado National Forest** operates a Douglas Ranger District office at Highway 80 and Leslie Canyon Road, north of town; (520) 364-3468; open weekdays 8 to 5.

There's not much to see in Douglas. The old but tidy-looking downtown is a good provisioning center, however, and Agua Prieta has the usual curio shops. Douglas does offer one grand jewel, which you'll encounter by following Highway 80 into town.

ATTRACTIONS

☺ **The Gadsden Hotel** ● *G Avenue and 11th Street; (520) 364-4481.* ⌑ This imposing five-story structure was built in 1907 by copper barons to provide suitable lodgings for visiting dignitaries. It was rebuilt in 1928 after a fire, and has undergone recent restoration. Particularly impressive is the atrium lobby with a grand curving Italian marble staircase. The ceiling, held up by rose marble columns with ornate gold-leaf capitals, contains barrel-arched stained glass skylights. A genuine Tiffany stained glass mural stretches 42 feet across the mezzanine. Arizona cattle brands are burned into the walls of its old fashioned saloon. Not surprisingly, the grand old Gadsden is a national historic monument.

Douglas Wildlife Zoo ● *Plantation Road, 1.5 miles north of Highway 80 (northwest of Douglas); (520) 364-2515. Daily 10 to 5; adults $3, kids $2. MC/VISA.* ⌑ This small zoo has a few big cats, deer, monkeys, llamas and those funny-looking pot-bellied Vietnamese pigs. It also functions as a pet and fish shop and dog grooming parlor.

ANNUAL EVENTS

For information on these and other events, contact the Douglas Chamber of Commerce at (520) 364-2477.

Two Flags International Arts Festival, third weekend of January.

Great American Bed Race, first weekend of June.

Douglas Fiesta Celebration, marking Mexico's independence, second weekend of September.

Cochise County Fair, third week of September.

WHERE TO RECLINE & DINE

☺ **The Gadsden Hotel** ● ☆☆☆ $$

⌑ *1046 G Ave. (11th Street), Douglas, AZ 85607; (520) 364-4481. Couples and singles $32 to $85. Major credit cards.* ⌑ Refurbished rooms with TV/VCRs, rental movies and phones; some suites, kitchenettes and apartments. Lobby lounge and old fashioned saloon. **El Conquistador Dining Room,** a handsome Spanish style dining room with outdoor terrace, serves American-Mexican fare 5:30 p.m. to 9 p.m. Sunday-Wednesday and 5:30 to 10 Thursday-Saturday; dinners $7 to $25; full bar service. Adjacent coffee shop serves breakfast and lunch.

Motel 6 ● ☆☆ $$ Ø

⌑ *111 16th St. (Highway 80), Douglas, AZ 85607; (520) 364-2457. Couples $28, singles $22. Major credit cards.* ⌑ Standard rooms with TV movies; phones, pool.

WHERE TO CAMP

Douglas Golf and Social Club ● *Off Leslie Canyon Road, north of Highway 80 (P.O. Box 1220) Douglas, AZ 85608; (520) 364-3722. RV sites, full hookups $12, golf $7, golf carts $9 on weekends and $6 weekdays. Reservations accepted; MC/VISA.* ☐ Combined RV park and golf course with paved sites, showers, laundry and pool. Golf clubhouse, 18-hole course with double tee markers.

Saddle Gap RV Park ● *Highway 80 at Washington Avenue (Route 1, Box 241), Douglas, AZ 85607. RV sites, full hookups $10. Reservations accepted.* ☐ Large gravel sites with picnic tables and cable TV, pull-throughs and a dump station.

GUEST RANCH

Price Canyon Ranch ● *P.O. Box 1065 (42 miles northeast on U.S. 80), Douglas, AZ 85607; (520) 558-2383. Couples $200 per day and singles $100, including all meals and unlimited horseback riding. Trailer park $10 for full hookups or $6 for tents (horses extra). No credit cards; personal checks accepted.* ☐ A century-old working cattle ranch where guests can help with the chores or relax. Riding, hiking, rockhounding, bird watching. Rowing and fishing in catfish pond. Lounge with TV, books and games.

THROUGH CHIRICAHUA COUNTRY TO WILLCOX

Backtrack briefly to U.S. 191 (shown as State Route 666 on some maps) and follow it north into the Sulfur Springs Valley, flanked by mountainous islands of Coronado National Forest. The route isn't very interesting—alternating between desert and brushy prairie—although it takes you near three historic sites. Two were havens haven for the Chiricahua Apaches, among the last of the American Indians to resist intrusion by outsiders and the other was an encampment for the army that pursued them.

Heading north on Highway 191, you'll pass through scruffy little **Elfrida,** and then **Sunizona,** both with fuel and provisions. In Sunizona, you'll see the turnoff to Chiricahua National Monument. Ignore it for the moment and continue nine miles on to another town with a contrived name—**Sunsites.** This planned desert community is a gateway to the hideout of one of America's most famous warrior chiefs:

Cochise Stronghold ● *In the Dragoon Mountains west of Highway 191, c/o Douglas Ranger District, Rural Route 1, Box 228-R, Douglas, AZ 85607; (520) 364-3468. RV and tent camping $6, with picnic tables and barbecues, water, composting toilets; RV limit 22 feet.* ☐ These rocky upcroppings in the Dragoon Mountain foothills served as Cochise's fortress during his 11- year battle with settlers and the U.S. Army in the valley below. Part of Coronado National Forest, it's now a recreation area with self-guiding nature trails, historic walks, and hiking trails into the surrounding mountains.

RV advisory ● Ten miles of dirt road—often bumpy—must be traversed to reach the stronghold. It's negotiable by RVs if driven slowly; check for road conditions after a storm.

Just below Sunsites, near the old cowtown of Pearce, travelers can play cowboy in this cowboy corner:

Grapevine Canyon Ranch ● *Highland Road (P.O. Box 302), Pearce, AZ 85625. Casitas $140 to $160 per person (double occupancy), cabins $120 to $140. Includes all meals, horses and guided sightseeing. MC/VISA, DISC.* ☐

This formation in Chiricahua National Monument's wonderland of rocks is called the Organ Pipe.

This working cattle ranch pampers guests with a swimming pool, cookouts and other activities, with overnight pack trips for the more adventurous. Casitas have a bedroom, refrigerator and a private porch or sun deck; cabins are single rooms with a private porch or sun deck.

Retrace your path to Sunizona and follow State Route 181 to the second Apache historic site. It's also one of the more interesting geological jewels of the national park system:

☺ **Chiricahua National Monument** ● *Dos Cabezas Route, Box 6500, Willcox, AZ 85643; (520) 824-3560. Admission $4 per family, $2 per hiker or biker. Camping $7 per night; shaded spots with barbecues and picnic tables, water and flush potties. Visitor center open daily 8 to 5.* ⊡ This pocket-sized preserve, covering only 12,000 acres, shelters some incredibly complex rock formations and five of the seven North American life zones.

Wind and rain have eroded a 27-million-year-old volcanic rhyolite deposit into fantastic shapes. Wander with your eyes and your camera and take your pick of descriptions: remnants of Greco-Roman temples, crowds of Easter Island statues and colonnades. Some formations, shrouded in trees, suggest jungle-clad Mayan ruins. The Apaches called this the "Land of standing-up rocks," which may be the best description of all. Some are precariously balanced, as if ready to fall at the slightest breath. But they have held those poses for tens of thousands of years.

A steeply winding eight-mile drive takes you up through Bonita Canyon—and through those five climate zones—to Massai Point high in the Chiricahua Mountains. From here, you can take in a grand expanse of the Chihuahuan Desert sweeping southeast into Mexico and the Sonoran Desert to the west. The best way to see the park is afoot. Hiking trails twist among the rock formations and climb up to vista points. A free shuttle leaves the visitor's center at 8:30 each morning to take hikers to Massai Point. From there, you can follow a complex of trails, leisurely working your way downhill, back to the center. Seventeen miles of trails wind through the park. Ranger hikes and talks at the amphitheater near the campground are scheduled periodically. Exhibits at the visitor center museum cover the area's flora, fauna, geology and human history. Some fine Chiricahua Apache artifacts are on display, including buckskin leggings, a pitch basket, war club and arrows.

These rocky ramparts were the refuge of the Chiricahuas during the 25-year war with the U.S. Army. Only when Geronimo surrendered in 1886 did settlement begin in earnest. One of the original homesteads, Faraway Ranch, is still intact, sitting in a pretty wooded glen of Bonita Canyon, near the park entrance. It remained in the original family until it was purchased by the park service in 1979. The ranch house, open periodically for tours, is furnished in a 1960s style. Check at the visitor center for the schedule. At other times, you can view ranch exhibits in a nearby outbuilding and prowl the grounds of the old homestead. The cabin of another pioneer family is just above the ranch; it's one of the oldest log structures in Arizona.

The other attraction in this desert basin requires a dusty drive. From Chiricahua, turn north onto State Highway 186 at its junction with 181 and head for Willcox. Nine miles from the junction, a dirt road takes you to one of the most remote preserves in the national park system:

☺ **Fort Bowie National Historic Site** ● *P.O. Box 158, Bowie, AZ 85605; (520) 847-2500. Visitor center open 8 to 5; free.* ☐ After eight miles of dirt road, you must invest in a 1.5-mile hike to reach the ruins of one of the West's most important army posts. Fort Bowie was built in 1862 to protect the vital Apache Pass during the army's war with the Chiricahuas. Patrols were launched from here to pursue the elusive Cochise and later Geronimo. When Geronimo surrendered, he and his band were brought to Bowie, then shipped in exile to Florida. Peace finally settled onto this lonely outpost. In fact, things were so peaceful, it was abandoned in 1894.

All that remains now are weathered ridges of adobe and stone walls—and a lot of history. The hike to the fort is a pleasant one—from a parking area up a gentle, winding incline to a remote high desert valley. Along the way, you'll pass the ruins of the old Butterfield stage stop, the fort cemetery and Apache Springs, still seeping water from the rough mountainside. At the fort, you can chat with the ranger on duty and wander among the ruins, reading signs that describe the spartan life at an army outpost. Books about the fort and the Apache wars are on sale in the small visitor kiosk.

RV ADVISORY ● Although the drive to Fort Bowie is rough in spots, it's straight and level for the most part. Any sized RV or trailer rig can make it.

You have two choices for continuing on to Willcox, the last stop in this tour of Cochise County. Either retrace your route to Highway 186 and head northwest, or continue 12 miles north on the Fort Bowie road until it intersects with Interstate 10. Both routes are equally dusty; the first is shorter.

Willcox

Elevation: 4,167 feet   **Population: 3,300**

Willcox began life in 1880 as a construction supply camp for the Southern Pacific Railroad, then it evolved into a small cow town. It still is a small cowtown, although it has become a major cattle shipping center, as well as a stopover for travelers on busy I-10. Townspeople like to brag about their na-

THE LAST WARRIOR APACHES

The Chiricahua Apaches were a fierce semi-nomadic warrior clan, pillaging, raiding and resisting white intrusion. "In all the wars for the North American continent, European invaders encountered no more formidable adversary than the Apache warrior," wrote Robert M. Utley in *A Clash of Cultures.*

From the ranks of these ferocious people emerged two leaders whose names would be known to every American school child—and every Hollywood script writer. Cochise was chief of a band of Chiricahuas that hunted, gathered and raided in the rough, thorny high desert below the mountains that now bear their tribal name. Geronimo, equally famous, was not a Chiricahua by birth and never wore the mantle of chief.

The Chiricahuas had been battling Spanish intruders since the 1700s, but it was white settlement a century later that pushed Cochise and his followers to their limits. Initially, he was friendly with the Americans. He even allowed the Butterfield Overland Mail Company to build a way station in Apache Pass in 1858. This low saddle in the Chiricahua Mountains, with a year- around spring, was a critical link to east-west migration.

Three years alter, Cochise came upon an army patrol camped at the pass. The unit's leader, young Lt. George N. Bascom, accused the chief of stealing livestock and abducting the stepson of a nearby rancher. Cochise denied the charges but Bascom ordered his arrest. In a scene right out of a movie script, the chief slit the wall of Bascom's tent with his knife and escaped. The incident escalated into bloody conflict that didn't end until 1872. Then, with assurances that his people could remain in the Apache Pass area, Cochise signed a peace treaty.

"Hereafter, the white man and the Indian are to drink of the same water, eat of the same bread, and be at peace," he said.

And then came Geronimo

He died less than two years later, still at peace with the whites. But harmony was short-lived. The government wanted all Apaches moved the San Carlos reservation to the north. In 1876, a brave named Pionsenay got drunk and killed a whiskey seller. That gave officials an excuse to declare all Chiricahuas as renegades and order them to San Carlos. Some went in peace but others escaped into Mexico. There, they joined with the Nednhi Chiricahuas and resumed raiding white settlements. Their chief was a man named Juh, but the Indians began rallying around a scowling, fierce Nednhi warrior named Geronimo. He had gained a reputation for terrorist raids in Mexico.

Juh and Geronimo raided settlements and clashed with the army for four years. Then, seeing that their fight was futile, they agreed to surrender and move their band to San Carlos. But it was a hot, miserable, disease-ridden place. Corrupt agents kept rations intended for the Indians and unrest grew. Geronimo and Juh fled the reservation in 1881 with about 70 followers. They took refuge in Mexico's Sierra Madre range and the war resumed.

Two years later, Geronimo agreed to return to the reservation, but he bolted again, in 1885. After more bloody skirmishes, he agreed to unconditional surrender in September of 1886. He and his entire band were loaded onto a train and shipped to Florida. Even those who had remained peacefully on the reservation and Apache scouts who had served with the army where shipped east. Treated like prisoners instead of reservation Indians, the men and women were separated and sent to different camps.

Generals O.O. Howard and George Crook, who had fought the Apaches, now pleaded with authorities to re-unite them with their families. It was finally done after a year's separation. Then in 1894, the tribe was moved to Oklahoma, where they remain today. Geronimo—the last warrior Apache—died there on February 17, 1909.

tive son, Rex Allen, a real cowboy who became a Hollywood cowboy. They've opened a museum to their sequined hero, who lives on a ranch in Sonoita. The downtown area retains an Old West look with false front stores and narrow brick and masonry buildings.

Approaching Willcox on I-10 from either direction, take exit 340 onto— what else?—Rex Allen Drive. Instead of heading downtown, go north to a frontage road to the **Chamber of Commerce,** which shares a modern structure with the **Museum of the Southwest.** Both are open Monday-Saturday 9 to 5 and Sunday 1 to 5; (520) 384-2272. You can pick up area maps and brochures, including a walking map identifying century-old structures in the Willcox Historic District. **Stout's Cider Mill,** adjacent to the visitor center/museum, is your kind of place if you love things applish.

Now, cross over the freeway on Rex Allen Drive, pass through the modest and modern business district, then turn right onto Steward Street. After a few blocks, turn left onto Maley Street, and then left again onto Railroad Avenue. This puts you in the one-block-long historic district, so look for a place to park. Railroad Avenue was the town's commercial center when the rails brought prosperity to the valley in the 1880s. Today's centerpiece is the **Rex Allen Arizona Cowboy Museum** and an adjacent Art Deco movie theater. Several other old brickfront and false front buildings, undergoing preservation, house gift and antique shops.

ATTRACTIONS

Museum of the Southwest • *1500 N. Circle I Rd., Willcox, AZ 85643; (520) 384-2272. Monday-Saturday 9 to 5, Sunday 1 to 5; free.* ☐ Exhibits in this small, nicely done museum feature the early Indian and cowboy life in this corner of Cochise County. It offers a fine display of Indian artifacts, graphics on Apache migration patterns and details of the Cochise-Apache Pass incident that started the long Chiricahua war. A wall graphic quoting Cochise is particularly memorable:

How was it, when I was young, I walked all over this country, east and west and saw no other people other than the Apaches. After many summers, I walked again and found another race of people had come to take it. How is it?

☺ **Rex Allen Arizona Cowboy Museum** • *Railroad Avenue near Malley Street (P.O. Box 995), Willcox, AZ 85644; (520) 384-4583. Daily 10 to 4; couples $3, singles $2, families $5.* ☐ They call him the "Arizona Cowboy," and he was that before he became a movie, TV and rodeo star. Rex Allen was born on a homestead ranch near Willcox. When he was 11, his father bought him a Sears & Roebuck mail-order guitar, and the rest is a press agent's dream. If you're too young to remember his many Republic Pictures horse operas, you surely can recall his resonant voice as narrator of nature films by Disney and other producers.

Exhibits in the storefront Rex Allen Museum trace his rise to stardom, with movie posters, some of his gaudy boots and cowboy clothes, sheet music and even a badly-done oil painted by Rex. Other displays trace the settling of the west by Spanish, Anglo and black cowboys. The building also houses the Willcox Cowboy Hall of Fame, with portraits of prominent local cattlemen. The next-door Rex Allen Theater, sporting an old-fashioned marquee, shows contemporary and Western films—including some of Allen's, of course. Across the street, in a park strip along the railroad tracks, is a life-sized bronze of Rex with his guitar.

WHERE TO DINE

Cactus Kitchen Restaurant ● ☆☆ $$

◻ *706 S. Haskell Ave. (I-10 exit 336); (520) 384-3857. American-Mexican; full bar service. Daily 5 a.m. to 9 p.m. MC/VISA.* ◻ Popular local place with Southwest décor; steaks, chops and chicken, plus Mexican entrées. Sunday buffet and all-you-can-eat Friday fish fry.

☺ The Dining Car ● ☆☆ $$

◻ *130 E. Maley (Railroad Avenue), Willcox; (520) 384-0515. American; wine and beer. Tuesday-Saturday 11 to 9. MC/VISA.* ◻ Housed in a bright red vintage railroad car, it features assorted specials that change weekly. Among regular menu items are mesquite grilled steak and chicken.

☺ Historical Saxon House ● ☆☆☆ $$$

◻ *308 S. Haskell (I-10 exit 336, then four miles south); (520) 384-4478. American; full bar service. Wednesday-Friday 11 to 2 and 5 to 9, Saturday 4 to 9, Sunday noon to 8, closed Monday-Tuesday. Reservations advised; MC/VISA.* ◻ Historic 1916 ranch home converted into an appealing restaurant with turn of the century décor. American menu with some continental entrées.

WHERE TO RECLINE

Best Western Plaza Inn ● ☆☆☆ $$$ Ø

◻ *1100 W. Rex Allen Dr. (I-10 exit 340), Willcox, AZ 85643; (800) 528-1234 or (520) 384-3556. Couples and singles $50 to $80. Major credit cards.* ◻ Attractive 92-unit lodge with TV movies, phones, refrigerators, some spa tubs; pool, spa, coin laundry. **Restaurant** serves 6 a.m. to 10 p.m.; dinners $6 to $13; full bar service.

Econo Lodge ● ☆☆ $$$$ Ø

◻ *724 N. Bisbee Ave. (I-10 exit 340), Willcox, AZ 85643; (520) 384-4222. Couples $85, singles $68. Major credit cards.* ◻ Seventy-two rooms with TV movies, phones; some microwaves, refrigerators and VCRs; pool, laundry.

WHERE TO CAMP

Magic Circle RV Park ● *700 N. Virginia Ave. (I-10 exit 340, then half mile northwest on Fort Grant Road), Willcox, AZ 85643; (800) 333-4720 or (520) 384-3212. RV sites, full hookups $19.50, no hookups $15.* ◻ Showers, coin laundry, groceries, Propane, dump station, kids playground, pool.

Heading back toward Tucson on I-10, you'll encounter an excellent Native American museum 22 miles west of Willcox:

☺ Amerind Foundation Museum ● *P.O. Box 400 (I-10 exit 318, then southeast one mile) Dragoon, AZ 85609; (520) 586-3666. Daily 10 to 4 September to May, Wednesday-Sunday 10 to 4 the rest of the year. Adults $3, seniors and kids 12 to 18, $2.* ◻ This fine museum, housed in Spanish Colonial buildings set into a rocky canyon, displays a treasure trove of early Native American lore. Exhibits feature Southwestern and Mexican archaeology, with pottery, basketry, projectile points and other implements unearthed in various digs. Other displays center on Northwest and Arctic bands and the Indian cultures of Mexico, Central and South America. More than 25,000 objects are in the collection, covering 10,000 years of history of the early people of the Western Hemisphere. Paintings and sculptures of past and contemporary Native American artists are exhibited in an adjacent gallery.

TRIP PLANNER

WHEN TO GO ● The high deserts and higher mountains of eastern Arizona are year-around havens, although some roads can be closed by winter snow. Show Low and Pinetop-Lakeside in the White Mountains and Payson below the Mogollan Rim are popular summer retreats for Valley of the Sun folks seeking heat relief. However, summers in some areas of middle eastern Arizona can be hot, hovering between 95 and 100. Winters are cool to cold, with occasional snow flurries. Spring and fall are nice times to visit.

WHAT TO SEE ● Discovery Park in Safford and the Museum of Anthropology at Eastern Arizona College in Thatcher; Casa Malpais Pueblo and Raven Site Ruin near Springerville; Apache County Museum in St. Johns; Petrified Forest National Park; Courthouse Museum in Holbrook; historic Fort Apache; Besh-Ba-Gowah Archaeological Park and Gila County Museum in Globe; Museum of the Forest in Payson.

WHAT TO DO ● Follow the Swift Trail below Safford into the heights of Mount Graham; poke about old town Clifton and Miami; take the Phelps Dodge mine tour at Morenci; schuss the slopes of Sunrise Ski Resort; hike the peninsula trails at Lyman Lake State Park; hike to the arch at Tonto Natural Bridge State Park; drive the Mogollan Rim Forestry Road.

☺ *Indicates an attraction, restaurant or lodging with special appeal.*

USEFUL CONTACTS

Apache-Sitgreaves National Forest, P.O. Box 640, Springerville, AZ 85938; (520) 333-4301.

Greater Globe-Miami Chamber of Commerce, P.O. Box 2539 (1360 N. Broad), Globe, AZ 85502; (800) 448-8983 or (520) 425-4495.

Greenlee County Chamber of Commerce, P.O. Box 1237, Clifton, AZ 85533; (520) 865-3313.

Holbrook-Petrified Forest Chamber of Commerce, 100 E. Arizona St., Holbrook, AZ 86025; (520) 524-6558.

Payson Chamber of Commerce, P.O. Box 1380 (100 W. Main St.), Payson, AZ 85547; (800) 6-PAYSON or (520) 474-4515.

Pinetop-Lakeside Chamber of Commerce, P.O. Box 266 (592 W. White Mountain Blvd.), Pinetop, AZ 85935; (520) 367-4290.

Round Valley Chamber of Commerce, P.O. Box 31 (148 E. Main St.), Springerville, AZ 85938-0031; (520) 333-2123.

Safford-Graham County Chamber of Commerce, 1111 Thatcher Blvd., Safford, AZ 85546; (520) 428-2511.

St. Johns Regional Chamber of Commerce, P.O. Box 178 (180 W. Cleveland), St. Johns, AZ 85936; (520) 337-2000.

San Carlos Apache Recreation and Wildlife Department, P.O. Box 97, San Carlos, AZ 85550.

Show Low Chamber of Commerce, P.O. Box 1080 (951 W. Deuce of Clubs), Show Low, AZ 85901; (520) 537-2326.

White Mountain Apache Enterprises, P.O. Box 220, Whiteriver, AZ 85941; (520) 338-4385 or 338-4386.

AREA RADIO STATIONS

KJJJ-FM, 102.1—Rock, popular.
KFMM-FM, 99.1—Country.
KZUA-FM, 92.1,—Country.
KRFM-FM, 96.5Rock and popular.
KVWM-FM, 93.5—Music, news.
KQAZ-FM, 101.7—Popular.
KNIX-FM, 102.5—Country.

KIXS-FM, 97.3—Light rock, news, talk.
KISS-FM, 98.3,—Country.
KIKO-FM, 106.1—Soft hits.
KNNB-FM, 88.1—Country, pops.
KCUZ-AM, 1490—Country.
KRVZ-AM, 1400—Country.

PETRIFIED FOREST

Chapter twelve

THE MIDEAST

Forests of wood; forests of stone

MIDEASTERN ARIZONA is a sampler of the rest of the state—high prairie, piney mountains, sculpted badlands, a large Indian reservation and craggy canyons—everything but a slice of the Sonoran Desert. Climate varies from the dry, hot Gila River Valley around Safford to cold and snowy winters of Show Low and the White Mountains.

With only one major attraction—Petrified Forest National Park—the mideast often is overlooked by outsiders. However, it has many lesser known lures that make a visit worthwhile. Particularly appealing are two major archeological sites near Springerville, recently opened to the public. The mideast has long been popular with sun belt residents who seek relief from summer heat while enjoying the trout streams, campgrounds and hiking trails of Coronado, Tonto and Apache-Sitgreaves national forests.

To cover all of the middle east's attributes, we've designed a rather convoluted route resembling a squiggly "S" that tipped over backward. You can cleverly climb into this chapter from the previous one by pressing eastward on Interstate 10 from Willcox. At exit 352, head north toward Safford on U.S. 191. The route passes through high basin country that alternates between desert, prairie and pasturelands. Filling the horizon to the west is the massive, ridge-like Mount Graham, one of the tallest peaks in Arizona at 10,713 feet. It's the dominate feature of Graham County's Gila Valley.

☺ If you're willing to climb to dizzying heights for some fine views, take the **Swift Trail** (State Route 366) up to Graham's ramparts. After passing the Safford Federal Correctional Institution with its double fences and nasty-looking rolls of concertina wire, the road begins a steep and quick climb into Coronado National Forest. It coils swiftly from desert through oak-chaparral woodlands to pines, offering ever widening views of the broad Gila Valley. You'll encounter a couple of picnic areas and forest service campgrounds along the way. (See "Where to camp" below.) About 17 miles up, the highway swings around to the mountain's southwestern side, providing vistas of the tiny blue ripple of the San Pedro River and the hazy blue shapes of the Galluro and Rincon Mountains near far away Tucson. Pavement ends after 22 miles at a wide turnaround; a gravel road continues another twelve miles, ending at Briggs Lake.

Early morning or late afternoon are grand times to make this drive, when the sun's slanting rays perform a light and shadow show on distant valleys and mountains.

RV ADVISORY ● Swift Trail has some steep hairpin curves although it's paved up the turnaround. Large RVs and trailer rigs should handle it. Beyond the turnaround, it's a rough forestry road; inquire before continuing.

Back down from the heights, continue on U.S. 191 toward Safford. If you're looking for a place to camp or recreate, you might want to stop just short of town:

Roper Lake State Park ● *101 E. Roper Lake Rd., Safford, AZ 85546; (520) 428-6760. Day use $3, camping $8 to $13 (details below, under "Where to camp").* ❑ This small park wraps around a reservoir stocked with catfish, bluegill and trout; only oars or electric motors are permitted. Facilities include swimming bays, hiking trails, picnic areas and a hot tub fed by a natural spring. The view of Mount Graham, sometimes reflected in the lake, is rather impressive.

Safford

Elevation: 2,920 feet   **Population: 7,710**

The seat of Graham County, Safford is the commercial centerpiece of a broad agricultural valley between the Pinaleno Mountains to the southeast and the Gila Mountains to the northwest. Sheltered from rainfall and sitting below 3,000 feet, it has a dry climate more akin to the desert than the mountains surrounding it. Hot summers provide the proper environment for cotton, one of the area's major crops. A well-tended town with a middle America look, Safford is a handy provisioning center and a stepping-off point for outdoor recreation in the Coronado National Forest that encloses Mount Graham and the Pinaleno range. Safford serves a trade area of 50,000 people, extending from mideastern Arizona into western New Mexico.

Entering town on Highway 191, turn left at a signal onto Thatcher Boulevard (Fifth Street) and drive several blocks into well tended old downtown district. Turn left onto Eighth Avenue, past the Greek-federalist yellow brick **Graham County Courthouse** and continue another block to the brick Colonial style 1921 library building, on your right. No longer in use as a library (the new one is at 800 Seventh Avenue), it houses the small **Graham County Historical Society Museum** on the upper floor. Go back to Thatcher Boulevard and drive a short distance to the **Graham County**

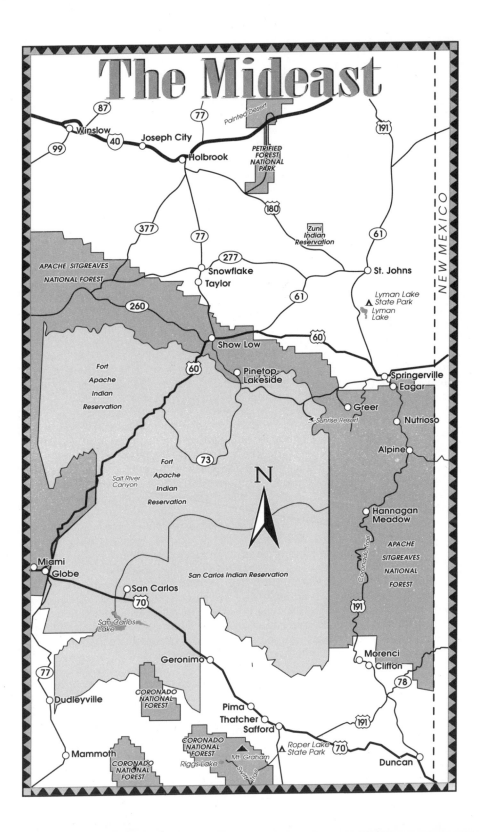

Chamber of Commerce and a small museum are housed in a modern adobe brick structure on your left, beside a small park. It's open Monday-Saturday 9 to 5; (520) 428-2511. Continue about half a mile to the next signal, near a suburban shopping complex and turn left onto 20th Avenue. Follow it about 2.5 miles into the countryside, past a couple of cotton fields to the fine new **Discovery Park Museum** at 20th and 32nd Street.

Return again to the main drag, turn left and drive about a mile toward the next-door community of **Thatcher.** Just short of its business district, take a half left onto Church Street and follow it several blocks to simple, attractive campus of **Eastern Arizona College.** Go to the public entrance of the administration building (right side) and ask for a campus map and directions to the excellent **Museum of Anthropology;** it's beside the girl's dorm. Return one more time to the main highway, backtrack through Safford and follow Highway 70/191 signs east.

ATTRACTIONS
In order of appearance

☺ *Mount Graham* • *In the Pinaleno range, Coronado National Forest.* ⛶ This long mountain ridge is the centerpiece of an alpine recreation area popular with hikers and campers; fisherpersons angle for trout in Riggs Lake. The dramatic Mount Graham Drive takes you through five climate zones to the 10,000 foot level. Hiking maps and such are available at the **Safford Ranger District** office in the Safford post office building on Thatcher Boulevard, just west of the Highway 191 junction, It's open weekdays 8 to 5; (520) 428-4150.

Mount Graham International Observatory • *Atop Emerald Peak in the Mount Graham wilderness. Not open to the public at press time, although tours may be arranged. Check with the Graham County Chamber of Commerce at (520) 428-2522.* ⛶ A joint effort of the University of Arizona and several other agencies, this new observatory was established in the mid-1990s. It houses the world's largest binocular telescope and other leading-edge astronomical gadgets.

Graham County Historical Society Museum • *Second floor of the old library, 808 Eighth Ave.; (520) 428-1531. Monday-Tuesday 1 to 4; free.* ⛶ This small museum (which may be moving elsewhere) has a limited exhibit of pioneer and Indian relics and old photos of Graham County.

Visitor Center museum • *Safford-Graham County Chamber of Commerce, 1111 Thatcher Blvd., Safford, AZ 85546; (520) 428-2511.* ⛶ More than an information center, the chamber building houses a nicely done museum with displays concerning area attractions and agriculture, and models of telescopes at the Mount Graham International Observatory. A state-of-the-art touch screen video directs visitors to area attractions.

☺ *Discovery Park* • *C/o Mt. Graham International Science and Culture Foundation, 1651 32nd St., Safford, AZ 85546; (520) 428-6260. Daily 10 a.m. to 10 p.m.* ⛶ Opened in late 1995, this discovery center is shaping up as one of Arizona's finest science museums. A planetarium section, operated in conjunction with the Mount Graham Observatory, features exhibits on latest technological developments, a 20-inch optical telescope for public use and a radio telescope. Other exhibits are "The Story of Cotton" in Gila Valley, "The World of Mining" with a model of an underground drift mine, "Wonders of the Land" featuring exhibits on the five climate zones found in Graham

County and "Lives of People," focusing on the area's pre-Colombian and various contemporary cultures. A wildlife habitat with exhibits of area flora and fauna surrounds the museum building.

☺ **Museum of Anthropology** • *On the campus of Eastern Arizona College, Church at College Avenue (P.O. Box 1186), Thatcher, AZ 85546; (520) 428-8310. Weekdays 9 to noon and 1 to 4 during the school year. Free; donations accepted.* ☐ Missed by most visitors, this is an impressive little museum focusing on the early peoples of central Arizona. Its focal points are two remarkably detailed dioramas—one showing life here 11,000 years ago when giant bisons and ground sloths roamed about; and another depicting a typical pueblo of 300 A.D. Extensive displays of pottery, basketry and other artifacts trace the development of various native groups in the area. At a hands-on exhibit, kids can try chipping arrowheads and making a fire with rubbing sticks.

Some nearby attractions

Eastern Arizona Museum • *Highway 70 at Main Street in Pima, seven miles northwest of Safford on Highway 70; (520) 485-2288. Wednesday-Friday 2 to 4 and Saturday 1 to 5.* ☐ Housed in a turn-of-the-century masonry store building, this museum has a rather large collection of pioneer and Native American artifacts.

Aravaipa Canyon • *Fifteen miles northeast of Safford.* ☐ A year-around creek, unusual in a desert climate, weaves through the bottom of rock-ribbed Aravaipa Canyon. Wilderness hikers are drawn to this area for its intriguing mix of hardwoods along the creek bed and saguaro in the steep hills. It's reached by the 24-mile dirt Klondyke Road, off Highway 70 northeast of Safford. Primitive campsites are available in this wooded riparian oasis. There's a modest day use fee and all hiking and camping require a permit from the Bureau of Land Management office across from the high school at 711 14th Avenue, Safford, AZ 85546; (520) 428-4040. It's open weekdays 7:45 to 4:15; permits also are available by mail.

ACTIVITIES

Cotton gin tours • Visits to a pair of area gins can be arranged by advance reservation: Safford Cotton Growers in Safford, (520) 428-0714; and Glenbar Gin in Pima, (520) 485-9255.

Golf • Safford Municipal Golf Course, 18 holes, pro shop and rental carts; (520) 428-1260.

ANNUAL EVENTS

For details on these and other events, contact the chamber at 428-2511.
Old Time Fiddlers Gathering, late February.
Gila Valley Rodeo in August.
Graham County Fair at the fairgrounds in October.
Cowboy Christmas Arts & Crafts Festival, November-December.

WHERE TO DINE

El Charro Restaurant • ☆ **$**

☐ *601 Main St. (two blocks from the courthouse); (520) 428-4134. Mexican-American; beer and wine coolers. Reservations accepted. MC/VISA.* ☐ Family café with typical smashed beans and rice fare, plus a few American dishes, including steaks and chicken. Old-time fiddlers entertain Wednesday nights.

Jumbo Restaurant ● ☆☆ *$*

❏ *817 Thatcher Blvd.; (520) 428-2888. Chinese; wine and beer. Daily 11 a.m. to 9 p.m. MC/VISA.* ❏ Airy, comfortable new restaurant brightened by lanterns and other Chinese regalia. The menu features mild Cantonese and more spicy Szechuan dishes, with family dinners starting under $10.

WHERE TO RECLINE

Prices reflect high season rates and may be lower at other times. Most were provided by the management and are subject to change; use them only as a guide.

Country Manor Motel ● ☆☆☆ *$$$*

❏ *420 E. Highway 70 (near downtown), Safford, AZ 85546; (800) 555-3664 in Arizona only or (520) 428-2451. Couples $48 to $68, singles $40 to $50, family units $85 to $125. Major credit cards.* ❏ Recently expanded inn with TV movies, phones, refrigerators, in-room coffee, complimentary cocktails; barbecue facilities, indoor pool, spa and saunas. **Restaurant** serves 24 hours; American and Mexican; dinners $6 to $15; full bar service.

Sandia Motel ● ☆☆ *$$* ∅

❏ *520 E. Highway 70 (near downtown), Safford, AZ 85546; (800) 950-SAND or (520) 428-1621. Couples $41 to $50, singles $39 to $45, family units $75 to $85. Major credit cards.* ❏ A 33-unit motel with TV and phones; some refrigerators and microwaves. Pool, spa, gift shop and coin laundry. **Aria's Ristorante Italiano** serves 11 a.m. to 10 p.m.; dinners $8 to $15; full bar.

WHERE TO CAMP

Roper Lake State Park ● *101 E. Roper Lake Rd., Safford, AZ 85546; (520) 428-6760. Water and electric $13, no hookups and tent sites $8, day use $3.* ❏ Campsites near a small reservoir; flush potties, tables and fire grills; some with hookups and showers. Other facilities include swimming bays, hiking trails, picnic areas and a natural spring-fed hot tub.

Mount Graham ● *No hookups; pit potties; $5. No reservations.* ❏ Several U.S. Forest Service campgrounds are along the Swift Trail that climbs Mount Graham. Two are on the paved section of the road, Arcadia, eleven miles up the highway, and Shannon, about 20 miles up, near the end of pavement.

NORTH TO CLIFTON/MORENCI

Head east about twelve miles on Highways 70/191, then branch northeast on 191. You soon leave Gila Valley farm country and begin climbing into the contoured desert foothills of the Gila Mountains. Some attractively buttes and other rocky upcroppings will break the monotony of the drive. In the fall, the region is brightened by blooming rabbitbrush.

At the junction of 191 and State Route 78, turn left and head for Clifton. If you want to stock up on Apache National Forest materials, first go briefly right to the **Clifton Ranger Station.** It's open weekdays 8 to 4:30; (520) 687-1314. Pressing on toward Clifton, you'll see a city limits sign long before you see signs of life. You'll also see what feeds the area's economy—multicolored tailing dumps, settling basins and other massive earth bruises from the world's largest copper mining operation. This brushy, mountainous country along the San Francisco River and Chase Creek was dramatic even before man took a hand, with its terraced cliffs and steep ravines. Further altered by mining operations, it is now—pick your own point of view—ugly or starkly beautiful.

Ore truck dwarfs its driver (far right) at a fueling station in the Phelps Dodge mine. The 240-ton rig stands 20 feet high.

The highway through here is called the Coronado Trail, in honor of the *conquistadore* who passed this way in 1540 in search of golden cities. One wonders why he picked such a rugged route and one chuckles at a bit of irony—there was gold here, in the gravels of the creeks. Mexican prospectors—it would be fun to fancy them as descendants of Coronado's men and local Indian women—found the gold in the 1860s. The small deposits soon played out, then American prospectors and entrepreneurs learned of copper in the area. This boom is still going on.

Clifton/Morenci

Clifton 3,502 feet/Morenci 4,080 feet   Area population: 4,700

Clifton was platted in 1873 as mines developed in the area. There are two theories concerning its name, depending on your historian: It's a derivation of "Clifftown" for the surrounding bluffs, or it was named after the Clifton copper mine. Henry Clifton was an early investor in the area. Morenci (*mor-EN-cee*), established in 1884, was named for the Michigan home town of an early mine official.

The Phelps Dodge Corporation came to the area in 1882 and—through the generations—it bought mining companies and claims until it was the sole operator. It eventually bought the town of Morenci, and then dismantled it because it sat on rich copper deposits. But no matter; company officials built a prim new community in 1969, with a shopping center, theater, bowling alley, swimming pool, motel, restaurants, video store—all of humanity's basic needs. Phelps Dodge now owns 22,000 acres and employs more than half of the area's population, 2,400 people.

Driving through a moonscape of tailing dumps and other unearthly gouges, you'll first hit Clifton which—despite its small size— is the seat of skinny, sparsely populated Greenlee County. It's a tough old working class mining town terraced into a brushy slope of Chase Creek and surrounded by the sights, sounds and smells of mining. Pause at the **Greenlee County Chamber of Commerce** in the restored 1913 Spanish style passenger depot of the Arizona and New Mexico Railway. It's open weekdays 9 to 5; (520) 865-3313. The Art Depot, a gallery displaying works of local artists, occupies one end of the building.

Just up the highway and to the left, you'll see the **Copper Head,** an 1880 narrow-gauge locomotive that hauled ore to the smelter. Nearby is the original town jail, hacked out of a cliff face in 1881. The story goes that the builder, Margarito Verala, spent his construction earnings on booze and women, shot a few holes in the town and became the jail's first occupant. But we've heard that tale before, in at least three other Western towns. (Our favorite involves jail builders in California's Lake County, who were thrown into their own slammer and escaped by lifting off the roof, which they'd neglected to bolt down.)

A few blocks beyond the chamber and jail, fork to the left, park in a wedge of a parking lot and stroll down Chase Street, Clifton's historic and decrepit business district.

RV ADVISORY ● Chase Street is very narrow and there's a big dip a few blocks up—guaranteed to drag the overhanging tail of a big rig. RVs can fit into one of the double length spaces at the beginning of Chase, or park on the highway shoulder.

☺ In stark contrast to primly planned Morenci, old downtown **Clifton** is about to fall apart. The decrepit brick and stone storefronts—some with elaborate friezes, pressed tin walls and rosettes—are fascinating to explore. With its narrow streets, high sidewalks and even some Roman arches, old Clifton almost suggests an abandoned European town. Chase street begs to be renovated into a tourist lure with boutiques and cafés and plaques telling of the town's rowdy past, but there's been little action thus far.

"Most of the buildings are owned by three guys in their nineties," a resident told us, "and have you ever heard of three ninety-year-olds agreeing on anything?"

A combination hardware store and mini-mart at the beginning of Chase is one of the few operating businesses. Farther up the street, the **Greenlee Historical Museum** occupies the yellow brick Eagles Hall, built in 1913. Most of the other buildings are inhabited only by ghosts of the fallen angels, tinhorn gamblers, randy miners and pompous mine owners who once walked these narrow streets.

From old Clifton, continue along Highway 191, which makes a wide sweeping turn up through terraced mining pits and tailing dumps. At a stoplight, you can continue straight ahead into town, or turn right, staying with the highway. Just up the highway, on the left and opposite the fire station, is the employment office of Phelps Dodge Corporation, where you can make reservations for a tour (see below).

If you continue into this planned company town, you'll see Phelps Dodge's appealing Spanish style shopping center on the right and the Morenci Motel and Restaurant on the left. (Mine tour groups form in the motel lobby and there's tour parking adjacent.) Staying with the main street, you'll hit a Phelps Dodge compound and the sign says you can't enter. As you turn around, notice the deep turquoise tailing pond where water is collected after processing copper ore.

PHELPS DODGE TOUR: THINK BIG

"We don't make jokes about women drivers around here," said our guide Julio Tavesin in his soft Latin accent. "The company likes them, because they're easier on the trucks."

He was talking about trucks that stand 20 feet high, weigh 240 tons and haul 70-ton loads of ore from huge open pit mines. Although the Phelps Dodge tour of the Morenci Mine facility rings with superlatives—it's the world's largest copper mining operation, producing about a billion pounds a year—the most impressive part of the tour was the equipment.

Tour guests can stand next to these monster trucks and kick an eleven-foot tire—each worth $18,000. The truck itself goes for about $1.5 million, so it's no wonder that the company likes its drivers to handle them with care. Even more gargantuan are the power shovels that load them. Priced at around $6.1 million each, they can scoop up 56 cubic yards of ore at a sweep. From a distance—on the rim of the ore pit—the trucks and loaders look like Tonka toys. Up close, they resemble larger-than-life creations for a Star Wars movie.

Copper from the Morenci mines is processed by two methods—conventional reduction mills, and a procedure called solvent extraction, developed recently to leach copper from low grade ore. The tours, which take more than three hours, cover both phases. Guests first see a video about solvent extraction and then they go to the facility itself. Water laced with kerosene and sulfuric acid is sprayed over piles of low-grade copper ore. What comes out is a brilliant blue fluid with a great name—pregnant leach solution. Copper is then reclaimed from the solution through an electrolysis process.

"What we get out of this process is 99.99 percent pure copper," our guide Julio pointed out. "The good thing about it is that we can re-work the old tailings profitably." He should know; he worked here for 42 years.

Big trucks; bigger pit

From the solvent extraction facility, we drove to the lip of the main pit, one of several giant holes being gouged into the earth by dynamite and monster machines. As we stared into the huge cavity, giant ore trucks were tanking up at a nearby fueling facility, taking on 1,200 gallons a gulp. The mine operates around the clock and a tank of fuel lasts about 24 hours. The drivers pull eight hour shifts although the trucks never stop working, except for maintenance. Every few thousand hours, their 16-cylinder diesel engines are changed.

We adjourned to the maintenance facility, where we were able to walk around and under—without ducking—these imposing beasts. They're so tall that mechanics use ladders to perform routine repairs. From there, we were taken into the bottom of the main pit to watch a huge shovel loading one of these trucks with a few swift scoops. The tour ended at the reduction plant, where crushed ore is pulverized to powder, diluted with water and then put through ceramic filters to extract the copper.

Back down in the pit, one of the giant shovels stood quietly with a load of ore in its scoop. It had finished loading a truck and another hadn't yet arrived.

"Somebody better get on the radio and get a truck down there. That shovel sittin' there is costing the company $32 a minute." Even though he was retired, Julio was still a company man.

ATTRACTIONS AND ACTIVITIES

Greenlee Historical Museum • 317 Chase Street, Clifton; (520) 865-3115. Tuesday, Thursday and Saturday 2 to 4:30; free; donations appreciated. ☐ Not fancy but interesting, the museum has the usual pioneer relics plus exhibits and photos of the mining days, which reached their peak early in this century. Of particular interest is a relief map of ore deposits and mines in the area.

☺ **Phelps Dodge mine tour** • *Free tours weekdays at 8:30 and 1:15. Call (520) 865-4521, extension 1435 for reservations, or stop at the Phelps Dodge employment office just above town on Highway 191, opposite the fire station. Tour groups meet at the Morenci Motel 15 minutes prior to departure.* ☐ These three-hour tours of the Morenci Mine operation include the world's second largest open pit mine and various ore processing facilities. Most tour guides are retired mine employees, so they know what they're talking about. (See box on previous page.)

Coronado Trail • Clifton's first visitor was Francisco Coronado, who trekked through here in 1540. The Coronado Trail—Highway 191—follows the *conquistador's* route north through the rugged mountains of Apache-Sitgreaves National Forest. Campgrounds and picnic areas line the winding roadway, and trailheads lure hikers deeper into the wilds. For a map and camping-hiking brochures, stop in at the **district ranger office** at the west end of Clifton, or write Apache-Sitgreaves National Forest, P.O. Box 698, Clifton, AZ 85533; (520) 865-2432.

WHERE TO DINE AND RECLINE

Kopper Kettle Café • ☆ **$$**

☐ *Morenci Plaza; (520) 865-2213. Mexican-American; full bar service. Monday-Friday 5:30 a.m. to 8 p.m., Saturday 5:30 to 2; closed Sunday. MC/VISA.* ☐ Basic, clean diner serving fajitas, chimichangas and other Mexican fare, plus Cajun chicken, steaks and chops; lounge adjacent.

Morenci Restaurant and Lounge • ☆☆ **$$**

☐ *At Morenci Motel; (520) 865-4111. American-Mexican; full bar service. Daily 5 a.m. to 9 p.m. MC/VISA.* ☐ Neat, spacious dining room. The menu includes gringo chicken, steaks and chops plus several Mexican entrées; lounge adjacent.

Morenci Motel • ☆☆ **$$**

☐ *One Burro Alley, Morenci, AZ 85540; (520) 865-4111. Couples $44 to $48, singles $38. MC/VISA.* ☐ Small, modern motel with cable TV; lounge and restaurant (see above).

ALONG THE CORONADO TRAIL

The twisting route north through Apache-Sitgreaves National Forest has a lot of titles. In addition to being U.S. Highway 191, it's the Coronado Trail, an Arizona scenic highway and a National Forest Scenic Byway. It's not quite as spectacular as all these labels suggest, although it's certainly an interesting route as it climbs from arid slopes above Morenci into Ponderosa pine highlands at more than 9,000 feet. The northern reaches offer grand displays of fall color, generally in middle October.

The highway climbs steeply from town, passing more mining gashes, terraced pits, settling ponds and a huge reduction plant. Near the top of a steep spiral, a scenic viewpoint invites you to pull over and see what the hand of man and his machinery can do to the landscape. A sign here identifies the Morenci Mining District as America's leading copper producer. Phelps Dodge had, when this sign was posted in 1993, moved 3.5 billion tons of ore to get at the copper. The rocks also yield gold, molybdenum and silver.

RV ADVISORY ● A sign at the start of this route warns that trucks over 40 feet shouldn't attempt this route. However, carefully driven RVs should be able to make it, despite some hairpin turns and steep spirals. Tank up before leaving Morenci, since a sign advises that the next services are 90 miles; that's in Alpine. Other place names appear on the map along the route, although they do not materialize into towns.

Beyond the Phelps Dodge turnout, the route goes into an even tighter set of spirals, coiling up from dry brushlands into oak-chaparral, juniper-piñon and finally Ponderosa forests. Rocky outcroppings and far away vistas add to the imposing setting. Seekers of solitude will love this area. Despite its scenic appeal, the twisting highway is lightly traveled. Picnic and camping areas are within easy reach, and there are several trailheads for those who brought their hiking shoes. The **Blue Range Primitive Area,** embracing the wooded canyons of the Blue River and its tributaries, lure those who really want to lose themselves.

The highway enters thick evergreen forest as it climbs up the Mogollan Rim, that grand ridge that marks the southern edge of the Colorado Plateau. The rim is more subtle here, cloaked in timber and without the dramatic cliff edges that are evident farther west. About 50 miles north of Morenci, watch on your left for the **Blue Vista Overlook.** From this 9,184-foot ridge on the edge of the Mogollan Rim, you can see forever—in two directions. Signs identify the overlapping peaks and ridges southeast toward New Mexico and west into Arizona. The long blue-gray ridge of Mount Graham is quite evident despite its great distance from here. A sort nature trail leads to other vista points. The views from the trail are no better than those from the parking lot, although it's a nice stroll through the woods; signs identify trees along the way.

Past Blue Vista, quaking aspens line the roadway and marble distant hills, presenting brilliant yellow displays in autumn. About seven miles from the vista point, you reach a bit of settlement: **Hannigan Meadow,** a recreation area with a store (no fuel), lodge, restaurant and campground. Several trails lead from here, and cross country ski trails are kept groomed from December through March. The lodge has rooms for around $65, and a dining room that's open daily from late spring through fall and Thursday through Sunday in winter. Contact Hannigan Meadow Lodge, P.O. Box 335, Alpine, AZ 85920; (520) 339-4370.

The first real community since Morenci, **Alpine** has fuel, lodging, restaurants and other essential services. The town's few stores and houses are littered over a high mountain meadow at the junction of highways 191 and 180. Although you've been losing altitude since Blue Vista, you're still high in the sky; Alpine's elevation is 8,046 feet. For forestry information, stop by the **Alpine Ranger Station,** on the left just past the junction. It's open weekdays 8 to 4:30; (520) 339-4384. The highway straightens out and loses elevation quickly beyond Alpine; the terrain lap-dissolves from Ponderosa to piñon-juniper and then rabbitbrush and other desert flora. Small **Nelson**

Reservoir, behind a rock and earthfill dam, offers a launch ramp, fishing docks and potties, courtesy of the forest service. A bit beyond, a five-mile dirt road leads left to the **Sipe-White Mountain Wildlife Area,** which is primarily an elk preserve. The road is narrow and not too bumpy, should you want to communicate with an elk herd.

Just beyond the wildlife turnoff, you approach the side-by- side towns of Eagar and then Springerville. Eager was named for 1871 settler John T. Eager, not for an ambitious beaver. The spelling has since been changed to "Eagar" for reasons that are lost to historians; maybe there were too many beaver jokes. Turn left from U.S. 180 onto State Route 260, following signs to Eagar. You'll shortly encounter a traffic light, where Eagar's Main Street leads north toward Springerville. However, before heading in that direction, we suggest that you continue straight ahead (west) on Highway 160 for a couple of interesting diversions.

Side trip to South Fork

No, this South Fork isn't a location setting for the old *Dallas* TV series. It's an attractively wooded ranching area on the south fork of the Little Colorado River. After traveling through five miles of bunchgrass prairie from Eagar, turn left at brown and yellow "Museum" sign and follow a chip seal road into the South Fork area. The route takes you from prairie into a handsome shallow wooded canyon.

☺ After just over two miles, fork right into the **South Fork Guest Ranch,** a woodsy resort with hiking, barbecues, horseback riding, fishing, boating and cross country skiing. Within the ranch complex is a delightful early American style restaurant called **Miss Ellie's.** Open to the public as well as South Fork guests, it regularly draws diners from nearby communities. The place is all done up in knotty pine, maple furniture and—a pleasing curiosity—Christmas wreaths. The guest ranch is open year around; Miss Ellie's serves from May through October. (Details under "Where to recline.")

From South Fork, continue straight ahead to X-Diamond Ranch, home to the unusual **Little House Museum.** It displays artifacts and photos of the area's pioneer days, plus early mechanical musical instruments. The museum and adjacent gift shop are open May 25 through Labor Day weekend, with 90-minute tours at 11 and 1:30 Thursday-Saturday and 1:30 only Sunday-Monday (closed Tuesday-Wednesday); by appointment the rest of the year. Adults $4, kids $1.50; (520) 333-2286.

Drive back through South Fork Guest Ranch and, if you need a place to camp, turn right and drive half a mile to **South Fork Campground** of Apache National Forest, with attractive wooded sites and flush potties; no hookups.

Back on Highway 260, you can return to Eagar or continue another few miles west and follow State Route 373 south to **Greer,** a small settlement in a pretty alpine setting. The route takes you through a gently rolling tree plain that's beautiful in fall when aspens add splashes of yellow to the evergreen forests. Founded by Mormons in 1879, Greer is now a popular retreat with several small resorts. Desert Arizonans head here in summer to escape the heat and fish in the Greer Lakes and Little Colorado River. In winter, they can follow several miles of cross country ski trails or commute to the Sunrise Ski Resort, about 15 miles farther west on the Fort Apache Reservation. (See below, on page 361.)

Upon returning to Eagar, turn north at the traffic light onto Main Street and head for Springerville. After a mile or so, the road becomes South Mountain Avenue, to avoid confusing it with Springerville's Main Street, which is perpendicular. Between the two towns, look to the right for the huge Round Valley Enosphere on the campus of **Northland Pioneer College**. This imposing sports and multi-use arena, shaped like a fat flying saucer, is just visible above the trees here, although it's easily seen from other vantage points.

Springerville

Elevation: 6,862 feet   **Population: 1,800**

About the time John T. Eager established what is now Eagar, Henry Springer opened a trading post four miles north. It was granted a post office in 1879 and has since outpaced Eagar to become the commercial center of a large cattle ranching region. The community has that moderately prosperous look typical of a rural trading center.

For the traveler, it can serve as a provisioning stop and base of operations for several area attractions, including two ancient Mogollan Indian ruins. Both can be toured by appointment only. Casa Malpais is a few miles from town, and tours begin at a downtown museum. Raven Site Ruin is off Highway 180/191 between Springerville and St. Johns. Our driving tour of the area will get you to both.

As you enter town from Eagar on Mountain Avenue, turn right onto Main Street, which puts you on U.S. Highway 60. Look to your right (beside a McDonald's) for **Madonna of the Trail**, a larger-than-life statue of a sunbonnet pioneer woman clasping her two children. Erected in 1928, it's one of a dozen identical statues throughout America, sponsored by the Daughters of the American Revolution to mark the country's significant pioneer trails. Highway 60 generally follows the route that early mountain man Jedediah Smith blazed to the Pacific Coast.

A short distance beyond, also on the right, is the **Casa Malpais Archeological Museum** which serves, through reservations, as the gateway to the ruin outside of town. A block beyond, housed in an old yellow school building, is the **Round Valley Chamber of Commerce,** open weekdays 9 to 5; (520) 333-2123. At the chamber, ask about the Renee Cushman Art Collection, which is on display at the local Mormon Church and can be visited by appointment only. A block beyond the chamber, turn right on Zuni Avenue and follow it two blocks up to the small **White Mountain Historical Park,** an outdoor museum with several pioneer buildings. For a nice view of Round Valley and that huge sports Enosphere dome, continue past the historical park a couple of blocks to a vista point adjacent to the town cemetery.

If you plan to visit the **Renee Cushman Art Collection,** return to Main Street, turn right onto Aldrice Burk Street and go a block and a half left to the Springerville LDS Church at 150 N. Aldrice Burk. Back on Main, head west on the combined highways 60/180/191. After about three miles, fork to the right and take 180/191 north toward St. John. Seven miles from the junction, look for a sign indicating **Raven Site** to the right. Go less than a quarter of a mile, turn right at a second Raven Site sign and follow a dirt road about half a mile to the site's headquarters, in a ranch complex. From here, if you've finished with this area, return to Highway 180/191 and head north toward St. Johns.

AREA ATTRACTIONS
In order of appearance

Note: For scheduling purposes, it's best to take the 9 a.m. Casa Malpais tour (about an hour an a half), check out the small historical park in Springerville, and then drive to the Raven Site for an afternoon tour, perhaps having lunch there (served at 12:30).

☺ *Casa Malpais Pueblo* • *Museum at 318 Main Street, open Wednesday-Sunday 9 to 5. Casa Malpais Pueblo tours depart here at 9, 11 and 2:30. Adults $3, seniors and students $2.* ⧠ The storefront visitor center contains a good selection of archaeology and regional history books, plus a few relics from the pueblo site. The real treasure is the site itself, on a volcanic mound about a mile from town and reached only by following your guide. Designated as a national historic site, it was occupied for about 200 years and abandoned around 1400 A.D. Although not large, it's one of the most intriguing such sites in the Southwest. A *New York Times* writer said that "few sites...in North America...have aroused so much curiosity and excitement."

Why all the excitement? The site contains two great mysteries. Its main feature is a huge kiva or ceremonial house, one of the largest in the Southwest. Yet the adjacent pueblo is very small, hardly adequate to support such a large kiva. Scientists theorize that this may have been a regional ceremonial site serving seven pueblos in this area. Mystery number two: A secret underground passage was discovered recently, containing basketry, pottery and more than a hundred skeletons. Such chambers are rare in Southwest archaeological sites. This mystery apparently will remain so. The passage ends at a wall, and officials of the Zuni and Hopi tribes, descendants of the Mogollan, have decreed that the area beyond the wall never be entered.

What visitors see are the four thick walls of the kiva and several pueblo rooms, which are being excavated. Although the site's existence was known to early settlers, little looting has occurred here because of its hilltop location and thick covering of rocky soil.

White Mountain Historical Park • *Zuni at Pima; (520) 333-2552 or (520) 333-4300. Weekdays 1 to 5 Memorial Day through Labor Day weekend; by appointment the rest of the year; admission $1.* ⧠ Several yesterday structures have been reassembled at this outdoor historical park, including a 1915 tourist cabin from a White Mountain resort, several log homes and a granary.

Renee Cushman Art Collection • *Springerville LDS Church, 150 N. Aldrice Burk. Open by appointment; call the chamber or one of these numbers—333-2170, 333-4514 or 333-4687.* ⧠ A fine selection of European art is on display in a three-room museum on the north side of the Mormon Church. Works range from European renaissance masters—including sketches by Rembrandt—to 19th century painters.

☺ *Raven Site Ruin* • *White Mountain Archaeological Center, HC 30, Box 30, St. Johns, AZ 85936; (520) 333-5857. Museum and gift shop open daily May through mid-October 10 to 5. Site tours at 10 and 11 a.m., then hourly from 1 to 4 p.m. Adults $3.50, seniors and students $2.50. Lunch served at 12:30 for $6 and dinner at 6 p.m. for $8.* ⧠ A private foundation was established in the early 1990s to protect and excavate an 800-room Anasazi-Mogollon ruin on a low hill above the Little Colorado River; it's one of the largest in the Southwest. The site had been brutalized by pot hunters for decades; one group even used a back-hoe to gouge at the buried pueblos.

Visitations begin at a ranch complex now serving as the foundation's headquarters. It's a busy place, with a small museum with artifacts from the site, a "chow hall" and a gift shop with several books on archaeology and regional history. Visitors then are directed to the nearby ruin. An informative 40-minute tour takes them to several excavated rooms; only 18 had been uncovered at this writing. This is an active site and visitors often see volunteer adults or school groups working archaeologists. Anyone interested can sign up for one or more days of hands-on work; the program can include meals and lodging. The tour ends at a realistically reconstructed pueblo, where visitors can slip through a narrow door, examine animal skins, pots and other artifacts and smell the spicy aroma of burning sage wood in the fire pit. (Close inspection revealed that it was fed by a Propane log lighter.)

ANNUAL EVENTS

For details on these and other events, contact the Round Valley Chamber of Commerce at (520) 333-2123.

Duck Race down the Little Colorado, early July.

Western Fourth of July Celebration, featuring a Rodeo.

Badlands Muster firemen's competition, mid-August.

WHERE TO DINE

The Red Bandanna Steak House ● ☆☆ $$

◻ 1223 E. Main St,; (520) 333-5465. American and Mexican; full bar service. Sunday-Thursday 11 to 9, Friday-Saturday 11 to 10. MC/VISA. ◻ Lively Western style café offering steaks and ribs, plus assorted Mexican entrées. Live music for dancing on Fridays and Saturdays.

☺ Safire Restaurant & Lounge ● ☆☆☆ $$

◻ Main Street at North Hopi; (520) 333-4512. American; full bar service. Daily 5 a.m. to 9 p.m. MC/VISA. ◻ Very appealing turn-of-the-century style restaurant with print wallpaper, copper drop lamps, brass and glass accents and plush booths. The menu features steaks, chops, chicken and seafood.

WHERE TO RECLINE
Springerville, Greer and South Fork

Greer Lodge ● ☆☆ $$$$

◻ Box 244, Greer, AZ 85927; (520) 735-7216. Couples and singles $60 to $95. ◻ Woodsy lodge and cabins tucked among the trees on the Little Colorado River. Bed & breakfast units and cabins with kitchens and fireplaces. Croquet, volleyball, horseshoes, riding and fishing in summer; skating, cross-country skiing and horse drawn sleigh rides in winter. **Restaurant** serves breakfast, lunch and dinner; entrées $11 to $18; wine and beer.

Reed's Motor Lodge ● ☆☆ $$ Ø

◻ 514 E. Main St., Springerville, AZ 85938; (800) 814-6451 or (520) 333-4323. Couples $32 to $40, singles $26 to $36, family units $52 to $70. Major credit cards. ◻ Attractive knotty pine 50-unit motel with TV movies, and phones, some microwaves and refrigerators; spa, coin laundry, gallery and gift shop, game room, free bicycle use.

South Fork Guest Ranch ● ☆☆ $$$

◻ P.O. Box 627, Springerville, AZ 85938; 333-4455. Cottages $35 to $90 for two to six people. ◻ Comfortably rustic cabins along the Little Colorado River, all with kitchen facilities and utensils; some with fireplaces. Ranch activities include horseback riding, fishing, boating and cross country skiing. **Miss Ellie's Restaurant** serves Monday-Saturday from 5 to 9 p.m. (plus Sundays in summer). The guest ranch is open year around; Miss Ellie's from May through October.

Super 8 Motel ● ☆ $$

☐ *138 W. Main St. (P.O. Box 1568), Springerville, AZ 85938; (520) 333-2655 or (800) 800-8000. Couples $41 to $46, singles $36 to $39, family units from $89. Major credit cards.* ☐ A 41-unit motel with TV movies and room phones; some refrigerators and microwaves; free coffee.

White Mountain Motel ● ☆ $ ∅

☐ *333 E. Main St., Springerville, AZ 85938; (520) 333-5482. Couples $26 to $40, singles $22 to $26, kitchenettes $27 to $40. No credit cards.* ☐ Basic 17-unit motel with room TV.

WHERE TO CAMP

Casa Malpais Campground ● *P.O. Box 726 (Highway 60, a mile west), Springerville, AZ 85938; (520) 333-4632. RV and tent sites; full hookups $16, water and electric $14.50, no hookups $10, camping cabin $18. Reservations accepted.* ☐ Pull-throughs, some shaded sites; showers, coin laundry, mini-mart and gift shop, dump station.

Lyman Lake State Park ● *P.O. Box 1428, St. Johns, AZ 85936 (Hwy. 180/191, 17 miles north of Springerville); (520) 337-4441. RV and tent sites; water and electric $13; no hookups $9.* ☐ Small state park on a reservoir on the Little Colorado River, with water view campsites; some pull-throughs. Flush potties and showers. Also boating, fishing, swimming and hiking; see park listing below.

NORTH TO THE PETRIFIED FOREST

From Springerville, drive three miles west and take the Highway 180/191 fork north toward Holbrook and Petrified Forest National Park. Several miles past the Raven Site turnoff, you'll see an inviting patch of blue in this beige bunchgrass prairie:

☺ **Lyman Lake State Park** ● *P.O. Box 1428, St. Johns, AZ 85936; (520) 337-4441. Day use $3; camping $13 with water and electric, $9 with no hook-ups (see "Where to camp" above).* ☐ Occupying the west shoreline of a reservoir on the Little Colorado River, this 1,180-acre park has camping, picnicking, swimming areas, boating and water skiing, plus a mini-mart and boat rental. Anglers try for planted bass, crappie and northern pike. Although the park is in an arid prairie, rocky outcroppings give it special appeal. A one-mile trail, starting at the campground, winds about a stony peninsula. One segment loops the peninsula shoreline; another takes hikers past several petroglyphs and leads to the top of this low, rugged hill. Park rangers conduct tours of the petroglyph sites in summer.

From Lyman Lake, Highway 191 delivers you to **St. Johns,** a small, ordinary prairie town dressed up a bit by tree-lined residential streets. A Spanish settlement called El Vandido was established here in 1873, then Mormon settlers came in 1879 and changed the name first to San Juan and then the Anglicized St. Johns.

As you drive into town, turn left at a T-intersection opposite St. John's Catholic Church and head west on U.S. 180 (Cleveland Street). A couple of buildings of interest are the brick and stone American Legion Hall on the left and cut stone Apache County Courthouse on the right. A block beyond the courthouse, on the left, is the combined visitor center and museum:

☺ *Apache County Museum and Chamber of Commerce* ● *180 W. Cleveland; (520) 337-2309 or (520) 337-2000. Monday-Friday 9 to 5. Free; contributions appreciated.* ❑ This nice little museum is a cut above most small town archives. Three dioramas portray an early Native American settlement, a ranching scene and downtown St. Johns in the 1880s. Other exhibits include assorted pioneer relics, lace dresses, photos and family trees of early settlers. Particularly interesting is a collection of nasty looking knifes and homemade guns taken from prisoners by the Apache County Sheriff's Department. A corner of the museum functions as the St. Johns Regional Chamber of Commerce visitor center.

Continue west and then northwest on U.S. 180. After 33 miles of bunchgrass desert interrupted occasionally by patches of junipers, you'll arrive at the south entrance to Petrified Forest National Park. Before entering, you'll encounter two elaborate rock and souvenir shops just outside the park gate—Petrified Forest Trading Post and Crystal Forest Museum and Gift Shop. They sell every conceivable petrified gimmick from bolo ties and bookends to polished table tops costing up to $8,500. Both have small museums with exhibits of petrifactions, Indian relics and fossils. Their rocks were gathered outside the park, incidentally. Not all of the petrified trees in this area are within the national park. Many are on private land, feeding a steady flow of souvenirs to gift and rock shops in and outside the park.

RV CAMPING NOTE ● Both rock shops mentioned above offer free overnight parking for self-contained RVs. There are no hookups, although RVers have access to their restrooms.

Petrified Forest & Painted Desert

☺ *Petrified Forest National Park* ● *P.O. Box 2217, Petrified Forest, AZ 86028; (520) 524-6228. Park gates and visitor centers open daily 8 to 5; longer in summer. Fees are $5 per car or $3 per hiker or biker. There are no lodgings or campgrounds within the park. The Rainbow Forest Museum, near the south entrance, has several exhibits on the park and its petrifactions, with a Fred Harvey gift shop and snack bar adjacent. The Painted Desert Visitor Center, just outside the north entrance, has a few museum exhibits and a book shop with a larger Fred Harvey complex that includes a gift shop and cafeteria, plus a service station and post office; open the same hours as the visitor center.* ❑

NOTE: Because of the vulnerability of these petrified wood formations to souvenir hunters, anyone attempting to remove material from the park will face a heavy fine and possibly a jail term.

Scientists say the odds of a tree becoming petrified are about a million to one, yet thousands managed to beat the odds in this high, grassy tableland. Petrified logs are scattered, like broken columns of fallen temples, over the preserve's 93,533 acres. Creation of these stone logs began about 225 million years ago in the late Triassic period when downed trees were washed onto a flood plain. Mud, silt and volcanic ash covered them, cutting off oxygen and slowing their decay. Eventually, ground water saturated with silica seeped in and replaced the wood cells with crystals. Some of the results are remarkably pretty. They have a luminous gemstone quality, with rich yellow, orange, gold and purple in their crystal patterns.

The author sits like a bump on a petrified log on the Giant Logs Trail.

Driving the park

Coming from St. Johns, enter the park's southern gate, follow a 27-mile scenic drive and exit the northern gate, at Interstate 40 about 25 miles east of Holbrook. You actually get two attractions for the price of one. The scenic drive takes you through a section of the **Painted Desert** north of the park. This multi-chromatic desert stretches for 200 miles across Arizona, along the northern edge of the Little Colorado River. Once inside the park, stop first at the **Rainbow Forest Museum,** which has excellent exhibits focusing on the beginnings of dinosaurs, including reconstructions of critters that roamed this area during the Triassic. The **Giant Logs Trail** behind the museum features the park's best examples of petrified trees.

Following the park road north, you can stop at turnouts for assorted points of interest. The first stop comes up immediately beyond Rainbow Forest—the **Long Logs Trail** and **Agate House.** The trail takes you half a mile through petrified logs—some of them long indeed—and past some pretty magenta colored eroded cones and buttes. Agate House is a partial reconstruction of dwelling built of petrified wood by Indians 700 years ago. Farther along the park road at **Jasper Forest,** logs are scattered in the desert sand like remnants of a sloppy lumbering operation. **Agate Bridge** is a remarkable petrified log that not only stayed intact but formed a natural span across a small wash. Supposedly, a cowboy won a $10 bet in 1886 by riding his horse across it. It has since been reinforced with a concrete beam, should anyone else be so tempted. At **Newspaper Rock overlook,** you can view squiggles, spirals, stick-men and hand prints left by some unidentified ancients. Fragmented walls of the **Puerco Indian Pueblo** are all that remain of a village that was occupied about 600 to 800 years ago.

The scenic route crosses over I-40 (no access) and travels six miles through the **Painted Desert** with its multi-colored, soft feminine contours. What you're seeing is an erosion of Chinle Formation clay; it was this same erosion that exposed the fallen stone trees nearby. Several turnouts invite you to pause and admire these splendid formations of magenta, beige, rust, orange, blue-gray and green. The route terminates at the park's north entrance visitor facilities. From here, you can hop onto I-40 and head west.

Holbrook

Elevation: 5,080 feet　　　　　　　　　　**Population: 5,890**

Founded in 1882 as a railroad terminal and ranching center, Holbrook is noted mostly as the gateway to Petrified Forest National Park. A century ago, it was better known as the shipping center for the Aztec Ranch, one of the largest cattle spreads in America. Running 60,000 head over a million acres of open range, it was nicknamed the Hashknife outfit because of its spade-shaped brand. Bad management and falling beef prices shut down the huge operation at the turn of the century.

Holbrook is an ordinary-looking community alongside the Little Colorado River with an old fashioned, clean-swept downtown. It has a few motels and restaurants and a lot of rock shops selling gems, thunder eggs and things petrified. Exit 289 or 286 three miles farther west will get you into downtown Holbrook; the first gives you a larger selection of service stations and motels, if that's important. Both deliver you to Navajo Boulevard, the main business street. Holbrook is the seat of sparsely populated Navajo County. The former yellow brick 1898 courthouse now houses a museum and Chamber of Commerce, which you'll encounter on your left, toward the west end of town:

Courthouse Museum and chamber office ● *100 East Arizona St. (Navajo Street); (520) 524-6558. Weekdays 8 to 5, plus evening hours of 7 to 9 from June through August.* ☐ A counter in the museum serves as the chamber, where you can get the usual brochures and maps. The museum itself, while interesting, is an unprofessional clutter. Its jumbled exhibits include old photos, pioneer relics, tortoise-shell combs, a turn-of-the-century living room, and a scene recreating the card game leading to the naming of Show Low (see below). An old-fashioned pharmacy displays such wonder drugs as Dr. Beaumont's tonic for snake bites, ticks and fleas, pneumonia, rheumatism, blood disorders, senility and fevers—something every travel writer needs. The most interesting exhibit is the original jail in the courthouse basement, where bad guys and Saturday night drunks were locked up; it was used from 1898 until 1976.

Historic downtown tour ● *Brochure available at the chamber.* ☐ Holbrook has a good selection of turn-of-the-century wood frame and stone buildings and this map-guide will lead you past several of them.

ANNUAL EVENTS

For details on these and other events, contact the Holbrook-Petrified Forest Chamber of Commerce at (520) 524-6558.

Pony Express Ride is the re-creation of the gallop from Holbrook to Scottsdale, late January or early February. You can have a letter carried and endorsed by the Pony Express by sending it to the Holbrook postmaster. It should be stamped, marked "Via Pony Express," and enclosed in another letter addressed to: Postmaster, Holbrook, AZ 86025.

Navajo County Fair in late April.

Holbrook Old West Days and Bucket of Blood Bike Races (named for a famous local saloon), mid-May.

Quilt Show and Old Time Fiddlers' Contest, early August.

All Indian Pow Wow, Labor Day weekend.

WHERE TO DINE AND RECLINE

Butterfield Stage Co. Restaurant ● ☆☆ $$

⊡ *609 Hopi Dr. (downtown), Holbrook; (520) 524-3447. American; full bar service. Monday-Saturday 11 to 1:30 and 4 to 10, Sunday 10:30 to 10. MC/VISA, AMEX.* ⊡ Western style restaurant with a stagecoach on display. Steak, prime rib and barbecue specialties; salad bar. Lounge adjacent.

Super 8 Motel ● ☆☆ $$ ∅

⊡ *1989 Navajo Blvd. (I-40 exit 286), Holbrook, AZ 86025; (520) 524-2871 or (800) 843-1991. Couples and singles $46.88 to $49.88, family units $51.88. Major credit cards.* ⊡ TV, phones, free coffee; pool.

Rainbow Inn ● ☆☆ $$ ∅

⊡ *2211 E. Navajo Blvd. (I-40 exit 289), Holbrook, AZ 86025; (800) 551-1923 or (520) 524-2654. Couples $43 to $47, singles $39. Major credit cards.* ⊡ A 40-room motel with TV movies, phones, room refrigerators.

Sahara Inn ● ☆ $$

⊡ *2402 E. Navajo Blvd., Holbrook, AZ 86025; (520) 524-6298. Couples $30, singles $24 to $30, suites $50 to $60. Major credit cards.* ⊡ Basic motel units with TV and room phones; pool.

WHERE TO CAMP

Holbrook KOA ● *102 Hermosa Dr. (I-40 exit 289), Holbrook, AZ 86025; (520) 524-6689. RV and tent sites, $16 to $21, "Kamping Kabins" $27. Reservations accepted; MC/VISA.* ⊡ Some pull-throughs, grassy tent sites; full hookups, TV hookups; showers, playground, rec room, miniature golf, minimart, Propane, dump station. Pancake breakfasts and chuck wagon dinners.

Two souvenir shops outside the south entrance to Petrified Forest National Park offer free overnight parking for self-contained RVs. There are no hookups, although RVers have access to the shops' restrooms.

SOUTH TO THE WHITE MOUNTAINS

Continue along Holbrook's main street across the railroad tracks and the Little Colorado River, following signs to highways 180 and 77 south. State Route 77 continues straight ahead toward Snowflake, returning you shortly to bunchgrass desert. After a dozen miles or so, you can see the hazy blue profiles of the White Mountains ahead. The highway climbs gradually into these hills and you're in a brushy juniper prairie by the time you reach the side-by-side communities of **Snowflake/Taylor,** at 5,630 feet. This surprisingly large complex of more than 4,000 residents stretches for a couple of miles along the highway. By the time you clear Taylor, the road begins to climb the White Mountains in earnest, completing a transition from juniper and sage to evergreens.

Pintail Lake waterfowl refuge, about four miles south of Taylor, is neither a natural lake nor a reservoir. It's a volcanic depression filled with treated water from a sewage facility, which has proven quite satisfactory for water birds. You can watch ducks and other fowl paddle contentedly about their treated water from an observation platform, reached by a short trail.

Show Low and Pinetop-Lakeside

Show Low elevation: 6,300 feet   **Population: 5,410**

Perched on the edge of the Mogollan Rim between the White Mountain Apache Reservation and Sitgreaves National Forest, these three communities have no specific tourist lures, although they're popular as alpine havens. Thousands of Arizonans have been lured to these cool summer heights and many have stayed, or they've built summer cabins. Thus, Show Low, Pinetop and Lakeside are fast growing resort communities. The highway linking them has become a rather untidy string of lodgings, restaurants, service stations and small businesses.

Show Low, the region's commercial center, originally was the hub of a ranching area. The unusual name comes from a low-ball poker expression; if you "show low"—have the lowest cards—you win. It seems that C.E. Cooley and Marion Clark had built up a 100,000-acre cattle spread in the 1870s. After six years, they decided to break up the partnership, and drew cards to see who would buy who out. Cooley drew the deuce of clubs; Clark moved on. Show Low's main drag is called Deuce of Clubs in honor of that draw.

Despite is colorful roots, Show Low offers no historic flavor. The business district is basically three miles of strip malls along Deuce of Clubs. Approaching town on State Route 77, you'll T-bone into that boulevard (U.S. 60). Turn right and, within half a mile, you'll see the junction of State Route 260, which takes you south to Pinetop-Lakeside and the Apache reservation. If you want to pick up some area information, follow the main street through town and you'll see the **Show Low Chamber of Commerce** on your left at 951 W. Deuce of Clubs. It's on the edge of the Northland Pioneer College campus; open weekdays 9 to 5 and weekends 10 to 2; (520) 537-2326.

Having done with Show Low, head south through the pines on Route 260. Between mileposts 347 and 348, watch for signs to the **Mogollon Rim Overlook,** reached by a one-mile nature trail. Signs along the path identify assorted flora, and the overlook provides views down into the thickly wooded Fort Apache reservation. Back on the highway, as you approach the woodsy communities of **Lakeside** and **Pinetop,** you can get forestry information at the **Lakeside Ranger Station** opposite Lakeside Campground. It's open weekdays 8 to 5; (520) 368-5111. The **Pinetop-Lakeside Chamber of Commerce** also is on the highway, at 592 W. White Mountain Blvd.; weekdays 8:30 to 5, Saturday 9 to 3 and Sunday 10 to 3; 367-4290.

ANNUAL EVENTS

For details, contact the Pinetop-Lakeside Chamber of Commerce at (520) 367-4290 or the Show Low Chamber of Commerce at (520) 537-2326.

Mountain Frontier Days, late June in Pinetop-Lakeside.

Square Dance Festival, mid-July in Show Low.

White Mountain Native American Art Festival, late July.

White Mountain Bluegrass Festival, mid-August, Pinetop- Lakeside.

WHERE TO DINE

Branding Iron Steak House ● ☆☆ $$

❑ *1261 E. Deuce of Clubs, Show Low; (520) 537-5151. American; full bar service. Lunch daily 11 to 2 daily, dinner Sunday-Thursday 5 to 9 and Friday-Saturday 5 to 10. MC/VISA.* ❑ Western style place with Native American artwork; specializing in prime rib, steak and seafood; Cowboy Bar adjacent.

Charlie's Steakhouse ● ☆☆ $$

☐ *Highway 260 (near First Interstate Bank), Pinetop; (520) 367-4900. American; full bar service. Daily 5 p.m. to 10 in summer, closed Mondays in winter. MC/VISA.* ☐ Locally popular place with hick Western atmosphere, serving steaks, seafood, ribs and prime rib

Casa Territorial ● ☆☆ $$

☐ *454 White Mountain Blvd., Pinetop; (520) 367-5050. Contemporary Mexican; full bar service. Daily 11 to 9:30; MC/VISA.* ☐ Cheerfully decorated Mexican *cantina* featuring fajitas, chimichangas, enchiladas and such.

WHERE TO RECLINE

Hidden Rest Resort ● ☆☆☆ $$

☐ *Off Highway 260, Route 3, Box 2590, Lakeside, AZ 85929; (800) 260-REST or (520) 368-6336. Couples and singles $45 to $82. MC/VISA, DISC.* ☐ Furnished knotty pine cabins, microwaves, TV and fireplaces; some spas.

KC Motel ● ☆☆ $$ ∅

☐ *60 W. Deuce of Clubs (downtown), P.O. Box 175, Show Low, AZ 85901; (800) 531-7152 or (520) 537-4433. Couples $45 to $62, singles $42 to $58. Major credit cards.* ☐ Large rooms with TV movies, phones and refrigerators; some suites; spa, free coffee.

Lake of the Woods Resort ● ☆☆☆ $$$

☐ *2244 White Mountain Blvd. (Highway 260), P.O. Box 777, Lakeside, AZ 85929; (520) 368-5353. All kitchenettes, $64 to $241 for two to ten people. MC/VISA.* ☐ Fully equipped housekeeping cabins, one to five bedrooms, with fireplaces; some with private boat docks. On a private trout fishing lake; boat rentals, playground, shuffleboard, horseshoes, spa and sauna.

The Pines ● ☆☆☆ $$$$ ∅

☐ *2700 S. White Mountain Rd. (Highway 260), Show Low, AZ 85901; (800) BEDTIME or (520) 537-1888. All condo units; one bedroom $69 to $89, two bedroom $89 to $109, three bedroom $109 to $119. Major credit cards.* ☐ Resort in woodsy setting; fully equipped condos with kitchens, fireplaces, spas, laundry facilities and barbecues.

WHERE TO CAMP

Camp Town ● *1221 W. McNeil St. (half mile west from Highway 60), Show Low, AZ 85901; (520) 537-2578. RV and tent sites, $15 with or without hookups. No credit cards.* ☐ Shaded sites in piney forest, some pull-throughs; showers, coin laundry; shuffleboard, horseshoes, golf chipping green.

Ponderosa Mobile Home Park ● *Route 1, Box 570 (144 Woodland Road), Lakeside, AZ 85929; (520) 368-6989. RV sites, full hookups $15. No credit cards.* ☐ Adult park with clubhouse, pool tables, card games, potlucks and other activities. Showers, coin laundry, Propane.

The Apache Nation

The Fort Apache Indian Reservation occupies one of the most scenic alpine areas of any Native American land in the country. Also called the White Mountain Reservation, it's Arizona's third largest after the Navajo-Hopi and Tohono O'odham. It sprawls over 1,664,872 acres of foothills, valleys and peaks of the White Mountains. More than 30 campgrounds offer 1,000 campsites; 25 lakes and streams are stocked with trout. Three lakes—Hon-Dah, Hawley and Reservation—have cabins, groceries, boat rentals and such. The reservation is home to **Sunrise,** probably Arizona's best ski resort. With all of this, the White Mountain Reservation has been called "the largest privately-held recreation area in America."

Modestly priced permits are required for most activities, including hunting, fishing, boating and camping. For information on permits and various activities available, contact: White Mountain Apache Enterprises, P.O. Box 220, Whiteriver, AZ 85941; (520) 338-4385 or (520) 338-4386. Since this is Native American land, a state hunting or fishing license isn't required; tribal permits serve that purpose.

Entering the Apache nation from Pinetop-Lakeside, you quickly encounter the thriving community of Hon Dah. What makes it thrive is the new **Hon-Dah Casino** at the junction of highways 260 and 73. It contains the usual ranks of slots and video poker machines, plus keno and a small snack bar. The complex also includes a service station, mini-mart and Hon-Dah RV Park with tree shaded sites; $17 for full hookups with phone and TV; 369-7400.

If you head east on State Route 260, you'll pass through the hamlet of **McNary,** little more than a handful of houses scattered in the woods. The highway travels 18 miles through a rolling tree plain to the Apache Nation's major visitor attraction:

☺ *Sunrise Park Resort* ● ☆☆☆ $$$

☐ *P.O. Box 217, McNary, AZ 85930; (800) 55-HOTEL or (520) 735-7676; snow report (800) 772-SNOW. Couples $56 to $110, suites $190 to $280. Ski packages with two nights lodging and two-lift tickets from $184 per couple. Lift tickets $29 all day, $23 half day and $15 for night skiing; senior lift tickets $10, age 70 and over ski free.* ☐ Sunrise is a year around resort with a full service hotel, including a restaurant, fireplace lounge, swimming pool, spa and a lake for swimming, sailing and fishing. In winter, it becomes one of the Southwest's largest ski areas with eleven lifts, 1,800 vertical feet and 65 trails on three mountains. Sunrise also has cross country skiing, snowmobile tours, sledding and tubing.

Back in Hon Dah, head south on State Route 73, following the wooded White River canyon to **Whiteriver.** It's the reservation's administrative and commercial center with a shopping complex and a motel-restaurant. At the tribal office here, you can get recreational information and permits. You also can dine and spend the night:

White Mountain Apache Motel and Restaurant ● ☆☆ $$

☐ *P.O. Box 1149, Whiteriver, AZ 85941; (520) 338-4927. Couples and singles from $50. MC/VISA.* ☐ Modern rooms with two double beds, TV. **Restaurant** serves 6 a.m. to 9 p.m.; American, Mexican and Indian fare; weekday noon and evening buffets; dinners $6 to $12.

Three miles below Whiteriver, you'll encounter what's left of a once legendary army post—**Fort Apache.** Now a small Indian community of weathered homes, it bears no resemblance to the Fort Apache made famous by Hollywood. A few shabby structures of the original fort survive, and it has been designated as a National Historic Park. Among surviving buildings are the imposing red brick Theodore Roosevelt Indian Boarding School, the 1871 commanding officers' quarters, an adobe adjutant's office and a few buildings along officers' row.

Apache Cultural Center ● *Fort Apache; (520) 338-4625. Monday-Friday 7:30 to 4:30 in summer, 8 to 5 the rest of the year. Free; donations appreciated.* ☐ In an ironic twist of history, a tattered log building that once housed

Geronimo pursuer General George Crook now shelters this small cultural museum. It displays some nice Apache beadwork, basketry and other crafts. Graphics and photos tell the story of the Apaches of yesterday and today. A drive is underway to build a new museum, which may be in place by the time you arrive.

From Fort Apache, Highway 73 swings west, taking you eight miles to the turnoff for **Kinishba Ruins.** Two miles off the highway, this crumbling but still intact adobe dates from 1300. It's too fragile to be entered but you can view it from outside. This is all that remains of a huge complex that once contained 700 rooms. University of Arizona researchers excavated a rich find of pottery, jewelry and other artifacts here during the 1930s.

A dozen miles from the Kinishba turnoff, Highway 73 terminates into U.S. 60. Follow it five miles south and then go northwest 14 miles to the remote Apache hamlet of **Cibecue.** There's not much to see here but you can hike, camp and picnic along Cibecue Creek, with a permit available from the Apache Traders store here. The Cibecue are a tiny band that once figured prominently in Apache history. A medicine man who taught a religion predicting expulsion of the whites was killed in 1880 when army troops tried to arrest him. The army's own Apache scouts mutinied and killed several soldiers. It was the only such revolt in the 75-year history of the Apache scout corps. The Cibecue incident sent a wave of unrest through the already restless Chiricahua Apaches on the San Carlos Reservation. It led eventually to Geronimo's departure to resume his campaign against the army.

South of the Cibecue, Highway 60 enters the 1,853,841-acre San Carlos Indian Reservation. It was here, in the arid Gila River Valley that Geronimo and his Chiricahua followers were crowded with other Apache tribes. Twice, he bolted to resume his long guerrilla war with the U.S. Army (see Chapter 11, page 335). A town named in his honor, 45 miles southeast of Globe, is now completely abandoned.

☺ A dozen miles below the Cibecue turnoff, you'll traverse the spectacular **Salt River Canyon.** The highway ribbons dizzily down into this rugged, terraced chasm, crosses the Salt River, then winds back up the other side. The rough-hewn peaks, buttes and fluted ridges with their wooded alluvial skirts rival Oak Creek Canyon in grandeur. Several turnouts and picnic spots along the way tempt you to spend more time admiring one of Arizona's most impressive ravines. The canyon crossing consumes ten twisting miles. Beyond it, you continue traveling through wild, remote and mountainous countryside until you approach a pair of old and still active mining camps.

Globe-Miami

Elevation: 3,544 feet   **Population: 6,265**

Set in the arid Cobre Valley, Globe is an old copper town with a turn-of-the-century main street, complete with an old fashioned J.C. Penney Store. Neighboring Miami has a similar old style downtown although it's a bit more weathered. Some of Globe's structures were "modernized" during the 30s to 50s decades, while Miami still retains its yesterday look. However, these are historic façades. Both are active communities, thanks to ongoing copper mining operations. The twin towns offer a good base for exploring the surrounding mountains and Indian reservations and Globe has one of the West's finest Indian archaeological sites. Tailing dumps and slag heaps tell of those busy days when eager men dug into these rough hills for their fortunes. But at least someone has a sense of humor about this brutalized landscape. They've erected three dummy camels that appear to be trudging up the barren slope of a large tailing dump between the two towns.

The seat of Gila County, Globe started life in 1886 after prospectors found silver on the Apache reservation. Their activities irritated the Indians, so the government merely carved off that chunk of the reservation and a town was laid out. The name Globe comes from a rounded silver nugget found in the area, with markings resembling the continents. The silver soon ran out, then rich copper deposits were discovered. The Depression shut down the mines, and Globe went to sleep until copper operations resumed several years ago.

Miami was established in 1907 at the site of a copper find. There are two versions for the name of this town, which bears not the slightest resemblance to the original Miami. Some historians say it was named for Miami, Ohio, not Florida. We prefer the second story—founder Black Jack Newman named it Camp Mima after his fiancé Mima Tune. Then it was distorted into "Miami" when the town was incorporated in 1918. The Cyprus-Miami Mining Corporation is still digging copper here.

Coming into Globe on Highway 60, you'll hit a stop light a Ash Street; turn right to follow the highway west into town. We're going to suggest touring the area backward since the well stocked **Greater Globe-Miami Chamber of Commerce** office is a mile and a half west, between the two towns. It's open weekdays 8 to 5 and Saturdays 8 to 2; (520) 425-4495. You can pick up, among other things, walking tour maps of old Globe and suggested area drives. To get there, stay on Highway 60, which bypasses old downtown on a viaduct. Your route becomes North Broad Street and you'll see the chamber on your left at 1360 North Broad; watch for the time and temperature sign. Next door, the **Gila County Historical Museum** occupies an old mine rescue station. The chamber office has RV parking in back.

Armed with proper directions, reverse your route on North Broad and, at the first traffic signal, turn left to get onto downtown Broad Street. This takes you past the old brick and masonry of the historic district. Note, among other interesting buildings, the **Gila County Courthouse** at Broad and Oak, now housing the Cobre Valley Center for the Arts. When you've finished with downtown, continue east on Broad, following signs to the excellent **Besh-Ba-Gowah Archaeological Park**. After a few blocks, watch for a sign directing you to the right across a railroad track. You'll pass through a residential area and then climb a low hill occupied by the archaeological park and the Globe Community Center.

RV PARKING ADVISORY ● The museum parking lot will accommodate small RVs. Larger ones can use a double parking space at the community center, which is a short walk away.

From the archaeological park, return to Broad and stay with it until it blends back into North Broad (westbound Highway 60). As you pass through the hamlet of **Claypool**, you'll head toward what appears to be a massive wall. It is instead a chalky white tailing dump, and Miami lies just beyond. To check out its old downtown district, drive past an abandoned smelter and turn right onto either Keystone or Miami street. When you've finished with this area, return to Claypool and turn north on State Route 88, headed past Roosevelt Lake to Payson.

A Salado Indian pueblo interior has been realistically created at Besh-Ba-Gowah Archaeological Park in Globe.

ATTRACTIONS
In order of appearance

Gila County Historical Museum • *1330 N. Broad St. (Highway 60, north of town), Globe; (520) 425-7385. Monday-Saturday 10 to 4. Free; donations appreciated.* ⌑ The museum occupies a 1914 Spanish style bungalow that served as the Dominion Mine rescue station. Exhibits include a furnished turn- of-the-century miner's cabin, a tack room with saddles and other cowboy stuff, an early bedroom setting with some floor-length dresses, a wet-plate camera and other relics. A vintage Seagrave fire engine, currently being restored, may be on display by the time you stop by.

Cobre Valley Center for the Arts • *100 Broad Street at Oak in the old Gila County Courthouse; (520) 425-0884.* ⌑ This sturdy brick, vaguely Spanish-style structure, completed in 1907, is the focal point of the downtown historic district. It contains art galleries and shops and a theater for the Copper Cities Community Players.

☺ **Besh-Ba-Gowah Archaeological Park** • *Near Globe Community center, a mile southwest of town, off Jesse Hayes Road; (520) 425-0320. Daily 9 to 5; adults $2, kids 12 and under free.* ⌑ Archaeologists and craftsmen have recreated Arizona's most realistic ancient Indian dwellings at Besh-Ba-Gowah. They're so believable that you almost expect to be greeted by the ghost of an occupant—hopefully a friendly one. Climb a rough wooden ladder and peer into a second-floor room where pottery, gourds, ears of corn and a plant fiber whisk broom are arranged as they might have been 600 years ago. A pot hangs over the fire pit and a loom with a half-finished blanket stands in a corner. In another area, a cutaway shows precisely how the roof was constructed of poles, yucca fiber, reed matting and mud. An adjacent museum has fine graphics and implements of the Salado people who occupied this pueblo. An advanced hunting and gathering band, they inhabited this area from 1100 to 1400 A.D. They were accomplished potters and weavers; the results of their handiwork are on display in the museum.

Historic downtown Miami • *Town Hall information desk is on Keystone Avenue, open 8:30 to 12 and 1 to 5; (520) 473-4403.* ❑ A walking map available at the Town Hall will direct you past Miami's historic structures.

ANNUAL EVENTS

For details on these and other events, contact the Greater Globe-Miami Chamber of Commerce at (800) 448-8983 or (520) 425-4495.

Gila County Gem and Mineral Show, last weekend of January.

Historic Home and Building Tour and antique show, third weekend of February.

Copper Dust Stampede, early April.

Old Time Fiddlers' Contest, late July.

Apache Day Celebration, third weekend of October.

Harvest Festival at Besh-Ba-Gowah, late October.

WHERE TO DINE

☺ **Blue Ribbon Café** • ☆☆ **$**

❑ *474 N. Broad; (520) 425-4423. American. Weekdays 6:30 a.m. to 9 p.m., Saturday 7:30 to 9, Sunday 7:30 to 8. MC/VISA.* ❑ Appealing café specializing in old fashioned fare, such as dinners with biscuits and gravy and home made pie. A specialty is the Cornish pastie, a beef, potato and onion pastry brought to America by Cornish miners.

Country Kitchen • ☆☆ **$**

❑ *Ash at South; (520) 425-2137. American regional; wine and beer. Daily 5:30 a.m. to 9 p.m. Major credit cards.* ❑ A franchised café with formula early American décor such as drop lamps, print wallpaper and Casablanca fans. The menu features regional specialties including chicken fajitas, old fashioned fried chicken and meatloaf.

Jerry's Restaurant • ☆☆ **$**

❑ *699 E. Ash St.; (520) 425-5282. American; no alcohol. Open 24 hours. MC/VISA, AMEX.* ❑ Family style restaurant serving steaks, seafood, meatloaf and other typical American fare, plus some Mexican entrées.

Irene's Real Mexican Food • ☆☆ **$**

❑ *1601 E. Ash; (520) 425-7904. Mexican-American; wine and beer. MC/VISA.* ❑ Long established café, now housed in a neat and prim new building with Spanish arch windows and comfortable booths. It offers assorted Mexican fare plus American steaks, seafood and hamburgers. Hot wings and *meneudo* are specialties.

WHERE TO RECLINE

Best Western Copper Hills Inn • ☆☆ **$$$** Ø

❑ *Route 1, Box 506 (Highway 60/70), Miami, AZ 85539; (800) 825-7151 or (520) 425-7151. Couples $62 to $75, singles $57 to $62, family units $85* to $105. *Major credit cards.* ☐ A 68-unit motel with TV movies and phones; free coffee, pool, gift shop, beauty salon. **Copper Hills Restaurant** and coffee shop serve 5 a.m. to 9 p.m., dinners $5 to $19; full bar service.

Cloud Nine Motel ● ☆☆ $$$ Ø

☐ *1699 E. Ash (Highways 60 and 70), P.O. Box 1043, Globe, AZ 85502; (520) 425-5741. Couples $52 to $55, singles $47 to $59, family units $62 to $85. Major credit cards.* ☐ A 71-room motel with TV movies, phones, some refrigerators and spa tubs; pool, spa.

El Rey Motel ● ☆ $$

☐ *1201 Ash St. (Highways 60 and 70), Globe, AZ 85502; (520) 425-4427. Couples $33 to $37, singles $25 to $27.* ☐ A 23-unit motel with TV, room phones; playground, picnic area; RV parking with no hookups.

NORTH TO PAYSON AND THE RIM

Traveling north on State Route 88, you're heading for Payson and a slice of the Mogollon Rim made famous by author Zane Grey. Designated as the Apache Trail Scenic Highway, it initially traverses an area of rural homes and mobile home parks. After a few miles, it lives up to its scenic billing, entering rough hill country dotted with saguaro cactus. Steep peaks and fluted ridges of the Apache Mountains mark the eastern skyline.

About 15 miles from Globe-Miami, the highway tops a rise and **Roosevelt Lake** appears before you: a ragged blue jewel in a mountain-rimmed desert basin. Keep left at a junction to follow the highway past the lake and Tonto National Monument, which we explored in detail in Chapter 8. Pressing northwest, the highway breezes through tiny **Punkin Center** and **Jake's Corner.** It then begins climbing out of a desert saguaro garden and into patches of junipers as it approaches a Payson. You first pass through tiny **Rye,** consisting mostly of a concentration of highway billboards. Just before reaching Payson, the highway tops a rise, offering a fine view of the Mogollon Rim. This high, pinkish cliff face, clearly marking the abrupt faulting of the Colorado Plateau, extends west to east from horizon to horizon.

Payson

Elevation: 4,930 feet   **Population: 6,500**

Payson first saw life in 1881 when prospectors found a bit of gold. But it was only a small bit, so the town—named by the first postmaster in honor of Senator Louis Payson to repay a political favor—grew up as a ranching center. Author Zane Grey loved the timbered land below the Mogollon Rim and built a hunting cabin about 20 miles northeast of town. Although he was never a permanent resident, he made frequent extended visits during the 1920s to hunt, fish, hike and write. He penned eleven of his 56 Western novels here. The Mogollon became the "Tonto Rim" in several of his books—a name still used hereabouts. Unfortunately, a reconstruction of his cabin, which was popular with tourists, burned in a 1990 forest fire.

Arrayed rather casually over juniper covered hills, Payson is now a commercial center and recreation area for folks drawn to the surrounding Tonto National Forest. It's also popular with retirees and several new subdivisions are a-building. Little of the original settlement remains. Modern Payson is mostly a commercial strip along State Route 97, called the Beeline Highway. It apparently earned its name because residents of Phoenix make a beeline to these cool juniper shaded heights to escape summer heat.

The first item of interest you'll encounter, just outside the city limits and on a small patch of the Tonto Apache Reservation, is the imposing **Matazal Casino**. It's done up in cut stone and dressed in bright Indian headdress design. The casino has the usual regiments of slots and video poker machines, plus a poker parlor, bingo parlor, keno, bar and restaurant, gift shop and kids' video game parlor.

Pressing through a string of motels and service stations, you'll see the **Payson Chamber of Commerce,** on your left in a brown wooden structure at Route 87 and Main Street. It's open weekdays 8 to 5 and weekends 10 to 2; (520) 474-4515. Turn left onto Main and follow it to the town's two museums. This isn't a typical main street, since it's lined mostly with small strip malls and an occasional open field. A small one-block stretch of false front stores—some occupied, some empty—are all that remain of old Payson. The first museum, part of an upstairs art gallery, is about a quarter of a mile from the chamber on the right; the second is a mile from the chamber, on the left, just beyond the brief old town section.

Zane Grey Museum ● In the Counseller Art Gallery, 408 W. Main St., Suite 8, Payson, AZ 85541; (520) 474-6243. Thursday-Tuesday 10 to 5; closed Wednesday; free. ◻ This small second floor gallery has several Zane Grey exhibits, plus Arizona books, collector books (Greys' and others), Western art and videos.

☺ *Museum of the Forest* ● 1001 W. Main St., Payson, AZ 85541; (520) 474-1541. Wednesday-Sunday noon to 4; $1. ◻ A statue of a woodsman out front marks this small, rather casually arrayed museum. Again, Zane Grey is a focus here, with several photos of the author hunting, fishing and hanging out with his buddies, plus displays of his writings and old posters of the many Western movies based on his books. Other exhibits include a blacksmith shop, a model of a late 1800s sawmill and some unusual miniatures of old farm equipment.

For information on **Tonto National Forest,** head for the district office about half a mile east of town on Highway 260. It's open weekdays 8 to 5; (520) 474-2269.

ANNUAL EVENTS

For details on these and other events, contact the Payson Chamber of Commerce at (520) 474-4515.

Payson Arts & Crafts Festival, late May.

Loggers, Blues and Crafts Festival, mid-July.

Payson Rodeo, second weekend in August (claiming, along with Prescott's, to be the oldest in the state).

Pine County Fair, mid-September.

WHERE TO DINE

Country Kitchen Restaurant ● ☆ *$*

◻ *210 E. Highway 260 (Walmart Shopping Center), Payson; (520) 474-1332. American; full bar service. Daily 6 a.m. to 10 p.m. MC/VISA.* ◻ Family restaurant serving homestyle American fare.

Heritage House Garden Tea Room ● ☆☆ *$*

◻ *202 W. Main Street, Payson; (520) 474-5501. Lunches only; weekdays 11 to 3. MC/VISA.* ◻ An attractive tea room in a 1925 tree-shaded bungalow with an outside patio; sandwiches, soups and salads.

Mario's Restaurant ● ☆☆ $

⊓ 600 E. Highway 260 (just east of Walmart), Payson; (520) 474-5429. *Italian and American; full bar service. Daily 10:30 to 9. MC/VISA, AMEX.* ⊓ Specialties include homemade lasagna and bread, pizzas, plus steaks and ribs. Adjoining lounge with off-track betting.

Ox Bow Inn ● ☆ $$

⊓ 607 W. Main St. (in old town area); (520) 474-8585. *American; full bar service. Daily noon to 10 p.m. No credit cards; personal checks accepted.* ⊓ This Western style café is more interesting outside than in, housed in a sturdy stone and log building. Heavy beam ceilings accent an otherwise spartan interior where steaks, pork chops, barbecued chicken and daily specials are served.

WHERE TO RECLINE

Best Western Paysonglo Lodge ● ☆☆☆ $$$ Ø

⊓ 1005 S. Beeline Hwy. (downtown), Payson, AZ 85541; (520) 474-2382. *Couples and singles $55 to $110. Major credit cards.* ⊓ Nicely kept 32-room motel with TV movies, phones, refrigerators, some fireplaces; pool, spa.

Holiday Inn Express ● ☆☆ $$$ Ø

⊓ P.O. Box 279 (206 S. Beeline Highway), Payson, AZ 85541; (800) HOLIDAY or (520) 472-7484. *Couples $59 to $129, singles $49 to $99, suites and family units $89 to $159; rates include continental breakfast. Major credit cards.* ⊓ Well-kept 44-unit lodge with TV and phones, some refrigerators, microwaves and spa tubs. Pool, spa and coin laundry.

Payson Pueblo Inn ● ☆☆☆ $$ Ø

⊓ 809 E. Highway 260 (half mile east of Highway 87), Payson, AZ 85541; (800) 888-9828 or (520) 474-5241. *Couples $44 to $59, singles $39 to $54. Major credit cards.* ⊓ A 39-unit motel with TV movies, phones, free coffee, refrigerators; some spa tubs; picnic areas.

NORTH TO THE RIM

North of Payson, Highway 87 continues toward the Mogollon Rim, passing from juniper into thick evergreen and oak country. About ten miles from town, a left turn takes you three miles across rolling forest land and then down into a thickly wooded ravine for a look at an historic lodge near a huge travertine arch.

☺ **Tonto Natural Bridge State Park** ● *P.O. Box 1245, Payson, AZ 85547; (520) 476-4202. Daily 8 to 6 April through October and 9 to 5 the rest of the year; $5 per car. For lodge tours call (520) 476-2264.* ⊓ The story goes that prospector Dave Gowan was chased into this rugged creek canyon by Apaches in 1877, and in his flight he discovered a huge travertine arch. Later, he convinced his nephew to come to America from Scotland and build a vacation retreat here. It operated under assorted owners until it was purchased recently by the state.

The wooden three-story lodge, built in 1927 and restored in 1987, doesn't overlook the arch, which is deep in a nearby creek canyon. It serves now as park headquarters and visitors can admire its grand main parlor with lofty ceilings, fireplace and print wallpaper hung with game trophies. Tours of the refurbished upstairs guest rooms can be arranged.

To reach the arch, go to the lower end of a large parking lot below the lodge and follow the McGowan Trail, which stair steps in a loop down to the base of the arch and back up. The Waterfall Trail, also mostly stairs, leads beneath a filmy drizzle from a travertine overhang—a fine place to be on a hot day. The Pine Creek Trail—misnamed, we think—is mostly a difficult boulder scramble along the rocky creek bottom. Those willing to struggle over rocks the size of mini-vans will eventually reach the arch. Incidentally, Tonto Natural Bridge isn't a free-standing arch, but more of a thick ridge with a hole through it.

North of here, the highway completes its climb up the Mogollan Rim, passing through the hamlets of **Pine** and **Strawberry.** They have no specific lures other than their woodsy settings, with a few lodges and motels for those who want to linger longer. The rim itself resembles an ordinary forested ridge here, although closer inspection reveals that it is indeed a wall that—unlike most ridges—is remarkably flat on top.

As you approach the top of the plateau, watch for the **Mogollon Rim Road** (Forest Road 300) that hugs the edge of the rim for about a hundred miles. It's gravel and dirt and generally well maintained, navigable by passenger cars and probably by carefully driven RVs. It starts near milepost 281, travels about 45 miles east and merges with State Route 260 between Kohls Ranch and Forest Lake; the last few miles are paved. It picks up again just east of Forest Lake and continues toward Show Low, hitting U.S. 60 five miles south of town. Before venturing forth, check with a forest service office for current conditions. Don't try the road during or after a rainstorm, and it's usually closed by snow in winter.

Meanwhile, as you persist northward on Highway 87, you'll leave the trees in favor of bunchgrass desert and wind up in **Winslow** on Interstate 40, which we visited in Chapter five. Staying with the highway will take you to Homol'ovi Ruins State Park, Little Painted Desert County Park and eventually into the next chapter.

INDIAN COUNTRY

Chapter thirteen

HOPI-NAVAJO CORNER
Exploring Four Corners country

THE GREAT HOPI-NAVAJO reservations in northeastern Arizona encompass some of the state's most interesting terrain, from starkly beautiful canyons to netherworld sandstone spires. They also provide an opportunity to witness two proud nations in transition—working to preserve their old ways while embracing many of our new ones.

The combined reservations cover about 29,000 square miles, encompassing all of northeastern Arizona and spilling over into Utah and New Mexico. That's nearly as big as New Hampshire, Vermont, Massachusetts and Connecticut combined.

The Navajo reservation, largest in America, covers 25,000 square miles. The Hopi reservation is much smaller, about 4,000 square miles. By an unfortunate whim of the federal government, Hopi turf is entirely surrounded by the Navajo reservation. The Hopi Nation does, however, encompass some of the tribe's ancestral lands. One pueblo, Old Oraibi, has existed for more than 800 years. Dating from 1150 A.D., it may be the oldest continually occupied settlement in America. Navajos are America's largest Indian tribe, numbering about 150,000 on the reservation, with several thousand more living elsewhere. Hopi population on the reservation is around 10,000. Navajos tend to live on their ranches and farms, while the Hopi prefer village life—commuting to the their agricultural lands.

TRIP PLANNER

WHEN TO GO ● Summers are busy in the tourist areas; reservations at the few motels should be made several months in advance. Campgrounds fill early. We prefer the spring and fall, when the weather is cool but not cold. Of course, many special events occur in the summers, but Hopi ceremonial dances are held year around. Some small gift shops—particularly in the Hopi pueblos—keep regular hours only in the summer, but larger ones are open all year. The reservations occupy a high plateau, offering warm summers and cool to cold winters. Expect an occasional dusting of snow if you visit in winter, although it rarely hangs around long.

WHAT TO SEE ● Hopi Cultural Center and Museum; Hubbell Trading Post National Historic Site; Navajo Tribal Museum in Window Rock; Canyon de Chelly National Monument; Monument Valley Tribal Park and Navajo National Monument.

WHAT TO DO ● Explore—politely—the ancient Hopi Villages; hike the White House Ruins trail at Canyon de Chelly National Monument; spread yourself into four states at Four Corners Monument; take a guided tour of Monument Valley; sign up for a hike to Keet Seel ruin in Navajo National Monument.

☺ *Indicates an attraction, restaurant or lodging with special appeal.*

USEFUL CONTACTS

Navajoland Tourism, P.O. Box 663, Window Rock, AZ 86515; (520) 871-6659 or (520) 871-6436 or (520) 6659.

Office of Public Relations, The Hopi Tribe, P.O. Box 123, Kykotsmovi, AZ 86039; (520) 734-2331, ext. 360.

AREA RADIO STATIONS

The Navajo-Hopi nations are served by powerful KTNN at AM-660 out of Window Rock. You'll get Indian news (and a chance to hear the fascinating Navajo language), Arizona and network news and plenty of "hit kickin' country music"—which must be said carefully.

As you travel, you'll pick up these stations on the reservation perimeter:

KXAZ-FM, 93.5, Page—Easy listening and new wave.
KMGN-FM, 93.9, Flagstaff—pop, light rock and country.
KAFF-FM, 92.9 Flagstaff—country.
KNAU-FM, 89.7, Flagstaff—National Public Radio.
KTLF-FM, 99.1, Gallup, N.M.—country, light rock.
KIWN-FM 92.9, Farmington, N.M.—light rock, pop, oldies.

When you enter reservation lands, you technically leave Arizona and enter sovereign nations. You don't need a passport, of course, and both tribes welcome visitors. But they are self governing and some of their laws differ from those outside. Alcohol is prohibited in Hopi-Navajo land; you cannot buy a drink at any reservation establishment or a can of beer in a market. As on other reservations, permits are required for hunting or fishing, and you don't need Arizona licenses. These permits are readily available through tribal offices and at some trading posts and stores; fees are modest. Safety belt use is required, as it is in the rest of the state. Navajo police use radar to enforce the speed limit, although they aren't fanatics about it.

Here's a point of minor confusion: Arizona does not switch to daylight saving time, and neither does the Hopi Nation, but the Navajo Nation does.

The Hopi-Navajo terrain may surprise you. Much of it is barren grassland, punctuated by startling scenery. Canyon de Chelly is one of the most interesting chasms we've ever seen; Monument Valley looks even more dramatic than it appears in photos. After you've driven for hours, seeing nothing but an occasional farmhouse, a great redwall butte may appear on the horizon or a cathedral-like spire may crop up in a pasture. Don't expect quaint Indian villages. You'll see occasional log and mud hogans and some modern ones made of lumber. However, most Navajo towns differ little from ours.

Shopping ● Navajos have long been noted for their artistry with hand-woven wool blankets and turquoise and silver jewelry—particularly the squash-blossom necklace. The Hopi produce fine basketry, pottery, silver jewelry and detailed, brightly-colored *kachina* (or *katsina*) dolls, carefully whittled out of cottonwood. Traditional *kachinas* are regarded as spiritual messengers. Navajo and Hopi artistry, like all native crafts, has been altered by the tourist market. The Navajo turquoise and silver jewelry trade actually was created in the late 1800s by the Fred Harvey Company. Don't be surprised to see a Levi-clad Hopi *kachina* in a craft shop, or one toting a camera.

Scores of roadside stands offer a bewildering variety of Navajo crafts, particularly in the western part of the reservation on routes to the Grand Canyon. Prices generally are better than those in the shops, although quality control may be better in some of the established trading posts.

Night driving ● Most of the Navajo and Hopi reservations are open range and livestock exhibit a sometimes fatal disdain for motor vehicles. We prefer to drive during daylight hours.

THE HOPI NATION

The Hopi pueblos, while intriguing, are not models of neatness. The earthy style of these ancient dwellings does not blend well with non-biodegradable objects such as car parts and tin cans. The gentle Hopi are more into spiritual things than landscaping. Look beyond the litter and realize that you are seeing people and dwellings that were here before Columbus set sail, before the Spanish began their intrusions into this peaceful land. The Hopi may have occupied this area for as long as man has wandered in the Southwest. Most anthropologists agree that they're descendants of the Anasazi.

Spanish padres tried to sell them on Christianity in the 1600s. But tensions built over the years, exploding into a violent Hopi revolt in 1680. They wiped out Spanish settlements and ripped mission buildings apart. Men were killed and women and children were captured and distributed among the Hopi villages. That brought an abrupt halt to Spanish influence in the area. It was one of the few violent acts in the Hopi's recorded history. Wanting only to be peaceful farmers, they grudgingly retreated as Navajo raiders and later American settlers began moving in on their land. In 1882, the government granted the Hopi their own reservation—in the middle of the Navajo Nation. Border disputes between the two tribes continue to this day—fought in the courts and before Congress.

The present day Hopi villages, many of which are several centuries old, occupy three high peninsulas rising 7,200 feet above sea level in the heart of their reservation, simply called First, Second and Third Mesas. Hopi cling to the old ways much more than the Navajos, still occupying these ancient pueblos. Their ritualistic dances, unchanged for centuries, are a major tourist lure in this corner of Arizona. However, even though they welcome visitors, photographing and recording their dances is forbidden, because of excessive intrusion by visitors earlier in this century. In fact, photography in general is prohibited on the reservation.

THE HOPI CEREMONIAL DANCE:
In touch with the spirits

Ceremonial dances, shown here in 1930, can no longer be photographed.
— **Photo courtesy Arizona Department of Archives**

The Hopi are a highly spiritual people and they often conduct elaborate ceremonial dances, garbed in brightly colored beaded costumes and jewelry. The dances may be to appeal for rain, or to ask for good health and seek harmony with nature. They're held throughout the year, some in private and others on village plazas, where visitors may observe them. Most dances open to the public are held on weekends, beginning at sunup and continuing all day, with stops for lunch and rest.

Plazas are small and not really set up for visitors, so crowds aren't encouraged. Dance schedules aren't posted, but you can check at the Hopi Cultural Center, or call these village community development offices. They're open Monday through Friday, 8 to 5: Bacavi, (520) 734-2404; First Mesa, 737-2670; Hotevilla, 734-2420; Kykotsmovi, 734-2474; Mishongnovi, 737-2520; Moenkopi, 283-6684; Shungopavi, 734-2262 and Shipaulovi, 734-2570.

Photography, sketching and tape recording Hopi dances are strictly forbidden. You're expected to watch respectfully, aware that this is a sacred religious ritual and not a tourist gimmick. While this may sound ambivalent, the Hopi are very private about these public ceremonies and they don't encourage visitors to ask a lot of questions.

Hopi Ceremony Schedule

Specific dance schedules are determined by village elders, who must consider the sun and moon positions and suitable spiritual vibrations. This is determined only a few days in advance, so consult local sources.

January—buffalo dances; February—bean dances; March—*kachina* night dances; April through June—*kachina* day dances; July—social dances; August—snake and flute dances; September—social dances; October—ladies' society dances; November—men's society dances; December—men's Prayer Feather Ceremony.

Bean dances are for crop fertility; social dances concern inter-tribal relationships and *kachina* dances are the most colorful, when performers wear masks and costumes representing various spiritual messengers.

THE NAVAJO NATION

Compared with the Hopi, the Navajo are newcomers, descendants of no-madic Athabascan clans from Canada. They moved into the Southwest from 1300 to 1500 A.D. Navajo and Apaches are distant cousins. Like the Apaches, the Navajo resisted outside intrusion, raiding settlements and clashing with the army. They were rounded up in the 1860s and forced to make the ago-nizing "Long Walk" to Fort Sumner in a bleak area of New Mexico. Then in 1868, they were given most of northeastern Arizona as a reservation—a blow to the Hopi who had occupied these lands for uncounted decades.

The ruling that gave the Navajos the most of this land gave them—by a further twist of fate—most of the area's resources. Coal, oil, natural gas and even uranium are being tapped beneath the arid soil. Forests cover the Defi-ance Plateau around Window Rock and some of the highlands to the north-west. Canyon de Chelly and Navajo national monuments and Monument Valley Tribal Park attract tourists and their dollars.

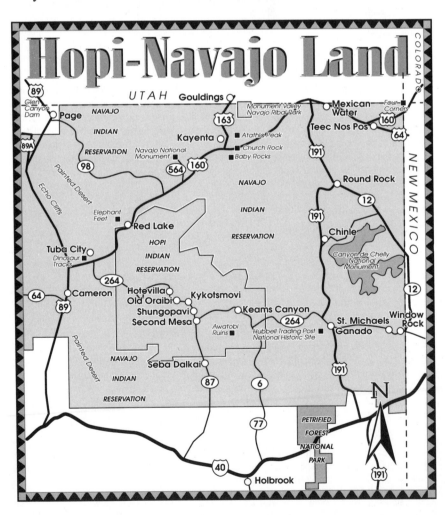

Driving tour: Hopi Nation

Points of interest are spread widely over this New England-sized land that comprises the Hopi and Navajo nations. We'll first explore the Hopi reservation, and then travel east, north and west through Navajoland. If you're dutifully following this book chapter by chapter, head north on State Route 87 from Winslow (Chapter twelve) and continue past Homol'ove Ruins State Park and Painted Desert County Park. You'll enter the Navajo Reservation just above Painted Desert. After 25 miles or so, you reach Hopi lands above a tiny Navajo village called **Seba Dalkai.** No sign marks your transition from Navajo to Hopi turf.

The straight-as-a-string road travels through high prairie, punctuated occasionally by buttes and spires, giving this spartan land an almost outerworldly cast. **Castle Butte** to the northeast is particularly imposing. Several miles into the Hopi Reservation, you'll perceive low ridges on the far horizon. These are the three mesas where most of the Hopi villages are located. They're small places, each with a few hundred residents.

Highway 87 bumps into Route 264 at **Second Mesa.** To view its ancient pueblos, go left (west) for a quarter of a mile and then turn right at a "Second Mesa villages" sign. You'll climb an imposing terrace where **Shipaulovi** (*Shih-PAW-lo-vee*) and **Mishongnovi** (*Mih-SHONG-no-vee*) have clung for centuries. These weathered pueblos were founded in 1680 when valley dwellers fled from the Spanish during the Hopi rebellion. If you turn right again at the "Mishongnovi community office" sign, you'll spiral to the uppermost terrace, where the road ends in a rocky plaza. A vision of an ancient Turkish village or medieval European mountain hamlet may come to mind.

RV ADVISORY ● Don't drive to the upper level in any vehicle larger than 21 feet. There's little room to turn around and your intrusion may not be appreciated.

Generally, it's best not to drive through these narrow village streets, even in a small car. Park and walk up to the villages, enjoying the lofty views. You can see the San Francisco peaks on the far Western horizon—to which the Hopi *kachina* spirits retreat each year.

From the high pueblos, return to Highway 264 and continue west, climbing rocky ramparts toward other levels of Second Mesa. You'll see several arts and crafts shops on both sides of the road, and signs indicating more on side streets. Most are in small rooms attached to homes, or in the homes themselves. As you drive past these scattered shops, the main Hopi visitor complex will appear on your right:

☺ *Hopi Cultural Center and Museum* ● *P.O. Box 7, Second Mesa, AZ 86043; (520) 734-6650. Museum and cultural center open Monday-Friday 8 to noon and 1 to 5 the year around, plus weekends 9 to 3 from May to mid-October. Museum admission $3 for adults and $1 for kids. Gift shops generally open daily 9 to 5; MC/VISA.* ☐ This handsome sandstone colored pueblo style complex includes a museum, gift shops, restaurant and motel (listed below). The nicely done museum has collections of modern and ancient pottery, murals portraying traditional villages, a hand-woven bridal robe and other things Hopi. A diorama of Keet Seel, a ruin in Navajo National Monument, shows how it appeared in 1200 A.D.

Walking Tours ● *Sign up at the cultural center or contact First Mesa Consolidated Villages, P.O. Box 260, Polacca, AZ 86042; (520) 737-2262.* ◻ Visitors can join 40-minute walking tours of First Mesa Villages, conducted Monday-Saturday 9 to 5 except on ceremonial days.

Hopi Arts and Silvercraft Center ● *Immediately beyond the Hopi Cultural Center (P.O. Box 37), Second Mesa, AZ 86043; (520) 734-2463. Daily 9 to 5; major credit cards.* ◻ Run by the Hopi Arts and Silvercraft Cooperative Guild, this is one of the best places to find Hopi art, with a good selection of *kachinas,* clay pottery, beautifully finished woven basketry and silver work such as watch bands, belt buckles and ladies' jewelry.

Pressing westward from the art center, you'll encounter some of the oldest of the Hopi settlements. **Shungopovi** *(Shung-O-PO-vee)* sits at cliff's edge with a view of the valley below. It's the largest Second Mesa village with about 750 residents. Down the hill, **Kykotsmovi** *(Kee-KOTS-mo-vee)* is the administrative center of the Hopi Nation. Begun in 1890, it's sometimes called "New Oraibi" because it's a spin-off from the older village. **Old Oraibi** *(Oh-RYE-bee),* just down the highway at the junction of Indian Route 2, is one of the more fascinating of the pueblos. Many structures are little changed from those you may see in reconstructed ruins. Other, more modern dwellings are being built upon the foundations of the old.

Hotevilla *(HOAT-vih-la),* to the left off the highway, is what you might call a "transition pueblo," a mix of adobe and cinderblock homes, perched on the edge of a mesa. It's a new village, established in 1906 by a group that left Oraibi to start their own community after an internal dispute. **Bacobi,** comprised mostly of prefab homes, is the last Hopi village you'll encounter.

Reverse your route through the reservation. You can get provisions at the large Fecakuku Market just beyond the highway 264/87 junction; there's a post office as well. Continuing east on 264, you'll drop down through some interesting rock formations to **First Mesa.** The only town on the highway is **Polacca.** It's a scatter of a modern settlement at the foot of the mesa, with none of the pueblo mystique. From here, a winding road leads up to three classic Hopi villages—the twin towns of Hano and Sichomovi *(si-CHO-MO-vee),* and charming little Walpi. **Hano** is occupied by a small group of Tewa Pueblo Indians from the Rio Grande. They were given refuge here after fleeing the Spanish in 1696. They still retain their own language and customs.

☺ Perched on the tip of a steep-walled peninsula like a village in the sky, **Walpi** is the most distinctive of all the pueblos. It could be an Anasazi village come to life. Timeless houses seem part of the narrow stone finger they occupy. The tiny village of 30 people is tied to the mesa by a 15-foot-wide strip of stone. Walpi is undergoing restoration to preserve its classic look.

Down off the mesas, you pass Keams Canyon, a government administrative center on the eastern edge of the Hopi Nation. **Keams Canyon Shopping Center** and small a motel sit alongside the highway. The main town, not a Hopi village, occupies an attractive wooded canyon north of the highway. It consists mostly of Bureau of Indian Affairs offices and a hospital.

WHERE TO DINE AND RECLINE IN HOPI LAND
☺ *Tunosvongya Restaurant* ● ☆☆☆ *$*

In the Hopi Cultural Center on Second Mesa; (520) 734-2401. American and traditional Hopi food. Daily 7 a.m. to 9 p.m. MC/VISA. ◻ This appealing restaurant is the best place on the Hopi-Navajo reservations to find traditional foods. Try Hopi dishes such as *chil-il ou gya va,* a lively blend of pinto beans, beef and chilies, or *nok qui vi,* stew with lamb, baked green chilies and Indian fry bread. The place serves good Indian tacos as well.

Hopi Land Café • ☆ **$**
In Keams Canyon Shopping Center; (520) 738-2296. Indian and American. Monday-Saturday 6:30 a.m. to 9 p.m., Sunday 8 to 6. MC/VISA. ☐ It's a simple little formica place serving light American fare and Indian tacos.

Hopi Cultural Center Motel • ☆☆ **$$ Ø**
☐ *P.O. Box 67, Second Mesa, AZ 86043; (520) 734-2401. Couples $55 to $60, singles $50 to $55, family units $60 to $70. MC/VISA.* ☐ Thirty-three attractive rooms with Hopi-Southwest décor; TV and phones. All smoke-free.

Keams Canyon Motel • ☆ **$**
☐ *Adjacent to Keams Canyon Shopping Center, P.O. Box 188, Keams Canyon, AZ 86034; (520) 738-2297. Couples or singles $42. MC/VISA.* ☐ Basic lodging with vaguely Indian décor.

WHERE TO CAMP

There are no organized campgrounds on the reservation, but you can park an RV at a site 100 yards from the Hopi Cultural Center (ask at the desk for directions), and across the highway from Keams Canyon Shopping Center. Both are fee free and both have two-day limits.

Driving tour: Navajo Nation

Leaving the Hopi reservation at Keams Canyon, you pass some interesting sandstone formations including **Steamboat Rock,** near the trading post of the same name. With a bit of imagination, this formation becomes an old sternwheeler; there's even a water line along the side. Eleven miles beyond is the Navajo town of **Ganado** and a historic site that's still functioning:

☺ **Hubbell Trading Post National Historic Site** • *P.O. Box 150, Ganado, AZ 86505; (520) 755-3475. Daily 8 to 6 in summer and 8 to 5 the rest of the year. Free.* ☐ Trading posts occupied a special place on the Western frontier. Traders formed a vital link between the Native Americans and the newcomers—a bridge between the two societies. They provided a market for Indian crafts while offering them essential white man's gadgetry such as tools, sewing machines and canned goods. Traders taught the Indians how to use these new tools; often, they interceded with government officials on the Indians' behalf. The trading post also was a social center, where both whites and Indians met to talk and swap gossip.

Hubbell, the oldest active post on the reservation, was established by John Lorenzo Hubbell in 1876. It's both an historic landmark and an active trading post. You can buy canned goods, bolts of cloth or harnesses, or curios, souvenirs and books. A large barn next to the venerable stone store once housed the post's livestock. Several old wagons are on display out back. At the visitor center museum, you'll learn about the vital role of the Western trading post. Navajo crafts people often come to demonstrate their skills at weaving and jewelry-making. Guided tours are conducted periodically, or you can buy a brochure that will steer you around the extensive grounds.

East of Ganado, Highway 264 climbs a high tableland and passes through piñons and Ponderosas of the Navajo Nation Forest. It tops out at 7,750 feet, then drops down to the Navajo tribal center.

Window Rock near tribal headquarters was sculpted in Kayenta sandstone.

Window Rock

Elevation: 6,764 feet   **Population: 2,200**

This community was established by whites; Indian Affairs Commissioner John Collier took a fancy to a natural sandstone arch and decided to locate the Navajo administration center here in 1934. It's now the Navajo Nation's tribal capital. Most of the administration buildings, many dating back to the 1930s, sit just below the arch near a wooded park.

The downtown area, at the intersection of highway 264 and Indian route 12, has the usual small town businesses. Continue through the intersection for the crafts center, on your left. Just beyond is an imposing new tribal structure, and behind that, a tired little zoo. At the Window Rock Parks and Recreation Department, next to the zoo, you can pick up camping and other recreational permits. It's open weekdays 9 to 5.

Navajo Arts and Crafts Center • *27002 Highway 264 (P.O. Drawer A), Window Rock, AZ (520) 871-4090. Daily 8 to 5; MC/VISA.* ◻ Operated by the Navajo Arts and Crafts Enterprise, the center has the largest selection of native handicrafts on the reservation. Products include silver and turquoise jewelry, unset turquoise stones, blankets, curios, bolo ties, squash blossom necklaces, dolls, sand paintings, pottery from Navajo, Jemez and Hopi tribes, and books on Indian lore.

☺ ***Navajo Tribal Museum*** • *In the Arts and Crafts Center (P.O. Box 308, Window Rock), AZ 86515; (520) 871- 4090. Weekdays 9 to 4:45. Free; donations appreciated.* ◻ This small, well-planned museum exhibits the skeleton of a 180-million-year-old *dilophosaurus,* plus displays tracing Indian occupation of the region from the basketmakers of 50 A.D. to the present. Artifacts include pottery, projectile points, metates and such. One exhibit traces the development of Navajo silvercraft. Contemporary life is shown in a clever display within a mockup of the Navajo's most useful tool, the pickup. (A new structure just beyond the craft center may house the museum in the near future, or the facility could be used for a visitor center and tribal offices.)

Navajo Nation Zoological Park ● *Just behind the new museum. Daily 8 to 5; free.* ⌑ The most interesting thing about this small, scruffy zoo is its setting—amidst several sandstone monoliths. The critters, some in cages, others in fenced-off areas against steep sandstone cliffs, are mostly from the Southwest. You first pass through an exhibit building with spiders, rattlesnakes, scorpions and other uglies. Outside, you can learn Navajo names of creatures as you pass their enclosures, such as *ma'ii* for coyote (which sounds like their howl) and *shash tazhinii,* a ferocious-sounding name for a black bear.

Return to the signal and head north briefly on Highway 12, then turn right onto Window Rock Road for the town's namesake:

☺ **Window Rock Tribal Park** ● *Near the tribal administration buildings.* ⌑ This is a pretty spot, with a landscaped park and picnic area shaded by junipers. Window Rock is a Kayenta sandstone ridge with a circular arch cut through it by wind and erosion. It's fenced off, but you can follow a trail beyond and behind it, where you will discover more weather-sculpted shapes.

WHERE TO DINE & RECLINE

Navajo Nation Inn and Dining Room ● ☆☆ $$$

⌑ *48 W. Highway 264 (P.O. Box 2340), Window Rock, AZ 86515; (800) 662-6189 or (520) 871-4108. Couples $67, singles $65, kings and suites $72. Major credit cards.* ⌑ Nicely decorated rooms with TV and phones. **Navajo Nation Restaurant** is open daily 6:30 a.m. to 9 p.m.; American, Navajo and Mexican fare; dinners $6 to $11. Entrées include Navajo mutton and beef stew, Navajo tacos, American chicken, steaks and chops.

From Window Rock, press northward on Highway 12, which takes you through more imposing beige and red rock formations. When you reach the town of **Fort Defiance,** stay alert for a right hand turn at a service station to stay with the highway. Otherwise, you'll continue straight ahead into the town. Pressing northward, you'll dip into New Mexico (marked by a sign) and then back into Arizona (not marked). This is an appealing drive into the pines of the Chuska Mountain foothills, offering picnic sites, campgrounds and a couple of fishing lakes. As further enhancement, the area is marked with occasional sandstone cliffs, buttes and spires. Particularly dominant to the east is a thick, towering butte with a wide alluvial skirt, called Black Pinnacle. Beyond small **Tsaile Lake,** you'll see the campus of Navajo Community College on your left. It has a fine little museum worthy of pause:

Hatathli Museum ● *Navajo Community College, just inside the east entrance of campus; (520) 724-3311. Weekdays 8:30 to 4:30; donations appreciated.* ⌑ This all-Navajo museum is housed in the octagonal Hatathli Center on the college campus. Exhibits trace Navajo and other Native American cultures. Handicrafts and artwork are available at a sales gallery.

Just beyond the college, you'll reach the hamlet of **Tsaile.** Highway 64 leads about 25 miles from here into the side door of Canyon de Chelly National Monument. However, before heading in that direction, we suggest that you continue another ten miles north on Route 12 to see a spectacular proscenium of red rock cliffs above the town of **Lukachukai.** Having done so, return to Tsaile Junction and head east toward the national monument.

de Chelly National Monument ● *P.O. Box 588, Chinle, AZ ⁷4-5436. Visitor center open 8 to 6 from May to September and ∂f the year; free. The center has a small museum with graphics ⸍occupation from basketmakers to Anasazi cliff dwellers of the 12th a·⸱ ⸱ centuries. Ranger programs, from late May through early September, include coffee talks at the campground amphitheater, canyon hikes, nature walks, lectures at Thunderbird Lodge and campfire programs.* ☐

Save a day for Canyon de Chelly, and yes it does rhyme. Canyon de Chelly and its adjoining Canyon del Muerto are unexpectedly beautiful steep-walled ravines, dropping a thousand feet to neat patchwork farms on the valley floor. Lining the banks of a meandering stream, these lands are still being tilled, as they have been since the 1300s. Knife-edged ridges and pinnacles rise from the valley floors and serpentine side canyons cut into the sheer walls. Cliff dwellings are tucked into hidden recesses, suddenly appearing as you scan the walls with your binoculars. There are few places on earth offering such a dramatic mix of natural formations and archaeological ruins.

Canyon hiking: Because the Navajo are even more sensitive than the rest of us about protecting prehistoric ruins, most of canyon cannot be entered without a guide. Free half-day ranger hikes leave the visitor center daily, usually from May through September. Also, you can hire a Navajo guide for $10 an hour and explore the canyon's inner secrets. This can be arranged at the visitors center.

Two rim drives take you to turnouts for an assortment of awesome views of the canyons and hidden Anasazi dwellings. If you're following our route from Tsaile, you'll first encounter the upper drive and run it in reverse:

North Rim Drive skirts the edge of Canyon del Muerto. Coming from Tsaile, you'll first encounter **Massacre Cave** and **Mummy Cave** viewpoints. Massacre Cave was so named because the Spanish slaughtered more than 100 men, women and children at a pueblo here. Go to the right, along the edge of the canyon, and you'll see remnants of a kiva, only 35 feet below. At Mummy Cave, you see a remarkably intact pueblo. **Antelope House** has two overlooks with views of a great free-standing wedge, formed where Canyon del Muerto and Black Rock Canyon merge. **Ledge Ruin Overlook** is a broad caprock peninsula with views up and down the chasm; two different viewpoints provide glimpses of canyon ruins.

The **South Rim Drive,** about 16 miles long, starts at the visitor center. To get there, continue east on Highway 64 toward Chinle, and then follow Canyon de Chelly signs. **Tsegi Overlook** provides a peek down the sheer canyon face to farm fields below. At **Junction Overlook,** you can see a tall, pie shaped peninsula where Canyon del Muerto joins Canyon de Chelly.

☺ **White House Ruins** can be reached by trail from White House Overlook, about six miles from the visitor center. It's the only trail into the canyon that can be taken without a guide. The broad path switchbacks 500 feet down to the canyon floor, where you skirt the edge of a farmer's field, wade an icy stream (take dry socks!), and cross to the dwelling. White House Ruin, named because the ancients whitewashed one of the structures, occupies a niche about 50 feet above you. Another ruin, fenced off from vandals, sits at its base. The walls here are so sheer and smooth that your voices bounce off them like vocal ping pong balls.

Back on South Rim Drive, you'll shortly encounter **Sliding House Overlook,** providing a view of ruins perched on a ledge so narrow that they

Spider Rock, incredibly slender and seeming to defy gravity, juts skyward in Canyon de Chelly National Monument.

seem ready to slip into the canyon. **Wild Cherry** provides more canyon vistas and **Face Rock Overlook** faces some cliff dwellings high in the opposite wall. **Spider Rock** overlook at the end of the route is the most impressive of all, with a half-mile rim trail with several vantage points. Here, the walls drop a thousand feet. Spider Rock is an unbelievably slender freestanding, spiked monolith rising 800 feet from the canyon floor.

Chinle

Elevation: 5,058 feet   **Population: approx. 2,000**

Spread thinly across a shallow basin, Chinle dates from 1882 as a Navajo trading post. It's now the commercial center for a surrounding ranching area and, for those who come in the front door, the gateway to Canyon de Chelly. It has a couple of motels, cafés and a fair sized shopping center called Tseyi.

ACTIVITY

Canyon de Chelly Tours ● *C/o Thunderbird Lodge, P.O. Box 548, Chinle, AZ 86503; (800) 679-2473 or (520) 674-5841. Major credit cards.* ☐ Half day tours depart at twice daily at 9 a.m. and 2 p.m.

WHERE TO DINE & RECLINE

Junction Restaurant ● ☆☆ *$$*

☐ *Highway 7, adjacent to Best Western Canyon de Chelly Inn; (520) 674-8443. Varied menu. Daily 6:30 a.m. to 10 p.m. (until 9 p.m. mid-November to mid-March).* ☐ Large, handsome restaurant serving an interesting mix of American, Southwestern, Mexican and some traditional Navajo dishes.

Best Western Canyon de Chelly Inn ● ☆☆☆ *$$$$* Ø

☐ *P.O. Box 295 (Highway 7), Chinle, AZ 86503; (520) 674-5875. Couples, singles and family units $75 to $102. Major credit cards.* ☐ Pleasant Southwest style motel surrounding a large lawn area; 102 units with TV and phones. **Junction Restaurant** listed below.

Thunderbird Lodge ● ☆☆☆ *$$$$*

☐ *Near Canyon de Chelly visitor center, P.O. Box 548, Chinle, AZ 86503; (800) 679-2473 or (520) 674-5841. Couples $83 to $88, singles $79 to $84, suites and family units $89. Major credit cards.* ☐ Well kept 72-unit inn with TV and room phones; gift shop. Family style **cafeteria** open 6:30 a.m. to 8:30 p.m. (to 7:30 in the off-season); American fare; dinners $8 to $12.

WHERE TO CAMP

Cottonwood Campground ● *Adjacent to Thunderbird Lodge, near visitors center. Tent and RV sites, no hookups.* ☐ Attractive sites shaded by cottonwoods; flush potties, picnic and barbecue areas, dump station. Water and restrooms shut down during winter; pit toilets available.

North from Chinle, Highway 191 travels through bunchgrass prairie accented by occasional redwall mesas. Two of the more impressive ones, visible to the northwest, are **White Top Mesa** and **Carson Mesa Red Rocks.** You pass Many Farms and Round Rock, little more than village trading posts, then turn east at Mexican Water onto Highway 160. Your destination: a cartographic novelty where the corners of Arizona, New Mexico, Colorado and Utah meet. We expected very little when we first traveled this spot and we weren't disappointed. A follow-up visit revealed more substance—dozens of arts and crafts stands and a chance to devour a Navajo taco:

☺ ***Four Corners Monument*** • This landmark is in a tribal park, with a small admission fee that goes to an educational fund. The precise spot where the four states meet is marked by a concrete slab with the state lines converging in the middle, like a sliced square pie. Each state's slice contains its name and seal. The gimmick here is to walk onto the concrete base and stand, squat or sit with parts of your anatomy in each of the four states. On a busy summer day, you'll have to wait your turn. You never have to wait long, since most folks feel silly and hold their poses only briefly. (A kind of frozen leapfrog position appears to be the most popular; not recommended for ladies in short skirts.)

Perhaps more interesting are the dozens of stalls selling Navajo jewelry, pottery, blankets, sand paintings and other crafts, plus T-shirts of course. You can watch demonstrations of sand paintings and other Navajo arts in a visitor center. Food stalls sell cold drinks, those notorious Navajo tacos and fry bread. (Fry bread looks and tastes like a pizza that lost all of its topping. It's best when dusted with cinnamon, which is a standard option.) Of interest only to trivia fanatics: Although you approach Four Corners via Arizona and then Colorado, the park entrance is through New Mexico.

From Four Corners, retrace your route west on Highway 160, past sandstone shapes that give promise of more to come at legendary Monument Valley. Along the way, you pass the serrated red limestone **Comb Ridge** on the right, just beyond Dennehotso, and a curious little formation called **Baby Rocks** near a now defunct trading post. Here, a mesa breaks into small columns of pinnacles that look like red clay soldiers marching off the end of the butte. A couple of miles farther, just west of the Navajo Route 59 junction, **Church Rock** juts from a nearby field like complicated cathedral spires.

Kayenta & Monument Valley

Elevation: 5,798 feet **Population: 3,400**

You've seen thousands of images of Monument Valley, in travelogues and Western movies, and on pretty posters. Ad agencies like to park cars atop the tall spires. However, you have to be there to get the full Cinemascopic impact of these awesome shapes. They rise from the desert in great tapered spires, unbelievably thin fins and broad-shouldered buttes, looking too alien to be earthly. From a distance, there is no more beautiful sight than a panorama of Monument Valley with puffy clouds rising to a high, blue sky.

Kayenta, gateway to Monument Valley Tribal Park, occupies an arid basin about 20 miles south, providing a few motels and restaurants for visitors. **Gouldings,** just opposite the Monument Valley park entrance on the Utah side, also offers lodging, shopping, a restaurant and campground. Driving north toward the monument from Kayenta, you'll pass **Agathla Peak,** the pointed black core of an ancient volcano that's nearly as impressive as the beige and rose sandstone shapes ahead.

☺ ***Monument Valley Tribal Park*** • *P.O. Box 360289, Monument Valley, UT 84536; (801) 727-3287. Daily 8 to 7 mid-March through September and 8 to 5 the rest of the year; last admission 30 minutes before closing. Adults $2.50, seniors $1, kids under 12 free. A campground near the visitor center has sites under shade ramadas, with picnic tables and grills, for $10. It has showers; no hookups. Also, there's a campground/RV park at Gouldings (see below)* ⌑

Before entering the valley, you must first pause at roadside kiosk to pay your fee, which allows you to follow the 17-mile drive among the park's formations. Just beyond is the small visitor center, perched on a ridge and providing great views of the valley below. A dozen or more tour operators parked nearby offer trips into the valley by jeep, flatbed trucks with seats affixed to the bed, or other rigs. They have two advantages: Your hosts describe what you're seeing and they're permitted to take back roads through the valley that aren't open to private vehicles. Prices range from $15 for an hour and a half to $50 for all-day trips. Gouldings Lodge also runs tours.

RV AND GENERAL DRIVING ADVISORY ● The road into the valley isn't recommended for trailers or motorhomes over 24 feet. We negotiated it in our 21-foot *Ickybod*, although we experienced considerable rocking and rolling. Folks with oversized vehicles or those who prefer not to drive the rough road can book a tour into the valley. Even in conventional cars, you may feel like you're doing the Baja 500 in slow motion, although the road gets better once you've descended the steep slope into the valley. Very low clearance vehicles such as sports cars might have a problem, particularly on the climb back out.

Although the formations are awesome, the valley is small, covering only a few square miles. We were slightly put off by the excess of signs telling you where you can't go and what you can't do. The Navajos are very protective of their natural areas. Hiking, rock-climbing and wandering off the designated route are prohibited. The scenic drive covers only a small part of the valley, although it does take you past many of its most striking formations. **Artist's Point,** a slight rise with views of the natural wonders around you, is a nice place to pause for a picnic. It's about midway through the drive.

These formations are remnants of an early Rocky Mountain range, eroded about 160 million years ago and fused into sandstone. The gradual uplifting of the Colorado Plateau created cracks and seams that eroded into canyons and gullies. As more of the land eroded, softer portions weathered away, leaving buttes and gravity-defying pinnacles. If you have time, spend a full day here—from sunup to sundown. Changing light and shadows cast their magic on these free-standing formations. Although the park is open only during daylight hours, you can see its shapes from many vantage points outside.

ACTIVITIES

Gouldings Tours ● *P.O. Box 1, Monument Valley, AZ 84536; (801) 727-3231.* ☐ These tours are booked out of Gouldings Lodge at Monument Valley or Wetherill Inn Motel in Kayenta. Full day with lunch, $60; half day, $30; two and a half hours, $25.

Monument Valley Tours ● *C/o Monument Valley Tribal Park, P.O. Box 93, Monument Valley, UT 84536; (801) 727-3287.* ☐ Make arrangements at the visitor's center; two and a half hours, $15; longer tours up to $50 a day. Departures on demand.

Multi-media show ● *Earth Spirit,* a presentation about Monument Valley, is shown at Gouldings Lodge nightly at 6:10, 7:10 and 8:10; adults $2, kids $1; free with Gouldings tour ticket; call (801) 727-3231.

WHERE TO DINE AND RECLINE

Golden Sands Café ● ☆☆ *$*

☐ *Uptown Kayenta on Highway 163, behind Wetherill Inn; (520) 697-3684. American. Daily 6 a.m. to 9:30 p.m. No credit cards.* ☐ Charmingly rustic place with checkered oilcloth, Western décor and a wood stove. American steaks, chicken and chops, Navajo tacos. You can book half-day Monument Valley tours at the café.

For quick bites, you'll find a pizza parlor, plus a deli and a bakery in Basha's supermarket at the Teeh'indeeh Shopping Center on Highway 163, near the junction with highway 160.

Gouldings Lodge ● ☆☆☆ $$$$$ Ø

❑ Six miles from the park entrance, P.O. Box 360001, Monument Valley, UT 84536; (801) 727-3231. Couples or singles $118, family units $124 to $130, cabins for one or two people $130. Major credit cards. ❑ Rooms have balconies or patios with views of Monument Valley. Nicely furnished with TV, phones; pool, gift shop. Very handsome **restaurant** serves breakfast, lunch and dinner; entrées $9 to $18. The Goulding complex also includes a service station and store, and it offers Monument Valley tours and a multimedia show; see "Activities" above. The original stone trading post has a small museum, with relics from the days when it was established by Harry and Lenore (Mike) Goulding in 1924.

Holiday Inn ● ☆☆ $$$$$

❑ On Highway 160, P.O. Box 307, Kayenta, AZ 86033; (520) 697-3221 or (800) 465-4329. Couples and singles $109. Major credit cards. ❑ A nicely appointed 160-room inn with TV and phones; pool, gift shop, coin laundry. **Monument Valley Restaurant** serves 6 a.m. to 10 p.m.; chicken, chops, steaks, fish, plus a Navajo "pocket sandwich"; dinners $7 to $14; Southwest style dining room.

Tsegi Canyon Anasazi Inn ● ☆☆ $$$$

❑ Eleven miles west on Route 160, P.O. Box 1543, Kayenta, AZ 86033; (520) 697-3793. Couples $90, singles $80. Major credit cards. ❑ Nicely kept motel between Kayenta and Navajo National Monument; nicely furnished rooms with TV movies. **Café** serves 24 hours in summer, 5 a.m. to 11 p.m. the rest of the year; American and Navajo fare; dinners $5 to $14.

Wetherill Inn ● ☆☆ $$$$ Ø

❑ P.O. Box 175 (on the highway to Monument Valley), Kayenta, AZ 86033; (520) 697-3231. Couples $78, singles $72. Major credit cards. ❑ A 54-room motel with TV movies, phones, free coffee; Monument Valley tours.

Back on Highway 160, head west toward Navajoland's second national monument, passing some handsome fluted cliffs en route. About 20 miles west of Kayenta, turn north on Route 564:

☺ **Navajo National Monument** ● HC 71, Box 3, Tonalea, AZ 86044; (520) 672-2366 or 672-2367. Visitor center open 8 a.m. to 4:30 p.m. Lookout trail open during daylight hours. Campground open mid-April through mid-October; RV and tent sites, no hookups; free. ❑ Navajo National Monument contains three of the most complete Anasazi ruins and one of the finest small museums in the state. It takes advance planning to visit two of the three ruins; the museum can be enjoyed any day. The visitor center occupies a piney ridge at 7,286 feet, so dress warmly for the off-season.

The three ruins sheltered by this small national monument are Betatakin, Inscription House and Keet Seel. Betatakin can be seen from an overlook not far from the visitor center, or visited by ranger-guided tours. Inscription House, 30 miles from the monument, is so fragile that it's closed to visitors. Keet Seel, the "star" of Southwest's Indian ruins, is eight miles away and can be visited only with an advance permit.

Two-and-a-half hour hikes to Betatakin leave the visitor center daily at 9 a.m. and 1 p.m. in summer and 11 a.m. in the off-season. It takes five to six hours, involving a difficult 700-foot descent into a canyon. You must sign up on the day of the hike; group sizes are limited, so arrive early. Hikes are conducted from early spring through October.

The hike to Keet Seel—a large, amazingly intact ruin with many roofs and timbers still in place—must be reserved early. Write or call two months prior to your trip; reservations aren't accepted before then. Visits are permitted only from Memorial Day through Labor Day weekend. Once at the site, you can't enter the ruin without a ranger, who will be on duty during visiting periods. When we last checked, the park service was considering limiting Keet Seel hikes to weekends because of personnel shortages, so permits may be *very* hard get. The permit also allows overnight stays at a primitive campground near the site.

Because these ruins were hidden from pot-hunters in a ruggedly beautiful canyon, they yielded a rich treasure of relics. Many have been used to create the excellent museum at the visitor center. Stone tools, implements and pottery are focal points of simple, uncluttered displays that teach us much about the Anasazi, perhaps the most dominant prehistoric tribe of the Southwest. They prevailed in this arid land for 13 centuries. You can crawl inside a reconstructed living unit that's so complete it seems the occupants just stepped out for a bit. A film about the Anasazi is shown periodically, and a ranger will activate a five-minute slide show concerning the monument. An adjacent gift shop open mid-April to mid-November sells Hopi, Navajo and some Zuni handicrafts, along with books and guides.

The nearest overnight lodging to Navajo National Monument, other than the campground, is Tsegi Canyon Anasazi Inn, listed above.

From the monument, continue southwest on Highway 160 toward Tuba City, passing a pair of sandstone buttes near Red Lake; they've earned the appropriate name of **Elephants Feet.**

Two attractions on the western side of the Navajo Nation—Little Colorado River Gorge and Cameron Trading Post, are on the highway to the Grand Canyon, and we covered them in Chapter three, page 74. The other attraction—of sorts—is the largest community on the reservation.

Tuba City

Elevation: 4,940 feet   **Population: 7,000**

Not an original Navajo town, Tuba City was established in 1877 when Mormon farmers settled around a nearby spring. The odd name comes from a Hopi chief, T Ivi, which settlers distorted to "tuba." After learning that they were nesting on Indian land, the Mormons tried unsuccessfully to gain title. They sold out to the government in 1903 and it became the U.S. Indian Agency's administrative center for the western Navajo reservation. Most of the stone government buildings still stand.

Tuba offers an interesting architectural mix. Many original buildings—including government offices—are of cut sandstone, standing alongside tree-shaded streets. Neighborhoods are a mix of ordinary bungalows, modular and mobile homes and some interesting "modern" prefab wooden octagonal hogans. The main part of the town is about a mile north of Highway 160.

Tuba Trading Post in downtwon Tuba City is worth a browse. It's an interesting hexagonal tufa block structure with a raised center floor, offering a good array of Indian crafts such as blankets, basketry, pottery and silver. The perimeter is a general store selling everything from groceries to VCR movie rentals to tricycles. It's open daily 7:30 to 8:30.

WHERE TO DINE & RECLINE

Tuba City Truck Stop Café ● ☆ $

☐ Highway 160-264 junction; (520) 283-4975. American, Navajo and Hopi fare. Daily 6 a.m. to 11 p.m. No credit cards. ☐ Basic formica café popular with locals. It has chicken, chops, sandwiches and excellent Navajo tacos.

Pancho's Family Restaurant ● ☆☆ $

☐ Downtown, between Tuba City Motel and trading post; (520) 283-3302. American, Mexican and Navajo. Daily 6 a.m. to 9 p.m. Major credit cards. ☐ Appealing place with pottery chandeliers, Navajo rugs on the walls; American and Mexican entrées plus Navajo fry bread. **CJ's Old Fashioned Ice Cream Parlor** behind the restaurant is open weekdays 2 to 9 p.m.

Tuba Motel ● ☆☆ $$$$

☐ Downtown, P.O. Box 247, Tuba City, AZ 86045; (520) 283-4545. Couples and singles $80 to $90. Major credit cards. ☐ Modern rooms with phones, TV; gift shop.

NAVAJO NATION ANNUAL EVENTS

July 4th Rodeo, Window Rock.
Eastern Navajo Fair & Rodeo, late July, Crownpoint, New Mexico.
Central Navajo Fair and Rodeo, late August in Chinle.
Navajo Nation Fair & All-Indian Rodeo, September, Window Rock.
Northern Navajo Fair, mid-October in Shiprock, New Mexico.
Western Navajo Fair, late October in Tuba City.

...and into the sunset

Just west of Tuba City on Highway 160, you'll see signs directing you to **dinosaur tracks.** They're a short distance north of the highway on a bumpy road. Reptilian critters strolled along a muddy shoreline here 200 million years ago, leaving hundreds of paw prints that have hardened in the sandstone. A few locals from the nearby village of Moenave are usually on hand to help you find them. They'll obligingly pour water into the tracks to accent them for photographs. A small offering for their helpfulness would be nice. Several jewelry stands are nearby.

Business was slow when we arrived late one March afternoon, so young Morris A. Chee, Jr., had plenty of time to spend with us.

"You're only my fifth and sixth people today," he said. "In summer, we get lots of people and go through maybe 80 gallons of water to make the tracks show up. We have to pack it from the village up there." He gestured toward tiny Moenave, across the sparse prairie. "When I'm done here, I'm going to celebrate my twentieth birthday. Sure wish more people had come."

We took the hint and doubled his gratuity, then we gave him a ride back to his village. We waved goodbye to this slender young man trying to make an honest dollar in a society that, in many ways, was still alien to him. Then, ending our Arizona adventure as all good Western epics should end, we put our faithful steed *Ickybod* into gear and headed off into the sunset.

WINTER IN THE SUN

Chapter fourteen

SNOWBIRD DIRECTORY
Finding a place in the Arizona sun

WHEN THE CHILL WINDS COME, millions of Americans and Canadians—mostly retirees—pull up winter roots and head for warmer climes. If you're one of these, you know that you've been nicknamed Snowbird. Arizona ranks second to Florida and ahead of California and Texas as a leading Snowbird retreat.

Exact figures are hard to find for this migratory flock, but Arizona may draw upwards of a million each winter. An Arizona State University survey indicated that most long-term winter visitors to the Valley of the Sun arrive in November (32 percent) and depart in April (55 percent). Sunbelt chambers of commerce report similar trends.

The ASU survey, taken at several Mesa-Apache Junction RV and mobile home parks, revealed some interesting statistics. About half of Arizona's long-term winter visitors occupy RVs or mobile homes; the others check into apartments or condos or they own winter homes in Arizona. A surprising 70 percent of mobile home park dwellers leave their unit there year-around; only 30 percent tow a trailer or drive a motor home to the state. And these are indeed migrants. Only five percent of those responding to the survey said they planned to stay permanently. The average length of a winter visit is between four and five months. Two-thirds of those surveyed have been doing the Snowbird bit for five or more years.

Where do you folks come from? A surprising 20 percent are from Canada. Most of the Americans surveyed came from Minnesota (13 percent), with Iowa and Washington tied for second at 11 percent. Number four was North Dakota with seven percent—an amazing figure, since it has a population of less than 700,000. Others were Colorado, six percent; Illinois, four percent; California, Oregon and Wisconsin, all three percent.

Since about half of the long term winter visitors lease apartments and condos, Tucson, Phoenix and some other cities list short-term lodgings in their tourist accommodation guides. Most Arizona RV parks offer special rates for long-term visitors. Many are elaborate resorts, with swimming pools, golf courses, marinas, recreational programs and other amenities.

Incidentally, whether you plan to winter in Arizona for two weeks or six months, remember to bring your sweater—perhaps even a down jacket. Compared with Bismark, North Dakota, and Edmonton, Alberta, much of Arizona is a winter paradise. But nighttime temperatures sometimes dip down to freezing in the Phoenix and Tucson areas. Days generally are in the balmy 60s, climbing often into the 70s. Tucson is more than a thousand feet higher than Phoenix and therefore slightly cooler. If you require balmier winter nights, the Colorado River corridor is warmer than the desert interior. Yuma, for instance, is less than 200 feet above sea level. Parker and Bullhead City often report the nation's highest temperatures—the year around.

Arizona offers a rich panorama of enticements for Snowbirds. If you're thinking about joining this flock, or if you'd like to find a new roost next winter, this directory of communities catering to Snowbirds should help. The list ranges from cosmopolitan Phoenix to dusty Quartzsite, and it includes some sun country places you may not be aware of. Chambers of commerce can provide more specific information. Most have lists of RV parks and mobile home resorts that cater to long-term visitors. All of the communities listed below are discussed in more detail elsewhere in this book. Chapter locations are shown at the bottom of each listing.

For complete details on moving to Arizona, either for the winter or permanently, get copy of our *Coming to Arizona* relocation guide. It's available at book stores or you can order it directly; see the back of this book.

RV ADVISORY ● Many RV parks with long-term rates—particularly those near metropolitan areas—book up early, so make your plans as soon as possible.

APACHE JUNCTION

Elevation: 1,715 feet　　　　　　　　　　　*Population: 19,175*

Location ● South central Arizona, 40 miles east of Phoenix, in the foothills of the Superstition Mountains.

Winter climate ● Warm and dry with cool evenings; less than eight inches annual rainfall. Average January high 65, low 35.

Characteristics ● A fast-growing community on the outer fringe of the Valley of the Sun's metropolitan core. It's a major Snowbird and retirement area, drawing about 40,000 winter visitors.

Attractions ● Phoenix and Scottsdale; Salt River Canyon reservoirs and Superstition Mountains with boating, fishing and other outdoor activities.

Long-term visitor accommodations ● About a hundred RV parks and resorts.

Advantages ● It offers a nice balance between cosmopolitan lures of Phoenix and a rural desert atmosphere with no traffic congestion.

Disadvantages ● Area recreational facilities become very crowded with Valley of the Sun residents on weekends.

Contact ● Apache Junction Chamber of Commerce, Box 1747, Apache Junction, AZ 85217; (800) 252-3141 or (602) 982-3141.   **SEE CHAPTER EIGHT**

BULLHEAD CITY

Elevation: 540 feet   *Population: 22,000*

Location ● Northwestern Arizona on the Colorado River, near the California-Nevada border.

Winter climate ● Warm and very dry with cool evenings; less than four inches of rain. Average January high 80, low 38.

Characteristics ● Fast-growing community scattered alongside Lake Mohave reservoir. The rising new casino town of Laughlin, Nevada, is just across the water. The area's economy is based almost entirely on tourism and water recreation.

Attractions ● Fishing, boating and swimming on Lake Mohave; casino shows and gaming in Laughlin. Lake Mead National Recreation Area is immediately north.

Long-term visitor accommodations ● Dozens of RV parks are along the river, mostly on the Arizona side, with some on the Nevada shore.

Advantages ● The area offers some of the most temperate winter climate in the Southwest; frost is rare. There's plenty of Nevada style amusement across the river.

Disadvantages ● Bullhead is not a well-planned city; the business area is rather scattered. There are few cultural opportunities here.

Contact ● Bullhead Area Chamber of Commerce, 1251 Highway 95 (P.O. Box 66), Bullhead City, AZ 86430; (520) 754-4121.   **SEE CHAPTER FOUR**

CAVE CREEK & CAREFREE

Elevation: 2,350 feet   *Population: Approx. 3,500*

Location ● About 15 miles north of Phoenix in central Arizona.

Winter climate ● Warm days, cool evenings; moderate rainfall (12 inches a year). Average January high 60, low 40.

Characteristics ● Cave Creek is a deliberately rustic Western style town; adjacent Carefree, a planned community, is more contemporary. They sit side-by-side, just beyond reach of the Valley of the Sun's congestion, in a scenic desert area.

Attractions ● Phoenix and its sundry lures, plus the golf courses, restaurants and elegant resorts of next-door Scottsdale.

Long-term visitor accommodations ● Conventional lodgings only; no RV parks in the area.

Advantages ● The cultural and night life offerings of Phoenix are nearby, yet the area is desert rural.

Disadvantages ● No RV facilities.

Contact ● Carefree-Cave Creek Chamber of Commerce, P.O. Box 734, Carefree, AZ 85377; (602) 488-3381.   **SEE CHAPTER SEVEN**

CASA GRANDE

Elevation: 1,398 feet   *Population: 20,000*

Location ● In south central Arizona, midway between Phoenix and Tucson, just off Interstate 10.

Winter climate ● Warm with chilly evenings, annual rainfall, eight inches. Average January high 66, low 35.

Characteristics ● An agricultural community; starting to catch a little of the Phoenix-Tucson growth fever, but still rural.

Attractions ● Nicely situated between the lures of Phoenix and Tucson.

Long-term visitor accommodations ● About 16 RV parks are in the area, plus apartment rentals.

Advantages ● This farm community, turning into an industrial, retail and tourist community, is ideally located between two metropolitan centers, linked by I-10.

Disadvantages ● Set in a farming area, it lacks the appeal of desert gardens, and it's a bit on the cool side in winter; it can get windy here.

Contact ● Greater Casa Grande Chamber of Commerce, 575 N. Marshall, Casa Grande, AZ 85222; (800) 916-1525 or (520) 836-2125.   **CHAPTER EIGHT**

LAKE HAVASU CITY

Elevation: 482 feet   *Population: 20,000*

Location ● On the Colorado River, at the Arizona-California border.

Winter climate ● Very warm with cool evenings; less than four inches of annual rainfall. Average January high 79, low 37.

Characteristics ● It was started several years ago as a planned community by the McCulloch Corporation, with the transplanted London Bridge as its centerpiece. It has since become the largest city on the Colorado River corridor between Arizona and California.

Attractions ● Adjacent Lake Havasu offers all sorts of water sports and of course, there's that bridge.

Long-term visitor accommodations ● There are many RV parks in the area, including a new full-service resort on Lake Havasu Peninsula.

Advantages ● Lake Havasu City is better planned than most river corridor towns. The winter climate is warm enough for all those water sports.

Disadvantages ● It's a long way from anywhere; the nearest freeway is 19 miles and that only gets you to Needles, California.

Contact ● Lake Havasu City Area Chamber of Commerce, 1930 Mesquite Ave., Suite 3, Lake Havasu City, AZ 86403; (520) 855-4115.   **SEE CHAPTER FOUR**

LAKE MEAD NATIONAL RECREATION AREA

Elevation (Boulder City, Nev.): 1,232 feet   *Population: 11,100*

Location ● Northwestern Arizona—Lake Mead and Lake Mohave.

Winter climate ● Similar to Bullhead City; warm and dry with cool evenings; less than four inches of rain. Average January high 80, low 38.

Characteristics ● A shoreline longer than the California coast provide water sports for more than eight million year-around visitors on Lake Mead above Hoover Dam and Lake Mohave below.

Attractions ● Colorado River corridor water sports; the glitter of Las Vegas is a short drive northwest.

Long-term visitor accommodations ● Nine marinas occupy Lake Mohave and Lake Mead shorelines and most offer long-term rental spaces. Others are in nearby Boulder City, Nevada.

Advantages ● Proximity to water sports; lower rental fees that urban areas.

Disadvantages ● There are no city services there. However, Boulder City is just seven miles away and Bullhead City is a short drive south.

Contacts ● For a list of marinas, contact: Lake Mead National Recreation Area, 601 Nevada Highway, Boulder City, NV 89005-2426; (702) 293-8907. For area information: Boulder City Chamber of Commerce, 1497 Nevada Hwy., Boulder City, NV 89005; (702) 293-2034.   **SEE CHAPTER FOUR**

MESA-TEMPE

Elevation: 1,200 feet   *Mesa: 340,000; Tempe: 150,000*

Location ● Just east of Phoenix in central Arizona.

Winter climate ● Balmy, with chilly evenings. Rainfall less than eight inches. Average January high 65, low 35.

Characteristics ● These two cities account for most of the Valley of the Sun's eastward suburban sprawl. They're primarily bedroom communities, among the fastest growing in the state.

Attractions ● Arizona State University in Tempe offers a fine cultural base and both communities have their own fine museums. Further, it's a short commute from here to the many lures of Phoenix and Scottsdale.

Long-term visitor accommodations ● Nearly 50 RV resorts and parks in the area, plus some winter apartment rentals (but scarce in Tempe because of ASU).

Advantages ● These large communities offer all essential services and plenty of shopping, plus their own cultural activities in addition to those in Phoenix.

Disadvantages ● This is suburbia with sunshine and traffic.

Contacts ● Mesa Convention & Visitors Bureau, 120 N. Center, Mesa, AZ 85201; (602) 827-4700; Tempe Chamber of Commerce, 60 E. Fifth St., Suite 3, Tempe, AZ 85281; (602) 894-8158. **SEE CHAPTER SEVEN**

PARKER

Elevation: 450 feet   *Population: 3,035*

Location ● Western Arizona, across the Colorado River from California.

Winter climate ● Warm with cool evenings. Rainfall less than four inches. Average January high 67, low 37.

Characteristics ● Parker, on the Colorado River Indian Reservation, covers a 16-mile strip along the Colorado River corridor. Compared with bustling Lake Havasu City and Bullhead City, it has more of a quiet, small-town America atmosphere.

Attractions ● Water sports are pretty much the main focus, with 16 miles of aquatic playground; Parker Dam is 20 miles north and Headgate Rock Dam is south, creating an offshore lake.

Long-term visitor accommodations ● The 20-mile "Parker Strip" between here and Parker Dam is practically a solid row of RV parks and resorts, lining both the Arizona and California shores.

Advantages ● Parker is a quiet community offering an abundance of rather inexpensive RV parks and miles of lake shoreline.

Disadvantages ● It's two to three hours from any city, with few cultural opportunities.

Contact ● Parker Area Chamber of Commerce, 1217 California Ave., Parker, AZ 85344; (520) 669-2174. **SEE CHAPTER FOUR**

PHOENIX-SCOTTSDALE

Elevation: 1,083 feet   *Phoenix: 1,036,000; Scottsdale: 165,000*

Location ● Central Arizona, in the heart of the Valley of the Sun.

Winter climate ● Balmy, with some chilly evenings. Rainfall, seven inches. Average January high 65, low 35.

Characteristics ● Phoenix and Scottsdale need no further introduction. Phoenix is the big, booming heart of the Arizona sunbelt and Scottsdale is a growing desert resort community.

Attractions ● Museums, major league sports, live theater, good restaurants, adjacent mountains, beautiful desert gardens—you name it. The Valley of the Sun is host to five of the eight Cactus League baseball clubs.

Long-term visitor accommodations ● There are many RV parks and resorts, particularly on the outskirts, plus winter apartment and condo rentals.

Advantages ● Phoenix offers a great mix of culture, night life, recreation and sunshine. Scottsdale, removed from the metropolitan core, is home to most of the area's resorts, surrounded by attractive desert mountains.

Disadvantages ● You may not care for the busy metropolitan bustle; RV park prices are on the high side.

Contacts ● Phoenix & Valley of the Sun Convention & Visitors Bureau, 400 E.

Van Buren St., Suite 600, Phoenix, AZ 85004-2290; (602) 254-6500; Scottsdale Chamber of Commerce, 7333 Scottsdale Mall, Scottsdale, AZ 85251-4498; (602) 945-8481. **SEE CHAPTER SEVEN**

QUARTZSITE

Elevation: 875 feet   *Population: 2,000*

Location ● Southwestern Arizona, 20 miles from the California border on I-10.

Winter climate ● Warm and dry; cool evenings. Rainfall less than four inches. Average January high 65, low 35.

Characteristics ● Quartzsite is a patch of desert that has become one huge RV park. Its population zooms to 200,000 in winter; it's probably the world's largest concentration of rec vehicle facilities.

Attractions ● Colorado River recreation areas are 20 miles west. Huge gem shows and flea markets from mid-January to early February draw up to half a million visitors to this dusty desert hamlet.

Long-term visitor accommodations ● There are wall-to-all RV parks; more than 70 at last count.

Advantages ● Quartzsite offers the cheapest RV rates in the state, and there's free RV parking out in the desert. More than 2,500 vendors set up camp during the annual gem and mineral show in February.

Disadvantages ● It's a cultural desert in the desert, sitting next-door to nothing. And it's just hound-dog homely.

Contact ● Quartzsite Chamber of Commerce, P.O. Box 85, Quartzsite, AZ 85346; (520) 927-5600. **SEE CHAPTER FOUR**

SIERRA VISTA

Elevation: 4,623 feet   *Population: 36,855*

Location ● Southeastern Arizona, 70 miles southeast of Tucson.

Winter climate ● Warm to cool days, chilly nights. Rainfall, 15 inches, snowfall 10 inches. Average January high 58, low 34.

Characteristics ● This is an Arizona surprise—a growing community the otherwise thinly populated southeast. This well-planned city is rimmed by mountains.

Attractions ● Historic Tombstone, Fort Huachuca Museum, Ramsey Canyon Natural Preserve, Coronado National Memorial, plus mountain and desert wilderness areas; short drives to Tucson and the Mexican border.

Long-term visitor accommodations ● Various apartment complexes, motels and hotels, plus several relatively inexpensive RV parks in next door Huachuca City.

Advantages ● It's away from the hustle, yet close to Tucson and the Mexican border. It's large enough to offer most services and conveniences.

Disadvantages ● Sierra Vista is a bit on the cool side for a winter retreat, although it offers one of the most temperate year-around climates in America.

Contact ● Sierra Vista Chamber of Commerce, 77 Calle Portal, #140-A, Sierra Vista, AZ 85635; (800) 288-3861 or (520) 458-6940. **SEE CHAPTER ELEVEN**

TUBAC

Elevation: Approx. 3,700 feet   *Population: 1,000*

Location ● South central Arizona, 40 miles south of Tucson and 20 miles north of Nogales, Mexico.

Winter climate ● Warm days, chilly nights. About 11 inches of rain; occasional traces of snow. Average January high 66, low 31.

Characteristics ● If you like history mixed with artistic funk, you'll like tiny Tubac. It's Arizona's oldest settlement and a popular artists' colony.

Attractions ● Less than an hour from Tucson and half an hour from the border. Tubac Presidio State Park and Tumacacori National Monument are nearby.

Long-term visitor facilities ● There are very few RV parks in the area.

Advantages ● Tubac is quiet, funky and remote, yet close to Tucson.

Disadvantages ● It's a bit cool for a winter resort, although it's warmer and closer to Tucson's attractions than nearby Sierra Vista, with an average January-March temperature of 69.

Contact ● Tubac Chamber of Commerce, P.O. Box 1866, Tubac, AZ 85646; (520) 398-2704. **SEE CHAPTER NINE**

TUCSON

Elevation: 2,584 feet   *Population: 667,000*

Location ● South central Arizona, 115 miles southeast of Phoenix and 64 miles north of Mexico (at Nogales).

Winter climate ● Balmy days, some cool to chilly evenings. Lots of cloud-free days; rainfall about 11 inches. Average January high 66, low 37.

Characteristics ● It offers the metropolitan lures of Phoenix, with more small city charm; the pace is a bit slower here.

Attractions ● Fine cultural offerings, good restaurants, skiing at nearby Mount Lemmon, surrounding desert gardens, excellent museums and galleries; good Mexican handicraft shopping in nearby Nogales.

Long-term visitor accommodations ● Tucson has a good selection of RV parks, winter apartments and condos. The visitor's bureau can recommend apartment locator services.

Advantages ● Think of it as a flat San Francisco with warm sunshine. (It's our favorite city in the Southwest.)

Disadvantages ● Large and spread out, with occasional traffic congestion. Also, RV parks are more expensive than in smaller communities.

Contact ● Metropolitan Tucson Convention & Visitors Bureau, 130 S. Scott Ave., Tucson, AZ 85701; (800) 638-8350 or (520) 624-1817. **SEE CHAPTER NINE**

YUMA

Elevation: 138 feet   *Population: 60,000*

Location ● On interstate 8 in Arizona's southwestern corner, 20 miles from Mexico (at San Luis).

Winter climate ● Warm days, cool evenings, occasionally chilly. It's the driest corner of the state; rainfall less than three inches. Average January high 68, low 37.

Characteristics ● Yuma is another Arizona surprise—a burgeoning mini-metropolis far from the rest of civilization. Snowbirds nearly double this fast growing sunshine resort's population each winter.

Attractions ● Occupying the site of Yuma Crossing—the old Colorado River gateway to California—it has several historic sites including the Yuma Territorial Prison, plus water recreation; Mexico shopping is 20 miles south.

Long-term visitor accommodations ● Several RV parks and resorts are on both shores of the Colorado River; many more are inland along I-8.

Advantages ● A small town atmosphere, with adequate facilities and services. Relatively inexpensive RV parks; water recreation. If you like your climate dry, Yuma's the place.

Disadvantages ● It's remote from any metropolitan center and offers limited cultural resources.

Contact ● Yuma Convention and Visitors Bureau, P.O. Box 10831, Yuma, AZ 85366-8831; (520) 783-071. **SEE CHAPTER TEN**

Chapter fifteen

AFTERTHOUGHTS
The very best of Arizona

THE ORIGINAL version of this book was called *The Best of Arizona.* Now, as the *Arizona Discovery Guide,* it's more comprehensive, listing not only the best, but all of the rest.

Of course, we have our preferred attractions, hikes, cafes, vistas and places to toast in the sun. We've picked our favorites in each category, followed by the other nine in alphabetical order. Thus, we have no losers in this Discovery Guide, only winners and runners-up.

THE TEN BEST OUTDOOR ATTRACTIONS

1. **Grand Canyon National Park,** which may be the grandest outdoor attraction in the world; Chapter three, page 59.
2. Arizona-Sonora Desert Museum, Tucson; Chapter nine, page 267.
3. Canyon de Chelly National Monument; Chapter thirteen, page 380.
4. Chiricahua National Monument; Chapter eleven; page 333.
5. Glen Canyon National Recreation Area; Chapter three, page 70.
6. Hoover Dam, particularly with its new visitor center; Chapter four, page 83.
7. Organ Pipe Cactus National Monument; Chapter ten, page 303.
8. Petrified Forest National Park; Chapter twelve, page 355.
9. Walnut Canyon National Monument; Chapter five, page 137.
10. Yuma Territorial Prison State Park; Chapter ten, page 296.

THE TEN BEST MUSEUMS

1. **The Heard Museum, Phoenix** is quite possibly the best Native American archive in America; Chapter seven, page 192.
3. Besh-Ba-Gowah Archaeological Park, Globe; Chapter twelve, page 364.
4. Desert Caballeros Western Museum, Wickenburg; Chapter eight, page 234.
5. Fort Huachuca Museum, Fort Huachuca; Chapter eleven, page 323.
6. Hall of Flame Firefighting Museum, Phoenix; Chapter seven, page 190.
7. Museum of Northern Arizona, Flagstaff; Chapter five, page 121.
8. Pima Air and Space Museum, east of Tucson; Chapter nine, page 270.
9. Sharlot Hall Museum, Prescott; Chapter six, page 172.
10. Titan Missile Museum, Green Valley; Chapter nine, page 284.

THE TEN BEST ACTIVITIES

1. **Hiking rim-to-rim**, which is the ultimate way to experience the Grand Canyon; Chapter two, page 43.
2. Cactus League baseball in Phoenix and Tucson; Chapter seven, page 201 and Chapter nine, page 272.
3. Canyon de Chelly ranger-led hikes, Chapter thirteen, page 380.
4. Chiricahua National Monument hike from Massai Point to the visitor center; Chapter eleven, page 333.
5. Hopi ceremonial dances, Hopi Reservation; Chapter thirteen, page 373.

Monument Valley, without question, offers some of the best views in Arizona.

THE TEN BEST VIEWS

THE TEN MOST INTERESTING TOWNS OR CITIES

8. Scottsdale; Chapter seven, page 210.
9. Sedona; Chapter six, page 142.
10. Wickenburg; Chapter eight, page 232.

THE TEN BEST RESTAURANTS

1. El Tovar Dining Room, Grand Canyon National Park; the perfect meal—excellent food and a view of the canyon; Chapter two, page 55.
2. Anthony's in the Catalinas, Tucson; Chapter nine, page 274.
3. Cafe Terra Cotta, Tucson; Chapter nine, page 274.
4. Chaparral Room at Marriott's Camelback Inn, Scottsdale; Chapter seven, page 216.
5. Chez Marc Bistro, Flagstaff; Chapter five, page 126.
6. Christopher's, Phoenix; Chapter seven, page 204.
7. El Chorro Lodge, Scottsdale, Chapter seven, page 216.
8. House of Joy, Jerome, Chapter six, page 166.
9. Murphy's, Prescott, Chapter six, page 175.
10. The Tack Room, Tucson, Chapter nine, page 276.

THE TEN BEST DESERT RESORTS

1. The Arizona Biltmore in Phoenix, the classic blend of history and luxury; Chapter seven, page 208.
2. The Boulders, Carefree; Chapter seven, page 219.
3. The Buttes, Tempe; Chapter seven, page 228.
4. Enchantment Resort, Sedona; Chapter six, page 154.
5. Inn at the Citadel, Scottsdale; Chapter seven, page 220.
6. L'Auberge de Sedona, Sedona; Chapter six, page 155.
7. Lodge at Ventana Canyon, Tucson; Chapter nine, page 280.
8. Marriott's Camelback Inn, Scottsdale; Chapter seven, page 220.
9. Scottsdale Princess, Scottsdale; Chapter seven, page 221.
10. Tanque Verde Guest Ranch, Tucson; Chapter nine, page 282.

THE TEN BEST HOTELS AND INNS

1. The Ritz-Carlton, a classic example of a luxury urban hotel resort, Phoenix; Chapter seven, page 207.
2. Arizona Inn, Tucson; Chapter nine, page 278.
3. Courtyard by Marriott, Tucson; Chapter nine, page 279.
4. Doubletree Suites at Phoenix Gateway; Chapter seven, page 206.
5. El Tovar, Grand Canyon National Park; Chapter two, page 50.
6. Fray Marcos Hotel, Williams; Chapter five, page 132.
7. Hyatt Regency, Phoenix; Chapter seven, page 207.
8. Lodge in the Desert, Tucson; Chapter nine, page 280.
9. Los Abrigados, Sedona; Chapter six, page 155.
10. Prescott Resort and Conference Center; Chapter six, page 176.

OTHER USEFUL BOOKS

Now that you've purchased this book and we've gotten your money—assuming you aren't still thumbing through it in the bookstore—we will recommend further reading. If you can't find them at a bookstore, they may be available directly from the publishers.

General travel information

Arizona Milepost Guide by William Hafford; Arizona Highways Books. A milepost-pegged guide to fifteen tours.
Arizona Scenic Drives by Stewart Greene; Falcon Press, P.O. Box 279, Billings, MT 59103. This book features a series of descriptive drives through the state.

avel Planner published by the Arizona Office of Tourism, 1100 W.
⸱., Phoenix, AZ 85007. A concise guide to the state, section by sec-
⸱tions, mileages, campgrounds, chambers of commerce, tour opera-
⸱⸱⸱ other essentials.

Grand Canyon National Park by John F. Hoffman, a National Parkways publication, World-Wide Research and Publishing Co., P.O. Box 3073, Casper, WY
82602. Attractive guide with background, visitor information, maps and lots of pretty
color photos.

The Grand Canyon: Temple of the World, an Arizona Highways Book, 2039
W. Lewis Ave., Phoenix, AZ 85009. Quotes from various authors who have been
moved to pen poetic prose about the canyon, along with the usual Arizona Highways style beautiful photos.

100 Best Restaurants in Arizona by Harry and Trudy Plate; Kelton Publishing
Co., P.O. Box 12521, Scottsdale, AZ 85267. It's just what the title says.

New Times Best of Phoenix Restaurant Guide by Howard Seftel; Gem
Guides Book Co., 315 Cloverleaf Drive, Suite F, Baldwin Park, CA 91706. A good
collection of restaurants compiled from Phoenix's *New Times* news weekly.

Roadside Geology of Arizona by Halka Chronic; Mountain Press Publishing
Company, P.O. Box 2399, Missoula, MT 59806. Scholarly yet highly readable guide
to geological formations that visitors see as they travel Arizona's highways.

RVing America's Backroads: Arizona by Kitty Pearson and Jim Vincent;
Trailer Life Books, Agoura, Calif. Full-color, attractively-illustrated guide to Arizona,
oriented to the RV set, with suggested driving tours in various areas of the state.

Scenic Sedona by Lawrence W. Cheek; Arizona Highways, 2039 W. Lewis
Ave., Phoenix, AZ 85009. Illustrated guide to Sedona and the Verde Valley area.

Travel Arizona by Joseph Stocker; Arizona Highways, 2039 W. Lewis Ave.,
Phoenix, AZ 85009. Sixteen tours, with illustrations, maps and color photos.

What Is Arizona Really Like: A Guide to Arizona's Marvels by Reg Manning;
Reganson Cartoon Books, P.O. Box 5242, Phoenix, AZ 85010. Humorously written
insider's look at Arizona with cartoon illustrations, by Pulitzer Prize-winning cartoonist for the *Arizona Republic.*

Retirement and relocation

Coming to Arizona by Don and Betty Martin; Pine Cone Press, P.O. Box 1494,
Columbia, CA 95310. A complete guide for future Arizonans: job-seekers, retirees
and Snowbirds, with details on housing, medical care, schools and leisure facilities.

The Phoenix Job Bank, Published by Bob Adams., Inc., 260 Center St., Holbrook, MA 02343. A "how-to" book for job-seekers, with lists of major Phoenix and
Tucson employers, job descriptions and techniques for successful job-hunting.

Retirement Living by Sally Ravel and Lee Ann Wolfe; Conari Press, 713 Euclid
Ave., Berkeley, CA 94708. Although it's oriented to northern California, it contains
useful information in planning for retirement and selecting a retirement community.

History, ghost towns and reference

Arizona Place Names, re-print of a 1935 edition by Will C. Barnes, University of
Arizona Press, Tucson. Thorough, comprehensive guide to the origin of Arizona's
geographic names.

Arizona's Best Ghost Towns by Byrd Howell Granger; Northland Press, P.O.
Box N, Flagstaff, AZ 86002. A helpful guide with maps and nice sketches.

Desert Wildflowers; Arizona Highways, 2039 W. Lewis Ave., Phoenix, AZ
85009. Gorgeous photos of desert blossoms, with descriptions and times to catch
peak blooming periods.

History of Arizona by Robert Woznicki, PH.D.; Messenger Graphics, 110 S.
41st Ave., Phoenix, AZ 85009. A highly-readable treatment of the state's history; not
comprehensive, but filled with interesting vignettes and personality sketches.

The Story of Superstition Mountain and the Lost Dutchman Mine by Robert Joseph Allen; Pocket Books, New York. A readable narrative of the Dutchman mine mystery, with some very questionable suppositions.

Travel Arizona: The Back Roads; Arizona Highways, 2039 W. Lewis Ave., Phoenix, AZ 85009. Lots of pretty color photos and route maps.

Hiking, camping, wildlife viewing

Arizona Day Hikes by Dave Ganci; Sierra Club Books. It describes a hundred day hike trails throughout the state.

Arizona Wildlife Viewing by John N. Carr; Falcon Press, P.O. Box 279, Billings, MT 59103. This small full-color book advises hikers and strollers where to see what kind of wildlife in the state's parks and recreation areas; compiled in cooperation with park and recreation departments.

A Hiker's Guide to Arizona by Steward Aitchison and Bruce Grubbs; Falcon Press, P.O. Box 279, Billings, MT 59103. A well-written guide with maps and black and white photos.

Hiker's Guide to the Superstition Wilderness by Jack Carlson and Elizabeth Stewart; Clear Creek Publishing, P.O. Box 24666, Tempe, AZ 85285. A fine little guide to trails in the Superstitions, brightened by the history and legends of the Lost Dutchman mine.

Outdoors in Arizona: A Guide to Camping by Bob Hirsch; Arizona Highways, 2039 W. Lewis Ave., Phoenix, AZ 85009. A good mix of campsite listings, color photos and history and vignettes about the state's out-of-doors.

Outdoors in Arizona: A Guide to Hiking and Backpacking by John Annerino; Arizona Highways, 2039 W. Lewis Ave., Phoenix, AZ 85009. Suggested hikes from desert to mountain to prairie, with maps and photos.

Native Americans

A Clash of Cultures: Fort Bowie and the Chiricahua Apaches by Robert M. Utley; for sale by the Superintendent of Documents, U.S. Government Printing Office, Washington, DC 20402. Also at national monuments and historic sites.

American Indians of the Southwest by Bertha P. Dutton; University of New Mexico Press. A good general guide to present and past Southwestern Indians.

The Complete Family Guide to Navajo-Hopi Land by Bonnie Brown and Carol D. Bracken; Bonnie Brown and Carol Bracken, P.O. Box 2914, Page, AZ 86040. It's a bit unprofessionally done, but helpful, with lists of attractions, places to dine and sleep; several children's pages to amuse the youngsters.

Geronimo: A Man, His Time, His Place by Angie Debo; University of Oklahoma Press, Norman, OK 73019. An award-winning biography of the famous Apache warrior; probably the most comprehensive Geronimo study ever written.

Hohokam Indians of the Tucson Basin by Linda M. Gregonis and Karl J. Reinhard; University of Arizona Press, Tucson. Scholarly, readable account of Tucson's early peoples.

Southwestern Indian Tribes by Tom Bahti; KC Publications, Inc., Box 14883-A, Las Vegas, NV 89114. Attractive guide to Arizona and New Mexico tribes with maps and color and black and white illustrations; nicely detailed photos of artifacts.

Visitor's Guide to Arizona's Indian Reservations by Boye De Mente; Phoenix Books/Publishers, P.O. Box 32008, Phoenix, AZ 85064. A thorough, well-written guide with lots of detail and maps.

HOW TO TALK LIKE AN ARIZONAN

Well, of course Arizonans speak English, but there's a sprinkling of Spanish and Indian words in there. And many Arizona place names have Spanish and Indian roots. This pronunciation guide—prepared with the aid of Brian C. Catts of the University of Arizona's Office of Public Service—will help you talk like a native.

Ajo *(AH-hoe)* — Town in southern Arizona; means "garlic" in Spanish.

Anasazi *(Ana-SAH-zee)* — Early Arizona Indian tribe; the name means "the ancient ones."

Apache *(Ah-PAH-chee)* — Central and southeastern Arizona tribe.

Athabaskan *(A-tha-BAS-kan; "a's" pronounced as in apple)* — Canadian Indian tribe; ancestors of the Navajo and Apache.

Bowie *(BOO-ee)* — Fort in southeastern Arizona, now a national historic site; also a tiny town on Interstate 10.

Canyon de Chelly *(du SHAY)* — Arizona national monument.

Canyon del Muerto *(MWAIR-toh)* "Canyon of Death," a ravine adjacent to Canyon de Chelly.

Carne *(CAR-nay)* — Meat.

"Cerveza fria, por favor" *(Sehr-VE-sa FREE-ah, por fah-VOR)* — "Bring me a cold one, please."

Chemehuevi *(Tchem-e-H'WAY-vee)* — Southern Colorado River tribe of Yuman origin; mostly in southeastern California. Meaning is unknown.

Chinle *(Chin-LEE)* Navajo town, the gateway to Canyon de Chelly.

Chiricahua *(Cheer-i-COW-wa)* — Southeastern Arizona Apache tribe made famous by Cochise and Geronimo's rebellions.

Cholla *(CHOY-ya)* — Large family of Arizona cactus.

Coconino *(Co-co-NEE-no)* — Arizona place name, given to a national forest, county and plateau south of the Grand Canyon.

Colorado *(Coh-lo-RAH-doh)* — Red.

El Tovar *(El To-VAR)* — Historic hotel at the Grand Canyon's South Rim.

Gila *(HEE-la)* — A river in southern Arizona.

Guadalupe Hidalgo *(Wa-da-LU-pay Hee-DAL-go)* The treaty ending the Mexican War, signed in 1848.

Havasupai *(Hah-vah-SOO-pie)* — "Blue-green water people" who occupy beautiful Havasu Canyon; also called Supai.

Hohokam *(Hoe-hoe-KAHM)* — Prehistoric tribe occupying deserts of Southern Arizona about AD 200 to 500; means "those who have gone."

Huachuca *(Hwa-CHOO-ka)* — Army fort in southern Arizona with an historic museum; also the name of a mountain range.

Hopi *(HOE-pee)* — Indian tribe, probably descended from the Anasazi.

Hotevilla *(HOAT-vih-la)* — Hopi village on Third Mesa. The name means "skinned back" or cleared off.

Hualapai *(HWAL-a-pie or WAH-lah-pie)* — Western Arizona Indian tribe; the name means "pine tree people."

Huevos Rancheros *(WHEY-vose ran-CHER-ohs)* — Popular Spanish style breakfast with eggs and picante sauce.

Javalina *(Ha-va-LEE-na)* — Wild boar.

Kykotsmovi *(Kee-KOTS-mo-vee)* — Hopi administrative center, on Third Mesa below Oraibi, also called New Oraibi. It means "the place of the mound of ruins."

Maricopa *(Ma-ri-KOH-pah)* — A name given to the Pipa tribe, which shares a reservation with the Pima.

Mescalero *(Mess-kah-LAIR-O)* — Arizona-New Mexico Apache tribe. The name is Spanish, referring to mescal cactus, a traditional food source.

Moenkopi *(Mu-en-KO-pee)* —Third Mesa Hopi village; "place of running water."

Mogollon *(MUGGY-yon)* — Ancient Indian tribe occupying eastern Arizona about AD 200 to 500; also Mogollon Rim, the abrupt southern edge of the Colorado Plateau.

Mohave *(Mo-HA-vay)* — Arizona place name, referring to Indian tribe and a county along the western border. Spelled "Mojave" in California.

Navajo *(NAH-VAH-hoe)* — America's largest Indian tribe, descended from the Athabascan band of Canada.

Nogales *(No-GAH-less)* Twin Arizona-Mexico border towns; the word is Spanish for "walnuts."

Ocotillo *(O-co-TEE-yo)* — Spiny-limbed desert bush with red blossoms.

Oraibi *(Oh-RYE-bee)* — Hopi settlement on Third Mesa; the name means "place of the Orai stone."

Paloverde *(PAW-lo-VAIR-day)* — Desert tree distinctive for the green bark of its limbs.

Papago *(PAH-pa-go)* — Spanish word for "bean eaters," referring to a Southern Arizona Indian tribe, which has since re-adopted its traditional name of "Tohono O'odham."

Pima (PEE-mah) — Central and southern Arizona tribe. The name was a Spanish mistake. When questioned by early explorers, they responded *"Pi-nyi-match,"* which means "I don't understand." The Spanish thought they were identifying themselves.

Prescott *(PRESS-kit)* — Town in central Arizona.

Quechan *(KEE-chan or KAY-chan)* — Indian tribe near Yuma area; also known as Yuma Indians.

Saguaro *(Sa-WHA-ro)* — Large cactus; its blossom is Arizona's state flower.

San Xavier *(Sahn Ha-vee-YAY)* — Spanish mission south of Tucson; some locals pronounce it *Ha-VEER.*

Sichomovi *(si-CHO-MO-vee)* — Hopi settlement on First Mesa; means "a hill where the wild currants grow."

Sinagua *(Si-NAU-wa)* — Ancient north central Arizona tribe; lived in the area about 900-1000 A.D. It comes from the Spanish words *sin agua*—"without water."

Shungopovi *(Shung-O-PO-vee)* — Hopi settlement on Second Mesa; means "a place by the spring where tall reeds grow."

Tempe *(Tem-PEE)* — City east of Phoenix.

Tohono O'odham *(To-HO-no ah-toon)* — Traditional Papago tribal name; it means "people of the desert who have emerged from the earth."

Tubac *(TU-bahk)* — Arizona's first settlement; below Tucson.

Tumacacori *(Too-mawk-ka-COR-ee)* — Spanish mission below Tucson.

Tusayan *(TU-sigh-yan or TUSSY-yan)* — Sinagua Indian ruin near Desert View in Grand Canyon National Park; also a town outside the south entrance station.

Ute *(Yoot)* — Large Great Basin Indian tribe; few members are in Arizona. It means "the tribe" in the Shoshoni and Comanche language.

Verde *(VAIR-day)* — Spanish for "green."

Wahweap *(WAH-weep)* — Ute Indian for "bitter water"; the name of a large marina at Glen Canyon National Recreation Area.

Wupatki *(Wu-PAT-key)* — National monument northeast of Flagstaff. The word is Hopi for "tall house."

Yaqui *(Ya-KEE)* — Small Indian tribe southwest of Tucson, near Tohono O'odham Reservation. Origin of name unknown; it might simply mean "the people," a self-reference commonly used by many early tribes.

Yavapai *(YA-va-pie)* — Central Arizona tribe. Origin of the name is not sure; it might mean "crooked mouth people" or "people of the sun."

Yuma *(YOO-mah)* — Large tribal group near the city of Yuma; the name is derived from *lum,* which means tribe. The original name is Quechan (see above), which the tribe is again using.

INDEX: Primary listings indicated by *bold face italics*

REMARKABLY USEFUL GUIDEBOOKS
from *PINE CONE PRESS*

Critics praise the "jaunty prose" and "beautiful editing" of Pine Cone Press guidebooks by Don and Betty Martin. In addition to being comprehensive and "remarkably useful," their books are frank, witty and opinionated. They're available from book stores, or directly from the publisher.

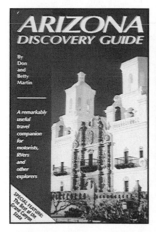  

ADVENTURE CRUISING
It's the first book of its kind—a guide devoted exclusively to adventure, specialty and other small ship cruises. Scores of cruise lines are listed, with hundreds of itineraries world wide. Special "Cruise closeups" provide an intimate look at more than a dozen different voyages. **— 352 pages; $15.95**

ARIZONA DISCOVERY GUIDE
This detailed guide covers attractions, scenic drives, hikes and walks, dining, lodgings and campgrounds in the Grand Canyon State. A "Snowbird" section helps retirees plan their winters under the Arizona sun, and special "RV Advisories" help steer RVers around the state. **—408 pages; $15.95**

THE BEST OF THE GOLD COUNTRY
It's a remarkably useful guide to California's gold rush area in the Sierra Nevada foothills and old Sacramento. This comprehensive book covers attractions, historic sites, dining, lodging and camping. **— 240 pages; $11.95**

THE BEST OF THE WINE COUNTRY
Where to taste wine in California? Nearly 300 wineries are featured, along with nearby restaurants, lodging and attractions. Special sections offer tips on selecting, tasting, serving and storing wine. **— 336 pages; $13.95**

COMING TO ARIZONA
This is an all-purpose relocation guide for job-seekers, retirees and winter "Snowbirds" planning a move to Arizona. It provides essential data on dozens of cities, from recreation to medical facilities. **— 232 pages; $12.95**

NEVADA DISCOVERY GUIDE
This guide covers all of Nevada, with a special focus on gaming centers of Las Vegas, Reno-Tahoe and Laughlin. A special section advises readers how to "Beat the odds," with casino gambling tips. **— 352 pages; $15.95**

More books and ordering information on the next page

NORTHERN CALIFORNIA DISCOVERY GUIDE

Our new Discovery Guide series focuses on driving vacations for motorists and RVers. We steer our readers to popular attractions and little-known jewels, along with great places to play, eat and sleep. — *356 pages; $12.95*

OREGON DISCOVERY GUIDE

From the wilderness coast to the Cascades to urban Portland, this book takes motorists and RVers over Oregon's byways and through its cities. It's another in the Martins' new Discovery Guide series. — *352 pages; $12.95*

THE ULTIMATE WINE BOOK

It's the complete wine guide, covering the subject in three major areas: wine and health, wine appreciation and wine with food. It's loaded with useful information for both casual and serious wine lovers. — *176 pages; $8.95*

UTAH DISCOVERY GUIDE

This remarkably useful driving guide covers every area of interest in the Beehive State, from its splendid canyonlands to Salt Lake City to the "Jurassic Parkway" of dinosaur country. — *360 pages; $13.95*

WASHINGTON DISCOVERY GUIDE

This handy book takes motorists and RVers from one corner of the Evergreen State to the other, from the Olympic Peninsula and Seattle to Eastern Washington's wine country and great rivers. — *372 pages; $13.95*

MARTIN GUIDES ARE AVAILABLE AT MOST BOOK STORES, OR YOU CAN ORDER DIRECTLY FROM THE PUBLISHER

VISA & MASTERCARD ACCEPTED

Phone, FAX, e-mail or write, giving us your credit card type, number and expiration date. Or you can mail us your personal check. For each book, add $1.05 for shipping ($3.05 for priority mail). California residents please include appropriate state sales tax.

**Send your order to: *Pine Cone Press*
P.O. Box 1494, Columbia, CA 95310
(209) 532-2699; FAX (209) 532-0494
e-mail: pinecone@sonnet.com**